Studien zum Internationalen Wirtschaftsrecht/
Studies on International Economic Law

edited by

Prof. Dr. Marc Bungenberg, LL.M., Universität des Saarlandes
Prof. Dr. Christoph Herrmann, LL.M., Universität Passau
Prof. Dr. Markus Krajewski, Friedrich-Alexander-Universität
Erlangen-Nürnberg
Prof. Dr. Carsten Nowak, Europa Universität Viadrina,
Frankfurt/Oder
Prof. Dr. Jörg Philipp Terhechte,
Leuphana Universität Lüneburg
Prof. Dr. Wolfgang Weiß, Deutsche Universität
für Verwaltungswissenschaften, Speyer

Volume 16

Nathalie Lendermann

# Procedure Shopping Through Hybrid Arbitration Agreements

Considerations on party autonomy in
institutional international arbitration

 **Nomos**

**The Deutsche Nationalbibliothek** lists this publication in the
Deutsche Nationalbibliografie; detailed bibliographic data
are available on the Internet at http://dnb.d-nb.de

a.t.: Konstanz, Univ., Diss., 2017

ISBN      978-3-8487-4599-9 (Print)
          978-3-8452-8944-1 (ePDF)


**British Library Cataloguing-in-Publication Data**
A catalogue record for this book is available from the British Library.

ISBN      978-3-8487-4599-9 (Print)
          978-3-8452-8944-1 (ePDF)


**Library of Congress Cataloging-in-Publication Data**
Lendermann, Nathalie
Procedure Shopping Through Hybrid Arbitration Agreements
Considerations on party autonomy in institutional international arbitration
Nathalie Lendermann
572 p.
Includes bibliographic references and index.

ISBN      978-3-8487-4599-9 (Print)
          978-3-8452-8944-1 (ePDF)


1st Edition 2018
© Nomos Verlagsgesellschaft, Baden-Baden, Germany 2018. Printed and bound in Germany.

*Meinen Eltern*

# Vorwort

Die vorliegende Arbeit wurde im Frühjahr 2016 von der rechtswissenschaftlichen Fakultät der Universität Konstanz als Dissertation angenommen. Änderungen von Schiedsordnungen konnten für die Veröffentlichung bis September 2017 berücksichtigt werden.

Mein besonderer Dank gilt meinem Doktorvater Professor Dr. Michael Stürner, M.Jur. (Oxford) für seine Aufgeschlossenheit gegenüber dem Thema sowie für Zuspruch und Unterstützung während der Promotionszeit und während meiner Zeit als wissenschaftliche Mitarbeiterin im Wintersemester 2010/2011 an seinem damaligen Lehrstuhl an der Europa-Universität Viadrina. Professorin Dr. Astrid Stadler danke ich für die sehr zügige und gründliche Erstellung des Zweitgutachtens und ihre herausfordernden Fragen, welche das Disputationsgespräch besonders spannend machten.

Herzlich bedanke ich mich zudem bei der Studienstiftung des deutschen Volkes für die finanzielle und ideelle Förderung während der Promotionszeit. Der Johanna und Fritz Buch Gedächtnis-Stiftung danke ich, dass sie die Veröffentlichung durch einen großzügigen Druckkostenzuschuss ermöglicht hat. Der Queen Mary University School of Law danke ich für die Ermöglichung meines Forschungsaufenthaltes in London im Herbst 2014. Den Herausgebern der Studien zum Internationalen Wirtschaftsrecht - Studies on International Economic Law danke ich für die Aufnahme in die Schriftenreihe.

Dem Singapore International Arbitration Centre sowie dem Internationalen Schiedsgerichtshof der Internationalen Handelskammer in Paris danke ich jeweils für die Möglichkeit, die Arbeit einer internationalen Schiedsinstitution als Praktikantin bzw. Rechtsreferendarin kennenzulernen. Die so gewonnenen Einblicke haben erheblich zur Themenfindung und Ausarbeitung beigetragen.

Julia Schneider danke ich sehr für die gründliche Durchsicht des Manusskriptes und ihre sprachlichen Korrekturanmerkungen. Von Herzen danke ich schließlich meinen Eltern sowie meinem Ehemann für ihren Rückhalt.

Berlin, Dezember 2017                                    Nathalie Lendermann

# Table of content

# List of abbreviations

| | |
|---|---|
| § / §§ | section / sections |
| AAA | American Arbitration Association |
| AAA-ICDR | International Centre of Dispute Resolution of the →AAA |
| ADCCAC | Abu Dhabi Commercial Conciliation and Arbitration Center |
| ADR | Alternative Dispute Resolution |
| AFA | Association française d'arbitrage |
| AG | Aktiengesellschaft (German stock corporation) |
| All ER | All England Law Reports |
| alt. | alternative |
| Am. Rev. Int'l Arb | American Review of International Arbitration |
| Am. Univ. Int'l L. Rev. | American University International Law Review |
| AR | Arrondissementsrechtbank (Dutch regional court) |
| Arb. | Arbitration; arbitral award / decision |
| Arb. Int'l | Arbitration International |
| art. | Article(s) |
| AS | Amtliche Sammlung (Swiss official legislation reporter) |
| ASA Bull. | Bulletin de l'Association Suisse de l'Arbitrage |
| ATF | Arrêts du Tribunal Féderal / Entscheidungen des Bundesgerichts (official reporter of the →BG) |
| AUT | Austria |
| Az. | Aktenzeichen (German for case →no.) |
| b2b | Business-to-Business |
| BE | Belgium |
| BeckRS | Beck-Rechtsprechung (German electronic case reporter at the fee based database http://beck-online.beck.de) |
| BG | Bundesgericht / Tribunal Fédéral (Swiss Federal Supreme Court) |
| BGB | Bürgerliches Gesetzbuch (German civil code) |
| BGBl. | Bundesgesetzblatt (German Federal Law Gazette) |
| BGH | Bundesgerichtshof (German Federal Supreme Court) |
| BöhmsZ | Zeitschrift für internationales Privat- und Strafrecht (founded by Böhm) |
| Buff. L. Rev. | Buffalo Law Review |
| Bull. | Bulletin (de la Cour de Cassation) (Bulletin of the →C.Cass.) |
| BV | Besloten Vennootschap (Dutch limited liability company) |
| C.Cass. | Cour de cassation (French Supreme Court) |

| | |
|---|---|
| C.Civ. | Code civil (French civil code) |
| C.H. | Confoederatio Helvetica / Switzerland |
| C.L.C. | Civil Law Cases |
| CA | Court of Appeals / Cour d'appel (appellate court, various jurisdictions) |
| Can. | Canada |
| CCI | Chambre de Commerce Internationale →ICC |
| CCIG | Chamber of Commerce and Industry of Geneva |
| CCIR | (Court of International Commercial Arbitration attached to the) Chamber of Commerce and Industry of Romania |
| CE | Conseil d'Etat (highest French administrative court) |
| CETA | Comprehensive Economic and Trade Agreement / Canada - EU Trade Agreement |
| Ch. | Court of Chancery (former court of equity of →EW) / Chancery Division (branch of the →EWHC); if used in titles of French publications also: chambre (French for: chamber) |
| ch. | Chapter |
| CIETAC | China International Economic and Trade Arbitration Commission |
| Civ. | Civil (division/chamber) |
| CJ | Code judiciaire |
| Colum. L. Rev. | Columbia Law Review |
| Comm. | Commercial (division/chamber) / (chambre) commerciale |
| CPC (FR) | Code de Procedure Civile (French Code of Civil Procedure) |
| CPC (RO) | Cod de procedură civilă (Romanian Code of Civil Procedure) |
| CPI (FR) | Code de la Proprieté Intellectuelle (French Code of Intellectual Property) |
| Ct. App. | Court of Appeals (appellate court) |
| DAS | Deutscher Ausschuss für Schiedsgerichtswesen (German Arbitration Committee; predecessor of the → DIS) |
| DCFR | Draft Common Frame of Reference |
| DDR | Deutsche Demokratische Republik → GDR |
| DIFC | Dubai International Financial Centre |
| DIN | Deutsches Institut für Normung (German Institute for Standardisation) |
| DIS | Deutsche Institution für Schiedsgerichtsbarkeit (German Arbitration Institute) |
| doc. | document(s) |
| DtZ | Deutsch-Deutsche Rechtszeitschrift (German law journal) |
| e.g. | for example |
| e.V. | eingetragener Verein (German registered association) |

| | |
|---|---|
| EC | EU, Council |
| ECHR | European Convention on Human Rights |
| ECJ | European Court of Justice |
| ECOSOC | United Nations Economic and Social Council |
| ed(s). | editor(s) |
| ed. | Edition |
| EGBGB | Einführungsgesetz zum (Introductory Act to the) →BGB |
| EGGVG | Einführungsgesetz zum Gerichtsverfassungsgesetz (Introductory Act to the German Law of the Organisation of the Judiciary) |
| ELR | Entertainment Law Review |
| Em. J. Int'l Disp. Res. | Emory Journal of International Dispute Resolution |
| ES | España / Spain |
| EU | European Union |
| Eur. Ct. HR | European Court of Human Rights |
| EW | England and Wales |
| EWCA | →EW Court of Appeals |
| EWHC | →EW High Court |
| EWPCC | →EW Patents County Court |
| F. App'x | Federal Appendix |
| F. Supp. | Federal Supplement |
| F.2d | Federal Reporter Second |
| F.3d | Federal Reporter Third |
| FAA | Federal Arbitration Act |
| Far East. Econ. Rev. | Far Eastern Economic Review |
| FETAC | Foreign Economic and Trade Arbitration Commission (predecessor of →CIETAC) |
| FIDIC | Fédération Internationale des Ingénieurs Conseils / International Federation of Consulting Engineers |
| FR | France |
| FTAC | Foreign Trade Arbitration Commission (predecessor of →FETAC and →CIETAC) |
| GDR | German Democratic Republic →DDR |
| Gen. Ass. Res. | General Assembly Resolution |
| GER | Germany |
| GRUR | Gewerblicher Rechtschutz und Urheberrecht |
| GRUR Int. | Gewerblicher Rechtschutz und Urheberrecht - Internationaler Teil |
| H.S.G. | Handelsrechtliche Schiedsgerichts-Praxis (German reporter for commercial arbitral awards→RKS) |
| Harv. L. Rev. | Harvard Law Review |

| | |
|---|---|
| HCCI | Hungarian Chamber of Commerce and Industry |
| HKIAC | Hong Kong International Arbitration Centre |
| HL | House of Lords |
| Hz. | Hangzhou, China |
| i.e. | id est (that is / that means) |
| I.L.M. | International Law Materials |
| IAA | International Arbitration Act |
| IACHR | Inter-American Convention on Human Rights |
| IBA | International Bar Association |
| ibid. | Ibidem (at the same place) |
| ICAC | International Court of Arbitration attached to the Chamber of Commerce and Industry of the Russian Federation |
| ICAI | International Federation of Commercial Arbitration Institutions |
| ICC | International Chamber of Commerce |
| ICC Bull. | Bulletin of the →ICC Court |
| ICC Court | International Court of Arbitration of the →ICC |
| ICCA | International Council for Commercial Arbitration |
| ICCPR | International Covenant on Civil and Political Rights |
| ICDR | International Centre for Dispute Resolution |
| ICSID | International Centre for the Settlement of Investment Disputes |
| idem | the same / by the same author |
| IHK | Industrie- und Handelskammer (German regional chamber of commerce and industry) |
| ILA | International Law Association |
| IN | India |
| Int'l Arb. L. Rev. | International Arbitration Law Review |
| IP | Intellectual and/or industrial property |
| IPC | Intermediate People's Court |
| IPRax | Praxis der Internationalen Privat und Verfahrensrechts |
| IPRG (C.H.) | Bundesgesetz über das internationale Privatrecht / Loi féderale sur le droit international privé (Swiss Act on Private International Law) |
| ITA | Institute for Transnational Arbitration |
| J. Int'l Arb. | Journal of International Arbitration |
| J. L. Econ. & Pol. | Journal of Law, Economics & Policy |
| J.D.I. | Journal du Droit International (Clunet) |
| JAC | Jerusalem Arbitration Centre |
| JIPL | Journal of Intellectual Property Law |

| | |
|---|---|
| JORF | Journal officiel de la République Française |
| juris | German fee based electronic database available at www.juris.de/jportal/index.jsp |
| JZ | Juristenzeitung |
| KG (C.H.) | Kantonsgericht (Cantonal court) |
| KG (GER) | Kammergericht (Higher regional court, Berlin) |
| L. & Soc. Rev. | Law & Society Review |
| LCIA | London Court of International Arbitration |
| LEXIS | Online law database of the company LexisNexis |
| LG | Landgericht (Germal regional court) |
| LJ | Lord Justice |
| LLC | Limited Liability Company |
| Lloyd's Rep. | Lloyd's Law Reports |
| LLP | Limited Liability Partnership |
| LMCLQ | Lloyd's Maritime and Comparative Law Quarterly |
| LMK | Kommentierte BGH-Rechtsprechung Lindenmaier-Möhring / Beck Fachdienst Zivilrecht LMK (German case reporter) |
| Lond. Rev. Int'l L. | London Review of International Law |
| LP | Limited Partnership |
| n. | note |
| n. d. | no date |
| N.Y. | New York |
| NAFTA | North Amercian Free Trade Agreement |
| NJOZ | Neue Juristische Online-Zeitschrift (German online law journal) |
| NJW | Neue Juristische Wochenzeitschrift (German law journal) |
| NJWE-WettbR | Neue Juristische Wochenzeitschrift - Entscheidungsdienst Wettbewerbsrecht (German online reporter of decisions on competition and unfair competition law) |
| no. | number |
| NV | Naamloze Vennootschap (Dutch stock corporation) |
| O.J. | Official Journal of the European Union |
| OGH | Oberster Gerichtshof (Austrian Supreme Court) |
| OLG | Oberlandesgericht (higher regional court in →GER or →AUT) |
| ONCA | Ontario Court of Appeal (Decisions) |
| p. / pp. | page / pages |
| P.R.C. | People's Republic of China |
| Pace L. Rev. | Pace Law Review |
| para. | paragraph(s) |

| | |
|---|---|
| PSI | Public Sector Information |
| pt. | part |
| QB | Queen's Bench (division) |
| R.P.C. | Reports of Patent Cases |
| RabelsZ | Rabels Zeitschrift für ausländisches und internationales Privatrecht - The Rabel Journal of Comparative and International Private Law |
| Rep. | Report(s) |
| Rev. | Review / Revue |
| Rev. Arb. | Revue de l'Arbitrage (French arbitration journal) |
| Rev. crit. DIP | Revue critique de droit international privé |
| Rev. Esp. Arb. | Revista de la Corte Española de Arbitraje |
| RG | Reichsgericht (Supreme Court of the German Reich) |
| RIDA | Revue Internationale du Droit d'Auteur |
| RIW | Recht der Internationalen Wirtschaft |
| RKS | Rechtsprechung Kaufmännischer Schiedsgerichte (German reporter for commercial arbitral awards →H.S.G.) |
| Rn. | Randnummer (German for numbered paragraph; →para.) |
| RO | Romania |
| S.Ct. | (Reporter of the) Supreme Court of the United States |
| S.D.N.Y. | Southern District of New York |
| SA | Société anonyme (French stock corporation) |
| SCC | Stockholm Chamber of Commerce |
| SCCAM | Swiss Chambers of Commerce Court of Arbitration and Mediation |
| SCCIETAC | South China International Economic and Trade Arbitration Commission, other name for →SCIA |
| SchiedsVZ | Zeitschrift für Schiedsverfahren (German arbitration journal) |
| SCIA | Shenzhen Court of International Arbitration |
| sent. | sentence |
| sess. | session |
| SG | Singapore |
| SGCA | Singapore Court of Appeals |
| SGHC | Singapore High Court |
| SHIAC | Shanghai International Arbitration Centre |
| SIAC | Singapore International Arbitration Centre |
| SIETAC | Shanghai International Economic and Trade Arbitration Commission, other name for →SHIAC |
| SLA | Softwood Lumber Agreement |
| SpA | Società per Azioni (Italian stock corporation) |

| | |
|---|---|
| SPC | Supreme People's Court |
| Stockh. Int'l Arb. Rev. | Stockholm International Arbitration Review |
| TCC | Technology and Construction Court (branch of the →EWHC) |
| TdC | Tribubal de Conflits (French court competent to solve conflicts of jurisdiction between administrative and ordinary courts) |
| Tenn. | Tennessee |
| TGI | Tribunal de Grande Instance (French court of first instance) |
| TRIPS | Agreement on Trade-Related Aspects of Intellectual Property Rights |
| U.S. | United States (Reports) |
| U.S. Dist LEXIS | Online reporter of →US district court cases maintained by →LEXIS |
| U.S.C. | United States Code |
| U.S.S.R. | Union of Soviet Socialist Republics |
| UAE | United Arab Emirates |
| UCP 500 | Uniform Customs and Practice for Documentary Credits, previous, 5th version (industry standards for letters of credit, adopted by the →ICC) |
| UK | United Kingdom |
| UNCITRAL YB | Yearbook of the United Nations Commission on International Trade Law (→UNCITRAL) |
| UNCTRAL | United Nations Commission on International Trade Law |
| UNSW L.J. | University of New South Wales Law Journal |
| UNTS | United Nations Treaty Series |
| URG (C.H.) | Urheberrechtsgesetz (Swiss law on author's and neigbouring rights) |
| UrhG (GER) | Urheberrechtsgesetz (German law on author's and neigbouring rights) |
| US | United States |
| UWG (GER) | Gesetz gegen den unlauteren Wettbewerb (German act against unfair competition) |
| v. | versus |
| V.U.W L. Rev. | Victoria University of Wellington Law Review |
| Vand. J. Trans'l L. | Vanderbilt Journal of Transnational Law |
| VFS | Vereinigung zur Förderung der Schiedsgerichtsbarkeit (German Association for the Promotion of Arbitration, predecessor of the → DIS) |
| Virg. L. Rev. | Virginia Law Review |
| W.D. Tenn. | Western District of Tennessee |
| WAMR | World Arbitration & Mediation Review |

| | |
|---|---|
| WIPO | World Intellectual Property Organization |
| WTO | World Trade Organization |
| YB | Yearbook |
| YB Arb. Med. | Yearbook on Arbitration and Mediation |
| YB ECHR | Yearbook of the European Commission of Human Rights |
| YCA | Yearbook of Commercial Arbitration |
| ZCC | Zurich Chamber of Commerce |
| ZIP | Zeitschrift für Wirtschaftsrecht und Insolvenzpraxis (German journal of business and insolvency law) |
| ZPO | Zivilprozessordnung (German Code of Civil Procedure) |
| ZZP | Zeitschrift für Zivilprozess (German journal of civil procedure) |

# Introduction

Worldwide, arbitration has become an established means to solve international commercial disputes.[1] Although it is difficult to quantify the significance of arbitration in comparison to state court litigation precisely,[2] there is agreement that arbitral tribunals decide a vast majority of international commercial disputes and that the impact of arbitration has grown in the process of globalisation.[3] It was even found that the cases published in official reports of the highest state courts become trivial and bourgeois in consequence of the development of arbitration.[4] In any case, commercial courts faced a sharp decline in case numbers in recent years while the business of international arbitration institutions keeps growing.[5] For the development of arbitration law and practice, arbitration institutions are key factors,[6] always striving to best serve parties' needs associated with the growing complexity and urgency of international business disputes.[7]

Confidentiality, international enforceability of the award,[8] the trust placed in the expert knowledge and neutrality of the selected arbitrators and

---

1   Blackaby et al., *Redfern and Hunter*, para. 1.01.
2   Arbitration awards are usually not published and proceedings often confidential. Consequence is a lack of statistical data (*see generally* Drahozal and Naimark, *Towards a Science of International Arbitration*; Coe, »From Anecdote to Data«; *see also* Hoffmann, *Kammern für internationale Handelssachen*, 32–39, summarising some statistical reports but regretting numbers to be not much more reliable than estimates; *see also* by the same author: »Schiedsgerichte als Gewinner der Globalisierung?«).
3   *E.g.* Schütze, *Institutionelle Schiedsgerichtsbarkeit: Kommentar*, V; Schwab, Walter, and Baumbach, *Schiedsgerichtsbarkeit*, 345–46.
4   Aden, *Internationale Handelsschiedsgerichtsbarkeit*, chap. 1, para. 7.
5   Hoffmann, *Kammern für internationale Handelssachen*, 39 (with further references).
6   *Cf.* Gottwald, *Internationale Schiedsgerichtsbarkeit*, 45, para. 24 (assuming that institutional arbitrations outweigh ad hoc arbitrations in number).
7   An aim, which motivates some institutions to frequently update their rules, which is why not all editorial changes to institutional rules made within the last year can be fully reflected herein (*see infra* at p. 50, n. 122).
8   Internationally, the widespread ratification of the New York Convention may make it easier to enforce a foreign arbitration award than a foreign state court judgment.

supposedly quick and possibly cost efficient proceedings[9] are some of the reasons named for the popularity of arbitration. Continued reluctance to allow another than a jurisdiction's official language in state court proceedings also contributes to the competitive advantage of arbitration.[10] A no less decisive factor is the liberty of the parties to structure and tailor the procedure followed in arbitration as they please.[11]

### §1 Problem identification and delimitation

When analysing extent and boundaries of the liberty to shape arbitral proceedings, it is crucial to differentiate between institutional and ad hoc arbitration. Ad hoc arbitral tribunals are constituted when a dispute arises. In principle,[12] they determine the procedure at their own discretion in cooperation with the parties. Equally, in institutional arbitration, the arbitral tribunal is usually set up only once a dispute has emerged. In addition, however, a permanent body exists - the institution - which assists the arbitration.[13] Such institutions commonly provide their own sets of pre-drafted rules for the constitution of the arbitral tribunal, the procedure and the rendering of the award.

This thesis intends to answer the question to what extent the choice of institutional arbitration in general and the choice of a specific arbitral institution in particular limits the parties' freedom to determine arbitral

---

9   Time and costs might be saved due to limited levels of review, but high fees for arbitrators and institutional fees make arbitration not usually the cheapest option (on this assumption, *see e.g.* Schwab, Walter, and Baumbach, *Schiedsgerichtsbarkeit*, 5, with further references).

10  *But see* Hau, »Fremdsprachengebrauch«, 58–60 (on a legislative project to introduce English as an optional language before German commercial courts).

11  Poudret and Besson, *Comparative Law of International Arbitration*, para. 522; Blackaby et al., *Redfern and Hunter*, para. 1.95; Lew, Mistelis, and Kröll, *Comparative International Commercial Arbitration*, para. 1.11, 1.16; Schwab, Walter, and Baumbach, *Schiedsgerichtsbarkeit*, 5.

12  Ad hoc arbitrations may also follow the UNCITRAL Rules (2010). The question whether ad hoc arbitration can follow institutional rules will be considered *infra* at pp. 151-156 (§7C.IV).

13  For elements relevant to define institutional arbitration, *see infra* at pp. 127-134 (§7A).

procedure. Is the choice of an arbitral institution decisive for the application of that institution's own rules or can parties opt out of these rules in favour of another institution's rules? If legally admissible and practically feasible, the question remains whether such a choice of rules different from those of the administering institution is recommendable in terms of costs, procedural efficiency and the recognition of the resulting award.

## A. The concept of hybrid arbitration clauses

Arbitration clauses which name one institution as administering[14] body and at the same time, distinct from usual practice, declare the arbitration rules of another institution applicable may be called hybrid arbitration clauses because they describe an arbitration procedure combining features of two different institutional systems.[15] A related problem, which shall be touched upon but not called hybrid arbitration for the purpose of this analysis, is whether ad hoc arbitration may be conducted pursuant to institutional rules.[16]

Hybrid arbitration clauses[17] are not entirely synonymous with so-called pathological arbitration clauses. Arbitration clauses that are pathological or defective/ambiguous/incomplete do not convey a clear agreement of the parties. In contrast, hybrid arbitration clauses are at the outset neither incomplete nor ambiguous. The parties' choice for arbitration and their specific choices of certain arbitration rules and an administering institution are clear. However, these choices collide with the rules and common practice

---

14  Herein, the terms »*administer*«, »*administering*«, »*administration*« are used in a merely descriptive sense, without prejudice to a possible qualification of some institutional actions as judicial, quasi-judicial, contractual or otherwise, *see infra* at pp. 435-438 (§16A.II.3.a) and pp. 444-447 (§16B.I).

15  On theslightly different use of the term by the Singapore courts, *see infra* at pp. 157-91 (§7D).

16  Herein referred to as »*wildcat arbitration*« (*see infra* at pp. 151-156 (§7C.IV).

17  Here not referring to the combination of elements of mediation and arbitration (»*med-arb-procedures*«), sometimes called »*hybrid*« (*see generally* Eidenmüller, »Hybride ADR-Verfahren«; *see also* Lögering, »VII. - Andere Verfahren: Schiedsgerichtsbarkeit«, para. 56) or clauses leaving a party the choice between arbitration and litigation that may also be called hybrid (*cf.* Draguiev, »Unilateral Jurisdiction Clauses«, 19, 20).

of the specified institution. As a hypothesis, such hybrid clauses are not incapable of being performed *per se*. Their operability depends decisively on the agreement of arbitrators and the chosen institution with the parties' choice. Therefore, it may be unjustified to label a hybrid arbitration clause as »*pathological*« if pathological is understood literally as meaning sick, defect, incurable.[18] Nevertheless, if the chosen arbitral institution refuses to administer the arbitration according to the parties' choice of another institution's rules, hybrid arbitration clauses can share the fate of pathological arbitration clauses. In this case, one may only try to save the arbitration agreement by supplemental interpretation, judicial contract adaptation or - which is preferable but unlikely after a dispute has arisen - by agreement of the parties to modify the clause. In any event, the label »*pathological*« shall not replace a thorough interpretation and analysis of the agreement concerned:

> »The concept of a pathological clause fulfils a descriptive function rather than a prescriptive function.«[19]

## B. Procedure shopping - Reasons for hybrid arbitration clauses

> »Flexibility can result in a multiplicity of procedures, rules, and institutions serving more to confuse the parties than to offer them a choice.«[20]

> »The wider the spectrum of choice available to the parties, the better able they are to shop for the arbitration process that most suits their needs.«[21]

A question worth asking is why parties would ever agree on hybrid arbitration clauses. The opinions quoted above indicate two possible causes which have to be kept strictly apart: confusion or conscious choice.

A motive for a conscious choice of hybrid arbitration is the attempt to combine the advantages of two different arbitration institutions and discard their disadvantages. Some arbitration rules, for example the arbitration rules of the ICC, are considered to be widely accepted, well-known and tested.[22]

---

18   Boo, »Arbitration«, 59.
19   *Insigma v. Alstom*, [2009] SGCA 24 [38].
20   Straus, »A Network of Arbitration Associations«, 487.
21   Trakman, »Arbitrating Options«, 293; *see also* Dezalay and Garth, »Merchants of Law as Moral Entrepreneurs«, 45 (observing an »*ability to forum shop - both in contractual negotiations and after disputes arise - among institutions, sets of rules, laws, and arbitrators*«).
22   *See* Stubbe and Hobeck, »Genese einer Schiedsklausel«, 17, n. 9 (recommending an ICC arbitration clause as internationally common standard).

However, tradition comes with a price tag: Arbitration administered by the International Court of Arbitration of the ICC (hereinafter »*ICC Court*«) is deemed to be rather expensive.[23] Hybrid arbitration clauses may be a way to choose a less-known institution in order for its more attractive schedule of fees to apply and to profit at the same time from the better-known and seemingly more reliable arbitration rules of a leading institution. Along this line, one hybrid arbitration clause providing that a smaller institution should administer the arbitration under the ICC Rules was judged as an »*effort to get the signature benefits of the ICC Rules without paying ICC prices.*«[24]

Another reason for such a choice may be that some institutions have a particularly good reputation in certain areas of the world only, like CIETAC in China or major Chambers of Commerce and Industry in their respective Eastern European home countries.[25] By agreeing to arbitrate before these institutions, a party from outside this area may want to ensure enforceability of the award by the courts and under the laws of that region, possibly deemed biased towards foreign institutions[26] or it may simply want to do the other contracting partner a favour. On the other hand, a businessperson from outside such region may be unfamiliar with these institutions' rules or little convinced by their effectiveness and quality.[27]

---

23   *Cf.* Queen Mary University of London, School of International Arbitration and White & Case, »Survey: Choices (2010)«, at 21. *See also infra* at p. 139 (§7B.III.1).

24   Kirby, »SIAC Can Administer Cases Under The ICC Rules?!?«, 325.

25   *See* Horvath, Konrad, and Power, *Costs in International Arbitration: A Central and Southern Eastern European Perspective*, 808 (Conclusion) (»*in every single CEE/SEE country a leading arbitral institution, which administers the majority of the arbitral proceedings and has extensive experience, can be found*«).

26   For example, there is a lot of uncertainty whether foreign arbitral institutions would qualify as »*arbitration commissions*« under Chinese law. Therefore CIETAC arbitration is often recommended as the safest option if the place of arbitration is in mainland China (Öhlberger, »What to Consider When Agreeing on CIETAC Arbitration«, 115).

27   Sometimes, reluctance to apply the institution's rules may be also be caused by incomprehensible drafting and/or translation (*see e.g.* CCIR Rules 2013 art. 1, 91 et seq., which appeared to simply repeat provisions of Romanian law or the European Arbitration Convention, thereby purporting to govern aspects which an institution should not be competent to regulate, like »*ad-hoc*« arbitration); clearer now: CCIR Rules, art. 82 (2014).

> »In a world sharply divided by many political, cultural and ideological differences, it is difficult for any one institution in one location to possess the universal acceptance of impartiality that is needed to serve all nations and all businessmen in this capacity.«[28]

Where such differences exist between two parties who nevertheless want to engage in common business activities and look for a suitable form of dispute resolution, an agreement on hybrid arbitration could at first glance seem like a viable compromise.[29]

Colloquially, one may refer to the motives behind the agreement of hybrid arbitration clauses as »*cherry picking*«, trying to get »*the best of both worlds.*« Legally this conduct may be qualified as »*procedure shopping*«, inspired by the term »*forum shopping*«. Forum shopping means to take advantage of the availability of several competing places of jurisdiction.[30] Forum shopping can be prepared by including choice of forum clauses in a contract. Often, a claimant also has a choice where to bring a case because several courts may be potentially competent according to competing conflict of laws rules in different jurisdictions. Tactical advantages may arise because there are no internationally uniform rules of private international law.[31]

Correspondingly, procedure shopping refers to taking advantage of the availability of several rules of procedure, more precisely of arbitral procedure. In contrast to forum shopping, relevant for the jurisdiction of both state courts and arbitral tribunals,[32] procedure shopping is primarily an issue in arbitration. Only in arbitration, the parties are largely free to determine the rules of procedure. In contrast, state courts follow mostly mandatory procedural law from which the parties cannot derogate.[33] Another

---

28  Straus, »A Network of Arbitration Associations«, 487.
29  Opting-out of the designated institution's rules in favour of UNCITRAL rules or other institutional rules appears to be relatively popular in contracts between parties from Socialist or former Socialist jurisdictions and Western parties (for contracts with Hungarian parties, *see e.g.* the remark by Eva Horvath reported by Labes, »Zusammenfassung der Podiumsdiskussion«, 573; for Chinese-Western contracts, *cf. also* Yuan, »Case study«, 3, available only in Chinese).
30  *See* Schack, *Internationales Zivilverfahrensrecht*, para. 251–52.
31  Gottwald and Nagel, *Internationales Zivilprozessrecht*, 32.
32  *See* Blackaby et al., *Redfern and Hunter*, para. 3.83, 11.30, 11.162; *see generally* Ferrari, *Forum Shopping in the International Commercial Arbitration Context*.
33  Rauscher, »ZPO, Einleitung«, para. 23.

difference is that procedure shopping in institutional arbitration is not unilateral conduct of one party but depends on an agreement of the parties. For this reason, some negative associations connected with the term forum shopping, *e.g.*, that it unilaterally favours the claimant party[34] or that the choice of a foreign place of jurisdiction may be abusive,[35] will not apply to the issue of procedure shopping.

Primarily, not be the respondent party should be interested to hinder such procedure shopping, but rather the arbitral institutions concerned: First, the administering institution has an interest in applying its own rules to the arbitration conducted under its auspices. This guarantees the quality of the procedure and the resulting award and thereby the institution's reputation. Furthermore, cost scales mirror the effort required to conduct arbitration under the institution's own rules, not the rules of another institution. Second, the institution which issued the rules may not appreciate another institution applying its rules without assurance that the administering institution has the necessarily organisational structure and experience to apply the rules as intended. In addition, a better-known and tested set of institutional arbitration rules is an important competitive advantage.[36] If parties can choose institutional rules without the issuing institution, this advantage decreases. Thus, it is predominantly in the interest of the institutions to oppose hybrid arbitration agreements and not in the interest of the parties. For this reason, it is questionable whether concepts to hinder forum shopping could also work to counter procedure shopping as here discussed.[37]

## C. The Insigma v. Alstom case

The leading case on the validity of hybrid arbitration clauses is the decision *Insigma Technology Co. Ltd. v. Alstom Technology Ltd.* of the Singapore

---

34  *See e.g.* Kropholler, »Anmerkung«, 905.

35  *But see* Schack, *Internationales Zivilverfahrensrecht*, 252 (criticising the demonisation of forum shopping, considering it to be legal and legitimate); *similarly* Gottwald and Nagel, *Internationales Zivilprozessrecht*, 166.

36  *Cf.* Queen Mary University of London, School of International Arbitration and White & Case, »Survey: Choices (2010)«, 22, chart 16 (available arbitration rules ranking third among the relevant criteria for choosing an arbitral institution).

37  *See e.g. infra* at pp. 434-435 (§16A.II.2.c) on anti-arbitration injunctions.

Court of Appeals of 2 June 2009 (hereinafter: »*Insigma v. Alstom*«).[38] Just as the Singapore High Court at first instance,[39] the Singapore Court of Appeals affirmed that an arbitration agreement is operative although the parties referred their dispute to one institution and at the same time chose another institution's rules to apply. In detail, the arbitration took place in Singapore under the auspices of the Singapore International Arbitration Centre (SIAC)[40] according to ICC Rules.[41]

The relevant part of the arbitration clause in dispute stated:

> »Any and all such disputes shall be finally resolved by arbitration *before the Singapore International Arbitration Centre in accordance with the Rules of Arbitration of the International Chamber of Commerce* then in effect and the proceedings shall take place in Singapore and the official language shall be English. The tribunal shall consist of three arbitrator(s) to be appointed in accordance with the Rules which are hereby incorporated by reference into this clause. The arbitration award shall be final and binding on both Parties. Both Parties shall perform the award accordingly [...] [*emphasis added*].«

This arbitration clause has been subject to a controversy between the ICC Court and SIAC: The ICC Court was of the opinion that no institution other than the ICC Court can apply the ICC Rules, as these refer to functions and actors specific to the ICC Court, with the consequence of the arbitration clause being inoperative.[42] SIAC nevertheless agreed to administer the arbitration according to the ICC Rules (1998) as best as possible. The functions of the Secretary General of the ICC Court and of the Court itself were carried out by the Registrar of SIAC and by its Board of Directors. The Singapore Court of Appeals, who finally dismissed a motion to annul the

---

38 *Insigma v. Alstom*, [2009] SGCA 24; for summaries of the decision, *see e.g.* Rana and Sanson, *International Commercial Arbitration*, 93–94, para. 4.40; Hwang, »Insigma Technology Co Ltd v. Alstom Technology Ltd, Court of Appeal, [2009] SGCA 24, 2 June 2009, *A Contribution by the ITA Board of Reporters*«. The arbitration proceedings preceding and continuing after this decision are herein also referred to as »*Alstom-Insigma*« arbitration.

39 *Insigma v. Alstom*, [2008] SGHC 134; *see also* Hwang, »Insigma Technology Co Ltd v. Alstom Technology Ltd, Singapore High Court, Originating Summons No 13 of 2008, 14 August 2008, *A Contribution by the ITA Board of Reporters*« (summary of the ruling).

40 *See* SIAC, »Website« (for additional information).

41 At the time referring to the ICC Rules (1998).

42 *Cf.* Kirby, »SIAC Can Administer Cases Under The ICC Rules?!?«, 326.

arbitral tribunal's ruling on jurisdiction, endorsed this practical approach.[43] However, a Chinese court later refused to recognise and enforce the awards rendered in this arbitration.[44]

## D. Other hybrid arbitration cases

*Insigma v. Alstom* is the most prominent case featuring a hybrid arbitration agreement but not a »one-off.«[45] A commentator remarked that

> »ICC officials have complained that the ›mixing and matching‹ scenario is something they have been faced with quite a bit.«[46]

In this context, a request for arbitration filed in 2012 with the ICC Court was based on an arbitration agreement that mentioned the ICC Rules but also referred to »*ad hoc*« arbitration. The ICC Court took the view that the clause was pathological but that the arbitration may still proceed.[47] It left it to the arbitral tribunal to decide on the validity and interpretation of the clause as an ICC arbitration agreement or an agreement on ad hoc arbitration.[48] Occasional inconsistencies between prospective arbitrators' acceptance statements[49] on the number of occasions they have acted as

---

43   *See Insigma v. Alstom*, [2009] SGCA 24 [35] (but confusingly referring to »*ad hoc*« arbitration with a »*substitute institution to administer the arbitration*« by carrying out the functions under the rules). *See infra* at pp. 157 (§7D) for a qualification of this hybrid arbitration as institutional and *infra* at pp. 344-400 (§14) on the substitution aspects.

44   *Alstom Technology v. Insigma Technology,* case no. 7 of 2011 [Chinese citation: (2011)浙杭仲确字第7号] (P.R.C. Hz. IPC, Zhejiang Province, 6 February, 2013) (hereinafter referred to as *Alstom v. Insigma [Hz. IPC]*). I thank Bianjingzi Lu, Di Wu and Christopher Bloch for their efforts to find the decision prior to its publication and to provide me with an English translation of the full judgment; now, an English summary is available at (2014) XXXIX ICCA Y.B. Comm. Arb. 380; herein the decision is summarised and discussed *infra* at pp. 480-487, §17C).

45   Kirby, »SIAC Can Administer Cases Under The ICC Rules?!?«, 325.

46   Mason, »Whether Arbitration Rules Should Be Applied by the Issuing Arbitral Institution«, 4 (full text currently unavailable; cited according to: Greenberg, Kee, and Weeramantry, *International Commercial Arbitration*, para. 4.176).

47   Pursuant to ICC Rules, art. 6 (4) (2012; 2017).

48   Unreported; soon after, the case was withdrawn, *see infra* at pp. 151-156.

49   ICC Rules, art. 11 (2) (2012; 2017).

arbitrator in »*ICC arbitration*« and the ICC Court's internal database have also raised speculation among ICC staff that such arbitrators might have added arbitrations under ICC Rules administered by other institutions or conducted ad hoc to the number indicated in their statement.

In 2013, the Singapore High Court referred to its previous jurisprudence in *Insigma v. Alstom* when deciding another case, upholding an arbitration agreement deemed pathological and suggesting that the parties should make the agreement workable by securing the acceptance of an Asian institution to administer hybrid arbitration under the ICC Rules.[50]

Recently, another case from Sweden transpired drawing back the arbitration community's interest[51] to the topic herein discussed: On 23 January 2015, the Svea Court of Appeal rejected to set aside an arbitral award rendered in 2013 in an arbitration conducted under the auspices of the Arbitration Institute of the Stockholm Chamber of Commerce (SCC) in application of ICC Rules.[52] The underlying contract referred in its Annex B in the form of a table to »*International Chamber of Commerce (ICC), Paris*« as »*Arbitration rules*« and to »*Chamber of Commerce and Industry, Stockholm, Sweden*« as »*Court of Arbitration.*«[53]

The Government of the Russian Federation had been respondent in the arbitration and had been ordered by the tribunal to pay a large sum of money to the claimant, a Moldovian company. The Government of the Russian Federation *inter alia*, argued before the Svea Court of Appeal that the arbitration clause was invalid, that the SCC lacked jurisdiction and that the SCC did not have the required organisational structure to administer proceedings under ICC Rules and failed to apply the ICC Rules as agreed between the parties correctly or in a satisfying manner - e.g. the Government of the Russian Federation complained that the SCC overlooked some calculation errors when scrutinising the award.[54] All of these objections were rejected and the award was upheld, relying on the principle of effective interpretation,

---

50  *HKL v. Rizq I*, [2013] SGHC 5; again justified in *HKL v. Rizq II*, [2013] SGHC 8; critical: Fry, »HKL v. Rizq«. *See infra* at pp. 174-177 (§8C.I.2) and pp. 433-434 (§16A.II.2.b).

51  *See e.g.* the discussion by Živković, »Hybrid Arbitration Clauses Tested Again.«

52  *Government of the Russian Federation v. I.M. Badprim S.R.L.*, T 2454-14 (Sweden Svea Ct. App., Stockholm, 23 January 2015) (reference is to the English translation published at http://www.arbitration.sccinstitute.com).

53  Ibid., 2.

54  *See* ibid., 7.

predominantly.[55] It is noteworthy that the SCC apparently, with its acceptance to administer the case, asked for the parties' agreement that it
would adapt the ICC Rules to fit its organisational structure.[56] Unfortunately, in its decision, the Svea Court of Appeal failed to address the consequence of the Government of the Russian Federation's failure to provide
the requested agreement with this approach. In fact, the most promising
challenge to the award,[57] arguing that by adapting the ICC Rules to the
SCC's structure, the SCC may have violated the parties' agreement on procedure, was rejected by the Svea Court of Appeal in one short sentence:

>»The arbitral tribunal cannot be deemed to have disregarded a joint instructions [sic]
>from the parties by adapting ICC's rules of arbitration to the organization of the
>SCC.«[58]

Although the brevity of the reasoning may be regretted, it shall be noted
with appreciation that the decision not only defends the attention given
herein to the topic of hybrid arbitration agreements in general but also this
thesis' main findings.[59]

E. Recent developments in institutional arbitration

Changes to rules of arbitral institutions made after *Insigma v. Alstom* also
underline the relevance and topicality of the issue of hybrid arbitration
clauses. The second sentence of article 1 (2) of the ICC Rules (2012), in
force as of 1 January 2012,[60] provides:

>»The Court is the *only body* authorised to administer arbitrations under the Rules,
>including the scrutiny and approval of awards rendered in accordance with the Rules
>[*emphasis added*].«

Article 6 (2) of the ICC Rules further stipulates:

---

55  Ibid., 13–14.
56  *Cf.* ibid., 7 (at least this is the way the Government of the Russian Feder-
    ation presents the procedural facts).
57  *See infra* at pp. 465-469 (§17A.II).
58  Ibid., 14.
59  As readdressed in the conclusion, *infra* at p. 495 (§19).
60  Unless otherwise indicated any reference to the ICC Rules refers to
    the 2012 version. Efforts have been made to indicate recent amendments
    made with the ICC Rules (2017), none of which are material to the issues
    herein discussed. Thereby = indicates the corresponding article in the 2017
    version.

»By agreeing to arbitration under the Rules, the parties have accepted that the arbitration shall be administered by the Court.«

The AAA-ICDR, followed the ICC's position and now provides in article 1 (3) sentence 4 of the latest version of its rules, in force since 1 June 2014:[61]

»Arbitrations administered under these Rules shall be administered *only* by the ICDR or by an individual or organisation authorised by the ICDR to do so [*emphasis added*].«

Conflictingly, since 1 May 2012, the arbitration rules of CIETAC,[62] stipulate in their article 4 (3):

»Where the parties agree to refer their dispute to CIETAC for arbitration but have agreed on a modification of these Rules or have agreed on the application of other arbitration rules, the parties' agreement shall prevail unless such agreement is inoperative or in conflict with a mandatory provision of the law as it applies to the arbitration proceedings. *Where the parties have agreed on the application of other arbitration rules, CIETAC shall perform the relevant administrative duties* [*emphasis added*].«

This provision still features in the CIETAC Rules 2015 that apply to arbitrations commenced after 1 January 2015.[63] While a similar provision was already part of the previous editions of the CIETAC Rules,[64] only the 2012 revision added the last sentence as clarification. Without mention of specific cases, it is reported that CIETAC has previously administered arbitrations under ICC Rules:[65]

»One leading institution has famously been telling people informally for a long time about its willingness to apply ICC rules (not something of which the ICC approves).«[66]

The diametrically opposed understandings of procedural party autonomy of the ICC Court and now also the AAA-ICDR on the one hand and CIETAC and SIAC on the other are a manifestation of the increasing competition

---

61    AAA-ICDR Rules (2014).
62    *See* CIETAC, »Website« (for further information).
63    *See* CIETAC Rules, art. 4 (3) (2015). *See infra* at n. 122, p. 50.
64    *See* (CIETAC Rules), art. 4 (2) (2005) (superseded); *cf.* Tao, *Arbitration Law and Practice in China*, 348.
65    Kniprath, »Neue Schiedsordnung der Chinese International Economic and Trade Arbitration Commission (CIETAC)«, 202 n. 60; *but see* D'Agostino, »Key Changes to the CIETAC Arbitration Rules« (assuming that this only meant administration by CIETAC under ad hoc rules). Unfortunately, cases are not publicly available.
66    Johnston, »Party Autonomy in Mainland Chinese Commercial Arbitration«, 553.

between well-established and smaller, emerging or mainly regionally operating arbitral institutions.[67] This demands an analysis of the background and
possible legal implications of exclusivity clauses on the one hand, like article 1 (2) of the ICC Rules in particular,[68] and clauses that explicitly allow
the application of another institution's rules on the other hand, *e.g.*[69] article 4 (3) of the CIETAC Rules (2012) and (2015).

Another development that brings the question of protection of arbitration
rules against competitive use by other institutions into focus is that
CIETAC's Shanghai and Shenzhen subcommissions separated from
CIETAC Beijing after a quarrel over the new CIETAC Rules and on administrative duties and privileges in May 2012. To CIETAC's discontent,
its most busy subcommissions announced the creation of new, independent
arbitration institutions now called Shanghai International Arbitration Centre (SHIAC)[70] and Shenzhen Court of International Arbitration (SCIA).[71]
The spin-offs continue to administer arbitrations under arbitration clauses
referring to CIETAC's former Shanghai and Shenzhen subcommissions, or
Shanghai and Shenzhen as places of arbitration, under both the CIETAC
Rules (2005) and under their own rules. SHIAC's and SCIA's Rules appear
to be largely inspired by the CIETAC Rules (2012), although both centres

---

67  Another regional arbitration institution, the Abu Dhabi Commercial Con-
    ciliation and Arbitration Center (ADCCAC), also follows a strategy to at-
    tract users by explicitly offering to administer arbitrations under different
    rules (*see* Blanke, »The New ADCCAC Arbitration Rules: Evolution or
    Revolution?«, referring to art. 2.2 of the ADCCAC's new rules in effect
    from Sept. 1, 2013, accepting this practice as »*not uncommon*« but seeing
    »*little sense*« in the supplementary application of the ADCCAC's rules).
68  Herein, ICC Rules, art. 1 (2) (2012; 2017) will be referred to as the prime
    example of an exclusivity provision in arbitration rules; however, the con-
    siderations apply to AAA-ICDR Rules, art. 1 (3) sent. 4 (2014) accord-
    ingly.
69  To the same effect but stressing the discretion of the institution and with
    legislative support (*see infra* at 98-101, §4C.II.2.b.ii; p. 106): CCIR Rules,
    art. 6 (2), 76 (2) (2014).
70  *See* Shanghai International Economic and Trade Arbitration Commission,
    »About Us« (but claiming to have been »*acting as an independent arbi-
    tration institute all along*«).
71  *See* South China International Economic and Trade Arbitration Commis-
    sion, »About Us«.

already revised its rules several times since the split to underline its autonomy from CIETAC.[72] In addition, the spin-offs declared that

> »if the parties agreed to apply the rules of other arbitration institutions, CIETAC Shanghai and CIETAC South China would recognise and respect their choice accordingly.«[73]

The controversy surrounding the CIETAC split raises the question if arbitral institutions could hinder their subcommissions or secretariat teams from engaging in competitive activities using the institution's rules, similar to commercial companies trying to protect themselves against future competition by partners or employees by way of contractual intellectual property and anti-competition provisions.[74]

Another notable development is the launch of new SIAC Rules on 1 April 2013.[75] With that version, SIAC introduced a completely new organisational structure, with a Court of Arbitration, composed of 16 »*leading arbitration practitioners*«[76] (hereinafter »*SIAC Court*«), somewhat resembling the ICC Court. The new names of actors within SIAC (*e.g.* »*Court*«, »*Committee of the Court*« and »*President*«) are now nearly identical to those within the ICC Court. Similar to the ICC Court, the SIAC Court now renders decisions on challenges to arbitrators[77] and on jurisdictional objections.[78] This shows that the ICC Court is a role model for other arbitral

---

72 *See* SHIAC Rules (2015) (current); *see also* SHIAC Rules (2014) (previous version); SHIAC Rules (2013) (again prior version); CIETAC Shanghai Rules (2012) (rules published before the renaming); *see also* SCIA Rules (2016) (current) and SCIA Rules (2012) (previous version).

73 CIETAC Shanghai Commission and CIETAC South China Commission, »Joint Statement«; *cf. also* SHIAC Rules, art. 2 (6) (2015); SHIAC Rules, art. 2 (5) (2014); SCIA Rules, art. 3 (3) sentence 2 (2012 and 2016) (but, cases where SHIAC and SCIA applied other than CIETAC's or their own rules are not yet reported).

74 While company and employment law issues thereby raised would surpass its scope, this thesis covers intellectual property and unfair competition law aspects of this question, *see infra* at pp. 272-344 (§13)

75 SIAC Rules (2013) (references to »*SIAC Rules*« without indicating a date are to this version, current at the time of writing). Efforts have been made to indicate further changes introduced with the SIAC Rules (2016).

76 »SIAC's New Governance Structure and Revised Rules of Arbitration«; *see also* Born, »New Rules at the Singapore International Arbitration Centre«.

77 SIAC Rules, art. 13 (2013) = art. 16 (2016).

78 Ibid., art. 25. *See infra* at pp. 392-394 (§14C.II.1).

institutions trying to stand up to the competition. Possibly, SIAC also tries to silence those criticising SIAC's administration of the arbitration in *Insigma v. Alstom* for lack of comparability between the ICC Court and SIAC.[79]

CIETAC followed suit and, with the 2015 edition of its rules, provides for an »*Arbitration Court*« to assume many functions. However, information on the structure and composition of this »*Court*« are not yet available. When comparing CIETAC Rules (2012) to CIETAC Rules (2015), the impression imposes itself that CIETAC's »*Secretariat*« was simply replaced by the term »*Arbitration Court*«, the Secretary General of CIETAC with »*President of the Arbitration Court.*« With some probability, CIETAC's new Arbitration Court may just the old secretariat with a more elaborate name. If this was the correct understanding, these revisions could indicate that CIETAC might have substituted the ICC Court simply with its secretariat when previously administering cases under ICC Rules.

## §2 State of discussion

Practitioners, including lawyers, arbitrators and employees of arbitral institutions, extensively discussed the problem of hybrid arbitration clauses following the Singapore courts' decisions in *Insigma v. Alstom*.[80] The issue was found to be »*novel and important.*«[81] Many welcomed the Singaporean rulings in favour of party autonomy.[82] Others approved in this particular

---

79   *E.g.* Kirby, »SIAC Can Administer Cases Under The ICC Rules?!?«, 327.

80   *See e.g.* Hill, »Hybrid ICC/SIAC Arbitration Clause Upheld in Singapore« (blog post); Kirby, »SIAC Can Administer Cases Under The ICC Rules?!?« (article by an ICC staff member); Ashurst LLP, »Singapore High Court Considers Use of Other Institutional Rules by SIAC« (post of law firm website).

81   Lau, »Singapore«, 698, para. 10.26.

82   *See* Lau and Horlach, »Party Autonomy«, 122 (stating that party autonomy covers hybrid arbitration clauses, if the right to fair hearing is not touched); *similarly* Lau, »Conference Report Madrid: Options for the Resolution of International Commercial Disputes, Including the Drafting of Dispute Resolution Clauses«, 13 (expressing that party autonomy should prevail »*as it is ›irresistible‹*«); *cf. also* Ashurst LLP, »Singapore High Court Considers Use of Other Institutional Rules by SIAC«.

case for reasons of waiver, bad faith or »*estoppel*«, but warned of considering these decisions as general »*precedent.*«[83]

Generally, practitioners consider hybrid arbitration clauses to be ill-ad-
vised. A court challenge of the resulting award would be more probable
than if a standard clause were used. Any expectancy to save costs could
therefore not be achieved.[84] It is largely undisputed that hybrid arbitration
agreements are not to be recommended.[85] Even the Singapore High Court
as a supporter of the validity and operability of such agreements admits:

> »In the ordinary course of things, hybrid arbitrations should be avoided. In fact, it
> is inconceivable that commercial parties with the benefit of legal advice will delib-
> erately choose to resolve disputes by way of a hybrid arbitration.«[86]

Several - ICC supportive - scholars and practitioners welcome the introduction of the exclusivity clause in article 1 (2) of the ICC Rules[87] as a clarification and some even consider it to be legally binding. For example, Barbara Helene Streindl[88] expresses the opinion that article 1 (2) of the ICC
Rules overrules any contrary agreement of the parties and asserts that administration by foreign arbitral institutions under ICC Rules is »*prohibited*«
and that the »*parties and other arbitration institutions*« have »*no say in*

---

83  Greenberg, Kee, and Weeramantry, *International Commercial Arbitra-
    tion*, para. 4.193, 4.195; *cf. also* Kirby, »SIAC Can Administer Cases Un-
    der The ICC Rules?!?«, 328. *See infra* at pp. 476-480 (§17B) on preclu-
    sion or waiver/estoppel issues.
84  *Cf.* Kirby, »SIAC Can Administer Cases Under The ICC Rules?!?«, 326;
    Hill, »Hybrid ICC/SIAC Arbitration Clause Upheld in Singapore«.
85  Kirby, »SIAC Can Administer Cases Under The ICC Rules?!?«, 326 (an-
    swering to the question if such a clause was advisable: »*That is easy: it is
    not*«). *See also infra* at pp. 145-146 (§7B.IV) and pp. 207-209 (§9).
86  *HKL v. Rizq II*, [2013] SGHC 8 [11]. For a discussion of this case, *see
    infra* at pp. 174-177.
87  A reaction to the case *Insigma v. Alstom*, [2009] SGCA 24; *see* Grierson
    and van Hooft, *Arbitrating under the 2012 ICC Rules*, 17 (on the history
    of the drafting of the 2012 ICC Rules). The similar clause in AAA-ICDR
    Rules, art. 1 (3) sent. 4 (2014) has not yet received any attention. It depicts
    the additional trait that the AAA-ICDR assumes a power to delegate ad-
    ministration services though cooperative agreements to other institutions,
    *see infra* at pp. 398-399 (§14C.IV) and pp. 495-513 (§20).
88  Barbara Helene Streindl was assistant counsel of the Secretariat of the ICC
    Court between 2001 and 2003 (BKP Rechtsanwälte, »Barbara Helene
    Steindl«).

*this.*«[89] However, she does not explain the legal basis for an authority of the ICC Court to bar other institutions from supporting and supervising arbitrations under the ICC Rules. Jakob Grierson and Annet van Hoft comment that parties ignoring article 1 (2) of the ICC Rules and agreeing on hybrid ICC arbitration »*may find that the resulting award is unenforceable.*«[90] Rolf Trittmann[91] deems even ad hoc arbitrations under ICC Rules to be excluded by article 1 (2) of the ICC Rules, or at least practically infeasible.[92] In relation to article 4 (3) of the CIETAC Rules, practicing lawyers also discourage parties to agree on CIETAC arbitration under another institution's rules. They fear potential conflict at least with ICC Rules.[93]

What all these comments have in common is that they lack reasoning to explain the supposedly binding nature of articles 1 (2) and 6 (2) of the ICC Rules. Only Jason Fry, former Secretary General of the ICC Court, acknowledges that »*it is hard to take issue*« with the argument that article 1 (2) of the ICC Rules »*cannot unilaterally restrict party autonomy*«, despite his initial warning about an »*already growing problem in Asia with so-called hybrid clauses.*«[94]

Apparently, the ICC Court intends neither to impose legal action upon other institutions applying ICC Rules nor to object to the enforcement of resulting awards for the time being.[95] Nonetheless, the enactments in articles 1 (2) and 6 (2) of the ICC Rules certainly have factually chilling effects. Whether SIAC would dare to administer another hybrid arbitration under

---

89  »Party Autonomy under the 2012 ICC Arbitration Rules«, 231.

90  *Arbitrating under the 2012 ICC Rules*, 17.

91  Currently, Rolf Trittmann is a member of the ICC Court (*cf.* International Chamber of Commerce, »List of Current Court Members«).

92  »Die wesentlichen Änderungen«, 48; *cf. also* Marenkov, »DIS-Herbsttagung ›Die neue ICC-Schiedsgerichtsordnung'*»* (reporting *Trittmann*'s comment); *similar*: Meeran, »The 2012 International Chamber of Commerce Rules of Arbitration«, 372 (»*making the ICC Rules ineffective in ad hoc arbitration*«).

93  *See* the client information of Herbert Smith Freehills LLP, »The New CIETAC Arbitration Rules: A Move towards Internationalisation?«

94  »HKL v. Rizq«, 460, 454.

95  *Cf.* Oon & Bazul LLP, »The New International Chamber of Commerce (›ICC') Rules 2012: Hybrid Arbitration Agreements & Emergency Arbitrator Provisions« (referring to a statement of John Beechey, President of the Court, and Jason Fry, at the time Secretary General of the Court).

ICC Rules is doubtful.[96] It will be explained whether such caution would be justified[97] and desirable.[98]

In contrast to the considerable discussion by practitioners, there is a lack of academic analysis of hybrid arbitration clauses. A reason may be the fluent transition from practitioner to academic in the field of arbitration, which leads to a number of publications that are - if not biased - superficial.[99] With a surprising lack of problem awareness, a certain guide to the SIAC Rules (2013), for example, simply advises that parties can provide for SIAC administered arbitration under another institution's rules if they do so expressly.[100] The authors, who are members of a London-based barrister chamber, mention neither the controversy surrounding the *Insigma v. Alstom* decision, nor the enforcement difficulties now faced by Alstom in China - let alone do they contemplate article 1 (2) of the ICC Rules. A publication on Singaporean jurisprudence in arbitration matters at least concludes its report on the *Insigma v. Alstom* decision with a short remark on article 1 (2) of the ICC Rules.[101] However, the author then refrains from further evaluation.[102] A German commentary on the ICC Rules mentions that the purpose of the exclusivity clause in article 1 (2) of the ICC Rules is to »*aim*« at clarity after the *Insigma v. Alstom* decision but it fails to elaborate further if such provision can achieve this aim.[103]

---

96  Izor, »Insigma Revisited«. In the *HKL v. Rizq* case, this issue became mute after the parties agreed on ordinary SIAC arbitration by way of novation, *see infra* at p. 433 (§16A.II.2.b).

97  *See in particular* the considerations on hybrid arbitration administration under the angle of intellectual property and unfair competition law, *infra* at pp. 272-344 (§13).

98  On the desirability of exclusivity of institutional rules, s*ee infra* at pp. 340-344 (§13D); on hybrid arbitration from a practical, institutional point of view, *see infra* at pp. 400 et seq. (§15).

99  Ginsburg, »The Culture of Arbitration«, 1340; Michaels, »Rollen und Rollenverständnisse im Transnationalen Privatrecht«, 19 (very critical on attempts of arbitrators to underline their elite status through publications); *but see* Dezalay and Garth, »Merchants of Law as Moral Entrepreneurs«, 43 (from a more economic perspective, seeing advantages in the mingling of arbitration scholarship and practice).

100 Brick Court Chambers, *SIAC Rules*, para. 1.2.

101 Sun, *Singapore Law on Arbitral Awards*, 20.

102 *See* Foxton, »Book Review on Singapore Law on Arbitral Awards by Chan Leng Sun«, 11 (also remarking this shortcoming).

103 Nedden and Herzberg, »Art. 1 ICC SchO«, para. 16.

Up to now, a monographic thesis has not been published on the subject. The most comprehensive and well reasoned analysis is provided in an article by Anthony Nicholls and Christopher Bloch, two Singapore based lawyers.[104] After presenting the *Insigma v. Alstom* case, including the ruling of the Singapore Court of Appeals[105] and the subsequent enforcement history in China,[106] they refer to the changes in articles 1 (2) and 1 (6) of the ICC Rules and the Singapore High Court's continued pro-hybrid arbitration jurisprudence in the decisions *HKL v. Rizq I*[107] and *II*.[108] Although - rightly - criticising the latter rulings as unnecessary applications of the hybrid arbitration idea,[109] they generally conclude that

> »[T]he ICC's administration cannot be forced upon parties to an arbitration if they choose to opt out. While the ICC does not believe that the ICC Rules 2012 are suitable for ad hoc or hybrid arbitrations [...] the ICC's position on the suitability of its Rules cannot be forced upon parties who have a right to develop their own procedures, including a procedure that is largely based on the existing ICC Rules 2012.«[110]

To a degree, hybrid arbitration agreements can be viewed as an extreme case of derogating from institutional arbitration rules through express party agreement.[111] However, even this broader subject of modifications to institutional arbitration rules has not yet attracted much scholarly interest. Legal literature contents itself with some warnings addressed to practitioners,[112] but academic writing appears to overlook the subject. In Germany, only Helmut Rüßmann recently started an analysis of the relationship between party agreements and institutional arbitration rules in a jubilee publication

---

104 »ICC Hybrid Arbitrations Here to Stay«.

105 *Insigma v. Alstom*, [2009] SGCA 24.

106 Referring to *Alstom v. Insigma (Hz. IPC)*. This decision is also subject to a short note by Liu and Cheng, »Enforcement of Foreign Awards in Mainland China«, 660. For a detailed discussion, *see infra* at pp. 480-487 (§17C).

107 *HKL v. Rizq I*, [2013] SGHC 5.

108 *HKL v. Rizq II*, [2013] SGHC 8.

109 *See infra* at pp. 175-177 (§8C.I.2.b)

110 Nicholls and Bloch, »ICC Hybrid Arbitrations Here to Stay«, 402.

111 *See* Chapter 3 for this opting-out aspect, *infra* at pp. 209 et seq.; *but see also* Chapter 4 for the additional opting-in aspect of hybrid arbitration agreements, *infra* at pp. 271 et seq.

112 *E.g.* Paulsson, Rawding, and Reed, *The Freshfields Guide to Arbitration and ADR*, 58.

for Rolf Stürner,[113] regretting that even a collection with the promising title »*Mandatory Rules in International Arbitration*« published in 2011[114] did not consider this issue.[115]

Whether hybrid arbitration agreements are capable of being performed also relates to the concept of institutional arbitration in general and its relationship to party autonomy. Yet again, despite the growing importance of institutional arbitration and the increase in number and variations of arbitral institutions, there is hardly any literature in this area going beyond practice guides to institutional rules. One more comprehensive but highly controversial analysis of ICC arbitration was attempted by Anthoine Kassis[116] and a more general dogmatic study of institutional arbitration was provided by Christian Wolf.[117] However, not only that these publications are already quite dated, they also do not sufficiently reflect the varieties of arbitration institutions and institutional activity existing in practice.[118]

*§3 Structure and research approach*

Due to the scarcity of previous scholarly analysis, this thesis can and will not follow a standard approach of describing and evaluating various existing opinions. Rather, it is necessary to first identify different problems of hybrid arbitration agreements by taking into account the main principles underlying institutional international commercial arbitration.

---

113 Rüßmann, »Zwingendes Recht in den Schiedsregeln einer Schiedsinstitution?«

114 Bermann and Mistelis, *Mandatory Rules in International Arbitration.*

115 Rüßmann, »Zwingendes Recht in den Schiedsregeln einer Schiedsinstitution?«, 481.

116 Kassis, *Réflexions*; summarised in English as: »The Questionable Validity of Arbitration and Awards under the Rules of the International Chamber of Commerce«.

117 Wolf, *Die Institutionelle Handelsschiedsgerichtsbarkeit.*

118 A shortcoming that a recent thesis by Rémy Gerbay on the »Functions of Arbitral Institutions« submitted at the School of International Arbitration, Queen Mary, University of London intends to cure. I am indebted to Rémy Gerbay for providing me with a copy of his submission prior to publication and for his valuable advice during my research visit to Queen Mary School of Law in September/October 2014. His thesis is now available for download at https://qmro.qmul.ac.uk/xmlui/handle/123456789/8143.

Starting point is the principle of party autonomy. Chapter 1 recalls content and limits of this principle in order to evaluate the phenomenon of hybrid arbitration from a normative perspective. Thereby, it also presents the legal framework of international commercial arbitration as the basis of the further analysis of hybrid arbitration agreements.

Chapter 2 then takes a closer look at the concept of institutional arbitration in comparison with ad hoc arbitration and various intermediate forms in order to qualify hybrid arbitration within these categories, reflecting common expectations associated with institutional arbitration. It further discusses common defects to which institutional arbitration agreements are prone, comparing hybrid arbitration agreements with arbitration agreements qualified as »*pathological*« by doctrine or jurisprudence. Thereby, Chapter 2 provides an overview of relevant cases other than the *Insigma v. Alstom* case. The purpose is twofold: First, the label »*pathological*« for hybrid arbitration agreements shall be justified or refuted. Second, ways to save pathological agreements are assessed, formulating expectations for an analogous treatment of hybrid arbitration agreements.

This analysis of institutional arbitration is supplemented in Chapter 3 with an enquiry into the practice of arbitration institutions faced with parties' attempts to modify the institutional rules or to opt out of them completely. Arbitration rules deemed essential (or »*mandatory*«) by leading institutions are identified. In addition, Chapter 3 analyses the right of arbitration institutions to refuse administering cases under modified rules on the basis of contract law. The assumption underlying this examination is that the operability of hybrid arbitration agreements largely depends on the flexibility of the administering institution.

A further focus lies on answering the question whether arbitral institutions are at all capable to meet the parties' expectations to administer arbitrations under another institution's rules. For this purpose, Chapter 4 discusses the legality of administering hybrid arbitration in view of intellectual property or unfair competition law concerns. This is followed by considerations on the practical feasibility of administering arbitrations pursuant to other rules, comparing special features of important arbitration rules, the organisational structures and human and other resources of different arbitral institutions. If an arbitral institution entrusts a task under its rules to a certain body, the expertise, internal democratic legitimisation and number of personnel of that body will be of relevance. Substituting this body with another body of another institution may be problematic.[119]

To limit its scope, the analysis in this thesis has to be restricted to some important institutions and their rules.[120] This includes the ICC Court and the ICC Rules and SIAC and its rules,[121] guided by the *Insigma v. Alstom* case. Further, a portray of the CIETAC Rules[122] including an explanation of corresponding aspects of Chinese arbitration law reacts to the addressed particularity in article 4 (3) of these rules.[123]

The comparison further includes the rules of the London Court of International Arbitration (LCIA)[124] and of the AAA-ICDR[125] owed to the relative importance of these institutions,[126] and of the German Arbitration

---

119 *Cf.* Kirby, »SIAC Can Administer Cases Under The ICC Rules?!?«, 327 (criticising the decision Insigma v. Alstom in this respect). Part of the analysis herein is guided by the criteria for substitution in private international law, *see infra* at pp. 344-355 (§14A).

120 Other institutions are occasionally referred to, where helpful for the discourse, but not systematically analysed. Moreover, the analysis is restricted to the main set of international rules of each institution as currently in force, unless otherwise indicated, without taking into account specialist rules on fast-track or expedited proceedings or for certain types of disputes that institutions have developed as alternatives to their general rules.

121 Generally, references are to SIAC Rules (2013) and SIAC Rules (2016), thereby = indicating the corresponding article in the 2016 version. Consistent with citations of other arbitration rules, references herein are made to article(s) (»*art.*«) of the SIAC Rules although SIAC itself proposes the locator »*Rule.*«

122 Most citations are to CIETAC Rules (2012) and CIETAC Rules (2015). All relevant material changes and CIETAC's new structure under CIETAC Rules (2015) and some editorial amendments are reflected; thereby = indicates the corresponding article in the 2015 version.

123 Quoted *supra* at p. 157.

124 LCIA Rules (2014); were appropriate, references are also made to the previous version: LCIA Rules (1998).

125 Again, as recently revised: AAA-ICDR Rules (2014); some references are to the previous version: AAA-ICDR Rules (2009).

126 LCIA places 2nd of the preferred and 3rd of the most used arbitral institutions, AAA ranges 3rd of the preferred and 3rd of the most used institutions (according to Queen Mary University of London, School of International Arbitration and White & Case, »Survey: Choices (2010)«, 23, charts 17, 18 [without differentiation between ICDR and other AAA-cases]).

Institution (*Deutsche Institution für Schiedsgerichtsbarkeit*) (DIS),[127] as this is the most prominent institution in Germany as the author's home jurisdiction. Moreover, tribute is paid to Switzerland's long tradition as an arbitration-friendly jurisdiction by also referring to the arbitration rules of the Swiss Chambers' Arbitration Institution,[128] which is comprised of the Chambers of Commerce and Industry of Basel, Bern, Geneva, Lausanne, Lugano, Neuchâtel and Zurich. The Swiss Rules are remarkable[129] because they are a result of a successful project to harmonise the arbitration rules of several cantonal Chambers of Commerce, which shows - at least on an inter-regional level - that cooperation may be a possible way to counter increasing conflicts and competition between different arbitral institutions.[130] Under the newest version of the Swiss Rules, administration services are no longer provided by the separate cantonal Chambers of Commerce but by a centralised institution called the Swiss Chambers Arbitration Institution, comprising the »*Arbitration Court*« and decentralised secretariats in each Canton.[131]

Chapter 5 finally draws procedural consequences from the prior analysis by evaluating the chances for enforcing or challenging hybrid arbitration agreements and resulting awards. The appropriateness of the current system of state court involvement in matters concerning institutional arbitration is reflected, including considerations on direct and indirect review of competences and decisions of arbitral institutions by supporting and controlling state courts. An overview of probable grounds to challenge hybrid arbitration awards is then completed with a detailed account of the Hangzhou Intermediate People's Court's refusal to enforce the *Alstom–Insigma* awards.[132]

---

127  All references are made to article(s) (»*art.*«) of the DIS Rules (1998) although the DIS itself uses a different locators for its provisions in various language versions of its rules (*e.g.* »*§*« for the German version, »*Section*« for the English version, »*Art.*« for the French version). The DIS intends to launch new rules in 2018.

128  Swiss Rules (2012); for illustrative purposes, occasional references are made to the previous version: Swiss Rules (2004).

129  *See* Oetiker and Burkhaler, »SCCAM,« 235 (»*unique in a Western European country*«).

130  For a general conclusion along this line, *see infra* at pp. 495-513 (§20).

131  *See* Swiss Chambers' Arbitration Institution, »Organisation«.

132  *Alstom v. Insigma (Hz. IPC)*; *see infra* at pp. 480-487 (§17C).

While the analysis is naturally written from the point of view of a legal scholar trained in Germany,[133] the aim is to cater to an international readership. For this reason, the thesis constantly refers to primary and secondary sources from different jurisdictions, understanding those as transnational »*persuasive authority*«[134] without following a classic comparative approach.[135] This means that the choice of jurisdictions covered is not standardised throughout the thesis but motivated for each singular issue by the following considerations:

- uniformity or harmonisation
- significance and comparability
- solution-orientation.

Based on criteria of uniformity or harmonisation, legal issues will be primarily discussed in relation to internationally or interregionally harmonised treaties or other enactments, including European Union (hereinafter »*EU*«) regulations and directives. Even where a particular instrument of harmonisation does not apply geographically, like in non-EU member states for EU directives and regulations, it is believed that these enactments can nevertheless provide guidance because they prove a broad consensus of several jurisdictions. At least, they may serve as a model for future law making. The same applies to the UNCITRAL Model Law on International Commercial Arbitration, which shall be the primary resource to illustrate statutory coverage of relevant arbitral issues.

If there is no or not sufficient uniform regulation to answer a given question, the thesis refers to national laws in view of their practical significance and comparability. Next to references to German law, which is not only of personal significance to the author but also a good example of an

---

133 Not presuming to yet meet the »*ideal*« of a comparatist without a national legal background (despite having participated in the valuable study program of transnational law at Geneva University recommended to that effect by Kadner Graziano, »L'européanisation du droit privé«, 323–24, n. 25).

134 Schlosser, *Das Recht der internationalen privaten Schiedsgerichtsbarkeit*, III.

135 Sharing the view of Schlosser, »Comparative International Commercial Arbitration (Book Review)«, 279 (rejecting the label »*comparative*« as unsuitable and out-of-date for modern legal studies not limited to one legal order); *reviewing*: Lew, Mistelis, and Kröll, *Comparative International Commercial Arbitration*.

UNCITRAL Model Law adaptation, effort is made to also cover positions under the laws of the United States (hereinafter »*US*«)[136] and England,[137] France and Switzerland as important places of arbitration. Not yet completely discarding the traditional idea of grouping jurisdictions in families of law,[138] English and/or US law may also be persuasive for other jurisdictions following a common law tradition, like Singapore, India, Australia and New Zealand and - to some extent - Canada,[139] whereas France, Germany and Switzerland exemplify civil law jurisdictions of the Roman, Germanic or Roman-Germanic tradition.[140] Unfortunately,[141] exhaustive considerations on legal orders with a socialist tradition would surpass the scope of this thesis. Nonetheless, occasional references concerning their specific arbitration traditions,[142] like mandatory arbitrator lists or state created, authorised (and possibly controlled)[143] arbitration institutions or »*commissions*«, shall provoke scholars more familiar with these legal orders to strengthen or refute the arguments made herein from their points of view. Due to the language barrier, attempts to cover aspects of the Chinese legal

---

136  With a focus on federal law but referring to state laws and court rulings occasionally.

137  In general, English law also applies in Wales, whereas Scotland and Northern Ireland are separate jurisdictions.

138  *See* Kadner Graziano, »L'européanisation du droit privé«, 320–21 (finding such grouping to be efficient at the outset).

139  Canada is often described as having a mixed civil-common law system, which further varies among states.

140  Kadner Graziano, »L'européanisation du droit privé«, 320 (with further references).

141  *Cf. also* ibid., 321 (hoping that legal systems with a socialist tradition are not left out of comparative exercises and harmonising projects).

142  On Chinese law, *see e.g. infra* at pp. 101-104 (§4C.II.2.b.iii); *see also* Fan, *Arbitration in China*, 115 (on the sophistication of the Chinese arbitration system away from the U.S.S.R. model of administrative arbitration and towards transnational standards). On aspects of Romania's modernised arbitration law, *see infra* at pp. 98-101 (§4C.II.2.b.ii); on the CCIR's arbitration practice, *see infra* at pp. 104-106 (§4C.II.2.c).

143  *But see* Arbitration Law art. 14 (P.R.C.): »*Arbitration commissions shall be independent from administrative authorities and there shall be no subordinate relationships between arbitration commissions and administrative authorities. There shall also be no subordinate relationship between arbitration commissions*«.

system[144] in this thesis are largely restricted to secondary materials and translations of legal provisions. Admittedly, such methodology cannot sufficiently account for possible divergences between the law as written and the law as it is actually applied,[145] but it may still provide a good starting point for future research.

The third guideline of solution-orientation has two dimensions: case-orientation and rule-orientation. Case-orientation means that it may be necessary to refer to certain legal orders, like Singapore and China, simply because the known cases of hybrid arbitrations transpired in these legal orders. In contrast, rule-orientation calls to refer to legislation or case law of jurisdictions that, although they may lack practical significance, stipulate a legal rule to apply to a certain problem posed. For this reason, the thesis for example discusses aspects of Romanian arbitration law, which, contrary to major arbitration laws, contains detailed provisions on institutional arbitration and the applicable institutional rules.[146] Such consideration of statutory stipulations only available in a few jurisdictions also serves as a corrective to the traditional approach of looking at representatives of families of law.[147] On the other hand, rule orientation also implies that even a significant arbitration jurisdiction will have to be treated step-motherly if its law does not contain a specific rule for a certain matter.[148]

While relevant rules on the conflict of laws are outlined,[149] the analysis tries, wherever possible, to identify principles common to most jurisdictions

---

144 Which is not only influenced by socialist beliefs but also by a historic emphasis on social habits and a culture of conciliation as opposed to a strict rule of positive law enforced by courts (*cf.* Zweigert and Kötz, *An Introduction to Comparative Law*, 286–88, taking leave from their previous categorisation of Chinese law into a »*Far Eastern legal family*«, admitting such construction to inappropriately neglect the tremendous differences among Chinese, Japanese and South East Asian legal systems).

145 *See* Bohnet, *Markenrecht in China und Russland*, VII (preface).

146 *See infra* at pp. 98-101 (§4C.II.2.b.ii).

147 Which is to some extent outdated, in particular when the aim is to further harmonise the law; regrouping by solutions may be more appropriate (Kadner Graziano, »L'européanisation du droit privé«, 321–23).

148 *See also* ibid., 332 (proposing to discard all legal orders not offering a precise solution to a problem). *See e.g. infra* at pp. 327-329 (§13C.III.3) on the lack of a specific law on unfair competition in England.

149 *See infra* at pp. 68-68) on the determination of the law of arbitration, pp. 75-86 (§4B.II) on laws applicable to the validity and operability of the arbitration agreement; pp. 236-243 (§11A.II) on the law applicable to the

in order to answer the research questions in a way that is appropriate no matter what the applicable law. This approach shall not negate the existing differences among legal systems.

> »If, however, a decision is given in [one] country which offends one's basic sense of justice, and if consideration of international sources suggests that a different and more acceptable decision would be given in most other jurisdictions, whatever their legal tradition, this must prompt anxious review of the decision in question. In a shrinking world [...] there must be some virtue in uniformity of outcome whatever the diversity of approach in reaching that outcome.«[150]

---

contract with the institution and pp. 297-304 (§13A.III) and pp. 333-340 (§13C.IV) for reflections on jurisdiction and applicable law for intellectual property and unfair competition aspects.

150 *Lord Bingham* in *Fairchild v. Glenhaven*, [2002] HL 22 (UK) [32].

# Chapter 1: Party autonomy and the legislative framework

»Quinimmo jus est in tacita et verisimili mente contrahentium.«[1]

Indeed, the law lies in the implied and probable will of the parties. The French legal scholar Charles Dumoulin (Latin name: Carolus Molineaus) employed this formulation in his 16th century treatise on the conflict of laws, claiming that the parties' (probable) will shall prevail with regard to the law applicable to a contact.

Party autonomy is also the first argument that springs to mind when discussing hybrid arbitration agreements: If parties are free to choose a *state's law* to apply to their contract, they should all the more be free to choose *rules* drafted by a *private* body, an arbitration institution, to apply to a contractually agreed arbitration. To the extent party autonomy in international arbitration is recognised, hybrid arbitration agreements are presumably valid.

The statement by Dumoulin quoted above also underlines one of the main difficulties arising when trying to solve a problem according to the parties' will: This will is often not clearly expressed but only implied. Party autonomy is therefore intrinsically linked to the issue of interpretation of agreements. This also applies to hybrid arbitration agreements, which can only be distinguished from clearly defective, pathological agreements by inquiring into the parties' intentions.[2]

This chapter highlights the importance but also the limits of party autonomy in international commercial arbitration (§4) and discusses the role of institutional arbitration rules within that framework (§5) in order to give a preliminary answer to the question if hybrid arbitration agreements are valid and operable (§6).

---

1   Molinaeus, *Conclusiones*; *reproduced by* Meili, »Argenträus und Molinäus«, 554; *also reprinted as Appendix II of* Savigny, *Private International Law and the Retrospective Operation of Statutes*, 452, 454; *discussed by* Gamillscheg, *Der Einfluß Dumoulins auf die Entwicklung des Kollisionsrechts*, 19, 25.

2   Discussed in detail in Chapter 2 (*infra* at pp. 157 et seq., §8).

*§4 Party autonomy to agree on hybrid arbitration under the law*

Notwithstanding all theoretical discussion as to concept and nature of party autonomy,[3] its acknowledgement in private law and more specifically arbitration law is uncontested (A). However, applicable laws (B), including arbitration laws (C) and other laws (D) limit party autonomy.

A. Importance of party autonomy in international arbitration

Party autonomy shapes international commercial arbitration proceedings.[4] Parties may not only choose their arbitrator(s),[5] they may also choose the place, language and procedural rules for the arbitration as well as the law applicable to the merits; they could even instruct the arbitrator to be guided by equity rather than by principles of law.[6] Some even say that party autonomy »*permits parties literally ›to make their own law‹.*«[7]

---

3    For a recent summary of the dogmatic discussion in Germany, *see e.g.* Habel, *Contract Governance*, 50–54.

4    *See e.g.* Blackaby et al., *Redfern and Hunter*, para. 6–08 (»*guiding principle*«); Varady, Von Mehren, and Barceló, *International Commercial Arbitration*, 69 (»*differentia specifica*«); Poudret and Besson, *Comparative Law of International Arbitration*, para. 522; Thorndon, »Party Autonomy«, 258 (»*concept* [...] *to dominate arbitration law*«); Böckstiegel, »Public Policy and Arbitrability«, 177 (»*well known condition*«); van den Berg, »Mandatory Rules: What's a Lawyer to Do?«, 352 (»*most highly touted advantage*«); *see also* Lau and Horlach, »Party Autonomy« (for further references).

5    Arbitral tribunals usually consist of either 1 or 3 arbitrators, although other, including even numbers are generally possible (*see* UNCITRAL Model Law 2006 art. 10 (1) [U.N.]; *see also infra* at pp. 367-368, §14B.III.1). In the following the use of the singular »*arbitrator*« includes the plural »*arbitrators*« and vice-versa, unless otherwise indicated.

6    Many jurisdictions allow for arbitrators acting as *amiable compositeur* or *ex aequo et bono* if the parties so agree (*cf.* Schütze, Tscherning, and Wais, *Handbuch des Schiedsverfahrens*, para. 584; Born, *Cases and Materials (2011)*, 962; *see generally* Sohn, »Ex Aequo et Bono«; *see also* Brower, »The Privatization of Rules of Decision«, 111 [explaining an award made ex aequo et bono to be »*a settlement, albeit one arrived at indirectly*«]).

7    Brower, »The Privatization of Rules of Decision«, 112.

I. An interplay of contract and private international law

Party autonomy is relevant both at the level of substantive law and at the level of private international law.[8] Concerning substantive law, party autonomy means freedom of contract.[9] Concerning private international law, it refers to the freedom of choice of law. The freedom of contract allows the parties to determine the content of their contractual relationship within the boundaries of mandatory law.[10] The freedom of choice of law may even enable the parties to circumvent mandatory rules of the otherwise applicable law by choosing a law not containing provisions like those intended to waive, subject to overriding mandatory rules of law or public policy.[11] In the following, the term party autonomy encompasses both the freedom of contract and the freedom of choice of law,[12] unless otherwise indicated.

The analysis of hybrid arbitration agreements starts from the premise that a reference to a set of arbitration rules is primarily an exercise of the freedom of contract because thereby the parties agree on the contractual terms of their arbitration agreement. Nevertheless, parallels to choice of law clauses cannot be denied since the parties refer to a comprehensive regulation drafted by an authority, thus similar to legislation, which has to be accommodated within an overall legal and factual framework. This becomes

---

8    Berger, »Aufgaben und Grenzen«, 14; Kropholler, *Internationales Privatrecht*, 292; *see* Kühne, »Methodeneinheit und Methodenvielfalt«, 136 (on party autonomy becoming a »*basic rule*« of private international law).

9    *Cf.* von Bar et al., *DCFR*, art. II.–1:102 (1): »*Parties are free to make a contract or other juridical act and to determine its contents, subject to any applicable mandatory rules.*«

10   Meaning ordinary or domestic mandatory law (»*einfach zwingende Normen*«, *see essentially* Schurig, *Kollisionsnorm und Sachrecht*, 58–64; praised by Michaels, »Die Struktur der kollisionsrechtlichen Durchsetzung«, 191).

11   Also referred to as »*internationally mandatory laws*« (*see e.g.* Kleinheisterkamp, »The Impact of Internationally Mandatory Laws on the Enforceability of Arbitration Agreements«, 91). On the doctrine of overriding mandatory rules of law (German: »*Eingriffsnormen*«), *see generally* Ungeheuer, *Die Beachtung von Eingriffsnormen. See infra* at pp. 470-476 (§17A.IV) regarding the related but not entirely synonymous concept of international public policy.

12   *See* Kropholler, *Internationales Privatrecht*, 293 (finding the details in terminology to be historically random); Böckstiegel, »Die Anerkennung der Parteiautonomie«, 141–42.

remarkably acute when parties choose other rules than those of the administering institution. If, contrary to the still prevailing opinion,[13] one accepted that parties could choose non-state rules as applicable *law*, the research topic would centre on the conflict of laws and not on contractual issues. For this reason, some concepts developed by private international law doctrine for the conflict of laws will also be valuable in the analysis of hybrid arbitration agreements, which may provoke a *conflict of rules*.[14]


II. Party autonomy in international arbitration conventions

International conventions respect party autonomy as the foundation of arbitration. Article V (1)(d) of the New York Convention stresses the importance of party autonomy in relation to the arbitral procedure at the level of recognition and enforcement of arbitral awards. Pursuant to this provision, courts may deny the recognition and enforcement of an award, if the procedure »*was not in accordance with the agreement of the parties.*«

The European Arbitration Convention, which is only applicable if the parties have their place of residence in different contracting states,[15] goes even a step further with its

> »conferral of an, at least at first sight, unlimited autonomy to the parties in organizing their arbitral proceedings [that] was revolutionary at the time.«[16]

Article IV (1) of the European Arbitration Convention has been referred to as the »*Magna Charta of Party Autonomy*«,[17] because it enumerates the parties' choices in respect of arbitral procedure in a positive and confirming manner. However, the question whether the provision may also be

---

13   *See infra* at pp. 110-116 (§5B).

14   *See e.g. infra* at pp. 344 et seq. (§14A) on the concept of »*substitution*«.

15   As of 4 March 2014: Albania, Austria, Azerbaijan, Belarus, Belgium, Bosnia and Herzegovina, Bulgaria, Burkina Faso, Croatia, Cuba, Czech Republic, Denmark, Finland, France, Germany, Hungary, Italy, Kazakhstan, Latvia, Luxembourg, Montenegro, Poland, Republic of Moldova, Romania, Russian Federation, Serbia, Slovakia, Slovenia, Spain, The former Yugoslav Republic of Macedonia, Turkey, Ukraine (UN, »Status - European Convention on International Commercial Arbitration«).

16   Kröll, »The Tale of a Sleeping Beauty«, 14.

17   Ibid.

interpreted as limiting party autonomy in institutional arbitration will require a closer look.[18]

III. Recognition of party autonomy by national arbitration laws

In principle, all national arbitration laws also recognise party autonomy.[19] When the UNCITRAL Model Law was drafted in 1985,[20] the principle of party autonomy was acknowledged without opposition.[21] Article 19 (3) UNCITRAL Model Law provides:

>Subject to the provisions of this Law, the parties are free to agree on the procedure to be followed by the arbitral tribunal in conducting the proceedings.«

Section 1042 (3) of the German code of civil procedure (*Zivilprozessordnung*) (ZPO)[22] adds instructively that the parties' agreement may also consist in referring to a set of pre-drafted arbitration rules. Similarly, Singapore's International Arbitration Act *(IAA)* provides that an agreement of the parties includes a reference to arbitration rules or to an arbitral institution to make a determination of a certain issue.[23] Similar provisions can be found in the statutes of all important places of arbitration.[24]

---

18   *See infra* pp. 95-97 (§4C.II.2.a.ii).
19   *See* Blackaby et al., *Redfern and Hunter*, para. 6–08 (*»principle that is endorsed worldwide*«); Poudret and Besson, *Comparative Law of International Arbitration*, 525.
20   First version cited as UNCITRAL Model Law 1985 (original version) .
21   Rep. of the Secretary-General: Possible features, WG II, 14th sess., para. 17 (1981) (*»most important principle*«).
22   Herein cited as ZPO (GER).
23   IAA § 15A (6)–(7) (SG).
24   *See e.g.* IPRG art. 182 (2) (C.H.): *»The parties may, directly or by reference to rules of arbitration, determine the arbitral procedure; they may also submit the arbitral procedure to a procedural law of their choice*« (English translation as published in Paulsson, *International Handbook on Commercial Arbitration*, Switzerland, Annex II, Suppl. no. 51, last updated March 2008; *also available at* Swiss Chambers' Arbitration Institution, »Federal Statute on Private International Law«). Similar: CPC art. 1509 (1) (FR) (Title VI on arbitration was fundamentally modified by the Décret portant réforme de l'arbitrage 2011 [FR]); Arbitration Act 1996 § 1 (b) (EW) (*»parties should be free to agree how their disputes are resolved*«).

The Federal Arbitration Act (FAA)[25] as the legislation primarily applicable to international arbitration with a place of arbitration in the United States[26] does not contain any *express* provision on the parties' autonomy to determine arbitral procedure. Nevertheless, case law unquestionably endorses the principle both in national and international arbitration.[27] The Tennessee Court of Appeals gave an intriguing description of the parties' procedural autonomy, stating that even »*splitting the difference‹, flipping a coin, or, for that matter, arm wrestling*« may be acceptable methods to solve a dispute.[28] Similarly, the Court of Appeals for the Seventh Circuit held:

> »Short of authorizing trial by battle or ordeal or, more doubtfully, by a panel of three monkeys, parties can stipulate to whatever procedures they want to govern the arbitration of their disputes [...].«[29]

In the same vein, the Supreme Court of Canada found that

> »the parties to an arbitration agreement are free, subject to any mandatory provisions by which they are bound, to choose any place, form and procedures they consider appropriate. They can choose cyberspace and establish their own rules.«[30]

---

25  Codified as Chapter 1 of the United States Arbitration Act §§ 1–16 (US). Hereinafter, the abbreviation »*FAA*« may also be used in a wider sense to refer to all chapters of the United States Arbitration Act in line with common practice (*see e.g.* Stein, »Polimaster Ltd. v. RAE Systems, Inc.«, 269: »*Chapter 2 of the FAA implements the New York Convention*«).

26  The FAA is applicable to arbitration arising from international transactions and overrides any inconsistent US state law (FAA § 2 [US]). Federal Circuit courts are competent for enforcing arbitration agreements and awards falling under the New York Convention (FAA §§ 203, 302 [US]). However US state laws may be applicable to »*contractual*« questions like existence and validity of arbitration agreements (*cf.* Holtzmann and Donovan, »National Report for the United States of America (2005)«, 4).

27  *See e.g. Volt,* 489 U.S. 468, 479 (S.Ct. 1989), 109 S.Ct. 1248, 1256 (US 1989) (»*Arbitration under the Act is a matter of consent, not coercion, and parties are generally free to structure their arbitration agreements as they see fit*«); *see also UHC v. Computer Sciences,* 148 F.3d 992, 995 (8th Cir. 1998).

28  *Team Design v. Gottlieb,* 104 S.W.3d 512, 518 (Tenn. Ct. App. 2002) (albeit clearly distinguishing such informal methods from enforceable arbitration agreements; *contra* Born, *Law and Practice (2012),* 147, 148, ambiguously citing this statement in relation to arbitration).

29  *Baravati v. Josephthal,* 28 F.3d 704, 709 (7th Cir. 1994).

30  Union des consommateurs v. Dell, 2007 SCC 34, 52 (Can.).

A persistent and relevant exception to the general acceptance of party autonomy may be the Arbitration Law of the People's Republic of China.[31] If the place of arbitration is in mainland China parties have to bear in mind that Chinese arbitration law is very detailed, and »*its provisions are to be considered mandatory and that party autonomy is somewhat limited*«[32] although China's foreign-related arbitration law permits »*substantially greater freedom and flexibility to contracting parties.*«[33] As one commentator wrote, there is a

> »(debatable) premise that under Chinese law it is better to have specific provisions providing permissions for acts and processes (rather than assume that they are allowed unless prohibited).«[34]

For foreign-related proceedings a number of such permissive provisions exist, *e.g.* allowing parties to choose a place of arbitration outside China - with the consequence that Chinese arbitration law would no longer apply except for enforcement issues –, appoint foreigners as arbitrators,[35] choose another than Chinese substantive law and even a foreign law to apply to the validity of the arbitration agreement.[36] Most relevant for the validity and operability of hybrid arbitration agreements is the lack of express recognition of ad hoc arbitration by Chinese arbitration law, even if the arbitration is foreign-related.[37] Even more restrictively, Chinese arbitration law requires arbitrations to be administered by a so-called »*arbitration commission*«, which has to be clearly designated in the arbitration agreement and which has to meet certain criteria that will be explained in more detail later.[38]

However, as international competition in the arbitration market increases, China gradually adapts to international standards. The latest news

---

31    Herein cited as Arbitration Law (P.R.C.).

32    Tao, *Arbitration Law and Practice in China*, para. 273.

33    Ibid., para. 329, 348 (but not clearly distinguishing arbitration *law* from CIETAC's arbitration *rules*).

34    Andrew, »Notable Characteristics of Arbitration in China«, 313.

35    Arbitration Law art. 67 (P.R.C.).

36    That this law is determined by the place of arbitration is only the default rule, *see* SPC's Interpretation of Arbitration Law, art. 16 (2006); *see generally* Tevini, »Besonderheiten des chinesischen Schiedsverfahrensrechts«, 26 (with further references). On the problematic distinction between law applicable to the arbitration agreement and law of the arbitration, *see infra* at pp. 75-86 (§4B.II).

37    *Cf.* Andrew, »Notable Characteristics of Arbitration in China«, 313 (»*has been interpreted widely to mean*«).

38    *See infra* at pp. 101-104 (§4C.II.2.b.iii).

is that the Supreme People's Court (SPC) considered an arbitration agreement valid that provided for arbitration administered in mainland China by an international institution, the ICC Court notably.[39] Now faced with such strong competition on the Chinese market, CIETAC also starts defying the rigorousness of Chinese arbitration traditions still reflected in the current wording of the law. *E.g.*, in a liberal interpretation of the arbitration law, CIETAC already allows parties to nominate foreign and non-listed arbitrators[40] or delegates competence-competence to the arbitral tribunal rather than exercising it itself as a an arbitration commission.[41] This practice seems tolerated or did not yet lead to any court challenges. For China, one may therefore conclude that there is still some official resistance against unconstrained party autonomy in international arbitration but that this resistance is in sharp decline the more China's traditional institutions design their system to become more flexible.[42]

IV. Reasons for the supremacy of party autonomy

Party autonomy is essential in arbitration because the arbitral tribunal derives its competence not from stipulation by law but from the parties'

---

39  *Anhui Longlide Packing and Printing Co. Ltd. v. BP Agnati S.R.L* (Reply), [2013] Min Si Ta Zi no. 13 (P.R.C. SPC, 25 March 2013) (hereinafter cited as »*Longlide*«; cited according to the English translation published by Sun, »SPC Instruction Provides New Opportunities for International Arbitral Institutions to Expand into China«, 695–700 (Appendix 3; also providing a translation of the reference for instruction by the Anhui People's Court in Appendix 4). But, the text of the law still suggests otherwise and uncertainties remain (on older decisions by lower courts along this line, *see* Andrew, »Notable Characteristics of Arbitration in China«, 313: »*logic of that enforcement is not entirely clear*«).

40  CIETAC Rules, art. 24 (2) (2012) = 26 (2) (2015); *cf. also* Arbitration Law pp. 66–67 (P.R.C.) (expressly allowing foreign arbitrators to be appointed by international arbitration commissions); *but see* ibid., art. 11 (4), 13 (providing that arbitration commissions must have listed arbitrators; the application to foreign-related cases being unclear).

41  CIETAC Rules, art. 6 (1) and (3) (2012; 2015); *but see* Arbitration Law art. 20 (P.R.C.) (only allowing the courts or arbitration »*commissions*« - not tribunals - to rule on arbitral jurisdiction).

42  On the regulating and modernising impact of Chinese arbitration commissions, *see generally* Ortolani, »The Role of Arbitration Institutions in China«.

agreement. It is a decisive feature of arbitration that it relies on a contract, two matching declarations of will.[43] In principle,[44] there is no arbitration without a contract.[45]

A different reason for party autonomy's leading role in international arbitration is that the parties tend to choose a place of arbitration in a neutral state, in which neither party has its place of residence or business.[46] These neutral venues may have little interest to regulate proceedings that mainly involve foreign parties and less their own citizens.[47] Moreover, as complex commercial legal disputes are a common subject matter of arbitration, the need for a tailor-made procedure is particularly high. Given that the parties are mainly companies and business people with economic experience, there is less need for state protection than in many state court procedures.[48] Nowadays, a reliance of party autonomy and contractual theories for new problems arising in international arbitration practice is also often a kind of lowest common denominator for those interested in the matter coming from different jurisdictions, backgrounds and cultures. In a world becoming more and more globalised at the economic level but being far from a universal system of law, it is often impossible to agree on an appropriate regulator other than the parties themselves.

For these reasons, procedural party autonomy is a concept predominant in arbitration, international commercial arbitration in particular. Hybrid arbitration agreements are at the outset an exercise of this procedural party autonomy. Therefore, the analysis will repeatedly recall the particular characteristics of international commercial arbitration:

---

43   Blackaby et al., *Redfern and Hunter*, para. 1–11 (*»the element of consent is essential«*).

44   This thesis excludes non-contractual, e.g. treaty-based arbitration, from its scope.

45   The contract does not have to be valid. According to the doctrines of separability and competence-competence, the arbitral tribunal may decide on the validity of the contract and the arbitration agreement.

46   *See* Queen Mary University of London, School of International Arbitration and White & Case, »Survey: Choices (2010)«, 20 (*» a third country for both/all of them and not otherwise disposed towards them«*).

47   *See* Petrochilos, *Procedural Law in International Arbitration*, para. 3.117.

48   *Cf.* Berger, »Aufgaben und Grenzen«, 14 (on this reason for the dominant role of party autonomy in arbitration).

- the contractual basis[49]
- the internationality of the dispute[50]
- the - often - »*neutral*« seat[51]
- the regulation and conduct of arbitration by private actors[52]
- the reduced control by state courts[53]

## B. Limits to party autonomy and applicable laws

> »It might seem as if parties and arbitrators inhabit their own private universe; but in reality the practice of resolving disputes by international arbitration only works effectively because it is held in place by a complex system of national laws and international treaties.«[54]

It is sometimes debated if international arbitration needs to abide at all by the rule of state law.[55] If derived from the parties' agreement and not from the authority of any state, one could argue that states cannot limit arbitrators'

---

49  *See infra* at pp. 232 et seq. (§11), in particular on the contractual relationship of the parties to the administering institution.

50  In domestic arbitration, more restrictions to party autonomy apply which would likely influence a verdict on hybrid arbitration agreements, but that have to be excluded from the scope of the thesis.

51  *See infra* at pp. 68-74 (§4B.I).

52  *See infra* at pp. 110-116 (§5B).

53  *See infra,* Chapter 5, at pp. 402 et seq.

54  Blackaby et al., *Redfern and Hunter*, para. 1.06.

55  For a recent debate, *see* Nakamura, »The Place of Arbitration«; *but see* Rubins, »The Arbitral Seat is No Fiction«; *see further* Pinsolle, »A Reply to Art. Published by Noah Rubins« (pointing out that, ironically, a certain *seat, e.g.* in France, would support the idea of *delocalisation*); *see already* Lew, 202 (»*floating award*«; reproduced in: Lew and Mistelis, *Arbitration Insights*, 455–85); expressing the same vision: Goldman, »Les Conflits de lois dans l'arbitrage international de droit privé«, 360; Paulsson, »Arbitration Unbound«; *idem* »Delocalisation of International Commercial Arbitration«.

powers. In theory, this may be correct, in practice it is not. Arbitration, even international arbitration,[56] does not take place in a legal vacuum.[57]

> »[A] completely denationalised law is of course a utopia. But it is a utopia not just in the broad sense of being unrealistic, at least for the present, and perhaps also for the future. No, it is a utopia in the very literal sense of the word. Recall what utopia means in Greek: *no place*. Delocalised arbitration, non-state law, is, quite literally, no-place law. It thus makes up a utopia in the central meaning of the term.«[58]

The reason why international arbitration cannot follow Utopian, »*no-place law*« is the want for enforceability. Despite the fact that many awards are complied with voluntarily,[59] enforceability of awards remains an essential concern for parties to arbitration.[60] Enforceability of awards is a decisive distinguishing factor to the growing competition of other alternative dispute resolution (ADR) mechanisms like mediation or conciliation. Of course, within the last years, ADR experienced a fast development in terms of numbers published by leading institutions,[61] but most ADR procedures only lead

---

56  For a widely accepted definition of *international*, *see* UNCITRAL Model Law 2006 art. 1 (3); for a more substantive definition, *see* CPC art. 1504 (FR) (an arbitration is international if it touches the interests of international trade); in the latter sense, *see also* Goldman, »Les Conflits de lois dans l'arbitrage international de droit privé«, 360 (preferring a substantive rather than procedural definition). Chinese law distinguishes between arbitration with and without a foreign element, the latter being governed by less stringent rules; disputes between Foreign Invested Companies and Chinese companies are not considered to have a foreign element (*see* Tevini, »Besonderheiten des chinesischen Schiedsverfahrensrechts«, 26- with further references). This thesis concerns international, non-domestic or foreign-related arbitration only.

57  *Cf.* Moses, *The Principles and Practice of International Commercial Arbitration*, 59.

58  Michaels, »Dreaming Law without a State«, 39.

59  *See* Queen Mary University of London, School of International Arbitration and PriceWaterhouseCoopers LLP, »Survey: Corporate Attitudes (2008)«, at 8 (Finding 4) (according to 34 % of the participants, more than 76 % of awards were complied with voluntarily by the opposing party; *but see* Blackaby et al., *Redfern and Hunter*, 11.02 (noting that reliable statistics are not available).

60  *See* Queen Mary University of London, School of International Arbitration and PriceWaterhouseCoopers LLP, »Survey: Corporate Attitudes (2008)«, i (introduction by Gerry Lagerberg) (referring to the previous, 2006, survey results).

61  *See* Wilske and Markert, »Entwicklungen 2010/2011«, 58.

to a compromise not easily enforceable in most jurisdictions.[62] Neither the UNCITRAL Model Law on International Commercial Conciliation[63] nor the European Mediation Directive[64] call for uniform enforcement mechanisms.[65] For this reason, the advantage of enforceability still makes arbitration the most important alternative to state court litigation. A national, completely autonomous arbitration would forego this advantage.

Although the New York Convention does not strictly require that awards can be attributed to the territory of a foreign state,[66] it cannot be denied that national arbitration laws provide for setting-aside actions before courts at the place of arbitration and that recognition and enforcement of awards are also tasks of national courts.[67] These state courts definitely have a natural forum and need to abide by applicable laws when exercising control over the arbitration. Accordingly, striving for enforceability in court is the reason why international commercial arbitration cannot be completely autonomous from the law. Hence, party autonomy always finds its limits in mandatory law - even if there is only very little mandatory law that applies to international arbitration agreements and procedure.[68] The following considerations

---

62   Cf. e.g ZPO § 794 (1) no. 4 (GER) (listing arbitration awards, but not other ADR results, as enforceable title). ADR results could be laid down as a settlement reached by attorneys (»*Anwaltsvergleich*«) or in a notary deed (cf. ZPO § 796a, 794 (1) no. 5 [GER]). At least within the EU, such authentic instruments are enforceable, cf. Brussels-Ia-Regulation 2012 art. 58; Brussels-I-Regulation 2000 art. 57 (see Eidenmüller, »Hybride ADR-Verfahren«, 5; Sussman, »Final Step«, 346).

63   UNCITRAL Model Law (conciliation) 2002; *see also* Sussman, »Final Step«, 346.

64   Mediation Directive 2008 (EU) *see also* Bundesministerium der Justiz und für Verbraucherschutz, »Gesetz zur Förderung der Mediation und anderer Verfahren der außergerichtlichen Konfliktbeilegung (Englisch)« (for an English translation of the German law implementing the directive).

65   *Cf.* Ulrici, »Anhang zu § 278a - Mediationsgesetz«, para. 9, Lembcke, »IV. - Andere Verfahren: Schlichtung«, para. 23. Many recommend conveying the mediation result into an arbitration award by consent (on agreed terms) (*see e.g.* Lörcher and Lörcher, »§ 45 - Durchsetzbarkeit von Mediationsergebnissen«, 1129, 1130).

66   New York Convention, art. 1 (1) sent. 2 (non-domestic award considered sufficient for application).

67   As the vision of an autonomous international arbitration court is merely an interesting fantasy (thereon, *see e.g.* Templeman, »Towards a Truly International Court of Arbitration«).

68   *See also* Renner, *Zwingendes transnationales Recht*, 79.

are made in search of mandatory law possibly refuting the presumption of validity of hybrid arbitration agreements as an exercise of party autonomy. Conceptually it is thereby necessary to distinguish the law applicable to the arbitration from the law applicable to the arbitration agreement.

## I. Law of arbitration: the seat principle

> »Das Schiedsgericht thront nicht über der Erde, es schwebt nicht in der Luft, es muss irgendwo landen, irgendwo erden.«[69]
>
> [The arbitration tribunal is not enthroned above the earth, it does not fly in the air, it has to land somewhere, to be rooted somewhere][70]

Arbitration laws and accordingly applicable mandatory provisions differ greatly. »*The idea of a universal lex arbitri is as illusory as that of universal peace.*«[71]

Hence, parties should make an informed choice, in particular if they want - for whatever reason - to opt for a procedure as unusual as hybrid arbitration. A problem that may come up is how to express such choice for a *lex arbitri*[72]. There is a controversy in theory[73] whether a direct choice of the applicable arbitration law, independent of the place of arbitration, is possible. Based on arbitration legislation,[74] many commentators discard such view.[75] Given that the place of arbitration is not necessarily the place

---

69    Raape, *Internationales Privatrecht.*, 557.
70    Unless otherwise indicated, all English translations in square brackets from non-English sources are by the author.
71    Blackaby et al., *Redfern and Hunter*, para. 3.72.
72    *Cf. infra* n.136 at p. 80.
73    *See* ibid., 3.63 (»*much theoretical discussion*«); Waincymer, *Procedure and Evidence*, 3.5.1, 3.8 (calling this a »*possible but undesirable scenario*« which is »*fraught with uncertainty and potentially raises a range of disputes and challenges*«).
74    *See* UNCITRAL Model Law 2006 art. 1 (2); *cf. also* ZPO p. 1025 (1) (GER); IPRG art. 176 (1) (C.H.), *but see also* ibid., art. 182 (1) (at the end) (parties may agree on a procedural law of their choice).
75    So-called territorial principle (*Territorialprinzip*) as opposed to the procedural theory (*Verfahrenstheorie*); for the German view, *see e.g.* Münch, »§ 1025 ZPO«, para. 3; Voit, »§ 1025 ZPO«, para. 3 (but differentiating between the tribunal and a court), *see also* Geisinger and Raneda, »Legislative Framework«, 4 (on Swiss law; *but cf.* IPRG art. 182 (1) at the end (C.H.), suggesting that a direct choice of the applicable arbitration law was

where hearings are held and the award is signed,[76] there are not many situations imaginable in which parties would want to choose a law of arbitration different from the place of arbitration, the seat.[77]

The place of arbitration, or the »*seat*«, is a central concept of international arbitration. The arbitration law of the seat is the applicable *lex arbitri*[78] and the courts of the seat exercise supporting and controlling jurisdiction.[79] The majority of international arbitration doctrine[80] accepts that the law of the seat applies to the arbitration.[81]

## 1. Choosing a place of arbitration

While the choice of a place of arbitration entails the applicability of that place's arbitration law, parties may not always have this in mind when drafting the arbitration clause. This has been nicely pictured by comparing arbitration law to traffic law:

---

possible); *see generally* Blackaby et al., *Redfern and Hunter*, para. 10.22 (finding the idea of choosing a procedural law other than that of the legal seat »*both unnecessary and unhelpful*«).

76  *See infra* at 2. (pp. 71-74) on the concept of a non-geographical seat; *but see* Schütze, »Die Bedeutung des effektiven Schiedsortes«, 1082– 83, 1086 (requiring some connection between the place of arbitration and the locations where procedural steps take place).

77  *See Peruvian Ins. Case*, [1988] Lloyd's Rep 116 (EW CA) 120 (»*The limits and implications of any such agreement have been much discussed in the literature, but apart from the decision in the instant case there appears to be no reported case where this has happened. This is not surprising when one considers the complexities and inconveniences which such an agreement would involve*«); *see also Karaha Bodas v. PPM Dan Gas Bumi Negra*, 364 F.3d 274, 291 (5th Cir. 2004) (with further references).

78  *But see* Urteil [Judgment], [1988] 41 NJW 3090 (GER BGH) at 3091 (on the earlier procedural theory - »*Verfahrenstheorie*«; with further references to early case law and commentary).

79  Waincymer, *Procedure and Evidence*, 3.3; *see also Peruvian Ins. Case*, [1988] Lloyd's Rep 120 (clarifying that an agreement to apply another than the seat's arbitration law, as rare it may be, would in no event give the courts of that other state jurisdiction over the arbitration and award).

80  *Cf.* Gaillard and Savage, *Fouchard, Gaillard, Goldmann*, 1428.

81  While the law governing substantive matters can and will often be different (Blackaby et al., *Redfern and Hunter*, para. 3.34, 3.38: »*an unconnected choice*«).

> »To say that the parties have ›chosen‹ that particular law to govern the arbitration is rather like saying that an English woman who takes her car to France has ›chosen‹ French traffic law, which will oblige her to drive on the right-hand side of the road, to give priority to vehicles approaching from the right, and generally to obey traffic laws to which she may not be accustomed. But it would be an odd use of language to say that this notional motorist had opted for ›French traffic law‹. What she has done is to choose to go to France. The applicability of French law then follows automatically. It is not a matter of choice.«[82]

While this observation may often be true, it is not a recommendable approach. Different from planning the next weekend trip, informed businesspeople should not ask whether they would rather go to France than to Switzerland when drafting an arbitration agreement. They should better consider which country's arbitration law and courts would most likely meet their expectations of extent of control and regulation and arbitration support. If the parties make no choice, it will be the arbitral tribunal's task to make an appropriate selection[83] or, in institutional arbitration, that of the institution,[84] failing which courts may need to select a place of arbitration, which may create conflicts of jurisdictions.[85] An informed selection requires analysis

---

82  Ibid., para. 3.61.

83  *Cf.* UNCITRAL Model Law 2006 art. 20 (1).

84  Such institutional selection can be final or provisional and subject to a final decision by the tribunal (*compare* ICC Rules, art. 18 (1) [2012; 2017]: »*fixed*«; similar: CIETAC Rules, art. 7 [2], sent. 2 [2012; 2015]; Swiss Rules, art. 16 [1] [2012]: »*determine*« *with e.g.* AAA-ICDR Rules, art. 17 [1] [2014] [»*initially*«]; AAA-ICDR Rules, art. 13 [1] [2009]). The arbitration rules may also provide for a default place of arbitration (*see e.g.* LCIA Rules, art. 16 [2] [2014]; LCIA Rules, art. 16 [1] [1998]: »*shall be London, unless*«; CIETAC Rules, art. 7 [2] [2012; 2015]: »*shall be the domicile of CIETAC or its sub-commission/arbitration center*«; SIAC Rules, art. 18 [1] [2010]: »*shall be Singapore, unless*«; *but see* SIAC Rules, art. 18 [2013] = art. 21 [2016], no longer stipulating a default seat). Problematic if court support was required before the constitution of the tribunal, the DIS Rules lack a provision on administrative determination of the place of arbitration (*see* DIS Rules, art. 21 (1) [1998]: »*shall be determined by the arbitral tribunal*«; *but see* Münch, »§ 1043 ZPO«, para. 7, even claiming that German law prohibits derogating this choice to an institution; *see also* SIAC Rules, art. 18 [2013] = art. 21 [2016]).

85  *See* Born, *Law and Practice (2012)*, 116, §6.03(C).

of both written arbitration law and court practice of the potential place of arbitration.[86]


## 2. Place of arbitration, place of hearing, seat of the institution

Geographical conditions, like the availability of an international airport, pleasant hotels or even of competent arbitrators and arbitral institutions technically need not play a role[87] when choosing a seat, if one understands the seat as a »*legal fiction.*«[88] It is now widely accepted that a geographical connection between the arbitration hearings and the seat of arbitration is not required.[89] Hearings may take place anywhere on the planet, the seat remains the one chosen by the parties or determined by the arbitral institution or tribunal.[90] It may nevertheless be prudent to hold at least one hearing at the place of arbitration to avoid any allegation of abuse.[91]

---

86 *See* Waincymer, *Procedure and Evidence*, para. 3.5.1 (warning of »*horror stories*« of court interference).

87 Born, *Law and Practice (2012)*, 119, §6.04(A)(6) (»*should virtually never be decisive*«); *see also* Poudret and Besson, *Comparative Law of International Arbitration*, para. 148 (»*secondary or even irrelevant*«).

88 Kaufmann-Kohler, »Globalization of Arbitral Procedure«, 1318; Berger, »Sitz des Schiedsgerichts«, 10 (»*formales Legaldomizil*«); Münch, »§ 1043 ZPO«, para. 3 (»*virtueller Schiedsort*«).

89 *Compare* UNCITRAL Rules, art. 18 (1), (2) sent. 2 (2010) (»*place of arbitration*«; »*the arbitral tribunal may also meet at any location it considers appropriate for any other purpose, including hearings*«) *with* UNCITRAL Rules, art. 16 (1)–(3) (1976) (still referring to the »*place where the arbitration is to be held*;« only allowing a different »*locale*« for witness hearings, evidence inspections and consultations among the tribunal but not for general hearings); *cf. also* Sanders, »Note« (on the traditional view).

90 *See supra* at notes 83–84.

91 Poudret and Besson, *Comparative Law of International Arbitration*, para. 134; *similar* Blackaby et al., *Redfern and Hunter*, para. 3.54; *see e.g.* Schütze, »Die Bedeutung des effektiven Schiedsortes«, 1080 (arguing that the choice of a place of arbitration in Papua-Neuguinea would be invalid if it was made only for the purpose of evading the application of mandatory provisions of the place of hearing); *contra* Waincymer, *Procedure and Evidence*, para. 3.5.1 (noting that few supervisory courts would take such a view).

In practice, most arbitration hearings are held at the place of arbitration and parties give important weight to geographical and logistical factors when making their choice.[92] Even arbitral institutions in the arbitrator selection process tend to pay attention to whether an arbitrator is located at or easily able to travel to the place of arbitration.[93] Cases of a purely legal or fictitious place of arbitration remain rare.

Generally, modern arbitration laws do not require a business presence of the administering arbitration institution at the place of arbitration anymore. Administration services can be provided from the offices of the institution even if the arbitration is seated and the hearing is held elsewhere.[94] Nevertheless, it is still very common that parties opt for the institution's seat as the place of arbitration and use the institution's facilities to hold hearings.[95]

It is occasionally assumed that Chinese law and jurisprudence would consider an arbitration clause inoperable that provides for arbitration to be administered by a Chinese arbitration commission in a city where that arbitration commission has no seat.[96] The SPC's Interpretation of 2006 also

---

92  »*Convenience*« of location and »*General infrastructure*« mentioned among the »*top* influences« for the choice of a seat by 45 % and 31 % respectively of the participants of Queen Mary University of London, School of International Arbitration and White & Case, »Survey: Choices (2010)«, 18, chart 14 (multiple answers possible).

93  *E.g.* within the ICC system, national committees at the place of arbitration are usually first asked to nominate a sole arbitrator or chairman, except where this is inappropriate in light of the parties' nationalities or for other reasons (*see* ICC Rules, art. 13 (3) [2012; 2017]; Born, *International Arbitration and Forum Selection Agreements*, 48).

94  Correctly stressed by Naciemento, »Konfliktlösung nach allgemeinen Schiedsordnungen«, 788; *but see* Straus to Sanders, »Comments on Draft ›Commentary on UNCITRAL Arbitration Rules‹«, 1 (suggesting that the place of arbitration should usually be the place where the appointing authority has its office, believing the same consideration to apply to the choice of both places); Hacking, »A New Competition«, 440 (finding the choice of an arbitration body and the choice of forum closely linked). The latter, older views are probably connected to a now outdated geographical understanding of place of arbitration, *see supra* at n. 89.

95  Johnston, »The Best Providers for Asian Arbitrations«, 46–47.

96  *Cf.* Kaplan, Spruce, and Moser, *Hong Kong and China Arbitration*, 312 (finding that »*CIETAC arbitration in Dalian*« would fail »*because CIETAC has no seat in this city*«; also reporting a case where clause referring to »*Guangdong Branch*« of FETAC - the CIETAC predecessor - was found inoperable); *but see* Ch'eng, Moser, and Wang, *International*

appears to suggest a connection between the location of an institution and the place of arbitration.[97] However, this interpretation only addresses the problem of unclear designation of an institution. It should not be itself understood as limiting the business of Chinese arbitration commissions to their municipality or the Chinese territory in general,[98] nor exclude administration services by foreign institutions in China in general.[99]

Constraints, whether real or imagined, to choose an arbitral institution located at the preferred place of arbitration may be a further reason to conclude hybrid arbitration agreements as a - in such a case unfortunate - compromise.[100] *E.g.*, if parties - mistakenly - assume that arbitrating in Singapore necessarily required the choice of a Singapore based institution they may be inclined to agree on hybrid arbitration administered by an institution based at the preferred seat but under the ICC Rules, with which they may be more familiar or in which they place more confidence. The same applies if parties want to choose ICC Rules and agree on a place of arbitration in mainland China but are uncertain, whether the ICC Court would be able or allowed to administer arbitrations there. Generally, one cannot recommend

---

*Arbitration in the People's Republic of China*, 79–80 (suggesting that this a a question of the applicable institutional rules only rather than the law).

97  SPC's Interpretation of Arbitration Law, art. 6 (2006): »*Where an agreement for arbitration stipulates that the disputes shall be arbitrated by the arbitration institution at a certain locality and there is only one arbitration institution in this locality, the arbitration institution shall be deemed as the stipulated arbitration institution. If there are two or more arbitration institutions, the parties concerned may choose one arbitration institution for arbitration upon agreement; if the parties concerned fail to agree upon the choice of the arbitration institution, the agreement for arbitration shall be ineffective*«; *cf. also* ibid., art. 12 (on the jurisdiction of the People's Court at the seat of the institution for applications under art. 20 of the Arbitration Law).

98  *But see* Andrew, »Notable Characteristics of Arbitration in China«, 314 (understanding that CIETAC was only allowed to administer arbitrations where »*hearings were held at another location*« but remaining »*seated in China*«; concluding that Chinese law »*would still apply to matters of oversight and supervision*«).

99  Which very recent jurisprudence now seems to acknowledge, *see Longlide*, [2013] Min Si Ta Zi no. 13; Dong, »Open Door for Foreign Arbitration Institutions?«; *cf. supra* at n. 39.

100 *Cf. also* Kirby, »SIAC Can Administer Cases Under The ICC Rules?!?«, 325, n.33 (noting that some consider ICC arbitration expensive due to the wrong assumption that it would require them to travel to Paris).

hybrid arbitration as a compromise in such a situation. First, it would be based on the principally outdated assumption that an arbitral institution may not render services for arbitrations seated abroad. Second, the wish to arbitrate at a certain place if often motivated by logistical and geographical concerns, which should play no role if one bears the now widely accepted notion of the legal, geographical place of arbitration in mind. It would certainly be a better solution to agree on the institution which parties trust most and this institution's rules. If parties then further agree on a place of arbitration in a jurisdiction with a well-considered arbitration law and supporting but little-interfering courts, where the notion of the non-geographical seat is accepted, they can freely agree, completely detached from the previous considerations, that hearings and meetings should take place at any location convenient to the parties.

3. Application of arbitration laws of states other than the seat?

If laws other than the *lex arbitri* limit the parties' procedural autonomy is a question still open to debate.[101] This issue has been named a »*third State mandatory rule problem.*«[102] In light of state courts' entitlement to refuse enforcement under article V (2)(b) New York Convention if the procedure was contrary to public policy,[103] the parties should in their own interest not completely ignore the law of the potential enforcement forum.[104] The public policy of the potential enforcement state therefore limits party autonomy. During arbitration, this may be merely a factual limit;[105] afterwards, it may

---

101  On this debate, *see generally* Lörcher, »Wie zwingend sind zwingende Normen?« and Schiffer, »Zwingende Normen«.

102  *E.g.* by van den Berg, »Mandatory Rules: What's a Lawyer to Do?«, 354; *see generally* Bermann, »Introduction: Mandatory Rules of Law in International Arbitration«, 7–15; *see also* Shore, »Applying Mandatory Rules of Law in International Arbitration«, 95.

103  *See generally* de Pfeifle, *Der Ordre Public-Vorbehalt als Versagungsgrund der Anerkennung und Vollstreckbarerklärung internationaler Schiedssprüche* (comprehensive comparative analysis on public policy challenges to arbitral awards).

104  On further conceivable connections based on conflict of laws theories, *see* Renner, *Zwingendes transnationales Recht*, 101–10 (mainly concerning mandatory substantive law).

105  Gaillard and Savage, *Fouchard, Gaillard, Goldmann*, para. 1193; Schiffer, »Zwingende Normen«, 23.

become a limit of legal nature as it entitles a court to refuse enforcement by law.[106]

At this stage, it is sufficient to highlight the difficulties arbitrators, parties and arbitral institutions face in determining appropriate procedural rules, reflecting both the law at the place of arbitration and the public policy of potential place of enforcement. Often neither the parties nor the arbitrators know the potential enforcement state at the time of arbitration - even less at the time of the drafting an arbitration agreement. There may be several conceivable states to seek enforcement of the future award. Very often, the place where the award will have to be enforced depends on the outcome of the case, as it is the winning party's task to enforce against the losing party. To require observance of the public policy of the enforcement forum may than create a vicious circle: The outcome of the case may depend on the place of enforcement, which in turn depends on the outcome of the case.[107]

For this reason, arbitration practice, as widely accepted by doctrine,[108] tends to avoid giving too much weight to the question where the award will be enforced and to the resulting public policy requirements.[109] When agreeing on or determining procedural rules, parties, arbitrators and institutions are mainly advised to pay attention to such demands of the potential enforcement state that are known, probable and easy to comply with.[110]

## II. Laws affecting the arbitration agreement

The previous considerations have defined the law applicable to arbitration *procedure* to be the arbitration law of the place of the arbitration. However, hybrid arbitration is not just procedure but *agreed* procedure. Such an agreement on procedure is part of the agreement to arbitrate. Therefore, it can be relevant to determine the law or laws applicable to the arbitration agreement itself. This conflict of laws question is closely connected to the

---

106 Discussed in more detail *infra* at pp. 470 et seq. (§17A.IV).

107 *See* Waincymer, *Procedure and Evidence*, para. 3.7.2 (altering the outcome of the award found »*hardly an exercise of the duty to render an enforceable award*«).

108 Ibid.; *see also* Platte, »An Arbitrator's Duty to Render Enforceable Awards«, 311 (»*arbitrator cannot be expected to consider the laws of all such places*«).

109 *See generally* Platte, »An Arbitrator's Duty to Render Enforceable Awards« (best efforts obligation).

110 *See* Waincymer, *Procedure and Evidence*, para. 3.7.2.

categorisation of the issue of hybrid arbitration: Does an agreement on hybrid arbitration raise *nullity/validity* concerns or does it raise only issues of *operability/performance?*

Article II (3) of New York Convention mentions both kinds of problems without further distinction and without an indication on the law applicable to these issues.

> »The court of a Contracting State, when seized of an action in a matter in respect of which the parties have made an agreement within the meaning of this article, shall, at the request of one of the parties, refer the parties to arbitration, unless it finds that the said agreement is *null and void, inoperative or incapable of being performed.*«

While legal doctrine enthusiastically discusses the problem of determining the law applicable to the validity of the arbitration agreement, the law applying to its operability, meaning whether an arbitration agreement is operative and capable of being performed, has not yet received any attention.[111] Often, creating additional categories of »*uncertainty*« or »*pathology*« circumvents the issue.[112] After quickly outlining the already much-advanced discussion on the law applicable to the validity of arbitration agreements, a proposal shall be made how these considerations may be transposed to the not yet widely considered problem of the law applicable to the operability of arbitration agreements - to the extent that this is a question of law and not only of »*fact and degree.*«[113]

---

111 *See only* Hill and Chong, *International Commercial Disputes,* para. 21.2.29 (finding that this question »*should also be governed by the proper law of the arbitration agreeement*« without specifying how to determine such »*proper law*;« also remarking a practice of English courts to »*determine these matters for itself, uninfluenced by foreign law*«).

112 *See in particular Insigma v. Alstom,* [2009] SGCA 24 [35, 37] (often synonymously employing terms like »*uncertainty*«, »*ambiguity*«, »*inoperability*«, »*invalid*« and »*pathological*« with regard to the challenges to the arbitration agreement raised by Insigma). However, as the place of arbitration was Singapore, the administering institution was Singaporean and the underlying licence contract contained a choice of Singaporean law, true conflict of laws questions did not arise there.

113 *Cf.* Tweeddale and Tweeddale, *Arbitration of Commercial Disputes,* para. 4.39.

1. The search for conflict of laws rules for validity issues

»[T]here is no other contract on earth that raises more difficult and complicated conflict of laws questions than the arbitration agreement.«[114]

Difficulties in determining the law applicable to the validity of the arbitration agreement have an obvious reason. The issue arises in different situations and at different stages: before arbitral tribunals and state courts, at the outset of the arbitration, during arbitration or before courts, when a party challenges the award either at the seat or at enforcement stage.[115] These instances do not have the same forum, the arbitral tribunal being said not to have a forum at all,[116] and therefore follow different conflict of laws rules or approaches.

Due to these difficulties, most arbitration scholars employ modern, »*materialised*«, as opposed to traditional conflict of laws approaches.[117] They do not strictly relate to concrete rules of the private international law of any forum.[118] This material or »*functional*« method[119] of evaluating available points of connection in consideration of outcomes and interests involved shall be applied because it best reflects the transnational approach followed herein.

---

114 Rüßmann and Timár, »The Laws Applicable to the Arbitration Agreement«, 859. However, determining the applicable law to the contract with the institution may be an equal challenge, which only received less attention, *see infra* at pp. 236-243 (§11A.II).

115 Ibid., 841 et seq.

116 *See supra* at pp. 65-68 on the delocalisation idea which is accepted to varying degrees.

117 *See* Picone, »Les méthodes«, 84 et seq.; *see also* Kühne, »Methodeneinheit und Methodenvielfalt«, 133. 138 et seq. (on materialisation as one of several trends in private international law); *cf. also* Wolf, *Die Institutionelle Handelsschiedsgerichtsbarkeit*, 15 (»*interessenanalytisch, statt nationalrechtlich dogmatisch*« [guided by an analysis of interests, not by the dogmas of national laws]).

118 Supported by Rome-I-Regulation 2008 art. 1 (2)(e) (EU) (excluding arbitration and choice of court agreements from its scope).

119 *See* Rühl, »Party Autonomy«, 154–55 (»*characterized by antidoctrinalism*«; referring to various works by *Arthur von Mehren*).

## 2. Initial considerations: substance v. procedure

As there is »*no universal consensus*« on what is procedural and what is substantive,[120] it is also difficult to assess the nature of the arbitration agreement.[121] Procedural contracts predominantly affect the parties' procedural status[122] whereas substantive (private law) contracts have their main effects in the private law domain.[123]

The arbitration agreement is often qualified as a procedural contract with the argument that its »*main*« effect is to exclude the jurisdiction of state courts.[124] Some courts, however, have stated that the arbitration agreement is a contract like any other.[125] In theory, the controversy goes back to the underlying dogmatic - almost philosophical - question of whether arbitration is more of juridical or of contractual nature.[126] In practice, the procedural or substantive nature of the arbitration agreement is of little relevance

---

120 Waincymer, *Procedure and Evidence*, para. 1.1.2.

121 *See* Lachmann, *Handbuch für die Schiedsgerichtspraxis*, para. 266; Rüßmann and Timár, »The Laws Applicable to the Arbitration Agreement«, 845–46 (with further references on the dispute); *see already* Walker, *Die freie Gestaltung des Verfahrens vor einem internationalen privaten Schiedsgericht durch die Parteien*, 8–11.

122 Musielak, »Einleitung«, para. 66; based on the theory founded by Schiedermair, *Vereinbarungen im Zivilprozess*, 43 et seq.

123 Schwab, Walter, and Baumbach, *Schiedsgerichtsbarkeit*, chap. 7, para. 37.

124 Ibid. (with further references on the controversy in German doctrine and case law).

125 *See e.g. Volt*, 489 U.S. at 478 (»*like other contracts*«); Urteil [Judgment], [1967] 48 BGHZ 35 at 44, [1967] 20 NJW 2057 (GER BGH) at 2059; *cf.* Rüßmann and Timár, »The Laws Applicable to the Arbitration Agreement«, 846 (finding this case law to support the substantive understanding; with further references); *but see now* Urteil [Judgment], [1987] 40 NJW 651 (GER BGH) (»*Unterfall des Prozeßvertrags*« [subcategory of the procedural contract]).

126 Jurisdictional theories are quite popular *e.g.* in Germany (*see* Saenger, *Handkommentar zur Zivilprozessordnung*, vor [before] 1025, para. 6; *cf. also* the introduction by Schwab, Walter, and Baumbach, *Schiedsgerichtsbarkeit*, 1, para. 1); in contrast, French jurisprudence and doctrine appears to favour more contractual or autonomous concepts (*cf. generally* Lew, Mistelis, and Kröll, *Comparative International Commercial Arbitration*, 5–4, 5–16 et seq., also on »*mixed*« or »*hybrid*« theories).

if one recognises both procedural and substantive implications.[127] Accordingly, the practice often resorts to one of the following - interchangeable - compromises: Either, the arbitration agreement is a substantive contract regulating a procedural relationship or with some procedural effects,[128] or the arbitration agreement is a procedural contract with some substantive effects.[129] In short: the arbitration agreement is »*a procedural and substantive contract, a contract of dual nature.*«[130]

An unambiguous decision in favour of one of the theories would only be required, if the nature of the arbitration agreement determined the applicable law. While the traditional view of procedure being governed by the *lex fori,* substantive issues by the *lex contractus* argues for such determination,[131] it is here suggested to discard this distinction as inappropriate in an international context.

First, it is unclear, which forum would be relevant - the place of arbitration or the forum of a state court rendering a decision on the validity and effects of the arbitration agreement.[132] Second, most codes of procedure do not regulate other than formal aspects of validity of the arbitration agreement, the question of their application is therefore mute where a resort to substantive contract law becomes necessary anyway.[133] That such substantive contract law is not necessarily the law of the place of arbitration but may be a law directly chosen by the parties is not only undisputed but also

---

127 Trittmann and Hanefeld, »Part II, § 1029«, 96, para. 7; *see already* Walker, *Die freie Gestaltung des Verfahrens vor einem internationalen privaten Schiedsgericht durch die Parteien.,* 9.

128 *E.g.* Urteil [Judgment], [1967] 48 BGHZ 44, [1967] 20 NJW 2059.

129 *See also* Trittmann and Hanefeld, »Part II, § 1029«, 96, para. 7; Münch, »§ 1029 ZPO«, para. 13–14.

130 Walker, *Die freie Gestaltung des Verfahrens vor einem internationalen privaten Schiedsgericht durch die Parteien.,* 11; Rüßmann and Timár, »The Laws Applicable to the Arbitration Agreement«, 849; *see also* Voit, »§ 1029 ZPO«, para. 4 (stressing the ambivalence of the arbitration agreement). Of the foundation theories on arbitration (*see supra* at n. 126), the so-called »*mixed*« or »*hybrid*« theory supports this understanding best (*see generally* Steingruber, *Consent in International Arbitration,* para. 4.17–4.22).

131 Rüßmann and Timár, »The Laws Applicable to the Arbitration Agreement«, 847.

132 Ibid.

133 *See* Münch, »§ 1029 ZPO«, para. 15–16.

clarified by the relevant conventions and legislation.[134] Therefore, the complex legal nature should not have any - practical - relevance for conflicts of law questions,[135] but may at most serve as their theoretical explanation.

Accordingly, the practical approach here followed is that any provision which the arbitration specific laws of a state, the *lex arbitri in strictu sensu*,[136] seeks to impose on arbitrations seated in its territory applies independently of the law chosen or otherwise applicable to the validity of the arbitration agreement.[137] This includes questions of form of the arbitration agreement, the *essentialia* of an arbitration agreement,[138] the arbitrability of the dispute and all questions of arbitration procedure, including non-waivable procedural guarantees of due process[139] but also specific framework conditions for institutional arbitration if regulated in the lex arbitri.[140] All questions that the lex arbitri does not address may be governed by a different law expressly or impliedly chosen by the parties.

To illustrate this approach with a controversial but accessible example: If parties provided for arbitration with a place of arbitration in mainland China, Chinese arbitration law would apply in its entirety,[141] including requirements pertaining to the validity of arbitration agreements like the need to specify an arbitration commission.[142] To require a clear designation of an arbitration commission is an arbitration specific policy choice of the Chinese legislator, which parties have to abide by - independent of the

---

134 New York Convention, art. V (1)(a); European Arbitration Convention, art. VI (2)(d); *cf.* UNCITRAL Model Law 2006 art. 34 (2) (a)(i). This is even acknowledged in China (*see* SPC's Interpretation of Arbitration Law, art. 16 [2006]).

135 *Contra* Rüßmann and Timár, »The Laws Applicable to the Arbitration Agreement«, 849.

136 Herein, terms like »*arbitration law*« and »*lex arbitri*« are used to refer to such arbitration specific laws of the place of arbitration only, to the exclusion of procedural laws inapplicable to arbitration and substantive laws of the place of arbitration.

137 An approach in practice largely accepted *see* (*see* Blackaby et al., *Redfern and Hunter*, para. 3.43, 3.60–63.61, on the dogmatic question if the *lex arbitri* is a procedural law).

138 *See supra* at pp. 158-161 (§8A).

139 Discussed *infra* at pp. 86§4C et seq. (at C).

140 *See infra* at pp. 91-106 (§4C.II.2).

141 *See also supra* at p. 69 (at §4B.I) on the determination or »*choice*« of the law of arbitration.

142 Arbitration Law art. 16 (2), 18 (P.R.C.).

questionable merits of such policy choice. Subjecting the validity of the arbitration agreement to another law, *e.g.* by express choice of *e.g.* Swiss law as the law of the arbitration agreement,[143] cannot validly circumvent this policy choice. Rather, a choice of Swiss law for the arbitration agreement would then have to be understood as a reference to the Swiss law of obligations to govern only those questions not specifically and mandatorily addressed by the law of arbitration.

3. Law of the arbitration agreement beyond the lex arbitri

Most arbitration laws do not govern general questions of the law of obligations, including formation, substantive validity and interpretation of contracts. Here, the discussion on the applicable law really becomes decisive.

Parties can of course directly choose the law applicable to the formation and substantive validity of their arbitration agreement,[144] but they almost never do and most institutional rules are silent on the matter.[145] Absent express choice, there are a number of conceivable views.[146] Many suggest applying either the law applicable to the main contract, including a law chosen to govern that contract,[147] or the contract law of the place of arbitration.[148]

---

143 *See also* Blackaby et al., *Redfern and Hunter*, para. 3.62: »*once a place of arbitration has been chosen, it brings with it its own law. If that law contains provisions that are mandatory so far as arbitrations are concerned, those provisions must be obeyed. It is not a matter of choice, any more than the notional motorist is free to choose which local traffic laws to obey and which to disregard.*«

144 *Cf.* New York Convention, art. V (1)(a); European Arbitration Convention, art. VI (2)(d).

145 *But see* LCIA Rules, art. 16 (4) (2014) (providing for the law of the seat to apply by default); *see also* Hong Kong International Arbitration Centre, »Model Clauses« (recommending an express choice in the new model clause).

146 *See generally* Lew, »The Law Applicable to the Form and Substance of the Arbitration Clause«.

147 Ibid., 143 (with further references, speaking of a »*strong presumption*« that a law chosen for the main contract shall also govern the arbitration agreement); *see also* Yuen, »Arbitration Clauses in a Chinese Context«, 584–85.

148 This view is backed by the relevant international conventions (*cf.* New York Convention, art. V [1][a]; European Arbitration Convention, art. VI

It is further proposed that the arbitration agreement is autonomous from all national laws, which is why its validity and interpretation should follow general principles without resort to a particular national law.[149]

There are arguments for and against each view. If the arbitration clause is part of a main contract, and not a separate submission agreement, it is likely that the parties assumed it to be governed by the same law. However, the principle[150] of separability, according to which an arbitration clause is an agreement distinct, »*independent*«, »*separable*«/»*severable*« or »*autonomous*«[151] from the main contract, weakens this presumption.[152]

Applying the law of the place of arbitration is reasonable as it already governs arbitration specific aspects.[153] However, when designating a neutral seat, parties would hardly ever consider that state's general law of

---

[2][d]; leaving the question open: Beschluss [Decision], [2012] 10 SchiedsVZ 337 [GER KG, Berlin]).

149 Leading case: *Dalico*, [1994] Rev. Arb. 116 (FR C.Cass) 116, 117; *see also* Petsche, *The Growing Autonomy of International Commercial Arbitration*, 79, 80 (with further references on this approach predominant in France).

150 Or »*doctrine*« or »*notion*« or »*presumption*« (*see* Born, *International Commercial Arbitration (2014)*, 352; Trittmann and Hanefeld, »Part II, § 1029«, 9).

151 On the variances in terminology, *see* Born, *International Commercial Arbitration (2014)*, 350–51 (autonomy reflecting the civil or Roman law concept, separability the common law understanding). This thesis prefers the term »*separability*« to avoid confusion with the discussion on arbitration's proposed autonomy from national laws (*see also* ibid., 351).

152 This is accepted in virtually all relevant jurisdictions *see e.g.* the codifications in: UNCITRAL Model Law 2006 art. 16 (1); ZPO § 1040 (1) sentence 2 (GER); Arbitration Act 1996 art. 7 (EW); IAA § 21 (2) (SG); IPRG art. 178 (3) (C.H.); CPC art. 1506, 1447 (FR); for US law, *cf. Prima Paint*, 388 U.S. 395 (1967); *Buckeye v. Cardegna*, 546 U.S. 440, 446 (2006); *cf. also* Graves and Davydan, »Competence-Competence«, 157 (finding competence-competence and separability to serve »*hand in glove*«); *see generally* Born, *International Commercial Arbitration (2014)*, 350 (§3.01) (»*separability presumption is of central significance in international commercial arbitration*«); for China, *see* Arbitration Law art. 19 (P.R.C.); Ch'eng, Moser, and Wang, *International Arbitration in the People's Republic of China*, 65–67; *see already* Kaplan, Spruce, and Moser, *Hong Kong and China Arbitration*, 314 (but remarking uncertainties as to the extent of the principle).

153 *See supra* at pp. 68-75 (§4B.I).

obligations and might thus be surprised to learn it being applicable. The third, »*French*«[154] way of resorting to general principles acknowledges that most contract laws are more or less aligned, in particular for commercial contracts, in that they rely on principles such as consent, intent, reasonable expectations, good faith and *pacta sunt savanda*. However, if common principles solving a certain question cannot be found or if there is disagreement on a certain consideration, this approach meets its limits.

Applying the mentioned connections alternatively[155] instead of exclusively eliminates most problems: If a question of formation, substantive validity or interpretation, which the *lex arbitri* does not regulate, can be solved by transnationally acknowledged principles of contract law, there is no need to search for the applicable law at all.[156] Otherwise, the law chosen for that contract, unless the main contract's validity or the validity of the choice of law clause is in doubt, primarily governs an arbitration clause in a contract. Then, or if the main contract does not contain any choice of law clause, the arbitration agreement is governed by the law of the place of arbitration, including its law of obligations.

### 4. Law applicable to the operability of the arbitration agreement

The here preferred approach regarding the law applicable to the formation and validity of arbitration agreements can be transposed to their operability. The operability of arbitration agreements may be in doubt for reasons specifically addressed by the *lex arbitri*. Then, this law applies, notwithstanding any contrary express or implied choice of law.

A modification of above example can illustrate this view:[157] The parties choose a place of arbitration in China and a specific arbitration commission and subject their contract to Swiss law. If the designated Chinese arbitration commission is dissolved, it is a question of Chinese arbitration law and not

---

154 *Cf.* Blackaby et al., *Redfern and Hunter*, para. 3.30.

155 *Cf.* UNCITRAL Model Law 2006 art. 34 (2)(a)(i) (on a state court's perspective in setting-aside proceedings; but leaving it open how to determine »*the law to which the parties have subjected*« the arbitration agreement); for an adoption of this rule, *see e.g.* ZPO § 1059 (2) no. 1 (a) (GER); clearer and more liberal: IPRG art. 178 (2) (C.H.) (expressly stipulating an alternative approach to the law applicable to the validity of the arbitration agreement).

156 *See infra* at pp. 161-65 (§8B) on the principle of effective interpretation.

157 *See supra* at p. 80.

Swiss law if such dissolution renders the arbitration agreement incapable of being performed. Even if the choice of Swiss law for the main contract were interpreted as an implied choice of Swiss law also for the arbitration agreement, it would only relate to aspects not specifically regulated in the arbitration law. As Chinese law requires arbitrations to be administered by arbitration commissions, does not support ad hoc arbitration and does not provide for means of court determination of an arbitration commission,[158] it seems that the verdict of inoperability cannot be avoided. To resort to Swiss law would of course bring a different result, as Swiss law accepts ad hoc arbitration and does not require the designation of an institution at all. Moreover, Swiss courts could support the arbitration process *e.g.* by appointing arbitrators or determining applicable arbitration rules.[159] However, if the place of arbitration is in China and not in Switzerland, a Swiss court could not provide such support. This exemplifies that it is usually unhelpful to have regard to arbitration laws of states other than the seat when assessing arbitration agreement's procedural operability - even if parties wanted to apply such laws to their arbitration agreement.[160]

If the operability of an arbitration agreement is challenged for reasons not contemplated by the law of arbitration, the impossibility to perform the arbitration agreement and its consequences should again be assessed under the transnationally acknowledged principles of law. Where such principles cannot be identified, any law expressly or impliedly also chosen for the arbitration clause or alternatively the law of obligations of the place of arbitration may be referred to. However, this only applies to grounds of inoperability that have their roots in the relationship of the parties to the arbitration agreement alone. What makes conflict of laws questions regarding the operability of arbitration agreements most difficult is that it may depend on the conduct of and relationships with third parties - notably arbitral institutions and tribunals.

In particular, it may be argued that a hybrid arbitration agreement was incapable of being performed because the designated institution refuses or would refuse to administer the case under other than its own rules or that the designated arbitration institution was not allowed to apply another

---

158  *Cf.* Arbitration Law art. 16 (2), 18 (P.R.C.).
159  *See* IPRG art. 185 (C.H.); *cf.* Kröll, »Commentary on Chapter 12 PILS«, 141 (»*catch all*« provision).
160  Although some jurisdictions allow their courts in exceptional circumstances to support foreign or potentially foreign arbitrations, *see infra* at p. 413, n. 48.

institution's rules *e.g.* for infringement of copyright or unfair competition allegations. The first argument, the arbitration institution's possible refusal to administer the arbitration, is governed by the law applicable to the contract to be concluded between such institution and the parties, discussed in more detail in Chapter 3.[161] The second argument, the possible illegality of administering arbitrations under another institution's rules, is to be considered under the law applicable to copyright infringements or unfair competition. Here, not only the place of arbitration but the seats of the administering institution and the institution that issued the applicable rules may be relevant connecting factors as elaborated in Chapter 4.[162]

Expressed concisely, the conflict of laws problem is this: There is not a single law applicable to the arbitration agreement. Rather, it is inevitable to apply the most appropriate law separately to each issue of validity or operability raised. That »*this piles up the proper laws absurdly high*«[163] cannot be avoided.[164] The pile becomes even higher if one also has to consider the position of institutions and arbitrators.[165] However, in order to keep the assessment manageable, it is useful to first look at the *lex arbitri* as the starting point. Where this law covers a particular question of validity or operability of the arbitration agreement, independent of the qualification of such question as formal, procedural or substantive, it applies directly.

Where an issue of validity or operability is not contemplated by the *lex arbitri* and not uniformly answered by transnational principles of arbitration and contract law, resort may be had to any law expressly or impliedly chosen to govern such question. Failing such choice, the place of arbitration will often be one relevant connecting factor to determine the applicable law.

---

161 *See infra* at pp. 236-243 (§11A.II).

162 *See infra* at 297 et seq.

163 As regretted by Mustill, J in *Black Clawson v. PWA*, [1981] 2 Lloyd's Rep 446 (EW Comm.) at 455.

164 *Cf.* Born, *Commentary and Materials (2001)*, 524 (at ch. 7 A.1.: »*peculiarly complex example of depecage*«).

165 Next to the »*lex fori, the proper law of the main contract, the proper law of the arbitration agreement, and the procedural law of the arbitration*« (Steingruber, *Consent in International Arbitration*, para. 4.19, n. 38), the laws of the arbitrator's contract, the institution's contracts with parties and arbitrators and even certain tort laws may affect the arbitration agreement's validity and capability of being performed (*see also infra* at pp. 236-243, §11A.II, pp. 297-304, §13A.III, and pp. 333-340, §13C.IV).

## C. Limits to party autonomy in arbitration laws

The general relationship between party agreement and arbitration law is proposed by article 19 (1) of the UNCITRAL Model Law (»*Subject to the provisions of this Law*«). Arbitration laws of all major arbitration jurisdictions incorporate this principle as well:[166] An agreement of the parties cannot overcome mandatory provisions of the law applicable to the arbitration proceedings, the *lex arbitri*, which is generally the arbitration law of the place of arbitration.[167]

A restricted factual exception to this proposition only applies if parties also expressly waive their right to setting-aside actions against the award in the arbitration agreement. Then, a disrespect of the *lex arbitri* might not have any legal consequence.[168] However, with regard to procedural irregularities,[169] this is only possible in a few jurisdictions like Switzerland,[170] Belgium[171] and Sweden.[172] For the majority of jurisdictions,[173] this consideration applies: Practically, the losing party may comply with the award without attempting any challenge - no complaint, no redress.[174] Legally,

---

166 *See supra* at pp. 60-63.
167 Waincymer, *Procedure and Evidence*, para. 3.7.1 (»*generally* [...] *accepted that mandatory procedural laws of the Seat apply*«); *see also* Merkin, *Arbitration Law1*, para. 14.2 (noting that the requirement of fairness is mandatory and »*not open to the parties to attempt to contract out of*«). *See supra* at pp. 68-74 on the seat principle.
168 At enforcement stage, the seat's law is then only of subsidiary importance (New York Convention, art. V (1)(d); *but see* Gaillard and Savage, *Fouchard, Gaillard, Goldmann*, para. 1183 - noting that any control of by the enforcement forum under the angle of the seat's law was both »*unsatisfactory*« and »*inappropriate*«).
169 English law only allows to waive substantive challenges, *cf.* Arbitration Act 1996 § 69 (EW); *see also* Born, *Law and Practice (2012)*, 335 n. 159 (naming Tunisia as another example of the »*few*« states providing for a complete waiver of recourse to state courts).
170 *See* IPRG art. 193 (1) (C.H.).
171 *See* CJ (BE.) art. 1718 (Belgium).
172 Lag om skiljeförfarande 1999 § 51 (Sweden).
173 All those not knowing a waiver of appeal (*cf.* Spohnheimer, *Gestaltungsfreiheit*, 66).
174 There is a German proverb saying »*Wo kein Kläger, da kein Richter*« [where there is no applicant, there is no judge]; *cf. also* Wagner, »*Part II*, § 1025«, para. 27.

however, the award can only resist challenges, if the arbitration procedure respected mandatory provisions of the law of the seat.

A mandatory provision

»is simply one where the relevant legislature wishes the norm to apply regardless of the will of the parties or regardless of any discretion otherwise given to an arbitrator.«[175]

For UNCITRAL Model Law countries, it can generally be said that all provisions concerning equal treatment of the parties and the right to be heard are mandatory.[176] These safeguards arguably already follow from international human rights conventions.[177] Besides, there are some variations in national arbitration laws about which provisions are mandatory.[178] The following overview pursues the task to shed some light on mandatory arbitration law in different jurisdictions - without aiming at completeness - before discussing the relevance of such mandatory law for the validity of hybrid arbitration agreements.

I. Mandatory arbitration law - an overview

As a rule of thumb, mandatory are only the provisions concerning the powers of state courts in relation to the arbitration (»*external relationship*«)[179]

---

175  Waincymer, *Procedure and Evidence*, para. 3.7.1.

176  *Cf.* UNCITRAL Model Law 2006 art. 18. Details on the extent of the right to be heard, e.g. if it encompasses the right to oral hearings or a contradictory debate, are disputed, *see* Waincymer, *Procedure and Evidence*, para. 3.7.1 (on perceived differences in various laws and arbitration rules between a »*full opportunity*« and »*reasonable opportunity*« to present its case).

177  *See in particular* ECHR, art. 6; IACHR, art. 8; *see also* ICCPR, art. 14 (1); Universal Declaration of Human Rights, art. 8, 10. The direct application of these guarantees to arbitration is debatable, (*see generally* Petrochilos, *Procedural Law in International Arbitration*, para. 4.07–4.08; Waincymer, *Procedure and Evidence*, para. 3.11.2; *see also* Clapman, *Human Rights in the Private Sphere*, 343, 356, favouring a direct horizontal effect of human rights treaties; *cf. also* X v. Germany, 5 YB ECHR. 94–96, 96 (1962), holding that an arbitration agreement does not waive the guarantee of a fair trial in art. 6 ECHR).

178  *Cf.* Horn, »Zwingendes Recht in der internationalen Schiedsgerichtsbarkeit«, 211.

179  Born, *International Commercial Arbitration (2014)*, 1532.

and all manifestations of due process rights like fair and equal treatment of the parties. This requires certain independence and impartiality of arbitrators and respect of the right to be heard.[180]

If one takes a look at Germany's arbitration law as an example of an UNCITRAL Model Law jurisdiction, one notices quickly that identifying mandatory provisions is not easy. While consulting the text of the law may be an enlightening exercise in many situations,[181] it is unfortunately rather fruitless here. The wordings of the provisions of the tenth book of the ZPO (GER) give no clear indication.

Of course, a great number of provisions expressly allow for derogating party agreements.[182] However, to conclude from such provisions expressly allowing for derogation that all other provisions of sections 1025 et seq. ZPO (GER) were mandatory would be a mistaken reversal - an inadmissible *argumentum e contrario*.[183] It is true that such a conclusion would be consistent with the logic of good drafting, but unfortunately,[184] the German legislator did not smooth out the uncertainties already embodied in the UNCITRAL Model Law. When drafting the UNCITRAL Model Law, the working group's discussion about labelling all dispositive and mandatory provisions ended without result.[185] Of the provisions not expressly open to an opt-out, some are mandatory, others not. Whether a

---

180 *Cf.* Nicholls and Bloch, »ICC Hybrid Arbitrations Here to Stay«, 404.

181 In line with the German saying »*Ein Blick ins Gesetz erleichtert die Rechtsfindung*«– which could be roughly translated as »*A look at the law simplifies the search for justice.*«

182 *E.g.* ZPO § 1034 (1) (GER) (number of arbitrators), ibid., § 1035 (arbitrator nomination); ibid., §§ 1037, 1039 (arbitrator challenge and replacement), ibid., § 1041 (provisional measures); ibid., §§ 1043, 1045 (choice of the place and language of arbitration), ibid., § 1046 (2) (preclusion); ibid., § 1047 (oral hearing), ibid., § 1048 (default consequences); ibid., § 1049 (tribunal appointed experts), ibid., § 1051 (law applicable to the merits); ibid., § 1052 (principle of majority decision), ibid., § 1054 (reasoned award); ibid., § 1057 (decision on costs), ibid., § 1058 (2), 1059 (3) (procedural delays).

183 *But see* Raeschke-Kessler and Berger, *Recht und Praxis des Schiedsverfahrens*, para. 128.

184 Khadjavi, *ICC-Schiedsordnung und deutsches Schiedsverfahrensrecht*, 9; Münch, »§ 1042 ZPO«, para. 15.

185 *See* Note by the Secretariat 1983 p. 79 (U.N.).

provision is mandatory or non-mandatory is supposed to be deductible from the legislative materials or the purpose of the provision.[186]

Clearer than Model Law inspired legislation, English law enumerates in Schedule 1 to its Arbitration Act exactly which provisions (25 of 100 provisions) are mandatory. Of course, Schedule 1 contains also the basic principles of fair and equal treatment and the right to be heard.[187]

In other, non-Model Law jurisdictions arbitration legislation restricts itself to simply naming these most important principles. It leaves all other questions to the agreement of the parties. *E.g.*, article 1510 of the French code of civil procedure (Code de Procedure Civile) (CPC) provides:

> »Quelle que soit la procédure choisie, le tribunal arbitral garantit l'égalité des parties et respecte le principe de la contradiction.«

> [Irrespective of the procedure adopted, the arbitral tribunal shall ensure that the parties are treated equally and shall uphold the principle of due process.]

Very similarly drafted is article 182 (3) of the Swiss federal act on private international law (Bundesgesetz über das internationale Privatrecht) (IPRG). Along the same line, US courts have held that only minimal requirements of due process limit procedural party autonomy in international arbitration.[188] Apart from such fundamental principles, these arbitration laws contain no additional rules on procedure. The parties are responsible to agree on sufficient procedural rules. Failing such agreement, they have to pay the price for this procedural freedom: far-reaching discretion of the arbitral tribunal.[189]

To be clear, one has to note that while there is broad acceptance of due process principles (right to be heard, equal treatment of the parties) as a limit to party autonomy, there are varied understandings regarding the detailed content of these principles. *E.g.*, there is no transnationally valid answer to the questions whether the right to be heard encompasses the right to

---

186 *Cf.* Entwurf eines Gesetzes zur Neuregelung des Schiedsverfahrensrechts, Bundestagsdrucksache 13/5274 at 46, 76 (1996).

187 Arbitration Act 1996 § 36 (EW).

188 *See e.g. Karaha Bodas v. PPM Dan Gas Bumi Negra*, 364 F.3d at 298–99; *see also Whittemore Overseas Co., Inc. v Société Générale de l'Industrie de Papier et al.*, 508 F.2d 969, 976 (2nd Cir. 1974) (arguing that, in the interest of efficiency and in light of the international character of a dispute, due process requirements are lower for arbitration proceedings); *see generally* Born, *International Commercial Arbitration (2014)*, 2169 (§15.04 [B][1]; quoting the just cited decisions, with further references).

189 Petrochilos, *Procedural Law in International Arbitration*, para. 3.78.

oral hearing and to what extent every aspect, including points of law, are to be dealt with in an adversarial manner.[190] There are also important differences in national arbitration laws concerning arbitrability, meaning the question which subject matters can be resolved by arbitration.[191]

## II. In particular: mandatory arbitration law against hybrid arbitration?

In their article on hybrid arbitration agreements and the Singaporean decisions in *Insigma v. Alstom*[192] and *HKL v. Rizq*,[193] Anthony Nicholls and Christopher Bloch noticed to be

> »*not* aware of *any* mandatory provisions in *any* national arbitration law that restrict the parties' ability to choose a hybrid form of arbitration [*emphasis added*].«[194]

### 1. No general due process concerns

In general, above overview of mandatory provisions underlines this negative finding. Especially, fair trial and due process rights appear not seriously at risk. At the outset, nothing suggests that the administration of an arbitration by another than the rules issuing institution would sacrifice the parties' right to be heard or that it would increase the risk of arbitrators acting partial.

However, if the administering institution is insufficiently prepared to administer arbitrations under the chosen rules, situations that put due process rights to a test are imaginable, in particular if state courts have a policy to

---

190 *See* Blackaby et al., *Redfern and Hunter*, para. 10.50.
191 Waincymer, *Procedure and Evidence*, para. 3.2.8 (also criticising the broader use of the term by US courts and authors covering all jurisdictional issues under this heading); *see also* Lew, Mistelis, and Kröll, *Comparative International Commercial Arbitration*, para. 9.4. According to the Supreme Court, arbitrability »*depends upon whether the parties agreed to arbitrate that dispute*« (*see First Options*, 514 U.S. 938, 938, 944 [1995], 115 S.Ct. 1920, 1921 1924 [US 1995] [although calling this a »*narrow question*«]; *see further* Shore, »The United States' Perspective on ›Arbitrability‹«, 69).
192 *Insigma v. Alstom*, [2009] SGCA 24.
193 *HKL v. Rizq I*, [2013] SGHC 5; *HKL v. Rizq II*, [2013] SGHC 8; *see supra* at pp. 38, 47.
194 »ICC Hybrid Arbitrations Here to Stay«, 404.

pay deference to institutional decisions. The argument that parties, by agreeing to a certain set of arbitration rules, waived their right to a reasoned decision or to an oral hearing concerning a challenge to jurisdiction or to an arbitrator[195] is less convincing if the institution rendering such decision is not the one contemplated by the applicable rules. The administering institution's organs and staff might be unable to warrant for the same degree of experience and care in rendering such decisions than the rules issuing institution.[196] It would be particularly worrying if an institution performed its services pursuant to a hybrid arbitration agreement in an intransparent way without consulting with the parties prior to taking relevant decisions, raising the question whether institutions have to abide by fair trial principles or if they can escape such duty by qualifying their decisions as merely »*administrative*« rather than judicial.[197]

However, even if hybrid arbitration increased the risk of due process violations in comparison to standard institutional arbitration, mere possibility of abuse by the institution, who is a third party to the arbitration agreement, would not invalidate the arbitration agreement itself. Only if a procedure in line with the mandatory provisions of the arbitration law cannot be expected at all, specific procedural arrangements could render the arbitration agreement invalid or inoperable. For hybrid arbitration agreements, one might expect that the administering institution would organise the arbitration in close cooperation with the parties and in respect of their rights. If this expectation were disappointed in a particular case, this would be a defect of the procedure but not of the agreement itself.[198]

## 2. The skeletal legislation on institutional arbitration

Opposition to hybrid arbitration may follow from principles governing institutional arbitration as distinct from ad hoc arbitration.[199] However,

---

195 *See Opinter v. Dacomex*, [1987] Rev. Arb. 479–80 (FR C.Cass) 480.
196 *See infra* at pp. 344-400 (§14) on requirements for substitution of institutional actors.
197 *See also infra* at pp. 435-438 (§16A.II.3.a) and pp. 444-447 (§16B.I).
198 *See also infra* at pp. 463 et seq. (§17A) on corresponding challenges to a resulting award.
199 As discussed in Chapter 2, *infra* at pp. 126-157 (§7).

international conventions or national arbitration laws do not focus much on this distinction at all.[200]

### a. Stipulations in international conventions

Neither does the New York Convention define institutional arbitration, nor does it contain any specific provisions on it. The reason for this is that the New York Convention does not regulate arbitration proceedings as such but only the recognition and enforcement of awards and to a limited extent that of arbitration agreements. In contrast, the European Arbitration Convention deals more extensively with arbitration agreements and proceedings and accordingly mentions the possibility of administered arbitration expressly.

### i. Article I (2) of the New York Convention

Only concerning the convention's scope of application, article I (2) of the New York Convention stipulates:

> »The term ›*arbitral awards*‹ shall include not only awards made by arbitrators appointed for each case but also those made by permanent arbitral bodies to which the parties have submitted.«

Historically, article I (2) New York Convention was meant to cover permanent arbitral bodies created by law or decree in the former U.S.S.R. and Czechoslovakia.[201] Today, the reference to »*permanent arbitral bodies*« might be understood to refer to arbitration institutions in general or only to those institutions like the International Commercial Arbitration Court of the Chamber of Commerce and Industry of the Russian Federation (ICAC),

---

200  *Cf.* Poudret and Besson, *Comparative Law of International Arbitration*, para. 93.
201  *See* ECOSOC, Enforcement Committee Report, para. 25 (1955) (rejecting the original Sovjet proposal); reintroduced by Czechoslovakia, Amendment to Art. 1; *cf. also* van den Berg, »111. Permanent Arbitral Bodies«.

considered a successor of FTAC,[202] some Eastern European institutions[203] and CIETAC that are still constituted by law or decree.[204]

However, not even the latter institutions render »*awards*« in need of recognition and enforcement. Only arbitral *tribunals* render awards. Neither the establishment of an institution by law, nor compulsory arbitrator lists, which only very few institutions still operate,[205] contradict the observation that the arbitrators are appointed »*for each case*« - not permanently - for about all commercial arbitrations.[206] Moreover, at least in theory, arbitrators are proclaimed independent from all institutions here considered and the states in which these are established.[207] If the second paragraph of the New

---

202 *See* Annex I to Law on International Commercial Arbitration art. 2, 4 (RF); *see also* ICAC's self-presentation: The Chamber of Commerce and Industry at the Russian Federation, »Commercial Arbitration in Russia (Historical)«.

203 For the CCIR, *see* Law on the Chamber of Commerce of Romania 2007 art. 29 (RO); with its Modifying Act 2011 (RO).

204 CIETAC's status can be traced back to the government's decision to create a Foreign Trade Arbitration Commission (*see* in anti-chronological order: Official Reply concerning the Renaming of FETAC into CIETAC [1988]; Notice concerning the conversion of FTAC into FETAC 1980 [P.R.C.]; Decision concerning the Establishment of FTAC 1954 [P.R.C.]; all published in English in *Selected Works of CIETAC*, xlv - xlvii; *see also* CIETAC, »About Us | Introduction« [historic self-presentation]).

205 Lists no longer mandatory under CIETAC Rules, art. 24 (2) (2012) = art. 26 (2) (2015) (allowing expressly agreed nominations of arbitrators outside the CIETAC panel »*subject to the confirmation by the Chairman of CIETAC*«); CCIR Rules, art. 17 (2) (2014) (appointment from the list only in case of default or non-agreement); *see also* ICAC Rules, art. 3 (4) (2010) (possibility to nominate co-arbitrators from outside the list); *but see still* CCIR Rules 2013 art. 18, 20, 91 et seq. (previous version; arbitrators could only be chosen from a fixed list, except when parties expressly agree on »*ad-hoc*« arbitration, for which the CCIR would provide some support); ICAC Rules, art. 17 (7), (9) (2010) (sole and presiding arbitrators to be appointed by ICAC from the list).

206 *Contra* Enforcement Committee Report, para. 25 (1955); as rightly pointed out by the UK delegate, *see* UNCITRAL and ECOSOC, »8th Meeting Summary Record«, 5; *see also* ibid., 6 (Swiss delegate Mr. Pointet seeing a necessity to clarify the validity of awards issued by institutions with mandatory lists).

207 ICAC's arbitrator list currently names more than 170 people to choose from, not all of which are of Russian origin (available at: The Chamber of Commerce and Industry at the Russian Federation, »List of Arbitrators«).

York Convention's article I has not always been obsolete, it is today.[208] Important for the Convention's application is only the voluntariness of the arbitration,[209] meaning that the arbitral tribunal's jurisdiction is based on an agreement of the parties.[210]

In any case, article I (2) of the New York Convention does not give any indication on the rules that should be applied before »*permanent arbitral tribunals*« independent of the question if today's arbitral institutions still belong to that category. Therefore, it cannot limit the parties' autonomy to refer a case to one institution by at the same time choosing another institution's rules.

---

In contrast, panels of communist/socialist institutions before the collapse of the U.S.S.R. were very restricted, making the choice »*more illusory then real*« (*see* Pisar, »The Communist System of Foreign-Trade Adjudication«, 1422, 1424, also doubting the independence of Soviet arbitrators then inevitably »*employed and paid by the government*«).

208 *Cf.* Bagner, »Art. I«, 21 (»*of much less interest*«); van den Berg, »111. Permanent Arbitral Bodies« (»*superfluous*«); *see already* Sanders, »111. Field of Arbitration - Permanent Arbitral Bodies« (calling the application of the convention to institutional arbitration »*obvious*«).

209 *See* »8th Meeting Summary Record« (for the delegates' discussion, whether arbitrations before permanent »*arbitration*« bodies meant by the proposal would be voluntary); *summarised by* van den Berg, *The New York Arbitration Convention of 1958*, 379–80; *cf. also* Glossner, »Institutionelle Schiedsrichterernennung«, 555 (remarking that the underlying conflict between planned and free markets was simply ignored in the parallel discussions to the European Arbitration Convention). Czechoslowakia's delegate agreed to adding »*to which the parties have voluntarily submitted*«, explaining that the proposal was merely supposed to cover awards rendered by »*independent arbitrators*« (*see* »8th Meeting Summary Record«, 5).

210 Decisions of the Russian Supreme Arbitrazh Court are, despite the confusing terminology, not arbitral awards (*see also* Yoshida, »History of International Commercial Arbitration and Its Related System in Russia«, 377). The court is a state court *inter alia* competent to review decisions of lower courts referred to as »*Arbirazh*« courts for historical reasons (*see* ibid., 378, explaining the system with failings of the people's courts in commercial matters). *Arbitrazh* should be translated with »*commercial*« rather than with »*arbitration*«.

## ii. Article IV (1)(a) of the European Arbitration Convention

The wording of the European Arbitration Convention suggests that party autonomy is limited if the parties submit their disputes to a »*permanent arbitral institution*«:

»Article IV - Organisation of the Arbitration

1. The parties to an arbitration agreement shall be free to submit their disputes:

(a) to a permanent arbitral institution; *in this case*, the arbitration proceedings shall be held in conformity with the rules of the said institution;

(b) to an ad hoc arbitral procedure; *in this case*, they shall be free inter alia

(i) to appoint arbitrators or to establish means for their appointment in the event of an actual dispute;

(ii) to determine the place of arbitration; and

(iii) to lay down the procedure to be followed by the arbitrators [*emphasis added*].«

From its wording, the provision assumes that the parties opting for arbitration before a permanent institution delegate all procedural decisions to the institution and that only in case of an ad hoc procedure (»*in this case*«) parties are granted further procedural choices. If this understanding were correct, hybrid arbitration would not be possible among parties to which the European Arbitration Convention applies.[211] It would not even be possible to agree on less radical derogations from only a few of the institution's rules.

However, such a strict literal interpretation contradicts not only arbitration practice, as most institutional rules allow for derogation albeit to varying degrees,[212] but was also not intended.[213] To the contrary, article VI of the European Arbitration Convention has to be seen in the context of its drafting history and purpose. The »*revolutionary*« idea was to enable a harmonised arbitration regime independent of the divergent procedural laws of the contracting states.[214] This idea stems from a draft by the ICC of 1953,

---

211  *See supra* at p. 59, n. 15.

212  *See infra* at pp. 209 et seq. (§10).

213  *Cf.* Moller, »Schiedsverfahrensnovelle und Europäisches Übereinkommen«, 63 (noting that drafters did not want to disadvantage institutional arbitration).

214  *See* Mezger, »Das Europäische Übereinkommen über die Handelsschiedsgerichtsbarkeit«, 255; *cf.* also Fouchard, *L'arbitrage commercial international*, para. 1184; Klein, »La Convention européenne sur l'arbitrage commercial international«, 634–35.

which had been basis of the discussion for the New York Convention.[215] However, the New York Convention could not achieve this goal, mainly since it only covers the recognition and enforcement of agreements and awards but not the arbitration itself.[216] The European Arbitration Convention then followed the original idea to create harmonised law on arbitration procedure by setting up a liberal regulation in article VI of the European Convention[217], which overrides, by force of an international convention, more restrictive arbitration laws of contracting states - unfortunately to date with only limited territorial scope.[218] Article VI of the European Convention is therefore only concerned with the relationship between national law and party autonomy, wanting the latter to prevail.

In other words, the default procedure set up in article VI of the European Convention has the force of a uniform, *non-mandatory* lex arbitri for arbitrations falling under the convention.[219] Despite the problematic drafting (»*in this case*«), the provision is not setting up a monopoly of the institution to determine procedure. Article XI (1)(d) of the European Arbitration Convention, according to which disrespect of the rules laid down in article VI is only a ground for setting-aside »*failing*« an agreement by the parties, finally makes clear that direct party agreement may trump institutional rules. Hence, a party agreement that other institutional rules shall apply may trump the rules of the administering institution also under the European Arbitration Convention.[220]

---

215 International Chamber of Commerce, Committee on International Commercial Arbitration, »Enforcement of International Arbitral Awards: Report and Preliminary Draft Convention«; *see also* Born, *Commentary and Materials (2001)*, 93–95, 100 et seq.

216 *Cf.* Glossner, »UN-Übereinkommen: 40 Jahre danach«, 221 (regretting that the world was not yet ready for former ICC Secretary General Frédéric Eisemann's idea of an »*international*« - as opposed to »*foreign*« - award); paper previously published in English: Glossner, »From New York (1958) to Geneva (1961) - a Veteran's Diary«, 6.

217 *Cf.* Klein, »La Convention européenne sur l'arbitrage commercial international«, 634 (explaining the purpose of the provision and its origins).

218 *See supra* at p. 59, n. 15.

219 *See* Klein, »La Convention européenne sur l'arbitrage commercial international«, 634.

220 Subject to any contractual priority as discussed *infra* at pp. 232 et seq. (§11).

## b. Rarity of national legislation on institutional arbitration

The UNCITRAL Model Law does not contain any reference to institutional arbitration at all and many other important arbitration laws simply provide for a free choice of arbitration rules, whether such rules are of institutional or other nature.[221] Apart from that, they do not contain any provisions attempting to regulate the practice of institutional arbitration in general, let alone the specific question of whether parties may choose one institution but another institution's rules.

### i. A regard to article 14 (2) of the Spanish arbitration law

A rare example of legislation on institutional arbitration of a Western state can be found in Spain's arbitration law, which stipulates notably in its article 14 (2):

> »Arbitral institutions shall exercise their functions in accordance with their rules.«[222]

Scholarly discussion of the provision is vague. Annotations to the provision do not mention the issue of hybrid arbitration agreements.[223] One could possibly understand that the principle that institutions shall exercise their functions under »*their*« rules opposes modification or opting-out of institutional rules. However, the provision first addresses arbitral institutions, not the parties. It should therefore not be interpreted as a mandatory provision but only as a default rule if parties refer to an institution in their arbitration agreement without making additional stipulations regarding the applicable rules.[224] The supremacy of party autonomy, which Spanish doctrine stresses

---

221  *See e.g.* ZPO § 1042 (3) (GER) (at the end); IPRG art. 182 (2) (C.H.) (at the end); CPC art. 1509 (1) (FR); Arbitration Act 1996 § 4 (3) (EW); IAA § 15A (6) - (7) (SG).

222  According to the consolidated translation by Cairns and Lòpez, »Spain's Consolidated Arbitration Law«; referring to: Ley de arbitraje 2003 (ES); as modified by: Ley de reforma 2011 (ES).

223  *Cf. only* Bachmaier Winter, »Art. 14«, para. 23 (just remarking that some institutions offer facilitated ad hoc arbitration services with limited influence on procedure, which is not of any concern).

224  *Cf.* ibid., para. 20.

to be »*lex prima*« for the administration of arbitration by an institution,[225] remains untouched.

This means that even rules deemed »*mandatory*« by the institution could not overrule the parties' will *by force of law*. Rather, the institution only has a choice between accepting to administer the case in accordance with the rule modifications agreed by the parties[226] and declining to administer the case in total.[227]

### ii. Exception: regulation of hybrid arbitration by Romanian law

Exceptionally, the new Romanian Code of Civil Procedure[228] now includes a whole chapter, Chapter VII, entitled »*Institutional Arbitration*«[229] and - much clearer than the Spanish arbitration law just touched upon - also addresses hybrid arbitration agreements.

Article 617 CPC (RO) regulates the general relationship between arbitration rules and derogating procedural agreements by the parties, stressing the supremacy of party autonomy:

> »(1) In their arbitration agreement, the parties may subject the resolution of their disputes to an arbitral tribunal belonging to institutional arbitration.
>
> (2) In case of disagreement between the arbitration agreement and the rules of institutional arbitration referenced in that agreement, *the arbitration agreement prevails* [*emphasis added*].«

However, most relevant for the admissibility of hybrid arbitration agreements, article 619 (2) CPC (RO) then provides an exception to the general supremacy of the arbitration agreement when it comes to completely opting-out of the administering institution's rules:

---

225 Ibid., para. 22; citing Lledó Yagüe, 141.

226 Bachmaier Winter, »Art. 14«, para. 22.

227 Muñoz Sabaté, »El reglamento de la institución arbitral a la luz de la Nueva Ley de Arbitraje«, 538; Bachmaier Winter, »Art. 14«, para. 22 (both unclear on the need for a stipulation in the rules for such a refusal right).

228 Herein cited as CPC (RO) (the revision entered into force more than two years after its enactment on 15 February 2013).

229 Romanian original: »*Arbitrajul instituţionalizat;*« all English translations by Ileana Smeureanu and Brooks Hickmann, published in: Paulsson, *International Handbook on Commercial Arbitration*, Romania, Annex I (supp. no. 74, last updated May 2013).

»By designating a certain arbitral institution as competent to resolve a specific dispute or a type of disputes, the parties automatically opt to apply the procedural rules of that institution. *Any derogation from this provision shall be null*, unless the management of the competent arbitral institution shall decide, depending on the circumstances of the case and the content of the procedural rules indicated by the parties, that the rules chosen by the parties may also be applied and shall establish whether they apply directly or whether they apply by analogy [*emphasis added*].«

The relationship between article 617 (2) CPC (RO) and article 619 (2) CPC (RO) has yet to be clarified. It seems obvious that article 619 (2) CPC (RO) would apply to pure hybrid arbitration clauses by which parties refer to a complete, different set of institutional rules. However, it remains to be seen if article 619 (2) CPC (RO) as an exception to the principal supremacy of party autonomy also covers cases of partial reference to other arbitration rules. A good example is an arbitration case where the parties opted for arbitration in Romania and for the arbitration rules of the Court of Arbitration attached to the Romanian Chamber of Commerce and Industry (CCIR) but wanted to apply ICC Rules with respect to arbitrator nomination and appointment only.[230] It seems that the Romanian legislator had that case in mind when drafting article 619 (2) CPC (RO).[231] However, in theory, such partial choice of another set of rules may arguably fall either under the permissive article 617 (2) CPC (RO) or under article 619 (2) CPC (RO), which would render such choice null, subject to a contrary decision by the administering institution.

The provision also does not distinguish between agreements on the application of other *institutional* rules and agreements to apply *ad hoc* rules like the UNCITRAL Rules.[232] It is *e.g.* very common that parties agree to constitute the arbitral tribunal according to the method stipulated in the UNCITRAL Rules, to this extent derogating from the rules of the administering institution.[233] Theoretically, it should not make a decisive difference,

---

230  Unpublished, *see* the blogpost by Dicu and Preda, »CCIR case summary« (in Romanian only).

231  *Cf.* Severin, »Consideratii«, 54–55; »Considerations«, 15 (finding that these provisions react to the »*real problem*« that parties' choices may be inoperable because *e.g.* ICC Rules provide for arbitrator nomination by National Committees to which the CCIR would not have access). On the issue of substituting institutional organs, *see infra* at pp. 344-400 (§14).

232  *See* Bobei, *Arbitrajul intern și internațional*, art. 619, para. 7 (mentioning the choice of UNCITRAL Rules as one possible application of the provision).

233  UNCITRAL Rules, art. 8 (2) (2010).

whether the parties directly agree on such as list method or just refer to article 8 of the UNCITRAL Rules in their agreement. If the place of arbitration is in Romania, the latter kind of agreement might nevertheless be disregarded by the institution pursuant to article 619 (2) CPC (RO), although there appears to be little rational justification for such decision. Different from a reference to other institutional rules, a reference to another set of non-institutional rules like the UNCITRAL Rules neither bears an apparent risk of inoperability nor of a conflict with another institution.

Romanian doctrine suggests to apply the legal exception under article 619 (2) sentence 2 CPC (RO) at the end routinely,[234] unless the parties' choice for different arbitration rules is evidently inoperable. According to this scholarly view, the institution would not have complete discretion whether to accept the parties' choice for different arbitration rules. Rather, there is supposed to be an assumption in favour of party autonomy, which is only rebutted if the institution finds that the particulars of the case or the content of the rules chosen by the parties make the parties' choice ineffective.[235] Without such restrictive interpretation, article 619 (2) sentence 2 CPC (RO) is deemed to contravene the voluntary character of arbitration.[236]

It remains to be seen how Romanian courts, institutions and arbitral tribunals will apply this provision in practice. In any case, it would not render a whole hybrid arbitration agreement invalid or inoperable but only the procedural modality of arbitration under another than the institution's set of rules. Essentially, this legislation places institutional arbitration rules at a level above ordinary contract terms, enabling the institution to impose its rules on parties choosing that institution. At the same time, Romanian law also restricts the autonomy of the institution. This becomes obvious if one reads article 619 (2) sentence 2 CPC (RO) together with the Code's definition of institutional arbitration:

> »that form of arbitration that is constituted and functions permanently under the auspices of an organisation or a domestic or international institution or as an autonomous non-governmental public interest organization, pursuant to the law, *based on its own rules that are applicable to all the disputes* that are brought before it for resolution under an arbitration agreement [*emphasis added*].«[237]

Accordingly, the application of the institution's own rules is a principle to which exceptions under 619 (2) sentence 2 CPC (RO) are only admitted on

---

234 Bobei, *Arbitrajul intern și internațional*, art. 619, para. 7.
235 *Cf.* Severin, »Consideratii«, 54; »Considerations«, 15.
236 Bobei, *Arbitrajul intern și internațional*, art. 619, para. 7.
237 CPC art. 616 sent. 1 (RO).

a case-by-case basis. A general policy according to which a certain institution would accept cases under different rules, as it is provided for in article 4 (3) of the CIETAC Rules, would probably conflict with this exigency.[238]

The fact that apart from the legislation of Romania, national arbitration laws currently miss particular provisions on the relationship between party autonomy and institutional rules could be an indication of little public interest opposing the admissibility of hybrid arbitration agreements. It may be assumed that the interests of arbitral institutions are sufficiently reflected by general principles of contract law as discussed in Chapter 3.

### iii. Specifics of Chinese law on institutional arbitration

As already touched upon, China's arbitration law is particular as it installs commission-administered arbitration as the standard form of arbitration. This particularity shall be elaborated on further in order to provide some background understanding for CIETAC's claim in article 4 (3) of its rules that it would administer cases under different institutional rules.

Article 16 (2) of the Arbitration Law of the People's Republic of China provides:

>»An arbitration agreement shall contain the following particulars:
>
>(1) an expression of the intention to apply for arbitration;
>
>(2) matters for arbitration; and
>
>(3) a designated arbitration commission.«

The reference to an »*arbitration commission*« means a permanent body. Articles 10-11 of the Chinese arbitration law define an arbitration commission as a body established in a Chinese municipality by the competent authority with:

- an own name, domicile and charter
- necessary property
- personnel forming the commission
- appointed arbitrators

Internationally operating arbitration institutions seated outside mainland China, such as the ICC Court and the other non-Chinese institutions here

---

238 In contrast to the situation under Chinese law, which somewhat provokes such general policy (*see infra* at iii).

considered do not meet these requirements.[239] Not only are they based outside China and therefore not controlled by Chinese authorities, but most also do not have »*appointed arbitrators*« as required under article 11. As a service, some may maintain arbitrator lists but the institutions do not permanently appoint these arbitrators.

Moreover, for foreign-related cases, articles 66 et seq. of the Arbitration Law (P.R.C.) contains specific provisions regarding the establishment of an international arbitration commission by the China Chamber of International Commerce, allowed to appoint foreigners as arbitrators. The law thus formally established a monopoly of CIETAC, as the commission founded by the China Chamber of International Commerce, to administer foreign-related cases.

However, factually, the separation between domestic commissions and CIETAC as the international arbitration commission established by the text of the law, has long been overruled by government order[240] and institutional practice. Today, CIETAC administers both domestic and foreign-related case whereas municipal commissions, most importantly the Beijing Arbitration Commission but now also SHIAC and SCIA, claim competence over international disputes as well.[241] Given this relaxation, the Chinese commission system may soon be outdated altogether. As noted, the SPC now appears to acknowledge this evolution and to find international arbitration institutions to be equal to »*arbitration commissions*« as required by the wording of Chinese law. However, - different from circulars and notices - its reply to the reference in *Longlide*[242] is not binding on courts deciding other cases and some uncertainties as to its meaning remain. It appears that the SPC applied article 16 (2) of the Arbitration Law (P.R.C.) as a formal rule only when assessing the validity of the arbitration agreement providing for ICC arbitration in Shanghai. The material side of the requirement of a »*designated arbitration commission*«, meaning whether the ICC Court would be

---

239 Yuen, »Arbitration Clauses in a Chinese Context«, 586; Andrew, »Notable Characteristics of Arbitration in China«, 313: »*Unfortunately the ICC, LCIA and others (including the SIAC and, possibly, the HKIAC) are not qualified in this regard.*«

240    *See* Notice Regarding Some Problems for the Implementation of the Arbitration Law 1996 para. 3 (P.R.C.) (allowing domestic commissions to accept foreign-related cases; *see also* Tao, *Arbitration Law and Practice in China*, 11, para. 29, n. 26).

241 Tao, *Arbitration Law and Practice in China*, 11, para. 29.

242 *Longlide*, [2013] Min Si Ta Zi no. 13. *See supra* at p. 63, n. 39.

allowed to operate in a China-seated arbitration without strictly fulfilling the conditions of articles 10-11 or 66 of the Arbitration Law (P.R.C) was surprisingly not addressed at all.

Article 18 further directs that

> »if an arbitration agreement contains no or unclear provisions concerning the matters for arbitration or the arbitration commission, the parties may reach a supplementary agreement. If no such supplementary agreement can be reached, the arbitration agreement shall be void.«

This provision underlines the designation of an arbitration commission as an essential requirement of an arbitration agreement under Chinese law. While not expressly prohibiting ad hoc arbitration seated in China, any ad hoc arbitration agreement will be difficult to enforce. The same applies where the designation of the arbitration commission is ambiguous. Chinese law does not provide for any means of court supplementation of arbitration agreements in this regard.

The express declaration of CIETAC in article 4 (3) of its rules, that it is prepared to administer arbitration under other than its own rules,[243] must be viewed in this context. It is an attempt to resolve a conflict between a designated institution and chosen rules without resorting to the verdict of invalidity under article 18 of the Arbitration Law (P.R.C.). If the place of arbitration is in China, the offer contained in article 4 (3) of the CIETAC Rules may be the only way to uphold an arbitration agreement that can be interpreted to refer to CIETAC but that mentions other rules, whether these are rules of a foreign institution or ad hoc rules like the UNCITRAL Rules. In most other jurisdictions, it is arguably the least controversial option to refer parties to ad hoc arbitration or to arbitration before the institution that issued the specified rules, in China it is not yet. CIETAC's approach to administering hybrid arbitration is therefore not just an attempt to benefit from the reputation of internationally leading institutions and rules but first and foremost a way to address a practical problem arising from the persistent constraints of Chinese arbitration law, in particular its strict »*commission*« requirement.[244] Without this exigency, a demand for CIETAC administered arbitration under other rules might never emerge, as parties could then easily chose *e.g.* ICC arbitration or ad hoc UNCITRAL arbitration with a seat in mainland China straightaway.

---

243  *See supra* at p. 40.
244  *See also supra* at p. 63 on attempts to flexibilise Chinese arbitration law through relatively creative institutional practice.

Whether the practice provided for by article 4 (3) of the CIETAC Rules would be accepted by Chinese courts remains unclear. Formally, its seems that hybrid arbitration administered by CIETAC remains arbitration conducted under the auspices of an arbitration commission established under article 66 of the Arbitration Law (P.R.C.), even if the rules of a Western institution or UNCITRAL Rules are applied. There are no reported cases on any CIETAC awards, whether upheld or annulled, rendered in arbitrations administered under other than CIETAC Rules.

c. The quasi-regulative force of institutional practice

Overall, it is remarkable that the practically important service of administering arbitration proceedings has hardly found the interest of the public legislator at all. Neither is there a consistent definition of institutional arbitration,[245] nor have legislating bodies engaged in the regulation of the relationship between institutional rules and the parties' direct agreements on procedure, conflicts between institutions, rights of institutions to refuse administering a case and the consequences of such refusal.

For better or worse, the practice of administered arbitration effectively develops *praeter* if not *contra legem*. Its market is self-regulated. It is therefore necessary to regard hybrid arbitration agreements from the perspective of institutional practice.[246]

However, it has been pointed out that a few jurisdictions, mainly those with socialist traditions,[247] do regulate institutional arbitration. Chinese arbitration law for example is formulated not as a law on what parties may agree on and how such an agreement would be performed and enforced but rather as a law on the establishment of institutions - arbitration commissions - and on the competences of such institutions seen as competition to the courts. However, in practice, the Chinese arbitration system departs more and more from its legislative roots. Institutions such as CIETAC, SCIA and SHIAC not only draft and revise their own rules, they even purport to be willing to apply UNCITRAL Rules or the rules of other institutions without that this practice would have found any clear offence with the Chinese courts yet.

---

245  *See infra* at pp. 126 et seq. (§7).
246  *See infra* at pp. 209(§10).
247  But to some extent also Spain, *see supra* at p. 97 (§4C.II.2.b.i).

The new Romanian arbitration legislation also tries to regulate the status and activities of arbitral institutions. However, even where it would be objectively desirable, the effectiveness of such regulation remains questionable. In fact, Romania's leading institution organising arbitration proceedings, the CCIR, first appeared little impressed by the legislator's attempts. *E.g.*, first ignoring the new law,[248] under its 2013 rules of organisation, the management of the CCIR still assumed exclusive power to establish mandatory lists of arbitrators and an even more restricted list of presiding arbitrators.[249] However, with the launch of the 2014 versions of both the arbitration rules[250] and the organisational rules,[251] party autonomy seems to be given more emphasis, now aligning more with both the status of the law and international standard.

As a side note: While one may notice that institutional practice used to differ for a long time and occasionally still differs from the wording of the law both in Romania and in China, the historical-legal background is different in both jurisdictions. In China, the arbitration law is quite dated, as it has not been formally revised since 1994.[252] This creates a necessity for practical improvement if Chinese institutions want to endorse the principle of party autonomy in order to compete in a global market. International arbitration practice therefore welcomes it, if Chinese institutions claim more

---

248 *See* CPC art. 616 (2), 618 (RO).
249 *Cf.* CCIR Organisational Rules 2013 art. 4; *see* Severin, »Consideratii«, 63, 65, para. 9, 11, ibid., 25, 27 (qualifying both the insufficient financial separation of accounts of the CCIR Court from those of the CCIR and the practice of arbitrator appointment as »*illegal*«). *See* CCIR Rules 2013 art. 89, 1 (2); if parties want to nominate an arbitrator not on the list, the CCIR Court requalified the arbitration as ad hoc (CCIR Organisational Rules 2013 art. 6; critical: Severin, »Consideratii«, 63; »Considerations«, 26, n. 32: »*more than questionable*«; *but see* Bobei, *Arbitrajul intern și internațional*, art. 618, para. 1 (only seeing an »*option*« for open lists but expecting manifest reservations against the future of closed lists).
250 *Cf.* CCIR Rules, art. 17 (1), (2) (2014) (now restricting the »*Court*'s« power to appoint arbitrators from the list to cases of default of disagreement by the parties).
251 *See now* CCIR Organisational Rules 2014 art. 4 (3) (expressly allowing appointments of arbitrators from outside the list for individual cases).
252 Although interpretations and notices of the SPC provide for some clarity and reform.

liberties than the wording of the law could suggest.[253] In contrast, the Romanian legislation on institutional arbitration is a quite recent attempt to bring the institutional arbitration system in Romania in line with international practice, raising the expectation for an institution like the CCIR providing services within that jurisdiction to respect the legislator's intentions where these are clearly expressed (like the rejection of mandatory arbitrator lists).

Regarding the discretion to disregard the choice of other than the institution's rules granted under article 619 (2) CPC (RO), there remains some uncertainty at present on both how such discretion would be exercised by institutions and whether and to which extent it would be reviewed by the courts. However, one indication for future institutional practice is provided by the CCIR's newest, 2014 version of its rules, providing in their article 6 (2):

> »Where upon requesting the organisation of the arbitration, the parties have already agreed, in writing, on other arbitration rules, the Court of Arbitration Board, taking into consideration the case conditions and the content of the rules of arbitration indicated by the parties, may decide for the rules chosen by the parties to be applicable, and the same are accepted by the arbitral tribunal.«

In a chapter applying only to international cases it is then emphasised:

> »The parties shall be free to decide either for these Rules, or for other rules of arbitral procedure. The provisions of Article 6 shall remain applicable.«[254]

This seems to indicate that the CCIR assumes that internationality of the dispute is a decisive element to be considered by the institution when exercising its discretion about whether to accept the parties' agreement on hybrid arbitration.

## D. Relevant limits to party autonomy outside arbitration laws

Having found that arbitration laws generally do not oppose hybrid arbitration agreements but rather accept them as procedural arrangements supported by the principle of party autonomy, this does not yet mean that a hybrid arbitration agreement is in any case enforceable, let alone advisable.

---

253 A dogmatic, public or democratic perspective shall not be taken herein as the author admits to not know enough about the Chinese understanding of concepts such as division of powers or the public-private distinction.
254 CCIR Rules, art. 76 (2) (2014).

Rather, it will be necessary, as indicated, to also have regard to laws, principles and practices outside the *lex arbitri*.[255] In particular, applicable intellectual property or unfair competition laws might prohibit the implementation of the parties' wish to have an arbitration administered by a certain institution under another institution's rules or the designated institution may be unwilling or incapable to provide such service.

Chapters 3 and 4 will discuss these aspects in detail. Here, it suffices to note that they primarily concern the question whether an arbitration agreement is capable of being performed as they relate to the conduct of the arbitral institution as a third party to the agreement. If a verdict of illegality of hybrid arbitration procedure was reached due to intellectual property or unfair competition concerns, this should not yet render the parties' agreement thereon null and void. The conclusion of the agreement is itself obviously not an act of copyright infringement or unfair competition. Rather, potential intellectual property or unfair competition issues could only result from the performance of such agreement through an institution, which would require the conclusion of a contract with such institution as an intermediate step.

## *§5 Private rules and party autonomy*

A hybrid arbitration agreement, just like an ordinary institutional arbitration agreement, contains an express reference to a pre-drafted set of arbitration rules. As noted, this right to select or draft procedural rules follows from the recognition or party autonomy.[256] The UNCITRAL Model Law provides:

> »where a provision of this Law refers to the fact that the parties have agreed or that they may agree or in any other way refers to an agreement of the parties, such agreement includes any arbitration rules referred to in that agreement«.[257]

However, the UNCITRAL Model Law does not expressly answer the question if the parties are completely free in their reference to arbitration rules or if this freedom is restricted to the choice of rules offered to them by the institution designated. The enactments in articles 1 (2) and 6 (2) of the ICC Rules certainly attempt to impose such restriction and thereby appear to

---

255 Possibly, from a jurisdiction other than the seat of arbitration, *see supra* at pp. 65-86 (§4B).

256 Waincymer, *Procedure and Evidence*, para. 3.9.

257 UNCITRAL Model Law 2006 art. 2 (e); *cf. also* ibid., art. 2 (d).

limit party autonomy to agree on hybrid arbitration under ICC Rules. The following considerations discuss types (A) and status of arbitration rules (B) and the interaction with soft law and arbitrator discretion (C-D) in order to evaluate this approach.


## A. Types of arbitration rules

In principle, there are two ways of determining specific rules on arbitral procedure. The parties may individually agree on all aspects they consider important, with gaps left to fill by discretion of the arbitral tribunal. More often parties refer to a set of pre-drafted rules. While the first variant may be suitable for well-experienced parties, lawyers and arbitrators and complex, largely technical disputes, the latter has the great benefit of convenience. Although theoretically, parties can agree on procedural aspects at any time, also after the dispute has arisen and the arbitration commenced, it is advisable to include the most important aspects already in the arbitration agreement to avoid any later delay and obstruction.[258]

Essential is an agreement on the number and method of appointment of arbitrators and the place of arbitration. Stipulations may further concern the form of statements of claim and response, the number of and delays for written submissions, confidentiality, representation, the need for an oral hearing, consequences of default, rules on evidence, the need for a reasoned award and the language of arbitration.[259] However, such detailed provisions on procedure can easily inflate an arbitration clause in a contract and create disagreements that may even endanger the contract conclusion as a whole.[260] This is another reason why most parties opt for pre-drafted rules.

---

258 *But see* Paulsson, Rawding, and Reed, *The Freshfields Guide to Arbitration and ADR*, 59 (*»but parties should avoid establishing every detail of the arbitral procedure as this is best left to be decided once a dispute has arisen«*).

259 *See* Voit, »§ 1042 ZPO«, para. 33.

260 An arbitration clause with six long paragraphs is suggested by Born, *International Arbitration and Forum Selection Agreements*, 64 (warning that such clause »*addresses a number of issues that may arise in relation to the agreement to arbitrate, while not addressing numerous other issues*«) (recommending the agreement on pre-drafted rules); *see also* Paulsson, Rawding, and Reed, *The Freshfields Guide to Arbitration and ADR*, 151–53 (Appendix 3) (even proposing an ad-hoc clause with up to eleven paragraphs).

The inclusion of a set of pre-drafted rules in a contract will often pass without much controversy.[261]

There is a great variety of pre-drafted arbitration rules from which to choose. These fall into two categories: Rules contemplated for institutional arbitration and rules suitable for ad hoc arbitration. While the market for ad hoc arbitration rules is relatively sparse - best known are the UNCITRAL Rules[262] - there are hundreds of institutional rules from which to choose.[263] In about every jurisdiction there is at least one[264] arbitral institution plus those operated by industry associations[265] and many of these institutions provide their own arbitration rules. Institutional rules are regularly updated or revised and, subject to express agreement to the contrary, usually apply in their most recent version as in force at the date of commencement of the

---

261 *See* Born, *International Arbitration and Forum Selection Agreements*, 67 (»*rule-by-rule bargaining over individual procedural points*« would be »*unrealistically expensive*«); similar: Paulsson, Rawding, and Reed, *The Freshfields Guide to Arbitration and ADR*, 9; Varady, Von Mehren, and Barceló, *International Commercial Arbitration*, 69; Münch, »§ 1042 ZPO«, para. 86; Paulsson, »Vicarious Hypochondria and Institutional Arbitration«, 245 (calling the view that custum-made rules were preferable in any case an »*utopian exhortation*«).

262 For an alternative consider *e.g.* Paris Arbitration Rules.

263 *See* Wolf, *Die Institutionelle Handelsschiedsgerichtsbarkeit*, 8 (already in 1992: »*nahezu unüberschaubar*« [almost uncountable]); *but see* Born, *International Arbitration and Forum Selection Agreements*, 47 (warning that institutions »*often lack the experience and track records that sophisticated users require*«); similiar fears are expressed by: Coulson, »The Future Growth«, 81 (calling for the adaptation of »*minimum criteria*« and »*standards*« to regulate the market).

264 This is likely an understatement. A extreme example is Latvia, the Latvian Register of Enterprises currently listing more than 100 institutions in the arbitration sector (*see* Republic of Latvia, »Šķīrējtiesu«; a number which used to be even higher, *see* Schewe, »Schiedsgerichtsbarkeit in Lettland«, 164). Very similar names of several registered institutions create a multitude of problems, including parallel proceedings and awards (ibid.).

265 *Cf.* Happ, »Arbitration Institutions and Centers« (for illustrational purposes; non-comprehensive list, not regularly updated); *see also* Pendell, »The Rise and Rise of the Arbitration Institution« (»*Exactly how many arbitration institutions exist and how many arbitrations they actually administer is unclear*«) (talking of a »*growing*« list of at least »*118 organisations*«); *see also* Born, *International Arbitration and Forum Selection Agreements*, 193–201 (App. D: non-exhaustive list with addresses).

arbitration.[266] However, a number of arbitral institutions do not publish arbitration rules and refer to the UNCITRAL Rules,[267] which were primarily designed for ad hoc cases.[268]

Sometimes rules published by institutions are referred to as institution-bound rules while rules for ad hoc proceedings, like the UNCITRAL Rules, are characterised as institution-free rules.[269] Such characterisation, which is not shared herein, assumes that ad hoc arbitration cannot take place under institutional rules and that an arbitration agreement excluding the institution's competence to administer the case would automatically be incapable of being performed.[270]

## B. Legal status and regime of arbitration rules

»Notice these words: *private* law. [...] Using the label of law in such a way is, admittedly, a fair marketing strategy for arbitration. But a marketing strategy it is.«[271]

In a recent publication, Thomas Schultz starts his thoughts on stateless law in international arbitration with the consideration that the label »*law*« is often used to »*achieve something honorable*« that »›*counts*‹ *beyond its sheer bindingness*« but may also be employed »*for darker purposes*« by those

---

266 *See* Münch, »§ 1042 ZPO«, para. 88 (incorporation by dynamic reference) (»*dynamische Verweisung*«); *cf.* ICC Rules, art. 6 (1) (2012; 2017); DIS Rules, art. 1.2 (1998); AAA-ICDR Rules, art. 1 (a) (2009); *but see* LCIA Rules (1998) (not containing such clarification); *see also* Born, *International Arbitration and Forum Selection Agreements*, 62 (recommending to indicate the applicable version in the arbitration clause in any event).

267 *See* Pendell, »The Rise and Rise of the Arbitration Institution« (»*A good number of the institutions have their own rules but a great deal more do not; unsurprisingly the UNCITRAL Rules make the most appearances as the preferred rules of institutions*«); *contra* Lörcher, Pendell, and Wilson, CMS Legal, »International Arbitration - an Overview«, para. 2.1.5 (»*Most arbitral institutions have published their own arbitration rules*«).

268 *Cf. UNCITRAL Recommendations to Institutions*, para. 20–22 (making recommendations on how to communicate adaptations without frustrating the parties expectations).

269 Münch, »§ 1042 ZPO«, para. 86.

270 *See e.g.* Rawert, »Schiedsklausel (institutionsgebunden) - Anmerkungen«, n. 3; Lachmann, *Handbuch für die Schiedsgerichtspraxis*, para. 416. *But see infra* at pp. 112-114 (B.I) and pp. 151-156 (§7C.IV).

271 Schultz, *Transnational Legality*, 3.

dependent on the recognition of a particular system or idea.[272] Arbitral institutions are certainly »*arbitration dependents*« interested in protecting arbitration by labelling it »*as a law-creating institution.*«[273]

To continue with this general philosophical characterisation of privately-made arbitration »*law*« including institutional rules would go beyond the scope of this thesis which has a more practical approach, being, distinct from Schultz' reflections, about »*doing law*« rather than »*thinking about law.*«[274] There is also no suggestion that institutions' motives behind presenting arbitration rules as law-type regulation are not noble ones of aiming to provide the best and most efficient service. However, the undeniable observation that leading arbitration institutions as dependents on the arbitration system would be the first to benefit from their rules »*counting*« beyond sheer (contractual) bindingness argues in favour of a more conservative, formal understanding of their status.

From such a formal point of view, arbitration rules, whether designed for ad hoc or for institutional arbitration, are not supported by the authority of the legislator. Therefore, they are not laws.[275] Laws are only stipulations that require observance independent of whether the addressee agrees to them.[276] The application of arbitration rules follows solely from party agreement as reflected by many arbitration rules.[277] Accordingly, arbitration rules are simply contractual stipulations.[278] By referring to a set of pre-drafted arbitration rules, the parties make such rules part of their agreement.[279]

---

272 Ibid.
273 Ibid.
274 Ibid., vii (Preface).
275 *See e.g.* Blackaby et al., *Redfern and Hunter*, para. 3.48 (»*great difference*«). Left undecided by Urteil [Judgment], [1988] 104 BGHZ 178, [1988] 41 NJW at 3091 (considering the ICC Rules to be either foreign law or foreign standard business terms).
276 Spohnheimer, *Gestaltungsfreiheit*, 104.
277 *See e.g.* DIS Rules, art. 1 (1) (1998); ICC Rules, art. 6 (1) (2012; 2017); AAA-ICDR Rules, art. 1 (1) (2014); AAA-ICDR Rules, art. 1 (a) (2009); LCIA Rules (2014); LCIA Rules (1998) (preamble); SIAC Rules, art. 1 (1) (2013, 2016). Implied reference by naming the institution is sufficient agreement.
278 Lachmann, *Handbuch für die Schiedsgerichtspraxis*, para. 416.
279 Wolf, *Die Institutionelle Handelsschiedsgerichtsbarkeit*, 105; *cf.* also Spohnheimer, *Gestaltungsfreiheit*, 102.

I. Lacking legislative or regulatory power of arbitral institutions

A legislative status of institutional rules appears indefendable, as arbitral institutions are not vested with legislative power by any state. This is obvious in Western legal systems where both the separation of powers at the state level and the distinction between public and private actors is well established. Here, arbitral institutions act as fully independent non-governmental associations or as private companies. However, even the institutions in the »*state sponsored*«[280] arbitration system of the People's Republic of China, of which CIETAC is the most important, are considered »*non-governmental arbitration commissions*« which are »*not subordinate to any administrative agency*«,[281] only their creation is subject to state approval and registration under Chinese law.[282] Accordingly, their enactments should not have the force of law but be considered as instruments of mere self-regulatory and contractual nature.[283]

Nevertheless and despite their private law nature, institutional rules resemble statutes.[284] Generally, arbitral institutions understand themselves as »*formulating agencies*«,[285] a term to describe private institutions whose

---

280 Johnston, »The Best Providers for Asian Arbitrations«, 44.

281 Stricker-Kellerer and Moser, »CIETAC Rules«, para. 26; Arbitration Law art. 14 (P.R.C.) (»*shall be independent from administrative authorities*«); on the historical development, *see* Fan, *Arbitration in China*, 115, 116.

282 *See* Arbitration Law art. 10 (P.R.C.); *see also* Fan, *Arbitration in China*, 117 (explaining that government support and organisation was only supposed to »*to help them get on the horse*« before arbitration commissions were able to operate independently; referring to Plan for the Reorganisation of Arbitration Organs 1995 [P.R.C.]). However, a survey conducted by the Beijing Arbitration Center in 2007 revealed »*much confusion*« about the nature of arbitration institutions in China with only about 14 % of local institutions considering themselves to belong to the private sector (Fan, *Arbitration in China*, 134–35).

283 Ch'eng, Moser, and Wang, *International Arbitration in the People's Republic of China*, 13.

284 Schöldström, *The Arbitrator's Mandate*, 404; Habel, *Contract Governance*, 103 (describing arbitration rules as *quasi codes of procedure* [»*quasi-Prozessordnungen*«], noting processes of juridification [»*Verrechtlichungprozesse*«] in arbitration).

285 Concept going back to Schmitthoff, »Nature and Evolution of the Transnational Law of Commercial Transactions«; as reprinted in: Schmitthoff, *Clive M. Schmitthoff's Select Essays on International Trade Law*, at 239;

rules are so widely used, that they effectively influence the law although the institution itself does not have law making competence.[286] Such private law making is of little concern to the extent rules can gain effect through contract, it is however more problematic, where state interests[287] or the interests of third parties are affected. The latter hurdle relates to a number of systematic inconsistencies in institutional arbitration rules. It is already regrettable that institutional rules do not clearly address the different contractual relationships in which they apply, but their legal effectiveness is most doubtful where they attempt to create rights and obligations of persons, which are not parties to any of these relationships.[288] In particular, confidentiality rules[289] and some liability exclusions[290] often encompass persons other than the parties to the arbitration, the institution and the arbitrators, without explaining how and by whom such duties or privileges should be transferred to these external persons.

When under article 1 (2) of the ICC Rules, the ICC Court attempts to prohibit the use of its rules outside ICC arbitration, this falls into the same category: Obviously, other arbitral institutions are not bound by any contract with the ICC to which the ICC Rules may apply. In relation to the ICC Rules, Menno Aden speculated whether such systematic shortcomings

---

see also Berger, *The Creeping Codification of the New Lex Mercatoria*, 88–90.

286 *See* Michaels, »Rollen und Rollenverständnisse im Transnationalen Privatrecht«, 36.

287 *Cf. also* ibid., 47–50 (on the allocation of tasks between formulating agencies and states).

288 Aden, *Internationale Handelsschiedsgerichtsbarkeit*, pt. B, Introduction, para. 21–22.

289 *See e.g.* Swiss Rules, art. 44 (1) sent. 2 (2012) (»*This undertaking also applies to*« tribunal-appointed experts, the secretary of the arbitral tribunal etc.; not addressing that such persons will have to agree to the rules in order to be bound by them); even more far-reaching: CIETAC Rules, art. 36 (2) (2012) = art. 38 (2) (2015) (including also witnesses, interpreters and »*other relevant persons*«, without clarifying how such contractual duty shall be transferred to them); *but see* DIS Rules, art. 43 (1) (1998) (only imposing a duty to »*obligate*« any persons *acting on behalf of any person involved in the arbitral proceedings*« to confidentiality; unclear whether experts, tribunal-appointed or party-appointed, and witnesses fall under this provision).

290 *See e.g.* ICC Rules, art. 40 (2012) = art. 41 (2017) (extending the liability exclusion *inter alia* to tribunal appointed experts and ICC National Committees and groups).

indicated an understanding of the ICC Rules as actual, sovereign legislation by ICC supportive circles, himself obviously - and correctly so - not sharing such view.[291]

Corresponding criticism applies to CIETAC's reaction to the spin-off by the Shanghai and Shenzhen subcommissions: The authority of CIETAC to declare the new institutions' activities »*null and void*«[292] in a regulatory manner and language is dubious.[293] Either Chinese law allows SHIAC and SCIA to operate as independent arbitration commissions or not but a simple announcement of CIETAC as a non-governmental commission should not itself have the effect of invalidating any awards rendered under the auspices of the spin-offs.

## II. Arbitration rules as standard terms of the arbitration agreement?

As pre-drafted arbitration rules are incorporated by reference into a large number of contracts, they could[294] - but not necessarily do[295] - qualify as standard business terms of the arbitration agreement with the respective higher requirements concerning fairness and transparency in some jurisdictions.[296] Concerning the relationship between the parties to the arbitration agreement, decisive criterion is whether one of the parties is a *supplier* who

---

291 Aden, *Internationale Handelsschiedsgerichtsbarkeit*, pt. B, Introduction, para. 22.

292 China International Economic and Trade Administration Commission, »Announcement of 31 December 2012«.

293 *Cf.* Arbitration Law art. 14 sentence 2 (P.R.C.): »*There shall also be no subordinate relationship between arbitration commissions.*«

294 *But see* Wolf, *Die Institutionelle Handelsschiedsgerichtsbarkeit*, 105; Aden, »Auslegung und Revisibilität ausländischer AGB am Beispiel der Schiedsverfahrensordnung der Internationalen Handelskammer«, 610 (arguing that the agreement on pre-drafted arbitration rules as a procedural contract - »*Prozessvertrag*« - should not be controlled under the angle of the law on standard business terms).

295 *Contra* Raeschke-Kessler and Berger, *Recht und Praxis des Schiedsverfahrens*, para. 630 et seq. (qualifying arbitration rules as standard business terms without regard to the circumstances of contract conclusion).

296 For Germany *cf.* BGB § 305 et seq. (GER); *see* Bundesministerium der Justiz und für Verbraucherschutz, »German Civil Code BGB« (for an English translation).

induced the rules on the other party.[297] Another matter is the characterisation of the arbitration rules as standard business terms in the relationship between the parties and the institution, an aspect that merits a closer look in Chapter 3 of this thesis.[298]

III. Law applicable to arbitration rules

There is ample discussion on whether arbitration rules can be chosen by the parties as an *alternative* to the *lex arbitri*.[299] That such assumption is dangerous[300] already follows from the need for enforceability and state court control of the award. Generally, the choice of non-state rules as »*law*« is not yet accepted; here, party autonomy in private international law has a limit.[301] While arbitration laws accord a lot of liberty to the parties to regulate their arbitration proceedings and to agree on suitable rules, complete opting-out of the law in favour of arbitration rules is not yet supported:

> »It may well be that the lex arbitri will govern with a very free rein, but it will govern nonetheless.«[302]

It should be clarified however, that as a mere publication by an institution, arbitration rules by themselves are not subject to any applicable law, they

---

297 Spohnheimer, *Gestaltungsfreiheit*, 106, 107.

298 *See infra* at pp. 255-264 (§11B.III); *see also* Rüßmann, »Zwingendes Recht in den Schiedsregeln einer Schiedsinstitution?«, 486; Spohnheimer, *Gestaltungsfreiheit*, 109; Schlosser, *Das Recht der internationalen privaten Schiedsgerichtsbarkeit*, 404; Lachmann, *Handbuch für die Schiedsgerichtspraxis*, para. 1367.

299 Toope, *Mixed International Arbitration*, 41 (stating that arbitration was »*not necessarily governed by the lex loci arbitri but* [...] *by another system of rules chosen or designed by the parties*«); *cf. also* Aden, *Internationale Handelsschiedsgerichtsbarkeit*, chap. 6, para. 17–18 (discussing this problem under the misleading heading of »*Statut*« [Applicable Law] of arbitration rules).

300 Blackaby et al., *Redfern and Hunter*, para. 3.50.

301 Rühl, »Party Autonomy«, 164–65 (noting that non-state rules are only given effect at the level of contract); *but see* ibid., 166–67 (on trends in newer codifications, *e.g.* in statutes of Louisiana and Oregon, to allow a choice of non-state *law*).

302 Blackaby et al., *Redfern and Hunter*, para. 3.50; *see also* de Ly, »Conflict of Laws - Overview«, 8.

do not belong to any private international law *regime* (German: »*Statut*«).[303] Rather, the law governing their validity, inclusion and interpretation is determined by the context in which they are referred to and become legally relevant. For procedural aspects, they are subject to the *lex arbitri*; to contractual aspects, dependent on the legal relationship at issue, the law of the arbitration agreement[304] or the contract with the arbitrator or with the institution applies.[305] Finally, the law applicable to the question whether such rules may be subject to copyright would have to be determined under relevant theories on the conflict of intellectual property laws.[306]

C. Soft law and arbitrator discretion

In addition to the rules by arbitral institutions, there is an increasing amount of soft law on arbitration, meaning guidelines[307] and codes of conduct[308] of non-state actors. Despite restrictive binding effect of these instruments,[309] such intensified para-regulation is sometimes criticised as »*legislitis*«[310] or »*modern disease of overregulation*«,[311] diminishing the advantage of

---

303 *Contra* Aden, *Internationale Handelsschiedsgerichtsbarkeit*, chap. 6, para. 17.

304 As discussed *supra* at pp. 75-86(§4B.II).

305 *See infra* at pp. 236-243 (§11A.II); *see also* Wolf, *Die Institutionelle Handelsschiedsgerichtsbarkeit*, 243.

306 *See infra* at pp. 301-304 (§13A.III.2), pp. 333-340 (§13C.IV).

307 *E.g.* IBA Guidelines on Conflicts of Interest (2004); IBA Guidelines on Party Representation (2013).

308 *See* Wilske and Markert, »Entwicklungen 2010/2011«, 59.

309 The IBA Rules on the Taking of Evidence have a status similar, although only supplementary, to institutional arbitration rules, if expressly agreed by the parties, *otherwise* they function only as guidelines (*see* the foreword to the IBA Rules on the Taking of Evidence, 2 [2010] [recommending model language to add to the arbitration clause]). The IBA Guidelines on Conflicts of Interest are »*not legal provisions and do not override any applicable national law or arbitral rules chosen by the parties*« (IBA Guidelines on Conflicts of Interest, introduction, no. 6 [2004]). Regarding the legal status of institutional arbitration rules, *see supra* at pp. 110-116 (at B).

310 Wilske and Markert, »Entwicklungen 2010/2011«, 60; Landau, »The Day Before Tomorrow«.

311 Lalive, »Arbitration - The Civilized Solution«, 484.

flexibility of arbitration and arguably the need for independent thinking.[312] Some fear that arbitration is being »*colonized*« by litigation.[313] Serge Lazareff even suggested ironically that we might soon be at the stage to prescribe the number of times parties' counsel may leave the hearing to go to the toilet and the admissible colour of the label of the case file.[314]

Most soft law, like the IBA Rules on Taking of Evidence or the IBA Guidelines on Conflicts of Interest in International Arbitration, primarily seeks to limit the discretionary power of arbitrators and less the flexibility and autonomy of the parties. If parties seek to depart from such privately enacted provisions, they can.[315] Not all such promulgated soft law is internationally accepted and it does certainly not amount to international public policy only because the drafting committees were composed of lawyers from different backgrounds.[316] Although there is now a development of drafting soft law addressed to the parties or their representatives, the counsel in the arbitration, exemplified by the »*IBA Guidelines of Party Representation*«[317] or the Annex to the new LCIA Rules entitled »*General Guidelines for the Parties' Legal Representatives*«,[318] such »*Ethics*« rules can also not directly limit party autonomy. Even though the IBA Guidelines of Party Representation proclaim that arbitrators might apply them *without* express

---

312 *Cf.* the ironic contribution by *Michael Schneider* with the telling title »The Essential Guidelines for the Preparation of Guidelines, Directives, Notes, Protocols and Other Methods Intended to Help International Arbitration Practioners to Avoid the Need for Independent Thinking and to Promote the Transformation of Errors into Best Practices«.

313 *See* Kathpalia, »Is Arbitration Being Colonized by Litigation?«, 263.

314 Lazareff, »Le bloc-notes: de l'excès de réglementation«, 11 (ironically suggesting this question to be referred to an international commission, personally preferring a very visible orange).

315 *Cf. e.g.* IBA Rules on the Taking of Evidence, preamble, no. 2 (2010) (»*The Rules are not intended to limit the flexibility that is inherent in, and an advantage of, international arbitration, and Parties and Arbitral Tribunals are free to adapt them to the particular circumstances of each arbitration.*«); *see also* Park, »Arbitration's Protean Nature: The Value of Rules and the Risks of Discretion« (arguing in favour of detailed default soft law of which the parties can opt out).

316 *See* Voser, »Harmonization by Promulgating Rules of Best International Practice«, 116.

317 IBA Guidelines on Party Representation (2013).

318 To LCIA Rules, art. 18 (5), (6) (2014).

party agreement, if appropriate,[319] they could not apply them *contrary to party agreement.*[320] Regarding the Annex to the new LCIA Rules, the considerations regarding institutional rules in general apply: they do not have the force of law but only of contract. Accordingly, the LCIA might refuse to administer a case based on an arbitration agreement expressly derogating from the application of these Guidelines or rather from the duty to ensure that party representatives agree to them.[321]

At present, most soft law instruments concern arbitration procedure in the narrower sense, meaning the procedure to be followed before an arbitral tribunal in both ad hoc and institutional arbitration. The administration of arbitration by an institution is arbitration procedure in a wider sense, a kind of framework procedure. The problems and conflicts that may occur in this framework and the duties of institutions towards the arbitrators and the parties and vice-versa have not yet been addressed by the arbitration community through any soft law instrument. It is an open question whether guidelines on »*best practices*« regarding the administration of arbitrations could help to elucidate issues surrounding hybrid arbitration agreements. It is likely, that stakeholders, different arbitral institutions in particular, would have a hard time finding a common position. Nevertheless, if such a project was ever to be initiated, this thesis may serve as a starting point to identify relevant concerns and arguments.

Like soft law, arbitrator discretion can never trump party autonomy. This follows directly from article V (1)(d) New York Convention, according to which an award may be refused enforcement if the procedure was not in accordance with the agreement of the parties.[322] For this reason, arbitrators

---

319 *See* IBA Guidelines on Party Representation, art. 1 (1) (2013) (»*or the Arbitral Tribunal, after consultation with the Parties, wishes to rely upon them after having determined that it has the authority to rule on matters of Party representation to ensure the integrity and fairness of the arbitral proceedings*«).

320 The IBA's comments to art. 1-3 of the guidelines leave it to the tribunal to determine the extent of its authority to apply the guidelines »*in absence*« of an agreement of the parties (ibid., 5).

321 LCIA Rules, art. 18 (5) (2014). The formulation prudently takes into account that the institution does not enter into a contract with the representatives but only with the parties, avoiding inconsistency as regretted *supra* at p. 113.

322 *See* *also* UNCITRAL Model Law 2006 art. 19 (1), 34 (2)(a)(iv), 36 (1)(a)(iv); *cf.* Waincymer,

have to be very careful not to ignore any procedural agreements unilaterally. Sometimes it may be difficult to ascertain whether a procedure was organised by party agreement or by exercise of arbitrator discretion. In the latter case, an arbitrator could easily depart from his or her previous proposal if it proves unsuitable in a given case while the parties' consent would be necessary to change party-agreed procedures. In practice, various methods are used to determine details of arbitral procedure, including Terms of Reference,[323] pre-hearing conferences, procedural orders.[324] However, the name and form of an instrument is often not sufficient indication to draw the line between arbitrator discretion and a party-agreed rule.[325] This problem proved a fatality for an award rendered in 2010 by an arbitral tribunal under the auspices of the DIS.[326] There, the arbitrator recorded a specific agreement on expert evidence in a document entitled as »*Procedural Order*« but later chose to ignore this agreement for reasons of efficiency. The Higher Regional Court of Frankfurt am Main annulled the award for non-compliance with party-agreed procedure.[327]

## D. Interplay of institutional and arbitral discretion and party autonomy

Similar to an arbitrator, an arbitral institution only has discretion how to organise proceedings to the extent parties have not expressly or by reference to arbitration rules agreed on a certain administrative aspect. Generally, administrative aspects of arbitration are also part of arbitration procedure[328] and, accordingly, non-compliance with the parties' agreement thereon

---

*Procedure and Evidence*, para. 2.10.3 (remarking that »*any well developed lex arbitri*« will provide this).

323 ICC Rules, art. 23 (2012; 2017).

324 *Cf.* Waincymer, *Procedure and Evidence*, para. 6.9, 6.12; *see* Wolf and Hasenstab, »Hybride Verfahrensgestaltung«, 614, 615.

325 *See* Wolf and Hasenstab, »Hybride Verfahrensgestaltung«, 614 (using the term »*hybride Verfahrensgestaltung*« [hybrid determination of procedure] to characterise the grey zone between arbitrator discretion and party agreement).

326 Endschiedsspruch, DIS-SV-B-724/07 (DIS, 19 March 2010) (unpublished).

327 Beschluss [Decision], [2013] 11 SchiedsVZ 49 (GER OLG, Frankfurt am Main).

328 *But see* Aden, »Der Verfahrensverstoß des Schiedsgerichtsinstituts«, 762 (differentiating between contractual and procedural acts of an institution).

could, if it affected the award, lead to successful challenges at the seat of arbitration or allow resistance against enforcement.[329]

When administering hybrid arbitrations, compliance with party agreement will often be difficult for institutions to warrant for. Misunderstandings and disagreements are likely as an institution not having the same actors, functions and experience than the institution that issued the rules can never implement them strictly. Some adaptation will be necessary. This consideration dictates the approach institutions should follow if they agree to administer hybrid arbitrations: They should make their approach transparent on how and if institutional actors will be substituted and how functions will be performed, obtain written approval by the parties thereon and strictly adhere to the approach thus agreed on.

It seems that SIAC, when administering the Alstom–Insigma arbitration, made an effort in this respect when the secretariat informed the parties by letter that it was prepared to administer the arbitration

> »under the SIAC Rules with the ICC Rules to be applied as a guide to the essential features the parties would like to see in the conduct of the arbitration, e.g., use of the Terms of Reference procedure, the scrutiny of the awards«,

that for the purposes of performing Terms of Reference procedure and scrutiny of awards

> »the equivalent functions of the ›Secretary-General‹ and ›Court‹ would, under the SIAC system, be the Registrar and the Chairman, respectively«

and that arbitrators' fees will follow an »*ad valorem scale along similar lines to that applied by the ICC.*«[330] However, it may be controversially discussed whether Insigma accepted this approach by conduct. An express agreement by Insigma is not reported but neither is a clear objection.[331] Moreover, in its letter, SIAC did not clearly address if arbitrator appointment was part of the »*essential features*« to which the ICC Rules should apply or if it would fall under »*other* [...] *administrative aspects*« that »*would necessarily have to be done* [...] *in accordance with the SIAC*

---

329 *Cf.* UNCITRAL Model Law 2006 art. 19 (1), 34 (2)(a)(iv), 36 (1)(a)(iv); New York Convention, art. V (1)(d).

330 *See Insigma v. Alstom*, [2009] SGCA 24 [9] (citing the secretariat's letter of 17 November 2006).

331 *See* ibid., para. 11 (on Insigma's wish to make the SIAC arbitration contingent on the withdrawal of the previously commenced ICC arbitration by Alstom); *Alstom v. Insigma (Hz. IPC)* (finding that it was Insigma's suggestion to transfer the case to SIAC).

*practices and procedures.*«[332] This uncertainty later proved fatal for the enforcement of the award in China. The Hangzhou Intermediate People's Court took the - to this extent defendable - view[333] that arbitrator appointment should have followed ICC Rules while the SIAC Secretariat - by mistake or due to a different understanding of the reference to ICC Rules - referred to the SIAC Rules when inviting the co-arbitrators nominated by the parties to designate a chairman.

It is also noteworthy that SIAC later had to modify its earlier stance to apply the ICC Rules only as a »*guide*« because the arbitral tribunal interpreted the arbitration agreement to require a more precise application of ICC Rules »*to the exclusion of the SIAC Rules*« and requested SIAC to confirm that it was prepared to abide by this interpretation.[334] SIAC confirmed and slightly revised its proposition regarding the substituting of ICC actors, announcing that roles will be performed as follows:

»SIAC Secretariat=ICC Secretariat

SIAC Registrar=ICC Secretary General

SIAC Board of Directors= ICC Court.«

Upon this confirmation and a hearing on jurisdiction, the tribunal assumed jurisdiction.[335]

This cause of events highlights an important problem relating to the interplay of institutional discretion, arbitrator discretion and party autonomy. According to the tribunal's interpretation, the parties had agreed in the arbitration clause that SIAC should apply ICC Rules directly and not only as a guide, accordingly, there was no room for institutional discretion to perform some functions under ICC Rules and others under SIAC Rules. Implicitly, the tribunal also appears to have assumed that the earlier correspondence between the secretariat and the parties does not amount to a modification of this agreement. However, the parties did not agree on which SIAC actors should replace which respective ICC actors. The manner of substitution was therefore left to the procedural discretion of the institution and the arbitrators. The probable interests of the parties should guide the exercise of such

---

332 *See Insigma v. Alstom*, [2009] SGCA 24 [9].

333 *Alstom v. Insigma (Hz. IPC)*. Less convincing is of course the court's complete ignorance of the requirement of outcome-relevance of procedural irregularities. The decision is summarised and critically discussed in Chapter 5, *infra* at pp. 480 et seq. (§17C).

334 *Insigma v. Alstom*, [2009] SGCA 24 [18].

335 Ibid.

discretion, implying that the substituting actors should be as comparable as possible to the actors replaced. Party autonomy therefore directs the exercise of arbitrator and institutional discretion. The problem of meeting the parties' expectations when substituting institutional actors is discussed in Chapter 4.[336]

*§6 Hybrid arbitration from a normative perspective*

Departing from the principle of party autonomy, this chapter outlined a hierarchy of legal rules, including treaties, laws, institutional rules, soft law and arbitral directions governing arbitration procedure relevant for the validity and enforceability of hybrid arbitration agreements (A). Such hierarchical perspective, which is based on the possibly conservative but still prevailing view that international arbitration fits into a framework of applicable laws and rules rather than being governed by completely autonomous concepts and practical conventions alone,[337] pleads in favour of the validity of hybrid arbitration agreements (B).

A. Arbitral procedure and the hierarchy of norms

To sum up, this is the hierarchic scheme of laws and rules governing arbitration procedure:[338]

On the lowest level are directions of arbitrators and institutions as well as instruments of soft law, which - in principle - are not binding on arbitrators or parties. In principle, arbitrators and institutions are bound to fulfil their mandate according to the parties will and the provisions of the *lex arbitri*, whether mandatory or not. Their discretion exists only where neither the parties nor the law have answered a particular procedural question.

---

336 *See infra* at pp. 344-400 (§14).

337 *See supra* at pp. 65-68 (§4B). Under autonomous theories or views guided by institutional practice alone, it may be easier to argue that arbitration institutions have a power to determine applicable rules even against the agreement of the parties (on this idea, *see generally* Gerbay, »The Functions of Arbitral Institutions«).

338 *Similiar*: Schmidt-Ahrendts and Höttler, »Anwendbares Recht bei Schiedsverfahren mit Sitz in Deutschland«, 268.

The non-mandatory rules of the *lex arbitri* create the second level. The parties can derogate from them by agreement, which can be a direct agreement or an agreement by reference to pre-drafted arbitration rules.

Party-agreed rules are on the next level, prevailing over non-mandatory law of the seat. Arbitration rules, whether published by arbitral institutions or designed for ad hoc arbitrations like the UNCITRAL Rules, are nothing but party-agreed rules. From a normative point of view, they are on the same level, neither superior nor inferior to direct agreements between the parties.[339] For this reason, any reference to »*mandatory*« arbitration rules - a term quite frequently used[340] - has to be put in quotation marks. Even institutional rules purporting to be mandatory are not mandatory in a normative sense. Mandatory is only a provision that a judge would apply to a private law relationship despite a contrary agreement of the parties involved in such relationship.[341] This does not apply to institutional arbitration rules because such rules only become applicable through party agreement. Any conflict between arbitration rules and individual stipulation by the parties is at the outset simply a conflict between two principally even-ranking contractual provisions.[342] Party autonomy is therefore not legally limited by the institutional rules themselves but only factually by institutions' conduct.

Mandatory provisions of the *lex arbitri*, to some extent harmonised by international conventions, are at the top of the hierarchy. Neither can the parties derogate from them, whether by agreeing on pre-drafted rules or otherwise, nor should the arbitral tribunal ignore them. They can also not be opted out of by subjecting the arbitration agreement to a law other than that of the seat. Any suggestion that the arbitrators should always follow

---

339 Rüßmann, »Zwingendes Recht in den Schiedsregeln einer Schiedsinstitution?«, 492 (»*kein höherrangiges Recht*« [no higher ranking law]); *see also* Schmidt-Ahrendts and Höttler, »Anwendbares Recht bei Schiedsverfahren mit Sitz in Deutschland«, 268; *contra* Berger, Center for Transnational Law, *Private Dispute Resolution in International Business*, para. 16–37 (assuming that arbitration rules rank above individual party agreements).

340 *See* Spohnheimer, *Gestaltungsfreiheit*, 104 (also criticising the use of this term); *cf. also* Rüßmann, »Zwingendes Recht in den Schiedsregeln einer Schiedsinstitution?«, 482 (reporting that the memoranda and pleadings of students in the 18th Willem C. Vis Arbitration Moot Court overemployed this terminology).

341 Renner, *Zwingendes transnationales Recht*, 33.

342 Spohnheimer, *Gestaltungsfreiheit*, 107 n. 30. *See infra* at pp. 243-264 (§11A.IIIIV; B) for the contract law analysis.

party agreement, even if this conflicts with mandatory law of the seat[343] is dangerous and not supportable given the evident risk of challenge of the award. If not successful in trying to persuade the parties to discard party agreements contradicting mandatory arbitration law of the seat, the arbitrators have to treat such conflicting agreements as invalid.[344]

To avoid a risk of non-enforcement, parties, arbitrators and institutions should also try to comply with known international public policy of the probable enforcement forum.[345] However, as there are various conceivable enforcement states,[346] only serious due process concerns limit party autonomy in this respect. Since ordinarily, the *lex arbitri* of the seat reflects these as well, compliance with mandatory law of the seat is usually sufficient.

## B. Validity of hybrid arbitration agreements in principle

From this overview of procedural party autonomy in international arbitration and its interaction with governing rules and laws, one can draw the following consequences for hybrid arbitration agreements:

Hybrid arbitration agreements are an expression of the parties will to determine the arbitral procedure as they please. The overall acknowledgement of party autonomy in international arbitration therefore favours the admissibility of hybrid arbitration agreements. Generally, mandatory arbitration laws that oppose hybrid institutional arbitration do not exist. The only jurisdiction that attempted a regulation of this phenomenon, Romania, did not exclude hybrid arbitration agreements in total but placed the validity of the choice of other institutional rules at the disposition of the administering institution.

In all other jurisdictions, arbitral institutions can, from a normative point of view, neither impose the application of their own rules on parties nor hinder parties to arbitrate under their rules without their supervision. Institutional rules are contract provisions on the same hierarchic level as direct party agreements. Therefore, institutional exclusivity provisions like article

---

343 *See e.g.* Voit, »§ 1042 ZPO«, para. 33 (separating the arbitration from award enforcement).

344 Wilske, »§ 1042 ZPO«, para. 17; Waincymer, *Procedure and Evidence*, para. 2.10.3.

345 Missing from the summary by Schmidt-Ahrendts and Höttler, »Anwendbares Recht bei Schiedsverfahren mit Sitz in Deutschland«.

346 *See e.g.* Waincymer, *Procedure and Evidence*, para. 2.10.3.

1 (2) of the ICC Rules cannot overrule the parties' choice for hybrid arbitration. Accordingly, hybrid arbitration agreements are valid and admissible under arbitration law.

The question if hybrid arbitration agreements are also capable of being performed (operable) requires further consideration of institutional practice[347] and legal principles not following from the *lex arbitri* but applying to the contract with the institution[348] or the activities of arbitral bodies in relation to other institutions.[349]

---

347 *See infra* at pp. 209 et seq. (§10) and pp. 344 et seq. (§14).
348 *See infra* at pp. 236 et seq. (§11A.II).
349 *See infra* at pp. 272 et seq. (§13).

# Chapter 2: Qualifying hybrid arbitration (agreements)

As outlined in Chapter 1, party autonomy implies that the parties are in principle completely free to choose whether to conduct the arbitration without or with - and with how much - support of an arbitral institution.[1] Nevertheless, the involvement of an arbitral institution as an additional player arguably changes the rules of the game and the role of party autonomy within it. It is the purpose of this chapter to reveal whether and how a hybrid arbitration procedure, if agreed, fits into the reality of institutional arbitration (§7).

Furthermore, by combining the features of one institution with the rules of another, hybrid arbitration agreements unquestionably raise issues of interpretation and performance. This provokes a regard at case law on »*pathologies*« of institutional arbitration agreements (§8).

On that basis, it will be possible to qualify hybrid arbitration procedure within the categories of institutional and ad hoc arbitration and to label corresponding agreements as pathological or non-pathological, identifying potential obstacles to the operability of hybrid arbitration agreements and ways to avoid or overcome these (§9).

## *§7 Categorisation of hybrid arbitration as institutional*

When deciding at first instance on the jurisdiction of the arbitral tribunal appointed under the auspices of SIAC for the *Alstom–Insigma* arbitration, the Singapore High Court simply qualified the agreed arbitration as ad hoc:

> »The present case, however, despite the nomination of the SIAC as the body to conduct the arbitration, is not an example of institutional arbitration by the SIAC, since the arbitration agreement specifically designated the use of ICC Rules instead. Thus, this is prima facie an agreement for *ad hoc* arbitration by the SIAC [*emphasis added*].«[2]

The Singapore High Court may have found such qualification necessary to support its pro-arbitration approach against any voices that understand

---

1    But *see supra* at pp. 101-74 (§4C.II.2.b.iii) and *infra* at pp. 97-104 (§4C.II.2.b) for exceptions under some arbitration regimes.

2    *Insigma v. Alstom*, [2008] SGHC 134 [34].

institutional arbitration to be *per se* a form of arbitration with limited party autonomy.[3] To understand or refute this trick, it is helpful to analyse the phenomenon of institutional arbitration by relating it to ad hoc arbitration. This section shall clarify the meaning of both concepts (A) and some advantages and disadvantages of institutional arbitration (B) before outlining various concepts of intermediate - semi-institutional - forms of arbitration (C). The practical variety of accepted forms of arbitration pleads in favour of allowing hybrid arbitration, whether as an institutional, ad hoc or intermediate form of arbitration (D).

## A. Hybrid arbitration as a problem of defining institutional arbitration

>»By *definition*, institutional arbitration requires the parties to a dispute to submit to the rules and administrative supervision of the chosen institution [*emphasis added*].«[4]

The premise that ad hoc arbitration allows for greatest flexibility, while institutional arbitration imposes more constraints, if accepted as true, intrinsically links the operability of hybrid arbitration clauses to the problem of defining institutional arbitration.

Herein, the definition attempt only contrasts institutional with ad hoc arbitration, answering the question when arbitration is institutional in character and when it is not. Other approaches would be to relate institutional arbitration to court litigation or the administration of court proceedings or to contrast the activities of institutions with those of arbitrators.

This section also refrains from defining »*arbitral institutions*«, in comparison to other organisations. It can simply be assumed for the purposes of analysing hybrid arbitration agreements that all bodies herein referred to - the ICC Court, SIAC, CIETAC, LCIA, AAA-ICDR, the Swiss Chambers' Arbitration Institution and DIS - are undisputedly arbitral institutions. They have a permanent organisation and offer services in relation to arbitration including arbitration rules and some - more or less - assistance in

---

3    *See e.g.* Schütze, *Institutionelle Schiedsgerichtsbarkeit: Kommentar*, chap. 1, para. 2 (concluding that institutional rules limit procedural options); *but see* Petsche, *The Growing Autonomy of International Commercial Arbitration*, 88–91 (defining »*autonomy*« as independence from state courts and laws and concluding that institutions increase this autonomy).

4    Enock and Melia, »Ad Hoc Arbitrations«, 91, para. 6–8.

their application.[5] The only question is whether it is institutional arbitration if one of these bodies applies the rules of another when assisting arbitration.

## I. Rejection of definitions based on the constitution of the tribunal

> »Most important is the principle that the arbitral tribunal is constituted *ad hoc* in every case in order to meet the requirements of jurisdiction and complete independence to the highest degree possible [*emphasis added*].«[6]

This quote is not, as one might instantaneously assume, a celebration of the advantages of ad hoc arbitration but rather an early comment on the functioning of the ICC Court. It underlines that it is unhelpful to draw the distinction between institutional and ad hoc arbitration with reference to the time or method of constitution of the arbitral tribunal.

To say that only ad hoc arbitral tribunals are constituted »*on the occasion*« of the dispute is incorrect, because when opting for institutional arbitration the parties refer their disputes to a permanent administering body but not to a permanent arbitral tribunal.[7] The arbitral tribunal is constituted ad hoc, but with the help of the institution which is itself permanent. Albeit to a lesser extent, this even applies to arbitration institutions with a compulsory list procedure. If permanence of the arbitral tribunal were the relevant criterion, »*every single arbitration would be ad hoc.*«[8] Any definition therefore has to centre on the involvement of an arbitral institution. Thereby, it is insufficient to consider the arbitral tribunal's constitution alone,[9] as this would ignore the differentiation between administered institutional arbitration and ad hoc arbitration with a predetermined appointing authority.

---

5   Meeting the minimal requirements set out by Gaudet, »La coopération des juridictions étatiques à l'arbitrage institutionnel«, 101.

6   Dietler, *Der Schiedsgerichtshof der Internationalen Handelskammer, seine Organisation und Verfahren*, 5 (original in German) (own translation).

7   *See supra* at pp. 92-95 (§4C.II.2.a.i) on the misleading terminology of New York Convention, art. I (2).

8   Greenberg, Kee, and Weeramantry, *International Commercial Arbitration*, para. 4.177.

9   *But see* Wolf, »§ 1025 ZPO«, para. 10 (defining ad hoc arbitration as arbitration without the involvement of an institution in the tribunal constitution process).

## II. Rejection of definitions focussing on the applicable rules

Another attempt to define institutional arbitration focusses on the applicable arbitration rules:

> »An ›institutional‹ arbitration is one that is administered by a specialist arbitral institution, *under its own rules of arbitration* [*emphasis added*].«[10]

This approach then considers ad hoc arbitration as

> »one which is conducted pursuant to rules agreed by the parties themselves or laid down by the arbitral tribunal.«[11]

Already at first glance, it is striking that hybrid arbitrations, like in the *Alstom–Insigma* case,[12] do not appear to match either of the just cited definitions. Neither does the institution administer the case »*under its own rules*«, nor did the parties agree the rules individually, nor did the arbitral tribunal lay them down. Rather, one institution drafted the rules and then the parties, the other, administering institution and the arbitral tribunal adapt them.

The very narrow definition of institutional arbitration as arbitration administered by an institution under its own rules is little convincing.[13] It mingles the definition of institutional arbitration with accepting - in pre-emptive obedience - the possible consequence of limited party autonomy without giving any reasons for this assumption. The availability of the UNCITRAL Rules for both ad hoc arbitrations and institutional arbitrations also contradict any differentiation relying on the criterion that the applicable rules have been pre-drafted.[14]

## III. Preference for definitions based on institutional involvement

Most convincing is a more literal approach: Arbitration administratively supported by an arbitral institution is institutional, all other arbitration only involving the parties and the arbitrators and largely depending on state courts for support, is ad hoc.

---

10  Blackaby et al., *Redfern and Hunter*, para. 1.158.
11  Ibid., para. 1.153.
12  *See supra* pp. 35-39 (Introduction, §1C).
13  *See also* Fry, »HKL v. Rizq«, 455 (speaking of an »*antithetic chimera of ad hoc administered arbitration*«).
14  Imprecise in this regard: Born, *Cases and Materials (2011)*, 64.

This means that only arbitrations not administratively supported by *any* arbitral institution are ad hoc arbitrations, independent of whether they follow tailor-made rules or UNCITRAL Rules or adapted rules published by an arbitral institution and originally designed for administration.[15] If *another* than the rules issuing institution proceeds with the administration, this is still an institutional arbitration.[16]

Characteristic element is the involvement of the institution as an additional actor in the arbitration proceedings.

In short, institutional arbitration is arbitration, which proceeds with the administrative support and under the supervision of an arbitral institution as an actor different from the arbitral tribunal.[17] Such a broad definition copes best with the practical reality of various institutions existing, available rules and differences in structure and process between administered arbitrations.[18] As a corollary, ad hoc arbitration means that parties agree to arbitrate a particular contract or dispute without referring to an arbitral institution for administrative support and supervision.[19]

Mere acting of a permanent body as appointing authority does not yet amount to administrative support, nor does the provision of hearing rooms and related facilities. Rather, administrative support means a certain *degree* of involvement in the arbitration as a process of dispute resolution.[20]

In the *Alstom–Insigma* arbitration, it is evident that SIAC was sufficiently involved in the arbitration to qualify it as institutional, in fact it was even

---

15  *See infra* at pp. 151 et seq. (§7C.IV) on ad hoc arbitration under institutional rules.

16  *Contra Insigma v. Alstom*, [2008] SGHC 134 [34].

17  Inspired by: Paris - the Home of International Arbitration, »Glossary of Arbitration Terms«; *cf. also* Schlaepfer and Petti, »Institutional versus Ad Hoc Arbitration«, 19 (§2.03).

18  *Cf.* Wolf, *Die Institutionelle Handelsschiedsgerichtsbarkeit*, 10 (describing institutional arbitration as an elastic grid of characteristics) (»elastisches Merkmalsgefüge«).

19  Adapted from Schlaepfer and Petti, »Institutional versus Ad Hoc Arbitration«, 13 (§2.02) (with further references); *but see* Trakman, »Arbitrating Options«, 293 n. 2 (criticising the use of the term ad hoc synonymously with non-institutional and wanting to restrict it to arbitration under a submission agreement concluded on the occasion of the dispute in contrast to arbitration under arbitration clauses).

20  *See* Fouchard, »Rights and Obligations of the Arbitrator with Regard to the Parties and the Arbitral Institution«, para. 38.

more involved as it would have been under its own rules,[21] agreeing *inter alia* to scrutinise Terms of Reference and the award pursuant to the ICC Rules (1998). The Singapore High Court's qualification of this arbitration as ad hoc[22] is therefore little convincing. This is even more so, if one bears in mind that the arbitral tribunal considered it necessary to readjust SIAC's approach to administering the proceedings and asked for confirmation that SIAC was prepared to substitute ICC actors in the process. Had the parties agreed on ad hoc arbitration, the arbitral tribunal would not have had any reason to do so.

IV. Degree of involvement of arbitral institutions

Having found that an arbitration is institutional if an arbitral institution is involved to some degree in the arbitration process, provides administrative support and supervision, this definition shall now be filled with life. This is not easy, as arbitral institutions and their rules differ considerably as to the level of organisation and control - or with a more negative connotation: bureaucracy.

At a glance, these are services provided by many arbitral institutions:[23]

- The institution receives the request for arbitration, notifies it to the respondent(s) and establishes the contact to the chosen arbitrators.
- The institution assists in fixing the place of arbitration.[24]

---

21  SIAC Rules (1997).
22  *Insigma v. Alstom*, [2008] SGHC 134 [34] (as quoted *supra* at p. 126).
23  *See also* Wolf, *Die Institutionelle Handelsschiedsgerichtsbarkeit*, 36–37 (§ 4) (developing a model of the typical arbitration institution). Herein, the focus lies on case related activities. Generally, arbitral institutions also undertake non-case related tasks like organising conferences and trainings on arbitration, promoting arbitration and developing arbitration law and policy.
24  Either finally or provisionally, *see supra* at p. 70, note 84 for details.

- In the exceptional case that the parties do not agree on the language of the proceedings, an institution may fix it.[25] However, more often this is left to the arbitral tribunal to decide.[26]
- The institution assists in fixing the number of arbitrators[27] and in nominating/appointing/confirming co-arbitrators and chairperson or a sole arbitrator.[28]
- The institution decides on challenges to arbitrators and replaces arbitrators.[29]
- The institution further controls the cost of arbitration including the arbitrator's fees and expenses[30] and requests the required advances/deposits from the parties.[31]

---

25  *See e.g.* LCIA Rules, art. 17 (2) (2014); CIETAC Rules, art. 71 (2012) = art. 81 (2015) (attention: Chinese is the default language for CIETAC proceedings).

26  *See e.g.* ICC Rules, art. 20 (2012; 2017); SIAC Rules, art. 19 (1) (2013) = art. 22 (1) (2016); AAA-ICDR Rules, art. 18 (2014); DIS Rules, art. 22 (1) (1998); Swiss Rules, art. 17 (1) (2012).

27  *See* ICC Rules, art. 12 (2) (2012; 2017) (sole arbitrator as default rule, discretion of the Court to appoint three arbitrators); similar: AAA-ICDR Rules, art. 11 (2014); LCIA Rules, art. 5 (8) (2014); SIAC Rules, art. 6 (1) (2013) = art. 9 (1) (2016); Swiss Rules, art. 6 (1), (2) (2012); *but see* DIS Rules, art. 3 (1998) (default rule of three arbitrators without any discretion given to the institution); similiar: CIETAC Rules, art. 23 (2) (2012) = art. 25 (2) (2015).

28  *See infra* at pp. 366-378 (§14B.III) on differences in terminology and requirements for institutional appointment.

29  *See* ICC Rules, art. 14, 15 (2012; 2017); SIAC Rules, art. 11–14 (2013) = art. 14--16 (2016); LCIA Rules, art. 10–11 (2014); AAA-ICDR Rules, 14–15 (2014); *but see* DIS Rules, art. 18 (2) (1998) (only the arbitral tribunal may decide on a challenge, not the institution and the decision is subject to control by the competent state court).

30  The administrative fixing of costs has to be separated from the tribunal's decision on who is to bear the costs of the arbitration, based on the outcome of the case or other criteria.

31  *See* ICC Rules, art. 36 (2012) = art. 37 (2017); AAA-ICDR Rules, 35–36 (2014); LCIA Rules, 24, 28 (2014); SIAC Rules, art. 30 (2013) = art. 34 (2016); DIS Rules, art. 7 (1) (1998) (initial deposit); *but see also* ibid., art. 25 (making the arbitral tribunal responsible for collecting deposits in addition to the initial deposit). The administrative fixing of costs is to be separated from the final decision on who is to bear the costs of the arbitration, based on the outcome of the case or other criteria, which is left to the arbitral tribunal.

- The institution may fix and control procedural time limits, e.g. for the final award.[32]
- The institution notifies the award to the parties.

The institution works most prior to the constitution of the arbitral tribunal. Once constituted, the arbitral tribunal controls the procedure in cooperation with the parties. However, institutions usually receive and file copies of all submissions and correspondence in the case.

Apart from these basic tasks and powers addressed above, institutional influence varies significantly. *E.g.*, for ICC arbitration, which is described as »*heavily administered*«,[33] one can note that the ICC Court has other significant tasks to fulfil prior to and after the constitution of the arbitral tribunal. These include a prima facie decision on objections to jurisdiction,[34] the approval of the Terms of Reference, if not signed by both parties,[35] and the scrutiny and approval of awards.[36]

It is generally not a task of arbitral institutions to decide the dispute.[37] Officially, only the arbitral tribunal decides whether the claim is justified and who should bear the costs of arbitration. Even if the institution applies a system of scrutiny of awards, only the draft award is subject to such review and the tribunal has the last say in it. However, one cannot deny the influence of some activities of institutions on the outcome of a dispute. Moreover, in the practice of some institutions, borders between arbitrators' tasks and institutional tasks may become blurred.[38]

The separation of tasks between the arbitral tribunal as the decision-making body and the institution as administrator may raise questions of competence concerning the application and interpretation of the arbitration rules. The AAA-ICDR Rules, exceptionally, attempt to clarify the responsibilities

---

32  *See infra* at pp. 381-384 (§14B.V) for details.
33  Lew, Mistelis, and Kröll, *Comparative International Commercial Arbitration*, para. 3–19; *cf. also* Schütze, *Institutionelle Schiedsgerichtsbarkeit: Kommentar*, 4 (ch. I, para. 8).
34  ICC Rules, art. 6 (3) (2012; 2017).
35  Ibid., art. 23.
36  Ibid., art. 33.
37  Nedden and Herzberg, »Art. 1 ICC SchO«, para. 11–12; *see also* Blanke, »Institutional versus Ad Hoc Arbitration«, 276 (remarking that despite the »*terminology that reflects a somewhat litigious heritage, neither the ICC Court nor the LCIA Court are courts in the archetypical sense*«).
38  *See infra* at p. 384 on - unverified - rumours of CIETAC staff participating in award drafting.

of the AAA-ICDR as administrator set against those of the tribunal in a single provision:

>»The arbitral tribunal, any emergency arbitrator appointed under Article 6, and any consolidation arbitrator appointed under Article 8, shall interpret and apply these Rules insofar as they relate to their powers and duties. The Administrator shall interpret and apply all other Rules.«[39]

In general, one may follow that arbitral institutions exercise important, procedurally relevant tasks for which they need certain powers. The parties refer powers to an institution through the arbitration agreement submitting the dispute to its administration and through the contract, which the parties conclude with the institution itself.[40] Arguably, the greater the powers and involvement of an institution, the greater is its responsibility for the proceedings. Accordingly, it will be difficult and undesirable for an arbitral institution to administer cases under the rules of another institution that do foresee a higher degree of involvement than the institution's own rules. On the other hand, an institution may also be little inclined to give up powers it commonly enjoys by agreeing to administer arbitrations under rules of a less-controlling institution. In practice, the feasibility of hybrid arbitration therefore depends on the flexibility of the administering institution to depart from its rules, to be discussed in Chapter 3,[41] but also by the comparability of its rules with those the parties want to apply instead, discussed in Chapter 4.[42]

B. Advantages and disadvantages of institutional arbitration

The following subsections shortly summarise and structure common arguments in favour and against institutional arbitration before concluding if and to what extent these apply to *hybrid institutional* arbitration.

---

39  AAA-ICDR Rules, art. 39 (2014); *see also* AAA-ICDR Rules, art. 36 (2009); *cf.* Gusy, Hosking, and Schwarz, *A Guide to the ICDR Rules*, para. 36.01 (finding the provision »*self-explanatory*« although »*it may not always be so clear*« what articles concern the tribunal's powers and duties).

40  *See infra* at pp. 235-236 (§11A.I).

41  *See infra* at pp. 209 et seq. (§10).

42  *See infra* at pp. 355 et seq. (§14B).

## I. Objective advantages

The parties may especially appreciate the support of an institution if they cannot agree on aspects of the procedure or if one party does not participate or tries to employ dilatory or obstructing tactics.

>>The creation of a self-sufficient dispute settling mechanism is dependent upon either further cooperation of the parties or on outside help.<<[43]

To employ an image introduced by a former colleague in a presentation about the ICC Court: If we compared arbitral proceedings to a train, the arbitrators would conduct the train upon instructions by the parties but the institution puts the trains on the rails and avoids any derailing if it spots obstacles on the tracks.[44]

Institutional rules usually provide that each party may apply to the institution to decide certain issues. In comparison, in ad hoc arbitration, the parties can only apply to state courts for such support. The necessity to apply to state courts for supporting decisions might entail several problems including the number of possibly competent *fora*, if the place of arbitration is not fixed[45] and the different attitudes of national legal systems and courts towards arbitration.[46] The parties may face possible or perceived partiality or lack of quality of available state courts that made the parties opt for arbitration in the first place.[47]

---

43 Varady, >>On Appointing Authorities in International Commercial Arbitration<<, 311; *reprinted in* Varady, Von Mehren, and Barceló, *International Commercial Arbitration*, 391–97 (at 391).

44 I thank Thomas Granier with whom I had the honour to work during an internship at the ICC Court; *cf. also* Jarrosson, >>Le rôle respectif<<, 394, para. 49 (using the image of a theatre play and comparing arbitral institutions with directors or sometimes prompters while the arbitrators and the parties are the actors).

45 *See supra* at n. 85.

46 Jurisdictions are commonly qualified as more or less *>>arbitration-friendly<<*. While no one has yet dared to propose a comprehensive list of arbitration-friendly jurisdictions, a good description is given by Aglionby, >>Arbitration Outside China<<, 685: >>*That means that in any proceedings where support is needed, the court will have the right powers and will apply enough, but not too much, oversight*<< (naming Hong Kong, Singapore, France, England, Switzerland and Sweden as positive examples).

47 *See also* Paulsson, >>Vicarious Hypochondria and Institutional Arbitration<<, 245.

Furthermore, while state courts may assist ad hoc arbitration by appointing an arbitrator or fixing the place and language of arbitration, the remuneration of the arbitrators there remains left to the parties' agreement, without the comfort of fee scales as are provided by many institutions.[48] The institutions' mechanisms to collect advances from the parties from which the arbitrators will be paid - the institution thereby acting as an intermediate between the parties and the arbitrators regarding fee issues - is considered a *»definite advantage«* of institutional arbitration also from an arbitrator's point of view, as it allows the arbitrators to *»maintain a certain level of material detachment.«*[49]

The parties to institutional arbitration may also appreciate to be able to contact the institution's personnel about the status of the case and about how to deal with procedural aspects without having to address such issue directly with the arbitrator. To this effect, institutions maintain more or less well-equipped libraries and databases.[50]


## II. Subjective advantages

> »Much scholarship on international commercial arbitration is difficult to distinguish from advertising.«[51]

While the services described above are objective, unquestionable advantages of institutional arbitration, there are other possible advantages occasionally mentioned that are more difficult to verify and that may just exist in the perception of the parties or the praise of practitioners under the wing of major institutions. As once regretted by Phillippe Fouchard, some arbitration institutions welcome a certain opacity or even public misinformation, in vanity or negligence, as this allows them to constantly affirm

---

48  *But see* LCIA, »Schedule of Arbitration Costs (LCIA)« (in LCIA arbitration, arbitrators are paid by the hour at rates freely agreed with the parties upon advise by the Registrar) (a maximum of £450 per hour is proposed).

49  Lew, Mistelis, and Kröll, *Comparative International Commercial Arbitration*, para. 3–23; *but see* DIS Rules, art. 25 (1998) (diminishing this advantage by making the arbitrators responsible for requesting advances on their fees).

50  Schütze, *Institutionelle Schiedsgerichtsbarkeit: Kommentar*, 2 (ch. 1, para. 2).

51  Michaels, »Dreaming Law without a State,« 37; referring to *idem*: »Rollen und Rollenverständnisse im transnationalen Privatrecht,« 192–93 (in the online version at p. 19).

their existence, reality and good functioning.[52] Being aware that practice, legal science and public relations often blend,[53] the following aspects are therefore classified as subjective advantages.[54]

These include the comfort of institutional rules, which, for being pre-set and tested, suggest to work well in practice. The fact that many cases have previously been decided under these rules and were administered by the institution may indicate a likelihood that the arbitration ends within a reasonable time.[55] However, as described by the image of a train referred to above, the parties and the arbitrators, not the institution, remain in conduct of the proceedings, two arbitrations are never the same[56] and *»the arbitration is only as good as the arbitrator.«*[57]

Some commentators suggest that the good name of the institution alone may favour the enforceability of the resulting award, even in countries with

---

52  Fouchard, »Typologie des institutions d'arbitrage«, 284.

53  Very critical recently: Fischer-Lescano, »Gutachten zu CETA,« 2 (*»Die Rechtswissenschaft ist in einer Weise mit dem globalen Schiedsgerichts-Business verflochten, die insgesamt doch sehr unappetitlich ist.«* [legal scholarship mingles with global arbitration business in a way which is truly appalling]; in the context of transatlantic free trade agreement projects).

54  Michaels, »Rollen und Rollenverständnisse im Transnationalen Privatrecht«, 20; *cf. also* Schlaepfer and Petti, »Institutional versus Ad Hoc Arbitration«, 13 (*»real or supposed«*); Johnston, »The Best Providers for Asian Arbitrations«, 41 (regretting that *»marketing presentations from institutions are increasingly slick«*); *see also* Poudret and Besson, *Comparative Law of International Arbitration*, para. 94 (on an not entirely unbiased *»fervour for institutional arbitration«*).

55  The same applies to arbitration under the UNCITRAL Rules (*see e.g.* Blanke, »Institutional versus Ad Hoc Arbitration«, 278). Probably, UNCITRAL Rules have been used more often than any of the major institutional rules but unfortunately, outside institutional arbitration, no statistics are available (*see* Schlaepfer and Petti, »Institutional versus Ad Hoc Arbitration«, 13, §2.01).

56  Lew, Mistelis, and Kröll, *Comparative International Commercial Arbitration*, para. 3–21.

57  LCIA, »The Case for Administered Arbitration« (calling this a *»truism«*); *see also* Dietler, *Der Schiedsgerichtshof der Internationalen Handelskammer, seine Organisation und Verfahren*, 5; Kassis, *Réflexions*, 285 (para. 411).

*»political interference or where the courts and law are not always arbitration-friendly.«*[58] Very optimistically, an author even alleges that an award

»issued e.g. by the ICC Court or the LCIA will almost certainly command the respect of an enforcing court, thus facilitating the enforcement process.«[59]

Another commentator mentions a perceived *»ICC stamp«* providing *»ICC insurance«* of enforceability.[60] Collecting empirical data backing such assumptions may be an interesting further research project since contracting states of the New York Convention are expected to enforce awards irrespective of whether they were made in institutional or ad hoc proceedings.[61] In any event, marketing activities of arbitral institutions strongly reflect this idea, purporting to provide awards of a particularly high quality,[62] although no arbitral institution would guarantee enforceability under a sanction of potential liability. In ICC arbitration, the high level of administration including features such as confirmation of party-appointed arbitrators and scrutiny of awards is intended to secure such *»quality.«*[63], The prestige of an institution may also be an argument to persuade the other party to arbitrate at all.[64]

---

58  Lew, Mistelis, and Kröll, *Comparative International Commercial Arbitration*, para. 3–20; *see also* Schlaepfer and Petti, »Institutional versus Ad Hoc Arbitration«, 20 (§2.03[B]) (*»higher quality award«*).

59  Blanke, »Institutional versus Ad Hoc Arbitration«, 277; a little more objective: Shiraz, »The New SIAC Rules 2007«, 1 (*»SIAC awards have received recognition and have been enforced in provinces such as Zhejiang, Guangzhou and Hebei«*).

60  Bühring-Uhle, Kirchhof, and Scherer, *Arbitration and Mediation in International Business*, 38.

61  New York Convention, art. I (2), II, V.

62  *See e.g.* ICC, »Ten Good Reasons to Choose ICC Arbitration« (*»Reputable«*); SIAC, »Why Choose Us« (*»SIAC arbitration awards have been enforced by the courts of Australia, China (Hong Kong), India, Indonesia and the USA amongst other New York Convention countries«*).

63  Similar: SIAC, »Why Choose Us« (*»We scrutinise the arbitral award, thus enforcement problems are less likely«*).

64  Lachmann, *Handbuch für die Schiedsgerichtspraxis*, para. 3050.

## III. Objective, possible and perceived disadvantages

The possible disadvantages of institutional arbitration should not be denied, some of which may have contributed to the emergence of the phenomenon of hybrid arbitration, while others relate to its handling.

### 1. Cost

The disadvantage of institutional arbitration mentioned most often is certainly the additional fee linked to the administration by the institution. All institutions charge administrative fees - in varying amounts.[65]

For example, the ICC Court charges a non-refundable filing fee of US $ 3,000.00[66] and further administrative expenses dependent on the amount in dispute. If the amount in dispute were US $ 1 Million, the administrative expenses would sum up to US $ 21,715.00 according to the cost calculator provided on the ICC website.[67] While, based on average arbitrator fees, this would be only about 15 % of the total costs in case of a three arbitrator tribunal,[68] the same administrative expenses would already add up to about one third of the total costs, if a sole arbitrator decided the case.[69] Moreover, the Court assumes a power to fix administrative fees at a higher amount than resulting from the scale, if the complexity of the case so requires.[70]

---

65  *See also* Horvath, Konrad, and Power, *Costs in International Arbitration: A Central and Southern Eastern European Perspective*, 811 (coming to the conclusion that amounts »*vary tremendously*«).

66  Which is an advance on the administrative costs.

67  ICC, »Cost Calculator«.

68  *See* ibid. (total costs: US $ 139850).

69  Ibid. (total costs: US $ 61094).

70  *See* ICC, »Cost of Arbitration in Detail (articles 36 and 37)« However, the ICC Rules only mention discretion to depart from the scales for »*fees of the arbitrators*« (ICC Rules, art. 37 [2] [2012] = art. 38 [2] [2017]).

For the same amount in dispute, other institutions - e.g. SIAC,[71] the DIS[72] or the AAA-ICDR[73]– would generally charge considerably less in administrative fees. However, many find that the features of ICC arbitration distinguishing it from pure »*Launching Systems*« are worth the difference.[74]

In contrast to the institutions just named, the LCIA calculates its administrative expenses at - non-negligible - hourly rates.[75] How many hours of work the institution's personnel or members of the LCIA Court would put into a US $ 1 Million case is of course impossible to estimate.

At this stage, it is sufficient to state that the administrative costs associated with the choice of institutional arbitration are considerable, but usually they do not nearly amount to the costs associated with arbitrators, legal representatives and experts - even for a rather expensive institution. Moreover, the limits set to the arbitrators fees by institutional rules can balance out additional administrative costs.[76]


2. Bureaucracy

The possible disadvantage of lacking flexibility of institutional arbitration is at the centre of this analysis. This can be a real disadvantage, depending largely on the institution's attitude towards allowing modifications of its rules.[77]

A related point of criticism is the perceived bureaucracy and resulting slowness associated with some institutional mechanisms. This becomes

---

71  *Cf.* SIAC, »Estimate Your Fees«.
72  *Cf.* Deutsche Institution für Schiedsgerichtsbarkeit (DIS), »Cost Calculator«. However, the complete amount has to be paid in advance, *see* DIS Rules, art. 7.1, 11.1 (1998) (*see also* Annex to § 40.5).
73  With some discretion for the institution to charge for additional services, *cf.* AAA, »Administrative Fee Schedules (Standard and Flexible Fee)«.
74  *E.g.* Karrer, »Naives Sparen birgt Gefahren«, 114.
75  For the LCIA's Secretariat staff at £150 to 250 per hour, dependent on function, for work of the LCIA Court »*at hourly rates advised by members of the LCIA Court*« (*see* LCIA, »Schedule of Arbitration Costs (LCIA)«).
76  *See* Lachmann, *Handbuch für die Schiedsgerichtspraxis*, para. 3057 (without differentiating between institutions); Karrer, »Naives Sparen birgt Gefahren«, 114 (recommending ad hoc arbitration only to experienced specialists); Craig, Park, and Paulsson, *ICC Arbitration*, 31 (§ 3.02) (finding ad hoc arbitration »*frighteningly expensive*«).
77  *See infra* at pp. 209 et seq. (§10).

most acute if institutional rules foresee a decision of a specific institutional body for several procedural steps. The most obvious examples stem from ICC arbitration.[78] First, the Court or at least the Secretary General has to confirm every member of the arbitral tribunal - even if the parties agree on its composition.[79] Second, ICC Rules require drafting and signing, or Court approval, of Terms of Reference. While Terms of Reference are a feature intended to finally save time by clarifying at an early stage of the proceedings the requests for relief and by listing the disputed issues,[80] they nevertheless require preliminary consultations and the drafting of an additional document, which has to be checked by members of the ICC Court's secretariat. The correspondence between the parties and the arbitral tribunal, between the members of the arbitral tribunal and with the secretariat might altogether take up to a few weeks in which the tribunal and the parties may not come any closer towards the resolution of their dispute.[81] Third, the process of scrutiny of the draft award initially requires a member of the ICC Court's secretariat to proofread the draft award for formalistic and stylistic errors and for serious material and enforceability concerns. At the second stage, the ICC Court has to decide whether to approve the draft award based on a summary and recommendation prepared by the competent team of the secretariat. If the Court refuses to approve the award, it refers the draft award back to the arbitrator(s) with a proposal of modifications. The modified award then has to go through the same scrutiny process again. In quite rare and probably justified cases, it may take around three or more court sessions until the Court finally approves an award.

>The arbitrators cannot be forced to accept any modifications. (Since arbitrators cannot force the Court to approve their award either, there is a theoretical possibility of a deadlock; but this does not occur in practice.)«[82]

---

78  *See* Paulsson, »Vicarious Hypochondria and Institutional Arbitration«, 251 (admitting »*room for improvement*«); *but see* Lachmann, *Handbuch für die Schiedsgerichtspraxis*, para. 3059 (estimating that the ICC Court's reaction time is surprisingly short).

79  ICC Rules, art. 12, 13 (2012; 2017).

80  Often, arbitrators only state in a general way that the »Issues« are what follows from the parties submissions because an agreement on an exhaustive list of issues proves difficult in practice.

81  *Cf.* Blanke, »Institutional versus Ad Hoc Arbitration«, 280 (warning that some parties »*abuse the negotiation of Terms of Reference as means to delay*«).

82  Craig, Park, and Paulsson, *ICC Arbitration*, 376, para. 20.01; *see also* Blanke, »Institutional versus Ad Hoc Arbitration«, 278 (warning that the

However, ad hoc arbitration procedures can be just as slow or even slower if one considered the delays that might occur if the parties fail to agree on the constitution of the arbitral tribunal and if an application to state courts was necessary - especially in states with a notoriously overloaded judiciary. As a rule of thumb, one can assume that the quicker the internal processes within an institution and the flatter its internal hierarchy, the less is there a concern of slowness associated with institutional arbitration. To react to criticism about the perceived stolidity of the ICC system, the ICC Rules have been streamlined for example with respect to arbitrator confirmation and the prima facie decision on jurisdiction.[83]


3. Intransparency and lack of control

Lack of control of institutional decisions is often mentioned as another disadvantage. In general, institutional decisions are not awards and therefore not subject to direct challenge before state courts, nor do institutional rules provide for any internal appeal against administrative decisions.[84] Nevertheless some supposedly purely administrative decisions may be quite far-reaching, notably the decision on challenges to arbitrators and the *prima facie* decision on jurisdiction.[85] A party may be very surprised to learn that (some of) its claims cannot be arbitrated before the institution,[86] without that the institution would communicate any reasons. Likewise, a party may be disappointed when an institution plainly rejects its objection to the nomination of an arbitrator or a challenge, supported by considerable legal

---

Court remembers unwillingness to accept modifications when pondering future appointments).

83   Now, the Secretary-General may confirm arbitrators in unproblematic cases under ICC Rules, art. 13 (2) (2012; 2017) or refrain from referring obviously unfounded jurisdictional objections to the Court (ibid., art. 6 [3]).

84   *But see* Walsh and Teitelbaum, »LCIA Court Decisions on Challenges to Arbitrators: An Introduction«, 310–12 (providing a digest of three LCIA decisions on challenges introduced against the LCIA or its secretariat; all rejected on the merits although *»there is no mechanism under the LCIA Rules for a party to challenge the institution itself*).

85   *See also infra* at pp. 384-386 (§14B.VI) on scrutiny of awards as exercised by the ICC Court, SIAC and CIETAC.

86   *Cf.* ICC Rules, art. 6 (4) (2012; 2017).

and factual submissions of its lawyers, without giving any explanation.[87] Consequently and in light of the growing number of arbitral institutions, some of »*whose institutional integrity and methods of governance are dubious*«,[88] voices begin to call that »*someone should police the police.*«[89]

The strongest critic of institutional arbitration is probably Antoine Kassis,[90] expressing the uncompromising[91] opinion that arbitration

»under the ICC Rules is not a true arbitration process and awards made in accordance with them are not true arbitral awards enforceable by State courts under national laws«[92]

While Kassis directs his criticism at the ICC Court, some of it applies to institutional arbitration in general. This concerns the argument that

---

87  *Cf.* ibid., art. 11 (4) (»*the reasons for such decisions shall not be communicated*«). While the LCIA furnishes reasoned challenge decisions to the parties, institutional decisions are rarely made available to the public (*see* Nicholas and Partasides, »LCIA Court Decisions on Challenges to Arbitrators« [arguing in favour of publishing challenge decisions]; Walsh and Teitelbaum, »LCIA Court Decisions on Challenges to Arbitrators: An Introduction« [about three years later answering to the request for publishment by summarising a few decisions]).

88  Paulsson, »Vicarious Hypochondria and Institutional Arbitration«, 226.

89  Ibid. (using this expression but not supporting such views).

90  Kassis, *Réflexions*; summarised in English as: »The Questionable Validity of Arbitration and Awards under the Rules of the International Chamber of Commerce«.

91  For the negative reception by the arbitration community, *see e.g.* Born, *Cases and Materials (2011)*, 62 (»*mixture of suspicion and hostility*«); Paulsson, »Vicarious Hypochondria and Institutional Arbitration«, 226, 251 (»*neither balanced nor constructive*«; »*fundamentally unsound*«); *but see* Lalive, »Note, CA Paris, 15.09.1998«, 115, para. 10 (acknowledging that the treatise was not without value: »*ne manquait pas de mérites*«). Critical but forgiving is the review by Fouchard, »Bibliographie - Réflexions«, 528: »*même s'il est lui-même injuste avec la C.C.I. [...] il n'existe aucun tabou en ce domaine, et une remise en question des habitudes ou des positions acquises n'est pas toujours inutile*« [although he is himself unjust to the ICC... a taboo does not exist in this field and questioning habits and acquired positions is not always useless] (fearing that Kassis' book may fall victim to a conspiracy of silence [»*victime d'une sorte de conspiration du silence*«]).

92  Kassis, »The Questionable Validity of Arbitration and Awards under the Rules of the International Chamber of Commerce«, 79; *Réflexions*, 6, para. 2.

institutional decisions, whether on jurisdiction or arbitrator nomination, confirmation and challenges are made »*hidden from the parties*«,[93] meaning without parties' access to the administrative correspondence in the file. If such decisions were taken without giving the parties' sufficient opportunity to comment, there would in fact be a concern with respect to the right to be heard. However, in practice most arbitration institutions invite parties' comments before any such decision and communicate all comments to everyone concerned, as does the ICC Secretariat. The only impediment is that the parties cannot follow the Court's deliberation process and cannot present their arguments orally. In most jurisdictions, this would not yet make a valid due process plea.[94]

In theory, the review of institutional decisions by state courts is much debated. Jan Paulsson, obviously an enthusiast about institutional arbitration, finds:

> »One of the crucial roles of these institutions is to try to keep disputes that have been referred to arbitration out of national courts.«

To him, control of institutional decisions by national courts »*would mean killing the system.*«[95] Others, including but not restricted to Kassis,[96] want to enable court review of at least some institutional decisions.[97] Chapter 5 will provide details on the reviewability of institutional decisions, notably under the angle of control of an institutional decision to accept or reject the administration of arbitrations under hybrid arbitration agreements.[98]

---

93  Kassis, »The Questionable Validity of Arbitration and Awards under the Rules of the International Chamber of Commerce«, 80, 88; *Réflexions*, 219, para. 303.

94  *See generally supra* at pp. 90-91 (§4C.II.1).

95  Paulsson, »Vicarious Hypochondria and Institutional Arbitration«, 251; *see also* Petsche, *The Growing Autonomy of International Commercial Arbitration*, 90.

96  *Cf.* Kassis, *Réflexions*, 190, 211, para. 291 (on challenge decisions).

97  *See e.g.* Khadjavi, *ICC-Schiedsordnung und deutsches Schiedsverfahrensrecht*, 98 (negative prima facie decisions found reviewable procedural awards); *cf. also* Wolf, *Die Institutionelle Handelsschiedsgerichtsbarkeit*, 122 (but with a different reasoning); *see also* Wilske, »Ad Hoc Arbitration in Germany«, 842, para. 17, n. 18.

98  *See infra* at pp. 435-442 (§16A.II.3).

## IV. Shopping for advantages with hybrid arbitration agreements?

Above summarised advantages and disadvantages differ from institution to institution and rules to rules. A motive to conclude hybrid arbitration agreements may therefore be for the parties to avail themselves of real or perceived advantages of a particular set of rules, *e.g.* to choose ICC Rules because there are well tested and efficient. At the same time they may want to avoid a particular disadvantage of the institution that issued these rules, e.g. the price tag attached to ICC arbitration.

When the case was still pending there, Insigma objected to the jurisdiction of the ICC Court to administer its dispute with Alstom expressly arguing that

> »arbitration administered by the SIAC costs less than one administered by the ICC.«[99]

It is not reported why the parties have not simply agreed on standard SIAC arbitration, but if one followed Insigma's slightly contradictory[100] arguments, there may have been an attempt to benefit from the »*hallmark of quality*« of the ICC Rules with this compromise.[101] If this was the motive behind the hybrid arbitration clause between Alstom and Insigma, »*an effort to get the signature benefits of the ICC Rules without paying ICC prices*«,[102] it is obvious that this effort failed. The only initial savings consisted in SIAC charging administrative fees according to its own scale, at the time certainly lower than those of the ICC Court. However, they should not even have taken that - overall negligible –[103] cost advantage for granted when concluding their hybrid arbitration agreement: SIAC could have arguably asked for higher administrative fees when agreeing to administer the proceedings given the additional effort associated with applying ICC Rules. Taking into account the arbitrators' fees, which SIAC calculated pursuant to ICC rates anyway,[104] and the legal costs incurred not only for the arbitration but also for the - expectable - state court applications in Singapore and China, the parties have certainly not made a good bargain. Moreover, the efficiency of

---

99   *Insigma v. Alstom*, [2008] SGHC 134 [29].
100  *See* ibid. (remarking the »*stark contrast*« between the position taken by Insigma before the ICC Court and then before SIAC and the Singapore court).
101  Which Insigma later described as »*disastrous*« (ibid., para. 24).
102  Kirby, »SIAC Can Administer Cases Under The ICC Rules?!?«, 325.
103  *See also* ibid., 326: »*Saving half a pittance is a pittance indeed.*«
104  *See Insigma v. Alstom*, [2009] SGCA 24 [9].

the ICC Rules is reduced if they are applied by an institution with a different structure and without experience in applying typical ICC features.[105]

In fact, it seems that parties agreeing for another than the rules issuing institution to administer their case jeopardise many objective and subjective advantages of institutional arbitration - predictability, experienced support, possibly greater likelihood of obtaining an enforceable award. At the same time, the disadvantages become more acute: costs are unlikely to be saved, the institutional involvement may become even more cumbersome and slow due to the difficulty to incorporate the unfamiliar rules and administration may be particularly intransparent, if functions have to be fulfilled by actors not contemplated by the rules.

By definition, an agreement on hybrid arbitration is thus an agreement for institutional arbitration but not in its most positive connotation. That does not mean that it should not be enforced:

> »In any case, inefficiency alone cannot render a clause invalid so long as the parties had agreed and intended for the arbitration to be conducted in this manner.«[106]

## C. Reality of intermediate forms of arbitration

Other intermediate forms of arbitration exist, which are neither institutional nor purely ad hoc[107] which shall be briefly portrayed, although they are not *in extenso* subject of this study.

As shown, hybrid arbitration agreements as discussed in this thesis are much closer to institutional arbitration agreements than to agreements on ad hoc arbitration. Nevertheless, their performance requires a much greater degree of flexibility and improvisation on behalf of parties, arbitrators and the institution than the conduct of a classic institutional arbitration based on a standard clause. Under this angle, hybrid arbitration loses a lot of the predictability associated with institutional arbitration, which could be a reason to qualify it as semi-ad hoc. In this respect, the expression »*hybrid*« might not only place hybrid arbitration in between two institutions[108] but also in between standard institutional and standard ad hoc arbitration. This

---

105 For this quasi-official position, *see also* Fry, Mazza, and Greenberg, *The Secretariat's Guide to ICC Arbitration*, para. 3–194.
106 *Insigma v. Alstom*, [2009] SGCA 24 [35].
107 Rubino-Sammartano, *International Arbitration: Law and Practice*, 4, para. 1.2.
108 *See* the explanation of the term in the Introduction, *supra* at p. 31.

hypothesis shall be tested by comparing hybrid arbitration with other intermediate, semi-ad hoc or semi-institutional forms of arbitration.

## I. Institutions acting as appointing authority

Parties may opt for ad hoc arbitration but designate a person, body or institution to appoint the arbitrator, a task that would otherwise be left to the competent state court at the place of arbitration.[109] The UNCITRAL Rules explicitly foresee that parties can agree on an appointing authority.[110] Most, if not all, arbitral institutions accept to act as appointing authority in ad hoc cases, a procedure that usually does not pose any particular problems. Some institutions published rules or practice notes on how they would treat such requests.[111]

## II. Facilitated ad hoc arbitration

Some institutions also offer certain additional services under UNCITRAL Rules as an alternative to administration under their own rules.[112] UNCITRAL recommends that institutions should make clear which kind of services they offer in this regard and distinguish these from merely acting as appointing authority.[113]

Following this recommendation, the DIS has published a document entitled »*UNCITRAL Arbitration Rules - administered by the DIS*« noting that:

> »The UNCITRAL Arbitration Rules, however, essentially provide for a non-institutional form of arbitration. Yet in practice, UNCITRAL encourages arbitral institutions and other interested bodies to offer administrative services and to act as appointing authority in order to facilitate arbitral proceedings conducted under the UNCITRAL Arbitration Rules.«[114]

---

109 *Cf.* UNCITRAL Model Law 2006 art. 11 (4)(c).
110 UNCITRAL Rules, art. 6, 7 (2010).
111 *See e.g.* ICC Appointing Authority Rules (2004).
112 *See UNCITRAL Recommendations to Institutions*, para. 16, 17, 18 (for examples).
113 Ibid., para. 21 (a).
114 DIS-UNCITRAL Rules (2012) (Introduction); *see also* SIAC Practice Note for UNCITRAL Cases (2014); *cf. UNCITRAL Recommendations to Institutions*, para. 16–18 (for more examples).

In this document, the DIS communicates a version of the UN-CITRAL Rules adapted to arbitration facilitated by the DIS, explaining the functions of DIS bodies in such context.[115]

The services that institutions offer under UNCITRAL Rules vary tremendously. While some, in addition to acting as appointing authority, only offer ancillary support services like hearing facilities, translation and correspondence services, others adapt the UNCITRAL Rules more to the system installed by the institution's own rules. According to SIAC's »*Practice Note for UNCITRAL Cases*« services include for example:

»a) Appointment of arbitrators;

b) Financial management of the arbitration;

c) Case management, which includes liaising with arbitrators, parties and their authorised representatives on proper delivery of notices, monitoring schedules and time lines for submissions, arranging hearing facilities and all other matters which facilitate the smooth conduct of the arbitration;

d) Exercising such supervisory functions under the UNCITRAL Rules as may be necessary; and

e) Scrutiny and issuance of awards made by the Tribunal, if requested by the Tribunal.«[116]

In particular, point e) is surprising since the UNCITRAL Rules do not normally foresee any scrutiny of awards by an institution.[117] Because of the range of services offered, SIAC charges the same fees that would apply for arbitration under SIAC Rules. Moreover, the President of the SIAC Court reserves the right to depart from the UNCITRAL list procedure if it was »*inappropriate*«, applying SIAC Rules on arbitrator appointment instead. Such far-reaching adaptations of the UNCITRAL Rules are not as problematic as one might assume in light of article V (1)(d) New York Convention. The SIAC Practice Note only applies if both parties expressly designated SIAC to »*administer*« the arbitration under UNCITRAL Rules, either in the arbitration agreement or subsequently. The parties' agreement therefore implies some measure of control by the institution. As UNCITRAL is not an arbitral institution competing in the market, there is also not the same opposition to institutions applying modified UNCITRAL Rules instead of

---

115 *See e.g.* DIS-UNCITRAL Rules, art. 10 (3), 11, 13 (2) (2012).

116 SIAC Practice Note, para. 3 (2014).

117 *See also* Craig, Park, and Paulsson, *ICC Arbitration*, 715, para. 38.08 (explaining that the ICC does not offer facilitation/supervision services under UNCITRAL Rules because of this inconsistency).

their own rules upon request of the parties than to institutions applying modified rules of another institution.

Nevertheless, arbitration agreements providing for arbitration administered or facilitated by an institution according to UNCITRAL Rules can cause uncertainty as to the extent to which the UNCITRAL Rules should be modified to fit the institutional scheme. According to one - problematic - decision of the Higher Regional Court of Celle (Germany), such uncertainty may even oppose the recognition and enforcement of a resulting award. The court refused to enforce an award rendered by an arbitrator appointed by the American Dispute Resolution Center Inc. who had assumed jurisdiction based on an arbitration clause providing in its second sentence:

> »The arbitration will be held in accordance with the United Nations Commission on International Trade Regulations and Law (UNCITRAL) Arbitration Rules administered by an arbitration agency, such as the International Centre for Dispute Resolution, an affiliate of the American Arbitration Association, at a hearing to be held in New York, USA«[118]

Resistance against enforcement of the award was successful on two grounds, the first of which shall not be discussed in detail.[119] Only the second successful challenge related to the problem of reconciling the UNCITRAL Rules with administration by an institution. The court held that the constitution of the arbitral tribunal was not in accordance with the parties' agreement because the sole arbitrator had been appointed by the American Dispute Resolution Center Inc. and not by an appointing authority determined by the General Secretary of the Permanent Court of Arbitration according to the chosen UNCITRAL Rules.[120]

This reasoning does not fully convince.[121] The terms »*administered by an arbitration agency*« indicate that the parties did not want pure ad hoc arbitration for which the appointment process in article 6 of the UNCITRAL Rules was designed. Rather, they agreed on support by an

---

118  Beschluss [Decision], 8 Sch 13/07 (GER OLG, Celle, 4 December 2008) [6] (cited according to the electronic database juris).

119  The arbitration clause was contained in standard terms of a franchise contract for fast food restaurants. In this context, the place of hearing (not: the place of arbitration) in the USA was held to unjustly disadvantage the German franchise partner (ibid., para. 29; thereon, *see* Schulz and Niedermaier, »Unwirksame Schiedsklausel in Franchiseverträgen«).

120  UNCITRAL Rules, art. 6 (2010); *see* Beschluss [Decision] [2008] Case no 8 Sch 13/07 (GER OLG, Celle, 4 December 2008) at [36–37].

121  *See also* Schulz and Niedermaier, »Unwirksame Schiedsklausel in Franchiseverträgen«, 203.

institution. The most important support provided by arbitral institutions, independent of whether these follow their own rules or UNCITRAL Rules, is to appoint arbitrators on behalf of the parties. Therefore, it is most probable that the reference to an *»arbitration agency«* was meant to be a choice of an appointing authority in the meaning of article 6 (1) of the UNCITRAL Rules. The decisive question should not have been *if* the parties had agreed on an appointing authority but *which* appointing authority they had agreed on - the AAA-ICDR or any institution at the claimant's choice as the wording *»such as«* suggests.[122] There would have been many good arguments to interpret the arbitration clause in a way that only the AAA-ICDR was meant to facilitate the arbitration and act as appointing authority. The AAA-ICDR was expressly mentioned, the - albeit not authoritative - German version of the arbitration clause did not contain facultative language in this respect,[123] the AAA-ICDR is a popular institution for transatlantic disputes and the AAA-ICDR is headquartered at the place of hearing in New York.[124] Such arguments validly support the finding that an arbitrator appointment by the American Dispute Resolution Center was not in line with the parties' agreement. In contrast, the Higher Regional Court's reliance on the default procedure under the UNCITRAL Rules despite the reference to an arbitration institution appears awkward and out of touch with arbitral practice.

III. Semi-institutional arbitration, e.g. Hamburg Friendly Arbitration

Some trade-specific rules and usages, for example arbitration under the Hamburg Local Commodity Trade Usage, the so-called *»Hamburger*

---

122 *Cf.* Beschluss [Decision], [2003] IHR 90 (GER BGH).
123 It read as follows: *»Die Schiedsgerichtsbarkeit findet entsprechend der Schiedsgerichtsordnung der UN-Kommission für internationales Handelsrecht (UNCITRAL-Schiedsgerichtsordnung) statt, ausgeübt durch das International Centre for Dispute Resolution, einem Mitglied der American Arbitration Association, bei einer in New York, USA abzuhaltenden mündlichen Verhandlung«* (missing the *»an arbitration agency, such as«* part of the English version) (*see* Beschluss [Decision] [2008] Case no 8 Sch 13/07 [GER OLG, Celle, 4 December 2008] at [4]).
124 In contrast, the American Dispute Resolution Center celebrates itself for its regional reputation as *»Conneticut's First Choice for Arbitration and Mediation«* (American Dispute Resolution Center, *»ADR Center | About Us«*).

*Freundschaftliche Arbitrage*« (Hamburg Friendly Arbitration), provide for an intermediate form of arbitration as well.[125] The Hamburg Local Commodity Trade Usage provides in § 20 that in case of a dispute each party may nominate an arbitrator and request the other party to do the same within a reasonable time limit. The two arbitrators shall render a decision and only if they cannot agree, they shall nominate an umpire. Only if a party is in default with nominating an arbitrator or if the two arbitrators cannot agree on an umpire or for the purpose of challenging and replacing arbitrators, requests have to be filed with the Hamburg Chamber of Commerce and Industry. In all other cases, the institution is not informed about the arbitration and, accordingly, it charges no fees. This is essentially a specific organised form of ad hoc arbitration with a predetermined appointing authority.[126]

IV. »Wildcat arbitration« - ad hoc arbitration under institutional rules

While for facilitated ad hoc arbitration the parties choose the institution without the institution's rules, parties may also choose institutional rules *without the institution* by appointing an ad hoc arbitral tribunal and instructing it to apply the arbitration rules of an institution.[127] Thereby, parties and arbitrators practically »*borrow*« institutional rules for their ad hoc proceedings.[128] Antoine Kassis even concludes his ICC critical treatise with the following recommendation:

> »Le meilleur des règlements est celui que est fait sur mesure […]. Ceux qui veulent en faire l'économie peuvent adopter un règlement tout fait, au besoin celui d'un centre d'arbitrage, mais sans la machinerie inutile, lourde, encombrante et coûteuse de ce centre.«[129]

> [The best procedural rules are tailor-made rules…Those that that want to save the effort may nevertheless adopt rules, if necessary such of an arbitration institution,

---

125 *See* Schlosser, *Das Recht der internationalen privaten Schiedsgerichts-barkeit*, 139, para. 180 (referring to *German type arbitration rules* [»*Schiedsordnungen deutschen Zuschnitts*«]).

126 *Contra* Urteil [Judgment], [1983] 36 NJW 1267 (GER BGH) 1268 (calling the Hamburg Friendly Arbitration a permanent arbitral tribunal) (»*in jedem Fall ein ständiges Schiedsgericht*«).

127 Rubino-Sammartano, *International Arbitration: Law and Practice*, 4, para. 1.2.

128 *See* Vidal, *Droit français de l'arbitrage interne et international*, 251.

129 Kassis, *Réflexions*, 285, para. 411.

> but without the unnecessary, heavy, burdensome and costly apparatus of this institution.]

Obviously, most other scholars and practitioners do not recommend such practice, sometimes named »*wildcat arbitration.*«[130] Ad hoc arbitration under institutional rules is undeniably impractical due to the need to modify the institutional rules, which refer in many provisions to tasks of the institution not available in ad hoc proceedings. Nevertheless, the practice is not perceived as outright impossible or inadmissible.[131] Arguably, such ad hoc arbitration under institutional rules is less controversial than hybrid arbitration as herein defined since it does not have an element of (potentially unfair) competition between arbitral institutions.[132]

1. Articles 1 (2) and 6 (2) of the ICC Rules & ad hoc cases

Then again, article 1 (2) of the ICC Rules suggests that the ICC Court is the only body competent to administer arbitrations under its rules and article 6 (2) of the ICC Rules underlines this by deeming parties that agreed on the ICC Rules to have accepted administration by the ICC Court. Arguably, these policy statements, their limited legal force being further discussed elsewhere,[133] also seek to exclude references to the ICC Rules in ad hoc proceedings. While the history of the provision, which has been introduced in reaction to the *Alstom–Insigma* arbitration,[134] indicates that it is mainly directed at other institutions, its precise intention and scope emerges not

---

130  *See e.g.* Wilske, »Ad Hoc Arbitration in Germany«, 827, para. 42; *but see* Rana and Sanson, *International Commercial Arbitration*, 88 (appearing to suggest that the adoption of institutional rules to ad hoc arbitration was a viable choice) (note: one of the authors, Rashda Rana, is identified as General Counsel of Bovis Lend Lease, a party itself once involved in such arbitration, *see infra* at 2., pp. 154-156).

131  *Cf.* Poudret and Besson, *Comparative Law of International Arbitration*, para. 93.

132  *But see Insigma v. Alstom*, [2009] SGCA 24 [26 f)] (finding hybrid arbitration with a substitution of institutional actors the less problematic option). *See infra* at pp. 272 et seq. (§13) on the intellectual property and unfair competition law aspects.

133  *See supra* at pp. 110-116 (§5B) on the status of arbitration rules.

134  *See supra* at pp. 35-39 (§1C); *cf.* Fry, Mazza, and Greenberg, *The Secretariat's Guide to ICC Arbitration*, para. 3–4, 3–193 (although not mentioning the Singaporean case expressly).

clearly from its wording. The use of the term »*administer*« in article 1 (2) of the ICC Rules could suggest that the ICC Court did not intend to hinder ad hoc arbitrations under its rules. The conduct of ad hoc proceedings by the arbitral tribunal can hardly be considered »*administration*.«[135] On the other hand, one should keep in mind the difficulties in differentiating between ad hoc and institutional proceedings[136] and the Singapore High Court's - herein rejected - characterisation of the *Alstom–Insigma* proceedings as »*ad hoc arbitration by the SIAC*.«[137]

In light of these developments, the general view that borrowing institutional rules for ad hoc arbitration proceedings was possible is subject to gradual change at least with respect to the ICC Rules. While the *Secretariat's Commentary* warns only that *no* institutional rules, particularly not the ICC Rules, were practically »*suitable*« for ad hoc arbitration,[138] first voices appear to postulate that articles 1 (2) and 6 (2) of the ICC Rules now legally exclude ad hoc arbitration under ICC Rules.[139] Moreover, if a party commenced ICC arbitration despite express provision for »*ad hoc arbitration*« under ICC Rules in the agreement, the ICC Court would probably accept the request and, in case of objections, render a positive prima facie decision under article 6 (4) of the ICC Rules.[140] Only this way, it could underline its policy of »*mandatory*« administration by the Court pursuant to article 6 (2) of the ICC Rules.[141] From a practical point of view, parties should therefore avoid referring to the ICC Rules for an ad hoc arbitration.

From a more theoretical point of view, it is more convincing not to understand articles 1 (2) and 6 (2) of the ICC Rules as excluding ad hoc arbitration under ICC Rules. As shown in Chapter 1, institutional rules, including articles 1 (2) and 6 (2) of the ICC Rules, can only become binding

---

135  *But see* Rubino-Sammartano, *International Arbitration: Law and Practice*, 4, para. 1.2.
136  *See supra* at pp. 127-134 (§7A).
137  *See supra* at p. 126, n. 2.
138  Fry, Mazza, and Greenberg, *The Secretariat's Guide to ICC Arbitration*, para. 3–193, 3–195.
139  *E.g.* Trittmann, »Die wesentlichen Änderungen«, 48; Meeran, »The 2012 International Chamber of Commerce Rules of Arbitration«, 372.
140  An argument rejected in the *Cubic* case was that the ICC Court did not tell the respondent that the arbitration clause may be understood to provide for ad hoc arbitration (*see Cubic v. ICC*, [1999] Rev. Arb. 103 (FR CA, Paris) at 110, *see also infra* at p. 247).
141  On such a case, *see supra* at p. 37, n. 48.

through contract.[142] Parties that prefer ad hoc arbitration under ICC Rules never conclude a contract with the institution and their own contract - the arbitration agreement providing for arbitration to be conducted ad hoc - would overrule articles 1 (2) and 6 (2) of the ICC Rules.

2. The Bovis Lend v. Jay-Tech case

In 2005, the Singapore High Court found an attempt by SIAC to impose its administration on parties to be ineffective.[143] In its arbitration rules for domestic cases then in force, SIAC had provided as follows:

> »The parties, by agreeing to submit or refer their dispute to the Centre for arbitration in any of the cases in Rule 1.1, agree that these Rules take precedence over any and all provisions in the underlying contract between the parties relating to dispute resolution by arbitration.«[144]

Against this background, the Singapore High Court decided on cross-applications by both parties for a declaratory ruling relating to their arbitration clause providing *inter alia* that unless otherwise agreed

> »the arbitrator will be appointed by the President of the Institute of Architects in Singapore (or such other body as carries on the functions of the Institute) or his nominee«

and that such

> »arbitrator must conduct the proceedings in accordance with Rules of the Singapore International Arbitration Centre.«[145]

*Jay-Tech Marine & Projects Pte Ltd* (hereinafter (»*Jay-Tech*«) first filed a notice of arbitration with SIAC, who opined that the parties could not have their arbitrator appointed by the Institute of Architects as SIAC's rules would take precedence over this agreement. *Bovis Lend Lease Pte Ltd* (hereinafter »*Bovis*«) then objected to SIAC's competence, taking the view that the arbitration should be ad hoc with an arbitrator appointed by the Singapore Institute of Architects. Jay-Tech's assent to this proposal crossed with Bovis' court application asking for an interpretative declaration in favour of ad hoc arbitration. Jay-Tech on the other hand expected

---

142  *See supra* at pp. 110-116 (§5B).
143  *Bovis Lend v. Jay-Tech*, [2005] SGHC 91.
144  SIAC Domestic Rules, art. 1.5 (2002).
145  *Bovis Lend v. Jay-Tech*, [2005] SGHC 91 [5].

practical difficulties in applying SIAC's rules in ad hoc arbitration and itself filed a court application for interpretation of the agreement.

The Singapore High Court interpreted this clause to refer to ad hoc arbitration under SIAC Rules with the Institute of Architects in Singapore as appointing authority. It held that such agreement was »*in accordance with the principle of party autonomy*«[146] and that there was »*no rule of law that prevents the parties from doing exactly what they did*« despite warning the parties that it was practically

> »difficult to fit an ad hoc arbitration into the format of an SIAC arbitration and if the parties do not intend the SIAC to carry out such functions, they will find that many of the SIAC procedural rules cannot apply to their arbitration.«[147]

The Singapore High Court also clearly rejected the idea that SIAC could dictate its rules to prevail as an »*unwarranted limitation on party autonomy*.«[148]

While the *Bovis Lend v. Jay-Tech* case was a first step on the route towards the Singapore courts' support of hybrid arbitration agreements in the latter decisions *Insigma v. Alstom* and *HKL v. Rizq*,[149] it seems much less controversial. Different from the *Insigma v. Alstom* case, an underlying policy issue of competition among institutions did not exist. The Singapore Institute of Architects is not an arbitral institution, it does not even propose arbitration rules, and it was only called upon to appoint an arbitrator. Accordingly, there was no accusation of unduly profiting from SIAC's rules.

Furthermore, the decision in *Bovis Lend v. Jay-Tech* effectively met the expectations of both parties, whose applications where not really opposing each other. Rather, both Bovis and Jay-tech simply sought to have clarity on how the courts would understand their agreement. The court even remarked that the parties' counsel could have avoided the whole suit »*if either of them had picked up the telephone and talked to the other*.«[150] However, it has to be borne in mind that SIAC's position, claiming that the parties could not have an arbitrator appointed by the Singapore Institute for Architects in SIAC arbitration, effectively limited the parties' options to find a compromise. This episode alludes to a difficulty in dealing with hybrid

---

146 Ibid., para. 19.
147 Ibid., para. 17.
148 Ibid., para. 20.
149 *See supra* at pp. 35-39 (§1C) and 174-177 (§8C.I.2).
150 An omission for which both parties are blamed, but Jay-Tech was charged with the costs as his arbitration notice led to the proceedings (*Bovis Lend v. Jay-Tech*, [2005] SGHC 91 [22d, 23]).

arbitration agreements before courts: The traditional court actions for control or support available to a party are always directed against the other party to the arbitration agreement and little appropriate where a disagreement on an arbitration agreement exists less with the other party than with an institution.[151]

V. »Switching« from institutional to ad hoc arbitration

Related to the just explained practice of wildcat arbitration is the question if parties may »*switch*« anytime from institutional arbitration to ad hoc arbitration.[152] First, it is clear that a clause providing for institutional arbitration does not hinder parties to conclude a new submission agreement to solve their dispute before an ad hoc appointed tribunal, preferably under rules suitable to ad hoc arbitration.[153] Before an institutional arbitration has commenced, this would not create any particular problems and should not even be labelled »*switching.*« Then parties simply base their arbitration on the new agreement.

The real »*switching*« problem is whether parties by way of agreement may take a case away from the administration and supervision of an institution and continue on an ad hoc basis, either because they are discontent with the institution's work or simply in order to save administrative fees. From a procedural point of view, there is no obstacle to such practice. The tribunal's competence is based on the parties' agreement, which they may modify at any time. However, of course, the parties can then no longer avail themselves of the institution's services for such arbitration and may also be barred from reintroducing the case to the institution should their ad hoc arrangement fail for whatever reason.[154] In addition, the institution might have contractual claims following the termination of its contract by the parties.

---

151 As discussed in Chapter 5, *infra* at pp. 430-435 (§16A.II.2).
152 Redfern and Hunter, *Law and Practice (1986)*, 115; in the current edition, »*switching*« is only rudimentarily touched upon (*see only* Blackaby et al., *Redfern and Hunter*, para. 2.105).
153 An institutional arbitration clause alone does not yet create obligations towards the institution, *see infra* at pp. 243-251 (§11A.III, IV).
154 *Cf.* Redfern and Hunter, *Law and Practice (1986)*, 115; referring to ICC case no. 2878, which is mentioned as the background to *Belgian Enterprise v Iranian Factory*, [1982] VII YCA 119 (ICC), original in French, published in [1980] 4 J.D.I. 978 (with annotations by *Yves Derains*).

D. Hybridity of arbitration administered under another institution's rules

The concept of »*hybrid*« arbitration is not an idea of this thesis but that of the Singapore courts using this term to describe the arbitration agreement between Alstom and Insigma. Herein, the term is employed because it provides a catchy identification of the topic. However, different from the explanation given in the introduction,[155] the Singapore courts characterised the form of arbitration agreed by the Alstom and Insigma as intermediate between ad hoc and institutional arbitration[156] and not as one in between two systems of institutional arbitration. Since SIAC's institutional influence on the *Alstom–Insigma* arbitration was not less but greater in comparison to standard SIAC arbitration, because the ICC Rules (1998) provided for more institutional control than the SIAC Rules (1997), the qualification as »*hybrid ad hoc arbitration*«[157] appears misleading. Hybrid ad hoc arbitration may be an appropriate characterisation if parties apply to an institution to provide less-controlling assistance to an arbitration to be conducted under tailor-made or UNCITRAL Rules.[158] In contrast, the *Alstom–Insigma* arbitration was clearly institutional. If it is herein described as hybrid, this should not indicate closeness to ad hoc arbitration but it rather alludes to the arbitration being an intermediate form of two different systems of institutional arbitration - of the institution asked to administer the arbitration and of the institution that issued the rules.

*§8 Qualification of hybrid arbitration agreements as pathological*

The first chapter came to the conclusion that hybrid arbitration agreements are usually valid but will very often raise some problems of both interpretation and performance. To describe arbitration agreements raising these and other problems, it is common to use the term »*pathological.*«[159] Frédéric Eisemann defined such agreements negatively as agreements that fail to meet one of these four objectives:

- to create effects which are binding on the parties

---

155 *Supra* at pp. 31-32 (§1A).
156 *Insigma v. Alstom*, [2009] SGCA 24 [26, 35].
157 Ibid.
158 Here referred to as facilitated ad hoc arbitration, *see supra* at pp. 147 (§7C.II).
159 *See e.g.* Schramm and Geisinger, »Art. II«, 58.

- to exclude the intervention of state courts in the resolution of the dispute, at least until the rendering of an award
- to grant jurisdiction to the arbitrators to decide likely disputes between the parties
- to put a procedure into place that, in the best conditions of efficiency, leads to the rendering of an award capable of being enforced.[160]

However, one commentator to the *Insigma v. Alstom* case found that

> »it does *not* appear that there is *any inherent ambiguity or uncertainty* in an agreement to resolve disputes before the Singapore International Arbitration Centre in accordance with the ICC Rules [*emphasis added*].«[161]

Aiming at justifying or refuting this finding, this section outlines minimum substantive requirements for arbitration agreements (A) and introduces the principle of effective interpretation (B). Then, the agreement between Alstom and Insigma is discussed in the context of arguably similar cases (C). This will help to either attach or detach the label »*pathological*« to hybrid arbitration agreements (III).

A. Essentialia and optional elements of an arbitration agreement

Party autonomy does not mean that parties *have* to agree on every detail of their arbitration, it only implies that they *may* do so. This understanding of party autonomy to agree on and shape arbitration proceedings influences modern approaches to interpret arbitration agreements. According to Redfern and Hunter's standard treatise on international arbitration, provisions in a contract that simply stipulate that any dispute »*is to be settled by arbitration in London*« or just »*Resolution of disputes: arbitration, Paris*« constitute valid arbitration agreements.[162] This proposition, which relates the issue of validity to the issue of supplementary interpretation, underlines that the only essential element of an arbitration agreement is a clear indication of the intention to refer disputes to arbitration.

---

160 Eisemann, »La clause d'arbitrage pathologique«, 130.
161 Joseph, *Jurisdiction and Arbitration Agreements and Their Enforcement*, para. 4.83.
162 Blackaby et al., *Redfern and Hunter*, para. 1.48, 2.64; *see also* Beschluss [Decision], [2003] 1 SchiedsVZ 284 (GER OLG, Hamburg) (»*Arbitration: Hamburg*« considered sufficient); Trittmann and Hanefeld, »Part II, § 1029«, para. 17. The use of the word »*arbitration*« is not decisive (Born, *International Commercial Arbitration (2014)*, 763 at § 5.04 [D.1.a]).

If a blanket clause like the examples just given states a place of arbitration in an arbitration-friendly jurisdiction, such clause will indeed be enforceable, even if there are many uncertainties as to the applicable arbitration procedure. Elements such as whether the arbitration shall be ad hoc or institutional, which procedural rules shall apply, the number of arbitrators and method of appointment, a choice of law and language are deemed *optional*[163] as they could be determined by the default provisions of the applicable arbitration law.[164]

The reference to an institution or a set of arbitration rules are such optional elements of an arbitration agreement by which the parties' derogate from dispositive provisions of the *lex arbitri*. Without such reference and failing a later agreement of the parties on these procedural issues, the arbitration agreement is commonly understood to provide for ad hoc arbitration in accordance with the law. This is decisive for the effective interpretation of not only arbitration agreements with ambiguous, inoperable, conflicting or otherwise problematic references to institutions and their rules and but also of hybrid arbitration agreements. Neither the determination of an institution nor the reference to specific rules are *essentialia* of an arbitration agreement, hence it seems difficult to support a position that hybrid arbitration agreements were invalid because there may be a conflict regarding these - merely optional - elements. Under modern arbitration laws, the question is therefore less if a hybrid arbitration agreement is a valid agreement on arbitration at all, but more if such agreement is workable as the parties intended or in need of interpretation or supplementation by the law.

---

163 Trittmann and Hanefeld, »Part II, § 1029«, para. 22; *see also* Lew, Mistelis, and Kröll, *Comparative International Commercial Arbitration*, para. 8–20 (»*other relevant issues*«); Saenger, »§ 1029 ZPO«, para. 13 (»*Fakultativer Inhalt*«); Born, *International Commercial Arbitration (2014)*, 763 (»*frequently (and advisedly) included*«); Born, *International Arbitration and Forum Selection Agreements*, 37 (»*critical*« from a practitioner's point of view).

164 Schwab, Walter, and Baumbach, *Schiedsgerichtsbarkeit*, chap. 6, para. 1 (but warning of the possible inappropriateness of the default provisions). The place of arbitration is decisive for the arbitration law, court support and control, making it a strongly recommendable element (*see also* Naciemento, »Konfliktlösung nach allgemeinen Schiedsordnungen«, 788; for references on case law, *see* Born, *International Commercial Arbitration (2014)*, 764, n. 734–35).

However, a few arbitration laws still pose higher demands as to the basic elements required for a valid arbitration agreement. For example[165] and as already mentioned,[166] Chinese arbitration law is exceptionally exigent in not recognising arbitration agreements with a place of arbitration in China but not clearly specifying an institution or rather arbitration commission.[167] Some Chinese courts found a reference to institutional rules to be insufficient to determine the institution.[168] The SPC only slightly eased its stance in this regard in its Interpretation issued in 2006,[169] according to which the institution may be inferred from the rules or the place of arbitration in some circumstances.[170] An argument of ambiguity in the sense that a hybrid arbitration agreement does not sufficiently indicate the competent institution,

---

165 *See* Born, *International Commercial Arbitration (2014)*, 765, n. 740 (§5.04[D][1][a]; with more references to laws with »*onerous*« conditions »*in a few developing jurisdictions*«).

166 *See supra* at pp. 101-104 (§4C.II.2.b.iii).

167 Arbitration Law art. 16 (2), 18 (P.R.C.).

168 *Zueblin v. Wuxi* [2004] Case no (2004) X.M.E.C.Z. 154 (P.R.C. Wuxi IPC, 2 September 2004) (clause in FIDIC standard contract referring to ICC Rules and Shanghai found invalid); here cited according to Beschluss [Decision], [2007] 5 SchiedsVZ 101 (GER KG, Berlin; recognising the Wuxi court's decision and refusing to enforce the ICC award). The Wuxi court, after consulting the SPC, had found the arbitration clause invalid for not clearly identifying an institution. It is unclear if it was seen as an additional obstacle that foreign institutions like the ICC Court are not strictly speaking »*arbitration commissions;*« also left open by the SPC's recent reply in *Longlide*, [2013] Min Si Ta Zi no. 13; Sun, »SPC Instruction Provides New Opportunities for International Arbitral Institutions to Expand into China«, 695 (Appendix 3); *see also* Dong, »Open Door for Foreign Arbitration Institutions?«

169 Two prior very strict and formalistic decisions of the SPC are summarised by Rana and Sanson, *International Commercial Arbitration*, 86, para. 4.15. On Interpretation Notices of the SPC, *see* Trappe, »Praktische Erfahrungen mit chinesischer Schiedsgerichtsbarkeit«, 145, n. 26.

170 SPC's Interpretation of Arbitration Law, art. 4 at the end (2006). In response, the ICC Court now suggests a China specific ICC clause: »*All disputes arising out of or in connection with the present contract shall be submitted to the International Court of Arbitration of the International Chamber of Commerce and shall be finally settled under the Rules of Arbitration of the International Chamber of Commerce by one or more arbitrators appointed in accordance with the said Rules*« (*see* International Chamber of Commerce, »Standard ICC Arbitration Clauses«; *see also* Hantke, »China ist anders: Neue ICC-Schiedsklausel«).

would therefore be more likely a validity problem under Chinese law with its strict commission requirement than under most other laws where the choice of institutional arbitration and the designation of an institution are just optional.

## B. The principle of effective interpretation and its limits

Hence, according to the prevailing opinion in arbitration doctrine and many arbitration laws, it is sufficient if parties agree to refer a definite dispute to arbitration. The question then arises how to treat additional but imprecise stipulations by the parties on optional elements.

A hybrid arbitration agreement usually suffers from some lack of precision on optional elements. For example, when the parties agreed that SIAC should administer the arbitration under ICC Rules in the *Alstom–Insigma* arbitration, the parties did not directly address the problem of SIAC substituting ICC actors like the ICC Court or Secretary General. It is a good and preferable solution if parties mutually agree on such particularities among themselves and with the administering institution.[171] Such an approach has the obvious advantage to protect party autonomy.

However, after a dispute has arisen, one of the parties - often the (potentially) respondent side - may be inclined to take every opportunity to avoid, delay or hinder the proceedings.[172] Moreover, national laws on state court proceedings and international civil procedure laws may be favourable to one party. Helping to implement an arbitration agreement will then be of little interest to such party benefitting from otherwise applicable laws and *fora*. Aware of these obstacles, most arbitral tribunals[173] and several

---

171 *E.g.* when SIAC took over the *Alstom-Insigma* arbitration, correspondence between the SIAC and the parties roughly laid down which SIAC actors would exercise which tasks (*see Insigma v. Alstom*, [2009] SGCA 24 [9], citing a letter of the SIAC's Secretariat; *but see also* ibid., para. 19, indicating a later change concerning the substituting organs).

172 *Cf. e.g.* the Petitioner-Appellant's brief in *ISC v. Nobel Biocare Investments*, 351 Fed. Appx. 480, 2009 WL 8037742 (Appellate Brief), at 5 (2nd Cir. 2009) (»*Nobel, however, refused to cooperate in choosing a set of rules for the arbitration before the AAA to which it had agreed, and instead refused to arbitrate at all*«).

173 X. v. Y., Award [2011] Case no 6210 (CAM, Milan, 4 May 2011), *summarized by* Coppo and Azzali, »X v. Y, Award, CAM Case no. 6210, 4 May 2011 (ITA Board of Reporters)«; *see also ICC Case no. 11869*,

jurisdictions' state courts[174] favour a pro-arbitration approach in accordance with the principle of effective interpretation (*in favorem validitatis*) when deciding on whether an arbitration agreement is valid and capable of being performed. When finding effective solutions, many courts even refer to rulings of other jurisdictions as transnationally persuasive authority and do not strictly apply their traditional interpretation rules.[175] Generally, effective interpretation means that an agreement that contains the essential element of consent to arbitration should be valid and operable notwithstanding any disagreement on the modalities of arbitration.

Nevertheless, effective interpretation has limits, which - again - follow from the underlying principle of party autonomy: The parties' procedural agreement needs to remain recognisable. Moreover, any interpretative solution to save an arbitration agreement has to respect applicable mandatory law.[176] Next to this general limit - a limit to the *if* of interpreting arbitration agreements effectively - there are specific limits to the acceptable methods and results - the *how* of effective interpretation. While it is commonly accepted that courts or arbitral tribunals can *discard* imprecisely agreed optional elements as mere »*surplusage*«, for example by interpreting an agreement with a reference to a non-existing institution as an ad hoc

---

[2011] XXXVI YCA 47 (ICC, Vienna) (positive decision on jurisdiction concerning a very poorly drafted contract, mentioning »*arbitration in Vienna, Austria in accordance to the rules of arbitration*« and various references to either non-existent ICC publications, e.g. *ICC 1995 Revision Publication N600* or ICC publications not related to arbitration, like »*ICC 500 UCP*«); *A v. B (Interim Award)*, [2001] 19 ASA Bull. 265 (CCIG, Geneva) [20] (»*favor arbitri*«; assuming that parties wanted to refer to the »*prominent*« arbitration institution in Geneva when designating both the »*Geneva Chamber of Commerce*« and »*the Geneva Court of Justice*«); *similiar X (Az.) v. Y (Lit.) (Award)*, [2006] 24 ASA Bull. 61 (CCIG, Geneva) [39, 40, 41] (»*arbitration court in Geneva*« considered a sufficient designation of the Geneva Chamber of Commerce and Industry based on parties' »*hypothetical intent*«); *but see M. v. K & W (Award)*, [1996] 14 ASA Bull. 290 (ZCC, Zurich) [11] (arbitrator declining jurisdiction due to a lacking reference to »*Zurich*« in a clause referring to the »*Arbitration Commission in Switzerland*«).

174 *See further infra* at pp. 163 et seq. (§8C.I); *see also HKL v. Rizq I*, [2013] SGHC 5 [21–23] (for further case law examples).

175 *See* Born, *Law and Practice (2012)*, 71–72 (with many examples and further references).

176 *Cf. e.g.* Beschluss [Decision], [2003] 1 SchiedsVZ 185 (GER KG, Berlin) at 186.

agreement,[177] it seems more problematic to *supplement* optional elements. Such supplementation exceeds the limits of interpretation if it amounts to »*rewriting*« the parties' agreement.[178] Furthermore, such rewriting raises difficult questions regarding the allocation of competence between controlling and supporting courts and the arbitral tribunal.[179]

## C. Case study: Pathological institutional arbitration agreements

The following subsections outline some notorious cases of arbitration agreements that were qualified as pathological, focussing on problematic references to arbitral institutions. One can distinguish *initial* pathologies and *subsequent* pathologies.[180] Both subcategories raise distinctive problems.

## I. Initial pathology: Drafting defects in the parties' sphere

> »The incorrect, unclear or contradictory designation of an arbitral institution is among the most frequent and critical flaws in international arbitration agreements.«[181]

At the time of contract drafting, the dispute resolution clause is often not of the highest priority. After day- and weeklong negotiations on commercial aspects, dispute resolution clauses are often included into the contract at the last minute. Colloquially, this is sometimes referred to as a »*Midnight*

---

177  *See* Born, *International Commercial Arbitration (2014)*, 778–79 (§5.04 [D][3]; with case law examples).

178  *See* ibid., 779, n. 814 (§5.04 [D][3]; with references on reluctant jurisprudence due to this concern).

179  *See infra* at pp. 413-430 (§16A.II.1).

180  Alternatively, one can distinguish arbitration agreements with drafting defects (German: »*redaktionell missglückte Schiedsvereinbarungen*«) and substantively defective arbitration agreements (German: »*inhaltlich missglückte Schiedsvereinbarungen*«) (*see* Hochbaum, *Mißglückte internationale Schiedsvereinbarungen*, 49 et seq., 142 et seq.).

181  Girsberger and Ruch, »Pathological Arbitration Clauses«, 136.

*Clause«* - problem.[182] *Frédéric Eisemann* metaphorically suggested building a »*Musée noir*« for these Midnight Clauses.[183]

The hybrid arbitration agreement featuring in *Insigma v. Alstom* does not appear to be such a Midnight Clause into which the parties invested not enough effort.[184] Rather, they may have thought about the clause too intensely, coming up with compromise then difficult to implement. Nevertheless, a party that wants to challenge a hybrid arbitration agreement - independent of its original intention - will certainly make an argument of ambiguity,[185] which brings the following case law into focus.


1. Ambiguous references to one or more institutions

Well-known examples of poorly drafted institutional arbitration clauses include references to the »*official Chamber of commerce in Paris*«[186] or the International Court of Arbitration in Austria (»*Internationales Schiedsgericht in Österreich*«).[187] Another clause stated, under the heading »*Arbitration*« in the contract's English version, that »*disputies and defferences are to be submitted without resourse to the ordinary court to Stockholm, Sweden* [sic].«[188] The Higher Regional Court of Stuttgart, after consulting various Russian and English dictionaries and consulting two translators, found this to refer to the Arbitration Institute of the Stockholm Chamber of Commerce.[189] A German case concerning an arbitration clause

---

182 *See e.g.* Dahm, »International Arbitration: Why Wearing A Good Suit Makes All The Difference«.

183 Eisemann, »La clause d'arbitrage pathologique«, 129, 132.

184 *Contra* Dahm, »International Arbitration: Why Wearing A Good Suit Makes All The Difference«. *See infra* at pp. 202 et seq. (at 3).

185 *Cf. also* Eisemann, »La clause d'arbitrage pathologique«, 129 (using the term pathological both for invalid arbitration agreements and agreements giving rise to challenge).

186 *Asland v. EEC*, [1990] Rev. Arb. 521 (FR TGI, Paris) (interpreted to refer to the ICC Court).

187 Beschluss [Decision], [2006] 4 SchiedsVZ 223 (GER OLG, Oldenburg) (finding the clause to validly designate the Vienna International Arbitral Centre).

188 *See* Urteil [Judgment], [2006] NJOZ 2836 (GER OLG, Stuttgart) at 2837. Apparently, both official contract versions, Russian and English, provided for similar uncertainties.

189 Ibid., 2840.

referring to the non-existent »*Anwaltsschiedsgericht*« is another such example.[190]

The courts in all of the above examples protect the parties' unequivocal choice for institutional arbitration by assuming that the defective designation of an institution refers to the most popular arbitration institution located in the region and/or the trade concerned.[191] Effective interpretation in this way is not considered undue »*rewriting*« if probable party expectations do not conflict with it. Accidental reference to a non-existent institution does not convey a detailed choice of procedure other than the choice for support by a respected institution.[192]

Cases where parties *by mistake* name more than one arbitration institution, or one institution and another institution's rules in the same contract or even in the same paragraph also belong in this category of defective arbitration clauses and are a little more difficult to deal with. At first sight, they are very difficult to distinguish from hybrid arbitration clauses that *deliberately* name one institution to administer the arbitration under another institution's rules. To decide whether parties just poorly drafted a clause or intentionally formulated it as a hybrid arbitration clause, the authority, whether it is a court, an arbitral institution or tribunal, would have to inquire into the intentions of the parties when agreeing to such a clause.

In the following, a summary of three cases shall highlight very contrasting approaches to arbitration agreements that refer to more than one institution and/or rules: one decided by the German Federal Supreme Court (BGH), one by the English Court of Appeals and one by the French Cour de Cassation.

---

190 Beschluss [Decision], [2011] 64 NJW 2977, [2011] 9 SchiedsVZ 284 (GER BGH).

191 *See also* Beschluss [Decision], [2012] 10 SchiedsVZ at 338; *but see* Urteil [Judgment], [1994] IPR-Rspr. 417 (GER OLG, Hamm) 418, English translation: [1997] XXII YCA 707 (GER OLG, Hamm) (agreement referring to International Chamber of Commerce in Paris with seat in Zurich found ambigous in an obiter remark; confusing seat of the institution, place of arbitration and place of hearing); similar: Urteil [Judgment], [1998] 6 RKS 17 (GER OLG, Dresden).

192 Possibly, it also expresses some geographical preference (*cf.* Urteil [Judgment], [2007] 7 NJOZ 5365 [GER OLG, Karlsruhe] at 5369); *see supra* at pp. 71-74 (§4B.I.2) on the common assumption of a connection between the seat of the institution and the places of arbitration and hearing.

## a. BGH judgment of 2 December 1982

On 2 December 1982, the German BGH rendered a noteworthy judgment.[193] The contract conditions in dispute, which were written in both German and Italian, provided *inter alia* for

> »Hamburger freundschaftliche Arbitrage aufgrund der Waren-Verein der Hamburger Boerse e.V./Arbitraggio amichevole in conformita alle condizioni del Waren-Verein der Hamburger Boerse e.V.«

> [Hamburg Friendly Arbitration according to the Hamburg Foreign and Wholesale Trade Association/ Friendly arbitration according to the rules of the Hamburg Foreign and Wholesale Trade Association]

The BGH held that this arbitration clause was contradictory and void because it could not be determined which permanent arbitral tribunal (»*ständiges Schiedsgericht*«) was competent. Consequently, the BGH annulled an arbitral award rendered by an arbitral tribunal constituted pursuant to Section 20 of the Hamburg Local Commodity Trade Usage providing for Hamburg Friendly Arbitration.

### i. Procedural history

The procedural background was as follows: The claimant initiated arbitration proceedings by sending a letter calling for »*Hamburg Friendly Arbitration proceedings as agreed*«, nominating an arbitrator and requesting the respondent to do the same.[194] The respondent replied on the merits without any objection to jurisdiction and without nominating an arbitrator. In line with Section 20 of the Local Commodity Trade Usage an arbitral tribunal was constituted consisting of the arbitrator nominated by claimant, an arbitrator nominated upon the claimant's request by the Hamburg Chamber of

---

193  Urteil [Judgment], [1983] 36 NJW 1267, [1984] IPRax 147 (GER BGH), French translation: [1983] Rev. Arb. 353 (GER BGH), English excerpts: [1990] XV YCA 660 (GER BGH).

194  As Hamburg Friendly Arbitration is initiated by a request for nominating an arbitrator sent to the other side, it seems inaccurate to speak of filing a claim with an arbitral tribunal (*see* Hamburg Local Commodity Trade Usage, § 20). This is correctly formulated in the English abstract published in [1990] XV YCA 661, *but see* [1983] 36 NJW 1267, [1984] IPRax 148 (German original: »*wandte sich* [...] *mit einer Klage an das ›vereinbarte Schiedsgericht der Hamburger freundschaftlichen Arbitrage‹*« [filed a claim with the »*agreed Hamburg Friendly Arbitration tribunal*«]).

Commerce on behalf of the respondent and an umpire agreed between the co-arbitrators.

The respondent first objected to the arbitral tribunal's jurisdiction in the oral hearing. The respondent asserted that it understood the arbitration clause to refer to arbitration in accordance with § 30 of the Conditions of Business of the Hamburg Foreign and Wholesale Trade Association (*Waren-Verein der Hamburger Börse e.V.,* hereinafter »*Waren-Verein*«), which provides for a different permanent arbitration court[195] with its own rules.[196] The claimant submitted that the clause meant to refer only to the substantive Waren-Verein Conditions, but not its arbitration rules.[197] The arbitral tribunal left the question of preclusion of the jurisdictional objection open, rejected it as unfounded and rendered an award against the respondent on the merits. The respondent filed a request to set the award aside, which was rejected in first instance but then accommodated in second instance by the Higher Regional Court of Hamburg whose judgment was finally upheld by the BGH.

ii. Critical comments on the decision

The BGH's decision to annul the award is problematic for several reasons. First, the BGH's reasoning that the jurisdictional plea was not precluded is little convincing. The respondent argued both before the arbitral tribunal and before the state courts in the setting-aside proceedings that it had only become aware of being before a Hamburg Friendly Arbitration tribunal rather than a tribunal of the Permanent Arbitration Court of the Waren-Verein in the oral hearing. The BGH accepted that excuse. However, the BGH failed to distinguish clearly between arbitral tribunal and arbitral institution. What the respondent may not have realised until the oral hearing concerns only the fact that the arbitration is not administered by the Permanent

---

195 German: Schiedsgericht des Warenvereins der Hamburger Börse e.V. (*see* Waren-Verein der Hamburger Börse e. V, »Permanent Court of Arbitration« ).

196 *See* Waren-Verein Conditions & Rules (2011).

197 *See* Timmermann, »Anmerkung zu den Schiedssprüchen B 1 Nrn. 38, 40, 44 und 47«, 54 (remarking that the clause had been used and interpreted in that sense for decades); *cf. also* Hamburg Local Commodity Trade Usage, § 20 (6) (which the BGH did not find applicable for lack of agreement and awareness by the Italian trader, *see* Urteil [Judgment], [1983] 36 NJW 1268–69, [1984] IPRax 148).

Arbitration Court of the Waren-Verein, the identity of the arbitrators was known to the respondent all along.

Second, the BGH qualified both Hamburg Friendly Arbitration and arbitration at the Waren-Verein as arbitration before a permanent arbitral tribunal (*»ständiges Schiedsgericht«*).[198] Notwithstanding the misleading use of that expression for an arbitral institution, which is based on the equally unclear article IV (1)(a) of the European Arbitration Convention,[199] this assessment is also substantively incorrect with respect to Hamburg Friendly Arbitration. Hamburg Friendly Arbitration is essentially ad hoc arbitration with an appointing authority.[200] There is no permanent arbitration court in Hamburg called *»Hamburger freundschaftliche Arbitrage.«*[201] The Local Commodity Trade Usage, § 20, primarily foresees that each party nominates an arbitrator to decide the dispute and that the arbitrators may nominate an umpire if they cannot agree. The Hamburg Chamber of Commerce is only involved in case of difficulties in the process of constituting the arbitral tribunal or in cases of challenges and does not exercise any supervising power.

Third, the BGH limited its reasoning to a mere literal interpretation of above cited arbitration clause. It noted that although the German version may, despite the incomplete syntax - missing the word *»conditions«* - be understood to refer to Hamburg Friendly Arbitration with the substantive conditions of the Waren-Verein applying, this was considered not sufficiently clear to a foreign contracting partner not familiar with the Hamburg Friendly Arbitration system.[202] The Italian version was found even less

---

198 Urteil [Judgment], [1983] 36 NJW 1268, [1984] IPRax 148.

199 *See supra* at pp. 92 et seq.

200 *See supra* at p. 147-147 (§7C.II); *see also* M., »Bibliographie - H.S.G«. (*»pas un arbitrage institutionnel mais ad hoc«* [not institutional but ad hoc arbitration]); Schwab, Walter, and Baumbach, *Schiedsgerichtsbarkeit*, chap. 41, para. 16 (*»typisches ad hoc-Schiedsgericht«* [typical ad hoc tribunal]); *contra* Schlosser, *Das Recht der internationalen privaten Schiedsgerichtsbarkeit*, para. 599; unclear: Timmermann, »Zur Auslegung der Klausel«, 145.

201 *Contra* Schwab, Walter, and Baumbach, *Schiedsgerichtsbarkeit*, chap. 41, para. 16.

202 Urteil [Judgment], [1983] 36 NJW 1268, 1269, [1984] IPRax 149, *see also* [1981] ZIP 170 (GER OLG, Hamburg); *Arbitral Award no. 38*, [1984] 3 RKS 42 (Waren-Verein, Hamburg) (positive award on jurisdiction despite formulation *»Arbitrage Amical à Hambourg«*); *Arbitral Award no. 40*, [1984] 3 RKS 44 (Waren-Verein, Hamburg); *Arbitral*

specific since it mentions »*Arbitraggio amichevole*« (friendly arbitration) without the prefix »*Hamburg*.«[203]

Without defying the finding of ambiguity as such,[204] it is regrettable that the BGH did not spent one further thought on the possibility of effective, supplementary interpretation of the arbitration agreement. This is surprising since the general intent of the parties to arbitrate their disputes in Hamburg under German law was clear.[205] In the interest of convergence of jurisprudence, courts controlling arbitral awards should follow the same pro-arbitration approach as courts deciding on an arbitration defence. Of course, it may be argued that there is no room for supplementary interpretation if the arbitration clause refers to two arbitral institutions without indicating a preference for one over the other. According to this view, perplexity of the arbitration agreement is a hurdle to effective interpretation.[206] However, it is little convincing to treat perplex arbitration clauses different from blanket clauses which are entirely silent on questions of the competent institution, *e.g.* clauses which only provide for »*Arbitration: Hamburg*«,[207] or arbitration clauses which refer to non-existent institutions. In case of blanket clauses or where the institution designated does not exist, courts usually

---

*Award no. 44*, [1984] 3 RKS 49 (Waren-Verein, Hamburg); *cf. also Arbitral Award no. 47*, [1984] 3 RKS 52 (Hamburg Friendly Arbitration, ad hoc, Hamburg) 53 (negative award on jurisdiction; arbitration agreement held to be contradictory); *but see* Urteil [Judgment], [1991] RIW 419 (GER LG, Hamburg) 419 (Waren-Verein award set aside; clause stating »*Hamburger freundschaftliche Arbitrage und Schiedsgericht in accordance with rules and conditions of the Waren-Verein der Hamburger Börse e.V.-Hamburg*« held to refer to Hamburg Friendly Arbitration with only the substantive Waren-Verein Conditions applying).

203 Urteil [Judgment], [1984] IPRax 149.

204 *But see* the distinction by Timmermann, »Anmerkung zum Urteil des BGH vom 2.12.1982«, 17; »Zur Auslegung der Klausel«, 136; »Anmerkung zu den Schiedssprüchen B 1 Nrn. 38, 40, 44 und 47«, 55 (pointing out that the term »*Hamburger freundschaftliche Arbitrage auf Grund der Waren-Vereins-Bedingungen*« - Hamburg Friendly Arbitration on the basis of the Waren-Verein Conditions -, if used completely, is sufficiently characteristic to be understood even by a foreign businessperson).

205 *See also* Timmermann, »Zur Auslegung der Klausel«, 136 (noting that the BGH did not respect the parties' intent to arbitrate their disputes in Hamburg).

206 *See* Münch, »§ 1029 ZPO«, para. 114.

207 Beschluss [Decision], [2003] 1 SchiedsVZ at 288; *see also* Schlosser, *Das Recht der internationalen privaten Schiedsgerichtsbarkeit*, para. 599.

refer the parties either to ad hoc arbitration or to the most prominent arbitration institution operating at the place of arbitration, assuming that this would still meet the essential expectations of the parties.[208] Even if an arbitration agreement suffers from perplexity with respect to the element of the competent institution, the remainder or the arbitration agreement is a result of a meeting of minds clearly giving arbitration the preference over state court litigation. This unambiguous choice should be respected.

The BGH also did not consider the question whether the arbitration clause in the case could be understood to refer to Hamburg Friendly Arbitration but under the Waren-Verein's arbitration rules.[209] In that case, a more justifiable ground for setting-aside would have been that the procedure was not in accordance with the parties' agreement rather than lacking jurisdiction of the arbitral tribunal. However, neither party had argued that point.

### b. Lovelock v. Exportles - a decision of the English Court of Appeals

The most relevant case concerning erroneous references to two different arbitral institutions - or rather: appointing authorities - decided by an English court dates back to the year 1967: the decision *Lovelock v. Exportles*.[210]

### i. Relevant case facts and procedural history

The case concerned a contract with two different arbitration clauses. The first provided that »[a]*ny dispute and/or claim* [...] *including disputes relating to the interpretation or execution of this contract*« should be decided by (ad hoc) arbitration in England under English law before English arbitrators. Should a party fail to appoint its arbitrator or should the co-arbitrators fail to agree on a chairperson, the chairman of the »*Particle Board*

---

208 *See supra* at p. 164. *See also* Kröll, »Die Entwicklung des Rechts der Schiedsgerichtsbarkeit 2005/2006«, 745.

209 In contrast, *see Schiedspruch*, [2007] 5 SchiedsVZ 55 (HCC, Hamburg) 56 (mentioning such a possibility in an obiter remark); *see also* Beschluss [Decision], [2009] 9 NJOZ 1218 (GER OLG, Schleswig) 1220 (rejecting a declaratory motion against Hamburg Friendly Arbitration under ICC Rules; suggesting the ICC Rules to apply supplementarily); *but see Arbitral Award no. 47*, [1984] 3 RKS 53 (discarding the possibility of Hamburg Friendly Arbitration under the Waren-Verein's rules).

210 *Lovelock v. Exportles*, [1968] 1 Lloyd's Rep 163 (EWCA Civ.).

*Section of the Timber Trade Federation*« was designated to make the required appointments. It was further stipulated that this clause »*shall not apply to any parcel shipped to countries other than the United Kingdom.*«[211] A next paragraph contained another arbitration clause providing for »[a]*ny other dispute*« to be referred to arbitration at the »*U.S.S.R. Chamber of Commerce Foreign Trade Arbitration Commission*« in Moscow.[212]

When a dispute arose, the parties could not agree whether to arbitrate ad hoc in England or before the commission in Moscow. The English party tried to initiate arbitration in England but the Russian defendants failed to cooperate in the constitution of an arbitral tribunal. The chairperson of the »*Particle Board Section of the Timber Trade Federation*« apparently refused to appoint arbitrators. Disappointingly, this aspect of refusal of the appointing authority is only mentioned *en passant* by Lord Justice Diplock, who finds that this would make the first arbitration clause unworkable.[213] He discusses neither the reasons for this refusal or the appointing authority's right to it, nor a possible cure by referring to default provisions of for court appointment of arbitrators.

The English party then started litigation before the English High Court, where the Russian party raised the arbitration defence, arguing that the case should be referred to arbitration in Moscow. Its request for a stay was rejected at first instance, a decision then upheld by the Court of Appeal. The Court of Appeal swiftly rejected a request by the Russian appellant to give leave to appeal to the House of Lords, agreeing with the respondent to the appeal, the English party, there to be »*no very great principle involved*«:

> »Lord Justice Diplock: It can so easily be cured by not doing the same silly thing again.
>
> Lord Denning M.R. No, we do not give leave.«[214]

Accordingly, the decision - despite its age - still reflects the current state of English jurisprudence on the matter.

---

211 Ibid., 163–64.
212 Ibid., 164.
213 Ibid., 167.
214 Ibid.

## ii. Critical comments on the decision

The Court of Appeal took the view that English courts have jurisdiction over the matter because the two arbitration clauses (there regarded as two parts of one clause) were irreconcilable. According to Lord Denning, at least five ways to interpret the clauses could be considered, all of which found »*untenable.*«[215] Independent of the question of how to interpret this specific agreement,[216] however, the decision fails to take into account that the parties in any event agreed on one thing: to arbitrate - and not to litigate - their disputes. Their disagreement only concerned the modalities« of arbitration: whether to arbitrate ad hoc or institutional, where, according to which rules, under which laws and before which arbitrators. From today's perspective, to agree on these modalities is not a requirement for a valid arbitration agreement; a blanket agreement may be supplemented.[217] From a ruling that sent the parties to the only forum they clearly derogated - a state court - one would have therefore expected at least some considerations why an arbitral tribunal could not have been court appointed.[218]

### c. Cour de Cassation, decisions of 20 February 2007 and 4 June 2009

The rulings by the German BGH and the English Court of Appeal contrast with newer rulings of the French Cour de Cassation of 20 February 2007[219] and 4 June 2009.[220]

---

215  Ibid., 166.

216  The understanding that arbitration in England should apply to disputes concerning goods delivered to the United Kingdom, arbitration in Moscow for goods to be delivered to other countries appears quite reasonable (*contra* Lord Denning, ibid.: *I cannot get that distinction out of the words*«, a view shared by Lord Justices Diplock and Davies, *see* ibid., 167).

217  *See supra* at pp. 161-163 (§8B); *but see also infra* at pp. 422-430 (§16A.II.1.d,iv) on the lack of provisions in arbitration laws to support institutional, rather than ad hoc arbitration.

218  *See* Arbitration Act 1950 § 10 (UK). However, the power of English courts to support arbitrations with an undetermined seat by appointing arbitrators was unclear at the time (*cf. now* Arbitration Act 1996 art. 2 (4), 18 (3) [EW]; on the connection requirement, *see* Steinbrück, *Die Unterstützung ausländischer Schiedsverfahren durch staatliche Gerichte*, 110).

219  *UOP NV v. BP*, [2007] Rev. Arb. 775 (FR C.Cass).

220  *Inéos v. UOP NV*, [2009] Rev. Arb. 652 (C.Cass).

## i. Facts, procedure and decisions

Both decisions relate to the same arbitration agreement, which the Cour de Cassation upheld although it contained contradictory references to two institutions. While one paragraph in the contract referred to the rules of the »*Association française d'arbitrage*« (AFA), another paragraph mentioned that the »*Chambre internationale de commerce de Paris*« - construed as referring to the ICC Court - should have exclusive jurisdiction. The Cour de Cassation reversed a judgment of the appellate court of Aix-en-Provence, which had previously held that the clause was null because it was impossible to determine the competent arbitral institution without a new agreement by the parties.[221]

According to the Cour de Cassation, the clause was, although contradictory, not manifestly incapable of being performed because the parties have unambiguously referred their disputes to arbitration. The supporting judge (»*juge d'appui*«) can help the parties to overcome difficulties in the constitution of an arbitral tribunal.[222] Due to the traditionally short reasoning of French court decisions, it is unclear whether the court considered the question if the arbitration clause could have deliberately referred to one institution and another institution's rules. Apparently, none of the parties has raised such an argument,[223] unlike in the Singaporean *Insigma v. Alstom* case where both parties eventually agreed that they intended to conclude a hybrid arbitration agreement.

## ii. Evaluation

The Cour de Cassation's pro-arbitration approach highlights the full effect French courts grant to the principle of competence-competence. The negative effect of this principle is understood to limit the powers of controlling courts to render a first ruling on the question of arbitral jurisdiction. It is the

---

221 *UOP NV v. BP*, [2006] Rev. Arb. 479 (CA, Aix-en-Provence).

222 *UOP NV v. BP*, [2007] Rev. Arb. 776 (C.Cass); *contra* [2006] Rev. Arb. 480 (CA Aix-en-Provence) (finding that the obstacles do not concern the constitution of the arbitral tribunal) (»*Un tel litige ne porte pas sur la constitution du tribunal arbitral*«).

223 *Cf. UOP NV v. Inéos*, [2008] Rev. Arb. 159 (CA, Paris) (subsequent decision; abstract).

French view that jurisdiction should be left to an arbitral tribunal, even where it is unclear *which* tribunal should rule thereon.[224]

Apart from this general controversy on the effects of competence-competence,[225] the decision underlines the connection between the inoperability caveat at the end of article II (3) of the New York Convention and the availability of court support: If a decision of a supporting court could help to implement the arbitration agreement, it is not incapable of being performed.[226] Overall, it is convincing to look into all available means, including resort to supporting courts, in order to uphold arbitration agreements referring, deliberately or by mistake, to two different arbitration institutions and/or rules. The parties' intent to refer to arbitration is clear, they »*actually refer to it twice.*«[227]

## 2. Hybrid arbitration a solution to ambiguity?

Probably for the better, none of the French courts concerned with the case just presented suggested that the contradictory references to two arbitration institutions could be reconciled letting the ICC Court administer the arbitration under AFA Rules. However, as introduced,[228] there is a peculiar[229] decision of the Singapore High Court along this line rendered in 2013.

### a. The case HKL v. Rizq

The problematic arbitration clause in this case provided for disputes to be »*settled*« by arbitration under ICC Rules by the »*Arbitration Committee at Singapore.*« In the High Court's opinion, such an institution does not exist and apparently, there was at the time no National Committee of the ICC in

---

224  *See* Cabrol, »UOP NV v. BP«, 160–62.
225  Discussed in more detail *infra* at pp. 413 et seq. (§16A.II.1).
226  *But see infra* at pp. 424-427 (§16A.II.1.d.iii) on the lack of a general duty to support arbitration if the arbitration agreement has defects not foreseen by the *lex arbitri.*
227  Cabrol, »UOP NV v. BP«, 162.
228  *See supra* at p. 38.
229  *See also* Fry, »HKL v. Rizq«, 453 (»*curious*«).

Singapore.[230] Nevertheless, the High Court, referring to the previous Singapore case law in *Insigma v. Alstom*,[231] found that the arbitration clause was

> »workable and not ›null and void, inoperative or incapable of being performed‹ [...] if the parties are able to secure the agreement of an arbitral institution in Singapore, such as the SIAC, to conduct a hybrid arbitration, applying the ICC rules.«[232]

In consequence, the High Court turned a pathological clause into a hybrid arbitration clause, suggesting to the parties that they should inquire with SIAC to administer the case,[233] although this was obviously not the parties' intent when concluding the arbitration agreement. In a subsequent ruling, the High Court defended this solution:

> »But, in this particular context, where parties are faced with the difficulty of overcoming a pathological arbitration clause, it is, in my view, appropriate to avail to them as part of a range of solutions, this solution of a hybrid arbitration, inelegant as it may be.«[234]

b. Critical comments of the decision

In principle, the decision to uphold the arbitration clause is in line with the concept of effective interpretation. However, the concrete conclusion reached by the Singapore High Court in this case is both dangerous and unnecessary:[235] The court could have easily construed the clause to refer to arbitration administered by the ICC Court,[236] even if it were true that no

---

230 *HKL v. Rizq I*, [2013] SGHC 5 [26] (granting a stay in favour of arbitration).

231 *Insigma v. Alstom*, [2008] SGHC 134; *Insigma v. Alstom*, [2009] SGCA 24.

232 *HKL v. Rizq I*, [2013] SGHC 5 [29].

233 *But see* ibid., para. 38 (alternatively recommending »*straightforward*« SIAC arbitration).

234 *HKL v. Rizq II*, [2013] SGHC 8 [11].

235 *See* Izor, »Insigma Revisited«: »*it is unclear whether the SIAC, or another arbitral institution, will now agree to administer a ›hybrid‹ arbitration under the ICC Rules given the introduction of Rules 1(2) and 6(2) in the 2012 ICC Rules, and the controversy that followed the earlier decision*«; *see also* Fry, »HKL v. Rizq«, 454 (»*fortuitous surgery*«; citing: Davis, »Pathological Clauses«, 386).

236 Fry, »HKL v. Rizq«, 456–57.

National Committee of the ICC existed or was operating in Singapore.[237] Under ICC Rules, the arbitration is administered by the ICC Court[238] and not by the National Committee, whose task is only to nominate arbitrators on behalf of parties.[239]

In addition, neither ICC National Committees nor the ICC Court »*settle*« disputes, this is the original task of the arbitral tribunal. Accordingly, the term »*Arbitration Committee*« probably did not designate an institution at all but only the arbitral tribunal, arguably consisting of three rather than a sole arbitrator, with the reference to the ICC Rules sufficiently indicating the parties' choice of administration by the ICC Court.[240] Different from cases of consciously agreed hybrid arbitration, the issue in *HKL v. Rizq* was not whether the »*ICC edict*« can override party autonomy but one of mere incorporation of article 6 (2) of the applicable ICC Rules (2012) into the agreement.[241] Although arbitration rules are merely contract terms, absent an individual agreement to the contrary, such terms must be giving a meaning when it comes to interpreting an agreement incorporating them.[242]

Therefore, the proviso of the clause being »*pathological*« and in need of »*saving*« appears questionable in the first place. Instead, the High Court should have referred the parties to ICC arbitration straightaway. As it stands, the decision has the bitter taste of a »*rather parochial approach in favour of Singapore's local institution.*«[243]

Although a provision in institutional rules like article 1 (2) of the ICC Rules

> »cannot curtail the freedom of parties to agree to be bound by the result of an arbitration administered by a different arbitral institution applying the ICC Rules«,[244]

---

237 *But see* ICC, »ICC Singapore« (listing the Singapore Business Federation as National Committee); *see also* Fry, »HKL v. Rizq«, 458.

238 ICC Rules, art. 1 (2) (2012; 2017).

239 Not to administer the proceedings (*contra HKL v. Rizq I*, [2013] SGHC 5 [26]); moreover, ICC Rules, art. 13 (3), (4) (2012; 2017) allow the ICC Court to make direct appointments if a National Committee is not functioning.

240 ICC Rules, art. 6 (2) (2012; 2017); *see also* Fry, »HKL v. Rizq«, 456–57.

241 Fry, »HKL v. Rizq«, 457.

242 Ibid., 460 (speaking of »*terms and conditions*«); *contra* Hochbaum, *Mißglückte internationale Schiedsvereinbarungen*, 61–62.

243 Fry, »HKL v. Rizq«, 459.

244 *HKL v. Rizq II*, [2013] SGHC 8 [10].

the court's subsequent finding that articles 1 (2) and 6 (2) of the ICC Rules can neither »*curtail the power of the court*«[245] in interpreting the clause at issue is dubious. Court *ordered* hybrid arbitration as opposed to party-*agreed* hybrid arbitration appears highly problematic. Generally, an arbitration agreement should only be interpreted as hybrid, if there is strong indication that the parties really wanted to depart from the standard practice of applying the rules of the institution designated to administer the case. If there is no such indication - in *HKL v. Rizq I* none of the parties even argued that they wanted to agree on hybrid SIAC arbitration under ICC Rules - an arbitration clause designating an inexistent arbitral institution and existing arbitration rules is best interpreted to refer to the institution that issued the rules. According to this understanding, names of locations combined with words such as »*Arbitration Committee*«, »*Arbitration Court*« or »*Arbitration Tribunal*« just indicate the place of arbitration and not an institution different from the one that issued the chosen rules.[246]

## 3. Distinction between deliberately hybrid & ambiguous clauses

*On their face*, the arbitration clauses in all cases just outlined hardly differ from the hybrid arbitration agreement leading to the Singaporean *Insigma v. Alstom* decisions.[247] The difference there lay only in the parties' intent appearing from their conduct and pleadings as both parties, upon withdrawing the arbitration initially commenced by Alstom before the ICC Court, agreed, at least at some stage, that the case should be administered by SIAC

---

245  Ibid.

246  Along this line, one ICC appointed arbitrator assumed jurisdiction pursuant to a clause referring to arbitration in Seoul before the »*Korean Commercial Arbitration Tribunal*« - an institution of that name does not exist - and the ICC Rules (award unpublished; first reported by Bond, »How to Draft an Arbitration Clause«, 67–68; *see also* Davis, »Pathological Clauses«, 376–78; *but see* Hochbaum, *Mißglückte internationale Schiedsvereinbarungen*, 62, arguing that the clause should have been read as referring to the Korean Commercial Arbitration Board as appointing authority with the ICC Court to administer the case under ICC Rules).

247  *Insigma v. Alstom*, [2008] SGHC 134; *Insigma v. Alstom*, [2009] SGCA 24.

but that ICC Rules should be applied.[248] Admittedly, it will often be very difficult for arbitral tribunals and courts to detect and prove such intent, the express pleading of the parties in *Insigma v. Alstom* that they deliberately opted for hybrid arbitration in - eventually frustrated - hope to save costs might remain exceptional. The difficulties in identifying hybrid arbitration clauses can be illustrated by two further decisions, the first possibly concerning a true hybrid arbitration agreement while the latter raising some serious doubts in this regard.

a. HCCI Court award of 18 April 2000

In 2002, a tribunal appointed under the auspices of the Court of Arbitration attached to the Hungarian Chamber of Commerce and Industry (herein: HCCI Court) rendered a decision effectively accommodating the idea of hybrid arbitration, the award in case no. VB/99130.[249] The positive ruling on jurisdiction, which was part of the award on the merits, was based on an arbitration clause providing that disputes should be resolved before the »*Court of Arbitration of Budapest, Hungary in accordance with the Rules of the International Chamber of Commerce.*«[250] Surprisingly, the editors of the *Revue de l'Arbitrage* categorised this as an »*ICC Case*« (»*affaire CCI*«) in the heading of both the case abstract and the case note.[251] The ICC Court would probably not share this view.

In his case note, Philippe Cavalieros approved of the tribunal's decision to assume jurisdiction and to apply some aspects (»*quelques doses*«) of the ICC Rules by analogy, although noting that the application of the complete set of ICC Rules, in particular its institutional aspects, would have been impossible.[252] In the terminology employed herein, Cavalieros thus

---

248 *See Insigma v. Alstom*, [2009] SGCA 24 [7–11]; although Insigma later tried to challenge this compromise it had proposed itself as »*disastrous*« (*cf. Insigma v. Alstom*, [2008] SGHC 134 [24, 29]).

249 *VB/99130*, [2002] Rev. Arb. 1019 (HCCI, Budapest) (original unpublished, translated extracts in French by Philippe Cavalieros).

250 Cavalieros, »Note, CCI No. VB/99130, 10.04.2000«, 1021.

251 *See VB/99130*, [2002] Rev. Arb. 1019; Cavalieros, »Note, CCI No. VB/99130, 10.04.2000« (possibly just an editorial problem of using CCI to abbreviate the Arbitration Court attached to the Hungarian Chamber of Commerce and Industy although the same abbreviation is commonly used to refer to the ICC Court in French).

252 »Note, CCI No. VB/99130, 10.04.2000«, 1032.

understood the arbitration clause to be *hybrid*, presenting, as in *Insigma v. Alstom,* a deliberate choice of arbitration conducted before one institution under another institution's rules.

However, »*Arbitration Court in Budapest*« is not the official name of the HCCI Court. Therefore, it would have been at least equally convincing to assume that the clause was just a pathological, poorly drafted reference to standard ICC arbitration with a seat in Budapest, similar to the interpretation here proposed for the arbitration clause in the Singaporean case *HKL v. Rizq*.[253] Nevertheless, the arbitral tribunal rejected the latter understanding for reasons of Hungarian law. Apparently, only the HCCI Court is - or was at the time - allowed to administer international arbitrations in Hungary according to section 46 (3) of the Hungarian Arbitration Law of 1994.[254] On that basis, an interpretation of the agreement in favour of this institution enjoying a monopoly in Hungary was therefore the only way to uphold the arbitration agreement in accordance with both the principle of effective arbitration and the law of the seat of arbitration. This case is therefore another example of hybrid arbitration as a phenomenon factually promoted by a restrictive arbitration law with regard to activities of foreign institutions.[255]

The case also highlights that the distinction between ambiguous, purely pathological arbitration clauses, meaning those *accidentally* containing conflicting references to two institutions and/or rules, and hybrid arbitration clauses purveying a *deliberate* choice for other rules than those of the administering institution is simply a matter of argumentation, proof and the interests involved. In this particular case, the respondent refused to take part in the proceedings while the claimant had an interest in arguing that the parties' meant to provide for arbitration at the HCCI Court. This way it could avail itself of the only institution allowed to administer international arbitrations in Hungary while benefitting from the more international

---

253 *See supra* at pp. 175-177 (§8C.I.2.b).
254 English translation of the provision: »*In international cases, the Institutional Arbitration Court attached to the Hungarian Chamber of Commerce and Industry shall act as institutional arbitral tribunal*« (translation published in: Paulsson, *International Handbook on Commercial Arbitration*, Hungary, Annex 1, supp. no. 19, last updated Aug. 1995). Hungarian law has become even more restrictive since then (*see generally* Cavalieros, »The Hungarian Arbitration Law«).
255 *See supra* at pp. 101-74 (§4C.II.2.b.iii) on a corresponding perception of the legal situation in China

character of the ICC Rules.[256] The tribunal accepted this pleading, certainly itself not entirely disinterested in keeping its mandate. However, often interests will lie differently. If the place of arbitration was a more arbitration-friendly or rather foreign-institution-friendly jurisdiction, the claimant would probably apply to the rules issuing institution directly, rather than an institution at the place of arbitration. A respondent choosing to defend its case before this institution or the tribunal would likely dispute any agreement on the mode of arbitration altogether while a tribunal appointed under the auspices of the rules issuing institution might be inclined to treat the conflicting reference to another institution as pathological and thus meaningless. The question whether an institution could administer a case under another institution's rules - a hybrid arbitration problem - would then not even arise.

Accordingly, hybrid arbitration clauses are at the outset very closely related to initially pathological clauses, meaning clauses with serious drafting defects. If, however, the deciding authority, whether a tribunal, a court or and arbitral institution, is convinced that the choice of one institution and another institution's rules was deliberate, entirely different issues arise. Such conviction is obvious where both parties unanimously claim their arbitration agreement to be hybrid. Then, party autonomy commands implementation as precise as possible as outlined above.[257]

The same conclusion is less pressing where only one party argues a case of hybrid arbitration as in the HCCI case no. VB/99130. Then, the principle of effective interpretation would usually argue in favour of interpreting the clause as designating the rules issuing institution, unless particular restrictions of the law of the seat - as in Hungary or, arguably, China[258] rendered such interpretation unworkable.

To interpret an agreement as hybrid is least convincing if none of the parties advances such an argument, if no obstacle to the arbitration being administered by the rules issuing institution exists and if a distinct

---

256 *See* Cavalieros, »Note, CCI No. VB/99130, 10.04.2000«, 1024. The claimant did not argue that the clause could refer to the HCCI *and* its rules (*cf. supra* at n. 251 on p. 178 on confusion about the abbreviation CCI).

257 *See supra* at pp. 119-122 (§5D).

258 *But see* for a potential factual opening of the Chinese arbitration market: *Longlide,* [2013] Min Si Ta Zi no. 13; Sun, »SPC Instruction Provides New Opportunities for International Arbitral Institutions to Expand into China«, 695 (Appendix 3); *see also* Dong, »Open Door for Foreign Arbitration Institutions?«

administering institution is not even clearly named as - to recall - it was the factual situation underlying *HKL v. Rizq.*[259]

b. The »ICC 500« case

In 2008, the AAA-ICDR refused to administer an arbitration under a dispute resolution clause quite obviously poorly drafted but also raising issues of compatibility between institutions and rules. In addition to an ambiguous reference to »*arbitration through The American Arbitration Association or to any other U.S. court*«, the contract called for application of »*the Rules and Regulations of the International Chamber of Commerce (ICC 500).*« The AAA-ICDR understood the clause to designate the ICC Rules and declined the case on that basis. In consequence, a motion to compel arbitration before US courts failed.[260]

In parallel, legal action was brought before Swiss state courts, which accepted jurisdiction and rejected the respondent's arbitration defence. In last instance, the Swiss Federal Supreme Court, like the US courts, based its decision predominantly on the alternative reference to »*any other US court*« contained in the dispute resolution clause, without focussing on the potential conflict between the designating institution and the applicable rules. Strikingly, the Swiss Federal Supreme Court understood the potential conflict to be a jurisdictional problem of finding the right tribunal (»*Schiedsgericht*«), failing to terminologically distinguish the tribunal from the institution.[261] It also avoided taking a position on whether arbitral institutions can or should apply another institution's rules.

---

259 *HKL v. Rizq I,* [2013] SGHC 5. *See supra* at pp. 174-177 (2).

260 *See ISC v. Nobel Biocare Investments,* no. 09–1442 (2nd Cir. 27 October 2009), 351 F. App'x 480 (US) (remand order; holding the clause to be »*ambiguous*« with respect to the reference to a »*US court*«; not discussing the issue of the AAA's refusal to administer under ICC Rules); affirmed by: *ISC v. Nobel Biocare Finance,* 688 F.3d 98 (2nd Cir. 2012).

261 *Cf.* X Holding AG, X Management S.A., A & B v. Y Investments N.V., 4 A 279/2010 (CH BG, 25 October 2010) (at consid. 3). The lower instance, the Higher Regional Court (Obergericht) of the Canton Zug, uses the term »*Schiedsstelle*« [arbitration board], which seems equally imprecise (*X Holding AG v. Y Investments NV* [C.H. OG, Zug, 8 April 2010], unpublished). I thank the Obergericht Zug for providing me with a copy of the unpublished decision.

The lower instances had made a few more observations on a possible conflict between arbitral institutions. The first instance, the Cantonal Court (*Kantonsgericht*) of Zug,[262] found that the arbitration clause created a conflict of jurisdiction between the two mentioned arbitral institutions, the AAA-ICDR and the ICC Court,[263] and was therefore incurably pathological.[264] The second instance, the Higher Cantonal Court (*Obergericht*) of Zug did not share this view, remarking that the parties' reference to the *»Rules and Regulations of the International Chamber of Commerce (ICC 500)«* only contains an agreement of the applicable arbitration rules:

> »Aus dem Verweis auf die ICC-Regeln zu schließen, die Parteien hätten - neben dem AAA und jedem anderen US-Gericht - auch noch die ICC als zuständig erachtet, ginge zu weit.«[265]

> [It would go too far to deduce from the reference to ICC Rules that the parties - next to the AAA and any other US court - also wanted to designate the ICC as competent.]

It remains unclear, whether the parties in this case deliberately wanted to agree on a hybrid arbitration clause - like in the *Insigma v. Alstom* case - or whether the reference to the AAA on the one hand and the *»Rules and Regulations of the International Chamber of Commerce (ICC 500)«* on the other hand was just accidental. The odd denomination *»ICC 500«* and the further ambiguities of the clause let assume that the drafting was not very well thought of.

It is even possible that *»ICC 500«* was originally not supposed to refer to the applicable arbitration rules at all.[266] Instead, it may have concerned the applicable substantive rules, namely the *»ICC Uniform Customs and Practices for Documentary Credits«* (or *»UCP 500«*),[267] a set of standards on the issuance and use of letters of credits published by the International

---

262 X Holding AG, X Management S.A., A & B v. Y Investments N.V., A2_2009_3 (CH KG, Zug, 14 December 2009) (unpublished).

263 *»Kompetenzkonflikt zwischen zwei institutionellen Schiedsgerichten (AAA oder ICC)«* (*as cited in* X Holding AG, X Management S.A., A & B v. Y Investments N.V., JZ_2010_9 [CH OG, Zug, 8 April 2010] [1.3]).

264 »[U]*nheilbar pathologisch*« (ibid.).

265 Ibid., para. 1.5.2.

266 *Contra ISC v. Nobel Biocare Investments*, 351 F. App'x 480; X Holding AG, X Management S.A., A & B v. Y Investments N.V., 4 A 279/2010 (CH BG, 25 October 2010); Girsberger and Ruch, »Pathological Arbitration Clauses« (not contemplating this likely interpretation of the dispute resolution clause).

267 International Chamber of Commerce, *UCP 500*.

Chamber of Commerce, sometimes wrongly referred to as »*ICC 500.*«[268] These standards do not concern arbitration.[269]

In any event, this case example illustrates the danger of an arbitral institution refusing to administer case due to the parties' odd procedural choices, whether made on purpose or by accident. The parties ended up before state courts of several instances and in two different jurisdictions - a fate which to avoid is usually the purpose of concluding an arbitration agreement in the first place.

While the interpretation problems associated with the clause belong to the category of initial pathology, the refusal of the AAA-ICDR to administrate the proceedings is an obstacle that materialised after the contract conclusion only once a dispute arose. Both the US and the Swiss courts ignored this problem of subsequent pathology, which shall be discussed in the following subsection.

---

268  *See* International Chamber of Commerce, »Traders Warned about Non-Existent ICC Instruments Quoted on Internet« (referring to the non-existent »*ICC 500*« possibly to be associated with »*UCP 500*«).

269  *See also* Takla, »Non-ICC Arbitration Clauses«, 7 (reporting a case where a party tried to base a request for arbitration on the ICC Uniform Customs and Practices for Documentary Credits, doubting that the counsel did not know that these rules do not contain a reference to arbitration).

II. Subsequent pathology: obstacles in the institution's sphere

Common examples of subsequent pathologies are the passing away of an expressly named arbitrator[270] or the dissolution or status change of an appointing authority[271] or arbitral institution as administering body.[272]

Herein, the situation of dissolution or status change of the designated arbitral institution shall be illustrated by one historical example, the dissolution of the Chamber of Foreign Trade of the former German Democratic Republic (GDR) with its attached Court of Arbitration, and by one very recent issue, the »*CIETAC split*.« An analysis of the case law pertinent to these situations may provide answers and hints to several important questions: To what extent are arbitration institutions interchangeable without violating the parties' agreement to arbitrate? Is the choice of an arbitral institution of such importance, that obstacles in this respect should render the whole arbitration agreement incapable of being performed?

These issues will likely gain attention because of the constant growth in number of more or less reliable arbitral institutions, increasing the risk of

---

270   *See* International Council for Commercial Arbitration, »Ch. II,« 53 (operability depends on national legislation); *see e.g. ACC Ltd. v. Global Cements Ltd.*, [2012] 7 SCC 71 (IN) (upholding an arbitration agreement despite the passing away of the persons named as potential arbitrators).

271   Well known is the example of the ad hoc arbitration case *Kuweit v. Aminoil*, where the original arbitration clause provided for chairman appointment by the »*British Resident of the Gulf*«, an entity no longer existing when the dispute arose (*as mentioned by* Blackaby et al., *Redfern and Hunter*, para. 2.182; *see also Kuweit v. Aminoil*, [1982] 21 I.L.M. 976, 980 [Final Award] [based on a new submission agreement now naming »*The President of the International Court of Justice*« as appointing authority]). Another historic example is RGZ 108, 246 (1923) (GER) (agreement which provided for appointment of the co-arbitrators by two merchants' organisations which had already merged at the time the dispute arose considered inoperative).

272   *See e.g. China Packaging v. SCA Recycling*, [1999] XXIV YCA 724 (Netherlands AR, Zutphen); *China Agribusiness v. Balli Trading*, [1998] 2 Lloyd's Rep 76 (EWHC Comm.), full text of decision: [1997] C.L.C. 1427 (EWHC Comm.) (CIETAC awards recognised based on agreements referring to FETAC); *see also Dalimpex Ltd. v. Janicki*, [2003] CanLII 34234 (Can., Ont., CA) (Polish National Chamber of Commerce considered successor of »*College of Arbitrators/ Arbitration Court at the Polish Chamber of Foreign Trade*«; also relying on an argument of preclusion).

»*stillborn institutions.*«[273] They are also insightful for evaluating hybrid arbitration agreements because it is not unlikely that an institution designated to administer arbitration under other than its own rules will eventually prove unavailable - not due to its dissolution but due to potential refusal or incapability to render such service. In addition, one scholarly proposal to solve cases of dissolution or status change of the designated institution by referring parties to another institution or body that may administer the arbitration under the unavailable institution's rules - which conceptually means hybrid arbitration - shall be discussed in this context.[274]

1. Retrospective: Dissolution of the GDR's chamber of foreign trade

After the German reunification, many continuing[275] contracts concluded between state owned enterprises of the German Democratic Republic (GDR) and West German companies still contained arbitration clauses[276] referring to the Court of Arbitration at the Chamber of Foreign Trade of the GDR.[277]

Before being dissolved in the process of the German reunification, the Chamber of Foreign Trade of the GDR concluded an agreement with the Association for the Promotion of Arbitration (*Vereinigung zur Förderung der Schiedsgerichtsbarkeit*) (VFS), dated 1 September 1990, on the transferal of the Court of Arbitration, renamed to »*Schiedsgericht Berlin.*« By further agreement of 4 November 1993, the DIS and the VFS decided to merge into one organisation, the DIS.[278]

---

273 Poudret and Besson, *Comparative Law of International Arbitration*, para. 95; Blackaby et al., *Redfern and Hunter*, para. 1–104.

274 *See infra* at pp. 202 et seq. (§8C.II.3) for a discussion of such suggestion by German academic Christian Wolf.

275 *See* Kirchner, »Schiedsgerichtsbarkeit in Berlin«, 270.

276 *See* Stumpf, »Probleme beim Abschluß von Verträgen mit Betrieben in der DDR«, 159.

277 *See generally* Heinz Strohbach, »Arbitration Between Foreign Trade Organizations of Socialist Countries and Parties from the Capitalist Economic Sphere« (for a contemporaneous insight into the activities of this and other socialist arbitration institutions from the point of view of a GDR arbitrator).

278 *See* Deutsche Institution für Schiedsgerichtsbarkeit (DIS), »DIS in eigener Sache«; Schwab, Walter, and Baumbach, *Schiedsgerichtsbarkeit*, chap. 41 para. 15; Hochbaum, *Mißglückte internationale*

a. BGH decision of 20 January 1994

In its decision of 20 January 1994,[279] the BGH had to decide whether the parties to a contract containing an arbitration clause naming the Court of Arbitration at the Chamber of Foreign Trade of the GDR[280] should still be referred to arbitration although the Chamber of Foreign Trade of the GDR had ceased to exist. The BGH found that the arbitration agreement was incapable of being performed and rejected the respondent's arbitration defence, allowing the claimant to bring its claims before German state courts.[281]

The decision is based on section 1033 no. 1 of the former version of the German code of civil procedure in force prior to the 1998 reform,[282] which stated that an arbitration agreement becomes invalid, unless otherwise agreed, if a named arbitrator dies, becomes unavailable, refuses to accept its mandate, withdraws of unduly delays his or her duties.[283]

Of course, the BGH realised that this provision was not directly addressing the issue of non-existing arbitral institutions. Rather, it referred to an arbitrator's death, refusal or incapability to fulfil his or her duties. The BGH nevertheless decided to apply this provision by way of analogy. Preconditions for such analogy are that the law contains a gap not foreseen by the legislator and that the interests involved are comparable in the situation governed by the law and the situation to be decided by the courts. The unintended gap in the law was found in the fact that at the time neither the parties to the arbitration agreement nor the legislative bodies could have predicted

---

*Schiedsvereinbarungen*, 187 n. 377 (referring to an unpublished letter of the Schiedsgericht Berlin).

279 Urteil [Judgment], [1994] 125 BGHZ 7, [1994] 47 NJW 1008 (GER BGH).

280 The arbitration clause simply stated: »*Als Gerichtsstand wird das Schiedsgericht bei der Kammer für Außenhandel der DDR vereinbart*«. [The Court of Arbitration at the Chamber of Foreign Trade of the German Democratic Republic is agreed as forum] (*see* Urteil [Judgment], [1994] 47 NJW 1008).

281 Ibid.

282 Herein cited as ZPO (old version) (GER).

283 *See* the English translation of the provision by Ottoarndt Glossner in: Sanders and van den Berg, *International Handbook on Commercial Arbitration*, Germany, Annex I (Suppl. 7, April 1987) (reprinted in: Böckstiegel, Kröll, and Nacimiento, »Annex II German Arbitration Law Prior to 1 January 1998«, 1117).

the far-reaching changes in political conditions that led to the dissolution of the GDR and its Chamber of Foreign Trade.[284] The BGH further considered this situation comparable to the case of an unavailable arbitrator named in the arbitration agreement. A choice[285] for dispute settlement at the Court of Arbitration at the Chamber of Foreign Trade of the GDR had considerable influence on the composition of the arbitral tribunal - comparable to the choice of a mandatory appointing authority[286] - because arbitrators could only be nominated from a limited list maintained by the institution (mandatory list procedure).[287]

The BGH further held that the DIS is not the legal successor of the Court of Arbitration at the Chamber of Foreign Trade of the GDR. According to the BGH, an arbitral institution performs exclusive (»*höchstpersönliche*« [highly personal]) duties.[288] For this reason, an arbitral institution was not entitled to transfer such duties unilaterally to another institution without the parties' consent.[289]

b. Evaluation and relevance for modern arbitration law

»The one charm of the past is that it is the past.«[290]

---

284 Urteil [Judgment], [1994] 47 NJW 1011.

285 To speak of a »*choice*« may be euphemistic. According to a recent DIS interim award the circumstances of the contract conclusion at that time of the East-West conflict were characterised by constraints for the foreign trade partners of the GDR [»*Zwangslage für Außenhandelspartner*«] and a complete absence of freedom of choice regarding the dispute settlement system (*Zwischenentscheid*, [2010] 8 SchiedsVZ 229 [DIS] 232; *contra* Habscheid and Habscheid, »Ende der West–Ost–Handelschiedsgerichts-barkeit?«, 370 [noting that some dispute settlement clauses favoured Eastern others Western arbitral institutions, always depending on which party held the whip hand] [»*am* ›*längeren Hebel*‹ *saß*«]).

286 *Relying on* RGZ 108, 246 (1923) (GER).

287 The arbitrators were part of the Arbitration Court, *cf.* §§ 4 (I) and 6 (I) of the Arbitration Rules of the Chamber of Foreign Trade of the GDR (*published in* Fellhauer and Strohbach, *Handbuch der internationalen Handelsschiedsgerichtsbarkeit*, 165, 167). To nominate non-listed arbitrators, parties had to agree on ad hoc arbitration (*cf.* ibid., 167 [at n. 10]).

288 Urteil [Judgment], [1994] 47 NJW 110.

289 *See already* Urteil [Judgment], [1994] 5 DtZ at 179.

290 Oscar Wilde, »The Picture of Dorian Gray«, 49.

With the modernisation of Germany's arbitration law,[291] section 1033 no. 1 ZPO (GER) (old version) was deleted. Sections 1038 and 1039 of the ZPO (GER) now call for the nomination of a replacement arbitrator if an arbitrator is incapable to fulfil its duties for reasons of death or serious illness or simple refusal.[292] In light of this, parties may even more be expected to arbitrate under the auspices of another institution, given that the institutions' functions - although not without value - are less crucial for the outcome of a dispute than the decisional powers of arbitrators. In a decision of 2011 regarding an agreement referring to a non-existent arbitral institution, the »*Anwaltsschiedsgericht*« (Lawyer Arbitration Court), the BGH clarified that the legal situation changed decisively with the 1998 reform and that effective, supplementary interpretation could now save such an agreement.[293]

In the historical context, however, the BGH may have come to the right conclusion. It is likely, that the arbitration agreements in contracts with GDR state owned entities were compromises reached due to a hint of mistrust of the foreign trade partners towards the GDR's state courts and because choice of court agreements in favour of a Western jurisdiction would not have been conveyable.[294] The BGH was probably correct in stating that, at the time, arbitration clauses mainly served to derogate from the jurisdiction of GDR state courts that lacked personal and organisational means to cope effectively with complex business disputes.[295] These motives to opt for arbitration arguably fell away with access to German courts after the reunification-

The same arguments are unlikely to apply in other less political situations of dissolution of arbitral institutions. In most cases, one may assume that parties could entertain the idea of administration by another, suitable institution. A DIS interim award of 2010 distinguishes the BGH's decision of 1994 to cases without a predicament (»*Zwangslage*«) having led to the choice of an arbitral institution.[296] Although section 1033 no. 1 ZPO (GER) (old version) was still applicable in the DIS case pursuant to transitional

---

291 By the SchiedsVfG 1997 (GER).
292 *See* Baumbach et al., *Zivilprozessordnung: mit FamFG, GVG und anderen Nebengesetzen*, § 1038, para. 4 (for further examples).
293 Beschluss [Decision], [2011] 64 NJW 2978, [2011] 9 SchiedsVZ 285.
294 *See also* Börner and Oehmke, »Schiedsgerichtsklauseln in fortgeltenden deutsch-deutschen Wirtschaftsverträgen«, 2217.
295 Urteil [Judgment], [1994] 47 NJW 1011.
296 *Zwischenentscheid*, [2010] 8 SchiedsVZ 232.

law, the arbitral tribunal dismissed the respondent's challenge to jurisdiction, who had argued that the German Arbitration Committee (*Deutscher Ausschuss für Schiedsgerichtswesen*) (DAS) named in the arbitration clause had been dissolved, rendering the arbitration clause incapable of being performed.[297] In spite of a merger of DAS and DIS in 1992,[298] the arbitral tribunal found that the DAS and its President were still available to make replacement appointments under the last available version of the DAS arbitration rules and that all other institutional functions could be assumed by the DIS. Moreover, as the arbitral tribunal correctly points out, the institution is not to be confused with the arbitral tribunal.[299] Shortly before, on 22 April 2009, another arbitral tribunal constituted under the auspices of the DIS[300] assumed jurisdiction although the arbitration agreement provided for arbitration before the DAS and rendered an award, which was subsequently declared enforceable in France. An appeal against the order of enforcement was rejected by the Paris Court of Appeal's decision of 20 March 2012 who considered the DIS do be the successor of the DAS and found the change of arbitration rules to be irrelevant for the validity of the arbitration agreement.[301]

From this line of decisions, starting with the BGH decision of 1994,[302] the DIS rulings of 2009[303] and 2010[304] and the BGH decision of 2011 on the non-existent »*Anwaltsschiedsgericht*«,[305] one can draw the following conclusion: The non-availability of a designated institution should only render the agreement inoperable if the following three conditions were cumulatively met:

---

297 Ibid., 230.
298 *See* Deutsche Institution für Schiedsgerichtsbarkeit (DIS), »About the DIS«.
299 *Zwischenentscheid*, [2010] 8 SchiedsVZ 232.
300 Unfortunately, the circumstances of the constitution of the arbitral tribunal - party-appointed or institution-appointed - are unknown.
301 *SAS v. Reo*, [2012] Rev. Arb. 805 (FR CA, Paris); *see* the case notes by Kühner, »Survie de la clause compromissoire«, 809 (in French); »Zur Wirksamkeit einer Schiedsklausel« (in German).
302 Urteil [Judgment], [1994] 125 BGHZ 7, [1994] 47 NJW 1008.
303 As finally declared enforceable in Paris, France (*see SAS v. Reo*, [2012] Rev. Arb. 805).
304 *Zwischenentscheid*, [2010] 8 SchiedsVZ 229.
305 Beschluss [Decision], [2011] 64 NJW 2978, [2011] 9 SchiedsVZ 285.

- The *lex arbitri* provides that the unavailability of arbitrators named in the agreement would render the arbitration agreement null (which is no longer the case under German law).
- The choice of an institution considerably influenced the expected composition of the tribunal.
- There are indications that one party would not have opted for arbitration at all, had it expected the circumstances leading to the unavailability of the institution.

The second condition will only be met if the parties referred to an institution with very formal rules on arbitrator nomination or even with a mandatory list procedure. In most other cases, it seems appropriate to give effect to the parties' general agreement to arbitrate by referring them to another institution or to ad hoc arbitration.[306]

## 2. A current issue: The CIETAC split

A new century, another continent but similar issues: The CIETAC split of summer 2012, that is the founding of independent institutions, SHIAC and SCIA, by CIETAC's former Shanghai and Shenzhen subcommissions, brings the questions of substitutability and succession of arbitral institutions back on the table.

### a. The background of the creation of SHIAC and SCIA

The reason or pretext[307] for the split was an internal quarrel on the CIETAC Rules (2012) and in particular on the allocation of disputes between the subcommissions and the headquarters in Beijing. In 2011, a large percentage of cases had been administered by the Shanghai subcommission (36 %) and a still significant number of cases had been referred to Shenzhen (15 %) - in relation to the 46 % of cases administered in

---

306 *See also* Kühner, »Survie de la clause compromissoire«, 810; »Zur Wirksamkeit einer Schiedsklausel«, 240 (drawing a parallel to cases of refusal of administration, like by the ICC in the *Qimonda* arbitration; *cf. Samsung Electronics v. Mr. Jaffe (Qimonda)*, [2010] Rev. Arb. 571 [FR TGI, Paris]).

307 *See* Rose, »The Tarnished Brand of CIETAC«, 142 (»[a]*necdotally*« mentioning tensions to date further back than the 2012 rules revision).

Beijing.[308] With the launch of the CIETAC Rules (2012), these subcommissions feared a substantial decline in cases, impact and - of course - fees as CIETAC introduced the following provision in its rules:

> »Where the subcommission/center agreed upon by the parties does not exist, or where the agreement is ambiguous, the Secretariat of CIETAC shall accept the arbitration application and administer the case. In the event of any dispute, a decision shall be made by CIETAC«[309]

While it was previously sufficient if the respective city was named as a place of arbitration in order to refer a dispute to the Shanghai or Shenzhen subcommission, the new provision was understood to allocate the majority of disputes to CIETAC Beijing. It was expected that only arbitration clauses naming the respective subcommission expressly, would not be considered »*ambiguous*« within the meaning of article 2 (6) sentence 4 of the CIETAC Rules (2012).[310] Arguably, such a rule is helpful in a legal system where arbitration clauses not clearly identifying an arbitration commission or providing for a place of arbitration where no such commission exists are likely considered invalid.[311] However, the Shanghai and Shenzhen subcommissions opposed the new allocation of cases connected with this clarification.

Consequently, the Shanghai subcommission declared its independence and abruptly released its own arbitration rules based on the CIETAC Rules (2005).[312] The Shenzhen subcommission followed soon after with an independence declaration according to which it would continue to apply the CIETAC Rules (2005).[313] CIETAC, in turn, announced on 1 August 2012 that

---

308  *See* Hirth and Munz, »CIETAC Schiedsvereinbarungen«, 9.

309  CIETAC Rules, art. 2 (6) sent. 4 and 5 (2012; 2015); *cf.* Hirth and Munz, »CIETAC Schiedsvereinbarungen«, 9.

310  Bert, »CIETAC Administered Arbitrations«.

311  *See supra* at pp. 101-104 (§4C.II.2.b.iii).

312  CIETAC Shanghai Rules (2012); *see* Wu and Sun, »CIETAC Issues 2012 Arbitration Rules but CIETAC Shanghai Issues Own Rules Too« (dating the »*independence*« announcement to 30 April 2012); *but see* Rose, »The Tarnished Brand of CIETAC«, 142 (»*10 July 2012*«).

313  Rose, »The Tarnished Brand of CIETAC«, 142 (the exact date of the Shenzhen subcommission's »*independence*« declaration appears not to be public knowledge); *cf. also* Wu and Sun, »CIETAC Issues 2012 Arbitration Rules but CIETAC Shanghai Issues Own Rules Too«; Bert, »CIETAC Administered Arbitrations«.

>»CIETAC's authorization to the CIETAC Shanghai Sub-Commission and the CIETAC South China Sub-Commission for accepting and administering arbitration cases is hereby suspended«[314]

and that parties shall submit their disputes under arbitration clauses referring to these subcommissions to CIETAC Beijing instead.[315]

In response, the Shanghai and Shenzhen subcommissions, purporting to have been independent arbitration commissions all along,[316] jointly declared that their competences are based on

>»the agreement of the parties, rather than the ›authorization‹ from any other institutions.«[317]

They also obtained approval from the municipal governments in their provinces for continuing their activities[318] and changed their names to SHIAC and SCIA respectively, although both - confusingly - also use alternative names: Shanghai International Economic and Trade Arbitration Commission (SIETAC) and South China International Economic and Trade Arbitration Commission (SCCIETAC).[319]

On 31 December 2012, CIETAC reiterated its position in another announcement, purporting to prohibit

>»the use of the name, brand and relevant logo of ›China International Economic and Trade Arbitration Commission,‹ either in Chinese or English, and to conduct any further arbitration activities in the names of CIETAC Shanghai sub-commission and CIETAC South China Sub-Commission«[320]

---

314 China International Economic and Trade Administration Commission, »Announcement of 1 August 2012«.

315 Ibid.

316 A true core of this is that the subcommissions had separate panels of arbitrators in the early days of CIETAC (*see* Kaplan, Spruce, and Moser, *Hong Kong and China Arbitration*, 308).

317 CIETAC Shanghai Commission and CIETAC South China Commission, »Joint Statement«.

318 *See* Chen, Cui, and Lui, »China - CIETAC ›Jurisdictional Turf War' Comes To An End?« (with references to the official Chinese publications of the administrative decisions); *see also* Rose, »The Tarnished Brand of CIETAC«, 145 (noting that the former subcommissions operated without official authorisation for a short time).

319 *See* Hirth and Munz, »CIETAC Schiedsvereinbarungen«, 9, 10; *see also* the ironic comment by Dresden, »Will the Real CIETAC Please Stand Up?« (*»if one new name was good, then two new names must be better«*).

320 China International Economic and Trade Administration Commission, »Announcement of 31 December 2012«.

At the same time, CIETAC objected to the continuation of the spin-offs' activities under a new name and institutional status, purporting to declare such changes »*null and void.*«[321]

SHIAC and SCIA subsequently implemented a number of reforms to underline their independence. These include the launch of SCIA's arbitration rules in December 2012,[322] new SHIAC arbitration rules published in May 2013,[323] revised with effect from May 2014[324] and again with effect from May 2015[325] and new panels of arbitrators including a large percentage of non-Chinese nationals from Taiwan, Macau and Hong Kong for both institutions and new model clauses.[326]

CIETAC reopened own offices in Shanghai and Shenzhen that may administer cases and, in the 2015 version of its rules, also assumes competence of the headquarters in Beijing over any cases submitted to subcommissions whose »*authorization has been terminated.*«[327]

b. Problems with »old« Shanghai or Shenzhen arbitration clauses

The new institutions claim to be competent on the basis of arbitration agreements referring to »*CIETAC Shanghai*« or »*CIETAC South China/Shenzhen*« respectively,[328] in particular during this transitional phase where contracts in dispute date back to a time where the subcommissions were still dependent on CIETAC (Beijing).[329]

---

321  Ibid.
322  SCIA Rules (2012).
323  SHIAC Rules (2013).
324  SHIAC Rules (2014).
325   SHIAC Rules (2015).
326  Chen, Cui, and Lui, »China - CIETAC ›Jurisdictional Turf War' Comes To An End?«
327  *See* CIETAC Rules, art. 2 (3), (6) and Appendix I (2015).
328  Hirth and Munz, »CIETAC Schiedsvereinbarungen«, 10.
329  *But see* Shanghai International Economic and Trade Arbitration Commission, »About Us« (claiming to have been »*acting as an independent arbitration institute all along*«); *see also* CIETAC Shanghai Commission and CIETAC South China Commission, »Joint Statement« (explaining CIETAC's history as a joint venture between institutions in Beijing, Shanghai and Shenzhen to »*promote the brand*« of China's foreign-related arbitration); *but cf.* Rose, »The Tarnished Brand of CIETAC«, 145 (calling this view »*revisionist*«).

This is not a major issue, if both parties agree expressly that SHIAC or SCIA shall now be competent to administer such cases submitted to them. Then, the issue of the competent institution is a »*moot point*«[330] for the parties. However, it is likely that a respondent party benefitting from the status quo would argue that whichever institution the other party approaches to commence arbitration is incompetent to handle the case.[331] Another, even more effective line of argument would be to find the arbitration clause invalid under article 18 of the Chinese arbitration law for failing to identify the competent commission.[332]

SHIAC and SCIA stress party autonomy to be the sole basis of their competence:

> »The selection of an arbitration institution through negotiation is a fundamental right of the parties; the jurisdiction of an arbitration institution over arbitration cases originates from the agreement of the parties, it is also one of the basic principles of modern commercial arbitration.«[333]

However, Chinese arbitration law is built less on the principle of party autonomy than on the traditional recognition of »*state sponsored*« arbitration by the law and government authorities.[334] If one nevertheless accepted party agreement as the basis of competence of SHIAC and SCIA in line with international standards, the existence of such agreement in favour of one of the new commissions remains doubtful, where the arbitration agreement was concluded at a time before the CIETAC split. In this respect, the creation of new arbitral institutions as spin-offs of a pre-existing institution, the dissolution and the merger of arbitral institutions all provoke similar questions: How does a change in circumstances concerning the chosen institution affect party agreement on arbitration? Is the effective interpretation of the arbitration agreement in such a case a support or a violation of party autonomy?

---

330 Dresden, »Will the Real CIETAC Please Stand Up?«; *see also* Rose, »The Tarnished Brand of CIETAC«, 174.

331 Dresden, »Will the Real CIETAC Please Stand Up?«

332 Ibid.

333 CIETAC Shanghai Commission and CIETAC South China Commission, »Joint Statement«.

334 Johnston, »The Best Providers for Asian Arbitrations«, 44; Rose, »The Tarnished Brand of CIETAC«, 175–76; *see also* Yu, »Arbitrators«, 12; *see supra* at pp. 101-104 (§4C.II.2.b.iii).

## c. Some local Chinese jurisprudence on the CIETAC split

Local courts in China have rendered divergent decisions in this regard. Some interpreted arbitration agreements mentioning the subcommissions expressly or Shanghai or Shenzhen as places of arbitration to now refer to the new commissions, others understood them to refer to CIETAC (Beijing), who continues to administer arbitrations in these provinces, and some even held such agreements to be invalid or inoperable altogether.[335]

### i. Court decisions in favour of SHIAC's or SCIA's jurisdiction

In a first decision of 14 November 2012,[336] the Intermediate People's Court of Guangdong Province in Shenzhen upheld a domestic arbitral award rendered in an arbitration administered by CIETAC's Shenzhen subcommission, which had commenced on 5 May 2012, therefore after the entering into force of the CIETAC Rules (2012) but assumingly[337] before the official independence announcement by the Shenzhen commission. The respondent challenged the award rendered on 22 August 2012 - after the rupture with the subcommissions but before CIETAC's »*suspension*« of the subcommissions' authority to administer CIETAC cases –[338] under article 58 of the Arbitration Law (P.R.C.). It alleged that the subcommission had failed to apply the CIETAC Rules (2012) and that it had not been notified in due time of the arbitration, however, the subcommission's competence to administer the case was not challenged. The Shenzhen court held that absent an agreement of the parties, the current rules of the competent arbitration commission should apply. Further finding the Shenzhen subcommission to be an independent arbitration commission, the court held the »*2005 edition*

---

335 *See generally* Bert, »CIETAC Administered Arbitrations«.
336 *Civil ruling in arbitration matter*, 2012, case no. 225 [citation in Chinese: (2012) 中法涉外仲字第225号] (P.R.C., Shenzhen IPC, Guangdong Province, 14 November 2012); excerpts in Chinese available online at South China International Economic and Trade Arbitration Commission, »SCIA Newsletter«, 2–5; *see also* Liu and von Wunschheim, »Judicial Side Effects of the CIETAC Split«, 5 (for an English summary but mentioning a different date of the decision).
337 Date unverified, *see supra* at n. 313 (p. 191).
338 *See supra* at p. 192.

*of the arbitration rules*« to be applicable to the proceedings.[339] Therewith, the Shenzhen court refers to the CIETAC Rules (2005) without reflecting the obvious contradiction between the Shenzhen commission's alleged independence from CIETAC on the one hand and the use of the rules - albeit of a former version - of CIETAC on the other hand.[340]

The Shenzhen court reiterated its pro-Shenzhen stance in a subsequent ruling of 20 November 2012.[341] This case concerned an application for the declaration of invalidity of an arbitration clause in an agency agreement referring to the »*South China subcommission*« and relating to a purchase contract containing a CIETAC arbitration clause. Arbitration proceedings had been introduced with SCIA in September 2012 around the time of the name change. Upon receiving the notice of arbitration, one of the respondents applied to the Shenzhen court to confirm that it was not bound by an arbitration agreement. However, the Shenzhen court rejected the application and held that following the name change, SCIA was the arbitration commission unambiguously designated by the arbitration agreement. Again, it seems that a lack of jurisdiction of SCIA as opposed to CIETAC was not actually put forward as a ground of invalidity or inoperability. Rather, the respondent only argued not to be a party to the relevant agreement.[342] Regarding the consequences of the CIETAC split, both Shenzhen court decisions just outlined are therefore only obiter dicta and do not present clear authority.

In contrast, lack of jurisdiction of CIETAC Shanghai following its independence declaration - but prior to its name change - was clearly argued before the Taizhou Intermediate People's Court. In its decision of 29 July 2013, the Taizhou court, granted enforcement of an award issued in the name of »*CIETAC Shanghai branch*« on 5 November 2012, rejecting the

---

339 Chinese original: »华南分会是独立的仲　机构，当事人协议将争议提交华南分会仲　即同　适用该会当 时适用的仲　规则。因此，仲庭适用2005 版《仲　规则》审理　圳市南×公司和张某之间 的纠纷符合法定程序«(»SCIA Newsletter«, 4) (translated with the help of Di Wu, law student at the University of Heidelberg).

340 *Cf. also* Liu and von Wunschheim, »Judicial Side Effects of the CIETAC Split«, 5.

341 *Civil ruling in arbitration matter*, 2012, case no. 226 [citation in Chinese: (2012)　中法涉外仲字第226号] (P.R.C., Shenzhen IPC, Guangdong Province, 20 November 2012) (here presented according to the summary by D'Agostino, »The Aftermath of the CIETAC Split«).

342 *See* D'Agostino, »The Aftermath of the CIETAC Split«.

argument that CIETAC Shanghai no longer had jurisdiction following its independence.[343] The courts rather formalistic argument that the award was issued in the name of »*CIETAC Shanghai*« as specified in the parties' contract, seems rather questionable. First, it is usually not the name of the administering institution that is important to the parties but the rules applied and the organisation and experience of the institution's staff. Second, after the declaration of independence, at least after the formal split in August 2012,[344] any issuance of awards in the name of CIETAC by the former Shanghai subcommission might even raise trademark infringement concerns.[345] However, more convincingly, the court also noted that the respondent had failed to address its jurisdictional objections to the arbitral tribunal, which were therefore precluded.[346]


ii. Court decisions against a former subcommission's jurisdiction

The Suzhou Intermediate People's Court also clearly addressed the consequence of the CIETAC split in a decision of 7 May 2013 but with a contrary outcome than the Taizhou ruling when it initially refused to enforce a domestic award rendered by CIETAC Shanghai after its declaration of independence but before the name change into SHIAC.[347] The arbitration based on two arbitration agreements referring to »*CIETAC Shanghai*« and »*CIETAC (place of arbitration: Shanghai, China)*« respectively had been commenced before CIETAC Shanghai already in 2010.

The Suzhou court held that CIETAC Shanghai, once it declared itself independent from CIETAC (Beijing) and received a registration certificate from the competent municipal authority in Shanghai, should have informed

---

343  *Civil ruling in enforcement matter*, 2013, case no. 2 [citation in Chinese: (2013) 浙台执裁字第2号] (P.R.C. Taizhou IPC, Zheijang Province, 22 May 2013) (*see* the summary by D'Agostino, »The Aftermath of the CIETAC Split«).

344  *See* China International Economic and Trade Administration Commission, »Announcement of 1 August 2012«.

345  *See infra* at pp. 308-310 (§13B.III).

346  *See* D'Agostino, »The Aftermath of the CIETAC Split«.

347  *Civil ruling in arbitration matter*, 2013, case no. 4 [citation in Chinese: (2013) 苏中商仲审字第4号] (P.R.C. Suzhou IPC, Jiangsu Province, 7 May 2013); *see* D'Agostino, »The Aftermath of the CIETAC Split«; Liu and von Wunschheim, »Judicial Side Effects of the CIETAC Split«, 9–10.

the parties to the arbitration thereof and asked for their approval of its continued administration of the case. Having failed to do so, CIETAC Shanghai as an independent commission was found to lack jurisdiction. Interestingly, although the decision supports the position of CIETAC (Beijing), it also supports the independence of SHIAC and the principle of party autonomy rather than state authorisation as the basis of jurisdiction of a Chinese arbitration commission.[348] However, the decision is no longer valid, as the Suzhou court revoked its ruling upon an order by the High Court of Jiangsu Province.[349]

A very similar decision of the Ningbo Intermediate People's Court refusing to enforce a CIETAC Shanghai award[350] shared the same fate: The decision had to be amended upon an order by the High Court of Zhejiang Province.[351] In difference to the case decided by the Suzhou court, the arbitration subject to the Ningbo court's decisions had been introduced much later, in August 2012 after CIETAC Shanghai's declaration of independence, and apparently, there was some evidence that the respondent had waived its initial objections to the subcommission's jurisdiction by participating in the proceedings.

d. The SPC's 2013 notice on the CIETAC split

The SPC first reacted to the CIETAC split on 4 September 2013 with a *Notice on Certain Issues Relating to the Correct Handling of Judicial Review of Arbitration Matters*, which was not officially published in a court bulletin or gazette but spread to municipal courts and lawyers associations.[352] According to the SPC's Notice, any court dealing with a

---

348 Rose, »The Tarnished Brand of CIETAC«, 170; Liu and von Wunschheim, »Judicial Side Effects of the CIETAC Split«, 12.

349 Liu and von Wunschheim, »Judicial Side Effects of the CIETAC Split«, 10; *see also* D'Agostino, »The Aftermath of the CIETAC Split«.

350 *Civil ruling*, [2013] Ningbo Intermediate People's Court no. 1 (P.R.C. Ningbo Intermediate People's Court, Zhejiang Province); *see* D'Agostino, »The Aftermath of the CIETAC Split«.

351 *Revised civil ruling*, [2013] Ningbo Intermediate People's Court no. 1 (P.R.C. Ningbo Intermediate People's Court, Zheijang Province); *see* D'Agostino, »The Aftermath of the CIETAC Split«; Liu and von Wunschheim, »Judicial Side Effects of the CIETAC Split«, 8–9.

352 Herein referred to as SPC's Notice on CIETAC split (2013); in English and Chinese available at: Peking University Law Department, »Notice of the

jurisdictional issue arising from the CIETAC split, whether in proceedings on the validity of arbitration agreement or regarding the setting-aside or enforcement of awards, has to refer the matter to the SPC for consultation.[353] The purpose is to ensure a consistency in the jurisprudence of the municipal courts.

e. Further guidance from the SPC: the 2015 reply

On 15 July 2015, with effect from 17 July 2015, the SPC issued a judicial interpretation (reply) binding on lower courts pursuant to which arbitration clauses referring to »*CIETAC Shenzhen*« or »*CIETAC Shanghai*« or similar should be interpreted by taking into account the date of the name change of the subcommission.[354]

Accordingly, if the arbitration agreement was concluded after the former Shanghai subcommission had declared that it would now operate under the names of SHIAC/SIETAC or, respectively, after the former Shenzhen subcommission had made it public that it would now call itself SCIA/SCCIETAC,[355] the parties are deemed to know that and refer to the newly independent centres by their new names. Apparently, according to the SPC's interpretation, the relevant dates of name change are 22 October 2012 for SCIA and 8 April 2013 for SHIAC.[356] If parties referred to CIETAC and the name of the city in their arbitration agreement concluded after these dates, this should be understood to refer to (the main) CIETAC (Beijing) in the SPC's view.[357] However, SHIAC or SCIA would have jurisdiction if the »*CIETAC Shenzhen*« or »*CIETAC Shanghai*« agreement was concluded prior to these dates - effectively assuming some sort of legal succession in favour of these centres.

---

Supreme People's Court«; *see also* Finder, »The Court's September 2013 Notice on the CIETAC Split« (criticising the lack of transparency).

353 Although not technically legislation, notices and interpretations of the SPC are respected like laws in China, *see* Ch'eng, Moser, and Wang, *International Arbitration in the People's Republic of China*, 12.

354 Here summarised according to Townsend, »New Judicial Guidance on the CIETAC Split.«

355 On the additional confusion caused by the alternative names, *see supra* at p. 192.

356 *See* Townsend, »New Judicial Guidance on the CIETAC Split.«

357 *See ibid.*

For pending cases filed with an institution prior to 17 July 2015, the interpretation installs a rule of preclusion in its second paragraph to the effect that challenges to the jurisdiction of the institution on the basis of the just mentioned interpretation rule (referred to as »*the golden rule*« by commentators)[358] should only be accepted by a court if the jurisdictional challenge was introduced to the court before the date of the first oral hearing in the arbitration. Further, the reply declares in its paragraph 3, that the interpretation rule should not serve as a ground to refuse the enforcement of awards, if the arbitration was commenced prior to 17 July 2015.[359]

Paragraph 4 then provides that if the »*same case*« was introduced with both CIETAC and SHIAC or SCIA prior to 17 July 2015, the courts may rule on interlocutory motions in accordance with the interpretation rule set up and decide which institution is competent. Failing the referral to a court prior to the first hearing, it provides that the institution that accepted the case first is competent.[360]


f. Evaluation


Overall, one can notice a pro-enforcement attitude of Chinese courts concerning awards based on old CIETAC Shanghai or Shenzhen arbitration clauses, at least of the higher courts.[361] The Suzhou and Ningbo Intermediate People's Court decisions initially denying enforcement had to be amended upon order of the respective province's High Court.[362] Remarkably, almost all cases reported prior to the SPC's clarifying interpretation concerned challenges to the enforcement of awards and not challenges to the validity or operability of the arbitration agreement pending arbitration.[363]

---

358 *E.g., see* ibid.

359 *See* ibid.

360 *See* ibid.

361 *But see* Liu and von Wunschheim, »Judicial Side Effects of the CIETAC Split«, 12 (criticising the higher courts' interventions as »*opaque*« and a »*de facto circumvention*« of the principle of finality of court rulings on award enforcement).

362 *See supra* at notes 343, 347, p. 197.

363 Except for *Civil ruling in arbitration matter*, 2012, case no. 226 [citation in Chinese: (2012)深中法涉外仲字第226号] (P.R.C., Shenzhen IPC, Guangdong Province, 20 November 2012); *see* D'Agostino, »The Aftermath of the CIETAC Split«.

However, even now, the SPC's position is not yet entirely clear, the notice issued in 2013 only set up a procedural reporting mechanism. The 2015 reply then concerns court challenges where the arbitration was commenced prior to 17 July 2015, however, it leaves a number of questions open: What actions - and at what stage of the proceedings - may be introduced in new cases, when arbitration is commenced after 17 July 2015 and accepted by either CIETAC or SCIA/SHIAC respectively in ignorance or contradiction to the »*golden rule*« rule set up by the SPC? Possibly, it is assumed that the Chinese institutions would feel bound by the SPC's interpretation just like courts so that this would not happen. Another open question is whether an award rendered by a tribunal appointed by the second institution - in contradiction to the »*first come, first serve*« rule set up by paragraph 4 of the 2015 reply - may or even should be set aside or refused enforcement even if jurisdiction was never challenged pending arbitration. And what does the SPC mean by »*the same case*«?

As time progresses since the independence declarations of SHIAC and SCIA, the initial question whether an arbitration agreement referring to the former subcommissions is capable of being performed and under the auspices of which institution it should be performed, CIETAC (Beijing) or one of the new commissions, will certainly come up more often.

To a degree, the issues raised resemble those discussed by the German jurisprudence on the fate of arbitration agreements referring to the Chamber of Foreign Trade of the GDR after the German reunification. To recall it, the BGH[364] had held that an arbitral institution performs exclusive (»*höchstpersönliche*«) duties, which cannot be transferred unilaterally to another institution. However, this jurisprudence, if applied to the CIETAC split situation, can lead both ways. Either one argues that the competences of the Shanghai or Shenzhen subcommission cannot be simply transferred to CIETAC (Beijing) following the split, or one may doubt the possibility of such transferal of competence to the newly independent institutions. With its reply of 15 July 2015, however, China's SPC indirectly accepted the transferral of old cases to SHIAC and SCIA in assuming some sort of legal succession between the former subcommissions and the new centres.

In the author's view, rather than setting a strict »*cut off*« date as done by the SPC, an interpretation of old CIETAC Shenzhen/Shanghai agreements should inquire into the hypothetic choice the parties would have made, had they already known of the CIETAC split situation at the time of concluding

---

364 Urteil [Judgment], [1994] 47 NJW 110; *see supra* at pp. 186-190 (§8C.II.1).

their arbitration agreement. Continuance in the staff handling the day-to-day administration pleads in favour of SHIAC/SCIA competence, since the parties may have chosen the respective subcommission because of a good experience with or a good reputation of their employees. On the other hand, CIETAC's historically acquired reputation,[365] a possibly greater consistency of its rules in comparison to the newer SHIAC and SCIA Rules and consistency in the CIETAC panel of arbitrators strongly support the assumption that the parties would have opted for CIETAC administered arbitration under CIETAC Rules. Given the importance of the composition of the arbitral tribunal and the specificity of the Chinese law and institutional practice of maintaining relatively fixed arbitrator panels, the latter considerations appear to outweigh the former.

In any case, mere objection to the institution who administered the case should at the outset not be sufficient to plead an irregularity in arbitral procedure or in composition of the tribunal serious enough to merit refusal of enforcement of an award already rendered.[366]

## 3. Hybrid arbitration as a solution to subsequent pathology?

To recall, the above criticism to the Singaporean decision in the case *HKL v. Rizq I* stressed that hybrid arbitration can hardly ever be considered the most effective interpretation to cure *initial* pathology of an arbitration agreement.[367]

Concerning *subsequently* pathological arbitration agreements, in particular such agreements that cannot be implemented because the chosen arbitration institution ceased to exist, one German author - Christian Wolf - suggests that such agreements should be saved by replacing the dissolved institution with another, existent institution. However, such other institution should then apply the dissolved institution's rules and perform the functions thereunder.[368]

---

365 *Cf.* Dezalay and Garth, »Merchants of Law as Moral Entrepreneurs«, 46: »[H]*istory is a key legitimator in the legal field. No one can compete with tradition without ending up underscoring that one group is a new arrival and another the established elite, akin to aristocracy*« (but there referring to the ICC Court).

366 *See infra* at pp. 476-480 (§17B).

367 *Supra* at pp. 174-177.

368 Wolf, *Die Institutionelle Handelsschiedsgerichtsbarkeit*, 199.

As noted, the DIS took this path when administering arbitration under the rules of the DAS that had been merged with the DIS.[369] This was possible because the DIS is still structured and equipped very similar to the former DAS and understands itself as the DAS' successor organisation. The same may be said about the relationship between SHIAC and SCIA to the former Shanghai and Shenzhen subcommissions of CIETAC. In these contexts, it seems feasible for the successor organisations to perform functions under the former institutions' rules.

However, *Wolf*'s proposal is not restricted to the situation that the dissolved institution has a successor organisation with similar actors. To the contrary, he considers any institution - or even an internationally experienced arbitration law firm - able to perform the functions under the chosen arbitration rules.[370] Wolf effectively proposes that an arbitration agreement, which becomes incapable of being performed due to a change in circumstances relating to the arbitral institution, should be adjusted into a hybrid arbitration agreement - without yet employing this term. Again, in line with the criticism addressed to the Singapore High Court's *HKL v. Rizq. I* ruling, such solution is impractical. While Wolf is right, that the parties' choice of institutional arbitration should be respected,[371] it is unlikely that reasonable parties who foresee the situation of a dissolution or change in status of the arbitral institution would provide that in such case another institution should apply the former institution's rules. It is much more probable - and advisable - that they would agree on a default institution *including this institution's rules*. The arbitration agreement should be adapted in accordance with the most reasonable solution. While hybrid arbitration may not be entirely impossible, it is usually unreasonable.

III. Are hybrid arbitration clauses initially or subsequently pathological?

Above overview of case law has shown that there is a general tendency to uphold arbitration agreements with problematic references to arbitral institutions. Hence, the category of »*pathological agreements*« may be misleading, in particular if used synonymously to invalid agreements. If agreements

---

369 *Zwischenentscheid*, [2010] 8 SchiedsVZ 229. *See supra* at p. 188.

370 Wolf, *Die Institutionelle Handelsschiedsgerichtsbarkeit*, 199.

371 Ibid.; unclear: Schlosser, *Das Recht der internationalen privaten Schiedsgerichtsbarkeit*, para. 444.

are described as pathological, these pathologies are often curable[372] by interpretation or court support.[373]

Therefore, one should use »*pathological*« merely as a descriptive, non-judgmental collective denominator for arbitration agreements that show some risk of inoperability that needs to be avoided or overcome by interpretation or adaptation, whether by courts, tribunals or the parties. *In that sense* and following Eisemann's criteria,[374] one can consider hybrid arbitration agreements as pathological since an increased likelihood of actions before supporting or controlling courts, jurisdictional objections before the arbitral tribunal or challenges to the award may jeopardise the functions of the arbitration agreement.[375]

Within the category of pathological agreements, cases of initial and subsequent pathology may be distinguished. Hybrid arbitration agreements show traits of both variants. At first glance, hybrid arbitration agreements display similarities to agreements accidentally referring to two different arbitral institutions, thus potentially justifying a categorisation as *initially* pathological. However, such qualification ignores that true hybrid arbitration agreements, by which parties undisputedly seek to designate one arbitral institution but another institution's rules as a matter of compromise or in view of expected cost or other advantages, as featuring in the *Insigma v. Alstom* case, are not due to a lack of care for the procedure to be followed.

Instead, the parties to such agreements consciously opted - for whatever reason - for a very specific kind of institutional arbitration. How and if such agreement is capable of being performed cannot be determined from a glance at the arbitration clause itself but only materialises once an arbitral institution is approached to administer the proceedings. It is then a matter for the parties and the designated institution to come to an understanding. Either such an agreement can be reached or the administering institution

---

372 On the distinction between curable and incurable pathologies, *see* Hochbaum, *Mißglückte internationale Schiedsvereinbarungen*, 56, 143; very vague: Davis, »Pathological Clauses«, 366, 379 (referring to »*slight*« or »*lesser*« in contrast to »*greater*« pathologies).

373 On the duty to avoid inoperability through court support, *see* Steinbrück, *Die Unterstützung ausländischer Schiedsverfahren durch staatliche Gerichte*, 76, 77 (with further references). *See also infra* at pp. 424-427 (§16A.II.1.d.iii).

374 *See supra* at p. 157.

375 *See* Davis, »Pathological Clauses«, 377 (»*Probably all four of the essential functions of the arbitration clause are placed in jeopardy by such a hybrid clause*«).

will refuse to administer the case.[376] An institution effectively declining to administer a case is unavailable just like an institution that no longer exists. Therefore, it can also be helpful to understand hybrid arbitration agreements as - potentially - *subsequently* pathological. The institution's unwillingness or incapability to apply the chosen rules is a circumstance that the parties would often not sufficiently consider when concluding a hybrid agreement.

One could possibly relate the just introduced subcategories of »*initial*« and »*subsequent*« pathology to the terms »*inoperative*« and »*incapable of being performed*« in article II (3) of the New York Convention. Some suggest that inoperativeness would refer to the subsequent expiry, termination or ceasing to have effect of the arbitration agreement while incapability of being performed applies to arbitration agreements that cannot be applied for practical, technical or legal reasons.[377] If one followed this reasoning, initial pathologies would more likely render an arbitration agreement incapable of being performed at the outset, while subsequent pathologies could render an arbitration agreement inoperative. However, overall, the distinction between »*inoperative*« and »*incapable of being performed*« appears to be more of literal than of practical nature as both defects eventually allow a state court to ignore an arbitration agreement.[378] In contrast, it is important to distinguish »*initial*« and »*subsequent*« pathologies when discussing how to avoid or overcome the verdict of inoperativeness or incapability of being performed (herein also referred to as inoperability).

For an initial pathology like an unclear or ambiguous reference to one or more arbitral institutions, effective interpretation is the method of choice to save such agreements. The relevant question is not a hypothetical. Rather, it is necessary to find out what the parties meant and wanted - not what they would have wanted - when they concluded their contract containing the arbitration clause.

In contrast, contract interpretation alone cannot save agreements by which parties initially made clear, unambiguous procedural choices that are no longer functional due to a change in circumstances. Instead, a pro-

---

376 *See infra* at pp. 232 et seq. (§11).
377 *See* Blackaby et al., *Redfern and Hunter*, para. 2.182; *cf. also* ICCA, »Ch. II«, 52, 53; with slightly contradictory examples: Tweeddale and Tweeddale, *Arbitration of Commercial Disputes*, para. 4.39, 4.44 (assuming that »*incorrectly cited*« rules would create inoperativeness while a »*vaguely worded*« arbitration agreement would be incapable of being performed).
378 *Cf.* ZPO § 1032 (1) (GER) (not separating both defects: »*oder undurchführbar*«).

arbitration approach to cases of subsequent pathology requires to ask the hypothetical question if the parties had still opted for arbitration - and what kind of arbitration and before which institution - had they expected this change in circumstances.[379] From a contractual point of view, this means to either resort to the idea of partial (in-)validity, or: partial (in-)operability, according to which an invalid or frustrated element leaves the remaining agreement untouched[380] or to adapt the arbitration agreement to the change in circumstances in line with frustration of contract principles (*clausula rebus sic stantibus*).[381]

These different approaches to cure - effective interpretation on the one hand, reduction to the operable part or contract adaptation on the other - are dictated by the principle of party autonomy. If parties exercised their autonomy through unambiguous procedural choices in favour a certain institution and identifiable rules, party autonomy requires respecting these choices without changing what the parties bargained for. This limits the room for interpretation. In contrast, if the parties failed to express a clear agreement for a certain institution or procedural rules in the first place, interpretation by arbitral tribunals and courts of such a vague or incomplete agreement would not unduly interfere with the autonomy of the parties. The risk of inoperability is therefore a factual limit to party autonomy but party autonomy also dictates how to avoid or overcome it. Inspired by but not entirely synonymous to the principle »*in favorem validitatis*«,[382] according to which courts and tribunals should seek ways to save arbitration agreements through interpretation or supporting decisions,[383] one may describe this as a »*favorem voluntatis*« principle, meaning that any solution first needs to correspond with the parties' expressed will, failing which their hypothetical will becomes relevant.[384]

---

379  A question answered negatively by the BGH in its decison concerning the dissoltuion of the Chamber of Foreign Trade of the GDR with the reunification, *see supra* at pp. 185-190 (§8C.II.1).

380  *Cf.* Draguiev, »Unilateral Jurisdiction Clauses«, 43 (suggesting to apply this concept to partially invalid unilateral arbitration clauses; with references to civil law statutes and common law case law).

381  For German law, *cf.* BGB § 313 (GER); *see* Wolf, *Die Institutionelle Handelsschiedsgerichtsbarkeit*, 198–99 (with further references).

382  *But see* Draguiev, »Unilateral Jurisdiction Clauses«, 42 (suggesting both terms to be interchangeable).

383  *See supra* at pp. 161-107 (§8B).

384  Referring back to the statement by Dumoulin cited *supra* at p. 56, n. 1.

*§9 The qualification's consequences: inadvisability and possible cure*

As used herein, the term »*hybrid*« refers to an agreed arbitration procedure combining features of the systems developed by two different arbitral institutions, it is less describing a hybrid between ad hoc and institutional arbitration. Although hybrid arbitration loses much of the predictability associated with institutional arbitration and requires a great deal of flexibility, the administering institution remains involved in the proceedings to a degree that opposes a qualification as ad hoc. To qualify hybrid arbitration as (semi-) ad hoc would not sufficiently take into account that parties obtaining an agreement of an institution to administer their arbitration, although under another institution's rules, submit to the control of such institution. At the outset, it also seems unnecessary to resort to such an artificial understanding of ad hoc arbitration in order to defend hybrid arbitration agreements. Given that institutional arbitration is at present largely unregulated,[385] there is room for the - albeit unusual - variation of hybrid arbitration even if qualified as institutional.

From a practical point of view, the history of the *Alstom–Insigma* arbitration, in particular its enforcement stage,[386] provides clear advice *not* to conclude hybrid arbitration agreements. That hybrid arbitration is inadvisable does not mean, however, that these kinds of agreements will not surface occasionally as attempts to combine advantages and eliminate disadvantages of different types of institutional arbitration. Such »*procedure shopping*« by agreement may prove unreasonably expensive,[387] but even a foolish agreement is an agreement and should be given some effect.

Above analysis of case law on pathological arbitration agreements provides a two-step answer to the question of »*how*« to uphold hybrid arbitration agreements without unduly »*rewriting*« them: First, it is necessary to interpret the parties' agreement. In particular, it is necessary to find out if they meant to apply only such provisions of the chosen rules that do not refer to the administering institution, provisions of procedure in the narrow sense.[388] Alternatively, they may expect or have expected the designated institution to perform administrative functions under the chosen rules,

---

385  *See supra* at pp. 91-106 (§4C.II.2)
386  Awards refused enforcement by *Alstom v. Insigma (Hz. IPC)*. *See infra* at pp. 480 et seq. (§17C) for a detailed discussion.
387  *Supra* at pp. 145-146 (§7B.IV).
388  *See* Cavalieros, »Note, CCI No. VB/99130, 10.04.2000«.

substituting the actors of the rules issuing institution.[389] As noted, in the *Alstom–Insigma* arbitration, SIAC first leaned towards the first, more cautious interpretation until the arbitral tribunal convinced it of the latter.[390]

Second, an issue of subsequent pathology may come up if and once the institution designated to administer the case proves incapable of performing or declines to perform services under the chosen rules. The idea of partial operability would then suggest referring the parties to either arbitration under the rules of the designated institution - striking out the unworkable rule derogation - or ad hoc arbitration - striking out the optional elements entirely. In contrast, a contract adaptation approach would allow referring the parties to another institution, preferably the one that issued the chosen rules. The more appropriate solution should be found on a case-by-case basis, depending on what was most important to the parties: the choice of administered arbitration, the choice of a certain institution or only the choice of particular rules.

---

389 The extent to which this is possible is analysed *infra* at pp. 344-400 (§14).
390 *Insigma v. Alstom*, [2009] SGCA 24 [18].

# Chapter 3: Opting-out aspect - derogation from institutional rules

An agreement on hybrid arbitration is a coin with two sides: On the one hand, parties opt out of the rules issued by the designated institution. On the other hand, they opt into the rules of another institution. Both aspects pose distinctive problems. This chapter shall first focus on the opting-out aspect, which to date has received much more attention by case law and doctrine, before the next chapter discusses the problem of opting-into the rules of another institution.

There is one main obstacle to effectively opting-out of an institution's rules: the risk that such designated institution would decline the case on that basis. Having already highlighted the quasi-regulative force of institutional practice,[1] it is prudent to first look at the positions revealed by different institutions on whether they would accept or refuse cases under modified or different rules (§10), before providing a legal analysis of an institution's right to such refusal (§11). On that basis, the relationship between the autonomy of the parties to choose *their* rules and the autonomy of the institution to determine *its* rules will be made clear (§12).

## §10 Institutions' flexibility in relation to their rules

Generally, there are some good policy reasons why arbitral institutions may be little inclined to accept major modifications of or even a complete opt-out of their rules by the parties. These reasons include:

- assurance of the quality of arbitrations held under the institutions auspices
- preservation of trust in the services of the institution
- promotion of distinctive features of the institution's own rules
- security in calculating effort and costs associated with administering the proceedings.

On the other hand, an institution not at all prepared to accept rule modifications may likely encounter the following reproaches (whether justified or not):

---

1    *Supra* at pp. 104-106 (§4C.II.2.c).

- not to respect party autonomy
- to be too bureaucratic
- to cause the parties' arbitration agreement to fail.

For this reason, most arbitral institutions show some flexibility when parties want to adjust their rules. However, flexibility depends on the designated institution's attitude in general (A), the specific rule modifications parties want to make (B) and the interests at stake (C).

## A. Institutional attitudes towards rule modifications: a case study

The following subsections shall give an overview of existing arbitral case law or statements of institutional representatives in order to characterise different institutions as to their rigorousness or leniency towards opting-out attempts by the parties.

### I. An example for the ICC's position: The Qimonda arbitration

The ICC Court is likely to reject a case if the parties want to depart from ICC Rules deemed essential[2] for the ICC's arbitration system.[3]

»[T]he attitude of the institution is not laissez-faire«.[4]

An example is the *Qimonda* case: An arbitration clause in a contract between Qimonda AG and Samsung Electronics provided for ICC arbitration to the exclusion of the ICC Court's confirmation of arbitrators and scrutiny and approval of awards.[5] After Qimonda AG's filing of insolvency and upon Samsung Electronics' request for arbitration against the liquidator Mr. Jaffé, the ICC Secretariat informed the parties that it would only administer the case and assist in the appointment of arbitrators if the parties waived the

---

2    *See infra* at pp. 219-220 (§10B.I).
3    *See* Craig, Park, and Paulsson, *ICC Arbitration*, 295, para. 16.01 (»*institutional bias of ICC arbitration*«); Schwartz, »Choosing Between Broad Clauses and Detailed Blueprints«, 111; Waincymer, *Procedure and Evidence*, para. 3.9.1 (with further references); *see also* Takla, »Non-ICC Arbitration Clauses«, 8–10 (with more examples).
4    Craig, Park, and Paulsson, *ICC Arbitration*, 1, para. 1.01.
5    *Contra* ICC Rules, art. 7 (4), 9, 27 (1998). *See infra* at p. 219-220 (§10B.I).

modifications of the ICC Rules (1998).[6] Mr. Jaffé, in his position as liquidator for Qimonda AG, refused to agree to such waiver and did not participate in the arbitrator nomination process. By letter of 10 December 2010,
the ICC Court's secretariat informed the parties of the administrative closing
of the proceedings.[7]

The case is the prime example for difficulties that may arise when parties
try to derogate from rules of the ICC Court as one of the more controlling
institutions.[8]

> »The ICC is unwilling to administer proceedings fundamentally different from its
> own basic concepts; it does not wish to lend its authority to an arbitration that does
> not allow the ICC Court to exercise its customary control.«[9]

However, the ICC Court has less problems with rule modifications that do
not relate to its own duties and powers but only to internal procedure before
the tribunal or parties' rights to apply to state courts.[10]

## II. SIAC's search for an acceptable position

SIAC's flexibility towards rule modifications by parties is difficult to assess.
One can notice the following - partially conflicting - developments. First,
SIAC changed its rules a number of times in recent years,[11] coming from a
system close to ad hoc arbitration with rules strongly resembling the UN-
CITRAL Rules to a system more and more controlling.[12] This suggests that
SIAC would now keep a strong hand on arbitrations conducted under its
auspices. SIAC's current Practice Note for UNCITRAL Cases supports this

---

6   *See Samsung Electronics v. Mr. Jaffe (Qimonda)*, [2010] Rev. Arb. 571
    (referring to the secretariat's letter of 12 October 2009).
7   Ibid., 575.
8   *See* Craig, Park, and Paulsson, *ICC Arbitration*, 41, para. 4.05 (»*super-
    vised institutional arbitration*«).
9   Ibid., 715, para. 38.08.
10  As exemplified by the ICC Court's administration of the *Kyocera* arbitra-
    tion despite parties' derogation from principle of finality of awards under
    the rules (*but cf. Kyocera*, 341 F.3d. 987, 1000 [9th Cir. 1997] - expansion
    of grounds for judicial review finally found invalid; overruling: *LaPine
    I*, 130 F.3d. 884 [9th Cir. 1997]).
11  The latest revision was launched in August 2016.
12  *See* Wegen and Barth, »Die neue Schiedsgerichtsordnung des SIAC«, 88
    (already making this observation for the SIAC Rules [2007]).

assumption since it effectively allows SIAC to closely control even arbitrations facilitated under ad hoc rules.

However, the available case law portrays a contrary development from a very rigid stance towards more flexibility. Concerning the arbitration clause underlying *Bovis Lend v. Jay-Tech*,[13] SIAC did not allow an outside appointing authority to step in, expressing the view that parties could not derogate from its rules at all, as it was at the time even expressly stipulated in SIAC's domestic arbitration rules.[14] A short while later, regarding the *Alstom–Insigma* arbitration,[15] SIAC's position changed to the opposite extreme, when it agreed to administer an arbitration under a completely different set of rules, the ICC Rules (1998).

About the motives for this change in position, one may only speculate:

- The *Alstom–Insigma* arbitration, in contrast to the *Bovis Lend–Jay-Tech* case, was international, arguably demanding more deference to party autonomy.
- The *Alstom–Insigma* arbitration was more lucrative, economically arguing in favour of accepting it.
- The Singapore High Court had disapproved of SIAC's lack of flexibility in *Bovis Lend v. Jay–Tech*.[16]

The latter, presumed motive for adopting a more flexible approach - obedience with local court authority - cannot be seriously criticised and the Singapore courts' subsequent jurisprudence certainly encourages SIAC to continue accepting rules modifications by the parties. Whether SIAC would again go so far to administer arbitrations under different institutional rules is another matter, relating to the opting-in aspect of hybrid arbitration.[17]

III. CIETAC's apparent position

CIETAC is said to be willing to administer cases under modified rules or even a completely different set of rules of another institution, as now clarified in article 4 (3) of the CIETAC Rules (2012 and 2015). Chinese author

---

13   *Bovis Lend v. Jay-Tech*, [2005] SGHC 91; *see supra* at pp. 154-156 (§7C.IV.2).
14   SIAC Domestic Rules, art. 1.5 (2002).
15   *See supra* at pp. 35-39.
16   *See supra* at p. 155.
17   *See infra* at Chapter 4, pp. 272 et seq.

Tao Jingzhou even takes the view that this was the only approach in line with international practice:

>>For example, prior to 1998, all disputes submitted to the CIETAC for arbitration were conducted pursuant to the rules of the CIETAC. This practice conflicted with international practice, which generally permits the parties to select not merely the applicable law, but also the procedural rules that will govern the arbitration.<<[18]

Although there are no reported cases, the Vice Chairman of CIETAC, Yu Jianlong, answered an interview question by Michael Moser as follows:

>>Mr. Moser: The Rules also allow the parties to agree to conduct arbitrations in China under rules other than the CIETAC Rules. Has this happened yet?

Mr. Yu: Yes. I think an agreement for such a procedure is usually a compromise between the Chinese party and the foreign party. CIETAC will in no way act against the principle of party autonomy, so long as the selected rules are neither inoperative nor contradictory to the mandatory provisions of the lex arbitri.<<[19]

## IV. The LCIA's flexibility proven in the Softwood Lumber Arbitrations

The LCIA's administration of the highly political and prominent dispute between the United States and Canada over trade duties and regulations concerning softwood lumber (the so-called *»Softwood Lumber Arbitrations«*) demonstrates that flexibility concerning the modification of institutional rules can be an important competitive advantage. In the Softwood Lumber Agreement (cited as *»SLA«*), the United States and Canada agreed to resort to LCIA administered arbitration to the exclusion of the dispute settlement mechanisms available under the WTO and NAFTA Agreements.[20]

Under the Softwood Lumber Agreement, the parties agreed on a considerable number of modifications of the LCIA Rules (1998), notably:

- They modified article 21 so that all experts shall be party-appointed rather than tribunal-appointed.[21]
- They changed article 5 (5) so that the LCIA Court shall *»endeavour«* to appoint the co-arbitrators to be nominated by each party and the

---

18  Tao, *Arbitration Law and Practice in China*, para. 348.
19  Moser and Jianlong, >>CIETAC and Its Work<<, 562.
20  *See* SLA, art. XIV (2), (6).
21  Ibid., art. XVI (6).

chairperson nominated by the co-arbitrators within five days from their nomination.[22]

- The arbitral tribunal was obliged to endeavour to render the award within 180 days from appointment.[23]
- Derogating from the default rule in article 28 (2), the arbitral tribunal was not supposed to render an award on costs.[24]
- The parties excluded the confidentiality obligation in article 30 in favour of transparency of matters of public interest.[25]

These modifications pay tribute to the fact that the Softwood Lumber Arbitrations concern public international trade law rather than commercial matters for which the LCIA Rules are designed. One of the more critical modifications was certainly the obligation of the LCIA Court to appoint the arbitral tribunal as nominated within five days. Since the LCIA Court was itself not a party to the Softwood Lumber Agreement, the parties could not have been sure of their agreement being operable.[26] This is probably the reason why the parties, well advised, formulated this aspect very carefully as a best-endeavours obligation only. The arbitrations then proceeded without encountering any administrative obstacles. Redacted versions of the awards rendered and submissions and exhibits are publicly available.[27]

However, despite the flexibility evidenced by the Softwood Lumber Arbitrations,[28] the LCIA would probably not accept a complete derogation of its rules in favour of other *institutional* rules - as opposed to UNCITRAL Rules[29] - as will be further explained in the next chapter about the problems relating to the opting-in aspect of hybrid arbitration.

---

22  Ibid., art. XIV (11).
23  Ibid., art. XIV (19).
24  Ibid., art. XIV (21).
25  Ibid., art. XIV (16)–(18).
26  *See* Turner, *A Guide to the LCIA Arbitration Rules*, para. 1.52.
27  *See* Department of Foreign Affairs, Trade and Development Canada, »Softwood Lumber - Dispute Settlement« (for all case materials).
28  »*Maximum flexibility for parties and tribunals to agree on procedural matters*« is also celebrated as first advantage on the LCIA's website (LCIA, »LCIA Arbitration«).
29  *See* LCIA, »LCIA Services in Ad Hoc Proceedings«; *see generally* Gerbay, »The LCIA«, para. 4–21, *see also supra* at pp. 147-150 (§7C.I, II) on appointing authority and other services under UNCITRAL Rules.

V. A recall of the »ICC 500« case to indicate the AAA-ICDR's position

Although perceived as little controlling, there are some limitations as to which derogations from its rules the AAA-ICDR would accept, as evidenced by the application filed with it referring to »*The American Arbitration Association or to any other U.S. court*« and »*the Rules and Regulations of the International Chamber of Commerce (ICC 500)*.«[30] As noted, the AAA-ICDR refused to administer these proceedings because it found the application of ICC Rules incompatible with AAA-ICDR arbitration.[31] This case evidences that the AAA-ICDR would not habitually accept arbitrations under other institutional rules, despite a few authors claiming in a very general way, without citing case references and without duly distinguishing between UNCITRAL Rules and institutional rules, that

> »AAA and the LCIA [would] also administer arbitrations using rules other than their own.«[32]

It appears decisive whether modifications are compatible with AAA-ICDR arbitration, a complete opt-out in favour of ICC Rules is certainly not.

VI. Recall of the DIS/DAS awards

As mentioned, two DIS-appointed *tribunals* showed some flexibility in 2010 when assuming jurisdiction under agreements relating to the DIS' predecessor, the DAS.[33] Here, however, the emphasis is on *tribunals* as it remains entirely unclear which position the DIS as an *institution* took in this respect, if any. Apparently, the DAS Rules were so similar to the then

---

30  *See supra* at pp. 181-184 (§8C.I.3.b).
31  *See* the Petitioner-Appellant's brief in *ISC v. Nobel Biocare Investments*, 351 Fed. Appx. at 4, 5; *cf. also X Holding AG, X Management S.A., A & B v. Y Investments N.V.*, 4 A 279/2010 (CH BG, 25 October 2010) (under A); *reported by* Girsberger and Ruch, »Pathological Arbitration Clauses«, 124.
32  Greenblatt and Griffin, »Towards the Harmonization of International Arbitration Rules«, 108, 109; *see also* Waincymer, *Procedure and Evidence*, 194, para. 3.9.2, n. 224; all referring imprecisely to Freyer, »Practical Considerations in Drafting Dispute Resolution Provisions«, 15 (stating that AAA and LCIA »*will now administer arbitrations using the UNCITRAL Rules*«).
33  *See supra* at p. 188.

current DIS Rules that a real issue concerning the administrative aspects of the arbitration did not arise.

As further elaborated in the next chapter, the DIS Rules are some of the least controlling, being very similar to ad hoc rules like the UNCITRAL Rules and giving the institution hardly any influence on the arbitration. This, of course, makes it easy for the DIS to react flexibly to opting-out attempts by the parties, as these will often not dramatically influence its own position.[34]

VII. The approach of one Swiss cantonal chamber of commerce

In an interesting decision, the Swiss Federal Supreme Court confirmed an interim decision (partial award) on jurisdiction[35] rendered by a tribunal appointed under the auspices of the Zurich Chamber of Commerce - prior to the founding of the Swiss Chambers' Arbitration Institution. The case concerned potentially conflicting references to three different sets of arbitration rules.[36] The arbitration agreement provided that all disputes should be finally

»[…] settled under the Rules of Conciliation and Arbitration of the Zurich Chamber of Commerce, Zurich/Switzerland, in accordance with the UNCITRAL Arbitration Rules. The number of arbitrators shall be three (3). ICC shall be the appointing authority acting in accordance with the rules adopted by ICC for that purpose.«

The Zurich Chamber of Commerce (hereinafter »ZCC«), different from what might have been the approach of the ICC or the AAA-ICDR in view of above cases,[37] had not refused to administer the arbitration entirely but had simply chosen to ignore the deviation from its rules with respect to arbitrator appointment. The President of the ZCC had appointed the chairman of the tribunal from a permanent list who had then appointed the co-arbitrators from a list of four provided by the President of the ZCC in line with

---

34  On the other hand, applying another, more controlling institution's rules - the opting-in aspect, *infra* at pp. 344-400 (§14) - would be a greater obstacle to DIS administered hybrid arbitration, since the DIS is not prepared to exercise far-reaching powers.

35  On the question if pure jurisdictional decisions can be considered awards, *see infra* at pp. 409-412 (§16A.I.4).

36  *S.A. AG v. B. NV*, [2003] ATF 130 III 66 (C.H. BG); *see also* Born, *Cases and Materials (2011)*, 289–92 (English translation of excerpts of the decision).

37  *See supra* at pp. 210 and 215-215 (§10A.I, V).

articles 11 (2) and 12 (4) of the ZCC Rules (1989).[38] The respondent party had later raised a jurisdictional challenge with the arbitral tribunal, which had been rejected.

Upon respondent's appeal claiming an irreconcilable conflict between arbitral rules, the Swiss Federal Supreme Court upheld this decision finding that - referring to good faith and effective interpretation principles - the primarily applicable ZCC Rules were to be complemented by the UNCITRAL Rules.[39] Concerning the constitution of the arbitral tribunal the court found that there was a potential conflict of jurisdiction as the ICC Rules provide for a different constitution procedure.[40] It deemed an appointment by the ICC Court impossible in institutional, non-ICC arbitration[41] and hence approved of the ZCC's disregard of the reference to ICC appointment:

>»[E]ine am Zweck der Vereinbarung orientierte Streichung der unmöglichen Er-nennungsbestimmung zu Gunsten der prioritären ZHK-Schiedsordnung [ist] durch-aus vertretbar [...].«[42]

>[Having regard to the purpose of the arbitration agreement, simply deleting the impossible appointment provision in favour of the ZCC Arbitration Rules, which enjoy contractual priority, is by all means reasonable.][43]

This case illustrates that in the interest of efficiency it could seem a practical option for an institution to accept a case despite feeling unable to attend completely to the parties' agreement and to proceed with the appointment

---

38  *S.A. AG v. B. NV*, [2003] ATF 130 III 68.

39  Ibid., 72 (at consid. 3.3). Translation adapted from Born, *Cases and Materials (2011)*, 291.

40  *S.A. AG v. B. NV*, [2003] ATF 130 III 73 (at consid. 3.3.), *see also* ibid. (at consid. 3.3.3.: »*Die beiden Ordnungen sind jedenfalls insoweit inkompatibel, als das konkrete Schiedsgericht nur einer der beiden Institutionen angehören kann*«; *cf.* the translation by Born, *Cases and Materials (2011)*, 289: »*The two regimes are thus incompatible insofar as the arbitration can only belong to one of the two institutions*«).

41  *S.A. AG v. B. NV*, [2003] ATF 130 III 74 (at consid. 3.3.3). Whether the ICC Court might act as appointing authority in institutional cases depends on how ICC Appointing Authority Rules, art. 1 (1), 4 (1), 5 (2) (2004) are interpreted.

42  The court further considered objections to the constitution of the arbitral tribunal to be precluded due to the respondent's non-reaction to the arbitral tribunal's notification of an »*order of constitution*« within a set time limit (*S.A. AG v. B. NV*, [2003] ATF 130 III 75–76 [at consid. 4.3]).

43  Translation adapted from Born, *Cases and Materials (2011)*, 292.

of the arbitral tribunal in accordance with its own rules, ignoring the derogation therefrom.[44]

The case is no clear authority on how the Swiss Chambers' Arbitration Institution, of which the ZCC now forms part, would react to modifications of its rules in general since it mainly raised issues of opting-into another institution's rules, here the ICC Rules, and potential inoperability of the procedural agreement arising therefrom.[45] Nevertheless, one may assume on the basis of this example case that the Swiss Chambers' would have reservations about any procedural agreement to opt out of essential features of the Swiss Rules for fear of inefficiency.

## B. A focus on essential (»mandatory«) institutional rules

The normative analysis provided by Chapter 1, underlined by the conceptual discussion of institutional arbitration in Chapter 2, contested the following kind of statement *in theory*:

> »[T]he mandatory rules established by the arbitration institution [...] constitute [...] procedural provisions by which the parties to an arbitration proceeding as well as their arbitral tribunal are absolutely bound.«[46]

Nevertheless, as the previous overview suggests, many institutions do not accept major derogations from their rules *in practice* - and have good reasons not to - in particular, when it comes to protecting features deemed essential. Accordingly, arbitration rules may be factually »*mandatory*.« Parties that do not want to risk that their arbitration agreement becomes incapable of being performed or that it can only be performed with a high number of adjustments should be aware of those rules whose derogation the issuing institution would likely object to.

As this risk is only a factual rather than a legal constraint to party autonomy, it seems more appropriate to speak of rules deemed »*essential*« by the institution instead of »*mandatory*« rules. The more rules an institution considers essential the less likely would it agree to administer hybrid arbitrations, in particular when the rules chosen by the parties differ considerably with regard to such essential elements. Unfortunately, institutional rules,

---

44  For the corresponding contractual analysis, *see infra* at pp. 263 et seq. (§11B.IV).

45  Discussed in detail in Chapter 4, *infra* at pp. 344-400 (§14).

46  Sandrock, »How Much Freedom Should an International Arbitrator Enjoy?«, 41.

similar to national laws, are not always self-explaining in this respect. They contain a »*no man's land*«[47] of rules of which parties are neither expressly permitted to nor not allowed to contract out of.[48] It is only sure, that all institutions will consider their administrative fee provisions and schedules essential. Like for almost every contract, the price is one of the *essentialia negotii*. Accordingly, the designated institution would usually not comprehend a hybrid arbitration agreement as derogation from its administrative fee scheme.[49] The following subsections describe the difficulty of identifying other possible essential rules of various institutions.

## I. Essential ICC Rules

The most commonly mentioned examples of essential institutional arbitration rules relate to ICC arbitration. The reason for this is not only the international importance of the ICC Rules and consequential familiarity of lawyers and scholars with them but also the ICC Court's reputation for being more controlling than other institutions.[50] Moreover, article 19 (1) of the ICC Rules tries to establish a preference of the ICC Rules over party agreements, allowing the latter only »*where the Rules are silent.*«

Most importantly, the ICC Court sees in its own the administration of the arbitration, as now regulated in article 6 (2) of the ICC Rules, an essential principle that cannot be derogated from.[51] However, logically, this can only become relevant if a party files a request for arbitration with the ICC Court despite an indication in the arbitration agreement that the ICC Court should not administer the arbitration.[52]

Doctrine further regards the Court's power to scrutinise draft awards, the need to draw up Terms of Reference and the requirement of a reasoned award as essential features of ICC arbitration.[53]

---

47  Schöldström, *The Arbitrator's Mandate*, 415.
48  Viewed critically by Kreindler, »Impending Revision of the ICC Arbitration Rules«, 56.
49  *Cf. Insigma v. Alstom*, [2009] SGCA 24 [9].
50  See *supra* at p. 210 (§10A.I); *see also* Waincymer, *Procedure and Evidence*, 195, para. 3.9.2.
51  Bassiri, »Art. 6 ICC SchO«, para. 53, 56.
52  *See also supra* at pp. 152-154 (§7C.IV.1).
53  *See e.g.* Schäfer, Verbist, and Imhoos, *Die ICC Schiedsgerichtsordnung in der Praxis*, 107–8; Craig, Park, and Paulsson, *ICC Arbitration*, 295, para. 16.01; Waincymer, *Procedure and Evidence*, para. 3.9.1; Landolt,

On the other hand, the ICC Rules undeniably also accord parties a great deal of flexibility. They can freely choose the place of arbitration,[54] the language,[55] the applicable law[56] and the method for constituting the arbitral tribunal.[57] These liberties follow directly from the wording of the rules.[58] Nevertheless, one should even regard such advance approvals of party derogations with caution. *E.g.,* under article 11 (6) of the ICC Rules, the ICC Court accepts if parties agree on a specific method for *nominating* arbitrators, for example by applying an UNCITRAL-type list procedure.[59] In contrast, the ICC Court is less inclined to accept any derogation from the requirement of Court *appointment* or *confirmation* of all arbitrators[60] as evidenced by the ICC Court's refusal to administer the *Qimonda* arbitration.[61]

II. Essential SIAC Rules

In light of SIAC's administration of the *Alstom–Insigma* arbitration under ICC Rules, one could assume that SIAC adopted a policy of utmost flexibility with respect to party derogations from its rules.[62] However, when taking a closer look, this conclusion does not impose itself. It has to be kept in mind that the ICC Rules (1998) applied in the *Alstom–Insigma* arbitration accorded SIAC, once it decided to substitute its organs for those of the ICC Court, the same if not greater control over the arbitration than it would have had applying the SIAC Rules then in force. Accepting to administer the arbitration under ICC Rules was therefore not connected to giving up any

---

»Antitrust Arbitration under the ICC Rules«, 1813, n. 368 (*»quasi mandatory«*; *»not certain whether the arbitrating parties can contract out of it«*); *see generally* Takla, »Non-ICC Arbitration Clauses«, 8–10.

54  ICC Rules, art. 18 (1) (2012; 2017).
55  Ibid., art. 20.
56  Ibid., art. 21 (1).
57  Ibid., art. 11 (6).
58  *See also* Schäfer, Verbist, and Imhoos, *Die ICC Schiedsgerichtsordnung in der Praxis*, 106–7.
59  *Cf.* UNCITRAL Rules, art. 8 (2) (2010).
60  *See* ICC Rules, art. 12 (3)–(5), 13 (2012; 2017).
61  *See Samsung Electronics v. Mr. Jaffe (Qimonda)*, [2010] Rev. Arb. 572. *See also supra* at pp. 210-215 (§10A.I).
62  *See supra* at pp. 210-212 (§10A.I)

privileges.[63] SIAC may have worried about increased responsibilities and additional workload but not about a lack of influence. The case therefore does not give a sufficient indication on whether SIAC would be open to all modifications of its rules, including those that would reduce its own involvement. Moreover, SIAC changed its rules significantly since the *Alstom–Insigma* arbitration. That the SIAC Rules are now more comparable to ICC Rules concerning the degree of institutional supervision implies that SIAC, whose personnel has also undergone changes, might now also take a more restrictive view concerning derogating party agreements, similar to that of the ICC Court.

Unfortunately, the SIAC Rules itself are not explicit in this respect. Article 1 (1) only provides that

> »[w]here parties have agreed to refer their disputes to SIAC for arbitration, the parties shall be deemed to have agreed that the arbitration shall be conducted and administered in accordance with these [SIAC] Rules [subject to any] mandatory provision of the applicable law of the arbitration.«

If and to what extent the parties may or may not derogate from the SIAC Rules is unclear. However, it is instructive to look again at the SIAC Practice Note on UNCITRAL Cases. The directives therein, which SIAC applies when providing facilitation services in arbitrations under UNCITRAL Rules, highlight which aspects of its own rules SIAC deems to be essential for effective administrative work. Therein, SIAC insists on the President's right to appoint arbitrators in accordance with the SIAC Rules should the UNCITRAL list procedure be inappropriate[64] and on controlling all financial aspects of the proceedings including the fixing and collection of advances and the fixing of the arbitrators' fees in accordance with the SIAC schedule.[65] Given that SIAC purports to apply these aspects of its rules even when the parties have chosen UNCITRAL rather than SIAC Rules, it is very likely that SIAC would also not welcome parties to modify SIAC Rules concerning these issues.

However, in contrast to the ICC Court, SIAC does not seem to consider its right to scrutinise awards as fundamental and non-derogatory. The Practice Note on UNCITRAL Cases provides that before issuing an award a tribunal »*may*« submit it in draft form to the Registrar,[66] giving the tribunal

---

63   *See already supra* at pp. 129-131 (§7A.III) and pp. 157-157 (§7D), rejecting a qualification as »*ad hoc*« for these reasons.

64   SIAC Practice Note for UNCITRAL Cases, para. 8 (2014).

65   Ibid., para. 12–31.

66   Ibid., para. 34.

discretion to use this service or not. Accordingly, the parties, whose agreements on procedure bind the tribunal in principle,[67] can exclude this option. In light of this, it is unlikely that SIAC would refuse administering arbitration under SIAC Rules only because parties exclude article 28 (2) - despite the imperative language of its last sentence:

> »No award *shall* be made by the Tribunal until it has been approved by the Registrar as to its form [*emphasis added*].«

This rule intends to protect the parties by limiting the powers of the arbitral tribunal and not to restrict party autonomy in favour of institutional control.

III. Essential CIETAC Rules

CIETAC Rules used to be subject to criticism for lacking recognition of party autonomy.[68] However, to compete successfully in an increasingly international market, CIETAC progressively allows parties' to make their own procedural choices.[69] CIETAC now lists »*Party Autonomy*« as first advantage of arbitration on its website.[70] When parties have agreed on CIETAC Rules, it is neither compulsory to conduct proceedings in Chinese nor to choose arbitrators from the CIETAC panel.[71] In principle, although this is uncommon in practice, parties could even agree on CIETAC arbitration seated outside mainland China.[72]

As pointed out, CIETAC Rules (2012 and 2015) now also allow the choice of a complete set of different rules. Since the revision of 2005, the requirement of an express approval of any modifications or choice of different rules by the CIETAC Commission does no longer exist.[73]

---

67  *See supra* at pp. 116-122 (§5C, D)
68  Tao, »CIETAC Rules Art. 4«, 519, para. 3–4.
69  *See* Born, *International Arbitration and Forum Selection Agreements*, 55.
70  China International Economic and Trade Administration Commission, »Advantages of Arbitration«.
71  *Cf.* CIETAC Rules, art. 24 (2), 28 (2012) = art. 26 (2), 28 (2015).
72  *See also* Brock and Feldman, »Recent Trends in the Conduct of Arbitrations«, 180 (but assuming that this could currently only apply to Hong Kong, where the first CIETAC subcommission outside mainland China is based); *cf.* China International Economic and Trade Administration Commission, »Home« (for further information of CIETAC's Hong Kong branch) and CIETAC Rules, art. 73 et seq. (ch. VI) (2015).
73  Tao, »CIETAC Rules Art. 4«, 519, para. 3–4.

Article 4 (3) of the CIETAC Rules stresses that the parties' agreement shall prevail over the rules only subject to mandatory *law* (not: rules).

Nevertheless and despite the wording of article 4 (3), one author finds it »*evident*« that not all CIETAC Rules may be modified, regrettably, without further specifications.[74] In contrast, another author stresses that

> »[f]ull effect is given to the parties' chosen arbitration rules, except where such an agreement is inoperative or in conflict with the Lex Arbitri«

and that such choice »no longer depends on the CIETAC's consent.«[75]

Article 13 (1) of the CIETAC Rules underlines this by providing that CIETAC shall accept a case in accordance with an arbitration agreement providing that disputes are to be referred to arbitration by CIETAC. This provision does not confer any discretion to CIETAC to refuse a case because of modifications to its rules. Articles 13 (1) and 4 (3) of the CIETAC Rules therefore extend CIETAC's offer to administer arbitrations also to cases where parties modified CIETAC Rules.[76] However, no one would deny that CIETAC could still refuse a case if parties imposed additional duties on CIETAC not contemplated by its rules and fee structure or if the parties tried to modify fee rules to CIETAC's disadvantage.

In any case, all modifications of standard CIETAC practice require an express written agreement by the parties and thus special care in drafting.[77] Moreover, it is entirely unclear how CIETAC would accommodate rule modifications in practice. In light of - unverified - reports on excessive factual influence by the institution's staff on award making,[78] it is not excluded that CIETAC could formally accept arbitration under less-controlling rules, *e.g.* UNCITRAL Rules, but would nevertheless exercise its usual supervision and, *e.g.* scrutinise awards possibly even without parties noticing. Instead of entering into an argument with the parties by insisting on applying rules granting it certain powers, CIETAC might possibly just exercise such powers anyway.

---

74  Lu, »The New CIETAC Arbitration Rules of 2012«, 314.

75  Tao, *Arbitration Law and Practice in China*, para. 599.

76  *See infra* at pp. 244-245 (§11A.III.1) on the prevailing and here preferred theory that the institution's offer to administer arbitrations is made to the public.

77  Born, *International Arbitration and Forum Selection Agreements*, 56.

78  Discussed *infra* at pp. 384-386 (§14B.VI).

IV. Essential LCIA Rules

>»The LCIA is known for its ›light-touch‹ approach. This approach seeks to give the parties and the tribunal maximum flexibility«[79]

However, slight changes to article 14 of the LCIA Rules indicate that the LCIA may now be more reserved towards party modifications of its rules than prior to the 2014 revision. Moreover, there is some uncertainty to which extent the proclaimed »*principle of overriding party autonomy*«,[80] if still valid, would apply to administrative aspects.

1. Party autonomy under article 14 of the LCIA Rules (1998)

The LCIA Rules (1998) were widely understood to stress the importance of party agreements on procedure more than any other arbitration rules.[81] The emphasis on party autonomy in article 14 has been labelled as the »*Magna Charta*« of the LCIA Rules (1998):[82]

>»The parties may agree on the conduct of their arbitral proceedings *and they are encouraged to do so* [...].«[83]

The way it is phrased, this provision expected parties to agree on the conduct of their proceedings individually. Moreover, party agreements expressly restricted the arbitrators' discretion pursuant to article 14 (2) of the LCIA Rules (1998) (»*Unless otherwise agreed by the parties*«), overruled only by the tribunal's duties to respect »*natural justice and procedural fairness*« and to avoid »*unnecessary delay and expense.*«[84]

---

79  Gerbay, »The LCIA«, para. 4–39.
80  On the LCIA Rules (1998), *see* Turner, *A Guide to the LCIA Arbitration Rules*, para. 1.41.
81  *Cf.* Nesbitt, »LCIA Arbitration Rules, Introductory Remarks«, 401 (listing this emphasis as a distinguishing feature).
82  Turner, *A Guide to the LCIA Arbitration Rules*, para. 1.41; *referring to:* Veeder, »London Court of International Arbitration - The New 1998 LCIA Rules«, 367.
83  LCIA Rules, art. 14 (1) (1998).
84  Ibid., art. 14.1 (i), (ii); *see also* Turner, *A Guide to the LCIA Arbitration Rules*, 1.42.

## 2. Revisions introduced by the LCIA Rules (2014)

Surprisingly, the LCIA Rules (2014) confine the previously celebrated reign of party autonomy, now only providing in their article 14 (2):

>»The parties *may* agree on joint proposals for the conduct of their arbitration for consideration by the Arbitral Tribunal. They are *encouraged to do so in consultation with the Arbitral Tribunal* and consistent with the Arbitral Tribunal's general duties under the Arbitration Agreement [*emphasis added*].«

The slight changes in sentence structure now indicate that the »*encouragement*« relates only to the consultation with the tribunal rather than agreements on procedure. Moreover, article 14 (5) of the LCIA Rules now attempts to place the tribunal's discretion above the autonomy of the parties, no longer containing the caveat »*Unless otherwise agreed.*«[85] These changes appear to be not merely editorial but rather seem to indicate a much greater emphasis on efficiency, possibly to the detriment of procedural flexibility for the parties.[86]

## 3. General restrictions to modify powers of the institution

Generally, it is unclear whether article 14 of the LCIA Rules (both in the 1998 and 2014 version) also applies to agreements on the tasks, rights and powers of the LCIA institutional organs. The fact that the article, next to addressing party autonomy, only mentions duties, powers and discretion of the arbitral tribunal suggests that »*conduct*« of the arbitral proceedings means the proceedings in the stricter sense only, like rules on submissions, hearings and evidence. Party autonomy concerning administrative aspects of arbitration procedure, like the appointment of arbitrators, challenges and other tasks of the LCIA Court and its Registrar may not be subject to this rule at all.[87] The systematic context of article 14 of the LCIA Rules backs

---

85    *Compare* LCIA Rules, art. 14 (2), (5) (2014) *with* LCIA Rules, art. 14 (1)–(2) (1998). *But see supra* at pp. 116-122 (§5C, §5D) (generally rejecting such order of preference).

86    *Cf.* Gerbay, »The LCIA«, para. 4–64 (expecting a balance »*between the two principles of flexibility (a corollary of the autonomy of the parties) and speed*«).

87    *But see* Greenblatt and Griffin, »Towards the Harmonization of International Arbitration Rules«, 108 (assuming »*complete autonomy*« of the parties without differentiation).

this understanding, being placed after the rules on the constitution of the arbitral tribunal.

Undeniably, limits to party autonomy by administrative powers under the LCIA Rules are less noticeable than under the ICC Rules. However, this is less a consequence of an emphasis of the LCIA Rules on party autonomy but rather owed to the fact that the LCIA Court does generally not exercise the same degree of supervision as the ICC Court. Elements like the scrutiny of Terms of Reference or awards, compulsory in ICC arbitration,[88] are unknown to the LCIA Rules, which renders the question moot if the parties could exclude such controlling features.[89]

However, a question that may come up under LCIA Rules just like under ICC Rules[90] is the possibility of restricting the respective Courts' power to appoint or confirm all arbitrators, including the party-nominated arbitrators. Article 5 (7) of the LCIA Rules (2014) states:

>»the LCIA Court alone is empowered to appoint arbitrators (albeit taking into account any written agreement or joint nomination by the parties).«[91]

If parties wished to exclude this requirement in general, this might not be accepted, even if the prospective arbitrators' impartiality and independence were not at issue.[92] A commentator remarks that the

>»LCIA's insistence that it alone is empowered to appoint an arbitrator, rejecting where appropriate the nominations of the parties, goes back at least as far as the 1915 edition of the LCIA rules.«[93]

---

88  *See supra* at pp. 219-220 (§10B.I).
89  *Contra* Turner, *A Guide to the LCIA Arbitration Rules*, para. 1.41.
90  *See supra* at pp. 210-215 (§10A.I) on the ICC Court's refusal to administer an arbitration where parties tried to exclude both scrutiny of the award and confirmation of party-nominated arbitrators, leading to *Samsung Electronics v. Mr. Jaffe (Qimonda)*, [2010] Rev. Arb. 571.
91  *See also* LCIA Rules, art. 5 (5) (1998).
92  On impartiality of party-appointed arbitrators *see generally:* Paulsson, »Are Unilateral Appointments Defensible?«; by the same author: »Moral Hazard in International Dispute Resolution«; Mourre, »Are Unilateral Appointments Defensible? On Jan Paulsson's Moral Hazard in International Arbitration«; Brower and Rosenberg, »The Death of the Two-Headed Nightingale«; Jiménez-Blanco and Iturmendi, »Los Llamados ›Árbitros de Parte.‹«
93  Nesbitt, »LCIA Arbitration Rules, Art. 5, Formation of the Arbitral Tribunal«, para. 9.

In contrast, to its proclaimed »*light touch*« in general,[94] the LCIA »*retains an extremely firm hand*« on the appointment of arbitrators.[95] If parties insisted on excluding LCIA appointment in advance, sacrificing the LCIA's ability to refuse arbitrators it deems not sufficiently independent or impartial or otherwise unsuitable, the LCIA Court might therefore refuse administering the case.[96] However, reports on cases where this happened are not known here.[97]

### V. Essential AAA-ICDR Rules

Article 1 (1) of the AAA-ICDR Rules highlights the general respect of party autonomy by providing that rules apply »*subject to modifications that the parties may adopt in writing.*«

The systematic position of this proviso in the first article of the rules suggests that such modifications can be agreed pertaining to all aspects of the AAA-ICDR Rules, including those concerning the administrative powers and duties of the AAA-ICDR.[98] It indicates that there are no limits to party autonomy under the AAA-ICDR Rules except for mandatory law.[99] By including such provision, the AAA-ICDR has certainly limited its discretion to reject cases because of modifications to the rules.[100]

However, it is noteworthy that the latest revision of the AAA-ICDR Rules weakened the emphasis on party autonomy. Under article 1 (a) of the AAA-ICDR (2009) Rules, parties were expressly allowed to agree on »*whatever*« modifications in writing. Based on this wording, one might have easily drawn the conclusion that the AAA-ICDR would consider none of its rules so essential - or a »*core characteristic*« - that it would refuse to

---

94   *See* Gerbay, »The LCIA«, para. 4–39.
95   Veeder, »London Court of International Arbitration - The New 1998 LCIA Rules«, 367.
96   *See generally* Nesbitt, »LCIA Arbitration Rules, Art. 1, The Request for Arbitration«, para. 6.
97   *See also supra* at pp. 213-210 (§10A.IV) on the Softwood Lumber Arbitrations where the LCIA Court exceptionally accepted a »*best-endeavors*« obligation to appoint all arbitrators as nominated, restricting its right to refuse appointment.
98   *Cf.* AAA-ICDR Rules, art. 1 (3), 39 (2014).
99   AAA-ICDR Rules, art. 1 (2) (2009).
100   Derains and Schwartz, *A Guide to the ICC Rules*, 8.

administer the arbitration if the rule was modified.[101] Obviously, the AAA-ICDR, similar to the LCIA as evidenced by its latest rule revisions,[102] realised that in the interest of efficiency, it could not realistically accept and implement all kinds of derogations from its rules.[103]

Officially, the AAA-ICDR exercises little control over arbitrations conducted under its auspices, even less than the LCIA. In particular, it does not reserve a right to confirm/appoint party-nominated arbitrators.[104] Therefore, rules which the institution would probably deem essential are difficult to identify. This is also due to the fact that administrative aspects of AAA-ICDR arbitration are less transparent than for example under the ICC Rules. Many administrative practices of the AAA-ICDR, like *e.g.* its informal scrutiny of awards by the secretariat, are not reflected in its rules at all.[105] For this reason, parties' wishes regarding the procedure and administration of the proceedings and the practice of the AAA-ICDR might occasionally conflict but such conflict would often go unnoticed.


VI. Essential DIS Rules

Article 24 (1) of the DIS Rules provides:

> »Statutory provisions of arbitral procedure in force at the place of arbitration from which the parties may not derogate, the Arbitration Rules set forth herein, and, if any, *additional* rules agreed upon by the parties shall apply to the arbitral proceedings. Otherwise, the arbitral tribunal shall have complete discretion to determine the procedure [*emphasis added*].«

Similar to article 19 (1) of the ICC Rules, the wording of this provision suggests that parties' autonomy to determine arbitral procedure is limited to

---

101  *Cf.* Gusy, Hosking, and Schwarz, *A Guide to the ICDR Rules*, para. 1.92.

102  As outlined *supra* at p. 224 (IV.2).

103  *See e.g. ISC v. Nobel Biocare Investments*, 351 Fed. Appx. at 4, 5; *cf. also X Holding AG, X Management S.A., A & B v. Y Investments N.V.,* 4 A 279/2010 (CH BG, 25 October 2010) at A, discussed *supra* at pp. 181-184 (§8C.I.3.b) and p. 215 (§10A.V).

104  *See infra* at pp. 368-371 (§14B.III.2) for details on institutional arbitrator confirmation.

105  *See infra* at pp. 384-386 (§14B.VI) for details on official and informal scrutiny of awards.

aspects not governed by the institutional rules, unless the rules explicitly allow party agreements.[106]

However, just like German arbitration law,[107] the DIS Rules do not exhaustively enumerate all dispositive provisions. The DIS accepts modifications of its rules even where the rules do not expressly contemplate an opting-out. One commentator even asserts that concerning all issues not determined« by mandatory arbitration law »*the parties' autonomy prevails*« and that parties choosing DIS Rules could »*amend or modify*« these rules at any time, even after the DIS accepted the case.[108]

The fact that the DIS Rules do not foresee any institutional decision on the validity of the arbitration agreement supports this understanding. The DIS would even proceed with the appointment of arbitrators under arbitration clauses with missing or ambiguous references to the DIS and leave all questions of jurisdiction and applicable rules entirely to the arbitral tribunal.[109] Given the overall reduced influence it exercises, a procedural rule that the DIS would consider essential to perform its services can at present not be identified, rather it would expect the arbitral tribunal to appropriately deal with any modifications to its rules. Certainly, however, the DIS - like any other institution - would take issue with attempts to opt out of the more *substantive* conditions regarding payment and limitation of liability for its services.[110]

## VII. Essential Swiss Rules

The Swiss Rules were originally inspired by the UNCITRAL Rules and accordingly reduced institutional influence on the proceedings to a minimum, which is certainly to the advantage of party autonomy.[111]

---

106 *Cf.* DIS Rules, art. 1 (2), 2 (2)–(3), 13 (1)–(2), 18 (2), 20 (1), 21 (1)–(2), 27 (2)–(3), 33 (3), 33 (4), 35 (1), 37 (2) (1998) (»*unless otherwise agreed*«).

107 *See supra* at pp. 87 et seq. (§4C.I).

108 Risse, »§ 24 DIS Rules«, para. 2.

109 Bredow and Mulder, »DIS Rules, § 1«, para. 12, 19, 20. *See also supra* at pp. 189 and 215 (§10A.VI) on the DIS' acceptance of notices based on DAS arbitration clauses.

110 *See* DIS Rules, art. 7, 44 (1998). *See generally supra* at p. 219.

111 Peter, »Die neue Schweizerische Schiedsordnung«, 59 (on the Swiss Rules [2004]).

> »The parties' freedom to derogate from the provisions of the Swiss Rules is hence the rule rather than the exception.«[112]

However, the latest revision has increased administrative control by the newly created Swiss Chambers of Commerce Court of Arbitration and Mediation (hereinafter »*SCCAM*«; sometimes the organisational body is also referred to as »*Swiss Court*«), possibly making the Swiss Rules more prone to rigidity. In particular, article 1 (4) of the Swiss Rules provides:

> »By submitting their dispute to arbitration under these Rules, the parties confer on the Court, *to the fullest extent permitted* under the law applicable to the arbitration, all of the powers required for the purpose of supervising the arbitral proceedings otherwise vested in the competent judicial authority, including the power to extend the term of office of the arbitral tribunal and to decide on the challenge of an arbitrator on grounds not provided for in these Rules [*emphasis added*].«

It is doubtful whether the SCCAM would happily agree to surrender these far-reaching powers.

It is also unlikely that a derogation from the SCCAM's right to confirm arbitrators under article 5 (1) of the Swiss Rules would be accepted without opposition. Already about the former Swiss Rules (2004), a commentator remarked that party autonomy to deviate from the Swiss Rules was limited where »*the powers of the Chambers, of the Arbitration Committee and of the Special Committee*« are touched.[113] The requirement to prepare a provisional timetable under article 15 (3) of the Swiss Rules is also considered essential.[114]

Unlike the AAA-ICDR Rules and the CIETAC Rules, the Swiss Rules do not contain a general provision on modifications being supported. Among Swiss authors, the view prevails that »*over-customization*« may be incompatible with institutional rules and that combining features of different rules should only be done in ad hoc arbitration.[115]

---

112 Zuberbühler, Müller, and Habegger, *Swiss Rules of International Arbitration*, Introduction, para. 30.
113 Ibid., art. 15, para. 6.
114 Geisinger and Ducret, »The Arbitral Procedure«, 80, n. 32.
115 Ibid., 77.

C. Controlling or lenient: negotiability of institutional services and rules

It is commonly suggested - and this section has largely supported that assumption - that some institutions are more controlling than others, making them less receptive to parties' wishes to individualise arbitration rules.

Among the institutions here compared, the ICC Court is certainly on the more controlling side whereas the DIS and the AAA-ICDR provide for a more lenient administration probably more inclined to accept party-autonomous rule modifications. The LCIA's administration is strictly organised at the beginning of the proceedings, keeping a firm hand on arbitrator appointments, but fades as soon as the arbitral tribunal is in office. Accordingly, rule modifications not affecting the appointment process would be relatively easy to accommodate.

SIAC's and CIETAC's positions regarding opting-out attempts by parties are most difficult to ascertain. On the one hand, one may assume considerable flexibility, with SIAC even agreeing to administer the *Alstom–Insigma* arbitration under ICC Rules and CIETAC officially proclaiming that parties may choose whatever set of rules they prefer for CIETAC administered arbitration. On the other hand, one also has to take into account that SIAC's and CIETAC's own rules give these institutions substantial influence they might not want to give up.[116] Since administration of the *Alstom–Insigma* arbitration under ICC Rules actually increased rather than decreased SIAC's control, the case may therefore not be an indication of a general leniency towards party-autonomous rules modifications. Correspondingly, for CIETAC it is unclear if its proclaimed willingness to accommodate the parties' wishes concerning the applicable rules involves a less-controlling exercise of its functions in practice. Possibly, CIETAC would only consider the arbitral tribunal bound by such rule modifications but less so its own actors and staff.

This overview of institutional practice has also shown that institutional flexibility depends largely on the bargain powers of the parties. If a particular arbitration is attractive, as a fee generator or to improve the visibility of the institution's services on a world market, an institution will accept more compromises as to the applicable rules than for small, unimportant cases. Not only SIAC's endorsement of the *Alstom–Insigma* arbitration,[117] a multi-million dollar dispute, exemplifies this but also the extraordinary

---

116 *See generally infra* at pp. 355 et seq. (§14B).
117 In contrast to the less compromising position taken regarding the *Bovis Lend-Jay-Tech* dispute, *see supra* at pp. 211-212 (§10A.II).

adaptations of its rules accepted by the LCIA for the highly prominent Softwood Lumber Arbitrations.[118] Accordingly, institutional rules, like other contract terms, are *negotiable*, even those herein identified as potentially deemed essential by the institution. It is just a question of the price to pay (in a literal and figurative sense). Correspondingly, accepting or declining to administer hybrid arbitrations is primarily an economic decision of evaluating benefits and costs - not only financially but also in consideration of effects on the institution's reputation and its relationship to other institutions.

## *§11 The institution's right to refuse the administration of a case*

»In our view, the only aspect of uncertainty or inoperability with regard to the Arbitration Agreement was the contingency of the SIAC declining to administer the arbitration according to the ICC Rules, a position it appeared to have taken originally [...], but one which it sensibly abandoned subsequently [...] (*internal cross-references omitted*).«[119]

The normative analysis in Chapter 1 has shown that arbitration institutions are not able to limit the parties' freedom to agree on the arbitration procedure by force of law.[120] To the contrary, institutional rules only become binding if the parties agree to them, they are therefore never mandatory in a formal sense.

However, it is commonly assumed that the institution can refuse to participate in the administration of arbitration[121] and the previous section has identified major derogation from an institution's rules as a likely ground for such refusal. A verification of the assumption that institutions are allowed to decline cases requires an analysis of the contract entered into between parties and an administering institution, in particular the manner and timing of the conclusion of such contract (A) and the right to terminate it (B). Moreover, the question arises how an institution's refusal to administer an

---

118 *See supra* at pp. 213-215 (§10A.IV)

119 *Insigma v. Alstom*, [2009] SGCA 24 [40].

120 *See supra* at pp. 122- 125 (§6).

121 *See e.g.* Schlosser, *Das Recht der internationalen privaten Schiedsgerichtsbarkeit*, 350, para. 452; Schäfer, Verbist, and Imhoos, *Die ICC Schiedsgerichtsordnung in der Praxis*, 107 (but noting this question to be not yet entirely settled).

arbitration, if contractually allowed, affects the parties' arbitration agreement and a pending or prospective arbitration (C).

## A. No duty of the institution to conclude a contract with the parties

»Avec l'entrée du centre d'arbitrage dans la danse arbitrale, les relations juridiques se compliquent.«[122]

[With the entry of the arbitral institution in the arbitral dance, legal relations get complicated.]

A distinctive feature of institutional arbitration lies in the multitude of the contractual relations. While ad hoc arbitration is based predominantly on the arbitration agreement concluded between the parties and the contract(s)[123] between the parties and the arbitrators, institutional arbitration brings another actor into the game - the arbitral institution. This complicates the contractual framework, which may be the reason why scholarly analysis of contractual relationships often discards institutional arbitration from its focus.

The difficulties already start at the linguistic level. The general term »*parties*« may refer to those who refer their dispute to arbitration (hereinafter also: »*arbitrants*«).[124] However, it can also mean the parties of one of the several contracts regulating institutional arbitration: the arbitration agreement itself, the contract between the arbitrants and the institution as discussed in the following or the contracts(s) of the arbitrants and/or the institution with arbitral tribunal.

Basis of the activity of an arbitral institution is a contract with the arbitrants.[125] Descriptively, this contact can be called a contract for the organisation or administration of an arbitration (hereinafter »*Administration*

---

122 Clay, *L'arbitre*, para. 695.

123 In a multi-arbitrator tribunal, there is a contract with each arbitrator.

124 Inspired by its corollary »*litigants*« and also the English title to the partially preserved Greek play »*Epitrepontes*« [The Arbitrants] by Menander, which features an arbitration-like scene (reproduced in: Capps, *Four Plays of Menander*, 25–127).

125 Clay, »Note, C.Cass., 20.02.2001«, 514, para. 4 (claiming to have first named this contract); Rüßmann, »Zwingendes Recht in den Schiedsregeln einer Schiedsinstitution?«, 483; Gottwald, *Internationale Schiedsgerichtsbarkeit*, 41, para. 21; *but see* Morgan, »International Arbitration in Hong Kong«, 448, para. 22.1 (»*no formal connection with their users*«).

*Contract*«).[126] For now, legal doctrine has hardly covered the Administration Contract at all.[127] It has to be clearly distinguished from the contract obliging an arbitrator to do his work (»*arbitrator's contract*«), which is not discussed herein in detail, as this would surpass the scope of this thesis.[128]

---

126 German: »*Schiedsorganisationsvertrag*« or »*Administrierungsvertrag*« or »*Institutionsvertrag*«, French: »*contrat d'organisation*« (*see e.g.* Wolf, *Die Institutionelle Handelsschiedsgerichtsbarkeit*, 70, 228 et seq.; Münch, »vor § 1034 ZPO«, para. 70; Lachmann, *Handbuch für die Schiedsgerichtspraxis*, para. 1587, 1723; Wilke, »Prozessführung in administrierten internationalen Handelsschiedsverfahren«, 18; Vogt, »Der Schiedsrichtervertrag nach schweizerischem Recht«, 84; Clay, *L'arbitre*, para. 699–700).

127 *See e.g.* Schäfer, *Die Verträge zur Durchführung des Schiedsverfahrens*, 1:204, 383 (incorrectly assuming this contract to be just a specific arbitrator's contract); more accurate but equally brief: Wilke, »Prozessführung in administrierten internationalen Handelsschiedsverfahren«, 18–19. For more thorough analyses, *see only* Wolf, *Die Institutionelle Handelsschiedsgerichtsbarkeit*, 70 et seq, 228 et seq.; Kuckenburg, »Vertragliche Beziehungen«; Clay, *L'arbitre*, 699 et seq.; with a special mention of Schöldström, *The Arbitrator's Mandate*, chap. 13, p. 399 et seq. (innovatively suggesting to regard each party's contract with the institution separately).

128 This »*enigmatic phenomenon*« (Lionnet, »The Arbitrator's Contract«, 161; *idem*, »Der Schiedsrichtervertrag«, 64: »*schillerndes Phänomen*«) already received a lot of attention, *see e.g.* Onyema, *International Commercial Arbitration and the Arbitrator's Contract*; Fouchard, »Final Report on the Status of the Arbitrator«; Derains and Lévy, International Chamber of Commerce and ICC Institute of World Business Law, *Is Arbitration Only as Good as the Arbitrator?*; Smith, »Contractual Obligations Owed by and to Arbitrators«; Clay, *L'arbitre*; Bucher, »Was macht den Schiedsrichter?«; Hausmann, »Der Schiedsrichtervertrag«; Hoffet, *Rechtliche Beziehungen zwischen Schiedsrichtern und Parteien*; Hoffmann, »Der internationale Schiedsrichtervertrag«; Oetting, *Der Schiedsrichtervertrag nach dem UML im deutschen Recht unter rechtsvergleichenden Aspekten*; Prütting, »Die rechtliche Stellung des Schiedsrichters«; Real, *Der Schiedsrichtervertrag*; Schwab, »Schiedsrichterernennung«; Strieder, *Rechtliche Einordnung und Behandlung des Schiedsrichtervertrages*; Vogt, »Der Schiedsrichtervertrag nach schweizerischem Recht«; *idem Der Schiedsrichtervertrag nach schweizerischem und internationalem Recht*.

## I. Nature and content of the Administration Contract

As remarked with regards to the arbitration agreement, it is questionable if the Administration Contract is a contract of procedural nature. However, for the Administration Contract such qualification is even less convincing. While the arbitration agreement has at least the one procedural consequence to exclude state court jurisdiction, the Administration Contract does not directly influence the procedural situation before state courts. Of course, if the institution refuses to enter into an Administration Contract or terminates this contract, state courts may again assume jurisdiction. However, this would not be a question of the existence or non-existence of the Administration Contract but rather of the operability of the arbitration agreement itself. The main effects of the Administration Contract are material: The institution is obliged to render administration services, the parties undertake to pay administrative fees.

Only of marginal practical relevance appears to be the determination of the contract type.[129] It is here assumed that the Administration Contract is essentially a specific contract for services, but a qualification as a *sui generis* contract appears equally appropriate.[130] In any case the Administration Contract, like the arbitrator's contract,[131] is not a contract for works. Of course, the arbitral institution does not owe a successful arbitration, an enforceable award or any rendering of an award by an arbitral tribunal at all. The arbitral institution only owes services. These services encompass but are not restricted to appointing an arbitral tribunal as outlined above.[132] In the *Cubic* case, one of the very rare lawsuits brought against an arbitral institution,[133] the Cour de Cassation clarified with respect to the duties of arbitral institutions under the Administration Contract that these are best

---

129 *See e.g.* Waincymer, *Procedure and Evidence*, para. 2.4, 3.14.1 (only speaking of »*some form of contractual arrangement*« without even mentioning controversies on the contract type); Fouchard, »Rights and Obligations of the Arbitrator with Regard to the Parties and the Arbitral Institution«, 15, 16, para. 15, 17 (noting that such classification is »*dear to lawyers of civil law countries*« but doubtlessly seen »*as a rather pointless operation*« by common law lawyers).

130 *See* Münch, »vor § 1034 ZPO«, para. 70.

131 *Cf. e.g.* Schwab, Walter, and Baumbach, *Schiedsgerichtsbarkeit*, chap. 11, para. 8.

132 *See supra* at pp. 128-129 (§7A.I); *contra* Vogt, »Der Schiedsrichtervertrag nach schweizerischem Recht«, 84.

133 Clay, »Note, C.Cass., 20.02.2001«, 513, para. 1.

efforts obligations (*»obligations de moyen«*) to strive for an effective arbitration in the interests of the parties.[134]

In detail, the arbitral institution's obligations follow from its arbitration rules, which can vary tremendously concerning the arbitral institution's tasks.[135] For example, the answer to the question if the arbitral institution has a best efforts obligation to ensure an enforceable award depends decisively on the supervisory functions the arbitral institution offers.

From an arbitral institution that offers scrutiny of awards also with respect to matters of substance, like the ICC Court, arbitrants can expect that it would advise the arbitral tribunal on issues, which may endanger the enforceability of the award. Whether the arbitral tribunal follows such advice is another matter. In this respect, article 41 of the ICC Rules explicitly provides that

> »the Court and the arbitral tribunal shall act in the spirit of the Rules and shall make every effort to make sure that the award is enforceable at law.«

In contrast, institutions that do not offer scrutiny services have no power and consequently no duty to influence the award making process. This applies to all other institutions here considered except for SIAC[136] and CIETAC.[137]

The main duty owed by the arbitrants under the Administration Contract is to pay the administrative fees charged by the institution.

## II. Law applicable to the Administration Contract

The few scholars that mention this contractual relationship do not[138] all agree on the law applicable to questions of conclusion and interpretation of the Administration Contract. Again,[139] the discussion will follow a modern,

---

134 *Cubic v. ICC*, [2001] Rev. Arb. 511 (FR C.Cass) 512.
135 Waincymer, *Procedure and Evidence*, para. 3.14.3; Gottwald, *Internationale Schiedsgerichtsbarkeit*, 42 (para. 21). *See supra* at pp. 131-134 (§7A.IV) and *infra* at pp. 355 et seq. (§14B).
136 SIAC Rules, art. 28 (2) (2013) = art. 32 (2) (2016); *see also* SIAC Rules, art. 37 (2) (2013) = art. 41 (2) (2016).
137 CIETAC Rules, art. 49 (2012) = art. 51 (2015). *See infra* at pp. 384-386 (§14B.VI) for details.
138 *Contra* Kuckenburg, »Vertragliche Beziehungen«, 80.
139 *See supra* at p. 78 (§4B.II.1).

material or direct approach, as most arbitral tribunals would pursue.[140] If such questions transpired in front of a state court, the following considerations may at least be helpful in the application of the forum's conflict rules, which usually provide for some flexibility and alternatives.[141]

Failing an unlikely direct choice of the applicable law,[142] the prominent views all more or less rely on a closest connection test, some proclaiming a *»better law«* approach notwithstanding the risks for legal certainty involved.[143] In detail, most see the Administration Contract governed by the law of the seat of the arbitral institution,[144] others by the law of the arbitration agreement.[145]

## 1. Law of the seat of the institution

The first view has the advantage of certainty if the place of arbitration is not yet determined. Moreover, the institution's staff and its decision-making bodies are usually located at the seat of the institution and provide their services from there; hence, the characteristic performance rule supports such finding.[146] However, this view is difficult to reconcile with the concept of arbitral institutions as international organisations administering arbitrations worldwide.[147] Furthermore, it complicates conflict of laws questions

---

140  Blackaby et al., *Redfern and Hunter*, para. 3.217, 3.218, 3.223 (on the so-called *»voie directe«*); a little more conservative: Schütze, *Institutionelle Schiedsgerichtsbarkeit: Kommentar*, chap. I, para. 13 (introduction) (referring to connecting factors accepted in civilised legal orders).

141  *See e.g.* Rome-I-Regulation 2008 art. 4 (1)(b), (3), (4) (EU).

142  In particular, institutional rules are silent on the matter.

143  *Cf.* Schöldström, *The Arbitrator's Mandate*, 425, 426.

144  *E.g.* Wilke, *»Prozessführung in administrierten internationalen Handelsschiedsverfahren«*, 18; Aden, *Internationale Handelsschiedsgerichtsbarkeit*, pt. B, para. 1; Schütze, *Institutionelle Schiedsgerichtsbarkeit: Kommentar*, chap. 1, para. 38; Lionnet and Lionnet, *Handbuch Schiedsgerichtsbarkeit*, 196; unclear: Nedden and Herzberg, *ICC-SchO/DIS-SchO*, Introduction, para. 14 (*»Recht am Tätigkeitsort der Institution«* [Law at the place of work of the institution]).

145  *Cf.* Schöldström, *The Arbitrator's Mandate*, 429; Müller-Freienfels, *»Der Schiedsrichtervertrag in kollisionsrechtlicher Beziehung«*, 153. *See supra* at pp. 75-86 (§4B.II).

146  *See* Schöldström, *The Arbitrator's Mandate*, 432.

147  Ibid., 432–33 (suggesting a distinction between regional arbitration institutions whose rules have been designed against the background of a

by adding a law of a jurisdiction possibly different from those determining the procedural lex arbitri, the substantive law applicable to the contract, the law applicable to the arbitration agreement and the law applicable to the relationship between parties and arbitrators and between arbitrators and the institution.[148]

## 2. Law applicable to the arbitration agreement

The method of collateral or accessory connection, in contrast to *dépeçage,* would argue in favour of applying the law of the arbitration agreement. However, criticism against this concept is twofold: First, if the parties chose the law applicable to the arbitration agreement,[149] its collateral application to the relationship with the institution would be critical because the institution did not actively participate in this choice of law and contracts cannot be concluded to the detriment of a third party. Even though the institution has the implied duty to administer the arbitration as agreed by the parties, the principle of privity of contract argues against imposing the parties' choice of applicable law upon the institution. Second, if the parties have not made a choice, another controversy intervenes on how to determine the law applicable to the arbitration agreement as outlined above.[150] In particular, the application of the law of the main contract may be justifiable for the relationship between the arbitrants, but for arbitral institutions, who have no connection with that contract apart from administering a procedure where it is in dispute, this would create unreasonable unforeseeability. Generally, the principle of privity of contract opposes the application of

---

particular national law and institutions whose rules are supposed to work under many laws, like the ICC Rules); *see also* Wolf, *Die Institutionelle Handelsschiedsgerichtsbarkeit,* 244; *but cf.* Turner, *A Guide to the LCIA Arbitration Rules,* para. 1.38–1.40 (remarking that, despite the LCIA's »*international pretensions*« even the LCIA Rules »*track the* [English] *Arbitration Act with utmost fidelity*«, »go hand in glove« with it).

148 *Cf.* Schöldström, *The Arbitrator's Mandate,* 433 (»*somewhat unsatisfactory*«); *see generally* Wolf, »§ 1025 ZPO«, para. 28. *See already supra* at p. 85 on similiar concerns.

149 Which used to be »*virtually unheard of*« (Petsche, *The Growing Autonomy of International Commercial Arbitration,* 77), *but see now* LCIA Rules, art. 16 (4) (2014); Hong Kong International Arbitration Centre, »Model Clauses«.

150 *See supra* at pp. 75-86 (§4B.II).

collateral connection considerations in multi-party, multi-contract situations. The theory of collateral connection departs from the idea of subjecting all connected contracts to one »*dominant contract.*«[151] However, a party to one of the connected contracts will understandably not welcome the presumption of a contract being dominant to which it is not a party.[152]

3. Law of the place of arbitration

Directly applying the law of the place of arbitration is equally problematic. First, parties may create a contractual relationship with the institution before determining the place of arbitration. Under many arbitration rules, the institution may fix the place of arbitration, which may again change during the proceedings if the parties or the arbitral tribunal so decide. It is little practical if obligations or breaches of contract are governed by a different law before and after the fixing or redetermination of the place of arbitration.

In this context, the law of the place of arbitration could not mean the *lex arbitri (in sensu strictu),*[153] because national arbitration laws, which are essentially procedural laws, usually do not contain provisions on material obligations of arbitral institutions.[154] Rather, the contract law of the place of arbitration would have to be applied which may be surprising to parties only having considered the arbitration regime of the place of arbitration. From the point of view of the institution, it would be equally unfortunate to be bound by and possibly liable under the contract law of a foreign jurisdiction with which it shares no further connection. Applying the contract law of the place of arbitration to the Administration Contract would entail unpredictability, which could seriously endanger the work of arbitral institutions. To be on the safe side, arbitral institutions would have to adjust their rules for every arbitration or provide different sets of rules depending on the place of arbitration, which seems virtually impossible.

---

151 Hoffmann, »Der internationale Schiedsrichtervertrag«, 150.
152 *But see* Schöldström, *The Arbitrator's Mandate*, 428 (concluding that arbitration doctrine favours collateral connection also in situations involving different parties).
153 *See supra* at p. 80, n. 136.
154 *See supra* at pp. 91-106 (§4C.II.2) for details.

4. Own view and determination of the administering institution's »seat«

To avoid such complications and given that courts in the jurisdiction where the institution is located have general (personal) jurisdiction over claims against it, it is preferable to apply the contract law of the seat of the institution notwithstanding the undisputable weaknesses of this view addressed above. In the famous *Cubic* affair, French courts have ruled accordingly and applied French law to the relationship between the ICC[155] and a party to an ICC arbitration,[156] surprisingly not considering an »*autonomous*« approach as proclaimed in France for the law applicable to the arbitration agreement.[157] This jurisprudence was confirmed in the following by the rulings of Paris' courts in the case *SNF v. ICC*.[158]

A few remarks are necessary to explain what is meant by »*seat*« of the institution. As the »*seat rule*« here favoured stems from closest connection and characteristic performance considerations under the private international law of contract,[159] doctrines on the personal regime governing a company like the real seat and corporation theory or any mixed theories[160] provide little guidance. Rather, it seems more appropriate to rely on the law of the place of business from which the relevant service is provided, either from the institution's headquarters, but possibly from a branch office.[161]

Often, this determination seems straightforward. For example, the ICC is incorporated as a non-governmental organisation under the laws of France and has its headquarters in Paris, where most of the secretariat's staff and in particular the ICC Court as the administrative decision-making body is located. Its seat is therefore principally in France, even though the ICC Court maintains representative offices in other jurisdictions. Likewise, the DIS is incorporated under the laws of Germany in Berlin and its secretariat

---

155 The ICC Court is a mere service of the ICC without legal personality (*Cubic v. ICC*, [1999] Rev. Arb. at 110).

156 Despite a place of arbitration in Zurich and laws of Iran applied on the merits (*see Cubic v. ICC*, [1997] Rev. Arb. 417 [FR TGI, Paris] at 421, to this extent not appealed).

157 *See supra* at pp. 75-86 (§4B.II).

158 *SNF v. ICC*, [2007] Rev. Arb. 847 (FR TGI, Paris) at 850; [2010] Rev. Arb. 314 (CA, Paris) at 318 (affirming). The place of arbitration was Brussels, Belgium.

159 *See supra* at p. 237, 146.

160 *Cf.* Eidenmüller, *Ausländische Kapitalgesellschaften im deutschen Recht*, § 1, para. 2–9.

161 *Cf. e.g.* Rome-I-Regulation 2008 art. 19 (EU).

administers arbitrations mainly from Cologne and Berlin, its seat is therefore in Germany. Correspondingly, SIAC is seated in Singapore, the LCIA in London, England.

For decentralised arbitral institutions, determination of the relevant place of business is a little more complicated: While the Swiss Chambers' Arbitration Institution itself is headquartered in Basel, the secretariats handling the cases are located at the different cantonal Chambers of Commerce and the SCCAM itself does not have a physical location. Similarly, the AAA-ICDR administers arbitrations through AAA Secretariats located across the United States. Although CIETAC is headquartered in Beijing, the regionally established subcommissions administer cases relatively independently.

The arising difficulties to determine the relevant seat of decentralised institutions within one state may not be decisive if the contract law of such state is relatively uniform even if the state - like Switzerland and the US - generally has a federal organisation. However, the assessment becomes difficult if one also takes into account that some institutions have created agencies or representative offices and subsidiaries in other jurisdictions in order to attract users in these areas. The ICC Court for example maintains an office in Hong Kong, accommodating a secretariat's team handling Asian cases, another in New York for North-American cases and a mere representative office, without case management staff, in Singapore. CIETAC opened a subcommission in Hong Kong.[162] While a former AAA-ICDR office in Dublin, Ireland, is now closed, the AAA-ICDR opened joint offices with other institutions in Mexico City and Singapore, the latter in cooperation with SIAC, and an independent institution created by legislative decree in Bahrain called the Bahrain Chamber for Dispute Resolution (BCDR-AAA).[163] The AAA-ICDR also maintains a number of cooperation agreements according to which it may provide arbitration services through facilities of other institutions - but the extent of such cooperation is unclear.[164] The LCIA created independent spin-offs, partly in cooperation with other institutions and government authorities, having their own

---

162 *See* China International Economic and Trade Administration Commission, »Home«.
163 Gusy, Hosking, and Schwarz, *A Guide to the ICDR Rules*, para. 1.36–1.39.
164 *See infra* at pp. 398-399 (§14C.IV).

rules and being located in India,[165] Mauritius[166] and the Dubai International Financial Centre (DIFC), a »*neutral*« zone within Dubai.[167]

In all these cases, it is decisive for determining the law applicable to the Administration Contract whether a branch is legally independent and where administrative decisions under the applicable rules are taken. For all ICC cases, including those handled by the secretariat teams in Hong Kong and New York, the relevant seat of the institution remains Paris, France, because the meetings of ICC Court are located there and because the offices in Hong Kong and New York are legally dependent branch offices only. Staff meetings take place in Paris and the Hong Kong and New York staff are connected by video conferencing with the Paris based teams and managing counsel. Similarly, Administration Contracts with CIETAC should follow the laws of the People's Republic of China as this subcommission, like the subcommissions in mainland China, is a dependent branch of CIETAC, Beijing.[168] For AAA-ICDR cases, the seat is New York, as the Mexico City and Singapore offices serve representative purposes only.

The BCDR-AAA however is a fully independent institution with its own rules that has no further connection to the AAA-ICDR except for having been opened by it. BCDR-AAA institutions are administered by the Bahrain Chamber of Dispute Resolution established under the laws of Bahrain and providing its services from its location in Manama, Bahrain.[169] Therefore, the laws of Bahrain rather than New York would be applicable.

To determine the law applicable to Administration Contracts with the LCIA's legally independent subsidiaries is slightly more difficult. Their status as independent subsidiaries, established under the laws of India, Mauritius and the DIFC respectively, and the fact that the responsible secretariat staff is based there indicate the application of the contract law of the subsidiaries' locations. However, under their respective arbitration rules, the LCIA Court, based in London, remains the official administrative decision-

---

165  LCIA India, »Home«.

166  LCIA-MIAC, »LCIA-MIAC Arbitration Centre«.

167  DIFC, »DIFC | LCIA Arbitration Centre«; *see* Gerbay, »The LCIA«, para. 4–33.

168  *Cf.* CIETAC Rules, art. 2 (3), (7) (2012; 2015).

169  *Cf.* BCDR-AAA Rules, art. 1 (c) (2010). Similarly, the Jerusalam Arbitration Centre, an ICC Palestine and ICC Israel joint venture, is not only »*wholly independent*« from the ICC Court but also has its own »*international arbitration committee (the JAC court)*« (*see* International Chamber of Commerce, »Historic Opening of Arbitration Centre Set to Advance Palestine/Israel Commercial Dispute Resolution«).

making body for arbitrations administered by these centres.[170] Nevertheless, this fact appears insufficient to apply English contract law to Administration Contracts with these centres. When rendering decisions in LCIA India, LCIA-MIAC and DIFC-LCIA arbitrations, the LCIA Court is not acting in its authority as an LCIA (London) organ but on behalf of the independent centres.

The following considerations on the formation of the Administration Contract are therefore subject to the governing law, dependent on the seat of the relevant business presence of the approached institution. However, there is some consistency among contract laws regarding formation questions, most departing from the idea of matching declarations of will, often described as offer and acceptance. In accordance with the transnational approach followed herein, such basic principles are applied without resorting to particular laws.[171] Nevertheless, the previous conflict of laws considerations may be helpful to evaluate specific cases.

## III. Contract formation theories

As noted, it is the essence of contract negotiation that even provisions designated as non-derogatory are open to discussion.[172] However, the conclusion of the Administration Contract is seldom the result of a real negotiation. Rather, the rules of the institution have been drafted for a large number of contracts and are induced by the institution as the provider. Therefore, they have all elements of standard business terms,[173] which the parties may

---

170 *See* LCIA India Rules, art. 3 (2010); LCIA-MIAC Rules, art. 3 (2012); DIFC-LCIA Rules, art. 3 (2008); Gerbay, »The LCIA«, para. 4–38.

171 Instead, private harmonising instruments like the UNIDROIT Principles or the Draft Common Frame of Reference (cited to the full edition as von Bar et al., *DCFR*) are referred to not as law but as doctrinal attestation of the transnational acceptance of a particular principle.

172 *See supra* at pp. 231-232 (§10C).

173 Rüßmann, »Zwingendes Recht in den Schiedsregeln einer Schiedsinstitution?«, 486; Spohnheimer, *Gestaltungsfreiheit*, 109; Schlosser, *Das Recht der internationalen privaten Schiedsgerichtsbarkeit*, 404; Lachmann, *Handbuch für die Schiedsgerichtspraxis*, 343. *See also supra* at p. 115 (§5B).

agree to or not. For this reason, many think institutional arbitration is a »*package deal*«.[174] Other commentators even claim that

> »[i]t is not necessarily the individual provisions of the chosen arbitration rules that apply contractually but rather the type of arbitration chosen, for example, ›*ICC arbitration*‹.«[175]

The following elaboration of the different theories on how and when the Administration Contract is concluded can help to support or refute this understanding.

### 1. Theory 1 - parties accept the institution's offer ad incertas personas

A widespread view assumes that the publication of arbitration rules is an offer of the institution to the public - *ad incertas personas* - to administer arbitrations under these rules.

Some advocates of this theory maintain that the parties accept this offer already with the conclusion of the arbitration agreement referring to a certain institution. The institution is deemed to have waived the requirement of a notice of acceptance.[176] However, there is no benefit in seeing the parties already bound by a contract with an arbitration institution long before a dispute arises. To the contrary, this concept would make it difficult for the parties to modify their arbitration agreement without the institution's

---

174 Picture used by Schöldström, *The Arbitrator's Mandate*, 413; *see e.g.* Takla, »Non-ICC Arbitration Clauses«, 7–9; Paulsson, »Vicarious Hypochondria and Institutional Arbitration«, 236.

175 Greenberg and Mange, »Institutional and Ad Hoc Perspectives on the Temporal Conflict of Arbitral Rules«, 213 (but correctly adding that a choice of an institution »*regardless of the content of its arbitration rules*« may only be assumed »[s]*ave indicating a contrary intention*«).

176 For German law: *cf.* BGB § 151 (GER); Schlosser, »vor § 1025 ZPO«, vol. 9, para. 12; Lionnet and Lionnet, *Handbuch Schiedsgerichtsbarkeit*, 197 (arguing that this would apply also under other laws); for French law :*cf.* Jarrosson, »Le rôle respectif«, 386–87; *see also* Ditchev, »Le ›contrat d'arbitrage‹«, 397–98 (but distinguishing for the ZCC between arbitrations introduced by members and non-members); *contra* Kuckenburg, »Vertragliche Beziehungen«, 83 (arguing that French law differs in this respect from German law); unclear: Kassis, *Réflexions*, para. 34; *cf. generally* von Bar et al., *DCFR*, II.–4:205 (3) (with notes at p. 342, para. 13--17 on different legal orders); *cf. also* UNIDROIT Principles, art. 2.6 (3).

consent or even to accept state court litigation by waiving the arbitration plea.[177] This limits party autonomy unwarrantedly and appears rather excessive, given that the majority of contracts with institutional arbitration clauses will never be in dispute. Furthermore, according to this view always the version of the rules in force at the time of the conclusion of the arbitration agreement would be applicable - a result neither in the interest of institutions,[178] nor of the parties since later revisions usually serve the business community better.

If the publication of arbitration rules was an offer by the institution, it is therefore preferable to assume that a party accepts this offer by sending a request for arbitration or notice of arbitration to the other party and/or the institution.[179] An arbitration agreement that designates that institution or its rules would give the party initiating arbitration the power to represent the other party when concluding the Administration Contract binding both parties.[180]

## 2. Theory 2 - request for arbitration as offer accepted by the institution

Another contractual model is to consider the publication of arbitration rules only as an *invitatio ad offerendum* and not yet a binding offer.[181] According to that view, the party initiating arbitration makes an offer to the institution, thereby also representing the other party, to arbitrate under the auspices of the institution and its rules and to pay the corresponding fees. The institution

---

177 *Cf.* Rüßmann, »Zwingendes Recht in den Schiedsregeln einer Schiedsinstitution?«, 485; Schütze, *Institutionelle Schiedsgerichtsbarkeit: Kommentar*, chap. I, para. 42.

178 *See* Rüßmann, »Zwingendes Recht in den Schiedsregeln einer Schiedsinstitution?«, 490; *cf. also* ICC Rules, art. 6 (1) (2012; 2017); LCIA Rules, Preamble (2014); AAA-ICDR Rules, art. 1 (1) (2014); DIS Rules, art. 1 (2) (1998); Swiss Rules, art. 1 (3) (2012) (all providing for application of the version in force at the time of the commencement of the arbitration); *see also* CIETAC Rules, art. 74 (2012) = art. 84 (2015).

179 *See e.g.* Jarrosson, »Le rôle respectif«, 387; Kuckenburg, »Vertragliche Beziehungen«, 82–84.

180 *See Cubic v. ICC*, [1997] Rev. Arb. 422; Born, *Commentary and Materials (2001)*, 1614, n. 120; Rüßmann, »Zwingendes Recht in den Schiedsregeln einer Schiedsinstitution?«, 485.

181 *See e.g.* Waincymer, *Procedure and Evidence*, para. 3.14.1; Aden, *Internationale Handelsschiedsgerichtsbarkeit*, pt. B, para. 3.

would be contractually bound once it expresses its consent to administer the arbitration. This may already be with the communication of the secretariat to the parties by which it forwards the request for arbitration to the respondent party and informs the claimant hereof.[182] At that time, the case will have received a case number and the parties are informed about the case managers in charge of the file, indicating that the institution will provide its services.

This cannot be different, where the institution's arbitration rules provide for a specific decision on the *prima facie* admissibility of the arbitration. Any idea of postponing the acceptance of the institution and the conclusion of the Administration Contract to the time of such a decision would cause unsupportable legal uncertainty. The Administration Contract assigns to the institution the genuine task to decide on its own competence.[183] A first instance court (*Tribunal de Grande Instance*) (TGI) in Paris held accordingly in the *Cekobanka* case,[184] finding that when deciding *prima facie* on ICC jurisdiction, the ICC Court acts in performance of the ICC's contractual obligations.[185]

The decision appears quintessentially correct with respect to the contractual foundation of the ICC Court's power and duty to assess the prima facie validity of the arbitration agreement. Unfortunately, the decision is nevertheless missing some logical links. In particular, the court left open whether the respondent party in the arbitration (Banque de la Méditerranée) was also part of the contractual relations with the ICC or if these only included the claimant (Cekobanka) and the ICC. Given that the ICC Court had decided that the arbitration should not proceed lacking a valid arbitration agreement, the conclusion of an Administration Contract including both arbitrants - if necessary - would have merited a comment.[186]

---

182 Schütze, *Institutionelle Schiedsgerichtsbarkeit: Kommentar*, chap. I, para. 42 (»*irgendeine affirmative Handlung*« [any affirmative conduct]); *cf. also* Aden, *Internationale Handelsschiedsgerichtsbarkeit*, pt. C, § 7 para. 1 (for the DIS); *contra* Clay, »Note, C.Cass., 20.02.2001«, 516, para. 10 (assuming this to be mere information, not acceptance).

183 Kuckenburg, »Vertragliche Beziehungen«, 81; *but see* ibid., 85 (contradictingly denying the ICC Secretariat's competence to declare an acceptance, thus negating an Administration Contract in case of ambiguous or derogating arbitration agreements until the Court's decision).

184 *Czekobanka v. ICC*, (1986) 1987 Rev. Arb. 367 (FR TGI, Paris).

185 Ibid., 368.

186 *See infra* at pp. 247 et seq.; *but see also* Schöldström, *The Arbitrator's Mandate*, 403 (validly criticising the »*implicit premise that there*

## 3. Theory 3 - contract only concluded with the respondent's answer

A third concept requires that both parties declare their consent to the administration by the institution not only in the arbitration agreement but also upon initiation of the arbitration. In contrast to the two theories outlined above, this presupposes that the arbitration agreement does not give a party the power to engage the other party in a contract with the institution.[187] Consequence of this theory would be that the Administration Contract is only completely concluded once the respondent party accepts the administration at least tacitly with its answer to the request for arbitration addressed to the arbitration institution.

At first sight, the appellate court (*Cour d'appel*) (CA) of Paris seems to have favoured this model in the *Cubic* case:

> »[E]*n adressant son mémoire en réponse* contenant demande reconventionnelle, la société Cubic qui avait reçu, le 3 octobre 1991, le règlement de conciliation et d'arbitrage de la CCI et les nouvelles règles et usages relatifs aux frais a ainsi donné son accord pour qu'un arbitrage soit organisé par la CCI [*emphasis added*]«[188]

> [*By filing its answer* with a counterclaim, the company Cubic who received the ICC's rules on arbitration and conciliation and the new schedule of fees on 3 October 1991 therewith declared its consent that the arbitration was to be administered by the ICC].

However, the particularities of that case have to be borne in mind. The arbitration clause was not a classic ICC clause but rather a blanket clause only providing for arbitration in Zurich in accordance with the laws of Iran without mentioning any institution at all.[189]

## IV. Conclusions for requests for arbitration under different rules

The third theory, requiring another expression of consent also by the respondent party, is impractical. In many cases, the respondent never reacts to the request for arbitration, which could obstruct the contract conclusion

---

> *necessarily must be a contract between both arbitrants on one side and the arbitral institution on the other*«).

187 *See e.g.* Ibid., 200, 401 (rejecting an »*agency reasoning*« as too complicated and little practical).
188 *Cubic v. ICC*, [1999] Rev. Arb. at 110.
189 *See* ibid., 104.

indefinitely pursuant to that view.[190] Usually, it is also unjustified to ask for such express acceptance since already the arbitration agreement creates an obligation of the parties *inter se* to accept the agreed procedure including the designated institution's administration.

However, in extraordinary cases, where the reference to the institution in the arbitration agreement is missing or unclear, an Administration Contract binding the respondent may not be concluded until the respondent expresses its consent expressly or by conduct. In such cases, the arbitration agreement can hardly be understood to confer a party a power to represent the other party in the conclusion of a contract with an institution not previously contemplated. In the particular circumstances of the *Cubic* case, the decision of the CA Paris was therefore correct.[191]

One could suppose that hybrid arbitration agreements were also so unusual to require another expression of consent to the administration by the respondent. However, it is more convincing to differentiate: a declaration of the respondent is unnecessary if the arbitration agreement conveys a clear choice of both arbitrants to the administration of the approached institution. Then, not the administration of the arbitration by the institution is an issue but the rules to be followed. For the arbitrants, the question is not if an Administration Contract should be concluded with this institution at all but how such a contract would be performed. In accordance with the arbitration agreement, the arbitrants should have parallel interests;[192] there is therefore no issue of lacking agency power. However, if the institution's declaration and conduct makes it clear that it is only willing to administer the case pursuant to its own rules without the modifications proposed in the request for arbitration, a party has no power of agency to bind the other party to these terms.[193] The same applies if the claimant approached the rules issuing institution although the arbitration agreement clearly provides for another institution to administer the case.

When the arbitration agreement contains a clear reference to an institution, the first two theories both have its merits. To assume that an institution

---

190 Clay, »Note, C.Cass., 20.02.2001«, 516, 517, para. 11.
191 *See also* ibid., 517, para. 12 (proposing a distinction between cases with clear and ambiguous/erroneous references to the arbitration institution).
192 *But see infra* at p. 268 (§11C.II) on difficulties for one party to terminate the Administration Contract on its own.
193 *Cf.* Rüßmann, »Zwingendes Recht in den Schiedsregeln einer Schiedsinstitution?«, 491 (on the parallel problem of the intertemporary application of institutional rules).

makes an offer to the public by publishing rules has the advantage of certainty for the users who can agree on institutional arbitration clauses without having to fear inoperability due to institutional refusal. The institution would need a valid cause to terminate the Administration Contract already concluded once it receives the request for arbitration; otherwise, it would be liable to the parties.

The second view pays more attention to the interests of institutions that may want to refuse administering even arbitrations under standard clauses, *e.g.* due to an unreasonable workload in relation to the expected fees and the amount in dispute. It cannot be estimated how many contracts with institutional arbitration clauses have been concluded in recent years and how many will be in dispute in the future. Most of these potential arbitrations will be profitable or at least cost effective for the institutions but there is a small chance that a large number of smaller but complicated cases might be filed with one institution at the same time. The second theory allows the institution to decline some of those cases. Even if one accepted that fundamental rights provisions like article 6 of the European Convention on Human Rights (ECHR) principally bind institutions,[194] this would not amount to a denial of justice. If novation or effective reinterpretation in favour of ad hoc arbitration is not possible, the parties can still litigate before state courts since, due to the institutional refusal, the arbitration agreement would then be incapable of being performed. Access to justice does not encompass access to arbitration.

Nevertheless, the first theory seems more correct. It corresponds to the current practice of major arbitration institutions to administer all arbitrations filed and based on their rules. A grant of a right to terminate the contract if the parties do not pay the filing fee or advance on cost under the rules sufficiently addresses the institution's interest to refuse administering arbitrations without security for costs.[195] Moreover, the parties trust in the services offered by the institution already when concluding the arbitration

---

194 *But see Cubic v. ICC*, [2001] Rev. Arb. 513 (completely rejecting the application of Art. 6 ECHR to institutional decisions); *rightly criticised by* Lalive, »Note, CA Paris, 15.09.1998«, 119, para. 28 (*»fort contestable«* [very contestable]).

195 Given the then obvious breach of contract by the parties, it seems that no jurisdiction would deny such right (*contra* Rüßmann, »Zwingendes Recht in den Schiedsregeln einer Schiedsinstitution?«, 485).

agreement, a trust that is generated by institutions encouraging parties to agree on their rules.[196]

Some of those authors preferring the second theory try to address the issue of parties' reliance on the availability of the institution's services by establishing an obligation to contract (German: »*Kontrahierungszwang*«) of the institution. Although they only see an *invitatio ad offerendum* in the publication of arbitration rules and standard clauses, they assume that an institution is obliged to accept any Administration Contract offered to it under its rules. That this proposition is imperfect already follows from the finding that there is no fundamental right to access to arbitration or in other words, the administration of arbitration is not so vital to justify an obligation to contract as a harsh restriction of contractual party autonomy.[197] Coming to the same result, but dogmatically defendable, this thesis therefore favours the first theory, according to which the publication of arbitral rules and description of services is an offer *ad incertas personas* which the parties accept with the request for arbitration.

The controversy between the two predominant contractual theories[198] is not really decisive for the question if an arbitral institution is obliged to administer the arbitration when the parties agreed on the application of different rules by way of a hybrid arbitration clause. Under both views, either the offer or the acceptance incorporates the institution's rules by reference. If the parties' arbitration agreement contains unforeseen modifications or, as in case of hybrid arbitration agreements, refers to a completely different set of rules, the institution is not required to accept such variations unless the rules expressly allow derogating party agreements.[199] If one assumes, in accordance with the first theory, that the publishing of institutional rules is an offer by the institution, the sending of a request for arbitration with an indication that the parties want to opt out of some or all of the rules is a modified acceptance. Most jurisdictions qualify modified acceptances as

---

196  *See e.g.* ICC, »Ten Good Reasons to Choose ICC Arbitration«; SIAC, »Why Choose Us«; LCIA, »The Case for Administered Arbitration«.

197  Rüßmann, »Zwingendes Recht in den Schiedsregeln einer Schiedsinstitution?«, 488; *see also* Aden, *Internationale Handelsschiedsgerichtsbarkeit*, pt. B, art. 1 ICC Rules, para. 15–17 (but considering a duty not to discriminate of the ICC Court under European competition law).

198  Theories 1 and 2 (*supra* at pp. 244-247).

199  Rüßmann, »Zwingendes Recht in den Schiedsregeln einer Schiedsinstitution?«, 487, 488.

counter-offers[200] unless the modifications are immaterial.[201] The institution can therefore refuse to accept that counter-offer with the consequence that an Administration Contract is not concluded.[202] The second theory, according to which the request for arbitration is the offer, comes to the same result. An institution can simply refuse to accept the offer if it does not agree with the parties' wish to derogate from its rules.

Hence, in theory, the contractual analysis is simple. An institution that does not want to administer an arbitration under different rules or with material alterations of its rules can refrain from concluding the Administration Contract.

## B. Practice test: refusal to administer as contract termination

In practice, one cannot explain the legal basis for institutional refusal to administer hybrid arbitrations or arbitration under modified rules so easily.

## I. Problem: Timing and communication of the institution's refusal

Often the problem is one of timing. Of course, a careful institution would address the parties' wish to derogate from its rules in the first letter and request the parties to waive any rule modifications it does not agree with. That way it would avoid entering into an Administration Contract under terms it does not want to support. However, many institutions' secretariats send standardised first letters simply acknowledging the filing of a request for or notice of arbitration, notifying it to the respondent party and informing both parties of the case number and the responsible case managers after collecting a filing fee. The fact that the arbitration agreement provides for opting-out of the rules is at that stage often ignored.

In fact, of the rules here considered only the Swiss Rules (2004) used to provide that the Chamber of Commerce, in consultation with the Special

---

200 *Cf.* von Bar et al., *DCFR*, II.–4:208 (1); for various legal orders, *see* notes, ibid., 352, para. 1; similar: UNIDROIT Principles, art. 2.11 (1).
201 *Cf.* von Bar et al., *DCFR*, II.–4:208 (2); UNIDROIT Principles, art. 2.11 (2).
202 *See* Díaz-Candia, »El Rol Jurisdiccional de Los Árbitros y Su Constructiva Evolución: Deberes y Responsabilidad«, 90; Kuckenburg, »Vertragliche Beziehungen«, 85.

Committee, shall refuse to accept a case as early as possible by refraining from forwarding the notice of arbitration to the respondent party if »*there is manifestly no agreement to arbitrate referring to these Rules*.«[203] However, this provision has been removed from the current version of the Swiss Rules. Instead article 3 (12) of the Swiss Rules (2012) requires a decision of the SCCAM to refuse to administer the case only when the respondent does not submit an answer or raises objections to the administration by the Arbitration Court. Similarly, in ICC arbitration, modifications of or a missing reference to ICC Rules will only be considered upon objection or lack of answer by the respondent in the *prima facie* decision under article 6 (4) of the ICC Rules, whereunder the Court might decide that the arbitration shall not proceed. At that time however, the institution has effectively started administering the arbitration, which suggests that the Administration Contract is already concluded.[204] Where institutional rules do not foresee a preliminary institutional decision on jurisdiction, even an arbitral tribunal may be constituted before a derogation from the institutional rules becomes an issue.[205] A decision, by the institution or the arbitral tribunal, that the arbitration may not proceed would then imply a termination of the Administration Contract.


## II. Solution: Flexible contract with a both-sided termination right

At present, arbitral doctrine appears to have overlooked the practical reality that disagreements between the arbitrants and the institution on the applicable rules would often not prompt an immediate rejection of a case by the institution. It seems inappropriate to solve such conflict by resorting to the idea of dissent, according to which a contract does not come into existence if declarations of will do not match. As shown, institutions effectively render services, such as deciding on the prima facie validity of the arbitration

---

203 Swiss Rules, art. 3 (6) (2004).
204 *Contra* Kuckenburg, »Vertragliche Beziehungen«, 85 (alleging a lack of authority of the ICC Secretariat as opposed to the ICC Court to conclude a contract with the parties). But, ICC Rules, app. II, art. 5 (2) (2012) (ICC Internal Rules) assumes that documents by the Secretariat have the Court's approval
205 As in the case *Chayaporn*, (1985) 1987 Rev. Arb. 179 (FR TGI, Paris): Before rendering the already drafted award, the tribunal ordered the parties to seek an order from the TGI as *juge d'appui* on the competence of the institution.

agreement or installing an arbitral tribunal even if the arbitrants' agreement on this institution or the applicable rules requires further clarification and assessment. To make the coming into force of an Administration Contract dependent on the result of such assessment would lead to significant uncertainty.[206]

## 1. Arguments for a right to terminate the Administration Contract

As a first attempt to deal with the practical reality outlined, it is here proposed that an Administration Contract, which comes usually into existence with the receipt of the request for arbitration,[207] first only obliges the institution to assess its own competence and the applicable rules in line with its standard practice. If, following such assessment, disagreement on the application of the rules of the institution, of a modified version or the rules even of another institution persists, both sides - that is the institution but also the arbitrants acting together - have a right to terminate the Administration Contract. This takes into account that administration of arbitration is a service of higher nature requiring mutual trust, which should lower the requirements for termination.[208] Where part of legal doctrine disputes that parties choose arbitral institutions based on such special trust,[209] it neglects the important role played by arbitral institutions in organising and supervising the proceedings and the significant influence of many institutions on the work of the arbitrators. Especially, if the rules authorise the institution to reject party-nominated arbitrators,[210] replace arbitrators even without a request by

---

206 One consequence of such view would be to deprive institutions of their right to keep the filing fee should the arbitration be terminated for lack of competence of the institution.

207 *See supra* at pp. 244-245 and 247-251 (§11A.III.1, IV)

208 For German law, this is stipulated in BGB § 627 (1); *cf. e.g.* Putzo et al., *Zivilprozessordnung*, before § 1029 ZPO, para. 11 (suggesting the application to arbitrator's services); *contra* Henssler, »§ 627 BGB«, para. 23 (quasi-judicial function« would oppose a qualification as »*service*«); *but cf. also* ibid., para. 20 (naming lawyer and tax adviser services as examples).

209 Wolf, *Die Institutionelle Handelsschiedsgerichtsbarkeit*, 248 (reasoning that such trust can only exist towards natural persons); *but see* Henssler, »§ 627 BGB«, 26 (with references on case law applying the provision to dating agencies, major law firms etc.).

210 *See e.g.* ICC Rules, art. 13 (2012; 2017); *cf.* LCIA Rules, art. 5 (7), 5 (9) (2014).

a party[211] or scrutinise arbitral awards,[212] parties have an interest that such far-reaching powers are only exercised by the staff of an institution in which they have confidence. Even the assignment of the task to nominate arbitrators in case of default of a party or disagreement between the parties, a typical obligation of all arbitral institutions, requires trust in the institution's competence to evaluate the suitability, independence and impartiality of the candidates. Therefore, the Administration Contract obliges arbitral institutions to render services of higher nature. Consequently, both sides should have a right to terminate that contract without pleading a particular cause other than a disagreement on how services shall be performed.

## 2. Limit to the right to termination

To account for their mutual reliance, there has to be a time limit within which the institution or the arbitrants *together* can exercise their termination right without being liable for damages.[213] This limit should be the time of the constitution of the arbitral tribunal. Until this time, the Administration Contract obliges the institution only to examine the arbitration agreement and procedural choices made by the parties and evaluate their operability and feasibility while the parties' are obliged to pay the filing fee as a handling fee. Once the institution formally or incidentally, by appointing or confirming arbitrators, decides that the arbitration shall proceed, the institution is bound to respect the parties' procedural choices. If the institution prior to appointing the tribunal clearly declares not to accept the parties' derogations from the institutional rules, both parties - *together* –[214] are free to withdraw the case before the tribunal is constituted,[215] failing which they would be bound by the institution's rules.

---

211 *See e.g.* ICC Rules, art. 15 (2) (2012; 2017).
212 *See* ibid., art. 33; SIAC Rules, art. 28 (2) (2013) = art. 32 (2) (2016); CIETAC Rules, art. 49 (2012) = art. 51 (2015).
213 *Cf.* BGB § 627 (2) (GER) (disapproving of an untimely notice of termination - »*zur Unzeit*«).
214 *See also* Fouchard, »Note, CA Paris, 04.05.1988, TGI Paris, 23.06.1988«, para. 8. *See infra* at p. 268 (§11C.II) on the problem of arbitrants as a plurality of persons on one side of the Administration Contract.
215 As happened in the *Insigma–Alstom* arbitration first filed with the ICC Court.

3. Contractual termination & jurisdictional decision of the institution

Generally, this contractual solution corresponds with the procedural practice of institutions providing for an institutional decision on jurisdiction in their arbitration rules.[216] Such a decision, that the arbitration shall or shall not proceed under the supervision of the institution, is usually taken before the appointment of arbitrators. However, it needs to be pointed out that the contractual termination of the Administration Contract by an institution, or generally its factual refusal to administer a case, and an institutional jurisdiction decision are conceptually different.[217] This is evident if one considers that institutional determination of jurisdiction only takes place upon objection or non-participation of the respondent, thus it seeks to regulate a conflict *among* arbitrants rather than the conflict between the arbitrants *on one side* and the institution *on the other* as here discussed.

III. Support of the solution: hybrid arbitration and the »battle of forms«

According to the solution proposed, the Administration Contract is a flexible contract, which first only provides for an assessment of the institution's competence and the applicable rules, which only become strictly binding once an arbitral tribunal is constituted without that either side has previously terminated the Administration Contract. The need for such a practice-friendly solution becomes particularly obvious under the hypothesis that parties approach an institution based on a hybrid arbitration agreement, expecting it to administer the arbitration under another institution's rules. This is, as it will now be explained, a kind of »*battle of forms*« problem.

1. The »battle« of institutional rules

One could assume that, contractually, modifications agreed by the parties would prevail over institutional rules since the latter are only incorporated by reference into both the arbitration agreement and the Administration

---

216  As it applies to the ICC Court, SIAC, CIETAC and the Swiss Chambers' Arbitration Institution, *see infra* at pp. 361-366 (§14B.II) for details.

217  *See infra* at pp. 362-363 (§14B.II.1) for details on this distinction, which appears to be ignored by Hofbauer et al., »Survey on Scrutiny of Arbitral Institutions«, 7.

Contract. The general rule that individual agreements prevail over standard terms would support this assumption.[218]

However, such argumentation ignores that institutions do not participate in the conclusion of the arbitration agreement. From the institution's point of view, the parties' terms in the arbitration agreement are therefore not individually negotiated. In the relationship between the parties on one side and the institution on the other, the institutional rules and the derogating terms of the arbitration agreement are therefore at the outset at the same level of contractual hierarchy.[219] When determining whether the institutional rules or the rules as agreed by the parties shall prevail, it is conceivable to apply theories developed for solving conflicts of colliding standard contract terms, also referred to as the »*battle of forms.*«[220]

Drawing this parallel is particularly convincing in case of hybrid arbitration agreements where the rules of the administering institution, as that institution's standard business terms, collide with the *pre-drafted* rules of another institution, which the parties refer to. In this case, all elements of standard terms are met:

- Both sets of rules are formulated in advance for »repeated use«/«several transactions.«
- Each side of the Administration Contract refers to them without negotiation.[221]

---

218 For German law *cf.* BGB § 305b (GER); on the transnational acceptance of this principle *see* UNIDROIT Principles, art. 2.1.21 (UN); Bar et al., *DCFR*, II. - 8:104; Restatement (Second) of Contracts 1981 § 203 (d) (US); *see also* Basedow, »§ 305b BGB,« para. 3 (with further references on this general principle of European private law).

219 As opposed to the relationship between the parties themselves, where individually negotiated terms definitely prevail (so held by *China Natural v. Apex*, 379 F.3d. 796, 800 [9th Cir. 2004]; *see already Cargill*, 25 F.3d. 223, 225 [4th Cir. 1994]).

220 von Bar et al., *DCFR*, 354 (commentary to II.--4:209); *see also* Schneider, *Die Kollision Allgemeiner Geschäftsbedingungen im internationalen geschäftsmännischen Verkehr*, 9.

221 *See* UNIDROIT Principles, art. 2.1.19; von Bar et al., *DCFR*, II.–1.109 (with references on many jurisdictions).

That the rules referred to by the arbitrants were not drafted by either of them but by another body, the rules issuing institution, is no obstacle. Terms drafted by a third party may also qualify as standard terms.[222]

The only element questionable in this respect is that of »*repeated use*« or formulation for »*several transactions*.« Most parties would - hopefully - not have concluded a larger number of hybrid arbitration agreements. Accordingly, they would not frequently address a request for arbitration to an institution referring to another than the institution's rules. Rather, this will usually remain a one-time issue. If it were a condition that the *supplying party* intended to use the terms several times, the rules referred to by the arbitrants, as opposed to the administering institution's rules, would not be standard terms. However, if it were sufficient that the institution that issued the chosen rules, as the *third party* formulating the terms, prepared these rules for repeated use, they would qualify as standard terms. Grammatically, definitions in legislation and harmonising instruments like the UNIDROIT Principles and the Draft Common Frame of Reference (DCFR) correlate the »*repeated use*« or »*several transactions*« element to the »*formulation*« or »*preparation*« of the terms, not to their supply or a party's intention to supply them.[223] Accordingly, if a third party formulated the terms, such third party's determination of the terms for several transactions is decisive. Terms formulated by a third party for several transactions are standard terms, even if the party supplying and using such terms for a contract intends to do so only in a single case.[224] Accordingly, both the administering institution's rules and other institutional rules parties refer to in their arbitration agreement are standard terms.

## 2. Solutions discussed for »battle of forms« problems

With respect to conflicting standard terms, doctrine has developed a multitude of solutions. These differentiate between different contract conclusion situations, the content of and extent of conflict between the standard terms

---

222  *See* UNIDROIT Principles, p. 66 (comment to art. 2.1.19); *cf. also* von Bar et al., *DCFR*, II.–1:110 (5) (but not covering b2b contracts).

223  UNIDROIT Principles, art. 2.1.19; von Bar et al., *DCFR*, II.–1.109; *see also* BGB § 305 (1) (GER) (»*für eine Vielzahl von Verträgen vorformulierten*« [formulated in advance for a plurality of contracts]).

224  *See* Urteil [Judgment], [2010] 63 NJW 1131 (GER BGH) [10] (with further references).

and with respect to the use of language in the standard terms according to which conflicting terms are not accepted (protective or »*paramount*« clauses).[225]

Ideally, these solutions accommodate the following interests:

- The parties expect to have concluded a valid contract.
- If to its disadvantage, each side generally wants its own standard terms to apply and to exclude the other side's standard terms.[226]

Based on these considerations, a solution negating a valid contract in case of conflicting standard terms (»*mirror-image rule*«) is no longer vigorously applied in any jurisdiction or by any authority.[227] A solution according to which always the standard terms of the party making the offer applies - referred to as theory of the first word or »*first shot rule*« - is also indefendable.[228] It contradicts the general rule that offer and acceptance have to be matching in principle and that a modified acceptance is a counter-offer unless the modifications are immaterial.[229] The only solutions sufficiently supported and worth discussing are the theory of the last word or »*last shot rule*«, the theory of partial dissent/validity or »*knockout*« rule and the »*characteristic performance theory.*«[230]

According to the *last shot rule*, a party is deemed to have accepted a counter-offer by conduct if it fails to object immediately. Consequently, the standard terms of the party last mentioning them before starting to perform

---

225 Schneider, *Die Kollision Allgemeiner Geschäftsbedingungen im internationalen geschäftsmännischen Verkehr*, 12–15, 17; Egeler, *Konsensprobleme im internationalen Schuldvertragsrecht*, 194; *cf.* von Bar et al., *DCFR*, 355 (explanation to II.--4:209).

226 Schneider, *Die Kollision Allgemeiner Geschäftsbedingungen im internationalen geschäftsmännischen Verkehr*, 17.

227 *See* ibid., 20 (considering 12 different legal orders); on the inappropriateness of such rule, *cf. also* von Bar et al., *DCFR*, 354 (explanation to II.--4:209).

228 Schneider, *Die Kollision Allgemeiner Geschäftsbedingungen im internationalen geschäftsmännischen Verkehr*, 21–22; *see also* Egeler, *Konsensprobleme im internationalen Schuldvertragsrecht*, 194.

229 *See supra* at p. 247-251 (§11A.IV).

230 *Cf.* Schneider, *Die Kollision Allgemeiner Geschäftsbedingungen im internationalen geschäftsmännischen Verkehr*, 20–24 (further theories are specific to certain contracts like contracts for sale).

the contract apply.[231] Some want to make an exception to this rule if the first offer's contract terms contain a protective clause.[232]

The *knockout rule* postulates that the parties have not reached an agreement on those standard terms that conflict, that are not »*common in substance.*«[233] Consequence of that rule is that non-agreed issues are dealt with in accordance with the dispositive provisions of the law.[234]

In the context of commercial contracts, the last shot rule is predominant in common law jurisdictions[235] while doctrine and jurisprudence in civil law jurisdictions tend to favour the knockout rule.[236] Despite the still persistent divergences, both the DCFR and the UNIDROIT Principles have adopted some version of the knockout rule, subject to a clear, prior or immediate declaration that a party does not want to be bound by a contract if its terms do not apply.[237]

The *characteristic performance theory* is inspired from corresponding principles in private international law.[238] Comparing the conflict of contract terms situation to a conflict of laws, the supporters of this view argue that the party rendering the characteristic performance not only knows best which terms are required but also relies and depends more on the application of its terms.[239]

---

231  Ibid., 20, 21 (colloquially called »*Ping Pong*« theory).

232  *See* Egeler, *Konsensprobleme im internationalen Schuldvertragsrecht,* 194.

233  von Bar et al., *DCFR,* II–4:209 (1), p. 356 (»*identity in result*« counts).

234  Schneider, *Die Kollision Allgemeiner Geschäftsbedingungen im internationalen geschäftsmännischen Verkehr,* 23.

235  *Cf.* ibid., 58.

236  *See* Grüneberg, in: Palandt, *Bürgerliches Gesetzbuch,* § 305, para. 54; *see also* Schneider, *Die Kollision Allgemeiner Geschäftsbedingungen im internationalen geschäftsmännischen Verkehr,* 52 (solution absolutely prevailing in Germany; with further references); *see generally* ibid., 119–20 (on Germanic and Roman legal orders). Nordic jurisdictions show a tendency towards case-by-case solutions (*see* ibid., 34–38, 121).

237  UNIDROIT Principles, art. 2.1.22; von Bar et al., *DCFR,* II.–4:209.

238  *See e.g.* Rome-I-Regulation 2008 art. 4 (2) (EU) (*cf. also* Recital 19).

239  *See* Schneider, *Die Kollision Allgemeiner Geschäftsbedingungen im internationalen geschäftsmännischen Verkehr,* 22.

3. Appeasing the battle of institutional rules

As a preliminary remark: None of the here discussed institutional rules contain an express protective clause that may be relevant for the evaluation. They do not clearly indicate which rules are deemed »*mandatory*«, in the sense that the institution would never accept a modification,[240] nor do they provide that the institutional rules shall generally prevail over the parties' individual procedural agreements.[241] Although institutions may prefer to see their rules to apply unaltered, they refrain from introducing protective clauses and from identifying essential rules in order to avoid the reproach of restricting party autonomy. With some restrictions introduced with the latest revisions, the AAA-ICDR Rules and the LCIA Rules even underline the parties' liberty to make their own arrangements[242] Therefore, the specific situation of a protective clause in one party's standard terms can be left out from the analysis.

As a transnationally accepted solution cannot be identified,[243] the above-mentioned theories will be evaluated according to their usefulness[244] in the specific situation of conflicts between the procedural rules chosen by the parties and the institution's rules without repeating general criticism to all solutions.

The last shot rule is only convincing when a performance of the contract by one party may lead the other party to think that its terms have been accepted. However, an arbitration institution starting to organise the proceedings, for example by inviting parties' arbitrator nominations and comments to jurisdiction, would commonly follow its own practice notwithstanding a derogating agreement by the parties. Although they are not law, institutional

---

240 *See supra* at p. 218 (§10B).
241 *But see* SIAC Domestic Rules, art. 1.5 (2002): »*The parties, by agreeing to submit or refer their dispute to the Centre for arbitration in any of the cases in Rule 1.1, agree that these Rules take precedence over any and all provisions in the underlying contract between the parties relating to dispute resolution by arbitration*« (not in force anymore).
242 *Compare* LCIA Rules, art. 14 (2) (2014) *with* LCIA Rules, art. 14 (1) (1998); *compare* AAA-ICDR Rules, art. 1 (1) (2014) *with* AAA-ICDR Rules, art. 1 (a) (2009). *See supra* at pp. 224-228 (§10B.IV-V).
243 *See* Schneider, *Die Kollision Allgemeiner Geschäftsbedingungen im internationalen geschäftsmännischen Verkehr*, 122 (negating a »*common core*« of legal orders).
244 Ibid. (»*better law approach*«).

rules are »*drafted as a piece of legislation*«[245] and most institutions apply them as such. Neither institutions nor parties think of institutional rules as standard business terms that can be waived by conduct - even though they should perhaps start considering this issue.

For this reason, degree of reliance on the performance of the Administration Contract is lower than with respect to ordinary contracts for works, services or goods. Moreover, the initial steps in arbitration are often similar, independent of the administering institution and its rules. The first steps in the arbitration procedure prior to the constitution of the arbitral tribunal can therefore hardly be interpreted as consent to particular rules on either side. An institution can also not reasonably understand the mere fact that one party pays a filing fee or advance as total submission under the institutional rules. In any case, such conduct by the party paying the advance can never bind the other party.[246]

Applying the knockout rule is equally unenlightening. Of course, one could assume that no agreement is reached where the rules agreed by the parties are different from the rules of the administering institution. However, the consequence of such solution would be that such questions have to be answered in accordance with the applicable law. This is problematic because most arbitration laws lack provisions on the functioning of institutional arbitration. Tasks and powers of arbitral institutions are defined neither by procedural nor by substantive law.[247] Many arbitration laws follow the basic model of ad hoc arbitration that is often not wanted by any of the parties when an institution is addressed to administer arbitration under rules derogating from its own.[248]

It is therefore necessary to find a solution to the issue of conflicting arbitration rules and party agreements that can cope with the reality of institutional arbitration. The most viable approach appears to be to give the institutional rules of the administering institution general priority over the parties' derogating agreements. This solution, which certainly facilitates the work of institutions, could be based on the characteristic performance theory. The arbitral institution undeniably renders the characteristic

---

245 Schöldström, *The Arbitrator's Mandate*, 404.
246 *See supra* at pp. 247 et seq. (§11A.III.3) on the agency problem when concluding an Administration Contract under rules deviating from the arbitration agreement.
247 *See supra* at pp. 91-106 (§4C.II.2)
248 *See supra* at pp. 207-209 (§9) on the preference for an interpretative solution to a pathology which meets the parties' intentions best.

performance under the Administration Contract. However, the characteristic performance theory has faced strong and justified criticism by contract lawyers. The most important argument against this rule is that it carves a presumptive dominance of one party in stone, preferring the stronger rather than the weaker party.[249] Applying the characteristic performance rule to conflicting terms of the Administration Contract also diminishes the force of the principle of party autonomy and risks to disadvantage institutional over ad hoc arbitration. Accordingly, it is untenable to give *general* preference to the administering institution's rules.

However, in line with the solution proposed above,[250] the characteristic performance rule has some merit for the purpose of determining the institution's obligations *up to the constitution of the arbitral tribunal*. This moment has already been identified as the point in the proceeding until which both the institution and the arbitrants have a right to terminate their relationship without assuming liability for damages. With that restriction to the initial steps in the administration of the arbitration, several arguments support the preference of the administering institution's rules (terms) in accordance with the characteristic performance rule:

- Inspiration from the corresponding conflict of laws rule is appropriate because, although not laws, arbitration rules are authoritative provisions drafted in a quasi-legislative manner.
- The principle of effective interpretation calls to applying the rules of the administering institution to avoid further obstacles and delays.
- The application of the administering institution's rules is almost a customary norm in international arbitration.[251]

Resorting to this solution is only required in case of a real collision of the rules and practices of the institution with the rules chosen by the parties already at this stage of the proceedings. Where both sets of rules regulate the initial steps in the arbitration in compatible ways, it is unnecessary to discard the application of either of them (principle of congruence, German:

---

249 *See e.g.* Egeler, *Konsensprobleme im internationalen Schuldvertragsrecht*, 195.
250 *Supra* at pp. 252-255 (at II)
251 *Cf.* Grüneberg, in: Palandt, *Bürgerliches Gesetzbuch*, § 305, para. 55–57 (on the particular contractual force of such trade-specific standard terms).

*»Kongruenzgeltung«*.[252] In this respect, the next chapter will discuss similarities and differences between institutional rules in detail.[253]

## IV. The institution's restricted right to disregard rule derogations

Accordingly, when faced with a request for arbitration requiring the application of another institution's rules, an arbitral institution may notify the request, assign a case file and assess its own competence according to its own, ordinary rules and procedures despite the modification agreed by the arbitrants. However, it has to inform the parties if or to which extent it is not prepared to accommodate the rules agreed by them prior to initiating the process of constituting the arbitral tribunal.[254] Usually, the arbitrants and the institution will then find an agreement. If not, the institution may terminate the Administration Contract and end its services; it should not, however, simply proceed with appointing arbitrators based on its own rules if the parties have not agreed to this approach.

Contractually, the institution therefore has a right to disregard such rule modifications agreed by the arbitrants that are incompatible with its services. However, this right is restricted to the very initial phase of the proceedings prior to the arbitrator appointment process. This proposed solution reflects the important role played by institutions until the constitution of the tribunal by granting institutions more autonomy and discretion how to administer the proceedings up to that point.[255] It also encourages institutions to take their role as a guardian of the regularity of the procedure seriously and to ensure that conflicts and disagreements on procedural aspects are solved early.

---

252 *See* ibid., § 305, para. 54 (on the application of this principle also in relation to the knockout theory).

253 *See infra* at pp. 344-400 (§14).

254 Similar: Schöldström, *The Arbitrator's Mandate*, 416–17 (noting that the ICC may be liable for imposing scrutiny of parties having opted out of this feature).

255 *See supra* at pp. 131-134 (§7A.IV).

## C. Effect on the arbitration agreement

A question left to discuss is what happens to the arbitration agreement when an Administration Contract is not concluded in the first place or terminated following a conflict over the applicable rules.

### I. Overview of the République of Guinée[256] cases

The relationship or question of dependence or independence between the Administration Contract and the arbitration agreement was a central issue of a line of jurisprudence concerning two urgency arbitral proceedings against the Republic of Guinea introduced by different companies before the Chambre arbitrale de Paris. The decisions do not concern refusal to administer a case or termination of the Administration Contract by the institution but an attempt by one arbitrant to terminate this contract (or rather to demand its »*résiliation judiciaire*«) against the will of the other arbitrant.

#### 1. The factual background

In substance, the dispute concerned several contracts concerning the construction of flats in Guinea which contained more or less ambiguous arbitration clauses, some of which were interpreted by the Paris court of first instance (*Tribunal de Grande Instance, TGI*) in its first decision in the matter (herein cited as *République de Guinée I*) to refer to the Chambre arbitrale de Paris.[257] During the arbitration proceedings, the Republic of Guinea

---

256  In chronological order, the court judgments in that matter herein referred to are the rulings of the TGI, Paris, in *République de Guinée v. Chambre arbitrale de Paris et al.* of 30 May 1986, 30 October 1986 and 28 January 1987 (cited as République *de Guinée I, II and III,* all reported in [1987] Rev. Arb 371), the rulings of the CA, Paris, in *Chambre arbitrale de Paris, Carfa Trade Group et Omnium de travaux v. République de Guinée et al.* of 18 November 1987 and 4 May 1988 (cited as *République de Guinée IV* and *V,* both reported in [1988] Rev. Arb 657) and the subsequent ruling of again the TGI in *République de Guinée v. R. & O. (arbitrators)* of 23 June 1988 (cited as *République de Guinée VI,* [1988] Rev. Arb. 657).

257  *République de Guinée I,* [1987] Rev. Arb. 371 (TGI, Paris); critical: Fouchard, »Note, CA Paris, 04.05.1988, TGI Paris, 23.06.1988« (»*assez douteux*« [quite doubtful]).

introduced an action against the claimants in the arbitration and against the Chambre arbitrale de Paris.[258] It requested *inter alia* the annulment of the arbitration agreements or, in the alternative, the judicial termination (*»ré-siliation judiciaire«*) of the contract with the institution, claiming to have erred about the arbitration institution and asserting faults committed by the Chambre arbitrale de Paris in the organisation of the two arbitrations. It also submitted to be willing to continue the proceedings ad hoc.

### 2. The decisions of the TGI, Paris

Partially following the requests, the TGI of Paris suspended the arbitration proceedings by interim order of 30 October 1986[259] and, by decision of 28 January 1987[260] and declared the resiliation of the contractual relations (*»liens contractuels«*) between the parties and the Chambre arbitrale de Paris, but not of the underlying arbitration agreements. The court found the institution to have raised serious doubts concerning its ability to ensure a fair and equitable process.[261] In consequence, the TGI ordered the arbitral tribunals to be replaced by ad hoc tribunals to be designated by the TGI as supporting judge (French: *»juge d'appui«*).

### 3. Partial annulment of the decisions by the CA, Paris

In its decisions of 18 November 1987 and 4 May 1988, the CA confirmed the decisions to uphold the arbitration agreements in principle, stressing the negative effect of competence-competence under French law.[262] Contrary to the TGI, however, the CA also found that a state court cannot suspend

---

258 Overall, there was some uncertainty if the Republic of Guinée sought procedural remedies against the opponent parties or wanted to engage the contractual responsibility of the arbitration centre; the distinction between both causes of action is discussed *infra* at Chapter 5, pp. 459-461 (§16C).

259 *République de Guinée II*, [1987] Rev. Arb. 371 (TGI, Paris).

260 *République de Guinée III*, [1987] Rev. Arb. 371 (TGI, Paris).

261 *Inter alia* finding that only three arbitrators were appointed although the rules provide for five and that the president of the Chamber had attended meetings with some arbitrators to the exclusion of the arbitrator nominated by the Republic of Guinea (ibid.).

262 *République de Guinée IV*, [1988] Rev. Arb. 657 (CA, Paris); *République de Guinée V*, [1988] Rev. Arb. 657 (CA, Paris).

ongoing arbitral proceedings because of a dispute concerning the arbitral institution nor, pending arbitral proceedings, declare the invalidity or resiliation of the Administration Contract. Rather, the arbitrators, whose personnel impartiality and independence was then not in doubt, should have considered these issues, including the allegations of disrespect of a fair and equitable process by the arbitral institution.[263]


II. Evaluation of the CA's ruling

A French commentator understood that the CA found the Administration Contract and arbitration agreement to be inseparable (*»pas dissociables«*).[264] This idea of *»inseparability«* could be understood to have the consequence that a defect of the Administration Contract would also affect the arbitration agreement. However, such idea of an inseparable connection between the arbitration agreement and the Administration Contract is little convincing and, essentially, the jurisprudence of the CA Paris does not seem to support it. Rather, the decision is not based on a contractual analysis at all but rather on the idea of judicial deference to institutional activity pending arbitral proceedings.[265] According to the policy predominant in France, state courts should not interfere with any aspect of arbitral procedure, including the administration by a permanent institution, until the rendering of the award. On a contractual level, the concept of separability, and not: inseparability, between the contracts underlying institutional arbitration supports this jurisdictional argument best. The alleged breaches of contract by the arbitration institution where neither attributable to the claimants nor to the arbitrators. Any hypothetical invalidity or termination of the Administration Contract could thus affect neither the agreement to arbitrate nor the arbitral tribunal's jurisdiction or proper constitution. Therefore, the TGI as supporting judge was not competent to put an ad hoc tribunal in place, as a difficulty in the constitution of the arbitral tribunal did - strictly speaking - not exist.

Still, the decision of the CA is critical insofar as it appears to install a quasi-total immunity of arbitral institutions administering arbitral

---

263 *République de Guinée V*, [1988] Rev. Arb. 657.
264 Boisséson, La constitution du Tribunal arbitral dans l'arbitrage institutionnel, 352.
265 Fouchard, »Note, CA Paris, 04.05.1988, TGI Paris, 23.06.1988«.

proceedings.[266] The CA confined its reasoning to the brief remark that the first instance court did not have the competence, under the cover of the alleged requirements of trust and serenity (*»sous le couvert de prétendues exigences de confiance et de sérénité«*), to break the contractual relations. The court perceived the lower court's decision to sanction mistakes to the detriment of the claimants although the alleged mistakes were not attributable to them but only to the Chambre arbitrale de Paris.[267] This reasoning lacks an explanation why a termination of the Administration Contract alone would have *»sanctioned«* the claimants, even if the arbitrations could have continued on an ad hoc basis arguably even with the same arbitrators. It is also based on the wrong assumption that the arbitral institution lost its ability to interfere with the arbitration (*»a perdu tout pouvoir d'action«*) with the constitution of the arbitral tribunal.[268] This finding conflicts with the reality of institutional arbitration.[269]

Despite the discussed weaknesses in reasoning, the outcome of the CA's decision is defendable because the Administration Contract is a multi-party contract that links the institution to at least two parties,[270] claimant and respondent, having partially opposing interests.[271]

> »Il est sûr que l'obstacle essentiel tient au désaccord des parties à l'arbitrage; si elles convenaient ensemble de mettre fin aux fonctions d'organisation de l'arbitrage qu'elles ont confiées à un Centre, ce dernier ne pourrait que s'incliner […].«[272]
>
> [Certainly, the essential obstacle had to do with the parties disagreement; had they decided together to end the functions to organise the arbitration assigned to the centre, the latter could not have done anything but to resign…]

---

266 Ibid.

267 *République de Guinée V*, [1988] Rev. Arb. 657 at II., second last paragraph.

268 Ibid. at II., fifth paragraph.

269 *See also* Fouchard, »Note, CA Paris, 04.05.1988, TGI Paris, 23.06.1988«, para. 13.

270 *Contra* Schöldström, *The Arbitrator's Mandate*, 403–11 (arguing that each arbitrant enters into a separate contract with the institution); *cf. also* ibid., 9. However, Schöldström admits that his model mainy works for a *»hypothetical run-of-mill ICC arbitration«* and not for attempts by parties to opt out of institutional rules (ibid., 410, 416).

271 *See generally* Leverenz, *Gestaltungsrechtsausübungen durch und gegen Personenmehrheiten*.

272 Fouchard, »Note, CA Paris, 04.05.1988, TGI Paris, 23.06.1988«, para. 8.

Generally, a plurality of persons on one side of a contract has to act together to terminate it.[273] Materially, such problem might be overcome by assuming a duty to cooperate between the arbitrants.[274] Procedurally, however, a claim *between arbitrants* based on such duty to cooperate in the termination of the Administration Contract falls within the scope of the arbitration agreement.[275] Consequence of the French prima facie approach to reviewing arbitral jurisdiction,[276] the CA Paris thus had to refrain from interfering.

III. Fate of the arbitration agreement: reconsidering the TGI's decisions

Only the TGI's first instance decisions in *République de Guinée*[277] addressed the problem of the fate of the arbitration agreement when the Administration Contract with the institution is, for whatever reason, null, void or terminated. In contrast, the CA Paris did not have to reconsider this question as it rejected the motion to annul the Administration Contract. According to the TGI, the arbitration agreement could survive the termination of the Administration Contract as an ad hoc agreement in line with the principle »*in favorem validitatis.*«[278]

As a side note, this corresponds with the procedural solution proposed by Romanian law, which –exceptionally - covers institutional arbitration extensively in its arbitration law:

> »If the organisation or institution specified in Article 616 refuses to administer the arbitration, the arbitration agreement shall remain valid, and the dispute between the parties shall be resolved pursuant to the provisions of the present Book.«[279]

---

273 *Cf.* Leverenz, *Gestaltungsrechtsausübungen durch und gegen Personenmehrheiten*, 154, n. 37 (on the example of a contract for lease with more than one lessee; with references to case law).

274 *See* ibid., 100.

275 *But see* Wolf, *Die Institutionelle Handelsschiedsgerichtsbarkeit*, 200–202 (suggesting procedural challenges against institutions by analogy to provisions on arbitrator challenges).

276 *But see infra* at pp. 415-419 (§16A.II.1.b) on divergent understandings of arbitral competence-competence.

277 *Supra* at pp. 265-265 (§11C.I.2).

278 *See supra* at pp. 161-163 (§8B) and pp. 207-209 (§9)

279 CPC art. 621 (RO); English translation by Ileana Smeureanu and Brooks Hickmann, published in: Paulsson, *International Handbook on Commercial Arbitration*, Romania, Annex I (supp. no. 74, last updated May 2013); *see supra* at pp. 98 et seq. (§4C.II.2.b.ii).

This obliges parties to arbitrate in ad hoc proceedings if the designated institution refuses to administer their arbitration.[280]

Another conceivable option would be to refer parties to another institution rather than to ad hoc arbitration. As already noted, striking out unworkable optional elements from an arbitration agreement like the reference to an unavailable institution, which can be based on the idea of partial (in-)validity, often appears less controversial than adding elements by way of contract adaptation for change of circumstances. However, party autonomy is endorsed best if a solution was found on a case-by-case basis in accordance with the principle »*in favorem voluntatis.*«[281] In many cases, ad hoc arbitration with state court support in the constitution of an arbitral tribunal will be an appropriate solution. If, however, it was of particular importance to the parties that the arbitration is overseen by a permanent institution, it may be more appropriate to adapt the arbitration agreement to designate another institution and rules able to meet the parties' expectations.[282] In case of a hybrid arbitration agreement, the rules issuing institution would be the most obvious substitute.

Then, there may also be - few, exceptional - instances where the administration by a particular institution was of such importance to the parties that the non-conclusion or termination of the Administration Contract with such institution would deprive the arbitration agreement itself of its basis.[283]

## *§12 Hybrid arbitration agreements and autonomy of the institution*

Concluding this chapter, one has to admit that the operability of hybrid arbitration agreements depends critically on the will of the institution designated to administer the proceedings. Institutional flexibility regarding rule modifications varies but most institutions do not welcome a complete opting-out of their rules.

---

280  The provision does not clarify when an institution has the right to refuse administering a case. Romanian doctrine recommends that arbitral institutions should adopt rules enumerating exemplary grounds for refusal (Bobei, *Arbitrajul intern și internaţional*, art. 621, para. 2).

281  *See supra* at pp. 161-163 (§8B) and pp. 207-209 (§9).

282  *Cf.* Wolf, *Die Institutionelle Handelsschiedsgerichtsbarkeit*, 199 (but, in detail, going a little too far with his proposal, *see supra* at pp. 202-203, §8C.II.3).

283  On jurisdictions hostile to ad hoc arbitration or with a monopolist institution, *see supra* at p. 180.

If an institution is unwilling to administer cases under modified rules or rules other than its own, it does not have to accept the parties' (counter-)offer to conclude an Administration Contract pursuant to their terms. Even were initial communication by an institution's secretariat amounts to acceptance, the institution should be able to terminate the Administration Contract prior to the constitution of a tribunal without liability consequences. Up to that point, an institution would usually follow its own practices in administering the arbitration and it has herein been argued that it is allowed to do so despite the agreement on other rules by the parties. Accordingly, the autonomy of the institution designated to administer an arbitration on the basis of a hybrid arbitration agreement is adversary to the principle of party autonomy calling to implement such agreements as precise as possible. The parties, in return, also have a termination right if they are not content with the institution's implementation of their agreement but they have to exercise this right together.

If the Administration Contract is not concluded or if it is terminated, the arbitration agreement can contractually survive as an agreement on ad hoc arbitration. However, for an originally hybrid arbitration agreement it may be even more appropriate, either for the parties themselves or a competent court,[284] to then adapt it to refer to the rules issuing institution.[285]

---

284 Chapter 5 discusses the extent to which arbitration laws provide supporting courts with the competence to install such solution, *infra* at pp. 422 et seq. (§16A.II.1.d).

285 *See already supra* at pp. 207-209 (§9).

# Chapter 4: Opting-in aspect - applying another institution's rules

The opting-out aspect of hybrid arbitration agreements just discussed concerned a number of general issues of flexibility of institutional arbitration and the contractual relationships in an institutional setting. Therefore, the observations made do not only apply to the specific issue hybrid arbitration but also to problems arising from other non-standard institutional arbitration agreements.

In contrast, the opting-in aspect, meaning the choice of institutional rules independent from the institution that issued these rules, is a characteristic feature of hybrid arbitration agreements only. This, the opting-in aspect, was perceived as the most contentious when SIAC agreed to administer the *Alstom–Insigma* arbitration under ICC Rules.[1] It is also what makes article 4 (3) of the CIETAC Rules so unusual in comparison to other rules' endorsements of party autonomy.[2] The ICC Court's and AAA-ICDR's reactions with exclusivity provisions in their own rules prove the controversy.[3]

A reason for such strong reaction may be a perception that institutions agreeing to administer cases under another institution's rules somehow unduly benefit from the reputation these rules have gained with the public, raising the question is such conduct was actually *legal* (§13).

A staff member of an arbitral institution and self-acclaimed »*Arbitration Activist*« once strongly rejected the »*accepted language*« of referring to an arbitration institution as a »›*service provider*‹ *in a* ›*highly competitive market*«, and recalled the original noble goal of arbitration pioneers to enable the »[p]*eaceful resolution of disputes.*«[4] Nevertheless, it cannot be denied that arbitral centres are indeed competing for users, their rules being important assets in such competition, which justifies considering the protection of their rules against use by competitors. However, not mainly commercial or financial interests motivate arbitral institutions like the ICC Court or the AAA-ICDR to strive for exclusivity in their rules. Protection of the exclusivity of institutional rules is also a form of quality control.

---

1   *See e.g.* Kirby, »SIAC Can Administer Cases Under The ICC Rules?!?«
2   *See supra* at pp. 224-228 (§ 10.B.IV, V) for the LCIA and AAA-ICDR Rules, at least in their former versions.
3   *See supra* at pp. 39-43§1E).
4   Magnusson, »A Call from an Arbitration Activist«.

Incorrect implementation of such rules by another institution could arguably not only damage the reputation of the rules but the trust in the institutional arbitration system altogether. Accordingly, this chapter shall also analyse if and how one institution can *factually* apply the rules of another (§14).

Having concluded the last chapter with the observation that the operability of hybrid arbitration agreements depends on the designated institution's will, this chapter will provide important information for institutions confronted with a request for hybrid arbitration to form that will (§15).

## §13 The legality of administering hybrid arbitrations

When looking article 1 (2) of the ICC Rules, according to which the ICC Court is »*the only body authorized to administer arbitrations under the Rules*«, one of the first ideas that spring to mind is that the ICC Court seeks to protect the exclusive use of its rules. Although, for the time being, the ICC does not make any efforts to enforce this exclusivity clause,[5] this subsection shall analyse if the ICC *could* take any legal action to keep other institutions from applying its rules or if the provision will remain simply a policy statement. As already sufficiently made clear, article 1 (2) of the ICC Rules itself - or the corresponding provision article 1 (3) sentence 4 of the AAA-ICDR Rules[6] - is not itself a sufficient basis for a legal claim against conduct of parties arbitrating before another institution or such other institution's conduct. With arbitration rules not having the status of law that would apply outside a contractual relationship and a contract between the rules issuing institution and these parties or the other institution not existing, the potential cause of action must lie elsewhere, possibly in intellectual or industrial property (IP) or unfair competition law.

The idea of IP or unfair competition law claims within the arbitration market has not yet received any scholarly attention, although it seems not entirely far-fetched.[7] The decision of the Singapore Court of Appeals in the *Insigma v. Alstom* case hinted at possible issues of exploitation of

---

5    *See supra* at p. 45, n. 95.

6    As quoted in the introduction, *supra* at p. 41.

7    *Cf. only* Redfern and Hunter, *Law and Practice (1986)*, 115 (warning about copyright issues when using institutional rules for ad hoc arbitration; no longer featuring in the current edition).

trademarks or goodwill, referring to the »*ICC brand of arbitration.*«[8] Moreover, former CIETAC Vice Chair and Secretary General Wang Shen Chang and former CIETAC staff member Lijun Cao also report to have encountered copyright claims by an English institution, whose rules the parties had chosen for arbitration administered by CIETAC:

> »In reality, the CIETAC handled several cases in which the parties agreed to refer the disputes to arbitration by the CIETAC in China, but under the Rules of an English institution. [...] Apart from that, the Rules are deemed copyright documents by the English institution, and the institution protested against the use of them in arbitration by the CIETAC, thus making the parties' agreement inoperative. In those cases, the CIETAC had to persuade the parties to reach an agreement, which they did reluctantly, to replace the Rules with CIETAC's.«[9]

Politically, it was certainly a wise decision to persuade parties to change to CIETAC Rules already to avoid any quarrel with the English institution.[10] Legally, however, the assumption that the use of another institution's rules would infringe copyrights (A) or any other form of protection (B-C) requires a more careful analysis to which this section will contribute; concluding with some remarks on the desirability of exclusive rules (D).

A. Institutional rules and copyright of the issuing institution

The first question asked is if arbitration rules are works protected by copyright law. Before addressing this issue, it is first necessary to launch a kind of *disclaimer*: At a conference entitled »*The Future of Copyright: If I could change just one thing*«,[11] one of the speakers, Cédric Manara, expressed his wish as follows:

---

8    *Insigma v. Alstom*, [2009] SGCA 24 [36].

9    Wang and Cao, »Towards a Higher Degree of Party Autonomy and Transparency«, 122.

10   *But see* Geiger, »Flexibilising Copyright«, 182 (regretting that a »*user, if he is not sure whether he needs an authorisation, rather than risk a law suit, might refrain from using free information*«); *cf. also* Logan, »The Emperor's New Clothes? - Part 2«, 92.

11   The conference was held on 7 October 2014 at King's College London, co-organised by the law firm Baker & McKenzie and WIPO on the occasion of the launch of the »Collecting Societies Handbook«. A video is available online (herein cited as »The Future of Copyright«).

»make.copyright.simple.«[12]

The problem is, copyright is currently far from being simple. Among the difficulties addressed at the conference just mentioned were:

- The problem of identifying copyrighted works, in lack of a formality requirement,[13] with different thresholds for protection in various legal systems.[14]
- The distinction between rights in form and expression, which are infringed only by close reproduction, and rights in content, which are only acknowledged to a limited degree (so-called *idea/expression* dichotomy).[15]
- The problem of internationally varying laws unable to cope with today's globalised and digitalised world and the corresponding conflict of laws and jurisdiction issues.[16]

When discussing the very specific problem of hybrid arbitration as a potential copyright issue, all these pitfalls of current copyright law coincide. The following considerations will address them in the just mentioned order. They start by identifying arbitration rules as copyrighted works, continue with an enquiry into the idea/expression dichotomy when assessing potential infringement by another institution using these rules and finish with highlighting jurisdictional and applicable law problems.

However, despite attempting an account on the basis of the current status of copyright law,[17] which, again, is not simple, the analysis will not be able to avoid a number of simplifications in order to remain within the scope of

---

12  »The Future of Copyright«, at 0:40:50. Cédric Manara is copyright counsel at Google.

13  *Cf.* Berne Convention, art. 5 (2).

14  *See* »The Future of Copyright«, from 0:34:07 (Cédric Manara naming photos of sausages or cats or posts in social networks as examples of protected »*works*«).

15  *E.g.*, Judge Colin Birss, said if he could change one thing it would be his - highly controversial - »*Red Bus*« judgment (*Temple Island v. New English Teas*, [2012] EWPCC 1 [EW Patents County Court]), not the result, but its reasoning on the »*signal*« v. »*content*« copyright distinction (»The Future of Copyright«, from 0:43:00, *see also infra* at pp. 284-288, §13A.II.2).

16  *E.g.*, Professor Bernt Hugenholtz wished for a uniform European copyright code (ironically adding: »*preferably of* [his] *own making*«, »*The Future of Copyright*«, at 0:24:23.).

17  As opposed to a discussion of how copyright should be regulated.

this arbitration-centred thesis. The discussion can only touch upon the main ideas of copyright law with a hope to motivate scholars from around the world to engage in a more thorough discussion of this topic and to test the proposals made against the background of various national laws.

I. Copyrightability of arbitration rules

The Berne Convention, as the most important convention on author's rights or copyrights,[18] covers *»literary and artistic works«*, requiring contracting states to protect *»every production in the literary, scientific and artistic domain, whatever may be the mode or form of its expression«*, and provides a long but still not exhaustive list of examples.[19] This wide definition principally encompasses texts for practical application like arbitration rules. *»The content of the work is never a condition of protection.«*[20]

Neither is an utilitarian, commercial purpose an obstacle to the application of copyrights under the convention.[21]

One prerequisite of protection, however, is answered neither by the Berne Convention nor by any other international instrument: Which texts qualify as *»works«* of an author? This concerns the thresholds of originality or creativity.[22] These criteria for granting copyright protection have to be considered pursuant to national law.[23]

Protection of creative works follows slightly different systems in Anglo-American and civil law systems. Anglo-American law uses the term *»copyright«* to describe rights granted by common law and statutes, originally restraining publication by copying of printed original works, later extended to also embrace public performance and non-original works.[24] These systems focus on *»concepts of advantages for society«*, economic incentive and *»reward for the author«*[25] while the civil law approach links authors'

---

18  Supplemented by the WIPO Copyright Treaty; *see* Lewinski, »§ 57 Grundlagen«, para. 18, 78.
19  Berne Convention, art. 2 (1).
20  *WIPO Guide*, 12, art. 2, para. 2.2.
21  Ibid., 13, art. 2, para. 2.4.
22  *See* Lewinski, »§ 57 Grundlagen«, para. 22.
23  Also, the Berne Convention, only concerns the legal position of foreign authors or works with a connection to a state other than the forum state. It belongs to the law of aliens (German *»Fremdenrecht«, see* ibid., para. 26).
24  *See* Sterling, *World Copyright Law*, para. 2.19, 2.20.
25  Ibid., para. 2.26; *cf. Feist v. Rural*, 499 U.S. 340, 349–50 (1991).

rights to the personality of the author, thereby focussing more on rights of the individual.[26]

In addition to these conceptual differences,[27] there are variances in legal systems as to whether original rights can be acquired by another person than the natural person intellectually creating the work, if the work is created on behalf of such other person. This is connected to the question if legal persons such as companies and institutions can be *authors* or *first owners* of rights, a question that shall be excluded from the scope of this thesis by assuming that the concerned arbitral institutions are at least entitled by assignment.

For reasons of simplification and unless otherwise specified the term »*copyright*« will in the following be used in its widest possible sense

> »as a catch-all phrase to describe rights granted to authors and related rights owners, in any system.«[28]

## 1. The originality/creativity threshold

It is generally acknowledged that copyright protection presupposes a certain level of originality[29] or even creativity[30] of the work. Because of the different philosophical approaches to copyright protection, which focus either on the effort involved or on the personality input of the author, criteria for protection are not (yet) uniform.[31] Civil law jurisdictions require »*a creation*«[32] or even a »*personal intellectual creation*«,[33] or at least »*an individual*

---

26  Sterling, *World Copyright Law*, para. 2.26.
27  *Cf. also* ibid., para. 2.09–2.14 (referring to classifications either as »*property*«, »*monopoly*« or »*personality*« or »*sui generis*« rights).
28  Ibid., para. 2.02 (10).
29  Ibid., para. 7.06; *see* Hilty and Nérisson, *Balancing Copyright*, 14 (»*all reports mention the originality requirement*«).
30  *But see* Hilty and Nérisson, *Balancing Copyright*, 14, 15 (most reporters rejected a condition of creativity, possibly for reasons of terminology).
31  *Cf.* Sterling, *World Copyright Law*, para. 7.06.
32  *See e.g.* CPI art. L. 111–1 (FR); *see also* Bertrand, *Droit d'auteur*, para. 103.38 (on the French understanding of »*création*«); *cf. e.g. Compagnie des Courtiers v Cellier des Halles*, [1991] 150 RIDA 147 (FR CA, Paris) (»*un apport original*«).
33  *See e.g.* for German law: UrhG § 2 (2) (GER) (»*persönliche geistige Schöpfungen*«).

*character.«*[34] Among common law jurisdictions, there are variances and some uncertainties as to the applicable test: Either the mere investment of skill, labour, judgment[35] - sometimes even reduced to the proverbial »*sweat of a brow*«[36] - may be enough or there has to be »*some minimal degree of creativity*« involved.[37]

To leave the depths of dogmatic differences among legal systems,[38] it appears most sensible to answer the question whether institutional arbitration rules enjoy copyright protection in any legal system by recalling a few illustrative and possibly analogous cases. As arbitration rules are a document for practical use, the following examples will be restricted to cases of utility works rather than pure literary or artistic works.

German courts have developed specific criteria to evaluate whether utility works like administrative or contractual forms or catalogues deserve copyright protection. According to this jurisprudence, the requirements for copyright protection are very reduced, except for works of applied art protectable by a design.[39] This jurisprudence is referred to as the »*Kleine Münze*« (small change) of copyright law, meaning that even less ground-breaking works are worthy of protection.[40] Already the *Reichsgericht* (Supreme Court of the German Reich) constantly held that copyrightability

---

34 *See* URG art. 2 (C.H.); on the evolution of Swiss jurisprudence towards a reduced, more objective individuality standard: Cherpillod, »Art. 2«, para. 15–22.

35 *See* Rahmatian, »Originality in UK Copyright Law«, 5 (with references on English case law); *see in particular: University of London Press v. University Tutorial Press*, [1916] 2 Ch 601 (EW) at 609 (only requiring »*that the work must not be copied from another work*«); for Singapore, *see* Allen, »Computer Software and Singapore's Law of Copyright«, 502; citing *Re AUVI Trade Mark*, [1992] 1 SLR 639 (SG HC) at 648.

36 Critical: Handig, »The Sweat of the Brow is Not Enough!«, vol. 35, n. 41.

37 For the US approach, *see Feist v. Rural*, 499 U.S. at 345–46.

38 *Cf.* Sterling, *World Copyright Law*, para. 7.20 (»*divergences may be less marked than at first sight may appear*«).

39 *See* Urteil [Judgment]: »*Silberdistel-Ohrclip*«, [1995] 97 GRUR 581 (GER BGH) at 582.

40 First used by Elster, *Gewerblicher Rechtsschutz*, 40 (»*ob es große oder kleine Münze ist*« [no matter whether it is big or small change]). The term may be inspired by the German proverb »*Wer den Penny nicht ehrt, ist des Talers nicht wert*« (Take care of the pence and the pounds will take care of themselves).

only requires a very small degree of personal creation.[41] The BGH partially follows this tradition, confirming *inter alia* the protectability of unofficial headnotes (summaries) to court decisions published in a review.[42] The BGH also acknowledged the general copyrightability of a lawyer's brief,[43] although the case was remanded to the lower instance for further factual assessment,[44] which is why the BGH's decision is constantly misunderstood as negating copyrightability.[45] The Higher Regional Court of Cologne justified the grant of an injunction against the use of standard business terms on eBay copied word for word from a competitor, but remarked that short, correct legal formulations should not be monopolised.[46] The Regional Court of Berlin admitted copyright protection of a model contract for »*host providing*«, finding that a clear and comprehensible definition of rights and obligations of parties to a contract not regulated in the civil code was an individual personal creation.[47]

However, there are also a number of contrasting decisions where German courts declined copyright protection of written works of legal nature. For example, the Regional Court of Stuttgart declined the copyrightability of a

---

41  *E.g.* Urteil [Judgment]*:* »*Kochrezepte*«, [1912] 81 RGZ 120 (GER RG) 123 (granting copyright to cooking recipes); *see also* Reimer, *Zum Urheberrechtsschutz von Darstellungen wissenschaftlicher oder technischer Art*, 575, n. 21.

42  *See* Urteil [Judgment]*:* »*Leitsätze*«, [1992] 94 GRUR 382 (GER BGH) at 386 (but there assuming a copyright exception as the headnotes were drafted by public judges) *see also* Beschluss [Decision], [2009] 9 GRUR-RR 164 (GER OLG, Cologne).

43  Urteil [Judgment], [1987] 40 NJW 1332 (GER BGH).

44  Ibid., at 1333 (stressing that the personal creation could only be denied if the brief's structure and language strictly followed the necessities of content, found unlikely in that case).

45  *E.g.* Kreutzer and Roger, »Copyright Protection of Standard Contracts« (annotation falsely labelling the BGH case with »*not copyrightable*«); *see also* Schack, *Urheber- und Urhebervertragsrecht*, para. 205 (finding the BGH's requirements for the protection of lawyer's briefs as scientific works to be very high); *contra* Wild, »Anmerkung: Zur urheberrechtlichen Schutzfähigkeit von Anwaltsschriftsätzen« 742 (finding that the BGH too quickly assumed copyrightability of lawyer's briefs, wanting to resort to unfair competition law).

46  Urteil [Judgment], 6 U 193/08, BeckRS 2009, 26171 (GER OLG, Cologne, 27 February 2009).

47  Beschluss [Decision], 16 O 83/05 (GER LG, Berlin, 4 August 2005) [26–28] (cited according to the database juris).

six-page standard contract for work placements of Polish nurses.[48] The decision was mainly based on the principle of freedom of ideas. Accordingly, the court held that some specific formulations might enjoy copyright protection, but not the ideas behind the contract provisions as such or the contract as a whole. Regarding the threshold of creativity, the court found that only such contract drafts are copyrightable that are exceptionally well-drafted products (German: »*Spitzen- bzw. Ausnahmeprodukt*«),[49] standing out from the mass of similar contracts.[50] The Higher Regional Court of Brandenburg decided similar, holding that model contracts usually do not have work quality, unless they are very complex, sophisticated and long.[51]

Overall, the German jurisprudence is confusing. On the one hand, works that show only a minimal degree of individual personal creation are considered protectable. That such »*small change*« has a practical purpose is acknowledged as a natural limit to creativity, thus reducing the requirements for protection.[52] On the other hand, it is deemed an obstacle to protection if the form follows the necessities of content, requiring a clear supremacy over the common, craftsman-like or mechanical-technical assortment of the material.[53]

These uncertainties, as well as the divergences from the standards established by the Berne Convention which oppose different levels of protection for utility works and pure artistic works,[54] could be easily overcome by addressing the underlying principle of freedom of ideas *only at the infringement level*. Equal protection of all works, independent of their artistic quality, can only be achieved by uniform and reduced requirements of creativity. A fear of blocking access to useful information is unfounded where courts

---

48   Beschluss [Decision], 17 O 68/08 (GER LG, Stuttgart, 6 March 2008); English summary: Kreutzer and Roger, »Copyright Protection of Standard Contracts«.

49   Beschluss [Decision], 17 O 68/08 (GER LG, Stuttgart, 6 March 2008) at [9].

50   Ibid., para. 5.

51   Urteil [Judgment], [2010] 10 GRUR-RR 273 (GER OLG, Brandenburg) 273.

52   Urteil [Judgment]: »*Bedienungsanweisung*«, [1993] 95 GRUR 34 (GER BGH) 35.

53   Ibid., 36 (»*ein deutliches Überragen des Alltäglichen, des Handwerksmäßigen, der mechanisch-technischen Aneinanderreihung des Materials*«); *see also* Urteil [Judgment], [1987] 40 NJW 1333.

54   *WIPO Guide*, 13, art. 2, para. 2.4.

consistently respect the idea/expression dichotomy at the infringement level.[55]

Two cases decided in the 1990s provide a good example of the equally confusing position of French courts on the level of originality/creativity needed for copyright protection of utility works. Both cases have very similar facts but contrasting outcomes. In the case *Compagnie des Courtiers v Cellier des Halles* the appellate court of Paris found that a map of wine regions in France was, at least partly, a protected work because the choice of colouring, typography and evaluation of wines were a sufficiently original contribution.[56] In contrast, in *Courtiers Jurés Piqueurs de Vins de Paris v. Needham (Sté DBB)* a table of wine regions in France with years and a short comment on the quality of each vintage, like »*petite année*«, »*année exceptionelle*« (poor year, exceptional year), was found to lack originality. Rejecting the appeal against the decision of the appellate court of Douai in this case,[57] the Cour de Cassation held that the wine listing, considering the presentation in form of a table and the comments on the vintages, only contained trivial information and expressions.[58] In their result, these decisions convey that the French courts in fact judged the quality and value of the wine guides, which is neither nationally[59] nor internationally an acknowledged criterion of protection.[60] Again, it would have been more appropriate to accept copyrightability but inquire more thoroughly into the question whether there was an infringement of existing copyright.[61]

Similarly, Swiss doctrine and jurisprudence reduce the individuality threshold to a minimum degree of individual labour if form and expression are dictated by functional necessities,[62] but deny protection to business texts like standardised letters, manuals or standard business terms for lacking individuality, nonetheless.[63]

The English standard for copyright protection is equally difficult to assess. While commonly the »*skill and labour*«-test is assumed to establish a

---

55   *See infra* at pp. 288 et seq. (§13A.II).
56   *Compagnie des Courtiers v Cellier des Halles*, [1991] 150 RIDA 147.
57   *Needham v. Vins de Paris*, [1997] 172 RIDA 189 (FR CA, Douai).
58   *Vins de Paris v Needham*, [1999] 180 RIDA 353 (FR C.Cass) at 357.
59   *Cf.* CPI art. L. 112–1 (FR).
60   *WIPO Guide*, 13, art. 2, para. 2.4.
61   *See infra* at pp. 288 et seq. (§13A.II).
62   *See* Cherpillod, »Art. 2«, para. 19 (with references to the relevant court decisions).
63   Ibid., para. 45.

rather low threshold not requiring any form of creativity,[64] there is some case law indicating that this standard would exclude some utility works from copyright. For example, in *Cramp & Sons v. Smythson,*[65] the House of Lords found a compilation of postal rates, weights and measures not worthy of copyright protection. It was considered too common[66] although, in contrast, it had been held in *University of London Press Ltd. v. University Tutorial Press Ltd.* that mathematics exam papers were protectable as »*what is worth copying is prima facie worth protecting*«, neglecting any quality threshold altogether.[67]

US case law developed towards restricting copyright protection for utility works at both levels: copyrightability and infringement. In 1986, the US Court of Appeals of the Eighth Circuit still found the insertion of page numbers from the reporter system of the West Publishing group (hereinafter »*West*«) into the database maintained by West's competitor Lexis to be an infringement of copyright not of the decisions, which are in the public domain,[68] but of West's compilation thereof.[69] The court followed the commercial argument that this »*would pro tanto reduce anyone's need to buy West's books*«, holding that the mere use of page numbers infringes copyright in the arrangement because a user could, *in theory*, reproduce an entire volume.[70]

However, the Supreme Court heightened the standard of originality in its *Feist v. Rural* decision, discarded the »*sweat of a brow*« doctrine according to which mere efforts in compiling data resulted in copyright protection, and declined copyrightability of phone book listings, as opposed to the phone book as a whole.[71] The court held that there is »*nothing remotely*

---

64   *But see* Rahmatian, »Originality in UK Copyright Law«, 12 (rejecting the lower v. higher standard assumption).

65   *GA Cramp & Sons Ltd v Frank Smythson Ltd,* [1944] AC 329 (UK HL).

66   Ibid., 335 (»*part of the ordinary contents of any pocket diary*«).

67   *University of London Press v. University Tutorial Press,* [1916] 2 Ch 601.

68   *See infra* at p. 284.

69   West's National Reporter System is the leading case law reporter in the United States (*see* Yen, »The Danger of Bootstrap Formalism in Copyright«, 462).

70   *West v. Mead,* 799 F.2d 1219, 1227–28 (8th Cir. 1986); severely criticised *inter alia* by Yen, »The Danger of Bootstrap Formalism in Copyright« (identifying the ruling as »*the ›worst‹ intellectual property opinion ever written*« in a symposium named accordingly).

71   *Feist v. Rural,* 499 U.S. at 361–64.

*creative about arranging names alphabetically.*«[72] This change in jurisprudence inevitably led West's claims to fail. In 1998, the Court of Appeals for the Second Circuit denied copyright protection in the publications of West, including page numbers, except for editorial features such as synopsis, digest topics, and key numbers.[73]. The decisions convincingly held that the page numbers and page breaks alone in West's reporters are not copyrightable and therefore the insertion of star pagination was not an infringing »*copy.*«[74] This jurisprudence, which cannot be understood as a complete denial of copyrightability of legal utility works, neatly underlines the connection between copyrightability and infringement when assessing copyright claims for utility works: Copyrightability of utility works only extends to such aspects which are not entirely prescribed by factual necessities, for this reason, many parts of such works are free to use. Infringement claims will therefore often fail unless the entire work is copied.

Singapore's jurisprudence, based on copyright law »*grandfathered*« in England,[75] appears now similar to that of US courts, requiring only a minimum degree of creativity for factual works but applying a strict test to determining infringement.[76] On a claim of copyright infringement by publishing tables of horse racing results similar to those published by a competitor, the Singapore Court of Appeals found the required level of creativity »*to be extremely low*«[77] although the information itself »*was freely available in the public domain.*«[78]

Quite convincing is the reasoning of the Higher Regional Court of Vienna in a decision of 2012,[79] who acknowledged that standard business terms enjoy copyright protection independent of their aesthetic or artistic value. The required individuality can follow both from the language used and from the intellectual construction of the text. However, the court rejected a claim for an injunction for lack of exact copy of the standard business terms.[80] The court thereby recognised the freedom of ideas and general

---

72 Ibid., 363.
73 Two decisions: *Bender v. West* (I), 158 F.3d 674 (2nd Cir. 1998); *Bender v. West* (II), 158 F.3d 693 (2nd Cir. 1998). The Supreme Court denied certiorari (*West v. Bender*, 526 U.S. 1154 [1999]).
74 *Bender v. West* (I), at 676; *Bender v. West* (II), at 693.
75 *Asia Pacific Publ. v. P & L*, [2011] SGCA 37 [17].
76 *See* Ng-Loy, »Singapore«, 829, 836.
77 *Asia Pacific Publ. v. P & L*, [2011] SGCA 37 [38].
78 Ibid., para. 97.
79 Entscheidung, 4 R 30/12d (AUT OLG, Vienna, 28 June 2012).
80 However, the court found an unfair competition law claim possible.

information underlying the copyrighted text. The Austrian Supreme Court confirmed the decision, and clarified that the less a model stands out from standard clauses used in a certain trade, the less likely will inspiration by it be an infringement of copyright. The original expression then just fades away (»»*Verblassen*‹ *des Originals*«).[81]

In light of the summarised jurisprudence by courts of various jurisdictions, many provisions in institutional arbitration rules will overcome the threshold of originality or creativity. Usually, teams of professionals draft such rules with great care and in a month if not yearlong process. Moreover, institutional arbitration rules, even individual articles and paragraphs, still vary greatly both in terms of language and content.[82] This indicates that their formulation is usually not entirely prescribed by factual necessities. They contain valuable contributions to the little detailed national arbitration laws. The verdict of a standard, mass product not worthy of copyright protection is therefore indefendable. To apply a formula suggested by the Swiss Supreme Court,[83] it seems excluded that a person asked to draft arbitration rules would draft rules identical to those of one of the existing institutions unless such person was copying from them. If one holds true to the principle that copyright protection should neither depend on the purpose of the work nor its artistic quality,[84] it is therefore undeniable that pre-drafted arbitration rules enjoy copyright protection, unless they are themselves copied from other rules.

The - albeit merely declaratory[85] - copyright notice imprinted on publications of many arbitration rules is therefore justified in principle. That of the ICC Rules shall here be quoted for illustration:

---

81   Entscheidung, 4 Ob 175/12g (AUT OGH, 18 October 2012).

82   *See infra* at pp. 355 et seq. (§14B) for a comparison of rules.

83   »*L'individualité se distingue de la banalité ou du travail de routine; elle résulte de la diversité des décisions prises par l'auteur, de combinaisons surprenantes et inhabituelles, de sorte qu'il paraît exclu qu'un tiers confronté à la même tâche ait pu créer une oeuvre identique*« [Individuality is distinguished from banality and rountine work; it results from a diversity of decisions made by the author, of surprising or unusual combinations of a kind that appear to exclude that someone else confronted with the same task would have created an identical work] (*Guide Orange*, [2010] ATF 136 III 225 [C.H. BG] at 229).

84   *See supra* at p. 275.

85   However, *de lege ferenda*, reintroduction of copyright notices was among the most popular proposals for change at the conference mentioned above

Nevertheless, it has to be borne in mind that copyright is designed to protect the author, not to protect investment by privatising information.[87] The interests of the public in free access to information have to be respected when determining when copyright in arbitration rules is actually infringed. Copyright concerns the formulations used, not the mere ideas behind a written work.[88]

2. Arbitration rules as works in the public domain?

The Berne Convention grants leeway to the countries of the Berne Union

»to determine the protection to be granted to official texts of a legislative, administrative and legal nature, and to official translations of such texts.«[89]

While arbitration rules are neither legislative nor administrative texts,[90] their »*legal nature*« is hard to deny. The question whether the Berne Convention requires to accord such rules the same protection as other literary works therefore depends on the meaning of »*official texts.*« From the wording, it is not entirely clear if this includes any texts of »*legal nature*« or only »*Public Sector Information*« (PSI), which means »*information produced, held, collected, commissioned by public entities or government controlled entities.*«[91] The latter understanding appears correct as the official WIPO guide mentions »*statutes, administrative regulations and court judgments*« (hereinafter »*state works*«) as examples falling under article 2 (4) of the Berne Convention.[92] In contrast, privately enacted texts, even if of legal nature, are not exempt from copyright.

---

as such requirement could simplify copyright law in today's globalised and digitalised age.

86  *See e.g.* ICC Rules (2012) (inside cover of ICC publication No 850 E).
87  Geiger, »Flexibilising Copyright«, 178 (introduction).
88  *See infra* at pp. 288 et seq. (§13A.II).
89  Berne Convention, art. 2 (4).
90  *See supra* at pp. 110-116 (§5B).
91  Jasserand and Hugenholtz, *Using Copyright to Promote Access to PSI*, 2, 5.
92  *WIPO Guide*, 20, art. 2, para. 2.18.

Many jurisdictions acknowledge exceptions for state works expressly.[93] Even without statutory stipulation to this effect, courts traditionally find state works to be in the *»public domain«*, meaning that the public interest to access, use and copy such works outweighs the interest of the author to restrict use.[94] Only a few states, notably France, repudiate a copyright exception for state works.[95]

Since arbitration rules are drafted on behalf of institutions that are commonly private actors, the question of exclusion of copyright for state works is not immediately relevant.[96] Arbitral institutions are not entrusted by the state to perform tasks of public authority.[97] However, some arbitration rules are published in official reporters or are authorised by government authorities, in particular in socialist or former socialist countries.[98] Moreover, the reason why many national laws exclude state works from copyright protection is the public interest to access and use authoritative works with mandatory or widespread application. This could raise the question if some of these interests would not also call for copyright exceptions for widely used arbitration rules, which - although not laws - have at least persuasive

---

93   *E.g.* UrhG § 5 (GER); Copyright Law § 105 (US); *see* Hilty and Nérisson, *Balancing Copyright*, 5 n. 17 (listing corresponding national legal provisions).

94   Under English law, the Crown or the parliament has copyright in state works (Copyright Act §§ 163–68 [EW]) but Crown copyright is waived for certain works such as parliamentary materials and laws, so that these are factually in the public domain (*see* Office of Public Sector Information, Minister of the Cabinet Office, and United Kingdom, *The Future Management of Crown Copyright.*, chap. 5).

95   CPI art. L. 111–1 (FR) (line 3, sent. 2).

96   This may be different for UNCITRAL, WIPO and ICSID arbitration rules because they are issued by international organisations within the meaning of public international law, their members are states (on this issue, *see generally* Kunz-Hallstein, »Die Beteiligung internationaler Organisationen am Rechts- und Wirtschaftsverkehr«).

97   *See supra* pp. 110-116 (§5B); on the official nature of works by state entrusted persons (German: »*Beliehene*«), *cf.* Albrecht, *Amtliche Werke und Schranken des Urheberrechts*, 64–65.

98   *E.g.* CCIR Rules are published in Romania's official monitor (»*Monitorul Oficial*«). CIETAC Rules were originally adopted by the China Council for the Promotion of International Trade, a government entity.

authority.[99] While copyright exceptions for arbitration rules are not yet a topic of academic debate, a few German authors discussed the suggestion that published arbitral awards, institutional arbitral awards in particular,[100] may be treated like court decisions as copyright exempt under § 5 (1) UrhG (GER).[101] Against this background, a proposal to treat arbitration rules like state laws for copyright purposes appears, at the outset, not entirely far-fetched.

Moreover, some scholars assert and even courts have held that there is no copyright in certain technical norms or standard business terms if these are officially published or authorised by the state[102] and in other privately authored works appropriated by the state.[103] However, a copyright exception for such privately drafted terms could only be assumed under these conditions:[104]

- The state includes or refers to[105] the terms in an official publication.
- Thereby, the state makes the content of the privately drafted terms its own (»*inhaltlich zu eigen machen*«).

---

99 *Cf.* Rehbinder, »Kann für Allgemeine Geschäftsbedingungen Urheberrechtsschutz in Anspruch genommen werden?«, 78 (on the normative effect of standard business terms).

100 *See* Arnold, *Amtliche Werke im Urheberrecht*, 125 (but in the result rejecting a copyright exception because arbitration is usually not public).

101 Against a qualification of arbitral awards as official works: Dreyer, »§ 5 UrhG«, para. 40; Schulz, »§ 5 UrhG«, para. 8; Albrecht, *Amtliche Werke und Schranken des Urheberrechts*, 52; *but see* Arnold, *Amtliche Werke im Urheberrecht*, 125 (arguing that the concept of precedent justified copyright exemptions for published ICC awards, failing to distinguish the institution from the tribunal; *see* Aden, *Internationale Handelsschiedsgerichtsbarkeit*, chap. 1, para. 8 correctly noting that »*jurisprudence of the ICC*« does not exist).

102 *Cf.* for German law: UrhG § 5 (2) (GER); *see also* Dreyer, »§ 5 UrhG«, para. 42 (but stressing that the exception has to be applied restrictively).

103 *See* most prominently Urteil [Judgment]*:* »*DIN-Normen*«, [1990] 5 NJW-RR 1452 (GER BGH) at 1452, 1453 (with further references); *see also* Urteil [Judgment]*:* »*Vergaberichtlinien*«, [2006] 108 GRUR 848 (GER BGH) at 849, 850. The *DIN-Normen* judgment caused the legislator to enact art. 5 (3) UrhG (GER) as an exception from the exception (Dreyer, »§ 5 UrhG«, para. 64).

104 Urteil [Judgment]*:* »*DIN-Normen*«, [1990] 5 NJW-RR 1453, 1454.

105 *But see* now UrhG § 5 (3) (GER) (mere reference insufficient).

- The terms have binding external effect (*»Außenwirkung«*), at least for a certain trade.

Similar principles apply in most jurisdictions: official publication only puts privately drafted rules in the public domain if the state treats these as a piece of state legislation.[106] Institutional arbitration rules do not meet the latter two conditions, even if authorised or published in an official reporter. Mere state authorisation or reference is not sufficient to give privately authored terms, including arbitration rules, a mandatory character that would put them on the same level as laws.[107] Arbitration rules, like other standard business terms, are only contractually binding. Absent contract, they are never mandatory.[108] A state publishing institutional arbitration rules also does not appropriate such rules as its own. In this context, appropriation means that the state refers to privately drafted texts for a subject matter for which it would otherwise have been required to draft own legislation.[109] However, states are not required to regulate institutional arbitration, because, for business disputes, there is neither an acknowledged right of access to arbitration in general nor to a specific institution.[110] For commercial disputes, it is acceptable if the role of arbitral institutions is determined by contract and party autonomy alone.

Generally, public domain copyright exceptions can be justified by preponderant public interests in free access to works. Of course, public interest in the free access to arbitration rules cannot be denied. Not only is the knowledge of the contents of these rules essential for drafting dispute resolution clauses but the rules of major institutions also indicate the current status of law and practice of international arbitration at a transnational level.

---

106 Albrecht, *Amtliche Werke und Schranken des Urheberrechts*, 211–12 (coming to this conclusion after a comparative analysis of the laws of 15 EU states).

107 *Cf. also* ibid., 59 (on trade specific standard business terms authorised by the government). *See also supra* at pp. 110-116 (§5B).

108 Ibid., 61.

109 *Cf.* Urteil [Judgment]*: »DIN-Normen«,* [1990] 5 NJW-RR 1452 (stressing that the authorities, had they not referenced the DIN standards, would have been required to draft similar regulations themselves); *see also* Albrecht, *Amtliche Werke und Schranken des Urheberrechts,* 70.

110 *See supra* at p. 250. In contrast, for consumer disputes, the EU's ADR directive appears to install a right to access an ADR entity (thereon, *see* Hofmann, »The Role of ADR Institutions« 112 et seq [by the author of this thesis]).

However, self-regulation in the arbitration market sufficiently accommodates that interest. For arbitration rules, different from technical standards, it is unnecessary to introduce copyright exceptions to ensure the free access of the users. While institutions enacting technical standards generate an income directly from the sale of publications of these standards, arbitration institutions profit from administering arbitrations.[111] In order to attract customers for their service, they need to publish their rules free of charge on their websites or through other relevant media. Currently, none of the major institutions charges fees for making its rules available. A copyright exception is unwarranted, if the general interest is already sufficiently satisfied through publication by the owner of copyright.[112] Accordingly, copyright in arbitration rules does not unduly obstruct access, even if arbitration rules are not generally considered to be in the public domain.

The extent of such copyright is a different matter sometimes discussed under the heading of »*free use*« or »*fair use.*«[113] While a public domain exception excludes whole categories of work from copyright, the concept of fair use only allows certain acts relating to generally protected works. Fair use is therefore not an exception to copyrightability but a limit to infringement. It is fair use if someone uses the work of an author only as an inspiration for its own work or cites a work for academic or other non-commercial purposes.[114] The concept of fair use serves to define negatively what amounts to copying, alteration and adaptation under copyright law as discussed in the next subsection.


II. Hybrid arbitration as infringement? - the idea/expression dichotomy

If one acknowledges copyrightability of arbitration rules, the question what amounts to an infringement comes into focus. The mere citing of such rules in scholarly works is of course not a violation, like the reproduction and dissemination for non-commercial purposes - as long as authorship is

---

111 *See also infra* at p. 341, n. 404 on arbitration institutions as »*by-product law makers*«.
112 Dreyer, »§ 5 UrhG«, para. 57.
113 The term free use is meant to include all acts in relations to a work which are not an infringement, whereas fair use is understood to refer to specific permissions like Copyright Law § 107 (US); Copyright Act § 30 (EW).
114 Loewenheim, »§ 8 Schutzumfang«, para. 8.

sufficiently indicated.[115] A little more delicate is the use of *e.g.* ICC Rules and its adaptation in an arbitration administered by another institution. On the one hand, one might suggest that this amounts to »*alteration*« or »*adaptation*«[116] of the ICC Rules. Moreover, administering an arbitration is commercial use, even if the administering institution is a non-profit organisation.[117]

On the other hand, for such use the ICC Rules as a written work do not need to be copied or physically changed, the administering institution would simply apply them - in a liberal way. As a matter of principle, copyright statutes do not condemn mere »*borrowing*«[118] since copyright traditionally protects the linguistic form of a work.[119] »*A fundamental point is that ideas, as such, are not protected by copyright.*«[120]

Johann Gottlieb Fichte, whom German doctrine appreciates as a founder of the concept of freedom of ideas in IP law,[121] once stated:

> »Dieses Geistige ist nehmlich wieder einzuteilen: in das Materielle, den Inhalt des Buches, die Gedanken, die es vorträgt; und in die Form dieser Gedanken, die Art wie, die Verbindung in welcher, die Wendungen und die Worte, mit denen es sie vorträgt.«[122]

> [This intellectual aspect is namely further divided: into the material, the contents of the book, the ideas it brings about; and into the form of these ideas, the manner and connection in which the phrases and wordings are brought forward.][123]

---

115 As often expressly clarified in respective notices, *see e.g.* ICC, »Copyright and Trademarks«.

116 *Cf.* Berne Convention, art. 12.

117 *See infra* at pp. 314-315 on the applicability of unfair competition law.

118 *Cf.* Kamina, *Film Copyright in the European Union*, 82 (on the rejected proposal to extend copyright protection in the UK to »*borrowing*« TV formats).

119 *Cf.* Rehbinder, »Kann für Allgemeine Geschäftsbedingungen Urheberrechtsschutz in Anspruch genommen werden?«, 76 (on the relevance of this principle for copyright protection of standard business terms).

120 *WIPO Guide*, 12, art. 2, para. 2.3.

121 *See e.g.* Oechsler, »Die Idee als persönliche geistige Schöpfung«, 1102.

122 Fichte, »Beweis der Unrechtmäßigkeit des Büchernachdrucks. Ein Räsonnement und eine Parabel«, 447.

123 Translation according to Tallmo, »Fichte«.

Today, this dichotomy of idea and expression is a universally accepted principle of copyright law.[124]

>Copyright assures authors the right to their original expression, but encourages others to build freely upon the ideas and information conveyed by a work.«[125]

The principle of freedom of ideas already influences copyrightability, having the effect that utility works do not enjoy copyright protection to the extent that they are conveyed in a form entirely prescribed by the necessities of content.[126] The Singapore Court of Appeals expressed accordingly:

>there cannot be a monopoly in facts or information, but only in the way of presenting or expressing them and it is always a question of fact whether the skill and labour involved in the presentation or expression justifies the incidence of copyright.«[127]

Even if a utility work, like rules for use in arbitration, is generally considered copyrightable, the idea/expression dichotomy requires assessing the question of infringement very carefully.[128] Using the idea behind a work is inspiration and not an infringement. If the expression is not copied, the copyright is not infringed.[129] The mere application of the information in a written utility work is therefore neither »*adaptation*« nor »*alteration*« of the work under copyright law, but free use of the idea behind the work.[130]

Since arbitrations rules have neither been covered by IP doctrine yet, nor been the subject of case law in this area, the following considerations make a little detour to other, possibly comparable works to illustrate this idea/expression dichotomy in order to incite discussion.

---

124 *See* Stamer, *Der Schutz der Idee*, 13, 180; *but see* Lin and Liu, »China«, 260 (noting reluctance by Chinese academics and legislators to draw the »*delicate*« distinction between idea and expression).

125 *Feist v. Rural*, 499 U.S. at 349–50.

126 Along this line, *see* TRIPS, art. 9 (2): *Copyright protection shall extend to expressions and not to ideas, procedures, methods of operation or mathematical concepts as such; but see* Oechsler, »Die Idee als persönliche geistige Schöpfung«, 1103 (qualifying the provision as a mere political declaration of intent for member states of the Berne Convention).

127 *Asia Pacific Publ. v. P & L*, [2011] SGCA 37 [100].

128 *Cf. also* Ng-Loy, »Singapore«, 829 (on this approach applied by Singapore courts).

129 *Hollinrake v Truswell*, [1894] 3 Ch 420 (EW) at 427.

130 *See* Oechsler, »Die Idee als persönliche geistige Schöpfung«, 1101; Laas, *Der wettbewerbsrechtliche Schutz von Geschäftsmethoden*, 29; *cf. also* Loewenheim, »§ 8 Schutzumfang«, para. 15 (change of work character usually amounts to free use).

1. A parallel: copyright infringement of game rules and show formats?

It is not always easy

>to tell whether what is sought to be protected is on the ideas side of the dividing line, or on the expression side.«[131]

It »*all depends on what you mean by ideas.*«[132] Courts often encountered this issue, which becomes acute where the alleged copy has another format/medium rather than being a slavish imitation, concerning the protection of entertainment industry products such as games and TV shows. Therefore, cases with such themes shall serve as illustration. Without implying that arbitration resembles a mere parlour game or show, similar considerations apply to the protection of arbitration rules developed by institutions

The German BGH in its »*Zahlenlotto*« [number lottery] decision of 1961 declined the copyrightability of specific game rules for a lottery altogether.[133] In contrast, a decision by the Regional Court of Mannheim[134] focussed also on the question of infringement. The claimant objected to the publication of rules for a dice game he had invented. The court rejected the claim, which aimed at hindering the publication of the rules so that readers of respondent's book could not play the game without buying the claimant's product. The court held that such goal contrasted with current copyright law:

»Denn an der - auch genialen - >Idee< wie der schlichten >Anweisung an den menschlichen Geist< existiert keine verfassungsrechtlich gesicherte Eigentumsposition.«[135]

[Because - even if brilliant - the >idea< as a >simple instruction to the human mind< is not a constitutionally protected property position].

This reasoning is convincing as it restores the original purpose of copyright: the protection of authorship not of investment.

---

131 *Baigent, Leigh v. Random House*, [2007] EWCA Civ. 247 [5].

132 *LB (Plastics) Ltd v Swish Products Ltd*, [1979] R.P.C. 551 (UK HL) at 629 (decision finding copyright infringement in building an object from another's drawing; in sharp contrast with US jurisprudence in *Muller v. Triborough Bridge Authority*, 43 F. Supp. 298 [S.D.N.Y. 1942]).

133 Urteil [Judgment]: »*Zahlenlotto*«, [1962] 64 GRUR 51 (GER BGH) at 52; *see also* Urteil [Judgment]: »*Golfregeln*«, [1996] 1 NJWE-WettbR 99 (GER OLG, Frankfurt am Main) at 100.

134 Urteil [Judgment]: »*Würfelspiel*«, [2008] 8 NJOZ 3551 (GER LG, Mannheim).

135 Ibid., 3555.

Similar considerations usually bring copyright infringement claims concerning TV show formats to fail, which shall be illustrated by the case *CBS v. ABC* decided by the District Court for the Southern District of New York in 2003:[136] The TV channel CBS alleged that its competitor's (ABC's) program »*I'm a Celebrity...Get Me Out of Here!*« infringed copyright in CBS' show »*Survivor.*« Both programs feature a group of people being outcast in a remote environment, who have to perform different physically or mentally challenging tasks in order to stay in the game and/or win food.[137] The court dismissed the copyright claim because of several dissimilarities in expression found between both shows, which overall lead to a more »*light-hearted*«, humorous tone of »*I'm a Celebrity ... Get Me Out of Here!.*«[138] The court stressed that the copyright claim did not fail because of lacking creativity invested in the authorship of the TV show »*Survivor*« but rather because such copyright did not extend to the underlying idea as such.[139]

Accordingly, copyright law does not sanction the use of facts and ideas first published by another author. It is only concerned with the protection of original expression. This principle seems equally fatal to any claim of infringement of copyright in arbitration rules as the »*stage directions*«[140] of institutional arbitration: like two game shows, which depend much on »*characters and their interactions*«,[141] two arbitrations never resemble each other.[142]

Administering arbitrations transposes arbitration rules as a written work into practical performance. Expressing an originally written work in another

---

136 *CBS Broadcasting, Inc. v. ABC, Inc.*, [2003] U.S. Dist LEXIS 20258 (S.D.N.Y. 13 January 2003).

137 However, a season of ABC's show is much shorter and the contestants are semi-prominent personalities - »*celebrities*« - while »*Survivor*« candidates are previously unknown.

138 *CBS Broadcasting, Inc. v. ABC, Inc.*, [2003] U.S. Dist LEXIS 20258 at [*34]-[*38].

139 *See* Logan, »The Emperor's New Clothes? - Part 1«, 40; referring to: *CBS Broadcasting, Inc. v. ABC, Inc.*, [2003] U.S. Dist LEXIS 20258 at [*5].

140 In a figurative sense, *see supra* at p. 135, n. 44.

141 *CBS Broadcasting, Inc. v. ABC, Inc.*, [2003] U.S. Dist LEXIS 20258 at [*34].

142 Lew, Mistelis, and Kröll, *Comparative International Commercial Arbitration*, para. 3–21.

than written form is usually free use,[143] unless the result still conveys the characteristic features of a »*tale*« or »*plot*« of the original work.[144] For pure utility works like arbitration rules, the proof of a distinctive narrative tale that could be transferred seems impossible.

### 2. Exceptional protection of the content and integrity of a work

The principle of freedom of ideas also applies to moral rights of authors. Moreover, the mere use of an idea is unlikely to damage the reputation of an author of a work reflecting that idea. The underlying idea as opposed to its expression cannot be attributed to any particular person. Nevertheless, the moral integrity right, the right of the author to

> »object to any distortion, mutilation or other modification of, or other derogatory action in relation to, the said work, which would be prejudicial to his honour or reputation«,[145]

is the *odd man out* of the protected rights because an infringement of this right neither requires an exact copy of expression nor alteration of expression. It is sufficient if the work is used *in another context* than imagined by the author.

Here, the personality related concept of *author*'s rights surpasses that of mere *copy*rights.[146] Yet, even in the English *copy*- rather than authors' rights system, »*content copyright*«, protecting not only against slavish imitation but already against use of substantial parts, requires the literary or artistic

---

143 *See also* Waelde et al., *Contemporary Intellectual Property*, para. 2.28: »*literary*« copyright »*knows no* [...] *concept of three-dimensional infringement*«); ibid., 4.26.

144 *See* Plassmann, *Bearbeitungen und andere Umgestaltungen in § 23 Urheberrechtsgesetz*, 143 (on the use of a tale - »*Fabel*« as substantive part of a work; with further references); on the borderline between free use of ideas and plot protection under US law, *see Nichols v. Universal*, 45 F.2d 119 (2nd Cir. 1930); for English law, *see Baigent, Leigh v. Random House*, [2007] EWCA Civ. 247 (rejecting infringement of copyrights in the »*Central Theme*« of a semi-historical book that inspired Dan Brown to his novel »*Da Vinci Code*«).

145 Berne Convention, art. 6bis (1).

146 *See supra* at p. 275; on the »*cautious*« approach of English courts regarding moral rights, *see* Waelde et al., *Contemporary Intellectual Property*, para. 3.41.

work to meet a standard of creativity substantially higher than investment of simple skill and labour to reflect the personality of the author.[147]

The moral integrity right protects the work as a whole and its reputation. This trait may be of interest for analysing copyright aspects of administering hybrid arbitrations since one ground of criticism voiced against such conduct is a possible damage to the »*hallmark*« features of well-known rules.[148] Illustrative examples for integrity infringements mentioned by doctrine[149] include:

- publishing a song on an album with music by nationalistic music groups[150]
- using the »*Bolero*« by Maurice Ravel as soundtrack to a porn movie[151]
- hanging a painting by Georg Baselitz the »*right*« way around[152]
- performing »*Waiting for Godot*« by Samuel Beckett with female actors.[153]

In a colloquial way, Samuel Beckett got to the heart of the integrity right with his answer to the question, why »*Waiting for Godot*« should not be performed by female actors: »*Women don't have prostates.*«[154] The Paris court formulated this more officially:

---

147 *E.g.* this appears to have been the ratio behind the notorious »*Red Bus*« judgment where Judge Birss applied a criterion of »*visually significant*« skill and labour guided by the photographer's »*own aesthetic sense*«, finding that the plaintiff's photograph met this threshold, qualifying it as a »*photographic work*«, not a mere photograph (*Temple Island v. New English Teas*, [2012] EWPCC 1 [33–34, 36]).

148 *Cf.* Kirby, »SIAC Can Administer Cases Under The ICC Rules?!?«, 324.

149 *See* Schack, *Urheber- und Urhebervertragsrecht*, para. 393.

150 Urteil [Judgment]*:* »*Springtoifel*«, [1995] 97 GRUR 215 (GER OLG, Frankfurt am Main) at 216; *but see Confetti Records v. Warner Music*, [2003] EWHC 1274 (Ch.) (derogatory treatment denied for lack of damage to reputation).

151 Nordemann, »Ersatz des immateriellen Schadens bei Urheberrechtsverletzungen«, 434.

152 Schack, *Urheber- und Urhebervertragsrecht*, para. 393.

153 *Jugement:* »*En attendant Godot*«, [1993] RIDA 225 (FR TGI, Paris); approving: Schack, *Urheber- und Urhebervertragsrecht*, para. 393 (but also mentioning a contrary decision by a Dutch court).

154 Quoted according to Ben-Zvi, *Women in Beckett*, x.

»Le respect est dû à l'œuvre telle que l'auteur a voulu qu'elle soit, qu'il n'appartient ni aux tiers ni au juge de porter un jugement de valeur sur la volonté de l'auteur, que le titulaire de droit moral est seul maître de son exercice.«[155]

[Respect is owed to the work like the author wanted it to be, it is neither for any third party nor for the judge to render a value judgment on this author's will, which the possessor of the moral right alone may exercise.]

Hence, the integrity right allows the author to determine and protect the character of his work as he or she pleases.

## 3. Application to the use of another institution's arbitration rules

The question now posed is whether the character of particular institutional arbitration rules is distorted if they are applied by another than the issuing institution. In tribute to the just quoted statement by Samual Becket about differences between body organs of men and women, one may be tempted to simplify that SIAC does not have »*ICC actors (by definition)*«[156] and that SIAC's application of ICC Rules in the *Alstom–Insigma* arbitration was thus derogatory treatment to a moral right vested by the ICC in its rules. However, such argumentation would disregard three essentials. First, arbitration rules are not works of pure literary quality like theatre scripts.[157] Second, they are not drafted by individual authors but by drafting committees on behalf of the institutions as legal entities. Third, arbitral institutions as service providers should subordinate their personal interests to those of the users. There is little room for moral rights in utility works because such rights protect personal intellectual interests, not commercial or public interests:[158]

»while copyright can subsist in simple or factual works and compilations, the copyright protection for such works is ›thin‹.«[159]

---

155 *Jugement:* »En attendant Godot«, [1993] RIDA 225.
156 Kirby, »SIAC Can Administer Cases Under The ICC Rules?!?«, 326.
157 Despite the illustrative allusions mentioned *supra* at p. 135, n. 44.
158 Schack, *Urheber- und Urhebervertragsrecht*, para. 387; Schulz, »UrhG § 14 Entstellung des Werkes«, para. 31; *cf. also* Waelde et al., *Contemporary Intellectual Property*, para. 3.42 (integrity right does not apply to works »*where the employer, Crown, or Parliament has the first copyright*«).
159 Ng-Loy, *Law of Intellectual Property of Singapore*, para. 10.1.30.

This also applies if one enquired pursuant to the common law concept of »*content copyright*« if the application of arbitration rules was a substantial reproduction of such rules. It is here argued that it is not. Applying such rules does not reproduce a *substantial part of their expression.*

This leads back to the outset: Without use of expression there is no infringement of copyright. Accordingly, any copyright in arbitration rules, as in game rules or show formats,[160] does not impede the use of the ideas expressed therein. Copyright in writings about a certain commercial method does not prohibit the *application* of such method.[161] It is therefore not a copyright infringement if other institutions adapt features such as scrutiny of award, Terms of Reference, emergency arbitrator proceedings and the like. Institutions may even include identical elements in their own rules, without indicating their source of inspiration, as long as they do not reproduce substantial parts of the language used. All the more, copyright does not forbid to freely apply such features without incorporating them in written form.

The correctness of this result becomes obvious if one draws a parallel to products more tangible than arbitrations: Nobody would claim the building of a machine in accordance with assembly instructions to be infringement of copyright in the instructions - whether accurately implemented or not.[162] Or in other words: »*you do not infringe copyright in a recipe by making a cake.*«[163]

Accordingly, applying copyrighted arbitration rules of another institution is not a copyright infringement - as disordered as the resulting arbitration may be.

---

160 *See supra* at pp. 291-293.

161 Laas, *Der wettbewerbsrechtliche Schutz von Geschäftsmethoden*, 29.

162 Ibid.; *Abraham Moon & Sons Ltd v Thornber & Ors*, [2012] EWPCC 37 (EW Patents County Court) [90–100] (on the reduced protection of literary works in comparison to artistic works in this respect); *see also* Lin and Liu, »China«, 260 (reporting the Chinese case *Chengming Meng v. Cotton-spinning Factory*, on an unsuccessful copyright claim concerning a spinning cone set based on a paper by the claimant).

163 *J & S Davis v. Wright Health*, [1988] R.P.C. 403 (EWHC Ch.) at 414 (per Whitford J).

III. Jurisdiction and applicable law problems: a hypothetical example case

In the interest of an easier access for lawyers whose main interests lie in arbitration rather than copyright law, the previous considerations have been simplified, assuming some sort of uniformity in principle among copyright laws.[164] Based on such streamlining, the question if hybrid arbitration infringed copyrights of the rules issuing institution is answered negatively. However, some differences regarding the thresholds for protection and infringement regarding utility works have been identified. Under some laws, a successful copyright claim may be slightly more probable than under others. Therefore, an institution based in one jurisdiction contemplating a possible copyright claim against an institution in another jurisdiction could be interested in an assessment of potential conflict of laws and choice of forum issues.

If copyright law is not simple, private international law of copyright is even more difficult. Here, it shall therefore suffice to give an abridged overview of possibly relevant considerations on the basis of only one, relatively straightforward, hypothetical[165] example:

> A Singaporean institution accepts to administer an arbitration under the ICC Rules (2012; 2017) ignoring the exclusivity clause in article 1 (2) of these rules. This arbitration takes place in Singapore, legally and physically,[166] and the ICC considers to claim damages based on an alleged copyright in its rules supposedly infringed by this act. The ICC further seeks an injunction against similar conduct in the future.

As an initial note: Traditionally, copyrights, like other IP rights, are considered territorial in application. This territoriality principle centres around the idea that copyrights are either domestic or foreign and that the former can only be infringed at home, the latter only abroad.[167] International treaties like the Berne Convention attempt to limit the discriminations of foreigners connected with this principle but accept its general application.[168]

---

164 Recall the »*disclaimer*« formulated *supra* at pp. 273-275 (§13A).
165 The ICC does presently not plan to enforce exclusivity in its rules by such means.
166 Meaning that the place of arbitration is Singapore and the hearings take place there as well.
167 *See* Schack, *Urheber- und Urhebervertragsrecht*, para. 915 (with further references).
168 But not irreversibly (ibid., para. 917).

1. Jurisdictional considerations

One may begin with a jurisdictional question: Where could or should the ICC file its action against the Singaporean institution? The most obvious - and easily defendable - choice would certainly be Singapore as this is the place where the targeted respondent is located and has its assets and it is also - in the relatively simple example - the place of arbitration and the place where the disapproved conduct took place.

Assuming that nevertheless the ICC preferred to introduce an action before a French court: Such court may first consider to apply the Brussels-Ia-Regulation[169] according to which claims relating to non-registered IP rights, like copyrights, can be tried at either the domicile of the respondent[170] or *»where the harmful event occurred or may occur«*[171] without regard to the origin of the work. However, the French court would soon realise that this is a third state situation; the respondent institution is not resident in a Brussels regime state.

Accordingly, the jurisdictional question would have to be answered under autonomous French principles of international jurisdiction. Thereunder, the French court would probably not inquire into the question of the origin of the arbitration rules as a work, as the mentioned territoriality principle does not concern jurisdiction in the Continental understanding. In contrast, common law courts might categorise the territorial principle also as a jurisdictional question, applying some kind of comity reasoning or the forum non-conveniens doctrine to the issue of subject-matter jurisdiction over claims of foreign IP rights.[172]

---

169 Implementation date: 10 January 2015; revision of the Brussels-I-Regulation 2000 (EU).

170 Brussels-Ia-Regulation 2012 art. 4 (1) (EU); Brussels-I-Regulation 2000 art. 4 (1) (EC); *cf.* Lundstedt, »Gerichtliche Zuständigkeit und Territorialitätsprinzip im Immaterialgüterrecht,« 103.

171 Brussels-Ia-Regulation 2012 art. 7 (2) (EU); Brussels-I-Regulation 2000 art. 5 (3) (EC). According to its wording, this provision should also have conferred mandatory jurisdiction on English courts in the *Lucasfilm* case (*see* Dickinson, »The Force Be with EU?«, 186–87; *contra Lucasfilm*, [2009] EWCA Civ. 1328 [129]).

172 *See e.g. Lucasfilm*, [2009] EWCA Civ. 1328 [183] (*»international jurisdiction over copyright infringement claims does not exist«*); *see also Voda v. Cordis Corp.*, 476 F.3d 887 (US 2007) (subject matter jurisdiction of US courts over foreign patents rejected). This approach may be based on the Anglo-American *»double actionability rule«* (*cf.* Walter, *»§ 58*

In accordance with autonomous French principles of international jurisdiction, the court in the example would consider that a tort action can be brought in France if the respondent resides in France, the harmful act occurred in France *or* the damage occurred in France.[173]

The institution in the example being based in Singapore and the place of arbitration being Singapore, the first two criteria for international jurisdiction of a French court are obviously not met. However, the ICC might argue that given its incorporation in France, economic or moral damage from the application of its rules occurred or is about to occur there. Of course, such an argumentation is slightly weakened by two facts: the ICC's status as a non-profit association[174] and the international reach of its activity.[175] On the first issue: non-profit does not mean that the association does not engage in commercial activity and cannot experience both economic success and damage; it only means that any profits are used to further the aims of the organisation rather than being distributed to its members. The second point is more problematic. Since the contested act mainly has implications for the ICC's success in the Asian market, the French court needs to consider if resulting damage (»*dommage subi*«) under article 46 (2) CPC (FR) also refers to mere financial loss and if such loss necessarily occurs where the victim's assets are located.[176] The ECJ's *Marinari* and *Kronhofer* rulings suggest differently[177] but, of course, French courts are not bound to follow these decisions in a third state situation when interpreting autonomous national law. However, the Cour de Cassation's interpretation of article 46 (2) CPC (FR) is similar. The place where the damage was suffered (»*dommage subi*«) is the place where primary damage occurred and not a place where merely financial consequences could be measured, because otherwise this

---

Anwendbares Recht«, para. 14; *see also* Sterling, *World Copyright Law*, para. 3.27). *But see* Private International Law Act 1995 § 10 (UK) (abolishing the double actionability rule); *see also* Dickinson, »The Force Be with EU?«, 186.

173  CPC art. 46 (2) (FR).

174  The ICC was established in 1919 under the Loi relative au contrat d'association 1901 (FR); *see* Derains and Schwartz, *A Guide to the ICC Rules*, 1.

175  *Cf.* Born, *Commentary and Materials (2001)*, 154 (stressing that the ICC Court »*has less of a national character than any other leading arbitral institution*«).

176  *Cf.* Hellner, »Unfair Competition and Acts Restricting Free Competition«, 53.

177  *Marinari*, C--364/93, [1995] ECR I–02719 (ECJ) [21]; *Kronhofer*, C--168/02, [2004] ECR I–06009 (ECJ) [21].

would always be the domicile of the victim (»*sinon, serait toujours le lieu du domicile de la victime elle-même*«).[178]

It is therefore decisive, where primary, rather than consequential, financial damage would occur if administration of arbitration in a foreign country infringed copyright in ICC Rules. It is in this respect an open question, if - in relation to their autonomous law - French courts would be persuaded by the ECJ's ruling in *Pinckney*.[179] To summarise, according to this jurisprudence, the place of primary damage to an IP right is the place under the law of which protection is sought. The consequence is a synchronisation between jurisdiction and applicable law,[180] meaning that in the example case jurisdiction would depend on whether the claimant relied on French law and on whether French law granted damages for infringements committed abroad. It shall here be assumed that French courts follow this approach. A synchronisation of jurisdiction and applicable law has the advantage of simplification, because the application of foreign law is reduced to cases of general jurisdiction, and it frustrates forum shopping, because a close connection to the territory of the court is assured. In the example case, the French court should therefore only accept jurisdiction to the extent French law applied as there is no general jurisdiction in France on the basis of the domicile of the respondent.

Conceptually, this solution locates copyrights, and accordingly the damage caused to such rights, at the place where these rights are protected by the applicable law. Another view stresses that non-registered IP rights, like copyrights, do not have any real location and that therefore the place where the damage occurs is always identical with the place of the infringing act.[181] According to this view, jurisdiction of French courts over the example case would be excluded, independent of the applicable law. Only the discussion of applicable law questions in the next subsection will therefore reveal differences in result between both views.

---

178 *See Padovano v. France 2*, (2000) Bull. 2000 IV, no. 48, p. 43 (FR C.Cass, Comm.) (but concerning local jurisdiction over a trademark claim).

179 *Pinckney*, C– 170/12, [2013] ECR I--00000 (ECJ) [43, 45].

180 Until a revision in 2007, such principle was explicitly enacted in Swiss private international law, *see* IPRG art. 109 (1) sent. 2 (old version) (C.H.). *But see now* IPRG art. 109 (2) (C.H.).

181 Schack, »Anmerkung«, 3630; *idem Urheber- und Urhebervertragsrecht*, para. 916 et seq.

2. Conflict of laws analysis

Relying on the example formulated above,[182] it is now assumed that the ICC sues the Singaporean institution in France and that the French court ties the question of jurisdiction to the question of applicable law, finding that damage in copyrights occurs at the place where the applicable law protects these rights. Accordingly, the court would have to apply the forum's conflicts of law rules to determine to what extent the claim is governed by French law. Only to this extent, the action would be admissible before French courts.

Considering article 8 (1) of the Rome-II-Regulation, which also applies to third state situations,[183] the French court would have to apply the law of the country for which protection is sought (*lex protectionis* principle).[184] The opposite concept would be the *lex originis* principle that submits copyrights to the law of their country of origin. Consequence of this idea, which is not yet widely accepted,[185] is that an IP right once it comes into existence in one jurisdiction would be universally protected, avoiding to a degree the current »*patchwork*«[186] of national copyright laws.[187]

---

182 *See supra* at p. 297.

183 *See* Rome-II-Regulation 2007 art. 3 (EU).

184 Which is not necessarily French law as the lex fori, *cf.* Drexl, »Internationales Immatrialgüterrecht«, para. 11. This is also consequence of the *falling apart of the Brussels and Rome Regime* (Schmidt-Kessel, Zeup 2004, 1021, 1031): Because the Brussels Regime does not apply to third state situations, autonomous provisions of jurisdiction apply, which do not always correspond to the applicable law provisions under the Rome-II-Regulation.

185 The majority of jurisdictions and the Berne Convention and the Rome-II-Regulation are still based on the lex protectionis rule, *cf.* Gottschalk, »The Law Applicable to Intellectual Property Rights«, 190 (with many references, also on exceptions in a few countries like Greece and Romania).

186 German: »*Flickenteppich*« (Lauber-Rönsberg, »Kollisionsrecht«, para. 4).

187 More and more voices defend a *lex originis* rule at least for some questions like who is first owner of a copyright: From German doctrine, *see e.g.* Schack, »Internationale Urheber-, Marken- und Wettbewerbsrechtsverletzungen im Internet«, 62; Klass, »Das Urheberkollisionsrecht der ersten Inhaberschaft«, 373; *idem* »Ein interessen- und prinzipienorientierter Ansatz fur die urheberkollisionsrechtliche Normbildung«. Hence, existence and ownership of copyright in ICC Rules - in contrast to their infringement - could arguably follow the law of the state of their first publication (*cf.* Berne Convention, art. 5 (4); *but see* Klass, »Ein interessen- und prinzipienorientierter Ansatz fur die urheberkollisionsrechtliche

The country for the territory of which protection is sought is often but not in any case identical to the country where an infringing act took place.[188] Accordingly, the law of the protecting country, lex protectionis, should not be confused with the law of the state where the tortious act was committed, the *lex loci delicti*. The country for which protection is sought is determined by the claimant's submissions. It is decisive on which territory the claimant wants to defend an alleged exclusive right.[189] If the ICC claimed damages allegedly incurred because of the Singaporean institution's acceptance to administer the arbitration in Singapore under ICC Rules, the French court would find Singapore's law to apply. To this extent, the country for the territory of which protection is sought is identical to the country of the infringing act.

If the institution was seated elsewhere in Asia, the assessment would become more complicated because the act committed in one state, the seat of the institution, then concerned another state, the place of arbitration. That the place of arbitration is a legal concept rather than a geographical place[190] does not facilitate the matter. In any case, French law does obviously not apply to any of these hypotheses, which should finally cause the claim to be inadmissible.

Determination of applicable law would be more complex if and to the extent the ICC sought to hinder the Singaporean institution from further administering arbitrations under ICC Rules anywhere, including but not restricted to arbitrations with a seat in France. Then, the territory for which protection is sought may arguably be the territory where the previous infringement took place or where an infringing act is likely to occur in the future or the place where the requested injunction shall be effective and enforceable. These places would fall apart if the ICC argued that the institution's administration of arbitration in Singapore under ICC Rules indicates that the institution would do likewise with other places of arbitration. Here, the question of applicable law is entangled with the procedural question of extraterritorial effects of court orders and leads back to the rapport between applicable law and jurisdiction. If a French court ordered an injunction supposed to cover administration of arbitrations legally but not factually seated in France, the extraterritorial efficiency of such order would

---

Normbildung«, 549, 557, proposing alternative criteria of first ownership). With publication online, this may even create further problems.
188 *Contra* Schack, »Anmerkung«, 3630.
189 Drexl, »Internationales Immatrialgüterrecht«, para. 12.
190 *See supra* at pp. 71-74.

depend on international recognition and enforcement cooperation.[191] However, at least French courts would consider it when exercising supporting or controlling jurisdiction over the arbitrations.

In general, and only as a starting point, it is here cautiously suggested to accommodate the interests involved as follows: For claims based on the allegation of copyright infringement by administering hybrid arbitrations, not only the seat of the institution but also the place of arbitration shall be deemed relevant protecting countries. The (legal) place of arbitration should be relevant as the allegedly infringing act has noticeable economic influence there. This solution is inspired by the so-called »*Bogsch theory*« for use in intangible form, according to which cross-border transmissions of works are also governed by the copyright law of the state of reception and not only of the state of emission.[192] The theory, which has found favour for the area of satellite radio and internet transmissions, seeks to hinder a »*hiding*« of servers or operators in jurisdictions with ineffective copyright regulation. The ensuing problem of a potential multitude of laws applying - a »*mosaic*« of laws - can be successfully countered by requiring a »*noticeable*« effect of the infringement at the level of substantive law (*de minimis* rule).[193] Transferred to a potential copyright problem when administering hybrid arbitrations, the place of arbitration is such a jurisdiction where at least *de minimis* effects of the alleged infringement result, its law should therefore be a protecting law in addition to the law of the seat of the administering institution.[194] An institution could thus base its potential

---

191 On the parallel problem of injunctions against multi-state acts of unfair competition, *cf.* Lindacher, «Die internationale Dimension lauterkeitsrechtlicher Unterlassungsansprüche«, 456 (assuming that a public policy caveat would apply if the conduct was legal under the foreign state's laws even where a convention on enforcement exists).

192 The theory is name after former WIPO Director General *Árpád Bogsch*. *See* Walter, »§ 58 Anwendbares Recht«, para. 71 (with further references); Schwarz and Reber, »§ 21 Rechte zur unkörperlichen Verwertung«, para. 100; Gottschalk, »The Law Applicable to Intellectual Property Rights«, 215.

193 *Cf.* Gottschalk, »The Law Applicable to Intellectual Property Rights«, 215–16; Metzger, »Zum anwendbaren Urheberrecht bei grenzüberschreitendem Rundfunk«, 246.

194 Effectively, this understanding leads to a choice between laws with a close connection to the dispute (*cf. also* Gottschalk, »The Law Applicable to Intellectual Property Rights«, 216–19, arguing in favour of the closest connection test as an »*escape clause*«).

claim of infringement of copyright in its rules alternatively on the law of the seat of the administering institution or on the law of the place of the arbitration causing offence. However, on the merits, such claim will likely fail under most laws.[195]


## B. Hybrid arbitration and trademark protection

»Many consumers know the quality of a product or a service by its brand, and that is why a *trade or service mark* may be a valuable asset. Motorists know the quality and prestige of a Rolls Royce by its name alone. Many business people in Asia might not know the precise structure of an ICC-administered arbitration, but certainly all commercial lawyers who are familiar with international arbitration would be familiar with the *ICC brand of arbitration*, and also with SIAC arbitration [*emphasis added*].«[196]

With these considerations, the Singapore Court of Appeals, upon *Insigma*'s argument that SIAC's administration deceived it of the »*ICC's hallmark of quality*«,[197] almost risked to fall into a vortex of challenging considerations of IP law. Fortunately, the court managed to find a quick escape route by rejecting the argument with bad faith concerns, since Insigma had originally argued before the ICC Court that the arbitration should be organised by SIAC.[198] Herein, some short remarks are nevertheless required on a possible relevance of trademarks for the legality of arbitrations administered by an institution under another institution's rules. Thereby, again,[199] only some basic - and widely accepted - principles of trademark law can be discussed in order to stay within the scope of this thesis.


## I. Trademark mentioning v. trademark infringement

For example, the ICC registered a number of word marks in »several countries«, including *inter alia* »ICC«, »CCI«, »International Chamber of

---

195 *See supra* at pp. 288-297 (II).
196 *Insigma v. Alstom*, [2009] SGCA 24 [36].
197 Ibid.
198 Ibid., para. 7, 36. *See also infra* at pp. 476-480 (§17B).
199 The »*disclaimer*« formulated in relation to copyright applies also to these trademark considerations, *see supra* at pp. 273-275 (§13A).

Commerce«, »International Court of Arbitration« and »ICC International Court of Arbitration.«[200] The ICC further claims that these trademarks

> »may not be used *in association* with products or services not from ICC without ICC's written authorisation [*emphasis added*].«

If the use of a word mark »*in association*« with another product or service really was a trademark infringement, one could easily conclude the service of arbitration administration under »*ICC Rules*« by other institutions to infringe the registered trademark »*ICC*.« However, the trademark notice published on the ICC's website is oversimplified. Generally, the mere *mentioning* (referring or editorial use) of a trademark,[201] even for commercial purposes, is not an infringement. Although a descriptive designation of another's product or service by its trademark name in order to identify it in relation to one's own product or service may qualify as »*use as a trademark*«, trademark holders may only prohibit such use if it creates the impression that there is a commercial connection between the other undertaking and the trademark proprietor.[202] Hence, it is a general principle that infringing use of a trademark requires some elements of confusion on the origin or licensing of the goods or services.[203]

There is no such confusion if an institution offers or accepts to administer an arbitration under the rules of another institution. Even if another institution openly asserts to be willing to administer arbitrations under ICC Rules, the users are aware that this service is not identical to ICC arbitration or offered with the authorisation of the ICC Court. Rather, »*ICC Rules*« is simply used to identify the rules applied as those drafted by and for the ICC. A false representation of the origin of the rules is excluded. While such conduct might still be a field of application for unfair competition law,[204] it is not a trademark infringement.[205]

---

200 ICC, »Copyright and Trademarks«.
201 *See* Ohly, »Schadensersatzansprüche wegen Rufschädigung und Verwässerung«, 927 (»*referierende Benutzung*«).
202 *Cf. BMW*, C--63/97, [1999] ECR I– 00905 (ECJ) [42, 64, 65] (on the interpretation of the European Trademark Directive).
203 *See* Nielen and Schork, »in: Marken- und Designrecht, G«, 287.
204 *See infra* at pp. 321 et seq. (§13C.III).
205 *Cf. generally* Marx, *Markenrecht*, para. 882; *cf. also* Ohly, »Schadensersatzansprüche wegen Rufschädigung und Verwässerung«, 927 (on the not yet fully clarified application of trademark law to product criticism and comparative advertising).

This also applies to the extent trademark protection includes company names and work titles independent of any registration.[206] For such commercial designations or *»business identifiers«*,[207] the threshold of infringement is not any lower than for other trademarks. A claim of infringement therefore involves that a work title or company name is used *»as a work title«* or *»as a company name«* without authorisation, again requiring an element of confusion.[208] Arbitral institutions administering hybrid arbitrations generally do not use the title of the rules issued by the other institution or that institution's name except for designating the rules applied. Rather, they apply the other institution's rules themselves, not just their title. Such conduct does not violate rights to the issuing institution's name or the work title nor would it - for lack of use of expression as explained above - infringe copyright.[209]

II. Dilution without confusion?

The issue of dilution of trademarks, which is at the border between trademark law and unfair competition law,[210] is usually discussed when a trademark infringement claim fails for lack of similarity between products or services. Then, a *»reputation«* of a well-known trademark achieved through *»brand image creation«* that surpasses the area of the trademarked good or service may justify protection against use of the trademark for dissimilar goods of services despite a lack of confusion on the identity and origin of the good or service.[211]

When trademark protection against hybrid arbitration is discussed, dissimilarity of services is not a major issue. Both the rules issuing institution

---

206  *See e.g.* MarkenG 1994 art. 5 (GER) (for German law).
207  *See* World Intellectual Property Organization and Paris Union for the Protection of Intellectual Property, »Recommendation on Well-Known Marks«, vol. 888 (E), art. 1 (iv).
208  *Cf.* Urteil [Judgment]: *»Würfelspiel«*, [2008] 8 NJOZ 3557.
209  *See supra* at pp. 288 et seq. (§13A.II).
210  *See* World Intellectual Property Organization and Paris Union for the Protection of Intellectual Property, »Recommendation on Well-Known Marks«, 18, para. 4.5 (*»Notes on Art. 4«: »third-party use of a well-known mark which is not contrary to honest commercial practice [...] does not constitute dilution«*).
211  Senftleben, »The Trademark Tower of Babel«, 49; regarding the international acceptance of this idea, *see* TRIPS, art. 16 (3).

and the administrating institution offer arbitration services.[212] Nevertheless, the question of potential trademark dilution without confusion arises because a classic trademark infringement claim would fail where it is clear that the rules the parties choose to apply are issued by another than the administering institution. Accordingly, not the identification function but only the reputation function of the issuing institution's trademarks may be at issue.

Therefore, trademark dilution concepts may play a role in assessing hybrid arbitration administration. The understanding of these concepts is not uniform, but the general parameters are:

- Only *»well-known«*[213] or *»famous«* trademarks or *»marks with reputation«* are protected against dilution.[214]
- Protection is against *»blurring«* and *»tarnishment«* of the trademark,[215] or broadly formulated against use that hurts the interests of the owner of the mark.[216]

Most titles of institutional arbitration rules or arbitration institutions would probably only be considered well-known or reputed, if a *»niche-knowledge«* standard was applied,[217] under which it would be sufficient if the mark was well-known among the business community likely to use arbitration services. Arguably, the trademarks *»ICC«* or *»International Chamber of Commerce«* could also meet a stricter, general knowledge standard in some markets.

*»Blurring«* concerns a conduct affecting the trademark's distinctiveness, while dilution through *»tarnishment«* means use of the trademark in a way

---

212 *But see infra* at pp. 344-400 (§14) on undeniable differences among institutions.
213 *See* TRIPS, art. 16 (3).
214 *See* Senftleben, »The Trademark Tower of Babel«, 54–55 (on the divergent terminology and standards applied by US and European law) (with further references).
215 Ibid., 56.
216 *See* TRIPS, art. 16 (3).
217 *See* Senftleben, »The Trademark Tower of Babel«, 54, 55 (concluding that European courts follow such approach, while US courts set a higher hurdle of fame in the general public); internationally, a niche approach prevails, *see* World Intellectual Property Organization and Paris Union for the Protection of Intellectual Property, »Recommendation on Well-Known Marks«, art. 2 (2) (*»relevant sector of the public«*).

that affects its reputation, power of attraction or »*goodwill.*«[218] A »*tarnishment*« claim requires proof of detriment or harm of the owner of the trademark.[219] Given the non-public nature of arbitration, any harm to the rules issuing institution's reputation through an arbitration administered by another institution is usually excluded. This could be different, if the resulting award was challenged on procedural grounds and the state court's decision mentioned the rules applied without clearly indicating the differing administering institution. However, such hypothesis appears quite unlikely and even then, a concrete harm will be difficult to prove let alone calculate.[220]

Distinctiveness of a trademark refers to the associate link between a trademark and particular products or services.[221] This link may be damaged if a trademark is used in a context of completely dissimilar, non-competing services or products, e.g. in case of »*the use of ›Mercedes‹ for bath tubs, cakes, cameras, shoes.*«[222] Administering hybrid arbitrations only involves the mention of trademarks of the rules issuing institution in a context of similar services. The association with arbitration services remains intact. Therefore, the »*blurring*« variant of trademark dilution appears also inappropriate to accommodate the interest of the rules issuing institution to oppose such conduct.[223]


III. Excursus: The CIETAC split as a potential trademark issue

A trademark controversy also surrounded the discussed spin-off of CIETAC's Shanghai and Shenzhen subcommissions, now SHIAC and SCIA, as CIETAC accused them of unlawfully using the »*name, brand and relevant logo*« of CIETAC.[224] Accordingly, one article was even entitled

---

218 Senftleben, »The Trademark Tower of Babel«, 55, 56 (with references to case law).
219 Ibid., 57.
220 *See generally* Ohly, »Schadensersatzansprüche wegen Rufschädigung und Verwässerung«, 930–31 (on difficulties and different approaches to calculate a dilution damage).
221 Senftleben, »The Trademark Tower of Babel«, 65.
222 Ibid., 69.
223 *See infra* at pp. 310 et seq. (§13C) on a possible application of unfair competition law.
224 China International Economic and Trade Administration Commission, »Announcement of 31 December 2012«.

»*The Tarnished Brand of CIETAC*« but regrettably refrained from a trademark law analysis.[225]

As this is a controversy between arbitration institutions all based in the People's Republic of China, it is quite obvious that Chinese law would apply to the trademark issues presented. The following reflections shall therefore outline a few basics of Chinese trademark law. Under Chinese law, trademarks, including service marks, are protected if they are listed in the trademark register.[226] Company names or work titles may also be registered as trademarks.[227] Without registration, only well-known (famous) trademarks are protected to the extent required by the Paris Convention for the Protection of Industrial Property (cited as »*Paris Convention*«)[228] but establishment as »*famous*« nevertheless requires an administrative or court decision, which may be difficult to obtain.[229] A trademark is only considered famous if it is well-known by the general Chinese public and if the products or services for which the trademark is used are of higher quality.[230] It is assumed that expressions like »*China International Economic and Trade Arbitration Commission*«, »*CIETAC*« are registered in China for arbitration services, so that the issue of their fame is mute.

Article 57 of the Trademark Law (P.R.C.) defines infringements very broadly[231] and although most examples appear to relate to trademarks for goods only, article 4 clarifies that all provisions shall be read to apply to service marks as well. Since SHIAC and SCIA provide services similar if not identical to those of CIETAC, at least any sending of letters, awards or

---

225 Rose, »The Tarnished Brand of CIETAC«.

226 *See* Trademark Law art. 1, 3, 4, 51 et seq. (P.R.C.).

227 In addition, municipally administered registration requirements apply (Provisions on Administration of Enterprise Name Registration 1991 [P.R.C.]; *cf.* Bohnet, *Markenrecht in China und Russland*, 57, 243, finding the relationship between company name registration and trademark registration unclear).

228 Paris Convention, art. 6bis.

229 Trademark Law art. 14 (P.R.C.); *see* Zhu, *Gewerblicher Rechtschutz in der VR China*, 36, 44–45; Bohnet, *Markenrecht in China und Russland*, 84; Liu, Tao, and Wang, »The Use and Misuse of Well-Known Marks Listings«, 689–90.

230 *See* Bohnet, *Markenrecht in China und Russland*, 82–83 (on the importance of the quality function under Chinese trademark law); *but see* Senftleben, »The Trademark Tower of Babel«, 51 (critical towards national approaches of assessing fame of a trademark).

231 *See* Zhu, *Gewerblicher Rechtschutz in der VR China*, 42.

other communication in the name of CIETAC or with a CIETAC logo might indeed infringe registered trademarks, subject to any usage rights possibly acquired during association or cooperation with CIETAC.[232] However, for lack of knowledge of the relevant facts, this cannot be fully evaluated here. As of yet, formal court or administrative action[233] by CIETAC against its former subcommissions is not reported. At a glance at the current websites of SHIAC and SCIA,[234] trademark-protected elements of CIETAC do not leap to the eye, although it is at least curious that a former web presence of SHIAC is, at the time of writing, still reachable via www.*cietac*-sh.org and SCIA's current domain is www.sc*cietac*.org.[235] However, these domains names seem to have been registered prior to the CIETAC split, which argues against infringement.[236]

## C. Administering hybrid arbitrations as unfair competition?

»As a fee-based service, arbitration already finds itself in highly competitive markets. The ICC competes with the ICDR to attract parties to adopt their rules, and they both compete against regional institutions like the Singapore International Arbitration Centre (SIAC). And together, the international institutions like ICC, ICDR, and SIAC all face competition from ad hoc arbitration under domestic procedural laws or UNCITRAL, as well as established and emerging national institutions. That competition is already fierce, and it is only the beginning.«[237]

---

232 *Cf.* CIETAC Shanghai Commission and CIETAC South China Commission, »Joint Statement«.

233 On the competence of the State Administration for Industry and Commerce to grant injunctions and fines and on courts' jurisdiction to grant damages *see* Zhu, *Gewerblicher Rechtschutz in der VR China*, 42; Bohnet, *Markenrecht in China und Russland*, 144.

234 Shanghai International Economic and Trade Arbitration Commission, »About Us«; South China International Economic and Trade Arbitration Commission, »About Us«.

235 *See also* Hirth and Munz, »CIETAC Schiedsvereinbarungen«, 9.

236 *Cf.* World Intellectual Property Organization and Paris Union for the Protection of Intellectual Property, »Recommendation on Well-Known Marks«, art. 6 (1) (establising a »*bad faith*« requirement).

237 McIlwrath, »Can Arbitration Keep Up?«

Statements by arbitration practitioners along this line are to be heard frequently.[238] One would assume that the *factual* observation that arbitral institutions severely compete in the global market[239] for administering arbitrations would entail a scholarly discussion of the *legal* consequences, in particular of the parameters set by the law on unfair competition. However, such debate has not yet set in. A reason may be that - fortunately - institutions try to solve their conflicts in an amicable manner, without tearing their competitors before courts. Open controversy between institutions is certainly not favourable to the reputation of institutional arbitration as a whole, as evidenced by the warnings of practitioners following the CIETAC split.[240]

Nevertheless, legal regulation of and remedies against hybrid arbitration may come into focus as competition increases. In fact, intensified competition among arbitral institutions was one of the motives for the 2012 revision of the ICC Rules.[241] Notwithstanding any hypothetical direct lawsuit of the rules issuing institution, an analysis under the angle of unfair competition is also relevant for the operability of hybrid arbitration agreements because a verdict of »*unfairness*« will detain institutions from accepting such cases. Furthermore, an award rendered in proceedings violating unfair competition principles might potentially be prone to a challenge for public policy violation.[242]

I. The problem to identify common principles among jurisdictions

As announced in the introduction,[243] this thesis tries to find transnationally acceptable answers to questions raised by the phenomenon of hybrid arbitration agreements. Admittedly, when researching on unfair competition

---

238 To the dismay of some (*see e.g.* Magnusson, »A Call from an Arbitration Activist«); *see infra* at p. 314 (§13C.II.1) on unfair competition law and non-profit entities.

239 *But see infra* at pp. 315-317 on hindrances to a worldwide arbitration market.

240 *See supra* at pp. 190-202 (§8C.II.2); *see e.g.* Dresden, »Will the Real CIETAC Please Stand Up?«: »*Would you hire a mechanic whose own car keeps breaking down?*«.

241 Böckstiegel, »Einführung«, 7.

242 *But see infra* at p. 475 (§17A.IV.3) on doubts on the well-foundeness of such challenge.

243 *See supra* at pp. 48 et seq. (§3).

law aspects, this approach met its limits. Regarding unfair competition law, international harmonisation has progressed even slower than concerning IP. The reasons are »*mainly historical*«: *E.g.,* intensely codified jurisdictions like Germany and Austria preferred the enactment of separate laws with individual offences while French jurisprudence developed an unwritten, generously applied tort of »*concurrence déloyale*«,[244] an approach that was again inappropriate for the English common law system, which relied on the very restricted tort of passing off and the idea of self-regulation.[245]

Article 10bis (2) of the Paris Convention only provides:

> »Any act of competition contrary to honest practices in industrial or commercial matters constitutes an act of unfair competition.«

Defining »*unfair*« with »*contrary to honest practices*« is of course not a definition at all. It is therefore left to the contracting states to fill these vague terms with life.[246]

The examples of unfair practices given in the third subsection of the same article have in common that they all require an act of deception (»*confusion*«, »*false allegations*«, »*indications or allegations* [...] *liable to mislead*«). For this reason, administering an arbitration under a hybrid arbitration agreement would usually not fall under the unfair practices defined by the convention. It can be assumed that arbitral institutions only agree to apply other than their own rules upon express wish of the parties who are aware that these rules were developed and drafted by another institution.

It is only worth discussing whether a public announcement of institutions to administer arbitrations under different rules[247] could be an indication

> »the use of which in the course of trade is liable to mislead the public as to [...] the *suitability for their purpose of the goods* [*emphasis added*].«

However, this last example listed in article 10bis (3) of the Paris Convention was deliberately phrased narrowly and only refers to misleading allegations about »*goods*.«[248] Whether allegations liable to mislead the public on the

---

244 On the basis of general tort law, C.Civ. art. 1382, 1383 (FR).
245 Henning-Bodewig, *International Handbook on Unfair Competition*, pt. A, § 2, para. 10.
246 Ibid., para. 28.
247 *E.g.* CIETAC Rules, art. 4 (3) (2012; 2015). *See also supra* at p. 212 (§10A.III).
248 Henning-Bodewig, *International Handbook on Unfair Competition*, pt. A, § 2, para. 61.

suitability of *services,* including the service of administering arbitration, are acts of unfair competition is left to national law.[249]

Within the European Union, several directives regionally harmonise some aspects of unfair competition law.[250] However, the scope of the Unfair Commercial Practices Directive in particular is limited to business - consumer contracts.[251] Since the vast majority of parties to international arbitrations are corporations and business people; it does not apply to the services here discussed.

Due to the lack of harmonisation, the following analysis will have to resort to national law concepts extensively. This makes an initial warning even more essential: The concepts discussed in the following are *not* universally valid; assessing if a certain institution's application of another institution's rules was illegal for being unfair will always require a more thorough, individual analysis than it can be provided herein.[252] When outlining some important considerations, the focus will again be on substantive aspects before addressing some jurisdictional and applicable law problems.

## II. Applicability of unfair competition law to arbitral institutions

Initial doubts against the general applicability of unfair competition law to arbitral institutions are threefold. First, many arbitral institutions are nonprofit associations operating to the benefit of the business society. Second, it is difficult to define the competitive market for services of arbitral institutions and third, the protection of commercial products and services by unfair competition law is subsidiary to IP rights protection as discussed above.

---

249 Ibid., para. 63.
250 Most important: Unfair Commercial Practices Directive 2005 (EU); Advertising Directive 2006 (EU).
251 *See* Henning-Bodewig, »Nationale Eigenständigkeit und europäische Vorgaben im Lauterkeitsrecht«, 556 (mentioning competence issues as a reason for this restriction). In contrast, the Advertising Directive applies at the b2b-level (ibid.).
252 *See supra* at pp. 273-275 (§13A).

1. Unfair competition in the non-profit sector

>One might wonder why international arbitral institutions, which are after all not-for-profit entities, might be so concerned about competing for a greater share of the arbitration market.«[253]

While above cited statement leaves no doubt about the reality of competition between arbitral institutions, the fact that these institutions are often incorporated as non-profit associations,[254] commands explanation why their activities should be subject to unfair competition law as relevant statutes often refer to activities by »*companies*« or »*economic undertakings.*«[255]

The answer is straightforward: Unfair competition law is concerned with commercial conduct and activities, not with legal status.[256] The terminology of the German act on unfair competition (*Gesetz gegen den unlauteren Wettbewerb*)[257] for example attempts to make this clear by referring generally to market participants (German: »*Marktteilnehmer*«).[258] Therefore, a status of an arbitration institution as a non-profit organisation, whether justified or not,[259] does not hinder an application of unfair competition law to its services. When non-profit institutions offer services against a fee within a market with other players, this is an act of competition. The intent to make profit is not relevant.[260] Arbitral institutions offer fee-based services. Their

---

253 Karton, *The Culture of International Arbitration*, 64.

254 *See* Waincymer, *Procedure and Evidence*, para. 3.14: »*Institutions range from non-profit to profit-making, government controlled to independent, parochial or truly international*«; *see e.g.* Fan, *Arbitration in China*, 122 (CIETAC is officially a »*not-for-profit company*«).

255 *Cf.* Cicoria, *Nonprofit Organizations Facing Competition*, 168–70 (on »*undertakings*« pursuant to European anti-trust law).

256 Voigt, *Idealvereine und andere Nonprofit-Organisationen im Wettbewerbsrecht*, 36.

257 Cited as UWG (GER).

258 Ibid., § 1, 2 (1) no. 2.

259 For criteria, *see* Cicoria, *Nonprofit Organizations Facing Competition*, 14–15; *see generally* Salamon and Anheier, *Defining the Nonprofit Sector*, 2, 70 et seq. (proposing an international classification of non-profits by sector).

260 Lettl, *Das Neue UWG*, para. 76; see also Brem, *Der ergänzende wettbewerbsrechtliche Leistungsschutz in Europa*, 36, 171.

commercial activity is indistinguishable from that of normal business firms.[261]

## 2. The market for administering arbitral proceedings

There can only be unfair competition if there is competition. Therefore, the application of unfair competition law usually requires some sort of a competitive relationship or competitive practice.[262] Even where unfair competition law is intertwined with consumer protection,[263] therefore surrendering the need for a direct competitive relationship, it still concerns »*market conduct*« in general.[264]

Concerning the market for services of arbitral institutions, one may suggest that the market is necessarily international if one acknowledges the free choice of the seat of arbitration, which can even be independent from the place of hearing according to the concept of the legal seat.[265] Moreover, many arbitral institutions strive to cater specifically to international parties. However, one should be careful with such general conclusion. Theoretically, the market of arbitral institutions is global. Practically, this is only true for some of the larger institutions. Perceptions of the users in the business community - whether based on truth or imagination - influence and

---

261 *See* Cicoria, Nonprofit Organizations Facing Competition, 170–71 (using the term »*commercial-nonprofits*«).

262 E.g. International News Service v. Associated Press, 248 U.S. 215, 235 (1918) (»*parties are competitors in this field*«); see generally, on the different requirements in other jurisdictions, Brem, Der ergänzende wettbewerbsrechtliche Leistungsschutz in Europa, 135, 172, 302, 351 (Italian law requires a direct competitive relationship, German law only an abstract competitive relationship and French law follows a case-by-case approach); but see ibid., 36, 79, 351 (Swiss and Spanish law do not require a competitive relationship; *cf. e.g.* UWG art. 1 [C.H.]); on the competition requirement under the Paris Convention, see Henning-Bodewig, International Handbook on Unfair Competition, pt. A, § 2, para. 40.

263 *See generally* Henning-Bodewig, International Handbook on Unfair Competition, V.

264 Henning-Bodewig, Unfair Competition Law, 1.

265 *See supra* at pp. 71-74 (§4B.I.2).

restrict this market.[266] While legal theory established distinctions between the place of arbitration, the place of hearing, the seat of the administering institution and the applicable law of the merits well, these concepts have not yet fully transpired into the minds of many advising lawyers and business people.

For now, only the ICC Court has been fully able to establish itself as a »*universal*« institution and has already administered arbitrations on every continent between parties from all regions of the world.[267] In contrast, the LCIA's main business is made with arbitrations in England and Wales, although parties come from various countries[268] and ICDR-AAA arbitration clauses usually provide for a seat of arbitration in the United States, less frequently in Europe or Asia.[269] SIAC's activities focus on Asian

---

266 *See* Johnston, »The Best Providers for Asian Arbitrations«, 41–42: »*The selection of an arbitral seat and institution is by no means rational: ignorance, emotion and prejudice, effective marketing - or its opposite, defamatory murmurings - and the charm, sophistication or otherwise of institutional representatives all play a part.*«

267 *See* Aden, *Internationale Handelsschiedsgerichtsbarkeit*, pt. B, art. 1 ICC Rules, para. 17 (assuming the ICC Court to have a dominant role within the European market and a important role worldwide); *see also* Dezalay and Garth, »Merchants of Law as Moral Entrepreneurs«, 46 (»*able to brag even about having becoming* [sic] *a sort of United Nations*«); *cf. also* Johnston, »The Best Providers for Asian Arbitrations«, 47 (noting the ICC Court to be the only traditional institution to promote seats of arbitration in Asia).

268 Turner, *A Guide to the LCIA Arbitration Rules*, para. 1.20 (until 2007 only 3 % of cases had their seat elsewhere); *ibid.*, para. 1.25 (admitting that the LCIA is seen as an institution »*to decide matters under English law, with English arbitrators and English lawyers, in London, in the English language*«); *but see ibid.*, para. 1.24, 1.28 (parties came from all continents with concentrations in Western Europe and the Caribean). The high number of »*Caribean*« parties is caused by statistics following incorporation theory. On efforts of the LCIA to become more international through establishing subsidiaries abroad *see* Gerbay, »The LCIA«, para. 4–32 to 4–38 and *supra* at pp. 240-243 (§11A.II.4).

269 Gusy, Hosking, and Schwarz, *A Guide to the ICDR Rules*, para. 1.35 (»*New York is by far the leading venue*«); *but see ibid.*, para. 1.38, 1.55 (on an »*increase of over 50 per cent in request for locales outside of the USA*«) (not distinguishing hearing locale from place of arbitration).

jurisdictions,[270] CIETAC currently only administers arbitrations in mainland China and Hong Kong,[271] the DIS has only very seldomly administered arbitrations outside Germany[272] and close to all cases under the Swiss Rules are seated in Switzerland with parties predominantly from Europe.[273] Of course, markets partially interconnect and activities of institutions will spread out further in future years. Nevertheless, the competitive relationship needs to be determined for each individual case, taking into account such aspects as nationalities of the parties, seat of arbitration, and type of dispute, *lex arbitri* and applicable law on the merits, language barriers and parties' perceptions of various institutions.

Regarding the *Alstom–Insigma* arbitration, a competitive relationship between the ICC Court and SIAC can hardly be denied, as the case was first introduced to the ICC and only after SIAC communicated that it would be willing to administer the case under ICC Rules, the case was withdrawn from the ICC.[274] This proves that both institutions were conceivable for the parties. In contrast, it might be more difficult to assume a competitive relationship between the ICC Court and CIETAC for arbitrations seated in mainland China, because there are still some uncertainties on whether Chinese arbitration law allows foreign institutions, which do not meet the criteria of an »*arbitration commission*«, to administer arbitrations in China.[275]

## 3. Relationship between unfair competition law and IP law

Many statutes contain general clauses condemning unfair competition, which vary in language but turn around the core of »*fairness of commercial*

---

270  *Cf.* Brick Court Chambers, *SIAC Rules*, vii (Preface: »*one of the leading regional international arbitration bodies in Asia*«).

271  *See* China International Economic and Trade Administration Commission, »Home« (for information on CIETAC's Hong Kong branch); *see also* Brock and Feldman, »Recent Trends in the Conduct of Arbitrations«, 180.

272  With parties mainly from Germany, followed by Central and Eastern European states (*cf.* Bredow, »Aus dem Tagebuch einer Schiedsgerichtsinstitution«, 23).

273  *See* Karrer, »Swiss Rules«, 366 (97% seated in Switzerland, with Zurich followed by Geneva and Lugano as main places of arbitration).

274  *See Insigma v. Alstom*, [2009] SGCA 24 [6–11].

275  *See supra* at pp. 101-74 (§4C.II.2.b.iii); *but see Longlide*, [2013] Min Si Ta Zi no. 13.

*practice.*«[276] For example, section 3 (1) of the German act on unfair competition (*Gesetz über den unlauteren Wettbewerb*) (UWG) provides:

> »Unlautere geschäftliche Handlungen sind unzulässig, wenn sie geeignet sind, die Interessen von Mitbewerbern, Verbrauchern oder sonstigen Marktteilnehmern spürbar zu beeinträchtigen.«

> [Unfair commercial practices shall be illegal if they are suited to tangible impairment of the interests of competitors, consumers or other market participants.][277]

However, reference to such general clauses must be handled with care because of the risk of undermining the decisions by legislators and treaty makers on the protectability of works by IP rights. Otherwise, the specific and restrictive requirements for IP rights as discussed would largely lose their meaning. If one could easily hinder use of another's work under general principles of unfair competition law, freedom of ideas and information would be seriously endangered.[278] Balances like the originality threshold, copyright exceptions and the idea/expression dichotomy for copyrights would be reduced to non-commercial creations, increasing the risk of monopolisation of ideas for profit-making and other commercial use. As competition itself is not unfair but the foundation of market-oriented societies, it should also not be itself decisive for the success of a claim of protection.

For this reason, the application of unfair competition law should not create exclusive rights that IP legislation deliberately refrains from granting. Unfair competition law may serve a »*gap-filling*« function but only where this does not conflict with the intent of the legislator.[279]

Accordingly, some jurisdictions[280] have developed doctrines of subsidiarity of unfair competition law, restricting its application to a reduced

---

276 Henning-Bodewig, *Unfair Competition Law*, 9 (within the European Union all states have enacted such general provisions, except for Great Britain, Irland, Cyprus and Malta); *idem* »New Initiatives for the Harmonisation of Unfair Competition Law in Europe«, 274 (finding general clauses to be »*the heart of every law on unfair competition*«).

277 Duffet, Bundesministerium der Justiz und für Verbraucherschutz, »The Act Against Unfair Competition« (hereinafter all English translations of the UWG (GER) are taken from this source unless otherwise indicated).

278 *Contra* Le Tourneau, *Le parasitisme*, 266–70.

279 Henning-Bodewig, *Unfair Competition Law*, 4–5; *but see* Le Tourneau, *Le parasitisme*, 269, para. 364 (finding that lacking coherence of IP law would justify an extensive application of unfair competition concepts).

280 However, *e.g.* the very broad concepts of unfair competition under French law appears to apply in parallel to or in supplementation of specific rights (*see generally* Schmidt-Szalewski, »Der Unterschied zwischen der Klage

number of cases meeting certain conditions.[281] Generally, these conditions, which fill out the open term »*unfair*«, stress the difference in purpose between IP law and unfair competition law: While IP law protects specific positions in works, results of the activity of the mind and achievements, unfair competition law seeks to hinder a specific behaviour.[282]

Under US law, the relationship between unfair competition law and IP law has an additional dimension: that of preemption of state laws and common law by federal statutes. Unfair competition, comprising the common law torts of passing off and misappropriation, generally belongs to the jurisdiction of the state courts whereas IP, including copyrights and trademarks, is regulated by federal statutes and falls into the competence of federal courts.[283] Accordingly, the US Supreme Court's jurisprudence limits unfair competition concepts, excluding their application to works and products that are not registered for patent, including design patent, trademarked, or copyrighted.[284]

However, there is a trend, which is followed herein, to no longer understand »*subsidiarity*« of unfair competition law in a formalistic way. It does not exclude unfair competition claims *per se* only because the claimant's product or service *is* or *is not* protected by a specific IP right. Rather, this principle only emphasises that unfair competition law should not

---

wegen Verletzung gewerblicher Schutzrechte und der Wettbewerbsklage in der französischen Rechtsprechung«, finding frequent combination of both causes of action). On parasitic behaviour which may be found even if the reproached conduct is not an infringement of IP rights (ibid., 6, with references), *see infra* at pp. 324-327.

281 For German law, *see e.g.* Urteil [Judgment]: »*Paperboy*«, [2003] 156 BGHZ 1 (GER) II.4, [2003] 56 NJW 3406 (GER BGH) at 3410 (with further references); on a gradual softening of the subsidiarity doctrine (»*Vorrangthese*«) under German law, *see* Köhler and Bornkamm, *UWG*, § 4, para. 9.6; for the modern understanding, *see e.g.* Urteil [Judgment]: »*Seilzirkus*«, [2012] 114 GRUR 58 (GER BGH) at 63.

282 Henning-Bodewig, *Unfair Competition Law*, 5.

283 *See* Pflüger, *Der internationale Schutz gegen unlauteren Wettbewerb*, 233–34.

284 *Sears*, 376 U.S. 225, 375–76 (US 1964) (» *But because of the federal patent laws, a State may not, when the article is unpatented and uncopyrighted, prohibit the copying of the article itself or award damages for such copying*«); *see also Compco*, 376 U.S. 234 (US 1964); preemption doctrine applied to the misappropriation concept, *e.g.* by *Barclays v. Theflyonthewall.com*, 650 F.3d 876 (2nd Cir. 2011); *NBA v. Motorola*, 105 F.3d 841 (2nd Cir. 1997).

circumvent specific conditions of patent, design, copyright or trademark law.[285] If certain additional requirements relating to unfairness of *behaviour* are met, categorisation as a tort may be justified independent of the status of specific protection for the claimant's product or service.[286] Whether »*subsidiarity*« is still the right term or whether one should now proclaim unfair competition law to apply autonomously and in parallel to IP law,[287] in a *concurring* way,[288] often appears to be just a dogmatic, terminological debate.

According to the previous findings, copyright infringement claims regarding hybrid arbitration would usually fail pursuant to the idea/expression dichotomy, although many arbitration rules would overcome respective originality or creativity thresholds.[289] Trademark law does not protect against use of institutional rules by other institutions unless, in exceptional cases, concomitant use of a trademark created confusion on behalf of the users regarding a potential relationship between the administering institution and the institution that issued the rules to be applied.[290] Even under a modern, restricted understanding of subsidiarity, the following considerations on unfair competition law will have to recall these findings to avoid conflicting results.

---

285 *See e.g.* Ohly, »Schadensersatzansprüche wegen Rufschädigung und Verwässerung«, 928 (on the relationship between trademark infringement and unfair competition).

286 *See* Urteil [Judgment]: »*Seilzirkus*«, [2012] 114 GRUR 63; *cf. also NBA v. Motorola*, 105 F.3d at 845 (*inter alia* establishing criteria of »*free riding*«, »*direct competition*« and reduction of »*the incentive to produce the product or service*« for a »*hot news*« misappropriation claim to survive preemption; *but see Barclays v. Theflyonthewall.com*, 650 F.3d at 903 (clarifying the limits of this exception to preemption; critically discussed by Shyamkrishna, »The Uncertain Future of ›Hot News' Misappropriation«).

287 Schreiber, »Wettbewerbsrechtliche Kennzeichenrechte?«, 115 (»*autonom vom und parallel zum*«).

288 *See e.g.* Stieper, »Das Verhältnis von Immaterialgüterrechtsschutz und Nachahmungsschutz nach neuem UWG«, 302 (»*in kumulativer Anspruchskonkurrenz*«).

289 *Supra* at pp. 275-297 (§13A.I, II).

290 *See supra* at pp. 308-310 (§13B.III).

III. Unfair competition concepts possibly applicable to hybrid arbitration

Just like IP law, the law on unfair competition does not hinder a competitor to build upon another's idea when offering a similar product or service. Economic, technical and cultural progress would otherwise be seriously hindered.[291] Protection of legal products like standard business terms, insurance policies[292] or, as here discussed, arbitration rules against exploitation by competitors is therefore limited.

Regarding the use of another institution's rules in arbitration administration, the following factors make the verdict of unfairness even more improbable:

- Arbitration rules are publicly available and published free of charge.
- Party autonomy pleads in favour of allowing such conduct.
- Institutions only exceptionally accept to administer hybrid arbitrations in order to meet the demands of the parties.[293]
- Administration of arbitrations is application, not imitation of rules.
- Inspiration from institutional best practices makes arbitration more efficient.

In the words of the arbitral tribunal in the *Alstom–Insigma* arbitration, as cited by the Singapore High Court, one may argue that

> »in any contest between the principles of freedom of contract and party autonomy, against competing claims based on ›institutional self-interest‹ the former should prevail.«[294]

With a view to either supporting or challenging this contention, the following subsections discuss categories of practices considered unfair in different jurisdictions, starting with civil law concepts, exemplified by German and French law, and continuing with a summary of the state of the common law on unfair competition before peeking at Chinese unfair competition law.

---

291  Lettl, *Das Neue UWG*, para. 322 (with further references).

292  *See* Hermes, »Die Schutzfähigkeit von besonderen AGB-Klauselwerken«, 153, 167.

293  As unfair competition law sanctions conduct, subjective elements are decisive. This is different for copyright claims (*see Baigent, Leigh v. Random House*, [2007] EWCA Civ. 247 [95 et seq.] on »*animus furandi*«).

294  *Insigma v. Alstom*, [2008] SGHC 134 [32]. However, it remains unclear whether this statement refers to the administering or the rules issuing institution.

1. The concept of exploitation or tarnishment of reputation

German case law has developed limited groups of cases in which the exploitation of a product or the ideas of a competitor can be considered unfair competition. These groups of cases have been implemented by the legislator into the UWG (GER) with the 2004 reform.[295] Most important are: illegitimate obtainment of documents/knowledge,[296] avoidable deception of origin,[297] exploitation of reputation[298] and tarnishment of reputation.[299]

To the administration of an arbitration under another institution's rules, the first two groups of cases are obviously inapplicable because arbitration rules are publicly and freely available and because the parties are aware that the rules have been drafted and published by another institution. However, the latter categories of exploitation or tarnishment of reputation may be relevant.

Under German law, a successful claim for exploitation of reputation requires that the respondent offers a *replication* (»*Nachahmung*«) of the claimant's product or service and that the following three prerequisites of unfairness are met:[300]

- The competitive characteristics of the claimant's product have afforded that product, not itself protected by trademark, with an exceptionally *good reputation*.
- The respondent's product or service alludes to the claimant's product or service *in order to unduly benefit* from its reputation.
- The parties' products or services are *similar*.

Some institution's services, ICC arbitration in particular, are arguably renown enough to meet the threshold of an exceptionally good reputation. More questionable is the similarity between services offered by different institutions. While such claim does not require liability to create confusion on the origin of the product or service, it is nevertheless excluded if the

---

295 Fock, *Der unmittelbare wettbewerbsrechtliche Leistungsschutz*, 92, para. 297; for prior case law, *see* ibid., 91, n. 381.

296 UWG § 4 no. 9 c. (GER).

297 Ibid., § 4 no. 9 a.

298 Ibid., § 4 no. 9 b, 1st alt.

299 Ibid., § 4 no. 9 b, 2nd alt.

300 Ibid., 4 no. 9 b, 1st alt.; *see also* Urteil [Judgment]: »*Tupperwareparty*«, [2003] 105 GRUR 973 (GER BGH) at 974–75.

difference between the products or services is obvious.[301] Arbitration professionals would certainly be aware of the differences between institutions and would know that, for example, ICC-administered arbitration and SIAC administered arbitration under ICC Rules do not provide the same degree of foreseeability.[302] However, assuming that not all arbitration clauses in contracts - not even the majority - are advised by arbitration lawyers, business parties, not arbitration specialists should be the group of reference for determining whether differences are obvious. In light of the great number of pathological arbitration agreements with missing, incorrect or ambiguous references to arbitral institutions, obviousness of the differences cannot be assumed.[303]

However, the administration of arbitrations under hybrid arbitration agreements is usually not an attempt to benefit *unduly* from the reputation of the rules issued by another institution. Like in the *Alstom–Insigma* arbitration, hybrid arbitration would usually take place only upon express wish by the parties. Imitation of a service or product is not exploitation of reputation if it is the appropriate solution to a given practical problem.[304] An institution accepting hybrid arbitration provides a solution to the problem of inoperability, which parties would otherwise have to face.

Tarnishment of reputation refers to bad quality imitations, which discredit the original product. Related fears have been voiced for the market for institutional arbitration:

»[T]he world may become flooded by imitations of the established arbitration institutions. Is that what we want?«[305]

In principle, a claim for tarnishment of reputation does not require confusion on behalf of the customer. However, the claim fails if the differences between the products or services are so great, that not even the public would

---

301  *See* Urteil [Judgment]*:* »*Handtaschen*«, [2007] 109 GRUR 795 (GER BGH) at 799.

302  *See also Insigma v. Alstom*, [2009] 3 SLR(R) 936 (SG CA) [36]: »*We would expect Insigma's legal advisers to have known about the ICC and the SIAC when they advised Insigma to accept the ICC Rules in an SIAC administered arbitration*« (but not mentioning any evidence that the agreement was in fact legally advised).

303  *See supra* at p. 163 (§8C.I).

304  Ohly, »UWG § 4«, para. 9.68.

305  Coulson, »The Future Growth«, 81.

mistake an imitator's product as the original.[306] The application of these criteria to the service of arbitration administration is difficult, because arbitration is usually confidential and therefore does not have a real public. However, this fact already indicates that tarnishment of reputation of arbitration rules by administering hybrid arbitrations is rather unlikely.[307]

Independent of the questionable exploitation or tarnishment of reputation by such conduct, occasional acceptance to administer a case under another institution's rules if so chosen by the parties in their agreement, should not be considered a *replication* in the first place. Offering a service *relying* on another's work product - here the administration of arbitration relying on another institution's rules - does not replicate such work product.[308] At least pursuant to German law, the intuition that »*ploughing with another man's heifer*« or »*sailing in the wake of a competitor*« was unfair competition is a widely spread misconception.[309]

## 2. »Parasitisme« - a concept of exploitation of efforts

French law of unfair competition is based on the general provisions of non-contractual responsibility in articles 1382, 1383 C.Civ.[310] In particular, doctrine and jurisprudence have developed the tort of parasitic behaviour (»*parasitisme*«), which can be defined as the illegal and intentional use of economic value created by another, that is the fruit of specific know-how and intellectual labour, or research and development (»*recherché-développement*«) not protected by any specific right.[311] In its judgment in *Parfum Ungaro v Viviers* of 1989, the Paris Court of Appeal compared such economic behaviour to parasitic behaviour in the animal world, whereby

---

306 Ohly, »UWG § 4«, para. 9.70; *cf.* Urteil [Judgment]*:* »*Handtaschen*«, [2007] 109 GRUR 799, para. 48.

307 *See supra* at pp. 306-308.

308 *Cf.* Urteil [Judgment]*:* »*Hartplatzhelden.de*«, [2011] 113 GRUR 436 (GER BGH) at 437; positively discussed *inter alia* by Ohly, »Anmerkung«.

309 Ohly, »Anmerkung«, 440, para. 5: »*Es entspricht einer weit verbreiteten Intuition, das ›Pflügen mit fremdem Kalbe‹ [...], das ›Abkupfern‹ oder das ›Segeln im Kielwasser eines Konkurrenten‹ als grundsätzlich unlauter anzusehen* [internal references omitted].«

310 Le Tourneau, *Le parasitisme*, 4.

311 *Cf.* ibid., 61–62; Logan, »The Emperor's New Clothes? - Part 2«, 88 (with further references).

the substance of another being is taken for one's own advantage, causing the other to suffer or even die.[312] In its result, the decision, which effectively condemned the respondent for plagiarism of the claimant's perfume, was upheld by the Cour de Cassation.[313]

In difference to the German concept of exploitation of reputation, not only the goodwill of a competitor but mainly its efforts and research put into the development of a product or service are protected. The tort of parasitism protects not only entire products but also techniques, commercial methods, know-how and studies.[314] A good reputation is not a condition for a claim of parasitic behaviour; it might only be an additional element to prove the respondent's intent and a resulting damage.[315] However, since reputation is always a result of efforts and does not fall from the sky (»*ne tombe pas du ciel*«),[316] this conceptual distinction is not as decisive.

If an institution administers arbitrations under rules developed by another institution this could principally fall under the fairly broad category of parasitic behaviour if one acknowledges that such rules are *innovative* and that their creation required considerable *investment*.[317] However, next to the requisites of innovation and investment on the part of the developer, it is further decisive that the competitor relies on this innovation and investment to save own efforts and investments.[318] According to the relevant case law, it is a condition that the competitor, instead of giving free rein to its creative

---

312 *Parfums Ungaro v. Viviers*, [1990] Receuil Dalloz 340 (FR CA, Paris).: »*il s'agit d'un parasitisme économique qui, à l'instar du parasitisme observé dans le règne végétal* ou *animal, s'analyse en une prise de la substance de l'autre ainsi appauvrie et parfois même conduite au dépérissement*« (approving: Le Tourneau, *Le parasitisme*, 63, para. 82).

313 *Jean Jaques Viviers v. Parfums Ungaro*, 89–16.048 (FR Comm., Paris, 6 May 1991) (leaving some doubt about whether confusion was not required or found to be established by the facts of the case). More clearly, *Neral v. Z & Y*, (2001) Bull. 2001 IV, no. 27, p. 24 (FR C.Cass., Comm.) appears to abandon the requirement of confusion.

314 Le Tourneau, *Le parasitisme*, 68, para. 88.

315 Ibid., 52, para. 68.

316 Ibid., 51, para. 67.

317 On the conditions of innovation and investment, *see* Henning-Bodewig, »Ausländisches Recht«, para. 192 (with further references); *see also* Le Tourneau, *Le parasitisme*, 62, para. 81.

318 *See* Henning-Bodewig, »Ausländisches Recht«, para. 192, n. 268 for references.

abilities, puts them to sleep (»*les met en sommeil*«) and restricts the development process to the imitation of another's work.[319]

Since institutions such as CIETAC and SIAC *have* developed their *own* arbitration rules, they never saved any efforts, never »*put them to sleep*«, by *additionally* accepting to administer arbitrations under ICC Rules for example. In the known cases, the offer to administer hybrid arbitrations was made in the apparent interest of the parties but not in the interest to save own investments. On this basis, a claim for parasitic behaviour would have to fail. Moreover, practical, technical or legal necessities to rely on another's efforts would exclude a claim for parasitism.[320] The need to accommodate party autonomy and save the arbitration agreement from inoperability may be such necessity.

The situation may be different if a newly created institution would not bother with developing any arbitration rules in the first place and offer to administer arbitrations under an established institution's rules instead. However, this is rare if not unheard of. Institutions relying on UNCITRAL Rules to administer arbitrations do not fall into this category, since UNCITRAL is not a competing institution. To the contrary, UNCITRAL expressly encourages the use of its rules by institutions.[321]

Only concerning SHIAC and SCIA, CIETAC's former subcommission spin-offs, an accusation of parasitical exploitation of CIETAC Rules might seem defendable during their current transitional phase - under the hypothetical assumption that the applicable Chinese law followed concepts similar to French law. Although both institutions have now officially published their own rules, they continue to administer arbitrations under CIETAC Rules if parties' so insist. Furthermore, the Shenzhen subcommission, now SCIA, did not publish its own rules until December 2012, relying only on the 2005 CIETAC Rules from June to November 2012,[322] and the Shanghai subcommission, now SHIAC, applied rules nearly identical to CIETAC's 2005 Rules until May 2013 before it published a new version of its rules.[323]

---

319 *Parfums Ungaro v. Viviers*, [1990] Receuil Dalloz 340; *see also* Le Tourneau, *Le parasitisme*, 63, para. 82.

320 *See* Le Tourneau, *Le parasitisme*, 67, para. 87 (citing various cases to this effect).

321 *See UNCITRAL Recommendations to Institutions*, para. 18 (calling the offer of institutional administration a »*measure of the success of the UNCITRAL Arbitration Rules*«).

322 *See* Hirth and Munz, »CIETAC Schiedsvereinbarungen«, 9.

323 *See* Chen, Cui, and Lui, »China - CIETAC ›Jurisdictional Turf War' Comes To An End?«

However, the CIETAC split raises many specific issues of corporate trans-formation - or joint venture dissolution, if one followed SCIA's and SHIAC's account of affairs –[324] and transfer of know-how that would influence the evaluation[325] and go beyond the scope of this thesis.

### 3. Common law: Passing off and misappropriation

Related to unfair competition, common law has developed the torts of *passing off* one's own good as that of a competitor[326] and *»misappropriation.«*[327]

The theory of misappropriation has principally a very broad scope of application. Comparable with French *parasitisme*, it comprises the idea that a competitor shall not exploit another's costs and efforts without employing similar efforts, shall not *»reap where it has not sown.«*[328]

The theory of misappropriation comes close to acknowledging direct protection of work results by unfair competition law and thus appears an obvious ground of action for the problem here discussed. However, one can notice a reduced field of application of the theory in present US case law. According to the preemption principle mentioned above,[329] federal law usually excludes a reliance on misappropriation if a work result is or could be protected by trademark or copyright.[330] Apart from cases falling under § 43(a) of the *»Lanham Act«,* which in all its variants, requires some element of

---

324 CIETAC Shanghai Commission and CIETAC South China Commission, »Joint Statement« (declaring to have been independent institutions all the time).

325 *Cf. also* Le Tourneau, *Le parasitisme*, 165, para. 214 (on the legitimacy of the use of know-how acquired by an employee for a new business; finding that only a brain wash - *»lavage de cerveau«* - could effectively hinder this).

326 In principle, a concept of trademark law but mentioned in the context of unfair competition (*see e.g.* Waelde et al., *Contemporary Intellectual Property*, para. 17.7, 17.69; *Irvine Tidswell v. Talksport*, [2002] EWHC 367, [2002] 2 All ER 414 [EWHC Ch.] [14]: *»underlying principle is the maintenance of what is currently regarded as fair trading«*).

327 *See* Fock, *Der unmittelbare wettbewerbsrechtliche Leistungsschutz*, 217, para. 768.

328 *International News Service v. Associated Press*, 248 U.S. at 239, 240.

329 *See supra*, n. 284 on p. 319.

330 *See* Fock, *Der unmittelbare wettbewerbsrechtliche Leistungsschutz*, 223, para. 792, p. 241, para. 861–64.

confusion or misrepresentation,[331] a real common law tort of misappropriation independent of confusion now only exists for the limited subject area of »*hot news*«, accounting to the time sensitivity of the newspaper industry.[332]

English courts and doctrine have never gone to the lengths of some US case law[333] towards protecting the use of another's work results by unfair competition law.[334] Rather, the misappropriation concept is largely unknown in the English legal system, whose concept of unfair competition law - to the extent it exists at all[335] - is entirely restricted to the tort of passing off, in its original form requiring misrepresentation,[336] or other confusion cases acknowledged under the Paris Convention. Categories of unfair competition without an element of confusion, misrepresentation or deception have not yet been acknowledged.[337]

The broader copyright protection for invested »*skill and labour*« under English law to some extent fills the gap of a non-existent unfair competition

---

331  The provision is codified in United States Trademark Act § 1125 (US).

332  *See NBA v. Motorola*, 105 F.3d 841; *Barclays v. Theflyonthewall.com*, 650 F.3d 876.

333  Prior to the US Supreme Court's decisions on preemption, *see supra* at p. 319, n. 284.

334  Very illustratively expressed by Jacob LJ in *L'Oreal SA & Ors v Bellure NV & Ors*, [2007] EWCA 968 (Civ.) [160]: »*I am not sure where I first saw the word used in this context, though I believe it to have come from the USA. I wish to state that I think it very unhelpful. We are all against misappropriation, just as we are all in favour of mother and apple pie. To use the word in the context of a debate about the limits of the tort of passing off and its interface with legitimate trade is at best muddling and at worst tendentious.*«

335  *See also* Hellner, »Unfair Competition and Acts Restricting Free Competition«, 67 (»*virtually non-existent*«); Logan, »The Emperor's New Clothes? - Part 1«, 40; *see generally* Waelde et al., *Contemporary Intellectual Property*, para. 17.69–17.72 (noting that the English understanding of passing off satisfies the requirements of the Paris Convention but does not go further than that).

336  On this »*present state of the law*«, *see* Wadlow, *The Law of Passing-Off*, para. 7-286.

337  *See L'Oreal SA & Ors v Bellure NV & Ors*, [2007] EWCA 968 (Civ.) [149–61]; Wadlow, *The Law of Passing-Off*, para. 7–281 to 7–285 (with further references).

law.[338] In fact, to describe a copyright infringement, Lord Davey used language that seems very similar to that used by the US Supreme Court's to characterise misappropriation in *International News v. Associated Press*:[339]

> »For the purposes of their own profit they desire to reap where they have not sown, and to take advantage of the labour and expenditure of the plaintiffs [...].«[340]

Similarly, on Singapore's law, doctrine also emphasises the purpose of IP law to prevent unfair competition and suggests, if necessary, to »*push past the boundaries of the traditional IP regime to stop this free loading.*«[341] From this overview, it thus seems that in the Commonwealth systems,[342] copyright could be a more probable cause of action whereas in Continental jurisdictions and in the US, some form of unfair competition appears slightly better suited to deal with an arbitral institution using the rules of another without authorisation. Overall, however, neither copyright[343] nor unfair competition claims are likely to be justified.

## 4. A glance at Chinese unfair competition law

Since mainly Chinese institutions openly announce in their rules to be willing to administer hybrid arbitrations,[344] it seems appropriate to give also a - very concise - overview on Chinese unfair competition law.

---

338 *See supra* at pp. 276-284 and 293-295 (§13A.I§13A.I,II); *cf. also* Rahmatian, »Originality in UK Copyright Law«, 12 (noting that English copyright law serves the purpose of countering free riding on a competitor's investment).

339 Quoted *supra* at p. 327, n. 328.

340 *Walter v. Lane*, [1900] AC 539 (HL) at 551.

341 Ng-Loy, *Law of Intellectual Property of Singapore*, para. 2.2.5, 2.4.1.

342 *See e.g.* for Australia: *Moorgate v. Philip Morris*, [1984] HCA 73 [40] (seeing in unfair competition a »*cause of action whose main characteristic is the scope it allows, under high-sounding generalizations, for judicial indulgence of idiosyncratic notions of what is fair in the market place*«).

343 *See supra* at pp. 273-304 (A).

344 CIETAC Rules, art. 4 (3) (2012; 2015); SHIAC Rules, art. 2 (6) and article 3 (3) (2015); SHIAC Rules, art. 2 (5) and article 3 (2) (2014); SCIA Rules, art. 3 (3) sentence 3 (2012).

Despite its orientation towards the self-proclaimed ideal of a »*healthy development of socialist market economy*«[345] the relatively young[346] unfair competition law of the People's Republic of China is nowadays quite similar in structure and content to many Western laws on the same subject - at least on paper.[347] A major difference concerns the enforcement aspect. Under Chinese law, mainly administrative bodies enforce unfair competition law through fines and penalties rather than courts through private law remedies like injunctions or damages.[348]

Similar to many European statutes,[349] China's unfair competition law centres on a general provision, its article 2:

> »A business operator shall, in his market transactions, follow the principles of voluntariness, equality, fairness, honesty and credibility and observe the generally recognized business ethics. »Unfair competition« mentioned in this Law refers to a business operator's acts violating the provisions of this Law, infringing upon the lawful rights and interests of another business operator and disturbing the socio-economic order. [...]«

In addition, a number of special torts of unfair competition exist. The relationship between the special torts and the general provision is - like in many other legal orders –disputed.[350] The prevailing opinion appears to be that the requirements of article 2 (2) of the Unfair Competition Law (P.R.C.) have to be met in addition to one of the specific provisions' requirements. The provision should not be resorted for gap-filling or creating unnamed torts of unfair competition.[351]

---

345 Unfair Competition Law art. 1 (P.R.C.) (cited according to the English translation published on the WIPO website); *see also* Ganea and Pattloch, *Intellectual Property Law in China*, 156.

346 On the legislative history, *see* Pflüger, *Der internationale Schutz gegen unlauteren Wettbewerb*, 263–72.

347 Ibid., 276; *but see* ibid., 304 (regretting a lack of willingness to enforce).

348 Pflüger, *Der internationale Schutz gegen unlauteren Wettbewerb*, 297–300.

349 *See supra* at p. 318, n.. 276.

350 *See supra* at pp. 317-321 (§13C.II.3).

351 Based on the wording »*in violation of this law*«, *see* Pflüger, *Der internationale Schutz gegen unlauteren Wettbewerb*, 278, 283; *see also idem* »Aktuelle Informationen: China«, 290 (regretting that the SPC's Interpretation on Unfair Competition [2007] leaves the question open).

Generally, the special torts in the Chinese Unfair Competition Act implement the basic requirements of protection under the Paris Convention[352] but do not go further than that. A special tort of misappropriation of another's efforts employed to develop a product or service, independent of any confusion, does not exist. However, *if confusing,* the use of another's company name can be an act of unfair competition,[353] which refers back to the considerations regarding the spin-offs conduct following the CIETAC split discussed above as a potential dilution of trademark issue.[354]

## 5. The tort of undue interference with contractual relations

Overall, the previous considerations found that existing concepts of unfair competition of various legal orders do not provide a clear legal basis for reproaching an institution for offering or accepting to administer arbitrations under another institution's rules. Only a very far-reaching understanding of parasitism or misappropriation concepts could achieve this but such reasoning would be prone to contradicting the findings regarding the legality of hybrid arbitration administration under copyright and trademark law made above.[355]

When considering the particular procedural facts of the *Alstom–Insigma* arbitration, however, a distinct aspect to raise concerns could be that of the timing of SIAC's entrance at the scene: When SIAC announced to be willing to administer the case under ICC Rules, a request for arbitration had already been filed with the ICC Court. Only *after* SIAC's letter on the position it would take,[356] the parties decided to withdraw the ICC application. From a perspective of pure causality, one could therefore get the idea that SIAC's conduct interfered with a contractual relationship and corresponding profit

---

352 Pflüger, »Aktuelle Informationen: China«, 287–96; *cf* Paris Convention, art. 10bis (3) and *supra* at pp. 311-313 (§13C.I).

353 According to Zhu, *Gewerblicher Rechtschutz in der VR China*, 47.

354 *Supra* at pp. 308-310, on the unclear relationship between Chinese trademark and unfair competition law, *see* Bohnet, *Markenrecht in China und Russland*, 38 (with references on Chinese doctrine); *cf.* Unfair Competition Law art. 5 (P.R.C.) (regulating a number of trademark related issues).

355 *See supra* at pp. 273-310 (§13A, B)

356 *See Insigma v. Alstom*, [2009] SGCA 24 [9] (citing the secretariat's letter of 17 November 2006).

expectations of the ICC.[357] If this happened again, an aggravating factor is that the ICC Court now expressed a claim of exclusivity in article 1 (2) of its rules, which applies, in principle,[358] in relation to parties commencing arbitration there and of which other institutions are certainly aware.

Although originally developed from general tort principles, it seems appropriate to refer to the tort of undue interference with a contractual relationship under the heading of unfair competition.[359] Such tort is, in one form or another, acknowledged in a number of jurisdictions.[360] Expressed simply, the main prerequisites for such tort are:[361]

- a breach of contract by a party to a contractual relationship
- enticement, procurement or provocation of that breach by the defendant
- damage caused by such breach.

In addition, some kind of subjective element of malice, knowledge[362] or intention to cause damage, will need to be proven.[363]

Already, in view of the enumerated basic objective elements and in disregard of any additional and subjective requirements, an assertion of tortious interference with the contractual relationship of the ICC with Alstom

---

357  On the conclusion of an Administration Contract, *see supra* at pp. 243-251 (§11A.III).

358  *See supra* at pp. 255-263 (§11B.III) on colliding terms in case of hybrid agreements.

359  For German law, *cf.* UWG § 4 no. 11 (GER) which turns general torts, including interference with contract, into acts of unfair competition if they affect competition (*see* Hasselblatt, »§ 58«, para. 138–41).

360  For EU states, *see generally* von Bar et al., *DCFR*, VI.–2:211, p. 3254 (A); *see e.g.* for English law: Rogers, *Winfield and Jolowicz on Tort*, para. 18–2 et seq. (mentioning *Lumley v Gye*, [1853] EWHC J73 [QB], 118 ER 749 at the origin of this tort); under German law, this is a variant of causing damage against good morals under BGB § 826 (GER) (*see* Wagner, »§ 826 BGB«, para. 59–64).

361  *See generally* von Bar et al., *DCFR*, VI.–2:211, p. 3254 (A); *Cf. Lumley v Gye*, [1853] EWHC J73 [10]; Wagner, »§ 826 BGB«, para. 60 (also additional requirements developed by German jurisprudence); *see also* Hasselblatt, »§ 58«, para. 146–50 (specifically on this tort as an act of unfair competition).

362  *But see* Hasselblatt, »§ 58«, para. 150 (turning a blind eye considered sufficient).

363  *See Lumley v Gye*, [1853] EWHC J73 [10] (»*who wrongfully and maliciously, or, which is the same thing, with notice, interrupts the relation*«); Wagner, »§ 826 BGB«, para. 60.

and Insigma is unfounded. First, it has been explained that parties to a contract with an institution may validly and legally terminate such contract at least until the constitution of an arbitral tribunal without cause,[364] which is exactly what happened when Alstom's request for arbitration was withdrawn from the ICC Court. This is not a breach of contract. Even if it were, mere declaration to be willing to administer the arbitration under ICC Rules would not yet amount to enticement, procurement or provocation of this withdrawal. Mere abetting or taking advantage of another's breach of contract should not yet be considered a tort, as such understanding would conflict with the principle of privity of contract,[365] although, again, French law would assume a tort in this respect more quickly than most others jurisdictions.[366]

IV. Jurisdiction and applicable law: three hypothetical situations

While overall, unfair competition concepts appear not to provide sufficient legal basis for a claim against administering hybrid arbitrations, a number of conceptual differences among jurisdictions have been highlighted to the extent that a transnationally applicable solution cannot be ascertained.[367] Notably, a broad concept of »*parasitisme*« or reduced requirements for tortious interference with contract could increase the chances of a successful claim under French law, if applicable. This makes considerations on jurisdiction and applicable law all the more important.

Again, it is impossible to treat this subject exhaustively,[368] which is why some thoughts on three hypothetical situations have to suffice to introduce relevant problems:

---

364 *See supra* at pp. 252-255 (§11B.II).

365 Hasselblatt, »§ 58«, para. 151; Wagner, »§ 826 BGB«, para. 59 (with further references on German case law); on other jurisdictions, *see* von Bar et al., *DCFR*, 3257–62 (notes to IV.--2:211).

366 *See* von Bar et al., *DCFR*, 3257, n. 1 to VI.–2:211 (with further references); on a »*principe d'opposabilité des conventions aux tiers*« gaining the upper hand, *see also* ibid., 3067, n. 80 to VI.–2:101 (with references to critical voices in doctrine; from case law, *see e.g. Prisma presse v. Michael Y Books & Plon*, [2000] Bull. 2000 I no. 246, p. 161 [FR C.Cass]).

367 *See supra* at I, pp. 311-313.

368 In particular, the analysis takes a predominantly European perspective, following the criterion of at least regional »*harmonisation*« as introduced *supra* at p. 52 (§3).

- An institution proclaims that it is willing and capable to administer arbitrations under the rules of another institution seated in another jurisdiction.
- Without having publicly communicated its willingness to do so, an institution occasionally accepts to administer cases under a hybrid arbitration agreement according to another institution's rules upon express party request.
- An institution offers to administer a case under the rules of an institution, seated elsewhere, which first received a request for arbitration. Upon this offer, the parties withdraw their case and file it with the other institution.[369]

Furthermore, it shall be assumed that the rules issuing institution considers to sue the other institution not (only) at that institution's seat but also at another (potential) place of arbitration.


1. Relevance of the market place for jurisdiction?

Like for other torts, including copyright infringement,[370] courts in many jurisdictions would accept international and local jurisdiction over unfair competition claims if the respondent is domiciled in their territory or if the relevant harmful act did or - for injunction against future conduct - will occur within their territory.[371] Within the Brussels Regime this follows from article 7 (2) Brussels-Ia-Regulation (article 5 (3) Brussels-I-Regulation) and article 5 (3) Lugano Convention respectively.

However, it is suggested that for unfair competition the place of the harmful act is not the place where a certain conduct *factually* took place but the place where the conduct affected a certain market or the place where the interests protected by competition law collide (hereinafter summarised as »*market place principle*«).[372] The consequence of this restriction is that an act committed on the territory of one state but only affecting competition in

---

369 As just discussed *supra* at pp. 331-333 (§13C.III.5).
370 *See supra* at pp. 298-301 (§13A.III.1).
371 *See generally* Glöckner, »Internationales Lauterbarkeitsprozessrecht«, para. 1–2 (also on the mixing of applicable law and jurisdiction questions by common law courts).
372 *See infra* at pp. 336-340 (§13C.IV.2) for details on the contents of the market place principle with respect to applicable law; *cf.* Geimer, *Internationales Zivilprozessrecht*, para. 1517a (on the relevance for jurisdiction).

another state (*distance tort*) could, subject to general jurisdiction based on the domicile of the respondent, not be brought before the courts of the former but only of the latter state.[373] According to this view, the *»market place«* determines not only applicable law but also jurisdiction (so-called synchronised jurisdiction - German: *»Gleichlaufzuständigkeit«*).[374] Their close connection to the factual situation at issue and to the applicable law argues in favour of the competence of the courts of the market place.[375]

Similar results are reached by common law courts applying principles of subject-matter jurisdiction, comity reasoning and the *forum non conveniens* defence.[376] However, a difference is that a common law court might decline its jurisdiction under *forum non conveniens* despite *personal* jurisdiction generally following from the domicile of the respondent. In contrast, the civil law concept of synchronised jurisdiction only restricts the *special* jurisdiction for torts of courts at the place where the harmful act occurred or will occur. Civil law courts would not - and courts in the EU are not allowed to - decline *general* jurisdiction at the respondent's domicile only because of the applicability of foreign law.[377]

However, the application of the market place principle already at the level of jurisdiction is not without opposition. Some argue that jurisdictional rules referring to the place of the harmful act, like *e.g.* article 7 (2) Brussels-Ia-Regulation (article 5 (3) Brussels-I-Regulation), have to be interpreted without regard to the kind of tort at issue. Accordingly, the claimant is given a choice between the courts at the place where the infringing act took place and the place where the damage occurred.[378] Nevertheless, even this traditional view declines already the admissibility of the claim if the claimant fails to plead an act of competition with a sufficient nexus to the forum.[379] Accordingly, the differences in result between both views are marginal. Without connection to the domestic market, a claim is inadmissible,

---

373 *But see* ibid. (criticising this as an inappropriate confusion between *»ius«* and *»forum«*).

374 Glöckner, »Internationales Lauterbarkeitsprozessrecht«, para. 40; *see also* ibid., para. 19, 20 (for references on variances of this theory). *See supra* at pp. 298-301 (§13A.III.1) on similar considerations for copyright claims.

375 Glöckner, »Internationales Lauterbarkeitsprozessrecht«, para. 40.

376 *Cf. supra* at p. 298, n. 172 on the same consideration with respect to intellectual property infringement cases.

377 Glöckner, »Internationales Lauterbarkeitsprozessrecht«, para. 2–3.

378 Ohly, »Internationale Aspekte«, para. 8 (with further references to this still prevailing opinion in Germany).

379 Ibid., para. 9.

whether for lack of jurisdiction or for lack of sufficient pleading of an unfair competition claim.

For the example situations, this means that, unless the rules issuing institution introduced its action at the other institution's domicile, not only the applicable law but also jurisdiction or at least admissibility of a claim would depend decisively on the market place affected by the reproached conduct, as further explained in the following.

## 2. Qualification of the reproached conduct and localisation of the market

From the outset, unfair competition is a tort.[380] Tort cases generally call to apply the law of the place where the damaged occurred, as the last event of the tortious act (*lex loci delicti commissi*), safe for a closer connection to another country.[381] However, as already noted with respect to jurisdictional aspects, legislation or case law in many jurisdictions adapted the *lex loci delicti* rule to the specifics of unfair competition.[382] Today, there is a worldwide tendency towards employing some variety of the market place principle,[383] understanding the place of the tortious act to be the place where the conduct affected a certain market or the place where the interests protected

---

380 *See* Hay, Borchers, and Symeonides, *Conflict of Laws*, 996, § 17.53 (for the American understanding).
381 *See generally* ibid., 795, § 17.2; for Europe, *cf.* Rome-II-Regulation 2007 art. 4 (EU).
382 Hay, Borchers, and Symeonides, *Conflict of Laws*, 997, § 17.53; *see also* Rome-II-Regulation 2007 p. recital 21 (EU) (»*Art. 6 is not an exception to the general rule in Art. 4(1) but rather a clarification*«); *see generally* Lindacher, »Die internationale Dimension lauterkeitsrechtlicher Unterlassungsansprüche«, 453–54.
383 *See* Hellner, »Unfair Competition and Acts Restricting Free Competition«, 52 (calling the »*the country whose market is affected*« to be a »*connecting factor*« of newer enactments, »*with modalities in the way of expressing this*«); *see also* Proposal for a Regulation of the European Parliament and the Council on the law applicable to non-contractual obligations, COM(2003) 427 final 15 (2003) (»*broad consensus*«).

by competition law collide[384] or more loosely »*the place where the claimant was injured in his business.*«[385]

However, such specific understanding of the place of the tortious act as the market place is only functional where market interests, rather than the personal interests of the claimant are affected. Exemplary of this consideration is article 6 (1) of the Rome-I-Regulation, which attempts[386] to express this distinction:

> »1) The law applicable to a non-contractual obligation arising out of an act of unfair competition shall be the law of the country where competitive relations or the collective interests of consumers are, or are likely to be, affected.
>
> 2) Where an act of unfair competition affects exclusively the interests of a specific competitor, Article 4 shall apply.«

Accordingly, the market place principle would apply to acts of competition affecting the interests of more than one competitor or also consumer interests, whereas bilateral acts of competition should be treated like ordinary torts.[387]

This relates to the question of qualification of the reproached conducts, which shall be elucidated by recalling the examples outlined above.[388] The conduct in the first two hypotheses affects not only the rules issuing institution but also the interests of the parties to the arbitration and possibly of other institutions as competitors. Therefore, the market place principle determines the applicable law. However, concerning the third hypothesis, it

---

384 These places are »*essentially identical*« (Hellner, »Unfair Competition and Acts Restricting Free Competition«, 59); *but see also* Nettlau, *Die kollisionsrechtliche Behandlung von unlauterem Wettbewerb*, 175–78 (on dogmatic differences between the market affection principle, »*Auswirkungsprinzip*«, and the interest collision solution, »*Interessenkollisionslösung*«).

385 Hay, Borchers, and Symeonides, *Conflict of Laws*, 996–97, § 17.53, n. 5–8 (with further references on US case law, which is often found to be »*inconclusive*« or »*not clear authority*« as to the applicable test).

386 But, »*the clarification might be in need of some clarifications*« (Hellner, »Unfair Competition and Acts Restricting Free Competition«, 52). Prior to the Rome-II-Regulation, several European jurisdictions, including Germany, the UK, Italy and France, did not have separate unfair competition regimes, while others did (*see* ibid., 51–52).

387 *Cf.* Proposal for a Regulation of the European Parliament and the Council on the law applicable to non-contractual obligations, p. 16.

388 *See supra* at p. 334.

seems justified to apply the general tort regime.[389] Tortious interference with contractual relations, which is there the most probable cause of action, mainly affects one competitor.[390] The alleged tortious act in that example would be the interference with a contract concluded at the seat of the first approached institution,[391] consequential loss of the expected full amount of the administrative fees results at the same place. If one locates primary damage at the place of the conclusion of the breached contract, the first approached institution might arguably rely also on its home law in its home jurisdiction to claim damages for enticement of breach of contract from the other institution in that example.[392]

A second difficulty is to determine the relevant market where a certain conduct potentially affects more than one jurisdiction's market (multi-state tort). Then, it appears most appropriate, in correlation with the *lex protectionis* principle applied to copyright infringements,[393] to refer to the claimant's position. If the claimant seeks an injunction for a particular market and if this market is one of the markets affected, then the law of this state should apply to the claim. Similarly, if the claimant submits that he has lost or will lose customers in a certain market and calculates the damage based on this loss, than the law of that market place should apply. This approach discards all laws of markets that are affected by a conduct but that are not relevant to the particular lawsuit. However, an inevitable consequence of this solution is that a court may have to apply different laws to different remedies claimed in one lawsuit based on the same case (so-called statute accumulation).[394] It also places a burden on competitors to comply with unfair

---

389 *See supra* at p. 332 on the existence of this tort both within and outside the context of competition; *see also* Lindacher, »Die internationale Dimension lauterkeitsrechtlicher Unterlassungsansprüche«, 457 (stressing that the mere fact that a general tort *also* affects the market, »*Auch-Marktbezug*«, should not disadvantage the claimant).

390 *See* Proposal for a Regulation of the European Parliament and the Council on the law applicable to non-contractual obligations, p. 16.

391 *Cf. supra* at pp. 236-251 (§11A.II, III, IV) on law applicable to and the conclusion of the Administration Contract.

392 *Cf. also* Lindacher, »Die internationale Dimension lauterkeitsrechtlicher Unterlassungsansprüche« (in favour of a localisation at the place of business of the claimant in this case, with supporting references); *but see supra* at p. 299 on the questionable relevance of pure economic loss.

393 *See supra* at pp. 301-327 (III.2).

394 Nettlau, *Die kollisionsrechtliche Behandlung von unlauterem Wettbewerb*, 187–88.

competition laws of all market places likely concerned. However, this challenge can be disregarded because predictability could not be assured anyway: Generally and virtually in all legal orders - to differing degrees –, unfair competition law is much more based on general clauses, principles and case groups, all of which are rather vague,[395] rather than on specific rights and prohibitions as is IP law.

Moreover, it can be unclear whether the advertising market, as the place where the potential customers are located, or the transaction market, as the place where provider and customer come together to meet demand, is relevant.[396] This controversy is decisive where either the product or service or the customers cross borders. In such cases, advertising market and sales market may differ. Generally, the advertising market is decisive because that is where the conduct first influences decision-making.[397] Advertising markets are all territories where potential customers can take note of the service or product.[398] However, the transaction market is relevant, if the provision of the product or service itself or the manner of such provision is the reproached act of unfair competition.[399]

These issues are all problems of localising the relevant market place(s). With a view to the hypothetical examples here discussed, it seems most appropriate to apply the law of the advertising market to the first hypothesis as the rules issuing institution would essentially want to hinder or react to the offering of hybrid arbitration in such a case. If an institution declares to be willing to administer arbitrations under the rules of other institutions on its website and in several languages or in a widely understood language like English, this act reaches the public worldwide. However, not all of the public are potential customers. The character of the service or product also influences the relevant advertising market.[400] Although major institutions

---

395  *See supra* at pp. 321 et seq. (§13C.III).

396  Critical on this distinction: Glöckner, »Erläuterungen zum Internationalen Lauterkeitsrecht«, para. 139–44.

397  Nettlau, *Die kollisionsrechtliche Behandlung von unlauterem Wettbewerb*, 211; *see also* Drexl, »Internationales Lauterkeitsrecht«, para. 134 et seq..

398  Nettlau, *Die kollisionsrechtliche Behandlung von unlauterem Wettbewerb*, 211; Drexl, »Internationales Lauterkeitsrecht«, para. 134 et seq.

399  Nettlau, *Die kollisionsrechtliche Behandlung von unlauterem Wettbewerb*, 211.

400  Ibid., 210 (with an example of the advertising market for fresh fruit being restricted to a local market, even if published on a website accessible worldwide).

offer arbitration services to the business community worldwide, some factual and legal restrictions apply as discussed above.[401] When determining the advertising market in an individual case, it is decisive where the customers are located, for which the institutions effectively compete.

In the second hypothesis, the advertising market is not pertinent because this is not even in a broad sense an act of advertising. Commonly the public would not even become aware of the institution's conduct, as arbitration is not public. Here, it becomes necessary to determine the transaction market, which could be either the seat of the institution as the place of contract conclusion and actual performance[402] or the places of arbitration as places of legal performance. As already discussed with regard to copyright claims, it appears sensible to consider both the institution's seat and any (potential) place of arbitration as relevant as the conduct has tangible (at least *de minimis*) effects on market conditions there.[403]


D. Concluding reflections on the economics of exclusive institutional rules

Above considerations have shown that institutional arbitration rules, the efforts put into the development of such rules and the reputation gained by an institution with its rules are assets with market value that only enjoy limited protection by IP and unfair competition law. The law does not appear to prohibit use of such rules in arbitrations administered by other institutions, making successful lawsuits on that basis unlikely. Like many other private

---

401 *See supra* at pp. 71-74 (§4B.I.2) and pp. 240-243 (§11A.II.4).
402 *See supra* at pp. 240-243 (§11A.II.4) for details.
403 *Cf.* Lindacher, »Die internationale Dimension lauterkeitsrechtlicher Unterlassungsansprüche«, 455–56. *See supra* at pp. 301-304 (A.III.2) (also on the corresponding problem of territoriality of court orders, injunctions in particular).

legal products, services, or »*by-products*«,[404] arbitration rules are therefore »*public goods*.«[405]

Although institutional arbitrations rules are usually creative and original enough to be copyrighted, such copyright is of limited value since it does not extend to the idea behind the rules. Therefore, it only protects against imitations of form and expression of specific rules. The mere application of another institution's arbitration rules in administering arbitration is not a copyright infringement.

Institutions can also not fully protect their rules through trademarks in names of the institution, institutional actors or the rules themselves. Trademark protection is only effective against the use of the protected named »*as a trademark*«, mere mentioning for reference is not an infringement.

The broadest protection may be achieved through instruments of unfair competition law. However, vague provisions or common law principles of unfair competition should not be used to circumvent balances and values of IP law. For this reason, the »*unfairness*« of a certain conduct requires special attention. When an institution only accepts to administer a hybrid arbitration in order to give meaning to the parties' agreement and in an attempt to avoid a verdict of inoperability - as it seems to have been SIAC's motivation in the *Alstom–Insigma* case - this should not be considered unfair. Then, the institution's conduct is an attempt to serve party autonomy and the institute of arbitration in general. It is not motivated by the desire to gain undue advantages, to parasitically exploit or misappropriate the reputation or efforts of the rules issuing institution. The fairness of administering hybrid arbitrations may be judged differently if an institution directly advertises itself as a cheaper alternative to the rules issuing institution by offering to apply such institution's rules. However, the formulation in article 4 (3) of the CIETAC Rules alone should not yet be understood as such advertising. First, it is not encouraging parties to agree on CIETAC arbitration under other rules, it only clarifies how such case would be dealt with. Secondly,

---

404 Term introduced by Kobayashi and Ribstein, »Law as Product and By-product«, 537 (qualifying privately drafted law-like provisions as such, if the drafter profits from other market activities rather than selling their legal drafts alone). Arbitration institutions are »*byproduct law drafters*« because they profit primarily from administering arbitrations and not from offering their rules as »*standards*« (*cf.* ibid., 538; *cf. also* Habel, *Contract Governance*, 119–26, on widely used contract terms as legal standards).

405 *See* Hermes, »Die Schutzfähigkeit von besonderen AGB-Klauselwerken«, 221 (with further references).

it primarily concerns cases where parties agreed on CIETAC administered arbitration under other non-institutional, in particular UNCITRAL Rules. This is unproblematic, since UNCITRAL is not a competing institution and further allows and encourages the use of its rules by arbitral institutions. Apart from that, this analysis refrains from evaluating any further narratives on statements by CIETAC staff with regard to the use of ICC Rules in particular, since such statements appear not to have been made officially and the accounts thereof[406] cannot be verified.

To come to these findings on the protection of arbitral services and rules by IP law and unfair competition law, it was necessary to resort to general principles of these fields of law and analogous examples because fully pertinent case law does not exist and classic legal writing on the protection of private legal services and products is scarce. In contrast, the discipline of law and economics seems to have found a liking in this topic. In particular, *Bruce Kobayashi* and *Larry Ribstein* published a series of impressive and elaborate articles on incentives for private law making through IP protection.[407] Therein, they find that law drafted by private initiatives and institutions valuably contributes to the legal environment as a »*feasible and powerful alternative.*«[408] However, inefficient IP protection for legal materials[409] reduces economic incentives and thus innovation, a conclusion they reach on the basis of sophisticated calculations of mismatch costs in various scenarios[410] that shall not be reproduced or questioned here. It shall only be highlighted that arbitration institutions are not in the same way confronted with a »*Hobson's choice*« between public enforcement and jeopardising IP

---

406 *E.g.* Johnston, »Party Autonomy in Mainland Chinese Commercial Arbitration«, 553, quoted in the introduction, *supra* at p. 40 at n. 66.

407 For the most recent, *see* Kobayashi and Ribstein, »Law as Product and Byproduct«; Kobayashi and Ribstein, »Private Lawdrafting, Intellectual Property, and Public Laws« (with more references on earlier publications on the subject); on state laws as »*products*«, *cf.* Renner, *Zwingendes transnationales Recht*, 67 (with further references).

408 Kobayashi and Ribstein, »Private Lawdrafting, Intellectual Property, and Public Laws«, 43.

409 In particular discussing the issue of private laws getting into the public domain through enactment or appropriation by the legislator (ibid., 44, 62 creations adopted as law not enjoying copyright identified as »*basic conundrum*«).

410 *See* ibid., 46–62 (distinguishing models with mere copyright protection, broader - patent like - IP protection and without IP protection).

rights as other private law makers,[411] because their rules, even though they are not »*laws*«, are enforceable through contract and highly demanded by users. The dilemma described by *Kobayashi* and *Ribstein* that »*uncertainty over enforcement*« can »*significantly lower both the demand for and the incentive to produce such products*« is less relevant for arbitral institutions considering the drafting of innovative arbitration rules. In fact, the significance of party autonomy in international arbitration law[412] appears to ease this problem.

A law and economics question worth asking would be whether broader protection of arbitration rules was desirable, providing exclusivity clauses like article 1 (2) of the ICC Rules with a legal effect towards other institutions or parties wishing to apply the rules in ad hoc proceedings. A consequence of non-exclusiveness of public goods is often the problem of »*free riding*«, which means that a continued taking of advantage of the good by competitors might stop the developer from further creations, enticing it to »*freeride*« on others' innovations as well until all innovation is brought to a hold.[413] Everybody relies on the other to save efforts and costs, with the negative result that nothing happens (so-called »*prisoner's dilemma*« in game theory).[414] From a strict economic point of view, it might therefore appear desirable if arbitration rules, including the idea behind these rules, were truly exclusive as proposed in article 1 (2) of the ICC Rules.

However, applying law and economics theories to arbitration institutions this way would disregard that these are not only motivated by saving costs, making profit and competing for a greater market share. Their self-perception as non-profit associations for the benefit of the international business community,[415] or even as »*Merchants of Peace*«,[416] distinguishes them from associations that draft legal texts for economic purposes like insurance companies. Similar to the regulatory competition between states, the competition between arbitral institutions is more a competition of ideas and

---

411 *See* ibid., 62.
412 In contrast to corporate law used by *Kobayashi* and *Ribstein* as example (ibid., 46).
413 Hermes, »Die Schutzfähigkeit von besonderen AGB-Klauselwerken«, 222.
414 Ibid.
415 *See supra* at p. 314.
416 International Chamber of Commerce, »The Merchants of Peace«.

reputation than in market shares.[417] It is highly doubtful whether the aim to provide the business community with an effective settlement mechanism would be furthered by exclusive rights of institutions in their arbitration rules. To the contrary, it seems that the effectiveness and consequential acceptance and reputation of a set of arbitration rules benefits from widespread use. The UNCITRAL Rules are the best example, as their effectiveness is undisputed although, or because, they have been applied by differently equipped institutions as well as in ad hoc arbitrations.

## §14 The feasibility of administering hybrid arbitrations

According to the previous section's findings, the application of institutional arbitration rules by another than the rules issuing institution poses more practical than legal problems. The practical problem of replacement of institutional actors may be dealt with by an analogous application of the *substitution* theory originally developed for the conflict of laws (A). Applying such theory requires comparing specific provisions of institutional rules and their purposes (B) and taking into account differences and similarities institutional actors (C). Finally, implementation of a hybrid arbitration agreement would always require some *adaptation* of the chosen rules to match the structure and organisation of the administering institution (D).

### A. The test: applying substitution theory to a conflict of arbitration rules

Rolf Schütze, in his praise of a practice handbook on international arbitration, noted that a German lawyer who has to represent a client in an arbitration in Singapore under SIAC Rules might feel like a Christian who, although he is aware of Islamic beliefs, will feel lost during a Friday prayer in a mosque or like a Muslim who studied Christian theology but does not know what to do at the holy mass.[418]

---

417 *Cf.* Renner, *Zwingendes transnationales Recht*, 69; *but see also* ibid., 71 (seeing more classic competition between fee financed arbitral institutions than between state courts).

418 Schütze, »International Commercial Arbitration, Commentary«, 30 (reviewing: Conrad, Münch, and Black-Branch, *International Commercial Arbitration*).

To continue on this road, like the Muslim and the Christ in this image would be even more puzzled should the priest or the muezzin then call to a Jewish service, the German lawyer could be quite astonished to learn that ICC Rules should be applicable in the SIAC administered arbitration. However, the lawyer's astonishment may not amount to complete bewilderment if the parties originally intended and agreed on SIAC administering the arbitration under ICC Rules and if the concrete way SIAC administered the case met the parties' expectations. Accordingly, hybrid arbitration agreements should be capable of being performed to the extent that the administering institution can *adequately* replace the institutional actors mentioned in the chosen rules. Adequacy of replacement of institutional actors may simply be seen as a question of contractual interpretation, or, alternatively or additionally, as a question of substitution and adaptation of the requirements of the rules.

## I. A contract perspective: general contract interpretation rules

The search for the parties' original intent and the interchangeability or substitutability of institutional bodies, concepts and processes may be viewed as a process of interpreting the arbitration agreement. Along this line, Jennifer Kirby reproached that the Singapore High Court in its *Insigma v. Alstom* ruling got around the problem if SIAC actors can perform ICC functions by interpreting the hybrid agreement »*to mean something other than it literally says.*«[419]

However, for contract interpretation, different from statute construction, a strict literal rule is indefendable; the wording is never the limit.[420] Rather, due consideration is to be given to the intent of the parties and the reasonable understanding and relevant circumstances of the case.[421] If regarded only as an issue of interpretation of the contractual terms of the arbitration agreement, the adaptation of the chosen arbitration rules to the facilities available at the administering institution is therefore not a major dogmatic concern. Freedom of contract allows replacing the institutional actors,

---

419 Kirby, »SIAC Can Administer Cases Under The ICC Rules?!?«, 327.

420 *See* Gaillard and Savage, *Fouchard, Gaillard, Goldmann*, 260–61 (with further references); also quoted by *Insigma v. Alstom*, [2009] SGCA 24 [32].

421 *Cf.* UNIDROIT Principles, art. 4.1–4.3; von Bar et al., *DCFR*, art. II.–8.101.

assuming that all parties and the administering institution agree. If the respondent party objects to such replacement, a contractual perspective may still provide sufficient arguments to reject such objections because inoperability of the arbitration agreement, with the consequence of reopening the path to state court litigation, is generally not perceived as a legitimate interest or reasonable expectation of any party pursuant to the principle *in favorem validitatis* as addressed above.[422]

In the following, it shall be assumed that both parties, as in the *Insigma v. Alstom* case, agree in principle that their original expectations were an arbitration administered by SIAC and its actors under ICC Rules but that they also expected concept, features and purpose ICC Rules to remain intact.

## II. A rule perspective: introduction to substitution and adaptation theories

Such probable expectations of parties agreeing on hybrid arbitration recall the question of qualifying the choice of institutional arbitration rules as exercise either of the freedom of contract or of the free choice of (rules of) law.[423] That institutional rules are commonly enacted by private actors and binding only through contract highlights the contractual traits of the problem. Nevertheless, the drafting process of a set of institutional rules undeniably resembles that of a piece of legislation.[424] The hurdles to rule adaptation and replacement of actors are higher if one regards arbitration rules as statute-*like* provisions.

Challenges of ensuring the *equality of different legal institutes*[425] and of smoothing *disharmonies in rule application*[426] pose themselves not only in association with the conflict of *laws* but also in respect of the conflict of arbitration *rules*. A solution can therefore be inspired by conflict of laws principles, as long as the private, contractual nature of arbitration rules does not get out of focus.

---

422 *See supra* at pp. 161-107.
423 *See supra* at pp. 58-59 (§4A.I).
424 Schöldström, The Arbitrator's Mandate, 404. *See supra* at pp. 110-116 (§5B).
425 Sonnenberger, »EGBGB, Einleitung«, para. 602 (German: »*Gleichwertigkeit fremder Rechtserscheinungen*«; with further references).
426 Ibid., para. 581 (German: »*Disharmonien der Rechtsanwendung*«).

German doctrine in particular applies theories of *adaptation* (German: *»Anpassung«*, *»Angleichung«*)[427] and of *substitution*[428] to meet the mentioned challenges in relation to foreign legal institutes. In private international law, adaptation means that an applicable rule of law of one jurisdiction may have to be modified if it conflicts with another, equally applicable rule of law of another jurisdiction to avoid an outcome incompatible with the purpose of both laws.[429] Such conflicts may for example exist between the procedural *lex fori* and the law applicable to the merits. The lack of a common jurisdictional framework then hinders an interpretative solution and requires a synthesis between both laws in order to deal with the disharmonies.[430]

As a corollary, substitution[431] means the replacement of a legal institute of the applicable law with a functional equivalent of another jurisdiction,[432] or more generally the concretisation of the conditions of the applicable law with institutes of another law.[433] A legal provision of one legal order is applied to a case situated within a different legal order, which does not know the same institutes.[434] A typical question of substitution is whether a notarisation by a foreign notary meets the requirements of notarised form under German law.[435] In a *»Resolution«* of 2007, the *Institute de Droit International,* an international association of scholars, formulated this objective of substitution:

---

427  *See* Kropholler, *Internationales Privatrecht,* § 34 I (preferring the German term *»Anpassung«* over *»Angleichung«*).

428  *See* Lewald, *Règles générales des conflits de lois,* at 132 (Lewald first named this theory).

429  Sonnenberger, *»EGBGB, Einleitung«,* para. 589.

430  Ibid.

431  *See generally* van Venrooy, *Internationalprivatrechtliche Substitution.*

432  Rauscher, *Internationales Privatrecht,* 117; Schotten and Schmellenkamp, *Das internationale Privatrecht in der notariellen Praxis,* § 3 para. 49a; *see also* Kropholler, *Internationales Privatrecht,* § 33 I.

433  van Venrooy, *Internationalprivatrechtliche Substitution,* 35, 136.

434  Sonnenberger, *»EGBGB, Einleitung«,* para. 602.

435  *See* Rauscher, *Internationales Privatrecht,* 119–20 (with explanations and case examples); Jayme, *»Report on Substitution«,* 3. Other examples concern the inclusion of foreign marriage and partnership regimes into the applicable tax, succession or social security law (*see* ibid., 52–53).

>»Substitution allows a legal relationship or act originating in a given State to entail all or part of the effects attached to a similar relationship or act under the law of another State.«[436]

Sometimes both concepts, adaptation and substitution, which are intertwined, are summarised under the heading transposition.[437] Generally, however, substitution, as a method of interpretation of the law,[438] prevails over adaptation, which results in a modified application of the law. First, it should be clarified through interpretation if and to which extent the legal institutes referred to by a particular provision may be substituted by those available. Only in a second step, other applicable provisions may have to be adapted to this interpretative result.[439]

Substitution analysis is commonly divided into two questions:

- Does the applicable provision's purpose exclude substitution of its requisites and legal institutes *per se*?
- If the answer to the first question is negative, what are the conditions for substitution?

For the second question, the relevant criterion is *equivalence,*[440] it is the key (»*la clé*«) to solve problems of substitution.[441] Doctrine argues in favour of a liberal application of the equivalence criterion because legal

---

436 Institut de Droit International - 1ère commission, »Resolution on Substitution«, art. 1; for drafting materials and deliberations, *see also* Jayme, »Report on Substitution«.

437 *Cf.* already Lewald, *Règles générales des conflits de lois*, 129 (»*même trait caractéristique*«); *see also* the questionary answer by Andreas Bucher, »Report on Substitution«, 30–35 (not recommending to distinguish between adaptation, transposition, equivalence and substitution on a transnational level); *but see* van Venrooy, *Internationalprivatrechtliche Substitution*, 137–38 (opposing such lack of differentiation).

438 *See also* Lewald, *Règles générales des conflits de lois*, 138 (understanding substitution as a method to interpret applicable law rather than to solve a conflict of laws).

439 Sonnenberger, »EGBGB, Einleitung«, para. 605.

440 Kropholler, *Internationales Privatrecht*, § 33 II (with references to German and French case law); Institut de Droit International - 1ère commission, »Resolution on Substitution«, art. 2.

441 Jayme, »Report on Substitution«, 7.

orders are structurally very diverse.[442] To establish equivalence, an exercise of comparative law is required.[443]

A comparative test, first inquiring into the purpose of a rule and then into the availability of equivalent actors to fulfil that purpose, appears also suitable for evaluating the factual operability of hybrid arbitration agreements, because such agreements can never be implemented one-to-one. By definition, actors such as the »*ICC Court*«, the »*ICC Secretariat*« or »*Secretary General of the ICC Court*« do not exist at other institutions and vice-versa.[444] In the ordinary meaning of replacement, the Singapore High Court frequently used the terms »*substitution*« or »*substitute*« in its *Insigma v. Alstom* decision.[445] The analysis if actors can be interchanged when applying institutional arbitration rules without impairing their purpose can therefore be called *quasi*-substitution or application of a *modified* substitution theory.

»*Quasi*« or »*modified*« because two caveats require attention: First, it has to be recalled that arbitration *rules* are not laws. Criteria developed for the conflict of laws[446] therefore do not apply directly;[447] the reference to such criteria only acknowledges that the *factual* statute-*like* character of institutional rules raises concerns similar to those in choice of law cases. Second, substitution is admittedly very much a civil law concept and a method apt in particular for highly codified legal orders like Germany. Generally,

---

442 Kropholler, *Internationales Privatrecht*, § 33 II; Institut de Droit International - 1ère commission, »Resolution on Substitution«, art. 3 (»*similarity between the aims and interests* [...] *sufficient*«).

443 Lewald, *Règles générales des conflits de lois*, 135; Vischer, *Die rechtsvergleichenden Tatbestände im internationalen Privatrecht*, 48.

444 Kirby, »SIAC Can Administer Cases Under The ICC Rules?!?«, 325.

445 *Insigma v. Alstom*, [2008] SGHC 134 [1, 24, 28, 35].

446 In a wider sense, without taking position on the dogmatical controversy if substitution is a method of applying substantive law to a case (German: »*Subsumtion*«) or a method of partial reference to a foreign law (German: »*Verweisung*«) (in the former sense: Lewald, *Règles générales des conflits de lois*, 138; *see generally* Sonnenberger, »EGBGB, Einleitung«, para. 606, 608–10; *see also* Currie, »The Law of the Forum«, 67, on foreign law as a »*datum*« having »*nothing to do with conflict of laws*«; *but see* van Venrooy, *Internationalprivatrechtliche Substitution*, 47, 226, 570, qualifying substitution as a reference rule of private international law).

447 Direct application would further contribute to the shapelessness of substitution theory as regretted by van Venrooy, *Internationalprivatrechtliche Substitution*, I.

private international law is characterised by a »*pluralism of methods.*«[448] Other jurisdictions were found to lack a similar »*culture*« of substitution,[449] although at least one American author mentioned the concept in his treatise.[450] The reference to this theory may therefore be questioned in light of the predominantly transnational approach of this thesis.[451] However, the mere observance that other legal orders have not yet consciously advanced a theory of substitution, does not mean that the problem does not exist and that the solutions provided by the theory would be rejected.[452]

In fact, the reason why many legal orders do not know substitution as a legal theory is probably due to a trend to answer concrete problems directly without searching for underlying principles and methods.[453] For those approving entirely of such direct approach, the foregoing reflections may be

---

448 Picone, »Les méthodes«, 25 (»*pluralité des méthodes*«); Kühne, »Methodeneinheit und Methodenvielfalt«, 144 (announcing the end of the period of monistic conflict of laws systems); *cf. also* Jayme, »Report on Substitution«, 46 (project of the resolution: »*pluralisme de méthodes*«); *but see* ibid., 57 (comment by Bucher considering this a banality).

449 van Venrooy, *Internationalprivatrechtliche Substitution,* IV, 564 (concluding that a transnational concept of substitution will never exist); *but see* Institut de Droit International - 1ère commission, »Resolution on Substitution«; *cf. also* Jayme, »Report on Substitution«, 9 et seq. (phenomenon exists in many jurisdictions without being named as such: *see e.g.* Gaudemet-Tallon at 10 and Lagarde at 26 for France, Vischer at 17--18 and Bucher at 30--31 for Switzerland, Struycken for the Netherlands at 19; *but see e.g.* North at 29, who sees no usefulness of substitution theory under English law).

450 Ehrenzweig, *Private International Law; a Comparative Treatise on American International Conflicts Law, Including the Law of Admiralty,* 119. Similar to the prevailing opinion in Germany, which understands substitution as a method of interpretation (*see supra* at n. 446), Brainherd Currie describes foreign law as a »*datum*« (»The Law of the Forum«, 67; further developed into a »*data theory*« by Ehrenzweig, »Local and Moral Data in the Conflict of Laws«).

451 *See supra* at pp. 48 et seq. (§3).

452 Accordingly, solution-orientation justifies inspiration by this concept, *see supra* at p. 52 (§3); *cf. also* Jayme, »Report on Substitution«, 7.

453 *See* ibid., 33, 70 (common law lawyers »*would certainly not use terms like substitution and equivalence* [but] *simply reach the appropriate result*«); *cf. also* Picone, »Les méthodes«, 25 (on »*false conflicts*« as an American concept relying on equivalence between laws); Jayme to Ehrenzweig, »Ausländische Rechtsregeln und Tatbestand inländischer Sachnormen«, 41 (on *data* cases as »*false conflicts*«).

unnecessary. For all others, a test *inspired* by substitution theory as just outlined helps to give a more structured answer to the question of how to implement hybrid arbitration agreements. Therefore, it is worthwhile to mention the theory of substitution as the source of inspiration for the following analysis, even if it is not yet a transnationally recognised method[454] and does not apply in its strict sense.[455]

After the following comparative, *quasi-substitution* analysis, an exercise of *(quasi)-adaptation* will ensue, if required and appropriate.[456] Adaptation in its strict sense of creating a synthesis between applicable laws could also help to accommodate the problem that interpretation of arbitration rules incorporated into the arbitration agreement may follow a different law than interpretation of same rules as incorporated into the Administration Contract.[457]

III. Parameter of equivalence: the applicable rule's purpose

Accordingly, the analysis of the operability of hybrid arbitration agreements requires a comparison between institutional actors, their legitimisation within the institution, their human and structural resources and qualification.

However, dependent on the degree of institutional influence under the chosen rules,[458] the need for substitution and the expectation regarding the legitimacy and qualification of the substituting actor varies. It is therefore useful to first compare the degree of institutional involvement and purpose

---

454  *Cf. also* Hübner, »Sinn und Möglichkeiten«, 246 (stressing that academic writing can only fulfill its role by also defending theories not yet generally accepted).

455  *But see* van Venrooy, *Internationalprivatrechtliche Substitution*, 566 (regretting widespread use of »*Substitution*« in a general sense).

456  *Infra* at pp. 399 et seq. (§14D); *cf. also Bucher* »Report on Substitution«, 35 (finding adaptation to be an imperative second step of any substitution).

457  *See supra* at pp. 110-116 (§5B); pp. 75-86 (§4B.II) and pp. 236-243 (§11A.II); *see also* Wolf, *Die Institutionelle Handelsschiedsgerichtsbarkeit*, 242–43 (proposing adaptation as a solution); *cf. also* Chan, »Of Arbitral Institutions and Provisional Determinations on Jurisdiction, Global Gold Case«, 179.

458  *See also supra* at pp. 131-134 (§7A.IV).

of institutional powers provided by different sets of institutional rules with a view to identifying or excluding potential for substitution.

Thereby, each phase of an arbitration shall be illuminated, beginning with its commencement, continuing with the potential institutional decision on jurisdiction, the appointment, challenge and replacement of arbitrators, the proceeding before the arbitral tribunal and finishing with provisions on the award and on costs.[459]

## 1. The functional equivalence test

Commenting on the remarkable[460] decision of the Singapore Court of Appeals in *Insigma v. Alstom*,[461] Réné-Alexander Hirth, a German lawyer, observed:

> »Diese, der sehr schiedsfreundlichen Haltung in Singapur weiter Geltung verschaffende Rechtsprechung findet wohl erst dort ihre Grenzen, wo keine Entsprechungen in den ›Organen‹ der jeweiligen Institutionen mehr zu finden sind.«[462]

> [This jurisprudence, which certifies Singapore's very arbitration-friendly approach, apparently has its limits only where equivalents to the ›organs‹ of the specific institutions cannot be found anymore.]

While this observation neatly stresses substitutability of »*organs*« as one of the main problems concerning hybrid arbitration agreements, it fails to provide guidance on which organs or actors of different institutions are deemed equivalents. In particular, Hirth's finding that SIAC, when administering the *Alstom–Insigma* arbitration, has exercised the functions of ICC actors through actors that *mirrored* those of the ICC Court, surprises in its generality.[463] At the time of this arbitration, which was introduced in 2006 when SIAC Rules (1997) were in force, SIAC did not have any body resembling

---

459 Provisions not relating to the institution are not covered herein; general reference is made to the growing number of practice commentaries to institutional rules, many of which are listed in the bibliography.

460 Hirth, »SIAC Rules«, para. 4; »Schiedsordnung des SIAC«, para. 4 (introduction).

461 *Insigma v. Alstom*, [2009] SGCA 24.

462 Hirth, »Schiedsordnung des SIAC«, para. 4, n. 9.

463 Ibid., para. 4; *see also* the newer English version, »SIAC Rules«, para. 4 (»*mirror images*«).

a Court,[464] nor a Secretary General.[465] Even SIAC itself appeared unsure whether it was more appropriate to let the SIAC Chairman exercise the ICC Court's functions or better SIAC's Board of Directors as it was eventually done.[466]

Obviously, SIAC and the Singapore courts did not see a need of identical or nearly *identical* actors to perform a hybrid arbitration agreement. Rather, they found it sufficient that *any* actors were willing to perform the required tasks under the applicable rules. The following considerations evaluate this very lenient stance.

## 2. Equivalence of actors or acts?

As this analysis is guided by substitution theory in private international law,[467] it is useful to highlight the parallel issue of equivalence between state actors like courts, judges and administrative bodies or actors with sovereign functions like notaries. In a conflict of laws analysis, this issue of equivalence between authorities is often mute due to the rule *locus regit actum,* meaning that the law of the state where the act was made governs its formal validity.[468] A discussion of equivalence only ensues if a certain type of authoritative act is entirely unknown in the jurisdiction whose law applies.[469] Then, classic substitution theory would focus on the functional equivalence of *acts* - not of *actors*. The reason is that a state actor would almost never issue a type of act not foreseen in its jurisdiction, even if asked to do so by parties.[470]

---

464 *See infra* at pp. 392-394 (§14C.II.1).

465 *See* SIAC Rules, art. 1 (2) (1997) (only mentioning the Registrar and the Chairman).

466 In an early letter, SIAC's Secretariat explained to the parties that the ICC »›*Secretary-General‹ and ›Court‹‹«* would »*under the SIAC system, be the Registrar and the Chairman, respectively*« (*see Insigma v. Alstom,* [2009] SGCA 24 [9]).

467 *See supra* at pp. 344-352.

468 Vischer, *Die rechtsvergleichenden Tatbestände im internationalen Privatrecht,* 52.

469 Ibid., 53; *see also* Institut de Droit International - 1ère commission, »Resolution on Substitution«, art. 6.

470 Vischer, *Die rechtsvergleichenden Tatbestände im internationalen Privatrecht,* 53; *but see* Allmeling, *Deutsche Scheidung mit Mullah*

In contrast, private institutions like arbitration institutions could issue acts not foreseen in their own rules upon the parties' wish. Different from state authorities, constraints of sovereignty and separation of powers or other »*policy considerations*« do not apply to them.[471] When SIAC administered the *Alstom–Insigma* arbitration, the question posed was therefore not if *acts* like arbitrator appointment or scrutiny of an award under SIAC Rules were functionally equivalent to similar acts under ICC Rules but if SIAC *actors* performing functions under ICC Rules were equivalent to ICC actors.

IV. Article 1 (2) of the ICC Rules - per se an exclusion of substitution?

A preliminary question, before discussing details of institutional rules and actors, is if an exclusivity clause in arbitration rules excludes any substitution by another institution *per se*.

The following reflections are based on article 1 (2) of the ICC Rules but apply correspondingly to similar provisions should other institutions follow this trend. However, they seem less pertinent to article 1 (3) sentence 4 AAA-ICDR Rules because its wording allows at least »*authorized*« individuals or institutions to apply AAA-ICDR Rules. Hence, different from the ICC Court, the AAA-ICDR appears to assume only a kind of exclusive right to apply or licence its rules[472] rather than also expressing practical concerns about substitution by other institutions.

The purpose of article 1 (2) of the ICC Rules is to hinder hybrid arbitrations[473] and first comments suggest the provision's effectiveness even in relation to other institutions.[474] Substitution theory could finally provide an

---

 (reporting a spectacular case, where a German court rendered a divorce judgment under islamic law in cooperation with a Mullah).

471 *See Insigma v. Alstom*, [2009] SGCA 24 [41] (only addressing arbitration specific policy considerations).

472 *But see supra* at pp. 272 et seq. (§13) on the lack of a convincing legal foundation for such claim.

473 Fry, Mazza, and Greenberg, *The Secretariat's Guide to ICC Arbitration*, para. 3–4.

474 Ghaffar, »Rules and Legislation: The 2012 ICC Arbitration Rules«, 171 (»*intended to militate against the enforceability of pathological clauses*«); *see also* Steindl, »Party Autonomy under the 2012 ICC Arbitration Rules«, 231; Grierson and van Hooft, *Arbitrating under the 2012 ICC Rules*, 17; Trittmann, »Die wesentlichen Änderungen«, 48.

argument for this opinion, because it is widely accepted that the possibility of substitution (substitutability, German: »*Substitutionsoffenheit*«), that is the question if a provision allows substitution, is determined by the law applicable to the *effects* of the legal relationship.[475] Transferred to the rule conflict at issue, ICC Rules, where applicable, could decisively determine if substitution of actors was possible. According to article 1 (2) of the ICC Rules it is not.

Here however, a first modification of the original substitution theory is justified and required. In private international law, the principle that the applicable law determines the possibility of substitution follows from state sovereignty and separation of powers. If the legislator expresses that a legal term in a statute means only the domestic institute, to the exclusion of foreign institutes, a judge cannot overrule such qualification. *Quasi-substitution* of institutes mentioned in rules enacted by private bodies like the ICC does not conflict with state sovereignty and powers, but only with unilateral, private stipulation which has to succumb to the principle of party autonomy. If, despite article 1 (2) of the ICC Rules, parties and another institution agreed that this other institution should administer the arbitration and, accordingly, that substitution of institutional actors shall take place, article 1 (2) of the ICC Rules cannot by itself render such agreement invalid.

However, article 1 (2) of the ICC Rules is a clear indication that many provisions in ICC Rules may only be adequately performed by ICC actors. Only ICC-administered arbitration is ICC arbitration. Absent a clear indication that the parties did not actually want ICC arbitration but arbitration administered by another institution under ICC Rules, a court should therefore not find a substitutability of actors. For this reason, the decision in *HKL v. Rizq*, in contrast to the *Insigma v. Alstom* rulings, must again be branded as flawed.[476]

## B. Rules referring to the arbitral institution and their purpose

To begin with, some general rules concerning the role of the institution in administering arbitration shall be recalled. Articles 1 and 6 (2) of the ICC Rules fall in this category as well as articles 1 and 36 SIAC Rules, articles 1 and 2, 4 (3)-(4) of the CIETAC Rules (2012, 2015) and article 73 (2) of

---

475  Institut de Droit International - 1ère commission, »Resolution on Substitution«, art. 4 sent. 2.

476  *See supra* at pp. 174-177 (§8C.I.2).

the CIETAC Rules (2012),[477] articles 1 (1) and (3) and 38 sentence 2 AAA-ICDR Rules, article 3 and 29 LCIA Rules and article 1 (4) Swiss Rules. The Swiss Rules further set out the role of the cantonal Chambers of Commerce in their introduction.

At least five purposes of such general rules can be identified:

- identification and definition of the status of the institution[478]
- confirmation of parties' consent to the powers of the institution[479]
- distinction of rights and duties of the institution from those of the arbitral tribunal[480]
- task allocation to various actors of the institution[481]
- exclusion of control of institutional decisions by state courts to the extent possible.[482]

Task allocation is also the subject of internal rules of the institution, that do not actually become part of the arbitration agreement, unless the institutional rules refer to them like article 1 (1) of the ICC Rules. Whether such internal rules become incorporated into the Administration Contract, with

---

477  = CIETAC Rules, art. 83 (2) (2015).

478  *See in particular*: CIETAC Rules, art. 1 (1) (2012; 2015); *cf. also* ICC Rules, art. 1 (1) (2012; 2017); Swiss Rules, introduction and art. 1 (1) (2012).

479  *See* ICC Rules, art. 6 (4) (2012; 2017); SIAC Rules, art. 1 (2013, 2016); CIETAC Rules, art. 1 (2) (2012; 2015); Swiss Rules, art. 1 (4) (2012); to the same effect: AAA-ICDR Rules, art. 1 (1) at the end (2014); LCIA Rules, art. 29, together with their preamble (2014).

480  *See in particular*: ICC Rules, art. 1 (2) sent. 1 (2012; 2017) (»*The Court does not itself resolve disputes. It administers the resolution of disputes by arbitral tribunals [...]*«); AAA-ICDR Rules, art. 39 (2014); *see also* AAA-ICDR Rules, art. 36 (2009).

481  *See* ICC Rules, art. 1 (2012; 2017); LCIA Rules, art. 3 (2014); CIETAC Rules, art. 2 (2012; 2015); SIAC Rules, art. 1 (3)–(5) (definitions) (2013, 2016); Swiss Rules, introduction, at (b) (2012); *but see* AAA-ICDR Rules (2014) (not explaining internal organisation in the rules) (*see infra* at pp. 398-399, C.IV).

482  *See only* LCIA Rules, art. 29 (1998); SIAC Rules, art. 36 (2013) = art. 40 (2016); *cf.* Swiss Rules, art. 1 (4) (2012) (»*to the fullest extent permitted*« may be interpreted as a waiver of appeal).

the consequence that their disrespect could entail claims of contractual liability, is open to debate.[483]

Of the here discussed institutional arbitration rules, DIS Rules clearly stand out because they do not contain any general provisions or definitions concerning the DIS as administering institution. This is due to the reduced administrative involvement of the DIS in arbitration proceedings, as the following analysis will show. All relevant issues are left to party agreement or the discretion and decision of the arbitral tribunal.

## I. Commencement of the proceedings

All of the rules here analysed provide for the *commencement* or *initiation*[484] of the arbitration that at least one party has to file a brief with the secretariat[485] of the institution and pay a filing fee.[486] Generally, such requirement of filing with the institution has the purpose of having a clear date for the commencement of the arbitration, confirmed by the secretariat,[487] relevant *e.g.* for the statute of limitation, *lis pendens* and interest and usually determining the applicable version of the rules. This is a notable difference to ad hoc arbitration, including arbitration with a predetermined appointing authority like Hamburg Friendly Arbitration, where arbitration is commenced by sending a notice to the other party only.[488] Practically, the institutions

---

483  *Cf.* Aden, *Internationale Handelsschiedsgerichtsbarkeit*, pt. B, para. 9 (introduction to ICC Rules, considering the reference to internal rules to be a drafting mistake).

484  Herein used synonymously; *but see* Roughton, »Commencing Arbitration: Contemporary Paradoxes and Problems«, 175–76 (on a possible divergence under the rules of the Japan Commercial Arbitration Association).

485  For the SCCAM, this means filing with any of the secretariat offices at the participating Chambers of Commerce (Swiss Rules [2012], Annex A).

486  *See generally* Roughton, »Commencing Arbitration: Contemporary Paradoxes and Problems«, 175 (on such requirement in »*almost all institutional rules*«).

487  ICC Rules, art. 4 (1)–(2) (2012; 2017); SIAC Rules, art. 3 (3) (2013, 2016); DIS Rules, art. 6 (1) (1998); CIETAC Rules, art. 11 (2012; 2015); LCIA Rules, art. 1 (4) (2014); AAA-ICDR Rules, art. 2 (2) (2014); Swiss Rules, art. 3 (2) (2012).

488  *Cf. supra* at p. 150-151 (§7C.III); this often entails problems of proof of receipt (*see also* Roughton, »Commencing Arbitration: Contemporary

here discussed testify the commencement of the proceedings. Essential is compliance with the filing fee requirement, failing which the arbitration may either not commence or be terminated by the institution.[489]

The terminology for the first brief initiating arbitration varies from »*Request for Arbitration*«[490] over »*Notice of Arbitration*«[491] to »*Statement of Claim.*«[492] Independent from the wording used, the requirements concerning content,[493] form and required copies[494] vary among institutions.

Some differences are connected to the function of the initiating brief only as a demand for arbitration or also already as a full statement of claim. Many institutions follow a two-step process, requiring a notice or request with limited requirements as to the substantiation of the claim in this initial phase and providing that the claimant shall submit its full statement only later to

---

Paradoxes and Problems«, 176, on this deficiency of UNCITRAL Rules and institutional rules replicating these).

489 ICC Rules, art. 4 (4), 3 (1) (2012; 2017) (also making the number of copies an essential requirement); DIS Rules, art. 7 (2) (1998); CIETAC Rules, art. 13 (3) (2012; 2015); LCIA Rules, art. 1 (1)(vi), (4) (2014) (without fee, request treated as not received); Swiss Rules, art. 3 (5) (2012); SIAC Rules, art. 3 (1)(k), (3) (2013, 2016) (without filing fee, the Registrar would not determine »*substantial compliance*«); *but see* AAA-ICDR Rules, art. 1 (2014) (not explicitly providing for consequences of failure to pay filing fee; only Administrative Fee Schedule provides for administrative closing of file).

490 ICC Rules, art. 4 (2012; 2017); LCIA Rules, art. 1 (2014); CIETAC Rules, art. 11 (2012; 2015).

491 SIAC Rules, art. 3 (2013, 2016); Swiss Rules, art. 3 (2012); AAA-ICDR Rules, art. 2 (2014).

492 DIS Rules, art. 6 (1998).

493 Many rules only mention »*shall*« requirements of substantiation and require only a more or less detailed summary of facts and claims, *cf. e.g.* ICC Rules, art. 4 (3) (2012; 2017); SIAC Rules, art. 3 (1) (2013, 2016); Swiss Rules, art. 3 (3) (2012); AAA-ICDR Rules, art. 2 (3) (2014); LCIA Rules, art. 1 (1) (2014); CIETAC Rules, art. 12 (2012; 2015); arguably more demanding: DIS Rules, art. 6 (1998) (»*shall contain*«; *but see* the German version: »*muss enthalten*« [must contain]; (2) »*specification of the relief sought*«, (3) *particulars regarding the facts and circumstances*«).

494 Most rules require sufficient copies to be sent to the institution but some provide for direct sending of a copy to the other party or parties (for the latter, *see e.g.* LCIA Rules, art. 1 (1) (vii) [2014]; AAA-ICDR Rules, art. 2 (1) [2014]).

the arbitral tribunal once appointed.[495] The answer to the Notice of or Request for Arbitration is treated accordingly. Of the institutions here discussed, this applies to the LCIA, the SCCAM, SIAC and, in practice, also to the ICC Court.[496] Some also describe ICC Rules as taking a »*middle road.*«[497]

In contrast, the DIS requires principally a complete statement of claim to commence proceedings, similar to what is required in German state court proceedings,[498] including *inter alia* a specified request for relief and a full statement of the facts. Moreover, the nomination of a co-arbitrator, unless a sole arbitrator is agreed, is required already with this statement of claim. After the constitution of the tribunal, it is directly for the respondent to reply, without another statement from claimant. The requirement for a complete statement of claim to initiate proceedings serves at expediting the proceedings.[499]

If the statement of claim is incomplete, the DIS Secretariat sets a time limit for additional submission; failing compliance, the proceedings are

---

495 *See e.g.* Turner, *A Guide to the LCIA Arbitration Rules*, para. 3.02; *cf.* Bühler, *Handbook of ICC Arbitration: Commentary, Precedents, Materials*, para. 4–24 (»*Claimant may choose to submit a less detailed Request, when the key point is to commence the proceedings*«); *but see* ibid., para. 4–20, 4–23 (finding it »*important that the ICC Court has from the outset more complete information*«; most claimants submit a detailed request with supporting documents).

496 LCIA Rules, art. 15 (2) (2014); Swiss Rules, art. 18 (2012); SIAC Rules, art. 17 (2) (2013) = art. 20 (2) (2016); *see* ICC Rules, art. 23–25 (2012; 2017) (further written submissions left to agreement of the parties or discretion of the tribunal); *see also* Schilling, »Art. 4 ICC SchO«, para. 1; *contra* Lachmann, *Handbuch für die Schiedsgerichtspraxis*, para. 2979 (assuming that the ICC, like the DIS, requires a statement of claim - »*Klage*« - already to initiate proceedings); Wilke, »Prozessführung in administrierten internationalen Handelsschiedsverfahren«, 29.

497 Wilke, »Prozessführung in administrierten internationalen Handelsschiedsverfahren«, 31; Bühler, *Handbook of ICC Arbitration: Commentary, Precedents, Materials*, para. 4–21, 4–23, 4–24, 4–25 (allowing the Claimant to decide »*which approach to adopt*«).

498 *See* Schilling, »§ 6 DIS SchO«, para. 1; *cf.* ZPO § 253 ZPO (GER).

499 Schilling, »§ 6 DIS SchO«, para. 2. Under LCIA Rules, the claimant has an option to have its request treated like a statement of claim (LCIA Rules, art. 15 [2]–[3] [1998]). Under Swiss and SIAC Rules, the statement of claim may accompany the Notice for Arbitration (Swiss Rules, art. 4 [b] [2012]; SIAC Rules, art. 3 [2] [2013, 2017]).

terminated by the DIS, without that an arbitral tribunal is ever appointed. These rather severe[500] requirements are problematic for two reasons. First, if the language of the arbitration is not determined in the agreement, it is uncertain in which language the statement of claim would have to be filed.[501] Second, the consequences for suspension of the statute of limitations are unclear.[502]

A similar procedure of combining the initiation of the arbitration and the written submissions on the claim is principally followed in AAA/ICDR and CIETAC proceedings. Both require a statement of claim with the request and do not foresee a second statement of claim once the tribunal is appointed. However, while AAA-ICDR Rules require only »*a description of the claim and of the facts supporting it*«,[503] CIETAC Rules even ask for an attachment of documentary or other evidence.[504]

From this rule comparison, the conclusion imposes itself that higher filing requirements and a double purpose of the initiating brief as a demand and statement of claim result in greater institutional control in the initial phase of the arbitration. However, when looking at the practice of scrutinising filing requirements, such finding cannot be fully supported. For example, although filing requirements under DIS Rules can be considered demanding, the secretariat hardly ever rejects a statement of claim for being incomplete.[505] Furthermore, a claimant curing initial incompleteness of the statement of claim within the additional time, benefits of the date of commencement with the first receipt of the (incomplete) statement of claim.[506]

---

500 *But see* Lachmann, *Handbuch für die Schiedsgerichtspraxis*, para. 3375 (noting the DIS Secretariat to act claimant friendly in general).

501 *See* ibid., 3366, 3367 (also noting that filing in languages other than German, English and French create additional administrative fees); *see also* Schilling, »§ 6 DIS SchO«, para. 8, 9 (suggesting to use, absent express agreement, the language in which the arbitration clause is drafted); *cf.* DIS Rules, Annex to art. 40 (5) no. 19 (1998) (on additional fees for translations).

502 Lachmann, *Handbuch für die Schiedsgerichtspraxis*, para. 3374.

503 AAA-ICDR Rules, art. 2 (3)(e) (2014). Further demand for written statements is in the tribunal's discretion.

504 CIETAC Rules, art. 12 (2) (2012; 2015).

505 Wilke, »Prozessführung in administrierten internationalen Handelsschiedsverfahren«, 29; Lachmann, *Handbuch für die Schiedsgerichtspraxis*, para. 3375; Aden, *Internationale Handelsschiedsgerichtsbarkeit*, pt. C, DIS § 6, para. 3–4.

506 DIS Rules, art. 6 (4) (1998).

In contrast, SIAC Rules pose less formal requirements for the notice of arbitration and the statement of claim only has to be submitted after constitution of the arbitral tribunal. Still, the compliance with the filing requirements is looked at more closely by SIAC. The arbitration only commences with a »*complete Notice of Arbitration*« or upon certification of the »*substantial compliance*« with the filing requirements by the *Registrar* –not by any ordinary case manager.[507] Under ICC Rules again only such filing requirements relevant for the institution to perform its tasks, like the identification of the parties and the reference to an ICC arbitration clause are checked by the secretariat, other requirements are a matter for the later appointed tribunal to consider.[508]

Overall, the differences in commencement rules appear manageable, even if an institution was asked to administer a case under another institution's rules. Neither different headings of the submissions should not be an obstacle, nor the varying requirements of content and copies. In principle, any institution's secretariat should be able to perform formal scrutiny of filing requirements of the initial brief for the purpose of legal certainty on the commencement of the proceedings. Specific competence is not required. As arguably all rules allow for some discretion in scrutiny of filing requirements, an institution may, in case of differences between the chosen rules and its own rules, apply the less demanding requirements according to the principle of congruence mentioned above.[509]

II. Institutional decision on jurisdiction

Some, but not all, arbitration rules provide for the arbitral institution to render a decision on institutional and/or arbitral competence.[510]

---

507 SIAC Rules, art. 3 (3) (2013, 2016); *cf. also* Roughton, »Commencing Arbitration: Contemporary Paradoxes and Problems«, 175, n. 3 (»*importance of strict adherence*«).

508 Bühler, *Handbook of ICC Arbitration: Commentary, Precedents, Materials*, para. 4-26.

509 *See supra* at p. 263, n. 252.

510 In the wider sense, this also concerns the questions if one or more disputes involving more than one contract and/or more than two parties can be tried together in a single arbitration, if additional parties may be joined and if proceedings can be consolidated. These specifics are left out herein as it is unlikely that a hybrid arbitration clause would ever be agreed between more than two parties or in more than one contract.

1. Distinction: review of filing requirements and contractual acceptance

Conceptually, scrutiny of filing requirements, contractual acceptance to administer a case and a (prima facie) ruling of the institution on jurisdiction are not identical.[511] As just discussed, scrutiny of filing requirements has the purpose of ensuring that an arbitration is only commenced, in particular in respect of statute of limitation concerns, with a brief that sufficiently informs the other party of the dispute. While institutional secretariats, when reviewing filing requirements, may draw the parties' attention to possible jurisdictional issues and cost consequences,[512] this does not amount to a provisional determination of jurisdiction.[513]

The acceptance of the case by the institution only concerns contractual duties and obligations between the institution and the parties. In contrast, an institutional decision on jurisdiction, even if on a prima facie and provisional basis has consequences for the continuation of the arbitration, and is therefore a procedural matter.[514] Different from the contractual decision whether to accept the administration of a case which is of course made *ex officio*, a ruling on jurisdiction only takes place upon objection or a lacking answer by the respondent. By the time the institution renders such a decision, the arbitration has already commenced[515] and the decision is rendered

---

511 *Cf.* Wolf, *Die Institutionelle Handelsschiedsgerichtsbarkeit*, 84 (distinguishing contract conclusion from the act providing the institution with its competence - »*Kompetenzbegründungsakt*«); *contra* Wilke, »Prozessführung in administrierten internationalen Handelsschiedsverfahren«, 35; Chan, »Of Arbitral Institutions and Provisional Determinations on Jurisdiction, Global Gold Case«, 410; Turner, *A Guide to the LCIA Arbitration Rules*, para. 3.08 (comparing the Registrar's review of filing requirements with the ICC Court's jurisdictional scrutiny, although noting »*important differences*«); unclear: Reiner and Aschauer, »ICC Rules«, para. 140 assuming the ICC's prima facie decision to be »*in fact a communication of private law/contractual nature*«).

512 *See* Chan, »Of Arbitral Institutions and Provisional Determinations on Jurisdiction, Global Gold Case«, 410–11 (concerning LCIA and ICDR practice).

513 *Contra* ibid.; Hofbauer et al., »Survey on Scrutiny of Arbitral Institutions«, 7.

514 Or »*administrative*« or jurisdictional matter, *see infra* at pp. 435-438 (§16A.II.3.a) and pp. 444-447 (§16B.I).

515 *Cf.* ICC Rules, art. 6 (4) (2012; 2017) (»*whether and to what extent the arbitration shall proceed*«); *contra* Roughton, »Commencing Arbitration: Contemporary Paradoxes and Problems«, 175–76; unclear: Wilke,

in performance of an already concluded Administration Contract. Its purpose is to solve a jurisdictional conflict *between the arbitrants* - not a potential conflict of the arbitrants with the institution.

CIETAC Rules highlight the difference between contractual acceptance of the case by the institution and the ruling on jurisdiction by mentioning these matters in two separate provisions of the rules.[516]

The latest revision of the Swiss Rules, deliberately or accidentally, appears to have replaced a provision governing the contractual acceptance of the case with an - albeit very limited - power to render an institutional decision on jurisdiction. Under the former version of the Swiss Rules, the Chamber of Commerce receiving a notice of arbitration, after consultation with the »*Special Committee*«, which was a centralised body already under Swiss Rules (2004),[517] could decide not to forward the notice to the respondent if there was »*manifestly no agreement to arbitrate referring to these Rules.*«[518] This can be understood as regulating a ground in which the institution may refuse to administer the case by not sending a notice amounting to acceptance of an Administration Contract.[519] In contrast, the new article 3 (12) Swiss Rules reminds more of a provision on jurisdiction/competence, with the caveat of being restricted to a decision on *institutional* (administrative) competence.

## 2. Rules on institutional decisions on jurisdiction and their scope

Article 6 (3) and (4) of the ICC Rules provides for a decision on whether the arbitration shall proceed if the following conditions are met:

- A respondent party either raised an objection to »*the existence, validity or scope of the arbitration agreement*« or did not submit an answer.
- The Secretary General decides to refer the matter to the Court.

If all respondents submit an answer without objections to jurisdiction or if the Secretary General finds the objection to jurisdiction obviously

---

»Prozessführung in administrierten internationalen Handelsschiedsverfahren«, 34–35.

516 Although, confusingly, in anti-chronological order, *see* CIETAC Rules, art. 6, 13 (2012; 2015).

517 *Cf.* Oetiker and Burkhaler, »SCCAM«, 239.

518 Swiss Rules, art. 3 (6) (2004).

519 *See supra* at pp. 243-251 (§11A.III) and pp. 269-272 (§12).

unfounded, a consideration for which the ICC Secretariat maintains an internal checklist, the case is transferred to the arbitral tribunal without a decision of the Court.[520] If the case is submitted to the Court for a decision on jurisdiction, such decision is only preliminary - *prima facie* - and not binding on the tribunal or a state court.[521]

Although article 6 (3) of the ICC Rules does not expressly mention an objection to the administration by the ICC Court, as opposed to objections to the overall validity of the arbitration agreement, such an objection would be treated as an objection pursuant to this provision. One of the points on the internal checklist asks if the arbitration clause contains a reference to the ICC. A hybrid arbitration agreement mentioning ICC Rules but another institution cannot be understood as a clear reference to the ICC Court despite article 1 (2) and 6 (2) of the ICC Rules, such question should therefore be referred to the Court by the Secretary General rather than being advanced to the arbitral tribunal directly.[522]

The first sentence of article 25 (1) of the SIAC Rules distinctly mentions objections to the institution's jurisdiction to administer the case:

> »If a party objects to the existence or validity of the arbitration agreement *or to the competence of SIAC to administer an arbitration* before the Tribunal is appointed, the Registrar shall determine if reference of such an objection is to be made to the Court [*emphasis added*].«

Even more clearly, the Swiss Rules restrict the institutional decision entirely to the question of administration by the Court.[523] The question of the tribunal's competence is left to the arbitral tribunal.[524] Article 3 (2) Swiss Rules provides:

> »If the Respondent does not submit an Answer to the Notice of Arbitration, or if the Respondent raises an objection *to the arbitration being administered under these Rules*, the Court shall administer the case, unless there is manifestly no agreement to arbitrate referring to these Rules [*emphasis added*].«

In sharp contrast, CIETAC Rules go a great step further and provide that CIETAC is originally competent to determine, not provisionally but with

---

520 ICC Rules, art. 6 (3) (2012; 2017).

521 *See* ibid., art. 6 (5), (7).

522 *Cf.* the mention of a similar - unreported - case, *supra* at p. 37, n. 48, on the lack of precision of the criteria for the Secretary General's decision, *see generally* Voser, »Die wichtigsten Neuerungen der revidierten ICC Schiedsordnung im Überblick«, 17.

523 *See* Ehle and Jahnel, »Revision der Swiss Rules«, 170 (»*gatekeeper*« role).

524 *See* Swiss Rules, art. 21 (1) (2012).

binding effect for the arbitral tribunal, »*the existence and validity of an arbitration agreement and its jurisdiction over an arbitration case.*«[525] Even after the arbitral tribunal is constituted, CIETAC stays competent to change its *prima facie* decision based on new evidence found by the arbitral tribunal,[526] with the somewhat odd consequence that the arbitral tribunal is responsible for examining the evidence on jurisdictional matters but CIETAC as institution renders the decision thereon.[527] This construction is due to commands of Chinese arbitration law, which provides that the power to decide on arbitral jurisdiction belongs to the arbitration commission rather than the tribunal.[528] While CIETAC can delegate its power to rule on jurisdiction to the arbitral tribunal according to its rules,[529] and often does when jurisdictional and substantive issues are intertwined, it is unclear whether this is in conformity with the arbitration law, which does not provide for such a possibility.[530]

All other rules here concerned do not provide for a *formal* institutional decision on jurisdiction and leave the question, including the question of institutional competence to administer the arbitration, entirely to the arbitral tribunal.[531] However, an institution might order a claimant to advance all costs, thus bearing the financial risk, until the arbitral tribunal renders its decision on jurisdiction if the arbitration agreement looks questionable.[532]

Substituting the competent actor to render a jurisdictional decision under the applicable rules when administering hybrid arbitration is a problem. SIAC did not face this dilemma when administering the *Alstom–Insigma*

---

525  CIETAC Rules, art. 6 (1) (2012; 2015); *cf. also* ibid., art. 6 (2).

526  CIETAC Rules, art. 6 (2) (2012; 2015).

527  *But see* Tao, »CIETAC Rules Art. 6«, para. 1 (remarking that CIETAC would consult with the arbitral tribunal if constituted before rendering a decision).

528  *See* Arbitration Law art. 20 (1) (P.R.C.).

529  CIETAC Rules, art. 6 (1), (3) (2012; 2015).

530  Tao, »CIETAC Rules Art. 6«, para. 2 (calling the rule »*daring*«).

531  *But see* Turner, *A Guide to the LCIA Arbitration Rules*, para. 3.09 (describing an informal practice of consultation between the LCIA Registrar and LCIA Court in such matters, which is »*difficult to summarize*«; in »*clear-cut cases*« the LCIA Court may »*refuse to set the arbitration in motion*«) (mingling commencement of arbitration with jurisdiction).

532  *See* ibid. (approving of such practice at the LCIA).

arbitration as at that time[533] Insigma explicitly agreed to arbitral jurisdiction in general and SIAC's jurisdiction to administer the case,[534] which made an institutional decision on jurisdiction - as opposed to the contractual acceptance to administer the case - unnecessary. Generally, for the administering institution to render an express or implied *positive* institutional decision on jurisdiction in substitution of the competent actor under the applicable rules seems less problematic than a negative one. Under most rules, except for CIETAC Rules, a positive decision by the institution determines the jurisdictional question only preliminarily and is therefore not subject to direct state court control.[535] If an institution faced with a hybrid arbitration agreement views the question of jurisdiction negatively it may be more appropriate for the institution to declare the *contractual* termination of the Administration Contract on the basis of the jurisdictional uncertainties, to which it is entitled in any case as argued above,[536] rather than to assume a procedural consequence to render a negative jurisdictional decision with questionable reviewability and on the basis of rules whose application is - in light of the objection or non-participation of a party - not clearly agreed.

III. Constitution of the arbitral tribunal

While it is a primary task of all arbitral institutions to assist in the constitution of the arbitral tribunal, the steps taken by institutions to that effect and the degree of control exercised in this regard vary tremendously.[537] Generally, institutional powers with respect to tribunal constitution seek to both avoid undue delay in case of non-participation or default of a party and ensure the independence and impartiality of appointed arbitrators.

---

533 However, Insigma later raised an objection with the arbitral tribunal, rejected by interim decision then unsuccessfully challenged before Singapore's courts (*see also infra* at p. 484, §17C.II.4).

534 It only objected formally to SIAC's apparent reliance on its own rules rather than art. 8 (1) of the ICC Rules (1998) for the tribunal's constitution, *see infra* at pp. 483-487 (§17C.II.3, IV).

535 As explained *infra* at pp. 438-439 (§16A.II.3.c).

536 *See* the conclusions to Chapter 3, *supra* at pp. 269-271 (§12).

537 Again, many rules also contain specific provisions for multi-party situations. For the reasons outlined *supra* at n. 510 at p. 361 they are not discussed herein.

1. Institutional determination of the number of arbitrators

In line with applicable conventions and most legislation,[538] all institutional rules here discussed allow parties to agree on the number of arbitrators, but prefer one or three arbitrators and oppose even numbers of arbitrators.[539]

All institutional secretariats would certainly draw the parties' attentions to possible issues with the choice of an even number of arbitrators. The ICC Court eventually accepts such choice where it does not conflict with the lex arbitri and if it is stipulated how a decision is made in case of disagreement between the arbitrators - be it that one arbitrator may decide alone or that an additional arbitrator shall then be appointed.[540] Large tribunals of five or more arbitrators are not only very expensive but also cause additional bureaucracy and delays. However, such choice is usually accepted,[541] even though institutional secretariats would first try to persuade the parties otherwise.[542]

Institutional determination of the number of arbitrators therefore only takes place in absence of a party agreement and only if an institution considers it appropriate to deviate from the default number provided by the

---

538  New York Convention, art. V (1)(d); European Arbitration Convention, art. IV (1)(d); *cf.* UNCITRAL Model Law 2006 art. 10 (1) : »*the parties are free to determine the number of arbitrators*«; for references on national law, *see* Born, *International Commercial Arbitration (2014)*, 1664, 1665, n. 160 (§ 12.02 [A]).

539  ICC Rules, 12 (1) (2012) (1 or 3); similar: CIETAC Rules, art. 23 (1) (2012) = art. 25 (1) (2015); AAA-ICDR Rules, art. 11 (2014) (no restriction); similar: Swiss Rules, art. 6 (1) (2012); LCIA Rules, art. 5 (2) (2014) (1 or »*more than one*«); *but see* Turner, *A Guide to the LCIA Arbitration Rules*, para. 4.07 (qualifying the rule as »*purely definitional*«); *cf.* Arbitration Act 1996 § 15.2 (EW) (presumption in favour of an uneven number); unclear: SIAC Rules, art. 6 (1) (2013) = art. 9 (1) (2016) (restriction to 1 or 3 may only apply to institutional determination); *but cf.* SIAC, »SIAC Model Clause« (*\*«State an odd number. Either state one, or state three»*).

540  Reiner and Aschauer, »ICC Rules«, para. 244; Grierson and van Hooft, *Arbitrating under the 2012 ICC Rules*, 127 (»*free to deviate*«); Derains and Schwartz, *A Guide to the ICC Rules*, 144 (not a »*mandatory rule*«); *but see also* ibid., 143, 145 (reporting decisions where the ICC Court did not allow parties to agree on an English style umpire system).

541  *Cf.* Born, *International Commercial Arbitration (2014)*, 1672–73 (§12.02 [F]).

542  *See e.g.* Swiss Rules, art. 6 (3) (2012).

rules. Most institutional rules here discussed provide for a sole arbitrator as default number[543] except for CIETAC Rules and DIS Rules, calling for a default three-member arbitral tribunal.[544] Swiss Rules always require an official Court decision in absence of party agreement, *»taking into account all relevant circumstances.«*[545] Nevertheless, when making that decision, the SCCAM's discretion is directed towards appointing a sole arbitrator.[546] The situation under Swiss Rules is therefore effectively similar to that under ICC, LCIA, AAA-ICDR or SIAC Rules.

The institution would appoint a three-member tribunal instead of a sole arbitrator, if this is warranted by the case's complexity and the amount in dispute given the additional arbitrator fees.[547] The purpose of rules providing discretion to the institution on the number of arbitrators to be appointed is to ensure the efficiency of the arbitration regarding time and costs. The decision on the number of arbitrators is rendered by the *»Court«* under ICC, LCIA and Swiss Rules, by the Registrar under SIAC Rules and - without specification - by the *»administrator«* under AAA-ICDR Rules.

Only under CIETAC and DIS Rules, the institution does not have any discretion to depart from the default rule of three arbitrators. A hybrid arbitration agreement providing for administration by these institutions but under other rules, could be interpreted as an agreement on a sole arbitrator as provided by default in such other rules.

## 2. Appointment upon agreed or unopposed party nomination

Differences among institutional powers under different rules are remarkable when parties agree on all of the arbitrators and their appointment.

In such case, the institution's involvement is not strictly necessary. In ad hoc arbitration, each party's nomination of a co-arbitrator, their joint nomination of a sole arbitrator or chairperson or the co-arbitrators' joint

---

543  ICC Rules, art. 12 (2) (2012; 2017); SIAC Rules, art. 6 (1) (2013) = art. 9 (1) (2016); LCIA Rules, art. 5 (8) (2014); AAA-ICDR Rules, art. 11 (2014).
544  CIETAC Rules, art. 23 (2) (2012) = art. 25 (2) (2015); DIS Rules, art. 3 (1998).
545  Swiss Rules, art. 6 (1) (2012).
546  Ibid., art. 6 (2).
547  ICC Rules, art. 12 (2) (2012; 2017); SIAC Rules, art. 6 (1) (2013) = art. 9 (1) (2016); AAA-ICDR Rules, art. 11 (2014); LCIA Rules, art. 5 (8) (2014); Swiss Rules, art. 6 (1)–(2) (2012).

nomination of a chairperson would at the same time be the appointment, without any involvement of a court or other appointing authority.[548]

A few institutions[549] maintain this concept of agreed or unopposed *nomination equalling appointment* also in the institutional situation. In the interest of party autonomy, they refrain from any institutional decision on the constitution of the arbitral tribunal. However, of the arbitration rules here analysed in detail, this concept only applies without restriction under the AAA/ICDR Rules. Under article 12 (1) and (2) of these rules, the parties are completely free to agree on the procedure to constitute the arbitral tribunal and may »*designate*« arbitrators completely »*without the assistance of the administrator*«, who would only »*communicate*« the appointment made by the parties to the arbitrator. CIETAC Rules appear to restrict direct party appointments through nomination to arbitrators listed on the CIETAC panel.[550]

In contrast, all of the other rules discussed require an institutional decision called »*confirmation*« or »*appointment*« even for party-agreed arbitrators.[551] However, such decision is usually a mere formality, which is why some rules leave it, if positive, to the »*Secretary General*«[552] of the institution's secretariat instead of the actor or body competent for the more problematic unilateral nominations.[553] Without party objection, an institutional refusal of confirmation is unlikely.[554] However, an institution might at times

---

548 *Cf.* UNCITRAL Model Law 2006 art. 11 (3) (a) (b); *see also* UNCITRAL Rules, art. 8 (1), 9 (1) (2010).

549 *See* Born, *International Commercial Arbitration (2014)*, 1681, n. 263 (for examples).

550 *See* CIETAC Rules, art. 25 (1), (2), 26, 28 (2012) = art. 27 (1), (2), 28, 30 (2015) (with confusing use of the words »*nominate*« and »*appoint*«); clearer: CIETAC Rules, art. 24 (2) (2012) = 26 (2) (2015) (only arbitrators not on CIETAC's panel require »*confirmation*« to be appointed).

551 ICC Rules, art. 12 (3)–(4), 13 (2012; 2017); SIAC Rules, art. 6 (3)–(4) (2013) = art. 9 (3)–(4) (2016); LCIA Rules, art. 5 (7) (2014); DIS Rules, art. 17 (1998); Swiss Rules, art. 5 (1) (2012); *see* CIETAC Rules, art. 24 (2) (2012) = 26 (2) (2015) (for other than panel listed arbitrators).

552 ICC Rules, art. 13 (2) (2012; 2017); DIS Rules, art. 17 (1) (1998).

553 *But see* SIAC Rules, art. 6 (3) (2013) = art. 9 (3) (2016) (»*President of the Court*« responsible for the appointment in all cases); LCIA Rules, art. 5 (8) (2014) (appointment by the »*LCIA Court*« in all cases); similar: Swiss Rules, art. 5 (1) (2012).

554 *Cf.* ICC, »*2012 Statistical Report*«, 5, 11 (96 % confirmation rate - not distinguishing cases with and without party objection).

refuse to confirm an arbitrator, even if jointly nominated, if that prospective arbitrator's independence is subject to serious and justified doubts. Impartiality and independence of arbitrators being considered aspects of due process in most jurisdictions,[555] institutions do not accept a waiver of these requirements.[556]

Other suitability concerns - like knowledge of applicable law and language - would only in very extraordinary cases cause an institution to refuse confirmation *ex officio*.[557] This might be different under CIETAC Rules, if an arbitrator from outside the CIETAC panel is nominated, which is allowed since the 2005 revision.[558] CIETAC Rules expressly make such nomination »*subject to the confirmation of the Chairman of CIETAC*.«[559] Some commentators still find this provision to pose higher hurdles to the confirmation of unlisted and foreign party-nominated arbitrators than the confirmation provisions in other institutional rules.[560] However, a Chinese scholar remarks such confirmation to be »*more of a formality*« that »*should not allow the CIETAC to refuse the appointment of a foreign arbitrator without good reason*.«[561]

Main reason for CIETAC's still notable but slowly fading prejudice towards complete party autonomy in selecting arbitrators is a stipulation in Chinese arbitration law:

> »Arbitration commissions shall draw up lists of arbitrators according to different professions.«[562]

As it is unclear whether this means that arbitrators have to be selected from such lists, confirmation of arbitrators from outside the panel may already be considered brave and revolutionary from a Chinese point of view.[563]

---

555 *But cf.* Born, *International Commercial Arbitration (2014)*, 1797 et seq., 1815 (§12.05 [B][1] and [C][2]; on reduced requirements for party-nominated co-arbitrators in the Anglo-American tradition and the possibility to agree on »*non-neutral*« co-arbitrators).

556 *See* ibid., 1681 (§ 12.03 [A][1]).

557 *See* ibid., 1663–64, 1682 (§§ 1201 [D] and 12.03 [A][1]).

558 *Cf.* CIETAC Rules, art. 21 (2) (2005).

559 CIETAC Rules, art. 24 (2) (2012) = 26 (2) (2015).

560 *E.g.* Born, *International Commercial Arbitration (2014)*, 1664 (§ 1201 [D]).

561 Tao, *Arbitration Law and Practice in China*, 131 (Chapter V - Arbitration Procedure).

562 Arbitration Law art. 13 (3) (P.R.C.).

563 Lu, »The New CIETAC Arbitration Rules of 2012«, 306 (»*ahead of the judicial practice*«).

In case of hybrid arbitration agreements, problems can arise from these differences if an institution refuses to confirm an agreed arbitrator. In contrast, an institutional confirmation declared but not required under the applicable rules is only superfluous but inoffensive.

3. Confirmation of a co-arbitrator nominated by one party alone

Accordingly, most institutional rules here discussed, except for AAA-ICDR Rules and CIETAC Rules for nominations from the panel, provide for an arbitrator *confirmation* procedure. This becomes most relevant, if a party objects to the nominee of the other party for a three-member tribunal. Then, the confirmation procedure serves the purpose of identifying issues with the prospective arbitrator's independence and impartiality prior to the appointment, giving each party a chance to comment and object. Without requirement of institutional confirmation, every objection has to take the form of a challenge, which then also affects the position of the already appointed arbitrator.[564]

To inform the parties about possible issues and thus to enable them to make an informed decision on whether to object - or challenge - an arbitrator, »*virtually all*« institutions require (prospective) arbitrators to disclose factors relating to the arbitrator's independence and impartiality prior to or when accepting a mandate and as soon as new circumstances arise. This concerns prior or ongoing connections of the arbitrator to any of the parties or to the dispute.[565] Some institutions also require a positive confirmation of independence and impartiality in a written acceptance and independence

---

564 *See* Born, *International Commercial Arbitration (2014)*, 1681 (§ 12.03 [A][1]). On challenge decisions, *see infra* at pp 378-381.

565 Ibid., 1903 (§12.05 [L][2]); *see* ICC Rules, art. 11 (2) (2012; 2017) (subjective standard: requiring disclosure of any circumstances that »*might be of such a nature*« to call independence into question »*in the eyes of the parties*«); more objective: SIAC Rules, art. 10 (4) (2013) = art. 13 (4) (2016) (»*any circumstance that may give rise to justifiable doubts*«); similar: CIETAC Rules, art. 29 (2012) = 31 (2015); AAA-ICDR Rules, art. 13 (2) (2014); DIS Rules, art. 16 (1) (1998); Swiss Rules, art. 9 (2) (2012); combining objective and subjective criteria: LCIA Rules, art. 5 (5) (2014) (*likely to give rise in the mind of any party to any justifiable doubts*«).

statement.[566] If the institution's staff is aware of further circumstances that should have been disclosed, it will usually inform the parties thereof on its own account.[567] The purpose of institutional oversight of disclosure obligations is to minimise miscommunication between the arbitrators and the parties and thereby reduce the risk of later challenges to arbitrators and/or the award on ground of lacking impartiality and independence.

Different from the confirmation of unopposed arbitrators as discussed above, the confirmation in case of objection is not a mere formality. Therefore, the decision on the suitability, independence and impartiality of the prospective co-arbitrator despite an objection is usually made by a higher or multi-person body - a »*Court*« or »*Committee*« - within the institution.[568]

In case of hybrid arbitration agreements, the question arises whether such confirmation decision should be made by the body of the administering institution ordinarily competent for this kind of decision or rather by a body whose composition is comparable to that of the body contemplated by the applied rules.[569]

## 4. Institutional selection of a co-arbitrator for a defaulting party

The institution's role is essential if a party fails to participate in the arbitrator nomination process. In such case, it is the institution's task not only to confirm but to select an arbitrator on behalf of the defaulting party. If a party fails to nominate a co-arbitrator in ad hoc arbitration within a reasonable or agreed time, the other party would have to apply to a court to make an

---

566 *See e.g.* ICC Rules, art. 11 (2) (2012; 2017) (statement of acceptance, availability, impartiality and independence); *see generally* Born, *International Commercial Arbitration (2014)*, 1904 (»*focus on independence*«; doubts to be resolved in favour of disclosure).

567 At least, the author knowns of such practice at the ICC Court and SIAC.

568 *See* ICC Rules, art. 13 (2), (3) (2012; 2017); *see also* DIS Rules, art. 17 (2), (3) (1998) (negative or problematic confirmation decisions up to the »*Appointing Committee*«); LCIA Rules, art. 5 (8) (2014) (»*LCIA Court*« appoints in all cases); Swiss Rules, art. 5 (1) (2012) (»*Swiss Court*« appoints in all cases); *cf.* SIAC Practice Note, para. 6 (2014); Brick Court Chambers, *SIAC Rules*, para. 6.3 (President of the Court to consult with two Court members); *but see* SIAC Rules, art. 6 (3) (2013) = art. 9 (3) (2016) (officially, »*President*« alone responsible).

569 *See infra* at p. 388.

appointment.[570] In institutional arbitration, the institution would select and appoint an arbitrator. All of the here discussed rules provide for this option.[571] However, DIS Rules only contemplate the more common situation of default of the respondent party, requiring the claimant to make its own nomination already with the statement of claim, failing which it will not be notified.[572]

The method of institutional selection of a co-arbitrator varies among institutions. CIETAC maintains a fixed arbitrator panel from which the Chairman would choose the arbitrator.[573] The CIETAC panel is often found to lack international diversity.[574] SIAC also maintains a - much more diverse - panel of arbitrators but the rules do not restrict the President's choice to it.[575] Similarly, the ICDR-AAA maintains a non-mandatory, publicly available list to which the institution would commonly resort although AAA-ICDR Rules do not expressly mention it.[576]

The DIS, SCCAM, LCIA, and ICC Court do not maintain official lists but rely on the experience of its staff, the competent body and an internal database.[577] The DIS has a specific body, the DIS Appointing Committee,[578]

---

570 *Cf.* UNCITRAL Model Law 2006 art. 11 (4) (solution adopted in most legal orders); *but see* Arbitration Act 1996 § 17 (EW) (non-defaulting party may elect to treat its nominee as sole arbitrator); Born, *International Commercial Arbitration (2014)*, 1692 (§12.03 [B][2]) (on due process and enforcement concerns raised by the English solution).

571 ICC Rules, art. 12 (4) (2012; 2017); SIAC Rules, art. 8 (2) (2013) = art. 11 (2) (2016); LCIA Rules, art. 7 (2) (2014); AAA-ICDR Rules, art. 12 (6) (2014); CIETAC Rules, art. 25 (1) (2012) = art. 27 (1) (2015); Swiss Rules, art. 8 (2) (2012); DIS Rules, art. 12 (1) (1998).

572 *See supra* at p. 359 (I); *see* Theune, »DIS Rules«, para. 94.

573 CIETAC Rules, art. 24 (2) (2012) = 26 (2) (2015).

574 China International Economic and Trade Administration Commission, »Panel of Arbitrators (Effective as from 1 May 2011)« (not even one third from outside China, Hong Kong, Taiwan and Macau); *see* Stricker-Kellerer and Moser, »Schiedsordnung der CIETAC« (reporting to have experienced frequent selection of Chinese arbitrators); *see also* Cohen, »Time to Fix China's Arbitration«, 32 (reproaching a practice to appoint even CIETAC's own staff as arbitrators).

575 *See* SIAC Rules, art. 10 (2013) = art. 13 (2016); SIAC, »SIAC Panel«.

576 *See* Gusy, Hosking, and Schwarz, *A Guide to the ICDR Rules*, para. 6.30.

577 Critical: Brower and Rosenberg, »The Death of the Two-Headed Nightingale«, 22, n. 104 (on the factual requirement of good connections to institutions).

578 *See infra* at pp. 395-397 (§14C.II.3).

only competent for appointments. The most elaborate and complicated procedure is followed by the ICC Court. First, the Court renders a formal decision on which National Committee[579] to invite for a proposal. Then the National Committee invited proposes one or more suitable candidates followed by the actual appointment of the Court of one of these candidates.[580] In some circumstances, the Court can make a direct appointment without relying on a proposal of a National Committee.[581]

It seems that in case of a hybrid arbitration clause, the selection process under the applicable rules would have to be followed, not the process the institution would usually follow. Otherwise, the constitution of the arbitral tribunal would not be in accordance with the parties' agreement, in particular since a defaulting party cannot be deemed to have accepted the method applied by the institution. However, to follow another institution's arbitrator selection process will usually be difficult. For example, ICC National Committees are unlikely to make a proposal to another institution than the ICC Court and other institutions do not have anything like National Committees.[582] Accordingly, a different administering institution might only resort to a »*direct*« appointment under ICC Rules, as if a suitable National Committee did not exist.[583] For institutions maintaining arbitrator lists, it is further unclear whether such lists are an element of the *institution* or of the *rules*. In the first case, arbitrators could be selected from the list although another institution's rules are applicable, in the latter case, the agreement on a hybrid arbitration clause would have to be understood also as derogation from the lists. Due to all of these uncertainties, it is justifiable to consider a hybrid arbitration agreement inoperable to the extent an institution has to *select*- not only *confirm* - an arbitrator on behalf of a party in default. Arguably, however, such inoperability might be overcome by court support.[584]

---

579  *See infra* at pp. 395-397 (§14C.II.3).

580  ICC Rules, art. 13 (3) (2012; 2017).

581  Ibid., sent. 2 and art. 13 (4).

582  *See infra* at pp. 395-397 (§14C.II.3); *cf.* Severin, »Considerations«, 15, para. 7.

583  *Cf.* ICC Rules, art. 13 (4) (2012; 2017).

584  *See infra* at pp. 422 et seq. (§16A.II.1.d).

5. Default rules for the designation of the chairperson

The presiding arbitrator is often »*the main figure in every arbitration*« regarding procedural directions and if co-arbitrators disagree.[585] The method of selecting this chairperson of a three-member tribunal is therefore of utmost importance. If the parties do not agree on a chairperson, some arbitration rules directly empower the institution to make a designation, other rules require selection by the co-arbitrators.

This specific difference between ICC Rules and the previous version SIAC Rules then in force[586] requires particular attention when evaluating SIAC's administration of the *Alstom–Insigma* arbitration. Under ICC Rules, the chairperson (called »*president*«) is generally chosen and appointed by the ICC Court based on a proposal made by an invited National Committee.[587] In contrast, SIAC Rules (1997) stipulated that the two co-arbitrators once appointed »*shall choose the third arbitrator who will act as the presiding arbitrator of the Tribunal.*«[588] A lack of attention of SIAC's secretariat to this difference may have been fatal to Alstom's later efforts to obtain an enforcement judgment in China.[589] After appointing the co-arbitrators, the SIAC Secretariat had invited the co-arbitrators to choose the presiding arbitrator pursuant to article 8 of the SIAC Rules (1997), instead of proceeding with an institutional nomination and appointment under article 8 (4) of the ICC Rules (1998).[590] However, it has to be stressed that the procedures for nominating the chairperson under both sets of rules are *default* provisions and that there is some evidence of an individual agreement of Alstom and Insigma on the chairperson or rather its nomination by the co-arbitrators.[591] Since then, SIAC changed its rules, the current rules no

---

585  Cohen, »Time to Fix China's Arbitration«, 33.
586  SIAC Rules (1997).
587  ICC  Rules,  art. 12 (5), 13 (3) (2012; 2017);  *cf.  also*  ICC  Rules, art. 8 (4), 9 (3) (1998).
588  SIAC Rules, art. 8 (1) (1997).
589  *Alstom v. Insigma (Hz. IPC), see infra* at Chapter 5, pp. 480 et seq. (§17C) for a detailed discussion.
590  *See Insigma v. Alstom*, [2009] SGCA 24 [14].
591  In fact, already when before the ICC Court, Insigma agreed to such nomination procedure - an agreement it later half-heartedly tried to withdraw (*see* ibid., para. 14–15).

longer providing for nomination of the chairperson by the co-arbitrators but by SIAC's »*President of the Court*«, thus for institutional nomination.[592]

Generally, the *default principle* of *institutional* nomination of the chairperson is also followed by AAA-ICDR Rules,[593] LCIA Rules[594] and CIETAC Rules.[595] CIETAC and AAA-ICDR Rules thereby primarily provide for a list procedure, similar to that contemplated by the UNCITRAL Rules,[596] to prepare the selection in cooperation with the parties, only in the last resort providing for direct institutional selection.[597]

In contrast, DIS Rules and Swiss Rules follow a *default principle* of *co-arbitrator* nomination of the chairperson,[598] similar to SIAC Rules (1997) as mentioned.

Given that the rules on the nomination of the chairperson of the arbitral tribunal are default rules under all of the institutional rules here discussed, the existing differences should usually not be relevant for the issue of substituting institutional functions when administering hybrid arbitrations. A problem would arise, however, in the following - cumulative - circumstances:

- An individual agreement of the parties on the applied method for nominating the chairperson does not verifiably exist.[599]

---

592 SIAC Rules, art. 8 (3) (2013) = art. 11 (3) (2016); *cf. already* SIAC Rules, art. 8 (3) (2010); SIAC Rules, art. 7 (3) (2007).

593 AAA-ICDR Rules, art. 12 (6) (2009) (»*if necessary* [...] *in consultation with the tribunal*«, which would mean co-arbitrators as a »*tribunal*« is not yet constituted without president).

594 *Cf.* LCIA Rules, art. 5 (8)–(9), 7 (2014).

595 CIETAC Rules, art. 25 (4) (2012) = art. 27 (4) (2015).

596 UNCITRAL Rules, art. 8 (2010); for CIETAC this method alleviates criticism of the earlier practice to frequently select Chinese nationals as presiding arbitrators (*see* Cohen, »Time to Fix China's Arbitration«, 33; *cf. also* Yuen, »Arbitration Clauses in a Chinese Context«, advising parties to explicitly agree on the condition that the presiding arbitrator shall be from a neutral jurisdiction).

597 CIETAC Rules, art. 25 (2), (4) (2012) = art. 27 (2), (4) (2015); AAA-ICDR Rules, art. 12 (6) (2014).

598 DIS Rules, art. 12 (2) (1998) (DIS Appointing Committee only asked if co-arbitrators do not agree); Swiss Rules, art. 8 (2) sent. 2 (2012) (Court designation only if co-arbitrators do not agree).

599 Which was the critical issue in the proceedings before the Hangzhou court on the enforcement of the *Alstom-Insigma* award (*see infra* at pp. 480 et seq, §17C).

- The administering institution follows another default method than contemplated by the applicable rules.

Then, the constitution of the arbitral tribunal would not be in accordance with the parties' agreement. However, this problem does not apply to hybrid arbitration agreements in general but only in case the administering institution fails to apply or incorrectly applies the other institution's rules.[600]

## 6. Institutional selection of a sole arbitrator or chairperson

In principle, the methods to select arbitrators referred to above also apply when an institution is required to select a sole arbitrator or chairperson under its rules. The main difference to the institutional selection of co-arbitrators are possibly elevated requirements that influence the way the institution would proceed with the selection.

For example, ICC Rules require the sole arbitrator or chairperson to be from a nationality other than all parties.[601] For this reason, the ICC Court would always ask a National Committee from a neutral state to make the required proposal. Subject to an agreement of the parties to the contrary, LCIA Rules and AAA-ICDR Rules also stipulate requirements of neutral nationality.[602]

In contrast, SIAC, Swiss, DIS and CIETAC Rules do not contain express nationality requirements although most would nevertheless avoid any violation of »*the basic principle of international neutrality.*«[603] However, some foreign users of CIETAC have made the experience to have been faced with a tribunal consisting of two Chinese and only one foreign arbitrator because of a - very common - selection of a Chinese national by the CIETAC Chairman.[604]

---

600 Possibly engaging institutional liability, discussed *infra* at pp. 447-457 (§16B.II).

601 ICC Rules, art. 13 (5) (2012; 2017).

602 LCIA Rules, art. 6 (1) (1998); AAA-ICDR Rules, art. 6 (4) (2009) (granting discretion to the Administrator).

603 Born, *International Commercial Arbitration (2014)*, 1738 (§12.04 [A][1]).

604 Stricker-Kellerer and Moser, »Schiedsordnung der CIETAC«, art. 19–24, para. 6.

Regarding qualification, only DIS Rules contain the express requirement of him or her being a lawyer.[605]

Generally, it seems that nationality or qualification requirements under institutional rules are not an obstacle to the operability of hybrid arbitration agreements as long as the administering institution duly respects them. However, the above-mentioned obstacles to substituting institutional actors when selecting arbitrators apply to the selection of sole arbitrators and chairpersons as well.[606]


IV. Challenge and replacement of arbitrators

Generally, institutional arbitration also has the advantage of providing relatively fast and efficient relief if a party is dissatisfied with an already appointed arbitrator, because a challenge can be addressed to the administering institution that has experience in dealing with such complaints.[607]

Almost all of the rules here discussed provide in a very similar way that a party can challenge an arbitrator by way of a reasoned written submission within a restricted time limit and that the party or the challenged arbitrator may accept the challenge, failing which the institution renders a decision on the challenge after inviting comments from the other party, the challenged arbitrator and, if applicable, the co-arbitrators.[608] Acceptable grounds for challenge are reasonable doubts as to the arbitrator's independence or impartiality, but other grounds related to qualification or effectiveness may suffice under some rules.[609] Challenge decisions are commonly taken by the actor competent for appointment and confirmation decisions.[610] While most

---

605  DIS Rules, art. 2 (2) (1998); *cf.* Theune, »DIS Rules«, para. 20 (legal education in any jurisdiction sufficient).

606  *See supra* at p. 374.

607  Born, *International Commercial Arbitration (2014)*, 1913 (§ 12.06 [A]).

608  ICC Rules, art. 14 (2012; 2017); SIAC Rules, art. 11–13 (2013) = art. 14–16 (2016); CIETAC Rules, art. 30 (2012) = art. 32 (2015); LCIA Rules, art. 10 (2014); AAA-ICDR Rules, art. 14 (2014); Swiss Rules, art. 10, 11 (2012).

609  *See e.g.* ICC Rules, art. 11 (1) (2012; 2017) (»*or otherwise*«); SIAC Rules, art. 11 (1) (2013) = art. 14 (1) (2016) (»*or if the arbitrator does not possess any requisite qualification*«); *see generally* Born, *International Commercial Arbitration (2014)*, 1916.

610  *But compare* SIAC Rules, art. 13 (1) (2013) = art. 16 (1) (2016) (challenge decided by the SIAC Court) *with* SIAC Rules, art. 6 (3) =

rules proclaim for such decision to be »*final and binding*«, the question of reviewability effectively depends on the applicable arbitration law.[611]

The only plain exception is article 18 DIS Rules.[612] Thereunder, it is not for the institution but the arbitral tribunal including the challenged arbitrator to decide on an unaccepted challenge.[613] Despite the principle that no one should be judge in his or her own cause (»*nemo debet essere judex in causa propria*«), this solution is found acceptable by German doctrine because of the mandatory court review of challenge decisions under section 1037 (3) ZPO (GER).[614] However, this provision only allows recourse to German courts if the place of arbitration is in Germany. While this will be true for a vast majority of DIS cases, it is not a necessity. The absence of an institutional challenge mechanism is thus detrimental to the acceptance of DIS Rules on an international level. Article 18 DIS Rules is particularly unsatisfactory when a sole arbitrator or the whole tribunal is challenged. In that case, a party will first have to submit its challenge to the DIS Secretariat only to find in the end that it has to apply to a state court anyway.[615]

If a challenge is accepted by the arbitrator, the other party or through decision, it becomes necessary to replace such arbitrator. Most rules provide for such replacement to follow the same procedure as the original appointment.[616] However, ICC and LCIA Rules give the respective Court discretion to appoint a substitute arbitrator directly in order to avoid further delays.[617]

---

art. 9 (3) (2016) (appointment made by the »*President*« of the SIAC Court).

611 *See infra* at pp. 435-438 (§16A.II.3.a); *see e.g.* ICC Rules, art. 11 (4) (2012; 2017); LCIA Rules, art. 29 (1) (2014); Swiss Rules, art. 11 (3) (2012); CIETAC Rules, art. 30 (6) (2012) = art. 32 (6) (2015).

612 Bredow and Mulder, »DIS Rules, § 18«, para. 18 (»*unique*«).

613 DIS Rules, art. 18 (2) sent. 3 (1998); *but see* Bredow and Mulder, »DIS Rules, § 18«, para. 12 (commenting that challenged arbitrators often abstain from participating in the decision in practice).

614 Theune, »DIS Rules«, para. 157.

615 *See* Bredow and Mulder, »DIS Rules, § 18«, para. 13.

616 Born, *International Commercial Arbitration (2014)*, 1921, 1922 (§12.06[A][6]); *see in particular* SIAC Rules, art. 13 (2) (2013) = art. 16 (2) (2016) (»*even if during the process of appointing the challenged arbitrator, a party had failed to exercise his right to nominate*«).

617 ICC Rules, art. 15 (4) (2012; 2017); LCIA Rules, art. 11 (1) (2014); *cf. also* Swiss Rules, art. 13 (2) (2012) (»*in exceptional circumstances*«).

Most of the rules here discussed also grant the institution a specific power to replace an arbitrator *ex officio* - without any challenge or party application - in exceptional circumstances if such arbitrator fulfils its function unsatisfyingly.[618] Before such replacement, the institutions would always consult with the parties and the other arbitrators. Nevertheless, this power to make an ex officio replacement is a very sharp sword interfering with the position of the parties and the replaced arbitrator. The only justification is the incorporation of the institutional rules into all three governing contracts: the arbitration agreement, the Administration Contract and the arbitrator's contract. In contrast, AAA-ICDR Rules and DIS Rules do not provide for such far-reaching supervisory power of the institution.

Generally, if an institution administers an arbitration under another institution's rules based on a hybrid arbitration agreement, it is well advised to refrain from exercising any unusual discretion regarding the replacement of arbitrators granted by such rules, in particular, from *ex officio* and direct replacements. Instead, it should replace arbitrators only upon justified challenge on grounds of independence and impartiality and follow the original appointment process for the replacement.

If the parties agree on arbitration under DIS Rules to be administered by another institution, in particular, this has to be understood as excluding any rights of the administering institution to decide on challenges and replacements as such rights are not foreseen by DIS Rules. The institution would have to forward any challenge to the arbitral tribunal under article 18 DIS Rules.

In return, a hybrid arbitration agreement providing for DIS administered arbitration under another institution's rules would cause serious problems at the latest when a party submits a challenge since a body ordinarily responsible to decide such challenges does not exist at the DIS. While the DIS Appointing Committee has experience to select arbitrators, it does not have any experience in evaluating independence and impartiality of already appointed arbitrators.

---

618 ICC Rules, art. 15 (2) (2012; 2017); SIAC Rules, art. 14 (3) (2013) = art. 17 (3) (2016); CIETAC Rules, art. 31 (2012) = art. 33 (2015); LCIA Rules, art. 10 (1) (2014); Swiss Rules, art. 12 (2012).

## V. Institutional control of the proceedings after the tribunal is constituted

As summarised, the role of arbitral institutions is most important until the constitution of the arbitral tribunal, who then takes over the file. However, to reuse the image introduced in Chapter 2,[619] some institutions do not only »*put the train on the rails*«, but also assume much of the »*steering.*« These institutions do not only control the arbitrator's work through *repressive* measures like replacement, they also employ *preventive* means to ensure a fair and efficient arbitration.

In ICC arbitration, as a more controlling system,[620] these include in particular:

- supervision of the draft of Terms of Reference and a procedural timetable
- shortening and extension of time limits for the rendering of an award.

Under article 23 (1) of the ICC Rules, the arbitral tribunal is required to draw up a document, the »*Terms of Reference*«, which shall contain the parties and arbitrators' names and addresses, a summary of claims and relief sought and defences including their estimate value, a list of issues to be determined, the place of arbitration and particulars of any additional or specifically agreed procedural rules. As mentioned, this requirement is deemed essential by the ICC Court and derogation is likely to result in a refusal of administration.[621] If all parties agree to the Terms of Reference, these are signed by them and the arbitral tribunal and submitted to the Court within two months from the transmission of the file. In such case, the institution officially only files the Terms of Reference but does not render any decision thereon or takes any influence on the content of the Terms of Reference.[622] In practice, however, the competent secretariat team would ask arbitrators to submit a draft of the Terms of Reference to it for comments prior to the signing by the parties and arbitral tribunal.[623] The ICC Secretariat maintains

---

619  *See supra* at p. 135.
620  *See* Schütze, *Institutional Arbitration*, para. 9–10 (Introduction); *cf. also* Schlaepfer and Petti, »Institutional versus Ad Hoc Arbitration«, 22 (describing administration under Swiss Rules as »*lighter*«).
621  *See supra* at pp. 219-220 (§10B.I).
622  ICC Rules, art. 23 (2) (2012; 2017).
623  *See also* Grierson and van Hooft, *Arbitrating under the 2012 ICC Rules*, 151.

a checklist on items that should and should not be contained in the Terms of Reference.

The Court only decides on Terms of Reference in case of default of a party to sign.[624] If this is required, the Court, based on a proposal prepared by the secretariat, has to verify that the Terms of Reference do not contain any procedural stipulation to which the defaulting party has not clearly agreed. The Court cannot replace a party's consent to a particular procedural issue by decision and would therefore refuse to approve Terms of Reference containing »*unresolved procedural questions*« that would be up to the tribunal to decide by procedural order.[625] The Terms of Reference checklist draws the secretariat's and Court's attention to possibly problematic procedural issues.

The purpose of the Terms of Reference procedure and its oversight by the ICC Court is procedural efficiency.[626] Its supervision, including the control of the two-month time limit, puts some pressure on the arbitral tribunal to deal with the case in a structured and speedy manner. The same applies to the requirement to submit a procedural timetable to the parties and the Court under article 24 (2) of the ICC Rules. Although the Terms of Reference procedure is not intended to hinder the parties from changing their arguments or withdrawing their claims at a later stage, modification of claims and submission of new claims will require the agreement of the parties or the approval of the arbitral tribunal after the signing or approval of the Terms of Reference.[627] Therefore, the Terms of Reference also have an effect of preclusion.

The other rules here considered do not contain any comparable provisions, leaving the conduct of the proceedings largely to the arbitral tribunal.[628] Only SIAC Rules (2007) introduced a feature comparable to the ICC Terms of Reference, the so-called Memorandum of Issues. This Memorandum of Issues had to be drafted by the arbitral tribunal after the written submissions of the parties and was supposed to be signed by both parties or approved by the Registrar.[629] The purpose was to help the arbitral tribunal

---

624 ICC Rules, art. 23 (3) (2012; 2017).

625 Reiner and Aschauer, »ICC Rules«, para. 497.

626 Ibid., para. 473.

627 ICC Rules, art. 23 (4) (2012; 2017); *see* Reiner and Aschauer, »ICC Rules«, para. 480–81, 498–504.

628 *See* Born, *International Commercial Arbitration (2014)*, 175 (»*a unique procedure under the ICC Rules*«).

629 SIAC Rules, art. 17 (2007).

to prepare the hearing or the award efficiently. However, this element was not well received and deleted with the next edition of the rules. At this stage of the proceedings, later than the ICC Terms of Reference phase, drafting and agreeing on such document might cause delay rather than improve efficiency.

If another institution administered an arbitration under ICC Rules, it seems little problematic if such institution's secretariat supported the tribunal and the parties to draft *agreed* Terms of Reference. If, however, one party refuses to sign the document, it is questionable which actor at such other institution could *approve* such terms given the lack of experience. In any case, such approval should not have any determinative effect on a procedural question; even more than the ICC Court itself, another institution should avoid any appearance of interfering with procedural party autonomy or arbitrator discretion at this stage.

A number of rules, but not all,[630] allow an institution to control the important time limit for the arbitral tribunal to render an award,[631] which is usually understood as limiting the tribunal's mandate with the consequence that an award rendered after expiry of such limit would be made by a then incompetent tribunal.[632]

Where such time limit follows from the arbitration rules or is set by the institution in the first place, it is logical that the institution may extend it. More problematic appears to be a power to override any time limit individually agreed by the parties, as article 38 (2) of the ICC Rules attempts to grant the ICC Court. It is then a matter of interpretation whether the individual agreement by the parties was meant to exclude such power, which argues in favour of obliging the institution to hear parties' positions prior to

---

630 *See* LCIA Rules, art. 22 (1)(ii) (2014) (only allowing the tribunal to extend any time limits); DIS Rules, art. 33 (1) (1998) (only providing for an award to be rendered within »*reasonable time*« without contemplating the situation that parties agreed on a time limit that could expire).

631 *See e.g.* ICC Rules, art. 30 (2) (2012; 2017); AAA-ICDR Rules, art. 30 (1) sent. 2 (2014) (determination of this limit arguably includes any shortining or extension); CIETAC Rules, art. 46 (2) (2012) = 48 (2) (2015); *see also* Swiss Rules, art. 2 (3) (2012); SIAC Rules, art. 2 (5) (2013, 2016) (generally on all kinds of time limits).

632 For example, a disagreement by parties on if and how to prolong a party-agreed time limit for the award proved fatal to the ad hoc procedure subsequent to the parties' withdrawal of ICC case no. 2878 (as mentioned *supra*, at p. 156, n. 154, there discussed under the heading of »*Switching*« from institutional to ad hoc arbitration).

exercising a perceived power to modify such limit. This should also be the route to take if a power to modify a time limit is unclear in light of an agreement on other than the administering institution's rules.

When institutional influence on the conduct of the proceedings is discussed, it is sometimes not sufficient to refer to what the wording of the rules provides. Instead, institutional practice may go beyond. In particular, those familiar with CIETAC's case management approach report that CIETAC's secretariat staff often supports arbitrators with tasks that would otherwise be performed by administrative secretaries: they arrange hearings, take notes of hearings, provide translations.[633] In addition, these services may even include tasks that should only be exercised by arbitrators such as site inspections, evidence collection or –occasionally - even the drafting of awards.[634] Should these reports (still) be true, such »*heavy administration*«[635] by CIETAC would be critical for its intransparency. When agreeing on arbitration, parties generally want the arbitrators to perform tasks that may influence the resulting award, any delegation to third parties, including staff of the administering institution, has to be specifically agreed on. In particular if administering arbitrations under other than its own rules, an institution should be very careful not to assume more competences than the parties have actually delegated to it with their agreement.

## VI. Institutional influence on the award

Some rules require that an arbitral tribunal submits a draft of any award it intends to issue to the institution for review (referred to as »*scrutiny*«). The purpose of such provisions is to aid enforceability and to control the quality of awards rendered under the auspices of the institution. Scrutiny also provides some assurance to arbitrators. Such scrutiny is often restricted to issues of form - although form and substance cannot always be clearly distinguished, e.g. when there is a question about the correct identification of the parties - but more often than not, rules also allow and require an institution to draw the tribunal's attention to possible material problems. Of the rules

---

633  Fan, *Arbitration in China*, 128.
634  Ibid., 128–29; Cohen, »Time to Fix China's Arbitration«, 36.
635  Fan, *Arbitration in China*, 128 (qualifying CIETAC's administration as heavier than that of the ICC Court).

here regarded, ICC, CIETAC and SIAC Rules expressly provide for such scrutiny.[636]

At the ICC, scrutiny of awards requires a decision by the Court, who is advised by a memorandum of the competent secretariat team. The possible results are either not to confirm the draft award and send it back to the tribunal, to confirm it subject to smaller modifications that are expected to be undertaken by the tribunal or to confirm the draft award as it is. The size and international composition of the Court may have the effect that critical issues are noticed more easily. In contrast, at SIAC, scrutiny is only provided at the secretariat level, by the Registrar, and accordingly, comments on substance are rare.

At CIETAC, scrutiny of awards is exercised by a team of case managers. The Expert Consultation Committee may be asked about certain legal issues.[637] In practice, the control exercised is reportedly quite extensive and goes beyond correcting formal errors and drawing the tribunal's attention to substantive issues. According to some allegations made by lawyers and CIETAC arbitrators, it is not uncommon that CIETAC would ask a tribunal to alter the outcome of a draft award; some even believe that entire awards are drafted by CIETAC staff to unburden some very busy arbitrators from this duty. However, this could not be verified.[638]

Other institutions also do exercise some but very limited review of the form of draft awards through their secretariat, even though the rules do not state so explicitly. This is for example reported for the AAA-ICDR[639] or the LCIA[640] but it can be assumed that it applies to most arbitral institutions.[641] Despite the lack of transparency resulting from the silence of these institutions' rules on this aspect, such informal review appears little problematic as long as the substance of the award is untouched and changes are not imposed on arbitrators. One may argue that the fact that an award is notified by the institution and bears its name entitles it to exercise such quality control.

On at least two grounds one may argue that in a hybrid arbitration exercising scrutiny of awards by substituting the competent actor of another

---

636 ICC Rules, art. 33 (2012) = art. 34 (2017); CIETAC Rules, art. 49 (2012) = art. 51 (2015); SIAC Rules, art. 28 (2) (2013) = art. 32 (2) (2016).
637 Fan, *Arbitration in China*, 132.
638 Cohen, »Time to Fix China's Arbitration«, 36.
639 *See e.g.* Appel, »International Centre for Dispute Resolution (ICDR)«, 84.
640 *See e.g.* Gerbay, »The LCIA«, para. 4–50, 4–81.
641 Hofbauer et al., »Survey on Scrutiny of Arbitral Institutions«, 7.

institution is a rather critical issue: First, the result of the arbitration is directly influenced by the institution's scrutiny, which makes successful challenges for procedural irregularity likely.[642] Second, the purpose of assuring consistency in rule application is difficult to fulfil by actors of another institution not experienced in applying and controlling these rules. However, the arbitral tribunal remains responsible for the award. If the institution only recommended but did not impose changes to the award, scrutiny would simply be a kind of editorial service, arguably exchangeable.

VII. Financial control

Many institutions also exercise significant powers in relation to costs, meaning the institutional and arbitrators' fees and expenses as opposed to the parties' costs and expenses for legal representation. ICC, LCIA and SIAC Rules and CIETAC's new rules applying from 2015 for example delegate the decision on the amount of fees - not: cost allocation - to the institution.[643] In contrast, Swiss and DIS Rules leave this task to the arbitrators, who, of course, have to comply with the institution's schedule of fees.[644] AAA-ICDR Rules take a middle road and enable the administrator to set the appropriate daily and hourly rate and to decide in case of a »*dispute*« on fees and expenses, but otherwise leave the assessment of the total amount to the tribunal.[645]

ICC, LCIA and SIAC Rules, Appendix B to the Swiss Rules and the AAA-ICDR Rules in their latest version also provide for a fiduciary role of the institution in collecting and forwarding advances on costs, including

---

642 *Cf.* Greenberg, »Arbitral Award Scrutiny Under Scrutiny«, 105. *See infra* at pp. 476-480 (§17B) on the criterion of outcome-relevance of procedural defects.

643 *See e.g.* ICC Rules, art. 37 (2012) = art. 38 (2017); LCIA Rules, art. 28 (1) (2014); SIAC Rules, art. 32 (2013) = art. 36 (2016); *see also* CIETAC Rules, art. 82 (1) sent. 2 (2015) (providing the new »*Arbitration Court*« with such power of determining the arbitrator's »*special remuneration*«); *but see* CIETAC Rules, art. 72 (2012) (not yet expressly providing for such power of the secretariat; although probably assumed in practice).

644 DIS Rules, art. 40 (2) (1998); Swiss Rules, art. 39 (2012).,

645 AAA-ICDR Rules, art. 35 (2014).

arbitrator's fees and expenses.[646] In principle, CIETAC Rules have to be understood in the same sense.[647] In contrast, the DIS does not assume such fiduciary role to the same extent. It only collects the administrative fee and a provisional advance in the amount of the fees for one co-arbitrator from the claimant but further advances are up to the tribunal to collect and keep.[648]

Under a number of rules, the institution also assumes a power to draw severe procedural consequences from a party's failure to make deposits, *e.g.* to treat a claim as withdrawn by the party responsible or to suspend proceedings,[649] other rules only allow the tribunal to draw such consequences.[650]

The purpose of rules on institutional cost control is to provide cost security to parties and arbitrators and to ensure that the arbitrators' adjudicatory function is not negatively influenced by cost considerations and disputes. Given the potential liability risk, it appears highly unlikely that institutions

---

646 ICC Rules, art. 26 (2012; 2017); LCIA Rules, art. 24 (2014); SIAC Rules, art. 30 (2) (2013) = art. 34 (2) (2016); Swiss Rules, Appendix B, para. 4 (2012); AAA-ICDR Rules, art. 36 (2014) (Administrator may demand initial and supplementary deposits); *but see* AAA-ICDR Rules, art. 33 (2009) (only the initial deposit was up to the Administrator to collect).

647 CIETAC Rules, art. 72 (1) (2012); *see also* CIETAC Rules, art. 82 (1) (2015) (with unusual terminology - »*CIETAC may charge the parties for*«; possibly, CIETAC understands arbitrators to be mandated by the institution rather than the parties.

648 DIS Rules, art. 7 (1), appendix to art. 40 (5) para. 17, art. 25 (1998).

649 *See e.g.* ICC Rules, art. 36 (6) (2012) = art. 37 (6) (2017) (after fruitless expiry of a time limit set by the tribunal); similar: SIAC Rules, art. 30 (5) (2013) = art. 34 (5) (2016); only for counterclaims: CIETAC Rules, art. 15 (3) (2012); *cf. also* ibid., art. 72 (2) (nomination of arbitrator treated as invalid in case of failure to deposit costs); to the same effect: CIETAC Rules, art. 82 (2) (2015); *see also* LCIA Rules, art. 24 (4) (1998) (»*may be treated by the LCIA Court and the Arbitral Tribunal as a withdrawal*«); *but see* LCIA Rules, art. 24 (6) (2014) (now only referring to the tribunal's power to treat a claim or crossclaim as withdrawn); unclear: AAA-ICDR Rules, art. 36 (4) (2014) (not indicating if the Administrator or the tribunal would decide that the failure to pay »*shall be deemed a withdrawal*«).

650 *See e.g.* LCIA Rules, art. 24 (6) (2014); DIS Rules, art. 25 (1998); Swiss Rules, art. 41 (4) (2012); *see also* AAA-ICDR Rules, art. 33 (3) (2009); *but see* now: AAA-ICDR Rules, art. 36 (4) (2014).

customarily exercising only very limited tasks in this regard, like the DIS, would be willing to assume more responsibility under another institution's rules providing for extensive fiduciary duties. If a hybrid arbitration agreement was interpreted that way, this aspect of it would probably not be capable of being performed.

## C. General comparison of actors of different arbitral institutions

Although the decisive question raised by hybrid arbitration agreements is one of the substitutability of *actors* rather than acts, the previous considerations have shown that this question can only be answered in consideration of the purpose and function of the institutional rule requiring such actor substitution.[651] The pertinent question is not if an actor like the SIAC's Board of Director at the time of the *Alstom–Insigma* arbitration or even the now established SIAC Court can be deemed equivalent to the ICC Court *in general* but if such actor can equivalently ensure the functions of the *specific* rules to be applied, *e.g.* to review impartiality, independence and qualification of arbitrators when performing appointment or challenge related tasks or to ensure the quality of decision and enforceability when scrutinising awards. Lack of experience with the kind of task is thereby an even greater issue than mere lack of comparability in number and qualification of staff.

However, such lack of organisational comparability of institutional actors may be a first indication of lacking functional equivalence, which is why the actors of different institutions shall in the following be grouped and compared in a general manner.

## I. The secretariats

The majority of work of an arbitral institution is certainly done within the institution's secretariat. Each of the institutions here discussed has a secretariat consistent of several case managers or counsel, i.e. persons with a legal background that are responsible for the correspondence with the

---

651 *See supra* at pp. 352-352 on the functional equivalence test developped (§14A.III.1).

parties and arbitrators including prospective arbitrators, the keeping of the file and required notifications under the rules.[652]

For institutions that have an additional, decision-making actor, like the ICC Court, the LCIA, the SCCAM and SIAC with their respective »*Court*«, the secretariat also serves as connecting link between users, meaning the parties and the arbitrators, with that actor. It further prepares the decisions to be taken through memoranda, which summarise the relevant positions, the legal situation and the issues at stake and which propose a preferred solution.

In terms of staff, institutional secretariats are quite differently equipped, due to the tremendous disparities in caseload among institutions. As one of the largest secretariats, the ICC Secretariat consists of about 40 legal and 40 non-legal employees currently organised in several teams according to jurisdictional or linguistic regions. Each team is headed by a counsel and includes two or three further deputy counsel and several assistants. Most teams are located in Paris, one in Hong Kong and one in New York.[653] In total there are more than twenty nationalities working at the ICC Secretariat and more than twenty languages spoken,[654] while main working languages are English and French. The secretariat is not part of the Court but its extended arm.[655] Once a week, preceding every meeting of the Court or Committee of the Court, the ICC Secretariat holds an internal meeting to discuss the recommendations to be made to the Court. The Hong Kong based and New York based staff usually join the staff meeting per video conference. At most times, there are also several short time interns that support the ICC Secretariat.

The fact that the AAA-ICDR, although a mere division of the AAA, is the second largest international arbitration institution in terms of caseload after the ICC Court,[656] suggests that the number of case managers within the AAA-ICDR secretariat would also be relatively large. However, the public information available in this regard is rather scarce, the webpage only mentions that fourteen languages are fluently spoken within the

---

652 While with the 2015 version of CIETAC's rules all references to the CIETAC secretariat have been replaced by references to an »*Arbitration Court;*« a qualification of this body as an institutional secretariat appears still appropriate despite the new name (*see infra* at p. 394 at II.2).

653 International Chamber of Commerce, »Secretariat of the Court«.

654 *See* Trittmann, »Die wesentlichen Änderungen«, 48.

655 Ibid., 50.

656 Thümmel, »ICDR-IAR«, para. 3.

AAA-ICDR.[657] It is reported that the AAA-ICDR as the »*administrator*«[658] assigns one case manager to each case responsible for the day-to-day work and communication and that the case managers are grouped into regional teams - similar to the ICC Secretariat in this respect - with one supervisor for each team.[659]

Similarly, the LCIA does not publish details on the number of personnel and team organisation within its secretariat located in London.[660] Commentaries to LCIA Rules mention that the LCIA Secretariat only consists of a handful of full time case managers, a Registrar and Deputy Registrar.[661] This »*lean*« organisation is said to reflect the LCIA Court's »*light*« hand in the case administration if compared to the ICC Court.[662]

In contrast to the AAA-ICDR and the LCIA, SIAC lists its entire legal secretariat staff, currently a Registrar and a Deputy Registrar, two managing counsel, two counsel and three associate counsel on its webpage with names, photos, brief biographical notes and direct contact details.[663] This indicates a very personal and transparent case management approach.

At the time of writing, the DIS Secretariat consisted of nine legal and non-legal employees including the Secretary General.[664]

CIETAC's organisation is special since its headquarters in Beijing and the subcommissions in Tianjin, Chongqing, the arbitration centre in Hong Kong and the offices in Shanghai and Shenzhen - the latter newly established after the spin-off of the former Shanghai and Shenzhen

---

657 AAA, »About the American Arbitration Association (AAA) and the International Centre for Dispute Resolution (ICDR)«.

658 *See infra* at pp. 397-399, at IV) on this concept.

659 Gusy, Hosking, and Schwarz, *A Guide to the ICDR Rules*, para. 1.98, 1.99.

660 LCIA, »Organisation«.

661 Gerbay, »The LCIA«, para. 4–7 (now mentioning »*seven legal counsel*«; unclear if this includes or excludes Registrar and Deputy Registrar); *see also* Turner, *A Guide to the LCIA Arbitration Rules*, para. 1.10 (then only counting three case managers, a Director-General, Deputy Director-General and Registrar).

662 Turner, *A Guide to the LCIA Arbitration Rules*, para. 1.10.

663 SIAC, »CEO & Secretariat«.

664 Information taken from the DIS website (DIS, »DIS Secretariat«, last accessed 31.12.2014; unfortunatly this page with information about the secretariat staff is now no longer accessible; the current website only contains general contact information).

subcommissions[665] - each have their own personnel to administer allocated cases very independently.[666] Each secretariat consists of a Secretary General,[667] two Deputy Secretary Generals and a large number of legal and non-legal staff. In total, about 100 staff members, 70 of whom are legally trained case managers, work for CIETAC, all of them bilingual in English and (Mandarin) Chinese.[668]

To this extent somewhat comparable to CIETAC, the Swiss Chambers' Arbitration Institution is also supported by decentralised secretariats at each of the seven participating Chambers of Commerce. Cases can be submitted to any of the secretariats and are then usually allocated according to places of arbitration.[669] If the place of arbitration is undetermined or outside Switzerland, aspects such as workload or language may play a role. The internal rules only mention the »*Secretariat of the Court*« to assist the SCCAM,[670] but do not outline its decentralised structure or the manner of case allocation to the staff based at the seven Chambers of Commerce.

## II. Multi-person bodies

Some institutions have a decision-making body, commonly named a »*Court*«, which is *separate* from the secretariat and which consists of

---

665 *See* CIETAC Rules, art. 2 (2)–(3) (2012); *see also* CIETAC Rules, art. 2 (3)–(4), Appendix I (2015) (locations of sub-commissions/centers moved to Appendix I; secretariats now called »*arbitration courts*«); *cf. also* ibid., art. 2 (6) (now providing that cases are administered in Beijing if a sub-commission's »*authorization has been terminated*«). For an account of the history and consequences of the CIETAC split, *see supra* at pp. 190-202 (§8C.II.2).

666 An independence which occasionally went too far, leading to parallel proceedings before two different subcommissions regarding claims and counterclaims with possibly conflicting results (*see China Natural v. Apex*, 379 F.3d. 796 [9th Cir. 2004] - on parallel proceedings in Beijing and Shanghai; CIETAC Beijing award enforced).

667 Now, renamed as »*president of the arbitration court*« (*see* CIETAC Rules, art. 2 (4) [2015]).

668 According to Fan, *Arbitration in China*, 124.

669 Swiss Chambers' Arbitration Institution, »Organisation«; *see also* Swiss Rules, Appendix A (2012).

670 SCCAM Internal Rules, art. 2 (2012).

multiple members elected for a certain time, which are not employed by the mother organisation. Such structure serves two purposes:

- Independence is ensured through separation of the procedural administration of arbitrations from the commercial activities and financial interests of the institution.
- An institutional decision can be more credible, if it is taken by a larger, multi-member body at best constituted by international arbitration experts.

In one form or the other, such »*Court*« exists under ICC, LCIA, Swiss and SIAC Rules. However, although CIETAC Rules (2015) also introduce an »*Arbitration Court*«, this body does neither appear to fulfil the general prerequisites just outlined nor to serve the same purpose as the »*Courts*« of the other institutions. »*Courts*« also have to be distinguished from bodies not concerned with case administration.

## 1. Comparison of the ICC, LCIA, SIAC and SCCAM

Despite the resemblance in name and some parallels in function, the ICC, LCIA, Swiss and SIAC Courts vary tremendously in size and organisation.

The ICC Court has more than 100 members and substitute-members of various jurisdictions[671] proposed by the ICC National Committees and appointed by the ICC World Council[672] with a President and a number of Vice Presidents.[673] All members are appointed for a term of three years in which they are not allowed to act as arbitrators in ICC arbitrations unless explicitly agreed by the parties.[674] The Court meets once a month in a general session in Paris open to all Court members and weekly in Committee of the Court sessions consisting of three Court members. Sometimes, Court members join the Committee via video or telephone conference only.

The LCIA Court comprises up to 35 members appointed for five years.[675] Like the ICC Court, the LCIA Court is very international with members

---

671 International Chamber of Commerce, »List of Current Court Members«.
672 *See* ICC Rules, Appendix II, art. 3 (1) (2012) (internal rules).
673 *See* ibid., Appendix II, art. 1 (1).
674 *See* ibid., Appendix II, art. 2 (2).
675 *See* LCIA, »Members of the LCIA Court« (for biographical notes of current members, including President, Vice Presidents, Honorary Vice Presidents and Registrar).

from a variety of jurisdictions.[676] Approximately every six months, the LCIA Court holds a general meeting to review the progress of pending cases and to render decisions.[677] In between, most decisions on individual cases are taken either by the President, a Vice President or - except for arbitrator appointments - by a Honorary Vice President on behalf of the LCIA Court or by a smaller panel of three to five members.[678] Different from ICC Court members who only receive some compensation for expenses, members of the LCIA Court are paid for their functions »*at hourly rates advised by members of the LCIA Court*« that add to the costs of arbitration.[679] Another difference is that members of the LCIA Court are not excluded from serving as arbitrators in LCIA arbitrations; they only have to refrain from decisions concerning their own cases.[680] Again different from the ICC Court,[681] the LCIA Court is also responsible for the development of the rules.[682]

SIAC now also features a »*Court of Arbitration*« with a cast that reads like a who is who of international arbitration but that is, with about fifteen members, notably smaller in number than that of the ICC and the LCIA Court.[683] While SIAC Court members may serve as arbitrators in SIAC arbitrations, the SIAC Practice Note on Administered Cases excludes them from being nominated by the institution. Similar to the ICC Court, the SIAC Court is now responsible for decisions on challenges to arbitrators[684] and, if the case is referred to it by the Registrar, for the prima facie decision on

---

676 *See* LCIA Constitution, A.1 (2011) (restricting the number of English nationals to six only).
677 At least once a year with an attendance quorum of seven members (ibid., E).
678 *See* ibid., D.2–3 (for details on the exercise of Court functions by officers of the LCIA Court); *see also* Konrad and Hunter, »LCIA Rules«, para. 26–29.
679 LCIA, »Schedule of Arbitration Costs (LCIA)«.
680 Further restrictions apply to the President, only allowed to act a party-nominated sole arbitrator or chair, and to Vice-Presidents, only eligible if nominated by a party (LCIA Constitution, F [2011]; *see also* Konrad and Hunter, »LCIA Rules«, para. 32).
681 In the ICC system, the ICC Commission on Arbitration, a division separate from the ICC Court, is responsible for the review and promotion of the ICC Rules.
682 LCIA Constitution, D.1 (c),(d) (2011); *see also* Konrad and Hunter, »LCIA Rules«, para. 28.
683 SIAC, »Court of Arbitration«.
684 SIAC Rules, art. 13 (2013) = art. 16 (2016).

jurisdiction.[685] When making arbitrator appointments, the President may but is not obliged to consult two further Court members.[686] In contrast to the ICC Court, the SIAC Court does not scrutinise arbitral awards. Scrutiny of awards is restricted to the secretariat's level, there to the Registrar, at SIAC.[687]

The SCCAM has currently 24 members plus a Chairman and two Vice chairmen elected for a three-year, renewable term. It is introduced as completely autonomous and independent,[688] which assumingly means independence from the individual Chambers of Commerce in the cantons, the arbitrators and any Swiss state authority. While many of the SCCAM's members appear to be of Swiss nationality and/or educated and working in Switzerland, they are undoubtedly highly experienced international arbitration practitioners.

Overall, institutional »*Courts*« have in common to provide a body of independent arbitration experts to decide relevant procedural issues and thereby assist the arbitral tribunal, which may generate particular trust in the proceedings. However, the outlined structural differences between the ICC, LCIA, SIAC and SCCAM can become relevant when evaluating their substitutability when it comes to implementing hybrid arbitration agreements.

## 2. The »Arbitration Court(s)«» under CIETAC Rules (2015)

As noted, CIETAC now also claims to have an »*Arbitration Court.*« However, a look at the CIETAC Rules (2015) quickly reveals that apart from the new name, this may not be a material change from the former system. In fact, the Arbitration Court assumes all functions previously assumed by the secretariat without that the rules provide for any additional powers or specific requirements as to the composition of that court, its term and meetings. Since further information has not yet been published, it is too early to speculate if this renaming of the secretariat into a »*Court*« will have any effect on CIETAC's case management approach in practice. It might be just a marketing idea. In any case, the term »*Arbitration Court*« appears somewhat

---

685  Ibid., art. 25.
686  SIAC Practice Note, para. 6 (2014).
687  SIAC Rules, art. 28 (2) (2013) = art. 32 (2) (2016).
688  SCCAM Internal Rules, art. 1 (2012); *see also* Swiss Chambers' Arbitration Institution, »Organisation«.

confusing as long as this body - as it currently appears - is composed of staff employed by CIETAC, lacking the relative diversity and independence of the members of the ICC, LCIA, SIAC and SCCAM.

This impression that the Arbitration Court was »*created*« by simply re-naming the former secretariat is underlined by the fact that the subcommissions/offices in Tianjin, Chongqing, Shanghai and Shenzhen also administer cases through their own »*arbitration courts*« whereas the term »*secretariat*« has completely disappeared from CIETAC Rules (2015).[689] Accordingly, day-to-day case administration and specific case related decisions making is, unless left to the chairman, still done by one and the same organisational body within CIETAC or its subdivisions, whether named a secretariat or an »*arbitration court.*«

This actor renaming with the 2015 revision of the rules could explain how CIETAC intends to »*perform the relevant administrative duties*« under article 4 (3) of the CIETAC Rules (2012 and 2015) in case parties agree on other institutional rules that do provide for a »*Court*« to decide certain aspects. Obviously, CIETAC assumes its »*Arbitration Court*« and former secretariat to be equivalent to any other institution's »*Court.*« For the dissimilarities just outlined, such assumption is incorrect. In addition, many important decisions, *e.g.* appointment[690] or challenge[691] and replacement[692] of arbitrators, are taken by the Chairman under the CIETAC system. Accordingly, a *functional* equivalence between the new »*Arbitration Court*« (≈ former secretariat) and the ICC, LCIA, SCCAM or SIAC Court is difficult to argue.

## 3. Other, multi-person bodies

Arbitral institutions also maintain multi-person bodies that are not responsible for procedural decisions in individual cases but for specific projects or the political or financial strategy of the institution. These bodies, which may be called »*board*«, »*committee*«, »*commission*« or »*institute*« are very diverse but have in common that they do not deal with individual cases. Such »*other*« bodies include for example:

---

689  CIETAC Rules, art. 2 (4) (2015).
690  CIETAC Rules, art. 24–26 (2012) = art. 26–28 (2015).
691  CIETAC Rules, art. 30 (6) (2012) = art. 32 (6) (2015).
692  CIETAC Rules, art. 31 (1) (2012) = art. 33 (1) (2015).

- The ICC Commission of Arbitration and ADR responsible for rule development and reports[693]
- The various Boards of Directors, *e.g.*, in the LCIA, DIS[694] and SIAC system, which are responsible for overall policy, or more commercially expressed: for business strategy, development and corporate governance[695]
- CIETAC's Specialized Committees: The Expert Consultation Committee, the Case Edition Committee and the Arbitrator Qualification Review Committee[696]

It seems obvious that such bodies not ordinarily participating in case administration will have trouble adequately substituting administrative bodies like Courts in hybrid arbitration. Nevertheless, after first proposing that the ICC Court's functions should be performed by the SIAC chairman,[697] as head of case management under the SIAC system at that time, SIAC announced during the *Alstom–Insigma* arbitration to substitute the ICC Court with its Board of Directors, apparently in contemplation of the tribunal's view on the matter.[698] Unfortunately, there is no account on how the SIAC Board of Directors actually dealt with tasks like scrutinising the final awards for example.

In the DIS system, a specific »*Appointing Committee*« exists that has the sole task of making default arbitrator nominations.[699] It consists of three members. While its task is roughly comparable to that of the National Committees under ICC Rules, its composition or mandate is not. ICC National Committees exists in most jurisdictions with a branch of the ICC as representative associations of the member companies. They are structured as independent associations with their own governance organisation.[700]

---

693 International Chamber of Commerce, »About the Commission on Arbitration and ADR«.

694 The DIS Board of Directors is further supported by an Advisory Board.

695 SIAC, »Board of Directors«.

696 China International Economic and Trade Administration Commission, »Organization«; *see* Fan, *Arbitration in China*, 124 (for details on tasks of and membership in these committees).

697 *See Insigma v. Alstom*, [2009] SGCA 24 [9] (citing the secretariat's letter of 17 November 2006).

698 Ibid., para. 18. *See supra* at pp. 119-122 (§5D).

699 DIS Rules, art. 12, 14 (1998).

700 International Chamber of Commerce, »National Committees Connections Gateway«.

## III. Individuals: President, Chairman, Registrar, Secretary General

In terms of case management experience it may have been more appropriate had SIAC followed the original proposal to replace the ICC Court with the SIAC Chairman during the *Alstom–Insigma* arbitration. However, the motivation in letting the Board of Directors step in was apparently to provide a multi-person body to match the multi-person ICC Court. Now that SIAC has its own Court under its current rules, the position of the former »*Chairman*« as the head of the institution no longer exists. However, there is a »*Chairman of the Board of Directors*« overlooking the financial and operational policies, a »*CEO*« connecting case management and operational management and a »*Registrar*« at the head of case management at the secretariat. Similarly, other institutions also have some individuals with an elevated position either within the secretariat, like *e.g.* the LCIA »*Registrar*« or the ICC or DIS »*Secretary General*«, or within the institution's Court, like the »*Presidents*« of the ICC or LCIA Court.

In the CIETAC system, also under CIETAC Rules (2015), the »*Chairman*« is the most important actor with decision-making powers similar to those of the Courts under ICC, LCIA, SIAC and Swiss Rules. It is unknown to how CIETAC would perform »*the relevant administrative duties*« pursuant to article 4 (3) of its rules if the parties opted e.g. for CIETAC administered arbitration under ICC Rules. Possibly, CIETAC's chairman would still assume all decisional powers, even though CIETAC now claims to have an »*Arbitration Court*« of its own - plus several »*arbitration courts*« at its subdivisions.[701] Alternatively, the »*Commission*« as a whole, which according to CIETAC's self-presentation consists of the Chairman and »*a number of Vice-Chairmen and Members*«[702] might assume the Court's responsibilities under ICC Rules. It is unclear if and how these »*Members*« ordinarily participate in CIETAC case administration as they do not feature anywhere in the rules. Overall, CIETAC's structure is currently not well communicated, with the newly revealed CIETAC Rules (2015) at the time of writing not yet reflected in the institution's presentation of its organisation on its website.

---

701 *But see supra* at pp. 394-395 (II.2) on the lack of organisational and functional equivalence of this new »*creation*« with the ICC Court.

702 China International Economic and Trade Administration Commission, »Organization«.

IV. The »administrator« under AAA-ICDR Rules

Unlike all of the other rules here discussed, AAA-ICDR Rules refrain from addressing internal actors and task allocation in their rules. Rather, AAA-ICDR Rules constantly refer to the »*administrator*«, who is not an individual person but the institution itself. Article 1 (3) AAA-ICDR Rules defines the administrator as »*the ICDR, a division of the AAA.*«[703] The rules allow the centre to provide services »*from any of the ICDR's case management offices or through the facilities of the AAA or arbitral institutions with which the ICDR or the AAA has agreements of cooperation.*«[704] The internal organisation is thereby entirely left to the AAA-ICDR, the parties do not know by whom a particular decision would be taken and if only a single case manager or a larger group of people would be involved. The AAA-ICDR may even delegate tasks to staff of another institution through an agreement of cooperation.[705]

Accordingly, the parties opting for AAA-ICDR arbitration cannot rely on a particular qualification or form of election of actors within the institution. While this makes AAA-ICDR Rules less transparent than the other rules here discussed, the discretion given to the centre as to its internal task allocation certainly reduces the risk of arguments on the performance by the institution, which may often be merely formalistic.

Due to the openness of the AAA-ICDR Rules regarding task allocation within the institution, a hybrid arbitration administered by another institution under AAA-ICDR-Rules should be less prone to criticism than for example a hybrid arbitration administered under ICC Rules. Any argument relying on parties' expectations as to the institutional actor competent for a certain decision is difficult to make in light of the vagueness of AAA-ICDR Rules in this regard. Although this did not hinder the AAA-ICDR in following the ICC's example in introducing some kind of declaratory exclusivity provision in the latest version of its rules, article 1 (3) sentence 4 AAA-ICDR Rules makes this exclusivity subject to express authorisation

---

703  *See also* Thümmel, »ICDR-IAR«, para. 17.
704  AAA-ICDR Rules, art. 1 (3) (2014).
705  The AAA-ICDR's cooperative agreements - about 60 in number with institutions in 43 countries - are confidential and unpublished. Many apparently only provide for the use of hearing facilities, but some even go as far as establishing common, unofficial arbitrator lists (*see* Thümmel, »ICDR-IAR«, 17; Gusy, Hosking, and Schwarz, *A Guide to the ICDR Rules*, para. 1.41).

by the AAA-ICDR. This implies that the AAA-ICDR's opposition to hybrid arbitration is less based on practical concerns of practical substitutability of actors[706] than on an alleged legal right to license the right to use its rules.[707]

## D. Adaptation of the rules to the administering institution's system

The tremendous differences between both institutional rules and institutional organisational structures just outlined highlight the difficulty to implement hybrid arbitration agreements. In particular for controversial institutional decisions, like jurisdictional decisions, (non-)confirmation, challenge and replacement of arbitrators, a finding of functional equivalence between actors of different institutions with often entirely different personnel structures, terms and experience will be very difficult to make. In particular, a combination of highly controlling rules with the administration by a more lenient institution or vice-versa will hardly work out well. The greatest potential to effectively implement hybrid arbitration agreements exists if parties agree on all procedural issues, however, then they would not need institutional administration at all.[708]

In any case, administering hybrid arbitration almost always requires far-reaching adjustments of the chosen rules to the structure of the designated institution. According to the conflict of laws concept of »*adaptation*« as introduced above,[709] disharmonies between different but equally applicable laws could be corrected by finding a result that meets the expectations of justice under both legal systems without prioritising one over the other. Negatively expressed, the idea of adaptation is to avoid a result deemed unjust in both legal systems.[710] Applied to the conflict of institutional arbitration rules and systems here analysed, one can argue that restoration of state court competence for inoperability of the arbitration agreement could be such unjust result.

However, even if avoidance of the verdict of inoperability was the motivation, any adaptation solution should respect the predominant justice

---

706 *See supra* at p. 352 (A.1).

707 *See supra* at pp. 354-355.

708 *See supra* at pp. 145-146 (§7B.IV).

709 At pp. 346-352 (A.II).

710 So-called material adaptation (»*sachrechtliche Angleichung*«, Schotten and Schmellenkamp, *Das internationale Privatrecht in der notariellen Praxis*, § 3, para. 50).

values applying to organising international arbitration: party autonomy and efficiency. According to the principle of party autonomy, any adaptation should not be imposed by the institution but be agreed among those concerned, that is the administering institution and both arbitrants, as it seems to have been at least attempted at the outset of the *Alstom–Insigma* arbitration.[711] If such an agreement cannot be reached, the expectation of efficiency of the proceedings should usually cause the institution to refrain from administering the arbitration by not concluding or terminating the Administration Contract.[712] As noted, it is usually much more efficient if a court referred the parties to arbitrate ad hoc or ordered them to agree on standard institutional arbitration[713] then to desperately attempt to implement a hybrid arbitration agreement by substituting actors that are not sufficiently equivalent.

### §15 Implementing hybrid arbitration: an institutional perspective

To conclude this chapter, one may note that it is not illegal for one institution to apply the rules of another institution if the parties so wish. Institutional arbitration rules are, despite contrary proclamations in articles 1 (2) of the ICC and 1 (3) sentence 4 of the AAA-ICDR Rules, effectively »*public goods*.«[714] However, given the great variations of institutional arbitration systems in terms of rules and organisation, hybrid arbitration almost always requires a lot of adjustments of the chosen rules which are only justified to the extent agreed by the parties. This underlines the finding of inadvisability of hybrid arbitration made above[715] and adds another dimension to it: Often, it will also be *inadvisable for the designated institution* to administer hybrid arbitration as the procedural regularity of the proceedings decisively depends on the parties' cooperation, which cannot be assumed at the outset. While it is appreciated if an institution wants to help parties to implement their agreement to avoid inoperability, it is here proposed that it should better convince the parties to agree on standard institutional arbitration. Should it fail with such persuasion, it should decline to administer the case to avoid potential malperformance of its services and disappointment of the parties'

---

711  *But see infra* at pp. 480-482 (§17C.I) on Insigma's later complaints.
712  As it is allowed to, *see supra* at pp. 269-271 (§12).
713  *See supra* at pp. 207-209 (§9).
714  *See supra* at pp. 340-344 (§13D).
715  *See supra* at pp. 157-209 (§8).

expectations.[716] It would then be up to the courts to decide if and how the agreement to arbitrate may still be enforced, which will be discussed in the next, final chapter.

This chapter also outlined some organisational changes made *within* arbitration institutions together with the rule revisions of recent years. In particular, the Swiss cantonal Chambers of Commerce reorganised themselves into one institution with an »*Arbitration Court*«, SIAC also created a »*Court of Arbitration*« as an independent body deciding *inter alia* on challenges to arbitrators and CIETAC, with the 2015 revision of its rules, introduces a body which is at least named an »*Arbitration Court*.« These kind of organisational changes reveal a proximity between the hybrid arbitration theme as herein discussed and the temporal conflict of arbitration rules:[717] If an institution changes its structure and actors from one version of its rules to the other, the hypothesis that parties could choose an older version of the rules[718] might provoke similar reflections on substitutability of actors since some of the actors mentioned in older versions may no longer be available.[719]

---

716  S*ee supra* at pp. 263-264 (§11B.IV) and pp. 269-272 (§12). On the serious risk of challenge to any award that is based on procedural rules other than those agreed by the parties, *see also infra* at pp. 465-469 (§17A.II).

717  Thereon, *see generally* Greenberg and Mange, »Institutional and Ad Hoc Perspectives on the Temporal Conflict of Arbitral Rules«; *see also* Rüßmann, »Zwingendes Recht in den Schiedsregeln einer Schiedsinstitution?«, 490–92.

718  As noted *supra* at p. 245, n. 178, most rules provide for the latest version at the time of the commencement of proceedings to apply. A reference to a set of rules is thus presumably dynamic (*see* Greenberg and Mange, »Institutional and Ad Hoc Perspectives on the Temporal Conflict of Arbitral Rules«, 200–210, citing case law, some conflicting). However, institutions *may* accept *express* references to former rules (but they are not obliged to, *see* Wolf, *Die Institutionelle Handelsschiedsgerichtsbarkeit*, 91–92, correctly stressing that party autonomy reigns procedurally but that, contractually, the institution's offer to administer cases is on the basis of its current rules only; *see also supra* at pp. 243-251 (§11A.III, IV).

719  *Cf.* Wolf, *Die Institutionelle Handelsschiedsgerichtsbarkeit*, 91 (generally mentioning reasons of organisation for a possible reluctance of an institution to apply former rules); *but cf. supra* at pp. 188 et seq. (§8C.II.1.b) and p. 215 (§10A.VI) on the DIS' administration of cases under the rules of the former DAS.

# Chapter 5: Hybrid Arbitration Clauses Before State Courts

Recognition of party autonomy as the underlying principle of arbitration *»does not mean that states (and their courts) play no role.«*[1]

> »[I]ndeed, the plea for autonomous international arbitration is, at the same time, the plea to state courts to support arbitration and enforce its results.«[2]

The foregoing analysis concluded that the principle of party autonomy supports the validity of hybrid arbitration agreements. If one focusses on the relationship between the parties to the arbitration agreement and the referenced institution, however, the same principle, in its manifestation as freedom to decide with whom and on which terms to contract, also serves as a limit to the operability of hybrid arbitration agreements. Generally, an institution is free to decline the administration of a case under another institution's rules. Hybrid arbitration agreements are therefore only operable if multiple actors cooperate: the two or more parties to the arbitration and the administering institution.

This last chapter shall now transpose above substantive findings into possible procedural legal actions between the parties to the arbitration agreement *inter se* and in relation to the institution designated to administer the case. First, state court action may be directed at the enforcement or challenge of the arbitration agreement as the basis of arbitral jurisdiction prior to or pending arbitration (§16). Second, even if, as in the *Alstom–Insigma* arbitration, an award is rendered, specific problems concerning the underlying hybrid agreement may be readdressed in setting-aside and enforcement proceedings (§17).

## §16 Enforcing & challenging hybrid arbitration agreements

When discussing procedural means to enforce or challenge hybrid arbitration agreements, it is useful to distinguish between the relevant relationships.

---

1 Michaels, »Dreaming Law without a State«, 41; referring to Lew, »Does National Court Involvement Undermine the International Arbitration Process?«, 492.

2 Michaels, »Dreaming Law without a State«, 41.

- First, the parties to the arbitration may disagree on the validity and interpretation of their agreement and on the role of the designated institution (A).
- Second, the parties may agree how their hybrid arbitration agreement should be implemented but the approached institution might not cooperate (B).
- Third, the rules issuing institution might also assert an interest in the matter.

However, the previous chapter, which outlined that a claim of the rules issuing institution against the administering institution under intellectual property or unfair competition law would often fail, has already touched upon relevant jurisdictional problems,[3] which is why the last mentioned inter-institutional relationship shall not be reiterated here.

A. Enforcement in relation to the other party

The introduction defined hybrid arbitration agreements as agreements by which parties *clearly* and *deliberately* refer to one arbitral institution but another institution's rules.[4] Accordingly, hybrid arbitration agreements do not suffer from the same ambiguity as other pathological arbitration agreements that name an inexistent arbitral institution or two arbitral institutions without stating an order of preference.[5] Nevertheless, there are at least three reasons why it is probable that questions of validity and operability of hybrid arbitration agreements may be addressed to state courts prior to or pending arbitration:

- First, hybrid arbitration agreements are unusual which increases the risk of non-compliance and chances of challenge by a party content with the status quo.
- Second, hybrid arbitration agreements undeniably raise interpretative questions concerning whether and which actors of the named institution could substitute the institutional functions under the referenced rules.[6]

---

3    *See supra* at pp. 297-304 (§13A.III) and pp. 333-340 (§13C.IV).
4    *See supra* at pp. 31-32 (§1A).
5    On arguments for and against a qualification as pathological, *see supra* at pp. 157 et seq. (§8).
6    *See supra* at pp. 344-400 (§14).

- Third, the designated institution may refuse to administer the arbitration,[7] in which case a court may have to decide if the parties may be referred to a) ad hoc or b) institutional arbitration before another institution.

## I. Overview of potentially available actions

Different state court competences correspond with these issues: competences to control arbitral jurisdiction and competences to support arbitral jurisdiction. Before entering into a procedural evaluation of issues specific to hybrid arbitration agreements, a short descriptive overview of state court competences over actions between (potential) arbitrants shall be given.

### 1. Action for dismissal or stay of litigation

The classic situation in which a state court may be required to control arbitral jurisdiction, or rather the arbitration agreement as a basis of it, is that a party introduces litigation on the merits, which the other party then seeks to avoid by raising the arbitration agreement as a defence (so-called arbitration plea or defence). The New York Convention then requires the seized court to »*refer*« the parties to arbitration unless the arbitration agreement is null, void, inoperative or incapable of being performed.

Most jurisdictions understand this as an obligation to enforce the negative effect of arbitration agreements and would order a dismissal or stay of litigation if the arbitration defence was justified. While civil law jurisdictions prefer a definite dismissal,[8] common law courts tend to order a stay only, keeping residue jurisdiction over the matter.[9] Practically, the difference is mainly one of terminology.[10]

---

7   *See supra* at pp. 209 et seq. (§10) on this practical risk and pp. 232 et seq. (§11) on the institution's right to refuse administering hybrid arbitrations.

8   *See e.g.* ZPO § 1032 (1) (GER); *cf.* Born, *International Arbitration and Forum Selection Agreements*, 63 (§2.07[B]) (»*principally civil law jurisdictions, including France, Switzerland and Germany*«).

9   *See e.g.* Arbitration Act 1996 § 9 (EW); *cf.* Born, *International Arbitration and Forum Selection Agreements*, 63 (§2.07[B]) (with references on other common law jurisdictions).

10  Born, *International Commercial Arbitration (2014)*, 1282–83 (at §8.03[C][2]: »*semantics*«).

2. Action for interlocutory declaratory relief

A distinct method for state courts to control arbitral jurisdiction is to accept a motion for declaratory relief on the admissibility or inadmissibility of arbitration prior to or pending arbitral proceedings. Such interlocutory action, however, is only available in some jurisdictions including *e.g.* Germany,[11] England[12] and China,[13] with some differences as to the conditions[14] and time limits for such action.[15]

---

11 ZPO § 1032 (2) (GER) provides: »*Bei Gericht kann bis zur Bildung des Schiedsgerichts Antrag auf Feststellung der Zulässigkeit oder Unzulässigkeit eines schiedsrichterlichen Verfahrens gestellt werden*« [Until the arbitral tribunal has been formed, a petition may be filed with the courts to have it determine the admissibility or inadmissibility of arbitration proceedings].

12 Arbitration Act 1996 § 32 (EW). Another motion to seek for a declaration on the validity of an arbitration agreement is granted to a non-participating party, *see* Arbitration Act 1996 § 72 (1) (EW). The extent of this right is somewhat unclear. The English Court of Appeal stressed that courts should be »*very cautious*« to accept jurisdiction on this basis since »*it will, in general, be right for the arbitrators to be the first tribunal to consider whether they have jurisdiction to determine the dispute*« (*Fiona Trust*, [2007] HL 40 [UK] [34]).

13 Arbitration Law art. 20 (1) (P.R.C.).

14 Relatively strict are the admissibility requirements under English law, *see* Arbitration Act 1996 § 32 (2) (EW): Either all parties have to agree or the arbitral tribunal has to grant leave and the court has to admit the action for reasons of efficiency. However, these conditions may be irrelevant to courts if an injunction is sought at the same time, *see e.g. The Hari Bhum I*, [2004] EWCA Civ. 1598 [63–65] (upholding a declaration that certain claims have to be arbitrated without even mentioning the conditions of § 32 of the Arbitration Act; at the same time setting an anti-suit injunction aside); applied by *Steamship Mutual v. Sulpicio*, [2008] EWHC 914 (Comm.) [34] (granting a declaration that the respondent was bound by an arbitration agreement and an injunction against parallel proceedings in the Philippines); for further references, *see* Joseph, *Jurisdiction and Arbitration Agreements and Their Enforcement*, 13.29, 13.30; Erk, *Parallel Proceedings in International Arbitration*, 150, n. 891.

15 While ZPO § 1032 (2) (GER) clearly restricts the availability of any such declaratory action to the time prior to the constitution of an arbitral tribunal, the correct construction of Arbitration Act 1996 § 32 (EW) is uncertain. One view is that prior the tribunal's constitution, declaratory relief would be available without conditions (*see generally* Joseph, *Jurisdiction*

Generally, an advantage of such interlocutory procedure is that it enables parties to seek an early, definite confirmation on the tribunal's jurisdiction to avoid that time and money is invested into proceedings that may lead to an award, which could be set aside. As long as arbitration may be commenced and continued in parallel pending the application to the state court,[16] the risk of slowing down the arbitration is relatively small.[17]

Many legal orders, however, do not accept motions for a declaration on the jurisdiction of the arbitral tribunal or the validity of the arbitration agreement.[18] This is obvious in jurisdictions according a negative effect to the principle of competence-competence, like France, and - to some extent - Switzerland,[19] as such actions would go against the principle that the arbitral tribunal should be the first to decide on its own competence. The same applies under US law, if parties »*clearly and unmistakably*« agreed to

---

*and Arbitration Agreements and Their Enforcement*, 13.25–13.31; *but see Vale do Rio*, [2000] 2 Lloyd's Rep 1 [EWHC Comm.] 53–54 - understanding that a party must always first await the constitution of the tribunal before being able to address an application to the court under § 32 and the conditions set out therein; disagreeing: *JSC v. AES*, [2010] EWHC 772 (Comm.) [22]).

16  Providing this expressly: ZPO § 1032 (3) (GER). In contrast, applications to Chinese People's Courts under art. 20 of the Arbitration Law (P.R.C.) put a parallel application before an arbitration commission on hold.

17  For the German Higher Regional Courts, it was also noted that these are relatively quick to decide within a period of six months (Sachs and Schmidt-Ahrendts, »Diverging Concepts of the Principle of Competence-Competence?«, 9).

18  However, one Canadian court allowed such motion on the basis of art. 8 (1) of the UNCITRAL Model Law itself, not requiring that the »*action*« brought before the state court is an action on the merits; (Jean Estate v. Wires Jolley LLP, 2009 ONCA 339, para. 40–43; *but see* Born, *International Commercial Arbitration (2014)*, 1081–82, n. 200, at 7.03[A][2][a] on opposite views expressed by other Canadian courts).

19  *But see UAE v. Westland Helicopters*, [1994] ATF 120 II 155 (C.H. BG) 164 (leaving it open whether declaratory relief would be available in exceptional circumstances) (at consid. 3 b.bb.); *see generally* Erk, *Parallel Proceedings in International Arbitration*, 146, n. 863–64 (with references to Swiss doctrine; the majority rejecting actions on the admissibility of arbitration, while views are divided on actions on the invalidity of the arbitration agreement).

arbitrate »*arbitrability*«, which in the US understanding includes the question of validity of the arbitration agreement.[20]

## 3. Actions for injunctive relief

In common law jurisdictions, it is generally possible to obtain a so-called anti-suit injunction in order to enforce an arbitration agreement.[21] Functionally different from a dismissal or stay of litigation in favour of arbitration and also different from a declaratory judgment on the validity of an arbitration agreement, such an injunction contains an enforceable order not to sue before a certain forum, usually a state court in a foreign jurisdiction, with a financial penalty in case of infringement.

In civil law jurisdictions, anti-suit injunctions are unavailable[22] and viewed critical as they may factually and indirectly intervene with the competences of foreign courts and because they favour the party that happens to be located in the jurisdiction that provides the most effective means of enforcement.[23] Most civil law courts do not recognise anti-suit injunctions ordered by common law courts and some even deny service of process if anti-suit injunctions are sought.[24] Just a few voices in legal doctrine want to

---

20   *See infra* at pp. 414-419 (§16A.II.1.b).

21   *See e.g The Angelic Grace*, [1994] 1 Lloyd's Rep 169 (EWHC Comm.), upheld by: [1995] 1 Lloyd's Rep 87 (EWCA Civ.) (leading English case on anti-suit injunctions to enforce arbitration agreements).

22   Born, *International Commercial Arbitration (2014)*, 1290 (§ 8.03 [C.6]); *see also* Schmidt, »Anti-suit injunctions im Wettbewerb der Rechtssysteme«, 493, n. 12 (on German law with further references); *but see* Schlosser, »Anti-suit injunctions zur Unterstützung von internationalen Schiedsverfahren«, 487 (on an exceptional decision of the Supreme Court of the German Reich, which prohibited the introduction of divorce proceedings in Latvia).

23   Pfeiffer, »Anmerkung« (characterising an anti-suit injunction as an anachronism born in the spirit of hegemonial thinking [»*ein Anachronismus, der aus dem Geist hegemonialen Denkens geboren ist*«]).

24   *E.g.* Beschluss [Decision], (1996) 109 ZZP 221 (GER OLG, Düsseldorf); *see also* Schlosser, »Anti-suit injunctions zur Unterstützung von internationalen Schiedsverfahren«, 487, n. 9–10 (with further references).

introduce this procedural means in order to enforce the obligation not to litigate arising from arbitration agreements effectively.[25]

Anti-suit injunctions have also faced considerable headwind from the ECJ within the boundaries of the Brussels regime. According to the *West Tankers* decision, the respect for sovereignty of the competences of other European courts required by the Brussels regime would be factually undermined if a court in one European jurisdiction could order a party not to sue before the courts of another European jurisdiction, even if such order seeks to enforce a valid arbitration agreement.[26] However, anti-suit injunctions can and are still ordered by US courts and courts in other common law jurisdictions[27] and - despite *West Tankers* - also by English courts at least if directed against lawsuits in courts outside the European Union.[28]

An *anti-arbitration injunction* is a special kind of anti-suit injunction seeking to hinder arbitration proceedings deemed in breach of a contractual or other obligation. Surprisingly, anti-arbitration injunctions face much more resistance, even by common law lawyers, than anti-suit injunctions in general. Apparently, it is considered more reproachable to intervene, at least indirectly and factually, with arbitral competence than with the competence of sovereign foreign state courts. Possibly, this is an indication of the overall arbitration-friendly tendency of legal writing that is often influenced by practitioner's interests.[29]

---

25 *E.g.* Schmidt, »Anti-suit injunctions im Wettbewerb der Rechtssysteme«, 498; Schlosser, »Anti-suit injunctions zur Unterstützung von internationalen Schiedsverfahren«, 491–92.

26 *West Tankers*, C-185/07, [2009] ECR I– 00663 (ECJ).

27 *See e.g. WSG Nimbus v. Cricket Sri Lanka*, [2002] SGHC 104 [91] (»*Once this court is satisfied that there is an arbitration agreement, it has a duty to uphold that agreement and prevent any breach of it*«); *see generally* Born, *International Commercial Arbitration (2014)*, 1292, n. 214 (§ 8.03 [C.6.b]); on the greater reluctance of US courts to grant such injunctions, *see* ibid., 1293 (at [c]) (citing a number of cases granting and denying anti-suit injunctions).

28 *See e.g. Midgulf. Int. v. Groupe Chim. Tunisien*, [2010] EWCA Civ. 66; for further references, *see* Illmer, »Anti-Suit Injunctions«, 406, n. 4; *see also* Pfeiffer, »Anmerkung« (noting a fear that London could lose attraction as an arbitration hub if English courts could no longer grant anti-suit injunctions following West Tankers).

29 *See supra* at p. 136, n. 51 on the intertwinement of arbitration doctrine and practice.

4. Actions for review of arbitral decisions on jurisdiction

»It is self evident [...] that an arbitral tribunal cannot be the final arbitrator of the question of jurisdiction; [...] this would provide a classic case of ›pulling oneself up by one's own boot straps.‹«[30]

State courts may control arbitral jurisdiction after an arbitral tribunal or institution has already a decision thereon. That such review is eventually available is clear and follows from provisions on the setting-aside and recognition and enforcement of awards.[31]

However, approaches vary regarding the availability of court review of *pure* jurisdictional decisions by arbitral tribunals and institutions. Whether courts can review them depends *inter alia* on the applicable arbitration law, on the type of arbitral body: tribunal or institution, and on whether arbitral body assumed or denied its jurisdiction.

According to article 16 (3) of the UNCITRAL Model Law, any party may request the competent court at the place of arbitration to review an arbitral tribunal's interim decision »*that it has jurisdiction.*« National arbitration laws of Model Law jurisdictions contain corresponding provisions.[32] The direct reviewability of an arbitral tribunal's positive decision on jurisdiction is therefore without doubt independent of the form such decision takes. The Singapore High Court's decision in the *Insigma v. Alstom* case was such decision under article 16 (3) of the UNCITRAL Model Law, as incorporated into Singapore law, against the tribunal's interim ruling on jurisdiction.[33]

Non-Model Law jurisdictions reach a similar result by characterising a ruling on jurisdiction as an award capable of setting-aside,[34] a question on which courts in Model Law jurisdictions are divided.[35] Connected to the

---

30    *The Johanna V*, [2003] EWHC 1655 [25], [2003] 2 Lloyd's Rep. 617 (Comm.) at 622.

31    *See infra* at pp. 470 et seq.

32    *See e.g.* ZPO § 1040 (3) (GER); *cf. generally* IAA § 3 (SG) (UNCITRAL Model Law having force of law in Singapore).

33    *See Insigma v. Alstom*, [2008] SGHC 134 [1].

34    *E.g.* IPRG art. 190 (3) (C.H.); Arbitration Act 1996 § 67 (EW); CPC art. 1520 no. 1 (FR); *but see* Born, *International Commercial Arbitration (2014)*, 1193, 1203 et seq. (at §7.03[E][7-8]; on the uncertainty of US law in this regard). *See also infra* at n. 67 at p. 417.

35    The text of art. 16 (3) sent. 1 of the UNCITRAL Model Law (»*either as a preliminary question or in an award on the merits*«) suggests that a pure interim decision on jurisdiction is not an award (so held by *Int'l Research*

question of the nature and type of review of positive arbitral rulings on jurisdiction, there are variations on the standard of review with some jurisdictions' courts applying a *de novo* standard[36] and others a deferential standard - at least if parties explicitly agreed to arbitrate jurisdictional issues.[37]

Very difficult to answer is the question how and if *negative* arbitral rulings on jurisdiction are reviewable because national arbitration laws do not take a clear position on it.

> »La sentence d'incompétence fait donc figure d'angle mort de la réflexion sur la compétence arbitrale.«[38]
>
> [The negative award on jurisdiction is the dead angle of contemplation on arbitral competence]

If the arbitral tribunal renders a negative decision on jurisdiction, such decision is necessarily final, because it ends the arbitration. This argues in favour of considering such decisions to be awards.[39] The paradox that an incompetent arbitral tribunal can render an award is overcome by the acknowledgement of competence-competence. However, that does not yet allow control of the jurisdictional finding. That an arbitral tribunal has wrongly negated its competence is not a ground for setting-aside under

---

      *v. Lufthansa Systems Asia Pacific*, [2012] SGHC 226 [111]; for further references from Hong Kong, *see* Born, *International Commercial Arbitration (2014)*, 1098–99, n. 287 at §7.03[A][4][a]; *but see* ibid., 1099–1100 - preferring the view that interim rulings on jurisdiction are awards; *cf. also* Beschluss [Decision], [2007] 22 NJW-RR 1008 (GER BGH) [5–6] - distinguishing the interim decision on jurisdiction from a decision on costs rendered at the same time, the latter part found capable of recognition as an award.

36   *De novo* review seems preferred *e.g.* in France, Germany and, for foreign arbitrations, in Switzerland, *see* Born, *International Commercial Arbitration (2014)*, 1114, 1119, 1124 (at §7.03[B][3], [C][2], [D][4]).

37   *See* ibid., 1232–33 (§7.03[I][4]; understanding US and English case law in that sense; with arguments in favour of a more deferential standard of review from the point of view of an arbitration practitioner).

38   Racine, »La sentence d'incompétence«, 731.

39   *See e.g.* Berger, Center for Transnational Law, *Private Dispute Resolution in International Business*, para. 28–40, 20–32; *see also* Kröll, »Recourse against Negative Decisions on Jurisdiction«, 63; *but see Persero v. Dexia Bank*, [2006] SGCA 41 [66].

many arbitration laws, those based on the UNCITRAL Model Law in particular.[40]

The German Federal Supreme Court for example held consequently that it is not possible to challenge an arbitral tribunal's finding that it does not have jurisdiction over the dispute.[41] However, the appellate court of Paris for example, took a different view and found that incorrect denial of jurisdiction was analogous enough to a wrong assumption of jurisdiction and should therefore be challengeable on the ground that the tribunal surpassed its mission.[42] This jurisprudence now entered the text of article 1520 no. 1 CPC (FR). However, a further problem may arise: Neither the arbitral tribunal nor an administering institution would commonly participate in court proceedings between arbitrants. Hence, it is difficult to explain how these bodies can be obliged to resume their contractual mandate and even from a purely procedural point of view, it seems that the annulment of a negative ruling on jurisdiction is not at the same time a positive decision on the jurisdiction of the arbitral tribunal.[43] These problems escalate in the discussion of the reviewability not of jurisdictional rulings of the arbitral tribunal but of an institution, which will be discussed below.[44]

---

40  *See* UNCITRAL Model Law 2006 art. 34; for some exceptions in non-Model Law jurisdictions, *see e.g.* IPRG art. 190 (2)(a) (C.H.) (wrong decline of jurisdiction as ground for setting-aside); *see also* CPC art. 1520 (1) (FR).

41  *See* Urteil [Judgment], [2003] 1 SchiedsVZ 39 (GER BGH) 40; *but see* Born, *International Commercial Arbitration (2014)*, 1236–37 (§7.03[I][5]; critical of this view, which is qualified as a minority view at the international level).

42  *SNCFT v. Voith*, [1997] Rev. Arb. 553 (FR CA, Paris) at 555: »*la convention des parties constituant le fondement légal de l'arbitrage, la décision des arbitres sur leur compétence est nécessairement soumise au contrôle de la Cour* [...], *ce contrôle portant, dans le cas où les arbitres se sont déclarés incompétents, sur le respect par ceux-ci de leur mission*« [since the arbitration agreement is the legal basis of arbitration, the arbitrators' competence decision is necessarily submitted to the control of the court, which concerns, if the arbitrators' wrongly declined jurisdiction, the respect of their mission]; *see already Swiss Oil v. Petrograb & Gabon*, [1989] Rev. Arb. 309 (FR CA, Paris) at 313.

43  *See infra* at pp. 430-435 (§16A.II.2) on the issue of limited res judicata effect.

44  *See infra* at pp. 435-442 (§16A.II.3).

## 5. Actions for state court support

Negative or reactive means of enforcement and declaratory relief may not be sufficient if the arbitration agreement is deemed valid but in need of interpretation or supplementation, *e.g.* when the parties' general intent to arbitrate is clear from the agreement but the mode of arbitration, the arbitrator appointment process or the designated institution is not. Then, state courts may have to enforce the arbitration agreement positively.

Here, US law is exceptional because the competences under the FAA do not formally distinguish between enforcing the negative obligation not to litigate through stay of the action before the state court and positively supporting arbitration. Under § 4 of the FAA the »*United States district court which, save for such agreement, would have jurisdiction*« is also competent for an order »*directing that such arbitration proceed in the manner provided for in such agreement*« (so-called motion to compel arbitration). Therewith, the US are virtually the only contracting state of the New York Convention that positively enforces agreements to arbitrate, understanding »*refer the parties to arbitration*« in such a way.[45]

Other national arbitration laws only provide for limited positive support of arbitrations, often restricted to measures relating to the appointment of arbitrators if the agreed arbitrator appointment process fails. Illustrative is the UNCITRAL Model Law. Its articles 11 (3) and (4) allow the competent court at the place of arbitration, as specified pursuant to article 6 of the UNCITRAL Model Law (the supporting court, »*juge d'appui*«), to appoint arbitrators on behalf of a party failing to do so.[46] It may also assist with other appropriate measures in case of obstacles to an agreed appointment procedure.[47]

---

45   *See* Born, *International Arbitration and Forum Selection Agreements*, 61 (§2.07[A][3]).
46   UNCITRAL Model Law 2006 art. 11 (3).
47   Ibid., art. 11 (4).

Some laws extend supporting jurisdiction to arbitrations with a yet undetermined place of arbitration, thus potentially seated abroad,[48] usually based
on some test of minimal connection with the court's territory.[49]

## II. Selected problems of enforcing hybrid arbitration agreements

It would surpass the scope of this thesis to cover all differences among legal
systems and persistent uncertainties regarding the enforcement of arbitration agreements through state courts. Therefore, the detailed analysis shall
be restricted to three interrelated themes potentially relevant in any lawsuit
concerning hybrid arbitration agreements: allocation of competence to determine the competent institution and applicable rules, the problem of *res
judicata* effect being limited to the parties and the question of control of and
deference to institutional decisions.

### 1. Allocation of competence

According to the view defended in this thesis, a state court in an arbitration-
friendly jurisdiction should usually reject the argument of *invalidity* of the
arbitration agreement in light of the principles of party autonomy and of
effective interpretation.[50] However, assessing the *operability* of hybrid arbitration agreements is less straightforward, in particular at a stage prior to
or at the outset of arbitration. Whether a hybrid arbitration agreement is
»*incapable of being performed*« within the meaning of article II (3) New
York Convention requires first an interpretation of the parties agreement
and second a prognostic evaluation of the likeliness that the chosen institution will accept to administer the case as agreed by the parties. This raises

---

48   *See e.g.* ZPO § 1025 (3) (GER); *see also* Beschluss [Decision], [2004] 2
SchiedsVZ 316 (even considering the German supporting judge competent when the arbitration agreement provides for arbitration in a foreign
state - Japan - but lacks an indication of the particular city or municipality);
criticised by Wagner, »Anmerkung« (warning of a generalisation of the
decision).

49   *See e.g. Israel v. NIOC*, [2005] Rev. Arb. 693 (FR C.Cass) (where it was
found sufficient that the President of the ICC was named as appointing
authority for the presiding arbitrator; the place of arbitration was undetermined).

50   *See supra* at p. 124 (§6B) and pp. 161-163 (§8B).

the important issue of standard of review of arbitration agreements exercised by state courts.

### a. Negative effect of competence-competence?

Much controversy concerns the standard of review state courts should apply to arbitration agreements. This debate, which relates to divergent understandings of the generally acknowledged principle of competence-competence of the arbitral tribunal,[51] is also connected to the question of appropriateness of interlocutory declaratory relief.[52]

To the extent that it is internationally accepted,[53] competence-competence simply means that the arbitral tribunal can decide on its own jurisdiction.[54] A valid arbitration agreement is not a requirement for the arbitral tribunal to be constituted and to rule on jurisdiction.[55] Equally undisputed, competence-competence does not mean that an arbitral tribunal is

---

51 *See* Born, *Commentary and Materials (2001)*, 853, 877 (*»remarkable and unusual diversity«*, *»wide variety of different approaches«*); Gaillard and Savage, *Fouchard, Gaillard, Goldmann*, 395 (*»subject of considerable divergence«*); Sachs and Schmidt-Ahrendts, »Diverging Concepts of the Principle of Competence-Competence?«, 2 (*»one of the most important concepts«* but *»also one of the most contentious ones«*).

52 *See supra* at pp. 405-407.

53 Codified in: UNCITRAL Model Law 2006 art. 16 (1); ZPO § 1040 (1) (GER) sentence 1; Arbitration Act 1996 art. 30 (1) (EW); IPRG art. 186 (1) (C.H.); CPC art. 1506, 1465 (FR); *see* Born, *Law and Practice (2012)*, 52 (§2.05) (*»almost universally accepted«*); *cf. also* Münch, »§ 1040 ZPO«, para. 4 (welcoming the clarification introduced with the 1998 arbitration law reform in Germany as overdue convergence with international standards). Under US law the doctrine is not codified but principally acknowledged by case law, if the parties' arbitration agreement covers jurisdictional matters (or *»arbitrability«*, *see supra* at p. 90, n. 191) (*cf. Prima Paint*, 388 U.S. at 404; more nuanced: *First Options*, 514 U.S. at 944, requiring *»clear and unmistakable evidence«*; *see generally* Graves and Davydan, »Competence-Competence«).

54 Gaillard and Savage, *Fouchard, Gaillard, Goldmann*, para. 653. Note again that Chinese law is again exceptional as it provides the arbitration commissions, rather than arbitral tribunals, with competence-competence (*see* Arbitration Law art. 20 (1) [P.R.C.]).

55 *See e.g.* Saenger, »§ 1040 ZPO«, para. 1; *see also* Voit, »§ 1040 ZPO«, para. 2 (goes without saying [*»selbstverständlich«*]).

necessarily the last to rule on its jurisdiction. Rather, courts at the seat and in the enforcement forum can review the arbitration agreement and the connected jurisdictional ruling. The disputed question is, if competence-competence means that the arbitral tribunal should always be the *first* to rule on its jurisdiction.

b. Overview of national approaches

Notably, French jurisprudence and doctrine[56] employs the term »*effet négatif de la compétence-compétence*« (negative effect of competence-competence) to limit court review of arbitration agreements.[57] According to this position, competence-competence also means that the arbitral tribunal can decide on its competence first. Before an award on jurisdiction is rendered, state courts can make a *prima facie* decision only. The court's review is restricted to whether the arbitration agreement is *manifestly* null or incapable of being performed (»*manifestement nulle ou manifestement inapplicable*«).[58] This view is now[59] also reflected in the wording of article 1465 CPC (FR):

> »Le tribunal arbitral est *seul* compétent pour statuer sur les contestations relatives à son pouvoir juridictionnel [*emphasis added*].«
>
> [The arbitral tribunal *alone* is competent to decide on objections concerning its jurisdiction.]

Consequently, French arbitration law does not provide for an interlocutory application to a state court for a declaratory judgment on the existence of a valid arbitration agreement.[60] Only once a final or partial award on

---

56  *See* Gaillard, »Note, C.Cass., 10.05.1995«, 619 (calling this a French specificity).

57  *See e.g. Coprodag v. Bohin*, [1995] Rev. Arb. 617 (FR C.Cass) (court seized on the merits incompetent to decide on objections to arbitration agreement; concerns domestic arbitration; *but cf.* Gaillard, »Note, C.Cass., 10.05.1995«, 618–19, stating that this decision is »*a fortiori*« relevant for international arbitration); *see generally* Delvolvé, Rouche, and Pointon, *French Arbitration Law and Practice*, para. 139 (with further references).

58  CPC art. 1506, 1448 (FR).

59  Since the Décret portant réforme de l'arbitrage 2011 (FR).

60  *Coprodag v. Bohin*, [1995] Rev. Arb. 617; *see* Gaillard, »Note, C.Cass., 10.05.1995«, 618 (*référé* to the TGI as *juge d'appui* also not available for that purpose).

jurisdiction is rendered, the question of arbitral jurisdiction is subject to court challenge.[61]

Although with very different terminology and arguments, US jurisprudence essentially comes to results similar to those under French law in most cases. Section 4 of the FAA assigns the question of validity and operability of the arbitration agreement to the courts. However, the US Supreme Court sees competence-competence of the arbitral tribunal as a contractual question of the scope of the arbitration agreement. If the arbitration agreement or the arbitration rules referenced therein show the parties' »*clear and unmistakable*« intent to refer the jurisdictional question to arbitration, the courts shall enforce such agreement without further assessing validity and operability issues.[62] By explicitly agreeing on the arbitral tribunal's competence-competence (competence-competence clause), parties can therefore opt out of the default jurisdiction of state courts under section 4 of the FAA.[63] Since most arbitration rules contain provisions on the competence of the arbitral tribunal to decide on its own jurisdiction[64] and since the reference to such rules is considered sufficiently »*clear and unmistakable*«,[65] state courts' competences under section 4 FAA are very limited. The state court is supposed to consider the validity of the competence-competence clause (or »*delegation agreement*«) but not of the whole arbitration agreement.[66] This restriction of US courts' review to the question of clear and unmistakable language is comparable to the prima facie review by French courts.

---

61  CPC art. 1520 no. 1 (FR).
62  *See First Options*, 514 U.S. at 943–45; *see also* Graves and Davydan, »Competence-Competence«, 162).
63  *See also* FAA § 208 (US) (on the application in non-domestic cases).
64  *See* Born, *Law and Practice (2012)*, 52 (§2.02) (with references at n. 26).
65  For references on US case law to this effect, *see* Born, *International Commercial Arbitration (2014)*, 1167, n. 640, 642 (§7.03[E][5][b][v]).
66  *Rent-A-Center*, 130 S.Ct. 2772, 2774 (US 2010) (»*Under the FAA, where an agreement to arbitrate includes an agreement that the arbitrator will determine the enforceability of the agreement, if a party challenges specifically the enforceability of that particular agreement, the district court considers the challenge, but if a party challenges the enforceability of the agreement as a whole, the challenge is for the arbitrator*«); *but see* Horton, »The Mandatory Core of § 4 of the Federal Arbitration Act«, 2 (fearing that the judiciary's role is limited to »*little more than rubber-stamping motions to compel arbitration*«).

Nevertheless, there is a notable difference between the French and the US approach: Different from French courts, US courts would fully review the arbitration agreement in absence of a clear contractual competence-competence clause. In France, a clear reference to arbitration even without a competence-competence clause suffices to refer parties to arbitration without detailed review of the agreement by the state court. This is important where the reference to the applicable arbitration rules, which may arguably contain a competence-competence clause, is unclear. US courts would probably proceed with a full review and interpretation of the arbitration agreement before referring parties to arbitration, French courts would not.[67]

The jurisprudence of the Swiss Supreme Court follows the French *prima facie* approach only if the prospective place of arbitration is in Switzerland,[68] but not if it is abroad.[69] This distinction is based on the consideration that parties should have access to Swiss courts at least at one point in time concerning the existence and validity of the arbitration agreement. If the place of arbitration is in Switzerland, setting-aside proceedings - unless validly waived - protect this right. If the place of arbitration is abroad, the Swiss courts fear to not have any further opportunity to rule on the arbitration agreement and therefore engage in a full review in case of an objection prior to or pending arbitration.[70] For arbitrations potentially seated outside Switzerland, Swiss courts assume comprehensive powers to review the arbitration agreement, similar to courts in Germany.

Before the legislative reform that came into force in 1998,[71] German jurisprudence followed an approach similar to that of the US courts based on a concept of contractual competence-competence clauses, which could

---

67  *See also* Born, *Law and Practice (2012)*, 53 (§2.05) (concluding that French courts *»will virtually never initially decide a jurisdictional objection«*). However, *a posteriori*, setting-aside proceedings enable a full review by French courts (*see supra* at p. 416). In contrast, § 10 of the FAA does *not expressly* allow vacation of the award on the ground of incompetence of the arbitral tribunal (*cf.* Graves and Davydan, »Competence-Competence«, 170, criticising the *Rent-a-Center* decision for this reason; *see* FAA § 10 (a)(4) [US], enabling vacation of the award only if the arbitral tribunal *»exceeded its powers«*).

68  *See A v. B.C., D.C. et al.*, [2004] ASA Bull. 145 (C.H. BG) (extracts in Italian, French, German and English).

69  *Mediterranean Shipping*, (1995) ATF 121 III 38 (C.H. BG) at 42.

70  Ibid. (consid. 2b).

71  SchiedsVfG 1997 (GER).

derogate the competence to rule on jurisdictional objections to the arbitral tribunal.[72] Now, however, German arbitration legislation, supported by doctrine and jurisprudence, grants courts a full right to decide on the existence, validity and operability of an arbitral agreement notwithstanding the arbitral tribunal's competence-competence.[73]

Overall, the same applies under English law, although doctrine advises courts to exercise some discretion *»which meets the justice of the particular case«* regarding the question whether to fully trial the issues raised concerning the existence, validity, operability and scope of the arbitration agreement or to grant a stay and leave this question to the arbitral tribunal.[74]

For other Model Law jurisdictions, there are divergent interpretations of article 8 (1) of the UNCITRAL Model Law concerning the standard of review.[75] Presenting all of these approaches in detail would surpass the scope of this thesis. Generally, it seems more convincing that courts in Model Law

---

72 *See* Urteil [Judgment], (1988) 3 NJW-RR 1526 (GER BGH) 1527 (with further references at II.1).

73 *See* ZPO § 1032, 1040 (3) sentence 2 (GER). *Cf.* Urteil [Judgment], [2005] 3 SchiedsVZ 95 (GER BGH) 96, 97 (first stating that competence-competence would no longer exist under German law, even if agreed, but then clarifying that this only meant *final* competence-competence); *see also* Voit, »§ 1040 ZPO«, para. 3; *but see* Schwab, Walter, and Baumbach, *Schiedsgerichtsbarkeit*, chap. 6, para. 9 (wanting to restrict the term »*Kompetenz-Kompetenz*« to a power of *final* decision on competence); along this line, *see* Graves and Davydan, »Competence-Competence«, 158 (»*the German form of Kompetenz-Kompetenz*«); clarified ibid., at 167 (»*absolute Kompetenz-Kompetenz was abandoned in 1998*«); *see also* Born, *Commentary and Materials (2001)*, 854 (explaining that »*Kompetenz-Kompetenz*« in German historically meant the right to a final, non-reviewable decision); Sachs and Schmidt-Ahrendts, »Diverging Concepts of the Principle of Competence-Competence?«, 5 (»*original concept* [...] *meant true competence-competence*«).

74 Joseph, *Jurisdiction and Arbitration Agreements and Their Enforcement*, para. 11.35–11.36.

75 For case law favouring full review, *see* Born, *International Commercial Arbitration (2014)*, 1007, n. 223–34; *but see* ibid., n. 236–39 (case law from a few, mainly common law jurisdictions favouring a prima facie review). Canadian courts now apply full judicial review to legal questions but prima facie review to factual questions (*Union des consommateurs v. Dell*, 2007 SCC 34, para. 68, 84).

jurisdictions are allowed - but not obliged –[76] to engage in a full review of the validity, operability and existence of the arbitration agreement, based on the natural reading of the wording (unless the court »*finds*«)[77] and the drafting history.[78] The risk of delay is minimised if arbitration can be introduced or continued pending the court action as provided by article 8 (2) of the UNCITRAL Model Law.

c. Plea for limited review of operability issues by state courts

One decision by the Singapore High Court[79] suggests that the standard of review and proof does not have to be identical for all kind of challenges to an arbitration agreement. Although Singapore is a Model Law jurisdiction, the Singapore High Court recently relied on the negative effect to the competence-competence principle with the consequence of only engaging in a prima facie review concerning a challenge to the *existence* of an arbitration agreement.[80] In an obiter remark, it found that the same, limited standard of review does not necessarily apply to arguments that the arbitration agreement was invalid.[81]

Without further commenting on the merits of this particular decision and the existence/validity distinction,[82] the idea of differentiating between

---

76  *See* Born, *International Commercial Arbitration (2014)*, 1084, 1085 (§7.03[A][2][b][i]; on court discretion to limit review if faced with dilatory tactics); similarly: Joseph, *Jurisdiction and Arbitration Agreements and Their Enforcement*, para. 11.36 (»*not an absolute rule*«).

77  Born, *International Commercial Arbitration (2014)*, 1081, 1082.

78  *See* UNCITRAL Working Group on International Contract Practices, Report, 5th session, 67, para. 77 (1983) (rejection of a proposal to add »*manifestly*« to the wording).

79  *The Titan Unity*, [2013] SGHC 28; *see* Hwang, »The Titan Unity« (for a summary).

80  *The Titan Unity*, [2013] SGHC 28 [14, 18].

81  Ibid., para. 15 (finding that the rejection of the proposal to include »*manifestly*« into the language of the UNCITRAL Model Law only concerned the »*null and void*« alternative; referring to UNCITRAL Working Group on International Contract Practices, Report, 5th session, 67, para. 77 [1983]).

82  *See generally* Born, *International Commercial Arbitration (2014)*, 1085–88.

objections to an arbitration agreement when assessing the standard of review to be employed by state courts and the standard of proof to be met by a party raising objections shall be developed further. It is here proposed that a distinction should be made between objections that the invoked arbitration agreement is allegedly »*null and void*« (herein also: invalid) and an allegation that the agreement is (only) »*inoperative*« or »*incapable of being performed*« (herein also: inoperable). In contrast to the existence/validity distinction[83] and a validity/scope distinction,[84] the validity/operability distinction has yet received little attention. However, there are better reasons for a prima facie standard of review regarding the operability of an arbitration agreement than regarding its existence or validity:

- Even if an arbitration agreement contains elements that are difficult to perform, the intention to arbitrate rather than litigate is clear.[85]
- Operability issues concern practical or procedural matters, which hardly ever touch public interests justifying court intervention.[86]
- Inoperability may be overcome by effective interpretation, adaptation or supplementation, best provided by an arbitral tribunal or by supporting courts.[87]
- The assessment of the operability of arbitration agreements often requires a prognosis of the conduct of an arbitration institution or an

---

83  This issue has received a lot of attention by US Courts, *see e.g. Rent-A-Center*, 130 S.Ct. at 2778; *Buckeye v. Cardegna*, 546 U.S. at 444; *see also again The Titan Unity*, [2013] SGHC 28 [15]; on the corresponding issue of »*standard of proof*«, *see* Born, *International Commercial Arbitration (2014)*, 751–59.

84  For references and discussion, *see* Born, *International Commercial Arbitration (2014)*, 1093 et seq. (§7.03[A.2.c]).

85  *See* ibid., 772 (with further references). *See also supra* at pp. 158-163 (§8A, B).

86  *Cf. Howsam v. Dean Witter Reynolds*, 537 U.S. 79, 80 (2002) (»*Parties to an arbitration contract would normally expect a forum-based decisionmaker to decide forum-specific procedural gateway matters*«); *see in particular Gone to the Beach, LLC v. Choicepoint Services, Inc*, 514 F. Supp. 2d 1048, 1051 (DC W.D. Tenn. 2007) (»[...] *the only issue for the court to resolve is not whether arbitration is appropriate, but what kind of arbitration is required under the contract. This issue of contract interpretation is not properly before the court*«); *see also* Born, *International Commercial Arbitration (2014)*, 776.

87  *See infra* at pp. 424-427.

arbitral tribunal to be appointed - all of whom are third parties to the controlling state court action.[88]

Accordingly, if existence and validity of the arbitration agreement in the strict sense are not disputed, state courts faced with an arbitration defence should refer the parties to arbitration unless the arbitration agreement is *manifestly inoperative or incapable of being performed.* »*Manifestly*« here implies that the party invoking such objections has to argue and, if disputed, prove that attempts to perform the arbitration agreement have already been made, if necessary with the help of supporting courts, and that these attempts failed despite such party's cooperation. A general invocation of ambiguities, inconsistencies or defects of the arbitration agreement not affecting the essential element of consent should be plainly rejected by the court. It seems that the problems arising from hybrid arbitration agreements can be best accommodated by this approach as it restricts the potential conflict between the institution and rules chosen to what it is: an issue of procedure rather than an issue of jurisdiction.

This should also apply where a state court, in a jurisdiction that allows it, is sought to make a declaration on the validity of an arbitration agreement or, as it is formulated by section 1032 (2) ZPO (GER) on the admissibility or inadmissibility of arbitration.[89] This controlling competence does not entitle such court to decide on specifics of the arbitration procedure to be followed. Rather, as it will be argued in the following, decisions on procedural aspects, including applicable arbitration rules, are more appropriately based on supporting competences, which only apply if the parties have not sufficiently determined an arbitral body to render such decisions. In this context, a decision of the Higher Regional Court of Berlin[90] deserves a slightly critical - but admittedly formalistic - note:[91] The case concerned an arbitration clause referring to the - non-existent - German Chamber of Commerce. The parties could not agree whether they should submit their case to the DIS or

---

88  *See infra* at pp. 430 et seq. (§16A.II.2)
89  *See supra* at pp. 405-407 (§16A.I.2).
90  Beschluss [Decision], [2012] 10 SchiedsVZ 337.
91  It is formalistic since the competence to support the constitution of an arbitral tribunal and the declaratory control of arbitral competence are both exercised by the same court, the Higher Regional Court at the place of arbitration under section 1062 (1) ZPO (GER). The issue becomes more acute when the competences of the court that would otherwise have jurisdiction over the dispute have to be distinguished from those of the supporting court, *see infra* at n. 97.

one of the German Chambers of Foreign Trade, which are part of a world-wide network and also provide arbitration services at each of their locations. Although the court correctly observed that the only question reviewable under section 1032 (2) ZPO (GER) is whether there is a valid arbitration agreement capable of being performed that covers the dispute in question,[92] it nevertheless accepted an application requesting to declare expressly that arbitration proceedings against the respondent are admissible *under DIS Rules*.[93] Neither the general preservation of the arbitration agreement, nor the interpretative solution found by the court, which made the requested declaration in favour of DIS arbitration, are prone to criticism. Nevertheless, the lacking reference to section 1035 (4) ZPO (GER), which adopts article 11 (4) of the UNCTRAL Model Law, as an arguably more appropriate legal basis for such ruling is regrettable.[94]

d. A case for court support

The limitation of competence of *controlling* courts in relation to operability issues just proposed can be balanced with an increase of court *support*. Traditionally, it is the role of supporting courts at the place of arbitration to overcome procedural problems, in particular those relating to the constitution of the arbitral tribunal.

While a failure to agree on an arbitral institution or the applicable rules is an issue distinct from a failure to constitute an arbitral tribunal, the choice of the institution nevertheless influences arbitrator appointment as a preliminary exercise.[95] For this reason, it should be considered to apply the respective national enactments of article 11 (3) and (4) of the UNCITRAL Model Law by analogy to cases where already the determination of the competent arbitral institution or the application of certain rules is at stake.[96] The French Cour de Cassation decided accordingly in its decision of 20 February 2007:

---

92  Beschluss [Decision], [2012] 10 SchiedsVZ at 338.
93  In German: »*festzustellen, dass ein schiedsrichterliches Verfahren gegen die Antragsgegnerin nach den Schiedsregeln der Deutschen Institution für Schiedsgerichtsbarkeit e.V. (DIS), Verfahrensort Berlin, zulässig ist*« (ibid., at 337).
94  *See also* Münch, »§ 1032 ZPO«, para. 23, n. 117.
95  *See supra* at pp. 366-378 (§14B.III) on institutional appointment procedures.
96  *See also* Münch, »§ 1035 ZPO«, para. 29, 32.

It is the task of the supporting judge (*juge d'appui*), not of the court otherwise competent for the dispute, to decide which institution is competent.[97]

### i. Concerns about extensive state court competences

However, applying the lex arbitri's provisions on competences of state courts extensively, even analogously, is problematic. Article 5 of the UN-CITRAL Model Law provides:

> »In matters governed by this Law, no court shall intervene except where so provided in this Law«

Most arbitration laws of Model Law and non-Model Law jurisdictions likewise oppose an extension of the jurisdiction of state courts.[98] Excessive state court intervention is generally seen as an obstacle to the effectiveness of arbitration agreements:

> »Protecting the arbitral process from unpredictable or disruptive court interference is essential to parties who choose arbitration (in particular foreign parties).«[99]

Therefore, some voices argue in favour of a strict literal interpretation of all provisions allowing state courts to decide in an arbitration context.[100] They reason that support and interference are often difficult to tell apart.[101] In consequence of this view, the supporting judge would not be competent to determine the arbitral institution if the arbitration agreement was ambiguous or otherwise defective in this respect because the respective provisions of most arbitration laws do not expressly cover this case.

### ii. Arguments for more competences of supporting courts

On the other hand, it is the supporting judge's original task to help arbitrations faced with obstacles. For this reason, broad interpretation of the assisting competences of state courts, in contrast to their controlling

---

97  *UOP NV v. BP*, [2007] Rev. Arb. 776.
98  Lew, Mistelis, and Kröll, *Comparative International Commercial Arbitration*, para. 15.12.
99  *Explanatory Note* to the UNCITRAL Model Law 2006 para. 17.
100  *See e.g.* Saenger, »§ 1026 ZPO«, para. 1.
101  *Cf.* Kreindler, »The Role of State Courts in Assisting Arbitral Tribunals Confronted with Guerrilla Tactics«, 103 (at [1]).

competences, faces weaker headwind.[102] Arbitration-friendliness means not only non-interference of state courts with arbitral decision-making but also the enabling of the arbitration process and the enforcement of arbitration agreements through the courts at the place of arbitration, if necessary.

In order to retain the balance between self-restraint and support, it appears most appropriate to allow the supporting judge to determine an appropriate institution who is then responsible for constituting the arbitral tribunal and for determining the applicable rules.[103] This way the parties' expressed wish that the arbitral tribunal shall be appointed in accordance with institutional rules rather than by a state court like in an ad hoc arbitration is respected.

### iii. General duty to support arbitration?

As argued, provisions regarding the appointment of the arbitral tribunal, if the agreed appointment process fails, *could* be applied analogously if the parties disagree on the designated institution or if this institution ceased to exist or refuses to administer the case, for example because the parties agreed on arbitration rules other than those issued by the designated institution. A supporting court of an arbitration-friendly jurisdiction would probably follow a request for a clarifying in order in such a case.[104] However, given the lack of specific provisions concerning problems of organisation of an arbitration other than mere appointment issues, a state court might also take the position that it is not under a general duty to render a decision to interpret or adapt the parties' agreement.

While it is agreed that effective, arbitration-friendly jurisprudence means that an arbitration agreement would not be found incapable of being performed if state court support *is* available in order to solve a particular

---

102  Lew, Mistelis, and Kröll, *Comparative International Commercial Arbitration*, para. 15.13.

103  As it has been done by the French *juge d'appui, see e.g. Asland v. EEC*, [1990] Rev. Arb. 521; *see also République de Guinée I*, [1987] Rev. Arb. 371.

104  *See e.g. UOP NV v. BP*, [2007] Rev. Arb. 775; *but see Chayaporn*, (1985) 1987 Rev. Arb. 179 (*juge d'appui* rejecting a motion to confirm the competence of the administering institution by ordonnance de référé after the arbitral tribunal was constituted); *see also* Beschluss [Decision], [2012] 10 SchiedsVZ 159 (GER OLG, Munich) 168 (underlining the reserve function of provisions on state court support).

problem with the agreement,[105] it is open to debate whether such support *has to* be available in every jurisdiction party to the New York Convention.[106] This is a matter of interpreting article II (3) of the New York Convention. A restrictive, literal reading suggests that states and their courts only need to respect arbitration agreements that are both valid and clearly capable of being performed. An arbitration agreement that would only be operative with state court support could arguably be ignored. A duty to enforce arbitration agreements through supportive orders is not expressly stipulated. If such an understanding of article II (3) of the New York Convention was correct, the respect of arbitration agreements could be subject to the proviso that parties and other actors concerned, like arbitrators and institutions, are willing to cooperate.[107]

The French Cour de Cassation once expressed a different view. According to its jurisprudence, it follows from the right to effective justice under article 6 of the ECHR and general principles of international arbitration that state courts *have to* provide support if the parties' agreement to arbitrate is clear but suffers from implementation defects:

> »[L]'impossibilité pour une partie d'accéder au juge, fût-il arbitral, chargé de statuer sur sa prétention, à l'exclusion de toute juridiction étatique, et d'exercer ainsi un droit qui relève de l'ordre public international consacré par les principes de l'arbitrage international et l'article 6.1 de la Convention européenne des droits de l'homme, constitue un déni de justice qui fonde la compétence internationale du président du Tribunal de grande instance de Paris, dans la mission d'assistance et de coopération [...].«[108]

> [The impossibility of a party to access the judge, including the arbitrator, who is competent to decide on its claim under exclusion of the competence of all state court jurisdiction, and thereby to exercise a right which follows from international public policy that is protected by principles of international arbitration and article 6.1 of the European Convention on Human Rights is a denial of justice which invests the President of the Tribunal de Grande Instance with international competence to provide assistance and cooperation...].

---

105 Schlosser, *Das Recht der internationalen privaten Schiedsgerichtsbarkeit,* para. 441.

106 Steinbrück, *Die Unterstützung ausländischer Schiedsverfahren durch staatliche Gerichte,* 76.

107 Ibid., 81.

108 *Israel v. NIOC,* [2005] Rev. Arb. 694.

The ruling is interpreted as granting a right to state court support of arbitration notwithstanding a lack of concrete competencies in arbitration laws.[109] Overall, such finding is questionable. If state court support is not provided, with the consequence that an arbitration agreement is found incapable of being performed, this does not yet consist in a denial of justice as access to state courts on the merits would then be available. The ruling of the Cour de Cassation just cited concerned a very specific dispute between the state of Israel and an Iranian Oil Company. There, effective relief from state courts in Israel, which would have been otherwise competent, may not have been available because of the participation of state actors and the treaty-based claim. To ordinary commercial disputes between private actors, the same ratio can hardly be applied. Concerning a decision by the ICC Court not to let an arbitration proceed regarding some of multiple respondents, French courts recently rejected a denial of justice claim finding that the claimant could still sue those respondents either in their home jurisdictions or reintroduce a better reasoned request for arbitration with the ICC Court.[110]

Hence, it is difficult to derive a general duty to provide state court support to arbitration from the right to access to justice where specific jurisdictional provisions to this effect are missing. A mere reference to article II (3) of the New York Convention is inconclusive. The wording of this provision does not stipulate a duty to provide support, nor is the New York Convention generally concerned with the enforcement of arbitration *agreements*. Its main aim is to harmonise the recognition and enforcement of arbitral *awards*.[111] The issue if and how to avoid inoperability of arbitration agreements is therefore left to national law. Accordingly, state courts are only obliged to order support to the extent that their national arbitration law contains corresponding procedural means. International law does not impose such duty.[112]

---

109 Muir Watt, »Note, C.Cass., 01.02.2005«, 702–3; *but see* Steinbrück, *Die Unterstützung ausländischer Schiedsverfahren durch staatliche Gerichte*, 77 (questioning this understanding).

110 *ABC v. ICC*, [2011] Rev. Arb. 991 (FR TGI, Paris) at 996–97; as upheld, *ABC v. ICC*, [2011] Rev. Arb. 997 (CA, Paris). On whether the ICC is the correct opponent in an action for court support, *see infra* at p. 432.

111 *See* Steinbrück, *Die Unterstützung ausländischer Schiedsverfahren durch staatliche Gerichte*, 86–87 (with further references).

112 *See also* ibid., 89.

## iv. Reawakening European Arbitration Convention's article IV?

»Is the European Convention buried in oblivion? [...] Or is it more a sleeping beauty which merely waits to be kissed awake?«[113]

As noted, national arbitration laws address institutional arbitration only rudimentarily[114] and provisions on state court support of the constitution of the arbitral tribunal rely on the model of ad hoc arbitration. Consequently, situations in which a party seeks help from a state court in designating a competent institution or in determining the applicable arbitration rules are not contemplated. As a matter of principle, it is here suggested that a supporting court addressed in such a situation can and should take only such measures that are necessary in order to make the parties' agreement workable and that its competence to do so follows from an analogous application of provisions on the appointment of arbitrators by state courts. Instead of treating deficient institutional arbitration agreements like *ad hoc* agreements, it is preferable to keep state court interference at a minimum by helping the parties to make their agreement workable as an agreement »on *institutional* arbitration. However, as the legal situation is unclear, such state court support may be refused. For this reason, it is worth discussing how future amendments of national arbitration laws or even an international treaty, for example a revision of the New York Convention or a modernisation of the European Arbitration Convention, concomitant with a desirable extension of its territorial scope,[115] could address this problem.

The procedure to remedy pathological arbitration agreements under the European Arbitration Convention's article IV[116] is in fact already a good model only requiring a few adaptations to be practically useful in today's context. According to articles IV (3), (5) and (6) of the European Arbitration Convention the claimant can request a decision of the president of the competent chamber of commerce[117] to decide whether the arbitration shall

---

113 Kröll, »The Tale of a Sleeping Beauty«, 3.

114 *See supra* at pp. 91-106 (§4C.II.2).

115 On the application only to arbitrations between nationals of contracting states, *see supra* at p. 59, n. 15; on the resulting limited practical impact of this convention, *see generally* Born, *International Commercial Arbitration (2014)*, 117–18 (at §1.04 [A][2]; nevertheless describing it as one of the »*most important regional commercial arbitration treaties*«).

116 *See already supra* at pp. 95-97 (§4C.II.2.a.ii).

117 The contracting states where required to provide a list of chambers of commerce competent under Art. IV (European Arbitration Convention, art. X).

be an ad hoc arbitration or institutional arbitration and to designate the competent *»permanent arbitral institution«*. Article IV (3) sentence 4 further allows the arbitrators or the respondent to make such a request on behalf of the claimant. If the president of the chamber of commerce did not react, the applicant could address the *»Special Committee.«*[118] Of course, this procedure is very complicated[119] as it was especially designed for the context of East-West trade in a time of political tension and had hardly been used.[120]. Moreover, for Western states, the Paris Agreement[121] drastically revised the procedure under article IV shortly after the coming into force of the European Arbitration Convention. It not only replaced the competence of the Special Committee with that of a supporting court at the seat - which seems sensible - but also deleted all the alternatives relating to institutional arbitration here of interest - which is regrettable. Despite all these defeats, the European Arbitration Convention is a good starting point because it explicitly addresses the problem of supporting institutional arbitration and provides a solution[122] which - when stripped of all the historical ballast and superfluous elements - can be broken down to the following ideas:

---

118 Consisting of a member designated by the chambers of commerce of *»Eastern«* states - then defined as states where no ICC National Committee existed -, a member designated by the chambers of commerce of *»Western«* states - then defined as states where an ICC National Committee existed - and a President (European Arbitration Convention, Annex; *see also* Glossner, »Institutionelle Schiedsrichterernennung«, 558, rightly remarking that this grouping of countries with and without ICC National Committees is now out-of-date).

119 *See also* Steinbrück, *Die Unterstützung ausländischer Schiedsverfahren durch staatliche Gerichte*, 68 (»*praxisfern*« [impractical]); Schlosser, *Das Recht der internationalen privaten Schiedsgerichtsbarkeit*, 599 (»*toter Buchstabe*« [dead letter]).

120 *See* Glossner, »Institutionelle Schiedsrichterernennung«, 557 (recalling only two applications to the Special Committee until 1993, both of which were subsequently withdrawn).

121 Paris Agreement, art. 1 (replacing the here relevant paragraphs 3, 5 and 6 with a very concise provision on state court support regarding »*any difficulties arising with regard to the constitution or functioning of the arbitral tribunal*«).

122 *Cf. also* Glossner, »Institutionelle Schiedsrichterernennung«, 558 (reasoning that mere existence of the procedure under Art. IV may have led to amicable solutions).

- Disagreement of the form of arbitration - institutional or ad hoc - or the competent arbitration institution should not render the arbitration agreement inoperable.
- Both parties and the arbitral tribunal[123] should be able to request a decision of an independent authority on the form of arbitration and, if applicable, the competent institution and applicable rules at an early stage of the proceedings.
- If possible, such a decision should be binding on the arbitral institution designated and the arbitral tribunal eventually constituted.

The authority competent to make such a decision can be the supporting judge (*juge d'appui*), that is the competent court at the place of arbitration, as it seems to be the view of the French Cour de Cassation[124] and the main idea behind article 1 of the Paris Agreement. A corresponding paragraph should be added to article 11 of the UNCITRAL Model Law, clarifying that the supporting judge shall also decide in case of disagreement on whether the arbitration shall be conducted as ad hoc or institutional arbitration and designate the competent arbitral institution and the applicable rules if the parties cannot agree. In order to avoid any abuse of this procedure to delay the proceedings or undue interference with arbitral competence, such application by a party should only be admissible prior to the constitution of any arbitral tribunal or upon application with the consent of the tribunal itself.[125]

---

123 Here lies one of the main shortcomings of the Paris Agreement (*compare* Paris Agreement, art. 1, giving only »*the claimant*« a right to apply to the competent authority, *with* European Arbitration Convention, art. IV [3]).

124 *UOP NV v. BP*, [2007] Rev. Arb. 776; *but see ABC v. ICC*, [2011] Rev. Arb. 991 (TGI) (where a decision by the ICC Court to not let the arbitration proceed with respect to four of eight respondents was not deemed a constitution problem falling within the jurisdiction of the *juge d'appui*«); upheld by: *ABC v. ICC*, [2011] Rev. Arb. 997 (CA) (with a slightly different reasoning; stressing that the ICC was the wrong respondent). *See supra* at p. 97.

125 *See supra* at pp. 405–407 (§16A.I.2) on similar considerations underlying the German and English provisions for interlocutory declaratory relief on arbitral jurisdiction; *cf. also supra* at p. 254 (§11B.II.2) on the same time limit to freely terminate the Administration Contract; *cf. also* Pluyette, »Le Point de Vue Du Juge«, 362–63 (wanting to allow recourse to the supporting court upon application by the tribunal or the institution in case of serious difficulties although this power for the state court to intervene is not derived from the law but the will of the parties, the arbitrators or the institution alone) (not explaining how *state* court competence could be based

After being constituted, it is usually more appropriate for the arbitral tribunal than for a supporting court to decide on the role of an administering institution and the applicable rules.[126] Concerning the issue of a desirable binding effect of the supporting court's decision on the arbitral institution, the court procedure should at least involve a consultation of the prospective institution prior to the decision and the court should only order measures which the respective institution is willing to support.

To create, by way of an international treaty, an independent international authority that can be addressed to decide these kinds of issues would naturally be an even better solution as it would also work if there were disagreement on the place of arbitration. Of course, this would be a very long-term project and is currently just a vision rather than a concrete proposal.

## 2. The limited subjective res judicata effect

Another insufficiency of arbitration laws *de lege lata*, arguing for a revision as just encouraged, is that all actions contemplated to enforce arbitration agreements, whether for dismissal or stay of litigation, declaratory relief, an injunction, review of arbitral jurisdictional decisions or state court support, are adversarial actions directed solely against the other party to the arbitration agreement. They do not take positions and interests of tribunals and institutions into account.

Impliedly, when wondering why the parties to the *Bovis Lend v. Jay-Tech* case had started court action although their positions were not that much apart, the Singapore High Court also observed this.[127] However, in that case, SIAC's opposition hindered a compromise the parties might have easily agreed on: SIAC administered arbitration with an arbitrator appointed by the Institute of Architects.[128] The Singapore High Court finally ordered

---

on party autonomy alone). *See also supra* at 199-200 (§8C.II.2.e) on a potential action for the determination of the competent institution by a state court in situations caused by the CIETAC split under the SPC's 2015 reply.

126 Determining whether a tribunal is already constituted for the dispute may be difficult regarding multi-party and or multi-contract situations where some claims or some respondents are excluded by the administering institution (there rejecting a competence of the supporting court: *ABC v. ICC*, [2011] Rev. Arb. 991 [TGI]; upheld on different grounds by *ABC v. ICC*, [2011] Rev. Arb. 997 [CA]).

127 *Bovis Lend v. Jay-Tech*, [2005] SGHC 91 [23].

128 *See supra* at pp. 154-156 (§7C.IV.2).

parties to arbitrate ad hoc and thereby avoided the issue that SIAC did not participate in the litigation, which would have made a solution in favour of such compromise SIAC had objected to difficult to implement.

a. Institutions not concerned by inter partes effect of court orders

The problem relates to the limits of the res judicata effect of controlling and supporting courts decisions on arbitration. Of course, such decisions have some res judicata effect on the parties to the proceedings. For example, if a state court decides that an arbitration defence is valid and therefore dismisses a litigation suit, the claimant is hindered to start another action on the same matter, subject to a change in circumstance.[129]

Some also argue that an arbitral tribunal appointed or to be appointed is procedurally bound to respect such a state court decision as implying positively that the arbitration agreement was valid.[130] For a dismissal or stay decision, this is already debatable since the dispositive section of such decision would only provide for litigation being (currently) inadmissible, nothing more. Therefore, it is more convincing that in subsequent arbitration proceedings a state court's grant of the arbitration defence only has a »*sui generis*« or »*factual*« *res judicata* effect, which is based on considerations of good faith. A respondent raising an arbitration defence opposing the jurisdiction of the state court is barred from objecting to the tribunal's jurisdiction in the following arbitration proceedings pursuing to the principle of *venire contra factum proprium*.[131] However, such an argument is only convincing if exactly the same jurisdictional conflict - arbitration versus litigation - is again at stake before the arbitral tribunal. It is a distinctive situation if the respondent party, after having successfully raised an arbitration defence before the state court, would object to the arbitral tribunal's

---

129  *Cf.* Voit, »§ 1032 ZPO«, para. 9 (assuming such change in circumstances if the arbitration tribunal subsequently denies its jurisdiction); *see also* Schwab, Walter, and Baumbach, *Schiedsgerichtsbarkeit*, chap. 7, para. 3.

130  *See* Schwab, Walter, and Baumbach, *Schiedsgerichtsbarkeit*, chap. 7, para. 3; Huber, »Das Verhältnis von Schiedsgericht und staatlichen Gerichten bei der Entscheidung über die Zuständigkeit«, 74 (assuming this to be the prevailing opinion in Germany).

131  *See Zwischenentscheid*, [2006] 4 SchiedsVZ 167 (IHK Kassel) 168; *cf. also* Beschluss [Decision], 8 Sch 6/06, BeckRS 2007, 10067 (GER OLG, Celle, 31 May 2007) (claimant who introduced arbitration acts in bad faith if disputing valid arbitration agreement in enforcement proceedings).

jurisdiction arguing not in favour of the jurisdiction of state courts but of another arbitral tribunal appointed or confirmed by another institution or under different rules. Then, the verdict of bad faith would not be so easy to reach.

In any case, a state court's interpretation of an arbitration agreement could in no event force an arbitral institution or a certain arbitrator to accept or resume a mandate. This issue of restricted subjective bindingness is particularly relevant to hybrid arbitration agreements: An arbitral institution will not necessarily accept administering a case under rules other than its own only because a state court took the view that this would be a good way to interpret the arbitration agreement.

Simply suing *both* the other party and the administering institution, as done by some applicants before French courts,[132] is not an appropriate solution. Due to the general shortness of French courts' reasoning, this consideration is difficult to detect from the respective decisions.[133] However, it seems obvious that an arbitral institution is not the right respondent in litigation seeking a judgment on the merits of the dispute between the parties or in an application for court support, whereas the other arbitrant appears to be the wrong respondent in an action to engage contractual liability of the institution.[134] Both kinds of actions may have to be brought before different courts and sometimes even in different jurisdictions, in particular if the seat

---

132 *See e.g. République de Guinée I*, [1987] Rev. Arb. 371; *République de Guinée II*, [1987] Rev. Arb. 371; *République de Guinée III*, [1987] Rev. Arb. 371; for a similar, unsuccessful attempt, *cf. already Japan Time v. Kienzle France*, case no. H2827 (FR CA Paris, 11 July 1980) (unpublished) (strongly rejecting a disguised appeal against the ICC's prima facie acknowledgement of jurisdiction; the applicant was even ordered to compensate the ICC for the »*abusive*« action against it); as discussed by Fouchard, »Les institutions permanentes d'arbitrage devant le juge étatique«, 232

133 *But see* more recently *ABC v. ICC*, [2011] Rev. Arb. 1000 (CA) (clarifying that actions for support in the constitution of the arbitral tribunal have to be directed against the opponent in the arbitration rather than the institution; not specifying whether this made the action inadmissible or unfounded); less clear: *ABC v. ICC*, [2011] Rev. Arb. 991 (TGI) (only reasoning that a negative prima facie decision regarding some of multiple respondents was not a difficulty to constitute the tribunal; not discussing the question of the correct opponent).

134 *See infra* at pp. 444-461 (§16B).

of the administering institution is not identical with the place of arbitration.[135]

### b. The decision HKL v- Rizq II

The Singaporean case *HKL v. Rizq*[136] underlines the problem of limited powers of state courts to render decisions binding on institutions neatly. To recall, the Singapore High Court granted a stay in favour of arbitration and went very far in suggesting that SIAC would be able to administer the arbitration under ICC Rules. The stay was granted under the condition

>»that parties obtain the agreement of the SIAC or any other arbitral institution in Singapore to conduct a hybrid arbitration applying ICC Rules.«[137]

Obviously, this condition meant to accommodate the problem that it was uncertain if SIAC would agree to another hybrid arbitration under ICC Rules, a conduct that the Singapore High Court could not oblige it to with its ruling.

Fortunately, the parties then quite wisely agreed on arbitration administered by SIAC under SIAC rather than ICC Rules. Nevertheless, the High Court had to explain at length in an additional opinion that the cited condition imposed was valid. Indeed, HKL Group, despite agreeing with Rizq on straightforward SIAC arbitration, had filed an appeal arguing that the imposed condition was impossible to fulfil in light of article 1 (2) of the ICC Rules. The High Court defended its decision stressing that its opinion was »*in no way a judicial endorsement of a hybrid arbitration*« and clarified that

>»if either party were able to procure a straightforward ICC arbitration in Singapore, the condition would be satisfied as would be the case if either party were to procure a hybrid arbitration administered by any other arbitral institution in Singapore.«[138]

Astonishingly, the High Court did not clearly address whether the agreement on straightforward SIAC arbitration as concluded by the parties fulfilled the condition imposed. This may have been taken for granted. In any event, this postlude to the High Court's decision suggests that controlling state courts should avoid directing the parties how to overcome pathologies

---

135 *See supra* at pp. 71-74 (§4B.I.2) on this distinction.
136 *See supra* at pp. 174-177 (§8C.I.2).
137 *HKL v. Rizq I*, [2013] SGHC 5 [37].
138 *HKL v. Rizq II*, [2013] SGHC 8 [12].

if there are several conceivable ways, of which - as argued - hybrid arbitration will hardly be the most appropriate.[139] This applies in particular for solutions requiring the cooperation of third parties such as arbitral institutions as long as there is no mechanism to let them participate in the proceedings among the parties.[140]

c. Anti-arbitration injunctions to solve institutional conflicts?

As explained, the lack of participation of arbitral institutions in proceedings between arbitrants on the validity and interpretation of their arbitration agreement has the consequence that such proceedings cannot create binding obligations for such institutions.

For the same reason, it is also entirely inappropriate to react with an anti-arbitration injunction[141] to conflicts of institutions and institutional rules possibly raised by a hybrid arbitration agreement. Even in the worst-case scenario, that one party understands such agreement to refer to the institution designated to administer the proceedings and files its case there while the other starts parallel proceedings before the rules issuing institution, prohibiting either party to continue its action is an unsuitable reaction. The competent institution and the applicable rules are procedural issues best decided by the approached institutions and tribunals once constituted. Conduct motivated by different interpretations of a potentially hybrid arbitration agreement, many of which are defendable,[142] will hardly ever meet the thresholds of being oppressive, vexatious or abusive or causing substantial prejudice or irreparable harm to the parties.[143] Rather, such an injunction

---

139 Similiar: Fry, »HKL v. Rizq«, 461 (»*it need not have gone so far*« and »*could simply have exercised its power to stay the proceedings*«).

140 *See supra* at pp. 427-430 on an idea for reform.

141 Independent of general concerns raised by such instrument, *see supra* at pp. 407-409 (§16A.I.3).

142 *See supra* at pp. 161-163 (§8B) and pp. 207-209 (§9).

143 On different criteria applied to grant anti-*suit* injunctions, *see* Born, *International Commercial Arbitration (2014)*, 1290, 1294 (§ 8.03 [C.6]); *see also* Illmer, »Anti-Suit Injunctions«, 406 (criticising the vagueness of alternative criteria such as that of a »*substantive legal or equitable right*« or the requirement that the foreign proceedings are »*vexatious and oppressive*«) (with many references to case law). *see e.g. Itabo v. CDEEE*, 2005 WL 1705080 (S.D.N.Y. 18 July 2005) (at *5-6); *The Angelic Grace*, [1994] 1 Lloyd's Rep 172; specifically on anti-arbitration injunctions, *see*

would mainly interfere with interests of the respective institutions, which themselves do not participate in the court action and therefore cannot properly defend these interests.[144]

### 3. Review of and deference to institutional decisions

If provided in the administering institution's rules, a disagreement between the parties on the competence of the institution will often first be decided by such institution. A discontent party may then want to attack such decision before a state court. However, it is commonly suggested that appeals to state courts against an arbitral institution's decision are not available. Arguments put forward for this view are *inter alia* that the institution's activity is of mere »*administrative*« rather than judicial nature and that the institutional decision on jurisdiction is only provisional rather than final. The following paragraphs address these arguments, restricted to the issue of control of jurisdictional institutional decisions.[145] The purpose is to determine the appropriate procedural means available to parties' discontent with an institution's rejection of jurisdiction, including indirect means, which raise the issue of deference to institutional decisions.

### a. Myth of the »administrative nature« of institutional acts - part I

»Contrôler l'administration paraît être une nécessité vieille comme le monde [...].«[146]

To control the administration appears to be a necessity as old as the earth and still, some, arbitral institutions themselves in particular, use an allusion to the »*administrative nature*« of their activity as a kind of magic key to

---

*generally* Tang, *Jurisdiction and Arbitration Agreements in International Commercial Law*, 170; *see e.g. J Jarvis & Sons Ltd v Blue Circle Dartford Estates Ltd*, [2007] EWHC 1262 (TCC) [40].

144 But, exceptionally, an institution could provide an *amicus curiae* opinion, *cf.* e.g. the opinion rendered by the chairman of SIAC in *Persero v. Dexia Bank*, [2006] SGCA 41 [66].

145 A parallel controversy exists concerning institutional challenge decisions.

146 Dupuis, Guédon, and Chretien, *Droit administratif*, 34.

exclude all judicial review.[147] This argument, although highly popular,[148] is of little value in the consideration of control of and deference to institutional decisions for at least two reasons.[149]

First, even though the institution does not - or should not - decide a case on its merits,[150] some institutional decisions do affect the procedural position of parties or arbitrators. Accordingly, the qualification as »*merely administrative*« is incorrect if administrative is understood as being synonymous to procedurally insignificant. This applies in particular to the decision on whether there is sufficient evidence of a valid arbitration agreement for

---

147 *See in particular* LCIA Rules, art. 29 (1) (1998) (»*decisions are to be treated as administrative in nature and the LCIA Court shall not be required to give any reasons*«); *but see now* LCIA Rules, art. 29 (1) (2014) (»*Save for reasoned decisions on arbitral challenges*«); *see also* ICC Rules, art. 1 (2) (2012; 2017) a little more descriptive, providing that the »*Court does not itself resolve disputes. It administers the resolution of disputes by arbitral tribunals*«); from doctrine *see e.g.* Fouchard, »Les institutions permanentes d'arbitrage devant le juge étatique«, 241, 247; *cf. also* Münch, »vor § 1034 ZPO«, para. 74 (»*stets nur Verwaltungsorgan*« [always only an administrative organ]) (unclear about the consequences following from this finding); critical of this view: Khadjavi, *ICC-Schiedsordnung und deutsches Schiedsverfahrensrecht*, 47; Schlosser, *Das Recht der internationalen privaten Schiedsgerichtsbarkeit*, 601 (rightly concluding that a qualification as administrative is insufficient to exclude institutional activity from control).

148 In particular with French authors and commentators on ICC arbitration, *see e.g.* Gaillard and Savage, *Fouchard, Gaillard, Goldmann*, 603; Derains and Schwartz, *A Guide to the ICC Rules*, 185; Delvolvé, Rouche, and Pointon, *French Arbitration Law and Practice*, 87; Clay, *L'arbitre*, 1053; *see also* Chan, »Of Arbitral Institutions and Provisional Determinations on Jurisdiction, Global Gold Case«, 412 et seq.

149 *See also* Schöldström, *The Arbitrator's Mandate*, 419 (»*proper analysis is not aided by that distinction*«) (with further references); *contra* Fouchard, »Les institutions permanentes d'arbitrage devant le juge étatique«, 240 (suggesting that the whole review scheme applying to institutional decisions depends on their qualification as judicial or administrative). However, for the Cour de Cassation, the argument of administrative nature suffices to defend the lack of reasons given by the ICC Court for its decisions, *see Opinter v. Dacomex*, [1987] Rev. Arb. at 480 (»*ne remplissait pas une fonction juridictionnelle*«).

150 On institutional influence on the award, *see supra* at pp. 384-386 (§14B.VI).

the arbitration to proceed and to arbitrator challenge decisions[151] but also to other decisions such as the prolongation of the time limit for the award or the determination of the number of arbitrators or of the place of arbitration. All decisions that involve conflicting positions of the arbitrants would ordinarily be rendered by the tribunal or by a court. If arbitration rules derogate these functions to the institution, this does not change their nature as procedurally relevant.[152]

Second, even if one followed the traditional view of an »*administrative*« nature of all activities of arbitral institutions, it remains unclear why such a characterisation should have the consequence that state courts should not control the institution's decisions or why they should even pay deference to them. Possibly, this argument goes back to a time where - whether as a residue from absolutism or in misunderstanding of the principle of separation of powers - administrative authorities could not be sued before courts.[153] Today, this argument is simply misleading. Arbitral institutions are private service providers and not part of the public executive power, but even if they were, that would not make them immune to court control.[154]

Review schemes under civil procedure acts do not distinguish between judicial and administrative activities but between awards and other kinds of decisions.[155] Awards are generally reviewable in setting-aside proceedings, other decisions only if the law provides so expressly. When considering the reviewability of institutional decisions, it seems therefore more appropriate to enquire whether such decision is (analogous to) an award or if the law provides for a review mechanism independent of the nature of the decision.

---

151 Thereon, *cf. now* LCIA Rules, art. 29 (1) sent. 2 (2014).

152 *See also* Khadjavi, *ICC-Schiedsordnung und deutsches Schiedsverfahrensrecht*, 45, 47, 48.

153 *E.g.* in France, a restriction of judicial control of administrative decisions was long understood as a necessary corollary to the principle of separation of powers, contrary to the understanding in the United States (*see* Dupuis, Guédon, and Chretien, *Droit administratif*, 38–39).

154 *See infra* at pp. 444 et seq. (§16B) on motions directed against the institution itself.

155 A controversy where the administrative-judicial distinction may be of greater interest could be the dogmatic question if arbitral institutions have to comply with due process requirements. Practically, however, procedural due process requirements apply to the arbitration as a whole, independent of whether the arbitration is ad hoc or administered. This results in a contractual obligation of the institution to ensure enforceability by not contravening fair trial prerequisites through its own actions.

The distinction between judicial and administrative activities appears unhelpful.[156]

### b. Provisional nature of the institution's decision on jurisdiction?

Generally, the argument of the provisional nature of the institution's decision on jurisdiction is more convincing than that of its administrative nature. If a decision is not yet final, it should not be reviewed to avoid disruption.[157]

If an institution's decision is only provisional, meaning that it is subject to a further decision by the same or another authority, then it is sufficient if state courts can review the final decision on the matter to safeguards parties' rights. Institutions usually base their decision on jurisdiction on a prima facie review of the arbitration agreement only as it is the case under ICC Rules, SIAC Rules and Swiss Rules.[158] For this reason, they are often qualified as provisional. However, it is a mistake to derive such provisional nature from the standard of review applied. Rather, a decision is provisional if it has no final effects on the procedural situation. If the institution *declines* its competence, even if only based on a prima facie review, such a decision is - subject to state court control - factually final, because an arbitral tribunal will then not be appointed under the auspices of the institution. The file is not transmitted to any arbitral tribunal.[159] Accordingly, a negative institutional decision on jurisdiction is always final, while a positive decision that the arbitration may proceed is merely provisional because the appointed

---

156 This distinction is also rejected by Gerbay, »The Functions of Arbitral Institutions,« 150 et seq.

157 *But see generally* Stürner, *Die Anfechtung von Zivil*Urteilen, 192 (on interlocutory appeals against provisional decisions, admissible *e.g.* under English law but usually not available in civil law systems like that of Germany).

158 In contrast to CIETAC Rules, *see supra* at pp. 363-366 (§14B.II.2).

159 The only exception applies in multi-party situations where an institution could decide that the arbitration shall proceed with respect to some but not all respondents. Then, a claimant may try to request the tribunal to extend its mandate over those respondents previously removed by the institution (*see e.g.* the case *X v. Y.*, [2009] 27 ASA Bull. 762 [C.H. BG]; *criticised by* Mourre, »Institutional Arbitration Rules: Do They Deserve More Deference?«, 150–51).

arbitral tribunal is not bound by it and decides on the jurisdictional objection anew - with the exception of CIETAC appointed tribunals.[160]

### c. No interlocutory review of institutional confirmation of jurisdiction

Accordingly, if the jurisdictional decision of the institution is positive, it is acknowledged that the parties cannot challenge this purely administrative, preliminary decision before state courts. The institution transmits the case to the arbitral tribunal, which decides finally on its jurisdiction, usually without being bound by the institutional decision.[161]

Due to its provisional nature, a positive decision by an institution that there is prima facie a valid arbitration agreement providing for the competence of an arbitral tribunal to decide the case under the auspices of said institution cannot be considered an award. Even if one did not require an award to decide the merits of a dispute, the institutional ruling on jurisdiction does even finally decide a procedural question. Accordingly, a setting-aside motion is unavailable against such a decision.

In close to all jurisdictions, specific judicial review is equally unavailable. Institutional decisions on jurisdiction are not expressly addressed by national arbitration laws[162] and provisions on the interlocutory control of interim decisions on jurisdiction, exemplified by article 16 (3) of the UN-CITRAL Model Law, only apply to decisions by arbitral *tribunals*. They should not be applied by analogy to decisions by arbitral *institutions,* as the situation is not comparable. Article 16 (3) of the UNCITRAL Model Law and corresponding national provisions aim to enable early court review of the tribunal's jurisdiction in order to save the parties from wasting time, money and effort into proceedings that may lead to an award that would eventually be set aside. For this purpose, it seems unnecessary to already submit the institution's positive prima facie decision to such review since the arbitral tribunal will fairly soon reconsider the same, often rather formalistic issue, which would not usually require extensive written submissions, let alone evidence. It is therefore sufficient if parties can apply to state

---

160 *See supra* at pp. 361-366 (§14B.II); *see also* SPC's Interpretation of Arbitration Law, art. 13 (2) (2006).
161 Nater-Bass, »Prima Facie«, 613.
162 On the general lack of regulation of institutional arbitration, *see supra* at pp. 91-106 (§4C.II.2).

courts at the place of arbitration to review the tribunal's ruling on jurisdiction.

The situation is different under Chinese law, where the arbitration law provides arbitration commissions rather than tribunals with the competence to determine the tribunal's jurisdiction fully and not only preliminarily. Such decision is then equal to an arbitral tribunal's decision on jurisdiction and should theoretically be reviewable as such. However, it is unclear if Chinese courts would treat such a decision as an award capable of setting-aside under article 58 of the Arbitration Law (P.R.C.). Arguably, a discontent party would have to await the award on the merits if it missed the opportunity to hinder the Commission's ruling by applying to a People's Court for interlocutory declaratory relief under article 20 (1) sentence 2 of the Arbitration Law (P.R.C.).

d. Indirect court »review« of institutional decline of jurisdiction

If the institutional decision is negative and if the applicable arbitration law foresees such procedure, parties retain the right to seek a declaratory judgment from a state court on whether a binding arbitration agreement exists[163] or, before US courts, apply for a motion to compel arbitration.[164] While article 6 (6) of the ICC Rules expressly clarifies this, the availability of state court relief does not depend on the institution's rules.[165] In other words, an arbitration agreement is not extinguished by an institution's negative ruling on it. However, the state court would not *directly* review the institutional decision but rather evaluate the validity and operability of the arbitration agreement. The competent court may take the previous decision by the institution into account or ignore it, but it would not correct it.

The issue is then not one of limited control of institutional decisions but rather one of deference to them. Some authors wish for the courts to exercise more »*judicial self-restraint*« in view of a prior institutional

---

163 *See supra* at pp. 405-407 (§16A.I.2).
164 Thereon, *see e.g. Global Gold v. Robinson*, 533 F. Supp. 2d 442 (S.D.N.Y. 2008) (where a motion to compel arbitration was considered the most appropriate action while an action directed at the control of the institutional decision was found inadmissible).
165 *Contra* ibid., 445 (discussing to which extent the ICC Rules permit interlocutory review; this is due to the US understanding of competence-competence as an issue of contractual arbitrability; *see supra* at p. 416)

decision.[166] However, courts are not obliged to exercise such deference.[167] Moreover, the fact that most institutions do not give reasons for their decisions considerably diminishes their persuasive force.[168] It would also lead to considerable legal uncertainty if the standard of review depended upon whether the institution's experience was supposedly »*universally recognized*« or not.[169] The quality control thereby implied would probably do more damage to institutional arbitration than help it as any state court's decision differing from the institution's assessment would then be understood as criticism to the particular institution. Better reasons therefore support the view that a state court, when asked for a declaration on the validity of an arbitration agreement or a motion to compel arbitration, should respect only such institutional decision of which it is substantively convinced, independent of the authority of the institution, and otherwise provide an independent reasoning for its decision. However, such reasoning should take the institution's factual opposition to administering the case into account when evaluating whether the arbitration agreement is still capable of being performed - if necessary before another institution or ad hoc.

As noted, many legal orders neither provide for declaratory relief regarding an arbitration agreement's validity, nor for a motion to compel arbitration. In the majority of jurisdictions, it thus seems that a party discontent with an institution's decline of jurisdiction would be left without remedy, except for the contractual remedies against the institution considered

---

166 Wilske, »Ad Hoc Arbitration in Germany«, 846 (para. 34); *see generally* Mourre, »Institutional Arbitration Rules: Do They Deserve More Deference?«.

167 *Cf. also* ibid. 148 (on the prevailance of public policy over institutional rules).

168 *See supra* at n. 87.

169 *But see* Wilske, »Ad Hoc Arbitration in Germany«, 846 (para. 34); *cf. also* Rubino-Sammartano, *International Arbitration: Law and Practice*, 367 (para. 13.1) (»*several arbitral institutions rightly enjoy judicial ›deference‹*«); *cf. also Carte Blanche*, 888 F.2d 260, 266–67 (2nd Cir. 1989) (»*ICC Court is the best judge of whether its procedural rules have been satisfied, and when it certified the award as final, it certified that the procedural rules had been complied with to its satisfaction*«) (internal quotation marks omitted). Such arguments risk to create special law for the ICC Court since it is doubtful if state courts are sufficiently »*acquinated with the field*« to tell other »*legitimate*« institutions from »*a constant stream of new entrants*« (*cf.* Paulsson, »Moral Hazard in International Dispute Resolution«, 19–20).

below.[170] In particular, a claimant cannot simply start an action on the merits before a state court and then invoke the arbitration agreement, as this would be contradictory. One very uncertain option would be to file the case with another institution, hoping it would assume jurisdiction in light of the previous institution's decline and the respondent's conduct. Another, and here preferred,[171] possibility is to treat the institution's negative decision on jurisdiction as an obstacle to the constitution of an arbitral tribunal. The supporting court would then have to consider if the arbitration agreement was and still is valid and workable in light of the negative institutional jurisdiction decision, again raising the issue of possible deference just addressed.

III. State court powers to enforce (hybrid) institutional arbitration clauses

This section identified three important problems affecting state court actions seeking to enforce or challenge arbitration agreements *appearing* to designate one institution but another institution's rules. »*Appearing*« since it has been highlighted all along that the border between a true hybrid arbitration agreement, by which both parties intentionally opt for such procedural arrangement, and uncertain and ambiguously drafted agreements is a very thin line drawn by the parties' interests, arguments and pleadings before the state court.[172]

These three main problems of state court procedure concerning possibly hybrid arbitration agreements are:

- Arbitration laws address the allocation of competence to determine or overcome operability issues of institutional arbitration agreements insufficiently.
- Arbitral institutions are not legally and technically bound by any state court decision between arbitrants.
- Uncertainties persist regarding the kind and extent of control of and deference to institutional decisions.

This is the approach herein proposed: Controlling courts including courts competent over the dispute in hypothetical absence of a valid arbitration agreement, should restrict their review of the question if an invoked

---

170  *See infra* at pp. 444 et seq. (§16B).
171  *See supra* at pp. 422-430.
172  *See supra* at pp. 177-184 (§8C.I.3).

arbitration agreement was capable of being performed to a prima facie test. If ambiguities, inconsistencies or defects of the arbitration agreement did not affect the essential element of consent, they should be plainly rejected by such controlling courts, as they are then only optional elements of procedure rather than of jurisdiction. Such optional elements of procedure, *e.g.* the competent institution or the applicable arbitration rules, are better determined by the courts responsible to support arbitrations. If and as long national laws do not clearly address obstacles in determining the competent institution and rules, supporting courts' competences can be based on an analogy to the provisions in national laws allowing state courts to help the constitution of an arbitral tribunal.

Such extensive competence of supporting courts does not yet overcome the problem that a dispute about the enforcement of an institutional arbitration agreement will often not only concern the parties to such agreement but also touch upon interests of both an institution designated to administer a case and, if different, an institution whose rules shall be applied. Orders by a state court made in proceedings between the arbitrants can logically never bind an institution to accept a case or allow the use of its rules. This limited subjective res judicata effect calls to consider additional dimensions of enforcing hybrid arbitration agreements: the parties'-institution[173] and institution-institution[174] relationships.

Finally, this section has already identified the common argument of a merely »*administrative nature*« of institutional decisions as confusing and unhelpful when considering possible state court actions available against them, an aspect that will be expanded in the next section.[175] However, when considering an institution's prima facie decision on jurisdiction, it is a valid argument to exclude such decision from direct review where it is only provisional, meaning a preliminary decision not binding on the arbitral tribunal. This generally applies to positive institutional decisions on jurisdiction.

For negative institutional decisions on jurisdiction, strict »*review*« is equally unavailable but that does not mean that a discontent party does not have legal means to enforce an arbitration agreement *despite* such decision. It may still apply for either a declaratory decision on the validity of the arbitration agreement or motion to compel arbitration, where the law so allows, or for state court support in constituting an arbitral tribunal. The state court would then not control the institutional decision as such but reconsider

---

173  As discussed *infra* at pp. 444 et seq. (B).
174  As discussed *supra* at pp. 272 et seq. (§13).
175  *Infra* at pp. 444-447 (§16B.I).

all jurisdictional arguments de novo. The idea of thereby paying considerable deference to the institution's prior decision is herein rejected. On the one hand, it has to be avoided that a special regime is created for decisions of a few reputed institutions like the ICC Court, only. On the other hand, state courts should not enter into a case-by-case evaluation of quality and reasoning - if any - of an institutional decision in proceedings in which the institution who rendered such decision would usually not even participate. The better approach seems to be to allow state courts to consider the relevant jurisdictional question de novo without judging the institution or the institutional decision as such.

## B. Enforcement in relation to the designated institution

The previous section concerned state court remedies available to parties to the arbitration agreement who do *not* agree on the interpretation and implementation of hybrid or of other unusual institutional arbitration agreements. Thereby, the lack of participation and consideration of interests of the administering institution was already identified as a potential problem. It is now time to consider if this problem loses significance if one regards the direct causes of action available to arbitrants who *do* agree on how their arbitration agreement should be implemented against the administering institution.

Contrary to the procedural remedies discussed above, such direct causes of action against the arbitral institution are predominantly contractual in nature. The main questions to ask are whether arbitral institutions' services are at all justiciable before ordinary courts, calling for a reconsideration of the »*administrative nature*«-argument already criticised, what standards apply to the liability of arbitral institutions and what remedies may be ordered by courts - only damages or also specific performance and termination.

## I. Justiciability - the myth of the »administrative nature« - part II

Another conceivable reading of the »*administrative nature*« argument refuted above,[176] is to draw a parallel to acts by administrative authorities belonging to the judiciary, like court registries for example, also called

---

176 *See supra* at p. §16A.II.3.a

administrative acts of the judiciary (German: »*Justizverwaltungsakte*«;[177] French: »*actes extrajudiciaires*« or »*d'organisation de justice*«). German doctrine defines these acts as all acts that are part of the administration of justice without being part of the jurisprudential function, meaning that they do *not* directly influence or prepare the decision-making process.[178] A similar concept also follows from French jurisprudence in the matter *Hénin* regarding the inadmissibility of an action for review (»*recours pour excès de pouvoir*«) of an instruction by the president of the court to a court clerk (»*greffier de la cour*«) regarding the handling of certain submissions and documents in pending proceedings. The case suggests that the answer to the seriously difficult question of the competence (»*question de compétence de difficulté sérieuse*«)[179] to review an act of a body belonging to the judiciary depends on whether the reproached act affected the decision-making process and outcome of the case. Acts potentially relevant for the outcome of a pending case are not subject to direct, interlocutory review, as this would interfere with the powers of the judiciary, whereas mere administrative acts of judicial bodies could be subject to review by administrative courts for excess of powers.[180]

While administrative acts of the judiciary would ordinarily fall within the jurisdiction of administrative courts, as it is the case in France for example,[181] German law provides for a special competence of ordinary courts found to be more closely associated to the issues at stake.[182]

---

177  *Cf.* EGGVG § 23 (GER).

178  Rathmann, »§ 23 EGGVG«, para. 1.

179  *Hénin,* Case no 95318 (FR CE, 5 November 1976).

180  *Cf. Hénin,* Case no 02051 (FR TdC, 2 May 1977) (where it was found decisive that the instruction to the court clerk concerned the admissibility of submissions; hence qualified as jurisdictional rather than administrative). On the difficult distinction between acts on the organisation of the judiciary which may be subject to review before administrative courts in France and acts concerning the administration of justice not subject to direct review, *see generally* Brown, Bell, and Galabert, *French Administrative Law*, 136–37 (with examples and references to court decisions).

181  *See* Aden, »Der Verfahrensverstoß des Schiedsgerichtsinstituts«, 760 (finding that an understanding of institutional acts as quasi-sovereign but non-judicial would theoretically have the consequence that French administrative courts were competent to review the ICC Court's decisions).

182  *See* Pabst, »vor § 23 EGGVG«, 1 (also stressing that the provisions on review of administrative acts of the judiciary specify the constitutional right to access to justice).

Based on these considerations, administrative acts of the judiciary are not reviewable and appealable in the same way as court decisions. However, they can still be subject to court action - either before administrative or ordinary courts - *directly* introduced against the authority or the state whereby the applicant could claim to be violated in its personal rights or that the authority exceeded its powers.

If one wanted to draw such parallel between decisions of arbitral institutions and administrative acts of the judiciary, the »*administrative nature*« argument commonly employed would therefore not exclude court control of institutional' acts but it would argue in favour of a direct control against the institution itself rather than an appeal-like control in proceedings between the arbitrants. Of course, such direct actions against an institution would clearly fall within the jurisdiction of ordinary and not administrative courts in light of the private status of modern arbitral institutions.[183]

Herein, it is preferred to stress the »*contractual*« rather than administrative nature of institutional decisions,[184] as this understanding seems less confusing and controversial and would also result in potential direct review. The arbitral institution rendering a decision on jurisdiction - whether positive or negative - acts in performance of contractual obligations, hence it could, in principle, be sued for breach of contract if it fails to fulfil this obligation with the required diligence.[185]

In no event could an emphasis on the non-judicial nature of institutional activity, even to the extent that this postulate was true, convincingly exclude arbitral institutions' activity from control altogether. To the contrary, only if the institution provided a judicial service, judge-like immunity may be arguable but otherwise it should be treated like any other service provider.[186] As Pierre Lalive suggested,[187] the argumentation of institutions trying to escape judicial control by on the one hand arguing to act as mere

---

183  *See supra* at pp. 110-116 (§5B).

184  *See e.g.* Reiner and Aschauer, »ICC Rules«, para. 140 (qualifying the ICC Court's prima facie decision as a contractual notice).

185  *See supra* at pp. 362-363 (§14B.II.1) on the preferable distinction of an institutional decision on jurisdiction from the institution's contractual acceptance of a case. However, if institutional obligations are understood as best efforts obligations only, an argument that the decision on jurisdiction was »*wrong*« should be insufficient to engage liability, *see infra* at pp. 452-455 (§16B.II.2).

186  *Cf.* Münch, »vor § 1034 ZPO«, para. 74 (wanting to allow contractual actions to enforce all institutional obligations deemed administrative).

187  »Note, CA Paris, 15.09.1998«, 117.

administration but on the other hand assuming privileges like the judiciary reminds of the fable of »*The bat and the two weasels*« by Jean de La Fontaine. There, a bat first argues to belong to the family of birds, then to the family of mice to save itself twice from being eaten.[188]

At the outset, institutional acts are therefore justiciable on the basis of contract. That does not mean however, that contractual actions against arbitral institutions are likely successful on the merits as the following considerations will underline. Moreover, the relationship between the procedural remedies addressed in the previous section and the direct remedies against institutional breaches of contract will have to be clarified.

## II. Liability of arbitral institutions

> »[T]oute partie à une convention, fût-elle une association chargée d'organiser un arbitrage, engage sa responsabilité dès lors qu'elle manque aux obligations contractées«[189]

> [Every party to a contract, even an institution with the task to organise an arbitration, is liable if it fails to meet its contractual obligations]

It astonishes a little that the Paris Court of Appeal in the famous *Cubic* case found it even necessary to express this thought, which is the basic idea of contract law in any jurisdiction: Who concludes a contract and fails to meet its obligations thereunder may be liable to the other party.

However, actions against arbitration institutions are still rare and the possible contractual liability of these institutions is a rather new phenomenon. Moreover, the jurisprudence in the *République de Guinée* affair, as discussed above, incidentally suggested that arbitral institutions might not need to fear any consequences for their wrongdoings.[190] Furthermore, while contractual theories on arbitration today prevail, residues of more jurisdictional, status-oriented approaches are still reflected in some jurisdictions' liability regimes for arbitrators and arbitral institutions as shall be outlined in the following.

---

188 An English translation of the fable is printed *e.g.* in de La Fontaine and Billinghurst, *A Hundred Fables of La Fontaine*, 66.

189 *Cubic v. ICC*, [1999] Rev. Arb. 111.

190 *See supra* at pp. 266-268 (§11C.II); *République de Guinée V*, [1988] Rev. Arb. 657.

## 1. Excursus: contractual liability of arbitrators

Although this thesis is more concerned with institutional conduct and responsibility in regard of parties' procedural arrangements, it is helpful to outline the basics of arbitrator liability first in order to better understand the institutional liability regime.

Generally, arbitrators are not fully liable for their acts and omissions committed in their quasi-judicial function.[191] Immunities or at least limitations of liability exist in all legal systems, either expressly provided by statute or developed by jurisprudence. Furthermore, institutional arbitration rules grant arbitrators protection from civil claims by the parties.[192]

### a. Statutory provisions limiting arbitrator liability

Some arbitration laws expressly provide that arbitrators are not liable except for intentional acts or acts committed in bad faith. An example is section 29 (1) of the English Arbitration Act, which provides:

> »An arbitrator is not liable for anything done or omitted in the discharge or purported discharge of his functions as arbitrator unless the act or omission is shown to have been in bad faith.«

Similarly, Singapore's Arbitration Act states that an arbitrator shall not be liable for

> »(*a*) negligence in respect of anything done or omitted to be done in the capacity of arbitrator; and

> (*b*) any mistake in law, fact or procedure made in the course of arbitral proceedings or in the making of an arbitral award.«[193]

Other common law jurisdictions contain alike limitations.[194]

A few civil law jurisdictions approach the issue the opposite way. Rather than expressly limiting arbitrator's liability, some statutes positively detail

---

191  *See* Götz, »Der Schiedsrichter zwischen Dienstleistungserbringung und Richtertätigkeit«, 313 (»*allgemeine Meinung*« [general opinion]).

192  Born, *Law and Practice (2012)*, 145 (§7.06).

193  IAA § 25 (SG).

194  For references, *see* Born, *International Commercial Arbitration (2014)*, 2028, n. 415–16 (§13.06[C][2][a]).

for which breaches of obligations the arbitrator may be liable.[195] It follows, by way of an *argumentum e contrario*, that the arbitrator is not liable for other oversights like rendering an award that is perceived as legally »*wrong*«, annullable or unenforceable.[196] This is also the approach taken by Chinese law, which provides that arbitrators, next to being removed from the competent commission's panel (if listed), shall »*assume legal liability according to law*«[197] in case or »*serious*« private engagements with a party or engaging in embezzlement, bribery, graft or rendering an award that »*perverted*« the law.[198]

Other arbitration statutes, including the UNCITRAL Model Law, German arbitration law, French arbitration law, the FAA (US)[199] and Swiss law, are silent on the matter. This may be due to the understanding that an arbitrator's contract, and hence arbitrator's liability, is not a procedural issue to be covered by the lex arbitri in the strict sense but a contractual question to be governed by the contract's terms, which may include arbitration rules, the regime of the arbitrator's contract and general contract law. Nevertheless, jurisprudence and or doctrine in these jurisdictions still recognise - to differing degrees as outlined below - a need to protect arbitrators from liability risks that could affect their independence.

b. Judicial rulings on arbitrator liability

Where arbitrator liability is not excluded by statute, courts have underlined the quasi-judicial function of arbitrators to protect them from being sued

---

195 *Cf.* ibid., 2028–29 (§13.06[C][2][a]; mentioning Spain, Italy and Austria as jurisdictions with an »*affirmative*« approach to liability with references to the relevant provisions).

196 *Cf.* ibid. (§13.06[C][2][a]; concluding that the purpose of such provisions is to limit liability to »*to a relatively narrow set of cases*«).

197 Which may refer to criminal and civil liability.

198 Arbitration Law art. 38, 34 (4), 58 (6) (P.R.C.).

199 *But see* Born, *International Commercial Arbitration (2014)*, 2034 (§13.06[C][2][b]; suggesting to refer to the policies underlying the Revised Uniform Arbitration Act, a widely adopted model law for state laws on domestic arbitration, also in international cases); *see* (Revised) Uniform Arbitration Act 2000 § 14 (a) (US): »*An arbitrator or an arbitration organization acting in that capacity is immune from civil liability to the same extent as a judge of a court of this State acting in a judicial capacity.*«

successfully. US jurisprudence in particular assumes that arbitrators enjoy a very broad immunity just like judges, extending even to intentional misconduct or gross negligence.[200]

In contrast, German courts have refused to apply the statutory immunity privilege for judges, which is enacted in the civil code,[201] to arbitrators. This is convincing. Since arbitration existed long before the enactment of the civil code, any gap in the code with respect to protecting arbitrators from liability is probably intentional. Moreover, given that the arbitrator is connected to the parties by contract, unlike a judge, the interests are not comparable. Different from a judge, an arbitrator could negotiate a limitation of liability clause for its contract.[202] Therefore, there is no room for judicial analogy requiring an unintentional gap in the law and comparability of the

---

200 *See e.g. Greyhound Lines*, 701 F.2d 1181, 1185 (6th Cir. 1983) (»*his purpose is ›functionally comparable‹ to a judge and, consequently, he is clothed with an immunity that is analogous to judicial immunity*«); *but see also Ernst v. Manhattan*, 551 F.2d 1026, 1034 (5th Cir. 1977) (clarifying that this immunity does not extend to the breach of the obligation to make a timely decision, considered as a contractual rather than quasi-judicial duty); *see generally* Townsend, »Recourse against the Arbitrator«, 115–16 (with further references to U.S. case law); *cf. also* (Revised) Uniform Arbitration Act 2000 § 14 (a) (US) (quoted *supra* at n. 199).

201 *See* BGB § 839 (2) (GER): »*Verletzt ein Beamter bei dem* Urteil *in einer Rechtssache seine Amtspflicht, so ist er für den daraus entstehenden Schaden nur dann verantwortlich, wenn die Pflichtverletzung in einer Straftat besteht. Auf eine pflichtwidrige Verweigerung oder Verzögerung der Ausübung des Amts findet diese Vorschrift keine Anwendung*« [If an official breaches his official duties in a judgment in a legal matter, then he is only responsible for any damage arising from this if the breach of duty consists in a criminal offence. This provision is not applicable to refusal or delay that is in breach of duty in exercising a public function]. The main criminal offences judges may make themselves guilty of under German law are accepting an undue advantage and corruption (»*Vorteilsnahme*«, »*Bestechlichkeit*«) or perverting the course of justice (»*Rechtsbeugung*«) (*see* Götz, »Der Schiedsrichter zwischen Dienstleistungserbringung und Richtertätigkeit«, 312).

202 Gal, *Die Haftung des Schiedsrichters*, 176–77; Strieder, *Rechtliche Einordnung und Behandlung des Schiedsrichtervertrages*, 72; Hausmann, »Der Schiedsrichtervertrag«, 151–52; *contra* Götz, »Der Schiedsrichter zwischen Dienstleistungserbringung und Richtertätigkeit«, 316 (ignoring this fact); Prütting, »Die rechtliche Stellung des Schiedsrichters«, 237 (arguing that arbitrator immunity is not predominantly an interest of the contract partners but a public interest).

problem not regulated to a situation governed by the law.[203] Nevertheless, the BGH, other German courts and the prevailing opinion in legal doctrine usually limit the arbitrator's liability to acts amounting to criminal offences.[204] They reach this result by assuming an implied term of the arbitrator contract, if liability is not already expressly limited for example by the referenced arbitration rules.

Some restriction of liability is, on the basis of contract law, therefore assumed even in jurisdictions rejecting general judge-like procedural immunity for arbitrators. This also applies in France, where the Cour de Cassation stresses that arbitrators should be independent in exercising their judicial function, that procedural means to challenge the arbitral award have priority over any actions for liability of the arbitrator and that arbitrators only have best efforts obligations in exercising their mandate, not owing a specific result or success of the arbitration.[205] Generally, a potentially »*wrong*« decision alone cannot engage liability.[206]

c. Arbitration rules excluding arbitrator liability

In the context of institutional arbitration, the question of arbitrator immunity granted by statute or jurisprudence is largely irrelevant. Close to all institutional rules provide for *contractual* exclusions of arbitrators' liability for the exercise of their procedural and quasi-judicial functions except in case of intentional wrongdoing,[207] although some rules also allow liability

---

203  Rüthers, Fischer, and Birk, *Rechtstheorie*, para. 888.

204  *See essentially* Urteil [Judgment], [1954] 15 BGHZ 12 (GER) at 14–15; from doctrine, *see e.g.* Wolff, »Grundzüge des Schiedsverfahrensrechts«, 111; Schwab, Walter, and Baumbach, *Schiedsgerichtsbarkeit*, chap. 12, para. 9; Gal, *Die Haftung des Schiedsrichters*, 194 et seq.; with a slightly different reasoning, *see also* Lachmann, *Handbuch für die Schiedsgerichtspraxis*, para. 4331.

205  *See* CNCA *v. Y, Z, B (arbitrators)*, [2011] Rev. Arb. 943 (FR C.Cass) at 945.

206  *Cf.* Poudret and Besson, *Comparative Law of International Arbitration*, para. 446 (referring to Swiss and Austrian jurisprudence to this effect).

207  *See e.g.* ICC Rules, art. 40 (2012) = art. 41 (2017); LCIA Rules, art. 31 (2014); SIAC Rules, art. 34 (1) (2013) = art. 38 (1) (2016); AAA-ICDR Rules, art. 38 (2014); Swiss Rules, art. 45 (1) (2012); DIS Rules, art. 44 (1998); *see generally* Born, *International Commercial Arbitration (2014)*, 2035–37 (§13.06[C][3]);        *but        see        CIETAC*

for gross negligence in case of ordinary breaches of contract (rather than quasi-judicial acts).[208] The terms of these provisions generally become incorporated into the arbitrator's contract. With respect to *arbitrator* liability, there is little dispute on the validity of these provisions. In light of the acceptance of restricted arbitrator liability under many statutes and by most courts, even without express agreement, it is unlikely that any court would deem such term unfair. This can be different for exclusions of liability for arbitral institutions, which will be discussed below.

2. Application of the same principles to arbitral institutions?

Some arbitration laws - mainly of common law jurisdictions - also exempt arbitration institutions from liability. An example is section 74 of the English Arbitration Act, which provides:

»(1) An arbitral or other institution or person designated or requested by the parties to appoint or nominate an arbitrator is not liable for anything done or omitted in the discharge or purported discharge of that function unless the act or omission is shown to have been in bad faith.

(2) An arbitral or other institution or person by whom an arbitrator is appointed or nominated is not liable, by reason of having appointed or nominated him, for anything done or omitted by the arbitrator (or his employees or agents) in the discharge or purported discharge of his functions as arbitrator.

(3) The above provisions apply to an employee or agent of an arbitral or other institution or person as they apply to the institution or person himself.«

A similar provision can be found in section 25A of Singapore's IAA and some US courts have equally applied a presumption of immunity to acts of arbitral institutions.[209]

---

Rules (2012; 2015) (not containing such restriction; *but see supra* at p. 449 and n. 198 on a limitation arguably following from an *argumentum e contrario* to Chinese statutory provisions positively providing for liability).

208 *Compare* DIS Rules, art. 44 (1) *with* (2) (1998); *but see e.g.* Swiss Rules, art. 45 (1) (2012) (not making such distinction and applying a »*gross negligence*« standard to all, including quasi-judicial acts).

209 *See e.g. Austern v. The Chicago Board Options Exchange*, 716 F. Supp. 121, para. 1, XVI YCA 191, 192, para. 1 (S.D.N.Y. 1989) (»*This quasi-judicial immunity has been expanded to protect associations, boards and other organizations sponsoring and administering arbitrations*«); officially left open by *Global Gold v. Robinson*, 533 F. Supp. 2d at 447–48

The main idea behind such legislation or jurisprudence is to avoid that parties discontent with an award circumvent the protection of the institutional arbitrators against liability as just outlined by simply suing the institution. However, if one understands the Administration Contract as a contract for services, rather than for works,[210] and if one accepts that even in institutional arbitration, the arbitrators' contracts are concluded with the parties (representation theory)[211] rather than the institution (performance theory),[212] there is no risk of such vicarious liability of the institution anyway.[213] The institution only has a best efforts obligation (*obligation de*

---

(»*recise contours of arbitral immunity are less important*«; but with some tendency towards quite broad immunity: »*If administrative institutions* [had] *to defend their decisions in the national courts of any country in the world, the expenses of defending such potentially far-flung suits could constrain their judgment*«); *see also* Born, *International Commercial Arbitration (2014)*, 2035–36, n. 472 (§13.06[C][3]); Gaillard and Savage, *Fouchard, Gaillard, Goldmann*, para. 1088–1, n. 166, 177 (with further references).

210 *See supra* at pp. 235-236 (§11A.I).

211 Assimilating the contractual model to that in an ad hoc arbitration, this theory seems to be the internationally prevailing opinion, *see e.g.* Waincymer, *Procedure and Evidence*, para. 2.04; Gaillard and Savage, *Fouchard, Gaillard, Goldmann*, para. 1106; Schwab, »Schiedsrichterernennung«, 508; Schwab, Walter, and Baumbach, *Schiedsgerichtsbarkeit*, chap. 11, para. 3–5. The institution's agency power follows from the Administration Contract (*contra* Rubino-Sammartano, *International Arbitration: Law and Practice*, 374–75, para. 13.5; Vogt, »Der Schiedsrichtervertrag nach schweizerischem Recht«, 79), procedurally supported by the *lex arbitri's* provisions on the appointment of arbitrators by third parties.

212 For this view quite popular in Germanic, civil law doctrine, *see e.g.* Hausmaninger, »Rights and Obligations of the Arbitrator with Regard to the Parties and the Arbitral Institution«, 37; Schäfer, *Die Verträge zur Durchführung des Schiedsverfahrens*, 1:204, 383; Schlosser, »§ 1025 ZPO«, vol. 9, para. 7; Saenger, »vor § 1025 ZPO«, para. 11; Münch, »vor § 1034 ZPO«, para. 68; Voit, »§ 1035 ZPO«, para. 22 (»*in der Regel*« [usually]); *see also* Vogt, »Der Schiedsrichtervertrag nach schweizerischem Recht«, 82, 83 (assuming the Administration Contract to be a contract for the benefit of a third party; a construction rightly rejected as unnecessary by Schöldström, *The Arbitrator's Mandate*, 411).

213 In contrast, under the performance theory - for this very reason herein rejected - arbitrators would conceptually be subordinates, with the consequence that the institution might have to stand up for their wrongdoings

*moyen*) to administer the arbitration in respect of the parties' agreement and the applicable rules. It is not responsible for potentially »*wrong*« decisions of the arbitrators.

Accordingly, civil law jurisdictions in particular see no need to grant general immunity or broad liability exclusions to arbitral institutions. However, liability limitations in arbitration rules usually extend to the institution as well. The current liability limitation provision under ICC Rules shall serve as an illustration:

> »The arbitrators, any person appointed by the arbitral tribunal, the emergency arbitrator, the Court and its members, the ICC and its employees, and the ICC National Committees and Groups and their employees and representatives shall not be liable to any person for any act or omission in connection with the arbitration, except to the extent such limitation of liability is prohibited by applicable law.«[214]

The efficiency of such provisions is often in doubt. If arbitral institutions do not exercise judicial functions, as many of them constantly stress,[215] they cannot enjoy judge-like immunity. Rather, they should be subject to contractual liability like any other service provider.[216] Already in the *Cubic* case, the Paris Court of Appeal remarked in an obiter dictum that the validity of the very broad liability exclusion under the ICC Rules (1998) was far from certain.[217]

Then, in January 2009, the Paris Court of Appeal, held in *SNF v. ICC*:

> »La clause élisive de responsabilité qui autorise la CCI à ne pas exécuter son obligation essentielle en tant que prestataire de services non juridictionnels doit être réputée non écrite dans les rapports entre la CCI et une partie dès lors que la clause contredit la portée du contrat d'arbitrage.«[218]

---

(*cf.* Münch, »vor § 1034 ZPO«, para. 70, on arbitrators as auxiliary persons [»*Hilfspersonen*«] of the institution).

214 ICC Rules, art. 40 (2012) = art. 41 (2017); even broader: ICC Rules, art. 34 (1998). For other institutions, *see supra* at n. 207 (all provisions extending liability restrictions to the institution and its staff).

215 *See supra* at pp. 435-438 (§16A.II.3.a) and pp. 444-447 (§16B.I).

216 *See also* Lalive, »Note, CA Paris, 15.09.1998«, 117.

217 ICC Rules, art. 34 (1998) was not yet in force and therefore not invoked by the ICC. *See Cubic v. ICC*, [1999] Rev. Arb. 111 (»*à la supposer même efficiente*« [even if we assumed such provision to be effective]); Lalive, »Note, CA Paris, 15.09.1998«, 116, 117 (judging the liability exclusion clause to be legally ineffective and politically erroneous).

218 *SNF v. ICC*, [2010] Rev. Arb. 314 (FR CA, Paris) 318, 319, *contra* [2007] Rev. Arb. 847 (FR TGI, Paris) at 849 (considering; ICC Rules, art. 34 [1998] to be valid under French law in international contracts).

[A provision excluding liability which allows the ICC to not meet its main obligation as a provider of non-jurisdictional services has to be considered non-written in the relationship between the ICC and a party since such a clause contradicts the purpose of the arbitration contract]

It follows from the circumstances that »*contrat d'arbitrage*« (arbitration contract) means the Administration Contract rather than the arbitration agreement (in French commonly referred to as »*accord compromissoire*«).[219]

In reaction to this judgment, the ICC added the restriction »*except to the extent such limitation of liability is prohibited by applicable law*« to article 40 of the ICC Rules (2012),[220] other institutions expressly reserve their liability for intent or gross negligence[221] to avoid the verdict of nullity of the provision under national contract law.[222] With such reservations, however, provisions in institutional rules limiting liability become largely superfluous. That an arbitral institution can only be sued successfully if it committed some rather grave fault already follows from the fact that the institution does not owe a certain result of the arbitration but only assisting services whereby it enjoys wide discretion on how to fulfil its obligations.[223]

## 3. Institutional liability risks connected to hybrid arbitration

A direct action to engage institutional liability on the ground that the institution - allegedly without reason - refused to administer an arbitration based on a hybrid arbitration agreement will not be successful. Dependent on the timing, the institution's refusal can have the consequence that an Administration Contract did not come into existence at all. Then, there is no

---

219  *Cf. also* the remark by M. Metais in Comité Francais de l'Arbitrage, »Débats«, 378.

220  Cited *supra* at n. 214 (= ICC Rules, art. 41 [2017]).

221  For references, *see supra* at n. 207

222  *See* Schöldström, *The Arbitrator's Mandate*, 412 (on different civil law systems; referring *inter alia* to BGB § 307 (2) [GER], but not even mentioning the rather strict »*Verbot der geltungserhaltenden Reduction*« [prohibition of saving the valid part of excessive terms] under ibid., § 306 [2]); *cf. also* Unfair Contract Terms Act 1977 § 3 (2)(a) and (b) (EW); *but see* Arbitration Act 1996 § 74 (1) (statutory liability limitation rendering this issue moot).

223  *See also* Gaillard and Savage, *Fouchard, Gaillard, Goldmann*, para. 1088–1; Lalive, »Note, CA Paris, 15.09.1998«, 117.

contractual claim in the first place. Moreover, a quasi-contractual or tort claim would also not exist since arbitral institutions are not under an obligation to contract for lack of a general right of access to arbitration.[224] Even if an institution first files and notifies the request and sends communication arguably amounting to acceptance,[225] it was here proposed that up to the constitution of the tribunal the institution can still terminate the Administration Contract and close the proceedings without engaging liability.[226] This again underlines that refusal to administer hybrid arbitrations is one of the safer options for the designated institution.[227]

The standard of liability under the applicable law of the institution's seat[228] and the institutional rules may become relevant in two situations. Either if the institution accepts to administer a hybrid arbitration and fails - at least in the discontent party's opinion - to apply the other institution's rules correctly or if the institution reacts to the hybrid arbitration request by simply ignoring the rule derogation and by imposing its own rules on the parties. In both cases, the award may be prone to challenge for failure to comply with the procedure agreed by the parties, including the method to constitute the arbitral tribunal.[229] In light of a hybrid arbitration agreement, determination of the applicable standard of institutional liability becomes very difficult should the liability limitations under the rules of the designated institution and under the rules of the other institution chosen by the parties differ. In accordance with the partial endorsement of the theory of characteristic performance to solve the battle of forms issue caused by a hybrid arbitration agreement, it is here suggested that the liability provision contained in the administering institution's rules should apply.[230] This solution does not seem to interfere with procedural party autonomy since liability is a purely contractual rather than procedural issue.

Generally, the threshold for liability (whether expressed as gross negligence, bad faith or otherwise) should not be whether the seized court would have interpreted the agreement differently or accommodated the parties'

---

224 *See supra* at pp. 247-251 (§11A.IV); *cf. also supra* at pp. 424-427 (§16A.II.1.d.iii), rejecting an allegation of denial of justice by not setting an arbitration in motion.

225 *See supra* at pp. 251-252 (§11B.I).

226 *Supra* at pp. 252-255 (§11B.II).

227 *See supra* at pp. 263-264 (§11B.IV) and pp. 269-271 (§12).

228 *See supra* at pp. 240-243 (§11A.II.4).

229 Subject to the criterion of outcome-relevance, *see infra* pp. 476-480 (§17B).

230 *See supra* at pp. 260-263 (§11B.III.3).

choice of rules in a different way. Rather, it should be decisive whether the approach taken by the institution is still defendable when weighing the interest of party autonomy against the interest of efficiency. The risk taken by the parties themselves in concluding a non-standard hybrid arbitration agreement may be regarded as contributory negligence. In no event should the mere fact that the award was annulled or refused enforcement engage the strict liability of the administering institution as such imposition of an obligation of result on arbitral institutions would severely damage the effectiveness of the institutional system.

In light of the outlined variances among legal systems and arbitration rules regarding institutional liability, it is recommended that an institution, if persuaded to administer arbitration under another institution's rules, agrees on an individual liability clause with the parties accommodating the specific implementation risks of the hybrid arbitration agreement.

III. Available remedies

If it were ever found - despite the mentioned reservations against justiciability of institutional conduct voiced in practice and the liability restrictions resulting from statute or the applicable arbitration rules - that an institution violated contractual obligations in relation to one or both parties by malperformance or non-performance of the Administration Contract, the question of the appropriate remedy would arise. Of course, an obvious claim would be one for damages, which would require proof that the institution's conduct - e.g. an incorrect implementation of the chosen arbitration rules - has resulted in economic loss or other harm. In addition to this factual difficulty of proving causality, additional legal obstacles exist if a party seeks either the (correct) performance of the Administration Contract or its termination.[231]

Independent of the general common law - civil law divide on the availability and prerequisites of the remedy of specific performance, it would be inappropriate for a court to order an arbitral institution to, and how to, perform its services. This follows from the fact that the services of an arbitral

---

231 *Cf. also* Fouchard, »Les institutions permanentes d'arbitrage devant le juge étatique«, 261 (finding that contract law, in theory, would allow claims for damages, termination of contract, specific performance and annullation of an institutional decision as reparation in kind).

institution are of higher nature requiring specific mutual trust;[232] for such kind of services, even civil law courts would not order specific performance or at least they would not order a penalty to enforce it.[233] For this reason, it already appears quite unlikely that a party would actually ever seek this remedy.[234]

The same argument - arbitral institutions offering services of higher nature - should often make court action for termination of the Administration Contract superfluous and thus inadmissible for lack of legal standing. Given the requirement of mutual trust, the arbitrants together can terminate the contract with the institution at any time without cause and thus without the help of a judge. Even if they decide to do so after the constitution of an arbitral tribunal, this might - dependent on the cause for termination - entail a damages claim of the institution but should not invalidate the termination as such.

As noted however, if there is a disagreement between the arbitrants on whether the institution should continue to administer the case, a decision on whether there is a duty to cooperate in the termination of the Administration Contract, which can only be derived from the arbitration agreement, falls within the competence of the arbitral tribunal, not a state court.[235] This

---

232 *See supra* at pp. 253-254 (§11B.II.1); *contra* Wolf, *Die Institutionelle Handelsschiedsgerichtsbarkeit*, 248–50 (rejecting the contractual qualification as services of higher nature but still arguing with the required trust to reject a claim for specific performance on procedural grounds).

233 *See e.g.* ZPO § 888 (3) (GER) (providing that a sentence to render personal services, which cannot be performed by another than the debtor, cannot be enforced).

234 It is a different, but here not relevant, question if specific performance was an appropriate remedy if a party sought performance of individual, non-judicial service acts by the institution, like the notification of the award. There are good reasons to allow contractual action for specific performance for such individual acts as opposed to the whole administration of an arbitration (*see* Wolf, *Die Institutionelle Handelsschiedsgerichtsbarkeit*; *but cf.* Schwab, Walter, and Baumbach, *Schiedsgerichtsbarkeit*, 12, para. 2–5- rejecting an action for performance even of mere service acts like signing and notifying the award against an arbitrator; not discussing institutions).

235 *See supra* at pp. 266-268 (§11C.II); *contra* Wolf, *Die Institutionelle Handelsschiedsgerichtsbarkeit*, 200–202 (seeking a solution in an analoguous application of provisions on the challenge of arbitrators).

applies even when an arbitral tribunal is not yet constituted,[236] subject to any future revision project for extended court support along the lines proposed made above.[237]

## C. The fork in the road to enforce hybrid arbitration agreements

Philippe Fouchard once stated that actions to control institutional activities take two forms. One is the traditional (or procedural) path, based on the interventionist and supporting powers of state courts in the matter of arbitration. The other »*new*« (or contractual) path is for a party to sue the arbitration institution directly and personally.[238] Both paths have been analysed in this section with a specific focus on problems arising from hybrid arbitration agreements. As to the relationship between the procedural and the contractual path, it seems sufficient and most practical to identify the proper parties and interests concerned. The procedural remedies of dismissal or stay of litigation, a declaration on the validity of the arbitration agreement, motions to compel arbitration, anti-suit injunctions, review of jurisdictional decisions or a plea for support of the arbitration react to a conflict between the parties to the arbitration agreement.[239] In contrast, the contractual path concerns a conflict between one or both parties to the arbitration agreement on the one hand and an institution on the other. To distinguish between »*jurisdictional*« decisions of institutions and »*administrative*« or »*contractual*« acts appears again unnecessary to find the most appropriate cause of action.[240]

The traditional ways to enforce arbitration agreements before controlling or supporting courts in proceedings between the parties to the arbitration agreement show three »*deficiencies*« in an institutional context. First, the

---

236 *See supra* at pp. 419-422 (§16A.II.1.c) on the limited competence of courts to determine operability issues.

237 *See supra* at pp. 427-430 (§16A.II.1.d.iv).

238 Fouchard, »Les institutions permanentes d'arbitrage devant le juge étatique«, 228–29.

239 *See also Global Gold v. Robinson*, 533 F. Supp. 2d at 448 (»*The real parties in interest to litigate the question of arbitrability are the parties seeking and resisting arbitration, not the arbitrators or arbitral administrators, whose role is solely to render neutral judgment*«).

240 *Contra* Fouchard, »Les institutions permanentes d'arbitrage devant le juge étatique«, 239, at para. 15 (suggesting that the whole system of judicial control of institutional decisions depends on the qualification).

standard of review for the question whether an arbitration agreement is capable of being performed is still undefined.[241] Second, there are conceptual and practical obstacles to bind an arbitration institutions not part of the proceedings between arbitrants to the result of such proceedings[242] and third, there is a lot of confusion about the procedural reviewability of institutional decisions.[243]

The potential availability of direct, contractual action against the arbitral institution does not entirely cure these »*shortcomings.*« As found, such action would have to overcome high hurdles of liability[244] and, reasonably, could only result in the remedy of monetary damages.[245] Next to the potential respondent, the remedy sought is therefore the decisive signpost at the fork of the road to enforce hybrid arbitration agreements before state courts. A party discontent with institutional conduct in this respect, *e.g.* with a refusal to administer the case under the chosen rules, with an institution's disregard of the parties' choice of rules or with the allegedly incorrect application of such rules should only directly sue the institution in exceptional circumstances and only if seeking damages. In all other cases, it should first try to find an agreement with the other party on how to proceed in light of problems to implement the arbitration agreement potentially aggravated by the institution's conduct. Even though a party could follow the traditional path to apply to a state court for declaratory or supporting relief, it may be unclear if the designated institution would be prepared to implement such court decision.

However, one may doubt whether the identified enforcement gap is really a »*deficiency*« or »*shortcoming*« of the legal framework of institutional arbitration, as just expressed in quotation marks. Maybe, it is better that parties and courts cannot *force* an arbitral institution to implement an arbitration agreement in the way they want - or in the way that a court finds the parties want. Access to (institutional) arbitration - as opposed to access to court - is not such an important value that it has to be enforced at any

---

241 Herein, a reduced review by controlling courts was considered appropriate, *see supra* at pp. 419-422 (§16A.II.1.c), if balanced by increased powers of supporting courts, *supra* at pp. 423 and 427-430 (§16A.II.1.d.ii,iv).
242 *See supra* at pp. 430-435 (§16A.II.2).
243 Herein, it was clarified that the problem is mainly one of possible deference to the institutional decision rather than one of review, *see supra* at pp. 440-442 (§16A.II.3.d).
244 *See supra* at pp. 447-457 (§16B.II).
245 *See supra* at pp. 457-459 (§16B.III).

sacrifice, in particular not at the sacrifice of the autonomy of arbitral institutions guaranteeing the efficiency of the institutional arbitration system. Of course, in the interest of party autonomy it would be preferable if a hybrid arbitration agreement could be saved without surrendering its institutional character; however, such solution should be found in cooperation with and consideration of the interests of the institution supposed to administer the case.[246]

## *§17 Challenging & enforcing hybrid arbitration awards*

As noted, parties often comply with arbitral awards voluntarily.[247] However, when controversies on the validity, interpretation or implementation of an arbitration agreement or procedural irregularities already transpired during the arbitral process, the losing party may be tempted to blame its defeat on the way these issues were dealt with by the arbitral tribunal or an administering institution. In this respect, an award based on a hybrid arbitration agreement (hereinafter also *»hybrid arbitration award«*), or any non-standard agreement for that matter, lays itself open to attack.

For a discontent party, there are two distinguishable opportunities - or fora - to challenge international arbitration awards: before the courts at the place of arbitration in setting-aside proceedings (also referred to as *»annulment proceedings«*) and before a court in the country where the winning party seeks to compel compliance with the award. The grounds for refusing to recognise and enforce arbitral awards listed in article V of the New York Convention are very similar[248] to the grounds for setting-aside under article 34 of the UNCITRAL Model Law and corresponding provisions of national law.[249] Therefore, they will herein be examined together and for that

---

246 *See supra* at pp. 427-430 (§16A.II.1.d.iv) on the idea of letting the designated or prospective institution participate in proceedings for court support.

247 Common assumption, *see e.g.* Berger, Center for Transnational Law, *Private Dispute Resolution in International Business*, para. 29–5. *See also supra* at pp. 86-87 (§4C).

248 Conflicting results between decisions by courts at the seat and the enforcement forum are nevertheless not uncommon (on uniform interpretation as a condition for a harmonising effect of the New York Convention, *see* ibid., 29–11; Sanders, *Quo Vadis Arbitration?*, 78–79).

249 On attempts by the drafters of the Model Law to mirror the grounds on non-enforcement under the New York Convention in the provision on

purpose be referred to as grounds for challenge, with due indication of relevant differences between both stages. One noteworthy procedural difference between setting-aside proceedings and enforcement proceedings is that the party that lost the arbitration, at least in part, would introduce the former while the winning party would introduce the latter. However, in both cases, the party challenging the award bears the burden of proof for irregularities in the arbitration, subject to any ground to be considered *ex officio*.[250]

To avoid entering into a discussion of general problems relating to arbitral awards, the following analysis is restricted to first identifying the most probable grounds for challenge of hybrid arbitration awards (A) before highlighting the following three specific issues (B):

- the relationship between grounds for challenge to be invoked by a party and those considered *ex officio*
- concepts of preclusion/waiver/estoppel of challenges
- the criterion that procedural irregularities need to have influenced the outcome of the arbitration to allow setting-aside or refusal of enforcement of the award

These issues are important for the enforceability of awards based on hybrid arbitration agreements if, as herein defined, the modality of designating one institution and another institution's rules was at the outset unanimously chosen by both parties.[251] In the event that this unanimity subsisted until the post-award stage, only *ex officio* grounds of challenge could oppose enforcement of the award. If a party's initial agreement to hybrid arbitration faded away during the cause of the proceedings, issues of preclusion/waiver/estoppel may arise. Finally, some of the differences between institutional rules and systems are of a rather formal nature.[252] If a party invokes procedural irregularities with reference to such formal issues, the criterion of outcome-relevance comes into focus.

---

setting-aside, *see generally* Poudret and Besson, *Comparative Law of International Arbitration*, 786; Born, *International Commercial Arbitration (2014)*, 3187 (§25.04) (with further references).

250 Born, *International Commercial Arbitration (2014)*, 3177–78, 3418–19 (§25.03 [A][4] and §26.03 [B][4]). *See also infra* at pp. 476 et seq. (§17B).

251 *See supra* at pp. 31-32 (§1A) and pp. 177-178 (§8C.I.3).

252 For a comparision of institutional rules, *see generally supra* at pp. 355 et seq. (§14B).

The Hangzhou Intermediate People's Court, when it refused to enforce the awards rendered in the *Alstom–Insigma* arbitration,[253] seems to have overlooked the issues of preclusion/waiver/estoppel and outcome-relevance entirely. This invites to summarise and criticise this decision as the preliminary unhappy end of this saga (C).[254]

## A. Probable grounds for challenge

When considering grounds for challenge of arbitral awards, it is important to bear the principle of finality of awards in mind. Accordingly, all grounds have to be interpreted restrictively.[255] The following subsections discuss probable grounds of challenge - and their merits - in relation to awards based on hybrid arbitration agreements.

### I. Invalidity of the arbitration agreement

With problems arguably rooted in the hybrid arbitration *agreement* itself, a challenge claiming that »*said agreement is not valid*«[256] is tempting.

---

253 *Alstom v. Insigma (Hz. IPC)*; *see infra* at pp. 480 et seq.

254 Alstom's claims were formally recognised in Hong Kong but, for lack of sufficient assets, not fully satisfied (*cf.* Dahm, »International Arbitration: Why Wearing A Good Suit Makes All The Difference«: »*It worked in Hong Kong*«). Alstom then initiated winding-up proceedings against Insigma in Hong Kong, the application was rejected in October 2014 for reasons of international comity only allowing Hong Kong's courts to wind-up of companies seated and listed in another jurisdiction (there meaning mainland China) in very extraordinary circumstances (*In the matter of Insigma Technology Co Ltd*, [2013] HCCW 224 [HK]).

255 General opinion, *see e.g* Berger, Center for Transnational Law, *Private Dispute Resolution in International Business*, para. 28–25.

256 For a motion to set the award aside, *cf.* UNCITRAL Model Law 2006 art. 34 (2)(a)(i); as a ground to refuse recognition and enforcement, *see* New York Convention, art. V (1)(a); on the existence of this ground of challenge, which gives effect to the basic rule of consent, »*under all national legal systems*«, *see generally* Born, *International Commercial Arbitration (2014)*, 3188 (§25.04 [A]); *see e.g.* ZPO § 1059 (2) no. 1 (a) (GER); IAA § 31 (2)(a)(b) (SG); Arbitration Law art. 58 (1) (P.R.C.); phrased slightly differently: CPC art. 1520 (1) (FR) (referring to a wrong upholding or decline of jurisdiction); similar: IPRG art. 190 (2)(b) (C.H.);

However, it is herein argued that such challenge to an award based on a hybrid arbitration agreement should usually not be successful. As exhaustively discussed in the first chapter, the validity of an arbitration agreement - as opposed to its capability of being performed - requires little more than the expressed consent to arbitrate rather than litigate the dispute. Disagreement of optional modalities - the administering institution or the applicable rules - does usually not affect the essentialia of the arbitration agreement and thus its validity.[257] Once an award has been rendered based on an agreement referring to one institution and another institution's rules, a party might credibly argue that the arbitration did not go as expected but it is less credible to claim that it never agreed to arbitrate at all. As explained, the question whether and how the arbitration agreement was capable of being performed - its operability - has become mute at the post-award stage or rather it is only reflected in the procedural grounds for challenge discussed below.[258]

As noted, a successful challenge on the ground that there was no agreement to arbitrate may be somewhat more probable in China than in other jurisdictions because the requirement that the arbitration agreement must unambiguously designate an arbitration commission under articles 16, 18 of the Arbitration Law (P.R.C.) could be understood as a condition for validity rather than operability.[259] Then again, the latest reply of the SPC in the *Longlide* case,[260] where an arbitration agreement referring to the ICC Court - which obviously does not meet the requirements of an arbitration commission under articles 10 and 11 of the Arbitration Law (P.R.C) - suggests that controlling courts should only formally review the commission requirement without questioning the characteristics of the designated entity

---

Arbitration Act 1996 § 67 (1) (EW) (referring to the substantive jurisdiction of the tribunal in general); less clear: FAA § 10 (a)(4) (US) (only mentioning the situation that »*the arbitrators exceeded their powers*«; *but see e.g. First Options*, 514 U.S. at 943, where a lack of an arbitration agreement binding on a non-signatory was found to be a ground to vacate the award).

257  *See supra* at p. 124 (§6B) and pp. 158-161 (§8A).

258  *See infra* at 465-470 (§17A.II-III)

259  *See supra* at pp. 101-104 (§4C.II.2.b.iii).

260  *Longlide*, [2013] Min Si Ta Zi no. 13; cited according to the English translation published by Sun, »SPC Instruction Provides New Opportunities for International Arbitral Institutions to Expand into China«, 695–700 (Appendix 3; also providing a translation of the reference for instruction by the Anhui People's Court in Appendix 4).

or the rules applied.[261] If a hybrid arbitration agreement clearly designates an institution, although it refers to another institution's rules at the same time, such formal test may be passed. To some extent, this interpretation of Chinese law justifies CIETAC's approach to dealing with hybrid arbitration agreements in performing the respective functions under the chosen rules.[262]

## II. Procedural irregularities

The most likely and potentially successful ground for challenge to hybrid arbitration awards is that the procedure was not in accordance with the agreement of the parties. This is an accepted ground for challenge under article V (1)(d) of the New York Convention at enforcement stage as well as a ground for setting-aside under article 34 (2)(a)(iv) of the UNCITRAL Model Law and the majority of national enactments.[263] Such challenge - to differing degrees - appears probable not only when the designated institution, as in the *Alstom–Insigma* arbitration, tried to administer the arbitration in accordance with the chosen rules of another institution, but also when the administering institution ignored part or all of the parties' agreement on such other institution's rules. For a court, this challenge creates the difficult task

---

261 *See supra* at p. 63, n. 39; *see also generally* Sun, »SPC Instruction Provides New Opportunities for International Arbitral Institutions to Expand into China« (on the debate and development of jurisprudence in China regarding agreements designating foreign institutions to administer cases in China). Wei Sun concludes that the SPC's *Longlide* ruling »*effectively ended the debate over the validity of such arbitration agreements*« and despite »*many questions yet to be answered* [...] *opened the door for foreign arbitral institutions*« (ibid., 689).

262 CIETAC Rules, art. 4 (3) (2012; 2015). *See supra* at pp. 101-104 (§4C.II.2.b.iii).

263 *See e.g.* ZPO § 1059 (2) no. 1 (d) (GER); Arbitration Act 1996 § 68 (2)(a) (EW); IAA § 31 (2)(e) (SG); for Chinese law, *cf.* SPC's Interpretation of Arbitration Law, art. 20 (2006); for further references, *see* Born, *International Commercial Arbitration (2014)*, 3260, n. 547–48 (§25.04 [C][1]; also remarking that case law in jurisdictions without express statutory provision to this effect considers disrespect of agreed procedures as either a due process ground or a variant of the *ultra petita* challenge; citing US, French and Swiss authorities). *See also infra* at pp. at pp. 473-475 (§17A.IV.2) on the French understanding of the contractual nature of arbitral procedure as a principle of international public policy.

of interpreting the parties' agreement at a post-award stage, an interpretation that would inevitably - and maybe rightly so - be influenced by the agreement's practical implementation.

The more the parties agreed on individual steps of the procedure during the course of the arbitration, the less likely would the fact that one institution administered the arbitration under the rules of another cause concerns. Wherever the administering institution had to take a decision on a procedural matter on which the parties disagreed, a discontent party may argue either that the institution applied the wrong rule or that the wrong actors applied the rule. The criteria for substituting institutional actors established above can help here to evaluate the appropriateness of the institution's conduct.[264] Many cases, however, may already be judged satisfyingly by correctly and strictly applying the criterion of outcome-relevance as discussed below.[265]

A violation of the applicable arbitration law is, as already exhaustively discussed in the first chapter, only a default ground for challenge. Party-agreed procedural rules usually prevail over the rules of the *lex arbitri*, save for the few rules that are mandatory - most of which are already reflected in the specific ground of challenge of an insufficient opportunity to present one's case (violation of the right to be heard).[266] Article 34 (2)(a)(iv) of the UNCITRAL Model Law, many respective national provisions[267] and article V (1)(d) of the New York Convention express this relationship accordingly; the New York Convention arguably even assumes a preference of party-agreed procedures over any law deemed mandatory at the seat of arbitration.

---

264 *See supra* at pp. 344-400 (§14).

265 *See infra* at pp. 476-480 (§17B).

266 *See* UNCITRAL Model Law 2006 art. 34 (2)(a)(ii); New York Convention, art. V (1)(b). On possible due process concerns raised by institutional applications of hybrid arbitration agreements, *see supra* at pp. 90-91 (§4C.II.1).

267 *E.g.* ZPO § 1059 (2) no. 1 (d) (GER); IAA § 3 (SG); phrased slightly differently: Arbitration Act 1996 § 68 (2)(a), 33 (EW) (referring to the tribunal's duty to respect mandatory law of the seat). However, some jurisdictions, *e.g.* the US, France and Switzerland, do not provide for challenges on the ground of disrespect of the law of the seat. Such challenge would have to be brought either as an invocation of the right to be heard or due process or on public policy grounds (*see generally* Born, *International Commercial Arbitration (2014)*, 3270–71, at §25.04 [D][1]; with further references). *See infra* at pp. 473-475 (§17A.IV.2) on »*ordre public*« as a catch-all phrase in the understanding of some French courts.

As established in the first chapter, express statutory provisions against hybrid arbitration agreements, procedures and awards cannot be found. The only arbitration law that explicitly governs this kind of situation, that of Romania, grants discretion to the administering institution on how to deal with the parties' choice of other than the administering institution's rules.[268] Of course, there is some uncertainty on how Romanian courts would understand this provision if asked to set aside an award because the institution exercised its discretion in one way or the other. Since the arbitration law there expressly provides for discretion of the institution, it seems unreasonable to fully review the institution's decision except for serious due process concerns.[269]

As for Chinese law, it allows setting-aside of a domestic (including a foreign-related) award on the ground that »*the arbitration procedure was not in conformity of statutory procedure*« without - which is of little surprise - establishing any prevalence of party agreements on procedure.[270] Given the discussed requirements for arbitrations seated in China to be administered by »*commissions*«,[271] and the official requirement that all arbitration rules are formulated by the »*China Arbitration Commission*« for domestic cases or the »*China International Chamber of Commerce*«[272] for international cases,[273] there are a number of arguments to find that hybrid

---

268 CPC art. 619 (2) (RO). *See supra* at pp. 98-101 (§4C.II.2.b.ii).

269 Here, some deference - in exception to the general view expressed *supra* at pp. 440-442 (§16A.II.3.d) - appears appropriate as the law expressly grants discretion to the institution.

270 Arbitration Law art. 58 (3) (P.R.C.); *but see also* SPC's Interpretation of Arbitration Law, art. 20 (2006): »*The term violation of legal procedures as prescribed in Article 58 of the Arbitration Law shall refer to violation of the arbitration procedures prescribed in the Arbitration Law or a circumstance under which the arbitration rules chosen by the parties concerned might affect the correct award for the case*« (internal quotation marks omitted).

271 *See* Arbitration Law art. 10–11, 16, 18 (P.R.C.).

272 Of which CIETAC is the dispute resolution arm (according to its self-presentation, *cf.* CIETAC, »About Us | Introduction«).

273 Arbitration Law art. 15, 73 (P.R.C.); *but see* ibid., art. 75 (allowing »*tentative rules of arbitration*« to be formulated by the commissions themselves). The China Arbitration Commission was effectively never established (*see* Tao, *Arbitration Law and Practice in China*, para. 92), which is why the temporary power of Chinese commissions to establish their own *domestic* rules under art. 75 of the Arbitration Law (P.R.C.) still applies. The legal basis - to the extent necessary - for commissions other than

arbitration awards violate Chinese arbitration law. However, in practice Chinese courts appear to pay a lot of deference to the activities of Chinese commissions - especially those of their municipality.[274] It also needs to be recalled that the SPC recently even approved of the enforcement of an ICC award rendered in Shanghai - which obviously did not correspond with any »*commission*« or rule formulation requirements of the *text* of the Arbitration Law (P.R.C.).[275] This indicates that an award rendered in China-seated hybrid arbitration could pass setting-aside and enforcement proceedings in China, in particular where the procedure was »*allowed*« under the administering institution's rules, *e.g.* under article 4 (3) of the CIETAC Rules. There is a lack of a strict separation between public law, private rules and party agreement in the Chinese legal system,[276] which is why the status of arbitration commissions may be described as somewhere between private, independent service providers and state registered and supported administrators of commercial dispute settlement.[277] This could result in article 4 (3) of the CIETAC Rules - or similar provisions established by other Chinese commissions[278] - *factually* overruling any contrary wording to the arbitration law. It goes without saying that a number of uncertainties remain here.[279]

---

CIETAC to establish own *international* rules is unclear but the practice appears nowadays largely accepted (*see* Zhou, »Arbitration Agreements in China«, 149: uncertainties stem from the permissive language in Arbitration Law art. 66 (P.R.C.): »*may*«).

274 *See e.g.* the decisions on the CIETAC split as discussed *supra* at pp. 190-202 (§8C.II.2).

275 *Longlide*, [2013] Min Si Ta Zi no. 13; Sun, »SPC Instruction Provides New Opportunities for International Arbitral Institutions to Expand into China«, 695 (Appendix 3); *see also* Dong, »Open Door for Foreign Arbitration Institutions?«

276 As exemplified by SPC's Interpretation of Arbitration Law, art. 20 (2006) (as quoted *supra* at n. 270).

277 *Cf. supra* at pp. 110-116 (§5B) and pp. 101-106 (§4C.II.2.b.iii; c).

278 *See e.g.* SHIAC Rules, art. 2 (6) and article 3 (3) (2015); SHIAC Rules, art. 2 (5) and article 3 (2) (2014); SCIA Rules, art. 3 (3) sentence 3 (2012).

279 *But see* Zhou, »Arbitration Agreements in China«, 148 (finding that even in China, »*courts' efforts are limited to making adjustments to fill in grey areas with a pro-arbitration approach*«).

III. Irregularity in the constitution of the arbitral tribunal

That the constitution of the arbitral tribunal was not in accordance with the agreement of the parties is a specific procedural ground for challenge which about all national laws explicitly mention.[280] When a party argues that the wrong arbitration rules were applied in respect of the composition of the arbitral tribunal it may be difficult to distinguish if it invokes a wrong constitution of the tribunal or disrespect of general party-agreed procedures as discussed above. Where the arbitration law allows for both kinds of challenges, this distinction is immaterial. However, where disrespect of party-agreed procedure is not an explicit ground for challenge - *e.g.* in France, Switzerland or the US - it may be more important to determine whether a certain procedural rule concerns the constitution of the tribunal. In particular, arbitration rules on challenges of already appointed arbitrators are here a grey area.[281]

As noted, in the *Alstom–Insigma* arbitration, the chosen ICC Rules (1998) followed the principle of institutional nomination of the chairperson,[282] but SIAC mistakenly asked the co-arbitrators for a nomination with reference to the SIAC Rules (1997) then in force.[283] The conformity of this procedure with the parties' agreement - and the outcome-relevance

---

280 *See again* New York Convention, art. V (1)(d) (first alternative); UNCITRAL Model Law 2006 art. 34 (2)(a)(iv) (first alternative); ZPO § 1059 (2) no. 1 (d) (GER) (first alternative); Arbitration Act 1996 § 68 (2)(c) (EW); IAA § 3, 31 (2)(e) (SG); CPC art. 1520 (2) (FR); IPRG art. 190 (2)(a) (C.H.); (*but see Hitachi Ltd v. SMS Schloemoann Siemag AG*, [1997] 15 ASA Bull. 99 [C.H. BG] at 103–4; applying high hurdles for a challenge on that basis if only party agreements on the tribunal's constitution rather than provisions of the law were violated); for case law and further references, *see* Born, *International Commercial Arbitration (2014)*, 3263–64 (§25.04 [C][3]).

281 *See Hitachi Ltd v. SMS Schloemoann Siemag AG*, [1997] 15 ASA Bull. 103–4 (at 4) (discussing but eventually rejecting the application of art. 190 (2)(a) IPRG to a complaint relating to a challenge under ICC Rules).

282 ICC Rules, art. 8 (4) sent. 3 (1998): »*The third arbitrator, who will act as chairman of the Arbitral Tribunal, shall be appointed by the Court, unless the parties have agreed upon another procedure for such appointment, in which case the nomination will be subject to confirmation pursuant to Art. 9.*«

283 *See supra* at pp. 375-377 (§14B.III.5).

of this formal mistake —[284] therefore depends on whether there was an individual party agreement on the method of co-arbitrator nomination. While the Singapore courts in the proceedings under article 16 found such agreement,[285] the Hangzhou Intermediate People's Court either ignored it or did not find it established by the evidence submitted.[286] In any event, this example warns that irregularities in the constitution of the tribunal are likely when an institution is supposed to follow other than its own rules in this respect. The previous chapter also highlighted that substituting institutional actors in the process of tribunal constitution is one of the most critical issues in the implementation of hybrid arbitration agreements.[287]

IV. Public policy

For substantive issues, public policy is already relevant at the setting-aside stage. Concerning procedural irregularities, the public policy ground is more decisive in recognition and enforcement proceedings, at least if the seat of arbitration was in a Model Law jurisdiction. The reason is simple: Any violation of applicable procedural law is a ground for setting-aside under article 34 no. (2)(a)(iv) of the UNCITRAL Model Law and respective national provisions.[288] Accordingly, the applicant in setting-aside proceedings would not need to argue that the violation of the seat's arbitration law meets the high threshold of a public policy breach.[289] In contrast, the enforcement state's demands can only be insisted on to the extent they are an expression of the right to be heard under article V (1)(b) of the New York Convention or to public policy in the meaning of article V (2)(b) of the New York Convention.[290]

---

284 *See infra* at pp. 476-480 (§17B).

285 *See Insigma v. Alstom*, [2008] SGHC 39, 42–43; *Insigma v. Alstom*, [2009] SGCA 27. *See also infra* at pp. 476-480 (§17B) on the concept of preclusion.

286 *See infra* at pp. 480 et seq. (§17C) for a detailed summary and discussion.

287 *See supra* at pp. 366-378 (§14B.III) and the conclusions at pp. 400 et seq. (§15).

288 *See supra* at n. 267 at p. 466.

289 However, this is different in jurisdictions like France, where non-conformity with the seat's arbitration law is not a ground for annulment, *see supra* at pp. 465-469 (§17A.II) and *infra* at pp. 473-475 (§17A.IV.2).

290 *See ILA, Committee on International Commercial Arbitration, Final Report to Public Policy as a Bar to Enforcement of International Arbitral*

1. What is public policy?

It is rather difficult to define the colourful term »*ordre public*« or public policy[291] as we are far from international consensus in this respect.[292] It is possible to differentiate, whether on a purely literal level or with legal consequences, between internal and international public policy or, in the French terminology, between »*ordre public interne*«, and »*ordre public international.*« While the former encompasses all national mandatory laws,[293] the latter refers to only a few principles of national law that shall apply even when the parties' choice or conflict of laws rules lead to the application of another jurisdiction's laws.[294] International public policy even limits party autonomy on a private international law level.[295] It is the prevailing opinion in international arbitration doctrine that article V (2)(b) New York Convention refers to international and not to internal public policy.[296] Not every

---

*Awards*, para. 19 (Recommendation 1 (c): »*International public policy includes both substantive and procedural violations*).

291 Herein, the terms are used synonymously (*cf.* Rome-I-Regulation 2008 art. 21 [EU]; *see also* Franz Schwarz and Helmut Ortner, »Procedural Ordre Public and the Internationalization of Public Policy«, 138, 139, also on attempts to distinguish the French and the English term).

292 *Cf.* Lalive, »Transnational (or Truly International) Public Policy and International Arbitration«, 273 (concluding that no common definition of the notion exists).

293 *See* C.Civ. art. 6 (FR): *On ne peut déroger, par des conventions particulières, aux lois qui intéressent l'ordre public* [...]« [One cannot derogate by individual agreement from laws touching public policy]); *see also* Franz Schwarz and Helmut Ortner, »Procedural Ordre Public and the Internationalization of Public Policy«, 152.

294 *Cf.* CPC art. 1520 no. 5, 1514 (FR) (breach of international public policy or even manifest breach of international public policy required to challenge international awards); *but cf. also* ibid., art. 1492 no. 5 (breach of internal public policy sufficient to challenge domestic award in France); *see also* Urteil [Judgment], [1986] 39 NJW 3027 (GER BGH) at 3028 (holding that German »*ordre public international*« is only violated if the award is based on a procedure that disrespected fundamental basic principles of German procedural law in such way that it cannot be considered an orderly, fair procedure anymore; for abstracts in English *see* [1987] XII YCA 489).

295 *See supra* at pp. 58-59 (§4A.I).

296 Another, possibly less misleading, term for »*international public policy*« is »*attenuated public policy*«. *See inter alia* Franz Schwarz and Helmut

non- or misapplication of mandatory substantive or procedural law of the enforcement state should allow a denial of recognition and enforcement of the award. Case law in several jurisdictions, although not always in identical terms, follows this approach in the sense that article V (2) (b) New York Convention is to be interpreted narrowly.[297]

However, despite the confusing terminology, international public policy does not mean anational, transnational or delocalised principles of law but concerns national principles that request for cross-border application - there is not one international public policy, but every jurisdiction has its own.[298] For this reason, this »*chameleon-like concept*« risks misapplication.[299] While there is some consensus across jurisdictions that equal treatment of the parties, the right to be heard[300] and impartiality of the arbitrators are part of international procedural public policy[301] a number of controversies and

---

Ortner, »Procedural Ordre Public and the Internationalization of Public Policy«, 153, 154 (»*now applied in many jurisdictions*«); ibid., n. 140 (»*nonwithstanding the differences in terminology*«); Poudret and Besson, *Comparative Law of International Arbitration*, para. 933; Gaillard and Savage, *Fouchard, Gaillard, Goldmann*, para. 1711; Raeschke-Kessler and Berger, *Recht und Praxis des Schiedsverfahrens*, para. 1038; *cf. also* ILA, Committee on International Commercial Arbitration, *Final Report to Public Policy as a Bar to Enforcement of International Arbitral Awards*, Recommendation 3(a).

297 *See e.g.* Urteil [Judgment], [1986] 39 NJW at 3028 (»*enge Grenzen*«); *cf. also Fincantieri-Cantieri v. Oto Melara*, [1992] ATF 118 II 353 (C.H. BG) (considérant 3c; on arbitrability and public policy); *UAE v. Westland Helicopters*, [1994] ATF 120 II 155 (at considérant 6b; noting that public policy is national by origin and international in effect, opposing a broad interpretation); *Whittemore Overseas Co., Inc. v Société Générale de l'Industrie de Papier et al.*, 508 F.2d at 974 (stating that the public policy defence is not a device to protect national interests); *Westacre v Jugoimport*, [1999] EWCA Civ. 1401, [1999] 2 Lloyd's Rep 65 at 75 (separating between »*English*« and international public policy, the latter applying to international arbitral awards).

298 *See also* Renner, *Zwingendes transnationales Recht*, 109 (concluding that the thought of transnational public policy has not much progressed yet).

299 Park, »Why Courts Review Arbitral Awards«, 605.

300 *See infra* at pp. 476-480 (§17B) on the problem to distinguish *ex officio* grounds from challenges to be invoked explicitly.

301 Lew, Mistelis, and Kröll, *Comparative International Commercial Arbitration*, para. 568; *cf.* Fernando Mantilla Serrano, »Towards a Transnational Procedural Public Policy«, 341; *see also* Franz Schwarz and Helmut

divergences exist. Regrettably, an in-depth discussion of these particularities would surpass the scope of this thesis. Generally, an award may be annulled or refused enforcement for breach of public policy, if it violates fundamental norms of public or economic life or if it unbearably contradicts elementary notions of the forum's legal order.[302]

## 2. Can private rules shape public policy?

When discussing the potential for public policy challenges to hybrid arbitration awards, one issue is of obvious relevance: whether arbitration rules, or party-agreed rules in general, can amount to international public policy. At first glance, such suggestion immediately surprises, given that arbitration rules only apply because of the parties' choice, are therefore on the same level with the parties' agreement. Accordingly, it is hardly conceivable that *privately* drafted and agreed institutional rules could amount to *public* policy.

Nevertheless, there is - rare - French case law suggesting that non-respect of party-agreed rules could result in annulment or refusal of enforcement of the award not only on the ground of non-respect of the agreed procedure[303] but also under the curtail of the public policy defence. In its decision of 15 June 1994[304] the Cour de Cassation confirmed a decision of the appellate court of Versailles, which refused enforcement of an arbitral award

---

Ortner, »Procedural Ordre Public and the Internationalization of Public Policy«, 181, 182 (describing due process as »another term for ›procedural public policy‹ itself rather than a subcategory«).

302  *Cf.* Beschluss [Decision], [2009] 7 SchiedsVZ 66 (GER BGH); *see also Persero v. Dexia Bank*, [2006] SGCA 59; *see generally* Born, *International Commercial Arbitration (2014)*, 3315 (§25.04 [H][1]).

303  *See Brasoil v. GMRA*, [1999] Rev. Arb. 834, [1999] XXIV YCA 296 (FR CA, Paris) (annulment of a decision called an »order« which the court requalified as an award; considering that the arbitral tribunal did not act in compliance with its mission when circumventing scrutiny by the ICC Court contrary to the 1988 ICC Rules; *cf.* ICC Rules, art. 21 [1988]).

304  *Dégremont*, [1995] Rev. Arb. 88 (FR C.Cass). The case is to be distinguished from cases where the ICC Court prolonged the delay for the award, without prior consultation of the parties (*see* Urteil [Judgment], [1988] 104 BGHZ 178, [1988] 41 NJW 3090 [GER BGH] [not finding a violation of public policy and the right to be heard]; reversing Urteil [Judgment], [1988] RIW 480 [GER OLG, Stuttgart]).

rendered in Rabat, Morocco, because the arbitrators ignored a six-month time limit for rendering the award stipulated in the applicable ICC Rules.[305] The Cour de Cassation reasoned:

> »[L]e principe selon lequel le délai fixé par les parties, soit directement, soit par référence à un règlement d'arbitrage, et dans lequel les arbitres doivent accomplir leur mission, ne peut être prorogé par les arbitres eux-mêmes, *traduit une exigence de l'ordre public aussi bien interne qu'international en ce qu'il est inhérent au caractère contractuel de l'arbitrage*; [...] les arbitres, en s'attribuant un pouvoir qui n'appartenait qu'aux parties ou, à défaut, à un tiers préconstitué ou au juge étatique, *avaient méconnu les exigences de l'ordre public international* [...] [*emphasis added*].« [306]

> [The principle that a time limit fixed by the parties, whether directly or by reference to arbitration rules, within which the arbitrators have to fulfil their mission cannot be unilaterally prolonged by the arbitrators *follows from both internal and international public policy, as it is inherent to the contractual character of arbitration*; by assuming a power which they did not have the arbitrators *have therefore violated the limits posed by international public policy.*]

This ruling of the Cour de Cassation overemploys the public policy defence without apparent need. Article V (1)(d) New York Convention covers the disrespect of party-agreed rules easily, which would be a more appropriate ground for refusal of enforcement. However, such detour[307] via the »*international public policy*« route is caused by the particularity that, from its wording, French arbitration law is more arbitration-friendly than required by the New York Convention. A *manifest* breach of public policy is thereunder the only available *intermediate* defence against recognition and enforcement of foreign and international arbitral awards.[308] Other grounds of

---

305 *Cf.* ICC Rules, art. 18 (1988). The ICC Rules (1988) were considered applicable only as reference (»*à titre d'inspiration*«) for the arbitral tribunal acting on an ad hoc basis (*see Dégremont*, [1995] Rev. Arb. 89; *cf.* Gaillard, »Note, C.Cass., 15.06.1994«, 96). On the application of institutional rules in ad hoc arbitration *see supra* at pp. 151-156 (§7C.IV).

306 *Dégremont*, [1995] Rev. Arb. 91; *see also Dubois et. al v. Boots Frites*, [1996] Rev. Arb. 101 (FR CA, Paris) 102 (repeating same reasoning, applying it to an award rendered in the Netherlands that disrespected a three-month time limit directly fixed by the parties).

307 *Cf. also* Waincymer, *Procedure and Evidence*, para. 6.3 (at p. 416) (»*roundabout way*«; also noting that the arbitral tribunal disrespecting such time limit might be considered »*functus officio*«, outside their jurisdictional mandate; *referring to Dubois et. al v. Boots Frites*, [1996] Rev. Arb. 101).

308 *See* CPC art. 1514 (FR).

challenge are only available in second instance, in specific appeal proceedings against the recognition and enforcement decision. Moreover, these grounds of appeal also do not expressly encompass a challenge corresponding to the second alternative of article V (1)(d) New York Convention.[309]

Generally, however, it is herein preferred to apply the public policy challenge restrictively and to prioritise other grounds of challenge as it will be explained below. When considering whether to allow or refuse enforcement of a hybrid arbitration award, neither exclusivity provisions contained in institutional rules,[310] nor the content of any particular rule, nor any alleged general principle that an institution should always follow its own rules should be elevated to the public policy level.

### 3. Public policy to protect interests of the rules issuing institution?

The possible intellectual property or unfair competition concerns discussed in the previous chapter could be viewed as possible grounds for challenge under the angle of a potential violation of substantive public policy.

However, independent of the difficult question which guarantees under national intellectual property laws or unfair competition concepts - if they covered the administration of hybrid arbitration–[311] could amount to international public policy, it seems inappropriate to allow a party to successfully challenge an award on this basis. First, it is essentially not the award itself that touches interests of the rules issuing institution in this regard but only the conduct of the administering institution in the proceedings leading to the award. Public policy should generally be understood as a concept of controlling the award as the *result* of arbitral proceedings, what happened during the proceedings is only relevant to the extent it is reflected in this result. Second, it would be unreasonable to deprive the winning party of its

---

309 *See* ibid., art. 1525–4; ibid., art. 1520. However, non-enforcement in these cases (*Dégremont*, [1995] Rev. Arb. 88; *Dubois et. al v. Boots Frites*, [1996] Rev. Arb. 101) could also have been based on the ground of challenge that the tribunal has acted outside its mission with the argument that the arbitration agreement had expired; *see* Gaillard, »Note, CA Paris, 22.09.1995, 11.01.1996«, 106; *cf. now* CPC art. 1520 no. 3 (FR).

310 Like ICC Rules, art. 1 (2) (2012; 2017); AAA-ICDR Rules, art. 1 (3) sent. 4 (2014).

311 For doubts regarding an alleged illegality of the application of institutional rules by another than the issuing institution, *see supra at* pp. 272 et seq. (§13).

enforcement option vis-a-vis the other party only because the conduct of a third party to this enforcement relationship, the administering institution, may have acted in a questionable way provoked by the hybrid arbitration agreement concluded by *both* arbitrants. In light of the current limitations to successfully engage the contractual responsibility of arbitral institutions,[312] the consequence of non-enforcement may not even be palpable to the institution whose conduct is reproached, compromising any aim of determent.

B. Party invocation, preclusion and outcome-relevance

To conclude the previous overview of probable grounds for challenge, it seems most likely - and most promising - for a discontent party to either invoke irregularities of arbitral procedure or in the constitution of the arbitral tribunal when challenging a hybrid arbitration award.

Without express invocation as a ground for challenge, however, a court should not reconsider the regularity of the arbitration procedure or the tribunal constitution according to the *principle of party invocation,* which is the procedural corollary to the principle of party autonomy as the basis of any arbitral procedure. Moreover, the party invoking such ground for challenge bears the burden of proof.[313] This general principle is important with regard to hybrid arbitration awards because, as just recalled, some of the issues raised thereby touch upon interests of arbitral institutions rather than those of the parties.[314] Annulment or enforcement proceedings may therefore not provide an appropriate setting to discuss them. However, some issues - those of arbitrability and public policy - may be raised by a controlling court *ex officio* in both annulment and enforcement proceedings.[315] Therefore, it is important to clearly identify the applicable ground for challenge, avoiding a resort to arbitrability or public policy where a more specific challenge applies. In particular, it is confusing and contradictory, to

---

312 *See supra* at pp. 444-459 (§16B).
313 *Cf.* UNCITRAL Model Law 2006 art. 34 (2)(a); New York Convention, art. V (1) (requiring the challenging party to »*furnish proof*«); *see generally* Born, *International Commercial Arbitration (2014),* 3177–78, 3418–19 (§25.03 [A][4] and §26.03 [B][4]).
314 *See generally supra* at pp. 272 et seq. (§13).
315 *Cf.* UNCITRAL Model Law 2006 art. 34 (2)(b); New York Convention, art. V (2) (»*finds that*«).

elevate the principle of *party* autonomy to international *public* policy as some French case law[316] suggests. That an institution administered the arbitration under another institution's rules should only be of concern to a court, if a party claims and proves in the particular case that the procedure or the constitution of the arbitral tribunal was not in accordance with the agreement of the parties. It is not the task of courts controlling arbitral awards to establish a general policy against hybrid arbitration.

A second consideration often decisive for the control of hybrid arbitration awards is that of potential *preclusion*. Assuming that at the outset, both parties deliberately opted for hybrid arbitration to avail themselves of the perceived advantages of one institution and of another institution's rules, any challenge of the award claiming the irregularity of such proceedings presupposes that one party changed its mind during the course of the proceedings. Dependent on the timing of such mind change, a party risks to be precluded with its challenge or it may be deemed waived. Conceptually, such preclusion or deemed waiver may follow from express procedural rules to this effect, from the substantive concept of good faith, which requires a party not to act against its own prior conduct (*venire contra factum proprium*) or equity (estoppel).[317] Article 4 of the UNCITRAL Model Law provides generally:

> »A party who knows that any provision of this Law from which the parties may derogate or any requirement under the arbitration agreement has not been complied with and yet proceeds with the arbitration without stating his objection to such non-compliance without undue delay or, if a time limit is provided therefor, within such period of time, shall be deemed to have waived his right to object.«[318]

The issue is most relevant for jurisdictional challenges, meaning the claim that the arbitration agreement was invalid.[319] A jurisdictional objection generally has to be brought early in the arbitration proceedings, which is

---

316 *E.g. Dégremont*, [1995] Rev. Arb. 88. *See supra* at pp. 473-475 (§17A.IV.2).

317 *Cf.* Lew, Mistelis, and Kröll, *Comparative International Commercial Arbitration*, para. 25–72. To discuss the proper dogmatic basis of preclusion or waiver with respect to different grounds of challenge under various jurisdictions would unfortunately surpass the scope of this thesis.

318 *See also* ZPO p. 1027 (GER); Arbitration Act 1996 p. 73 (1) (EW) (expressing the same principle).

319 *See supra* at pp. 463-465 (§17A.I).

expressly stipulated in the UNCITRAL Model Law and relevant national enactments.[320]

However, for procedural challenges or challenges with respect to the constitution of the arbitral tribunal some procedural concept of preclusion or material principle of waiver may apply as well if a party failed to raise its concerns with the arbitral tribunal and/or with the administering institution on time.

When participating in the constitution of the SIAC confirmed tribunal for the arbitration with Alstom, Insigma obviously attempted to avoid such preclusion or waiver of a potential future challenge on the basis of an improper constitution of the tribunal with this formulation in a letter to the secretariat:

> »While it is true that there was an agreement in previous correspondence that the third arbitrator be nominated by Mr Hwang and Professor Pryles jointly (with the caveat that [Insigma's] jurisdictional objections to the ICC would not be prejudiced), that agreement pertained specifically to the ICC proceedings, which are distinct from the present proceedings before the SIAC.«[321]

However, Insigma explicitly stated that it did not object to Mr. Moser acting as chairman, who was proposed by the co-arbitrators Mr. Hwang and Mr. Pryles, and repeated, by letter dated 6 February 2007, that its concerns only related to the formal application of article 8 of the SIAC Rules (1997) to the tribunal constitution.[322]

This correspondence is not easy to understand. One interpretation may be that Insigma did not doubt Mr. Moser's independence and impartiality but still wanted to safeguard its right to challenge the tribunal constitution. However, the formal insistence on applying article 8 of the ICC Rules (1998) rather than article 8 of the SIAC Rules (1997), without explaining what difference this would have made, suggests that Insigma only meant to reserve its right to challenge a perceived procedural irregularity raised by the SIAC secretariat's reference to its own rules rather than an irregularity in the tribunal constitution.[323] In any event, the Singapore courts

---

320 *Cf.* UNCITRAL Model Law 2006 art. 8 (1); *see generally* Born, *International Arbitration and Forum Selection Agreements*, 1239–40 (§7.05 [A]; with references to statutes and case law from various jurisdictions; concluding this to be a general principle with very few exceptions).

321 Letter of 24 January 2007, here cited according to *Insigma v. Alstom*, [2009] SGCA 24 [15] (insertions in brackets as in the decision).

322 Ibid.

323 *See supra* at p. 469 (§17A.III) on the difficult distinction between both kinds of challenge.

found that the parties have actually reached a subsequent agreement on the constitution of the arbitral tribunal, which made the differences between the *default* rules in the respective articles 8 of the ICC Rules and SIAC Rules (1997) immaterial.[324]

This illustrates the connection between party autonomy, preclusion and the *criterion of outcome-relevance*: Since Alstom and Insigma agreed on the constitution of the arbitral tribunal, a later challenge on this basis was precluded, whether on procedural grounds or because such challenge would have been in contradiction to the previous consent. This left Insigma only with the application of the wrong institutional rule when SIAC confirmed Mr. Moser as the chairman as a possible point of attack. However, independent of the qualification as an irregularity in the procedure or in the constitution of the tribunal, this issue was not outcome-relevant given the express agreement on Mr. Moser as the chairperson. Accordingly, the Singapore Court of Appeal highlighted that

> »whether the subsequent confirmation of the appointments by the SIAC was made with reference to SIAC Rules or to ICC Rules would have made no difference at all to the outcome.«[325]

Where an irregularity even left the tribunal's composition unaffected, it could not have affected the outcome of the award. In such a case, the principle of restrictive interpretation of grounds for challenge calls to uphold the award despite a minor procedural mistake identified.[326] While a court cannot be expected to enter into far-reaching hypothetical considerations on how the arbitration would have proceeded and ended, had the irregularity not occurred, a challenge on such ground should only be entertained where the party seeking annulment or resisting enforcement provides a substantial explanation of why this aspect was of importance.[327] At least from what is reported in the rulings by the Singapore courts and the Hangzhou

---

324 *See Insigma v. Alstom*, [2008] SGHC 39, 42–43; *Insigma v. Alstom*, [2009] SGCA 27.

325 *Insigma v. Alstom*, [2009] SGCA 24 [27 (c)].

326 Born, *International Commercial Arbitration (2014)*, 3268 (§25.04 [C][6]).

327 Under this angle, another reproach has to be made to the BGH's annulment of a Hamburg Friendly Arbitration award by Urteil [Judgment], [1983] 36 NJW 1267, [1984] IPRax 147, French translation: [1983] Rev. Arb. 353, English excerpts: [1990] XV YCA 660; *see supra* at pp. 166-170 (§8C.I.1.a).

Intermediate People's Court, Insigma's objections seem to lack such substantiation.[328]

## C. The Hangzhou Intermediate People's Court's ruling

These considerations on enforcing awards based on hybrid arbitration agreements would not be complete without finally presenting and discussing Alstom's failed attempt in mainland China[329] to obtain recognition and enforcement of the awards that were rendered in the hybrid arbitration administered by SIAC under ICC Rules.

In 2010, the SIAC confirmed arbitral tribunal rendered a partial award[330] with addendum[331] and a final award[332] with addendum[333] that ordered the Hangzhou located company Insigma Technology *inter alia* to pay a high multi-million dollar amount. Trying to enforce these awards, Alstom applied to the competent Hangzhou Intermediate People's Court, who, after obtaining the view of the SPC in accordance with the established reporting system,[334] rejected the application in February 2013.[335]

## I. Insigma's objections to recognition and enforcement

Before the Hangzhou court, Insigma brought forward a whole range of arguments in order to challenge the arbitral awards which Alstom sought to enforce. The following three allegations directly relate to the specific issue of the arbitration being based on a hybrid arbitration agreement:

---

328 However, the Hangzhou Intermediate People' Court here took a different view and refused enforcement of the awards rendered in the *Alstom-Insigma* arbitration as discussed below.

329 On Alstom's legally - but not practically - more successful enforcement action in Hong Kong, *see supra* at n. 254 on p. 463.

330 Dated 18 January 2010 (unpublished and unavailable).

331 Dated 14 April 2010 (unpublished and unavailable).

332 Dated 12 July 2010 (unpublished and unavailable).

333 Dated 11 October 2010 (unpublished and unavailable).

334 SPC's Circular on Foreign Arbitrations (1995).

335 *Alstom v. Insigma (Hz. IPC)*; *see also* Liu and Cheng, »Enforcement of Foreign Awards in Mainland China«, 658-660.

- The arbitration agreement was allegedly ambiguous for lack of agreement on the institution, on the applicable rules or on the kind of arbitration (ad hoc or institutional).
- The arbitration agreement was allegedly inoperative as SIAC administered arbitration under ICC Rules was impossible.
- The case had been pending before both the ICC Court and SIAC for two months before it was withdrawn from the ICC in alleged violation of both ICC and SIAC Rules.

In addition, Insigma argued that even if hybrid arbitration was theoretically possible, SIAC failed to apply the ICC Rules (1998) correctly, alleging that

- the arbitral tribunal was constituted according to SIAC Rules and therefore not in accordance with the parties' agreement on ICC Rules,
- the arbitration was formally commenced under article 3 of the SIAC Rules (1997) and not as agreed under ICC Rules,
- Terms of Reference were only signed by Alstom and not by Insigma contrary to article 18 (2) of the ICC Rules (1998).
- contrary to article 22 (2) of the ICC Rules (1998), SIAC did not announce the date for the final award when closing the proceedings and
- SIAC did not scrutinise and approve the award as required under article 27 of the ICC Rules (1998).

The other grounds of challenge to recognition and enforcement invoked by Insigma are not of interest for the specific issue of hybrid arbitration agreements as they can apply to arbitration under standard clauses as well. Mentioned for sake of completeness only, there were further allegations that

- a prerequisite of »*amicable consultations*« had not been fulfilled before the commencement of arbitration,[336]
- the arbitration agreement's scope would not cover the whole dispute,
- the decision on the merits violated Chinese public policy and that
- the awarding of interest and expenses lacked reasons.

---

336 The first sentence of Clause 18 (C) of the License Agreement in dispute provided for amicable consultation between the executives of the parties as a first tier of dispute settlement.

## II. The Hangzhou court's factual findings on the arbitration procedure

The Hangzhou court recapitulated that the arbitration of a dispute relating to a technology license agreement was based on an arbitration clause providing for arbitration before SIAC in Singapore in the English language under ICC Rules then in effect. The factual findings of the Hangzhou court, although they essentially correspond with those of the Singapore courts as discussed throughout this thesis, shall be presented in some detail because they give an illustrative account of many procedural issues that can arise from hybrid arbitration agreements.

### 1. The initial commencement of ICC arbitration

Based on the hybrid arbitration clause, Alstom first submitted a request for arbitration to the ICC Court in August 2006 and nominated Michael Pryles as its co-arbitrator. In its answer to the request for arbitration, Insigma objected to the ICC Court's jurisdiction, suggesting that SIAC should handle the case, Despite its jurisdictional objection, Insigma nominated Michael Hwang as its co-arbitrator for the arbitration.

### 2. The circumstances of the case transferral to SIAC

The procedural steps taken to transfer the case to SIAC were disputed between the parties in the enforcement proceedings before the Hangzhou court. In particular, Insigma alleged that the representatives of Alstom communicated with SIAC's secretariat privately, without informing Insigma, about the option of transferring the case to SIAC. However, after hearing evidence and cross-examination, the Hangzhou court could not confirm this allegation of unilateral conduct. To the contrary, it found that Insigma was copied into all correspondence between Alstom and the ICC Court's secretariat, SIAC's secretariat and the prospective co-arbitrators Mr. Pryles and Mr. Hwang without, at that time, voicing any objection.

In particular, in a letter dated 23 November 2006 sent to SIAC and copied to Insigma and the ICC Court, Alstom expressed that both parties wished to transfer the case to SIAC. Alstom's letter of the same date sent to Mr. Pryles and Mr. Hwang reiterated that »*both parties have reached an agreement on transferring the arbitration from ICC to SIAC.*« On 11 December 2006, Alstom formally requested the withdrawal of the arbitration from the ICC

Court. By letter of the same date sent to SIAC, the ICC and Insigma, Alstom asked SIAC's secretariat to deem the letter of 23 November 2006 as formal start of the arbitration at SIAC. SIAC then sent a first letter on 13 December 2006 to both Alstom and Insigma confirming that Alstom has initiated arbitration »*in accordance with rule 3 of the 1997 SIAC Rules.*«

## 3. The constitution of the arbitral tribunal

In a second letter dated 18 December 2006, SIAC's secretariat asked both parties whether the nominations of Mr. Pryles and Mr. Hwang made in the initial ICC proceedings should be treated as nominations for confirmation by SIAC. Both parties agreed by letters of 21 December 2006.

On 10 January 2007, SIAC informed the parties that it had confirmed the appointment of Mr. Pryles and Mr. Hwang as co-arbitrators and then invited the co-arbitrators to select a third, presiding arbitrator »*in accordance with rule 8 of the SIAC Rules.*«[337] At this point, Insigma first raised an objection by letter dated 11 January 2007: it complained about the commencement of arbitration at SIAC before the ICC arbitration was officially withdrawn and protested against the application of SIAC Rules to the constitution of the arbitral tribunal.[338] On 2 February 2007, the ICC Secretariat recorded the withdrawal of the ICC arbitration proceedings in its files.

SIAC then notified the parties that Mr. Pryles and Mr. Hwang agreed to designate Mr. Michael Moser as presiding arbitrator. As explained above, Insigma replied on 6 February 2007 that it did not object to the person of Mr. Moser as presiding arbitrator but expressed concern about the procedure of his designation. Asked by Alstom whether it nevertheless consented to the appointment of Mr. Moser as chairman of the tribunal, Insigma repeated in its letter to Alstom dated 14 February 2007 that it agreed to the appointment of Mr. Moser but that this consent »*shall not affect the viewpoint on the defects in the arbitration clause.*« By letter dated 23 February 2007, SIAC confirmed the constitution of the arbitral tribunal with Mr. Pryles and Mr. Hwang as co-arbitrators and Mr. Moser as chairman.

---

337 SIAC Rules, art. 8 (1) (1997): »*If three arbitrators are to be appointed, each party shall appoint one arbitrator. The two arbitrators thus appointed shall choose the third arbitrator who will act as the presiding arbitrator of the Tribunal.*«

338 *See supra* at p. 479 (§17B).

4. The hearing on jurisdiction and the Singapore courts' decisions

A first hearing on jurisdiction took place in Hong Kong[339] in September 2007 and the arbitral tribunal confirmed its jurisdiction in a decision dated 10 December 2007. As noted, Insigma challenged this decision before the Singapore High Court who rejected the challenge in a ruling upheld by the Singapore Court of Appeals.[340] During this interlocutory legal action in Singapore, the arbitration did not progress significantly until the Singapore Court of Appeals finally rejected the appeal on 23 March 2009.

5. The hearing on the merits and the awards

The hearing on the merits took place in April 2009. On 21 August 2009, SIAC declared the proceedings closed in accordance with article 22 of the ICC Rules (1998). SIAC also extended the time limit for issuing an award until 23 February 2010.[341] The first award on the merits was rendered on 18 January 2010, ordering Insigma to pay about 25 million US Dollar, to abstain from using certain technology of Alstom and to return confidential information. A decision on interest and expenses was reserved for later. Some formal errors in this first award were corrected by addendum decision of 14 April 2010. On 12 July 2010, the tribunal ordered Insigma in a final award on interest and expenses to pay another substantial amount of more than 30 million US Dollar in interest, legal fees and expenses. Again, this award had to be corrected by an addendum on 12 July 2010. Altogether, the arbitration thus took about four years.

---

339 Hong Kong was only the place of hearing while Singapore was the legal place of arbitration; *see supra* at pp. 71-74 (§4B.I.2) on the concept of a non-geographical or legal seat.

340 *Insigma v. Alstom*, [2008] SGHC 134; *Insigma v. Alstom*, [2009] SGCA 24. *See supra* at pp. 409-412 (§16A.I.4).

341 *Cf.* ICC Rules, art. 22 (2) (1998). It is not reported which actor at SIAC took this »*Court*« decision. It is also not reported if further prolongations were granted for the addendum to the first award and for the award on interest and expenses with addendum.

III. The ratio of the Hangzhou court's decision

The enforcement proceedings in China took another two years with a dev-astating outcome for Alstom since the Hangzhou court refused to recognise and enforce those multi-million dollar awards, which Alstom had spent so much time and money to obtain.

The Hangzhou court held that recognition and enforcement of the awards rendered in Singapore are governed by the New York Convention. It ac-cepted Insigma's challenge under article V (1)(d) that the composition of the arbitral authority was not in accordance with the agreement of the par-ties. In particular, the Hangzhou found it decisive that the chairman of the arbitral tribunal was selected by the two co-arbitrators, or even only by one co-arbitrator »*without objection from the other arbitrator*« rather than by the institution as required by ICC Rules. According to the reporting system established by the SPC notice of 1995, such decision to reject the enforce-ment of foreign arbitral awards needed the approval of the higher courts up to the SPC.[342] Therefore, it can be assumed, that the SPC shared the Hang-zhou court's view in the result. Unfortunately, the judgment itself does not mention the reference or the Supreme Court's reply in the matter.

The other grounds to refuse recognition and enforcement raised by In-sigma were not discussed since one challenge was found successful.

IV. Evaluation

Technically, the Hangzhou court's ruling is irreproachable. It gave a correct and exhaustive account of the procedural facts, applied the New York Con-vention and relied on the accepted ground for challenge of recognition and enforcement that the arbitral tribunal was not properly constituted. Moreo-ver, the SIAC secretariat's reference to its own rules when initiating and confirming the selection of a chairman certainly did give rise to concerns in this respect. As a positive note, the Hangzhou court also did not rely on some specific Chinese understanding of administered arbitration and the designation of arbitration institutions[343] when dealing with the enforcement of the foreign awards. Insigma's allegations of indefiniteness or inoperabil-ity of the arbitration agreement were wisely not entertained. In fact,

---

342  SPC's Circular on Foreign Arbitrations (1995).
343  *See supra* at pp. 101-104 (§4C.II.2.b.iii) on the specifics of Chinese law in this regard.

correctly so at this stage,[344] the Hangzhou court did not discuss at all whether SIAC was generally capable of and allowed to administer arbitration under ICC Rules. Rather, it restricted itself to controlling the correct application of the rules chosen by the parties.

That the Hangzhou court did not discuss the question whether hybrid arbitration was generally possible or the allegations of Insigma to have been deprived of the ICC »*branding*« to the same extent the Singapore Court of Appeals did[345] is owed to the procedural situation and not to be criticised: First, at this stage, the arbitration agreement was performed in some way, the operability issue is thus no longer relevant. Second, it would be for the winning rather than the losing party to express an interest in having an award reflecting the goodwill of a certain institution. When resisting enforcement, the argument that an award did not have the expected prestige seems somewhat odd. Moreover, in this case, Insigma had undisputedly agreed to - if not proposed –the transferral from the ICC Court to SIAC.

Despite all these positive points, the decision cannot be totally appraised because it overlooked the pressing issues of preclusion and outcome-relevance entirely.[346] It failed to give any reasons why the application of the principle of institutional selection of the chairman under the ICC Rules (1998) was of such importance to warrant the non-recognition of the award although Insigma had clearly indicated its consent with the composition of the tribunal as constituted. Here lies a major shortcoming and the reason why the Hangzhou Intermediate People's Court came to a result opposite to that reached by the Singapore Court of Appeals. Although some »*issues before the Singapore and Chinese courts were different*«[347] it seems prone to recall some of the Singapore Court of Appeals' correct observations as to tribunal's constitution:

---

344 *See supra* at p. 477 on annulment and enforcement proceedings as improper instances to install a policy against hybrid arbitration.

345 *Insigma v. Alstom*, [2009] SGCA 24 [35–36]. *See supra* at pp. 304-304 (§13B) and pp. 344-400 (§14) for these aspects.

346 *See also In the matter of Insigma Technology Co Ltd*, [2013] HCCW 224 [21]; *but see* the more appraising note by Liu and Cheng, »Enforcement of Foreign Awards in Mainland China«, 660: »*The decision shows that the Chinese courts attach great importance to the compliance of the arbitral process with the parties' agreement and are able to logically tackle complicated issues such as those arising in this case.*«

347 Liu and Cheng, »Enforcement of Foreign Awards in Mainland China«, 660.

- Insigma had acknowledged that the tribunal, including Mr. Moser as chairman, was properly constituted and only reserved its objections regarding the arbitration clause.
- Insigma agreed to Mr. Moser's appointment.
- Whether confirmation of the tribunal was made with reference to ICC or SIAC Rules would have made no difference regarding the tribunal's constitution.[348]

Without establishing essentially different facts, the Hangzhou Intermediate People's Court failed to discuss a possible preclusion or waiver of Insigma's challenge to the tribunal constitution. Moreover, it remains unclear why a reference by SIAC to its own 1997 rules and not to the ICC Rules (1998) when confirming the arbitrators should have influenced the award rendered in any way. Notably, Insigma did not argue that the confirmation should have been made by the ICC Court or Secretary General rather than a SIAC actor.[349] In addition, a confirmation decision only approves the tribunal as found according to party-agreed procedure; it does not concern a procedural issue in dispute between the parties. Accordingly, the hurdles to find functional equivalence between the respective actors should not be set too high.[350]

## §18 Enforcement risks of hybrid arbitration agreements

The foregoing discussion of procedural actions to challenge or enforce hybrid arbitration agreements and awards has underlined the substantive findings of the previous chapters that hybrid arbitration agreements, although not generally invalid,[351] are usually inadvisable[352] because they present serious difficulties of implementation.[353]

Prior to or pending arbitration, any dispute between the arbitrants on the interpretation of their agreement is difficult to overcome as controlling courts should not interfere with arbitral procedure[354] whereas the

---

348  *Insigma v. Alstom*, [2009] SGCA 24 [27].
349  It is not reported which SIAC actor took this confirmation decision.
350  *See supra* at pp. 368-371 (§14B.III.2).
351  Finding of Chapter 1, *see supra* at pp. 122-163 (§6).
352  Finding of Chapter 3, *see supra* at pp. 157-209 (§8)
353  Findings of Chapters 4 and 5, *see supra* at pp. 269-272 (§12) and 400-402 (§15).
354  As discussed *supra* at pp. 413-422 (§16A.II.1).

competences of supporting courts under most national laws do not suffi-ciently meet the demands of institutional arbitration.[355] As of now,[356] it seems that courts can only reinterpret a problematic institutional arbitration agreement as one for ad hoc arbitration, unless they understand their statu-tory powers extensively and analogously to allow court determination of a competent institution and applicable arbitration rules. As noted above,[357] reinterpretation as an ad hoc agreement is a rather intrusive interference with the parties' clear agreement of some form of *institutional* arbitration.[358] An agreement on hybrid arbitration may therefore not be entirely unen-forceable but, once it becomes necessary to apply to state courts, it will of-ten be enforceable only as something other than what the parties originally bargained for: an *ad hoc* arbitration agreement not supported by any insti-tution. This is also due to the fact that any agreement on institutional arbi-tration, even if a court finds it enforceable as such, would require the vol-untary cooperation of a designated institution.[359]

If, as in the *Insigma v. Alstom* case, the parties, the administering institu-tion and the tribunal managed to overcome implementation difficulties up to the rendering of an award, challenges of the award are still likely. Issues of operability of the arbitration agreement then transform to issues of pro-cedure. Correspondingly, the grounds of challenge with the highest chances of success are that the procedure or tribunal's constitution was not in ac-cordance with the agreement of the tribunal. It was the latter ground, which brought Alstom's enforcement efforts against Insigma in mainland China to fail. Although *dogmatically*, the Hangzhou Intermediate People's Court's decision to refuse recognition and enforcement of the *Alstom–Insigma* awards may be criticised as being somewhat formalistic, failing to consider aspects of preclusion/waiver and outcome-relevance, it is *practically* a per-fect warning against hybrid arbitration agreements.

---

355 As outlined *supra* at pp. 422-427 (§16A.II.1.d).
356 *See supra* at pp. 427-430 (§16A.II.1.d.iv) on a proposal to change this sit-uation.
357 *See* the expectations formulated in Chapter 2, *supra* at pp. 207-209 (§9).
358 *See* the finding of Chapter 3, *supra* at pp. 157-209 (§8).
359 *See supra* at pp. 430-435 (§16A.II.2) on the lack of a binding effect of the court decisions rendered in proceedings between arbitrants on the institu-tion, at pp. 435-442 (§16A.II.3) on the limited reviewability of institu-tional decisions and at pp. 444-461 (§16B) on the unlikely success of a direct, contractual action against an arbitral institution.

# Conclusion

The common assumption that party autonomy is restricted in institutional arbitration when compared to ad hoc arbitration[1] is not wrong but too general. It does not pay enough attention to the dogmatic foundations of limitations to party autonomy in institutional arbitration or to the different attitudes of arbitral institutions towards modification and opting-out attempts with regard to their rules. Moreover, such assumption does not give a satisfying answer to the practical question of how to deal with hybrid arbitration agreements or related procedure shopping attempts by parties without causing damage to the system of international arbitration, institutional arbitration in particular. After summarising the findings of this thesis regarding the *status quo* of the legal framework and institutional practice concerning hybrid arbitration agreements (§19), some suggestions on how to accommodate the issue of procedure shopping through hybrid arbitration agreements and related issues in the future shall be addressed (§20).

## *§19 Summary of findings*

This thesis has shown that the restrictions to the choice and modification of institutional arbitration rules are less of a legal than of a factual nature. Conventions and laws largely refrain from regulating institutional arbitration. Such regulation is left to private actors, the arbitral institutions. However, privately drafted arbitration rules do not have the force of law. They can only become binding through contract and contractual terms can be modified by agreement.

The reason why a modification of institutional arbitration rules or a complete opting-out of the administering institution's rules in favour of another set of rules is problematic lies not in any »*mandatory*« character of the rules as such but in the complex contractual structure of institutional arbitration. Institutional arbitration is not only based on an arbitration agreement and contracts between the parties and the arbitrators but on an additional agreement to be concluded with the arbitral institution. The conclusion of the

---

1    *E.g.* Patocchi and Niedermaier, »UNCITRAL-Schiedsordnung«, para. 13 (»*Einleitung*« [introduction]).

Administration Contract is free; the institution is not under an obligation to contract, in particular not if the parties do not accept its rules as standard terms. Therefore, neither arbitration agreements that provide for institutional arbitration but with major modifications of the rules nor hybrid arbitration agreements that refer to a completely different set of rules are invalid *per se*. However, their operability - their capability of being performed - depends decisively on the attitude, cooperation and flexibility of the institution designated to administer the case.

Regarding rule modifications, some institutions appear more flexible than others.[2]

Most adverse to party-agreed rule modifications is certainly the ICC Court.

In contrast, in the text of their rules, the AAA-ICDR and the LCIA used to underline party autonomy also in relation to the institution's rules, although this liberal stance was slightly restricted with the 2014 rule revisions of both institutions. The LCIA appears particularly concerned with safeguarding its control over the constitution of the arbitral tribunal but may be open towards other rule modifications by the parties.

Swiss arbitration has developed from little administered, decentralised arbitration systems organised at the various cantonal Chambers of Commerce to a large centralised, much more institutionalised systems under the Swiss Rules to be administered by the SCCAM. It can be expected, that significant rule modifications would be viewed more critical by the new centralised institution, which has an interest in increasing consistency to develop a brand of »*Swiss Arbitration*.« Although they provide some facilitating services under UNCITRAL Rules, all these institutions are unlikely to accept administering arbitrations under other institutional rules in fear of losing some of their traditional control and of damaging their relationship to the other institution and their own reputation in the arbitration world.

Under DIS Rules, party autonomy is arguably greater than under most other institutional rules because the DIS generally takes a very cautious stand in the administration of the proceedings. In fact, its role is not that different from that of institutions acting as appointing authority and facilitator in ad hoc arbitrations.[3] Relevant decisions, including the determination

---

2 *Contra* ibid. (drawing conclusions from the ICC's practice to arbitration institutions in general).

3 On intermediate forms of arbitration, *see supra* at pp. 146-157 (§7C); *cf. also* Schlosser, *Das Recht der internationalen privaten*

of the place of arbitration, challenge decisions and the assessment of the arbitrators' fees, are left entirely to the arbitral tribunal. A prima facie decision by the institution on jurisdiction is not foreseen. Therefore, the DIS might accept to administer cases with material changes to the DIS Rules and leave it to the parties and the arbitral tribunal how to accommodate such modifications. However, if parties agreed on hybrid DIS administered arbitration under another institution's rules, the problem materialises that the DIS does not have suitable, experienced actors to replace the required functions in particular under »*heavily administered*«[4] rules like those of the ICC Court. Accordingly, it is likely - and advisable - that the DIS would make it clear at the outset that it is not prepared to substitute any institutional actors or provide any services it would not provide under its own rules. However, if the parties agree or the arbitral tribunal so decides, provisions of the chosen rules that are compatible with DIS arbitration may be applied, meaning all rules not requiring institutional implementation. This would then be similar to the situation when parties agree on institutional rules for ad hoc arbitration (»*wild cat arbitration*«).[5]

SIAC and CIETAC are institutions of which it is reported that they have agreed to administer hybrid arbitrations in the past, hybrid arbitration under ICC Rules in particular. SIAC's flexibility in this respect gained notoriety with the *Insigma v. Alstom* case which received mixed critics from the arbitration community, while CIETAC's willingness to administer hybrid arbitration was long known only from hear-say but is now clearly addressed in article 4 (3) of the CIETAC Rules. SIAC and CIETAC have in common that they are based in Asian jurisdictions, however, their home jurisdictions still display divergent attitudes towards international commercial arbitration. While the principle of party autonomy is prominently enshrined in Singapore's IAA, flexibilisation and de-controlisation of Chinese arbitration law are still a work in progress. Their locale may have influenced these Asia-based institutions' flexibility towards hybrid arbitration in two ways: First, hybrid arbitration agreements appear to be more common in contracts with one Asian party. A hypothetical explanation for this - which should provoke further empirical research - may be the growth of Asia's economies

---

*Schiedsgerichtsbarkeit*, 139, para. 181 (qualifying the DIS predecessor, the DAS, as an institution for semi-organised arbitration of the »*German type*«).

4    Lew, Mistelis, and Kröll, *Comparative International Commercial Arbitration*, para. 3–19.

5    *Cf. supra* at pp. 151-156 (§7C.IV).

on the one hand and the traditional strength of Western businesses on the other. Such constellation can incite the parties to hybrid arbitration agreements as a compromise between the rules of a traditional, European institution and administration by an upcoming Asian-based institution. Confusion on the - in theory negligible - correlation between place of arbitration, place of hearing and seat of institution further encourages such hybrid arbitration compromise. Second and curiously, both a very liberal arbitration policy as maintained by Singapore's legislator and courts and a much more restrictive approach towards private arbitration as still residual in the arbitration law of China may entice arbitration institutions to innovatively apply hybrid arbitration agreements by substituting the actors and functions of the rules issuing institutions. From SIAC's point of view, the acceptance of the *Alstom–Insigma* arbitration was performance of the arbitration agreement in support of Singapore's pro-arbitration policy. The Singapore Court of Appeal's decision proved it right.[6] From CIETAC's point of view, administering hybrid arbitrations may be a way to circumvent restrictions under the Chinese arbitration law by enabling parties to choose the rules they want for their arbitration in China and to comply at the same time with the mandatory requirement of designating an arbitration »*commission.*«[7] In particular, it is still not entirely clear if and in which circumstances foreign institutions are allowed to administer arbitrations in China, although there is recent jurisprudence of the SPC indicating a revolution here.[8]

Certainly, to accept cases under another institution's rules, as SIAC did with the *Alstom–Insigma* arbitration, and CIETAC offers under its rules, may have the taste of these institutions trying to benefit from efforts other institutions invested into their rules and from their success and reputation. However, even with a view to this consideration, the administration of hybrid arbitrations is defendable. In particular, mere application, rather than reproduction, of another institution's rules is, although it is commercial use, neither an infringement of the copyright the issuing institution retains in its rules nor does such conduct infringe the issuing institution's trademarks. Intellectual property claims of the rules issuing institution against another institution administering arbitrations under its rules are therefore not

---

6    *Insigma v. Alstom*, [2009] SGCA 24.

7    Arbitration Law art. 16, 18 (P.R.C.).

8    *See Longlide*, [2013] Min Si Ta Zi no. 13; cited according to Sun, »SPC Instruction Provides New Opportunities for International Arbitral Institutions to Expand into China«, 695 (Appendix 3); *see also* Dong, »Open Door for Foreign Arbitration Institutions?«

available. More appropriate to react to the conduct of administering hybrid arbitrations may be an application of unfair competition law, with concepts of exploitation of reputation, parasitism or misappropriation springing to mind. However, the various concepts developed in different jurisdictions all require a verdict of »*unfairness*« regarding the conduct to be condemned. Such threshold is indispensable if one wants to avoid a dilution of the hard criteria, balances and values of primarily applicable IP law. If an institution's main motivation in accepting arbitrations under other institutions' rules was/is a desire to help parties to implement an otherwise inoperable arbitration agreement, such pro-arbitration attitude can positively outweigh less noble side motives. Against this background, administering hybrid arbitrations is not illegal. In this respect, it does not make a real difference, whether rules contain an exclusivity clause like article 1 (2) of the ICC Rules or article 1 (3) sentence 4 of the AAA-ICDR-Rules since these provisions do not have the force of law. Privately enacted, they can only become binding on contracting parties. A contract between the ICC or the AAA-ICDR with other institutions or with any parties asking such other institutions to administer an arbitration under ICC or AAA-ICDR-Rules does not exist.

The main and true obstacle to the performance of hybrid arbitration agreements is not a legal but a practical one: the problem of how to substitute actors foreseen in the rules, which the administering institution does not have. It was herein proposed to apply a test of functional equivalence[9] between actors to this issue: Only if the purpose of a particular rule can be adequately fulfilled by a certain actor of the administering institution, this actor may substitute the actor meant by the referenced rules. Functional equivalence is easier to find for any institutional acts required under the rules that simply confirm party-autonomous agreements on procedure, while it requires greater similarity between the respective actors when the institution has to take a controversial decision. In differentiation to the functional equivalence test herein developed, it seems insufficient to simply ask whether the administering institution has an actor named similar to that referred to by the applicable rules. In particular, a denomination like »*Court*« is not protected or defined and institutional »*Courts*« are constituted and work very differently. Tremendous differences already exist between the ICC's, LCIA's, SIAC's and the SCCAM. A perception that any institutional body named a »*Court*« might »*mirror*« *e.g.* the ICC Court is taken ad

---

9    Inspired by substitution theory developed for issues resulting from a conflict of laws, *see supra* at pp. 344-355 (§14A).

absurdum by the latest version of CIETAC's rules. It seems that with the CIETAC Rules (2015), the term »*Secretariat*« was simply replaced by »*Court*«, without at the same time enacting major changes in constitution or tasks of the former secretariat now named Court.

Harmonisation of institutional arbitration rules can be a suitable reaction to the phenomenon of procedure shopping through hybrid arbitration agreements but such harmonisation should not end at the merely terminological level as implied by the launch of the CIETAC Rules (2015). Rather, the fact that parties seek procedural compromises as controversial as the hybrid arbitration agreements herein discussed in order to avail themselves of the advantages of different institutional systems should motivate arbitration institutions to cooperate and exchange their experiences with certain features of their rules. Where both the imposition of mandatory rules and procedural remedies fail as reactions to such procedure shopping, cooperation and harmonisation - rather than competition and protectionism - may be key.[10]

In addition, if institutions want to protect the parties' autonomy to agree on institutional arbitration, they should join forces and exercise their influence towards a reform of arbitration laws that are almost entirely based on a model of ad hoc arbitration, which creates a number of uncertainties in the field of supporting and enforcing a choice for institutional arbitration.

In particular, different national courts asked to decide on the validity and operability of hybrid arbitration agreements have dealt with the tension between party autonomy and institutional autonomy in different ways. Singapore's courts deciding on the hybrid arbitration clause in *Insigma v. Alstom*[11] at an interim stage, after the tribunal's decision on jurisdiction but prior to the final awards, found that the principles of party autonomy and effective interpretation required to confirm both the parties' choice of hybrid arbitration and the way SIAC interpreted the underlying arbitration agreement. Similarly, the Svea Court of Appeal, at the post award stage, recently rejected a challenge to an award rendered in proceedings conducted before the SCC under application of at least some features of ICC Rules, although it was deemed

---

10  On the traditional remedies to the vaguely related (*see supra* at pp. 32-35, §1B) problem of forum shopping, *cf.* Renner, *Zwingendes transnationales Recht*, 57.

11  *Insigma v. Alstom*, [2008] SGHC 134; *Insigma v. Alstom*, [2009] SGCA 24.

»undisputed that the SCC lacks the required organizational structure to administer an arbitration fully compliant with ICC's rules«[12]

In deciding that way, both the Singapore courts and the Svea Court of Appeal put the focus on the parties' autonomy to choose arbitration over state court litigation and protected this general choice by granting the respective administering institution great liberty in performing the hybrid arbitration clauses.

In contrast, when deciding on the validity of the final awards rendered in the *Alstom–Insigma* arbitration, the Hangzhou Intermediate People's Court in China put the emphasis on details of what it considered to have been the parties' procedural agreement and refused to enforce the awards because it found that SIAC interpreted and performed the arbitration clause too liberally.[13]

These conflicting decisions show that the role of arbitral institutions as players among parties, arbitrators and courts is not yet sufficiently defined. It was herein recommended that institutions should generally try to work together with parties and arbitrators when adapting chosen arbitration rules of another institution to their own system and structure. However, even where an institutional interpretation and performance of a certain procedural rule was not expressly accepted by a party to the arbitration, courts should, in the interest of efficiency, only interfere when a challenging party proves that full compliance with such rule was of particular importance to it. While the Singapore courts and the Svea Court of Appeal followed this maxim, the Hangzhou Intermediate People's Court's decision to refuse enforcement of the awards on the basis of a minor irregularity in the procedure for the constitution of the arbitral tribunal appears disproportionate.

## *§20 Looking back for a way forward: A plea for institutional cooperation*

For the prospect of a bright future for institutional arbitration, it may be inspiring to take a look back to its childhood days. In the late 60s, early 70s, arbitral institutions sought to open foreign arbitration markets and to smooth out conceptual differences between Western and Eastern

---

12 Government of the Russian Federation v. I.M. Badprim S.R.L., T 2454–14 (Sweden Svea Ct. App., Stockholm, 23 January 2015) 13.

13 *Alstom v. Insigma (Hz. IPC)*, discussed in detail *supra* at §17C (pp. 480 et seq.).

institutions by developing policies of cooperation. The Third International Arbitration Congress held in October 1969 in Venice was devoted to this topic.[14]

In many respects, the aim of better cooperation was accomplished. For example, an international, supra-institutional organisation was created, the International Committee for Commercial Arbitration, now named International Council for Commercial Arbitration (ICCA), which organises congresses and conferences and coordinates common marketing and educational activities.[15] A similar project is the International Federation of Commercial Arbitration Institutions (ICAI) created a while later in 1985.[16] However, projects to coordinate arbitration institutions and to prepare uniform institutional rules[17] seem to have been given up - or maybe they have been overrun by the drafting of the UNCITRAL Model Law and the UNCITRAL Rules, which are independent of any institutional framework. The downside is that »*rivalry, confusion, and difficult-to-obtain information that* [...] *inhibit parties in making a reasonable choice*« seem to persist.[18] Only the AAA-ICDR Rules still display residues of the early concept of cooperating with other institutions to meet worldwide demand.[19] However, given the lack of transparency - the AAA's cooperation agreements are not publicly available - the claim that AAA-ICDR arbitration may be administered by other institutions on the basis of cooperation agreements appears detrimental to an informed exercise of party autonomy in choosing an institution and applicable rules as well.

Within the last 50 years, the harmonisation of legislation through the New York Convention and the UNCITRAL Model Law, with the wide acknowledgement of party autonomy and of concepts like the legal seat, not

---

14 Program available at International Council for Commercial Arbitration, »IIIrd Congress, Venice October 1969: Program of Congress Sessions«; *cf. also* Straus, »A Network of Arbitration Associations,« 491–92.

15 On ICCA's history, *see generally* Veeder, »ICCA 50th Anniversary Speech«.

16 Thereon, *see generally* Davidson, »The International Federation of Commercial Arbitration Institutions«.

17 *See* Straus, »A Network of Arbitration Associations«, 494 (on ICCA's former working committees on Coordination of Arbitration Institutions, Exchange of Information and Preparation of Uniform Rules).

18 Ibid., 488 (calling, already in the 1970s, for a network of arbitral institutions, allowing participants to administer arbitrations under the other participating institutions' rules).

19 *Cf.* AAA-ICDR Rules, art. 1 (3) sent. 3 (2014).

necessarily identical with the place of hearing or location of the institution, has increased flexibility and universality as »*primary advantages of arbitration.*«[20] Conversely, the same development created a potential for competition on a worldwide market for institutional arbitration services, which seems to have incited a mild form of protectionism of traditional institutions fearing for their »*pivotal*« role,[21] exemplified by provisions like article 1 (2) of the ICC Rules and article 1 (3) sentence 4 AAA-ICDR Rules. It would be regrettable, if such unilateral insistence on the exclusivity of institutional rules contradicted the achievements in creating a harmonised international arbitration regime made so far. The better approach may be for institutions to consult each other for a solution whenever parties attempt to combine features of different institutional systems by agreeing on a hybrid arbitration clause or the like. In addition, practical warnings against such »*mixing and matching*«,[22] in substance not contested herein, would be listened to more carefully if voiced unanimously and simultaneously by a number of institutions, not restricted to the traditionally leading ones.

> »[C]ooperation between the arbitration organisms, which today exist in the world may be enormously useful, and what is more it hardly seems an exaggeration to say it is this very cooperation which will prove to be the mainspring of all real progress.«[23]

## *§21 Recall of key propositions*

- The acceptance of party autonomy as the key concept of international arbitration supports the validity of hybrid arbitration agreements.
- From a normative-hierarchical perspective, an arbitral institution cannot forbid parties to choose its rules for an arbitration that is to be administered by another institution.

---

20 Straus, »A Network of Arbitration Associations«, 488.
21 *Cf.* ibid., 488, 493 (welcoming it, if a network of institutions would underline such role of the ICC; quoting a remark by Eugene Minoli to the same effect).
22 Mason, »Whether Arbitration Rules Should Be Applied by the Issuing Arbitral Institution«, 4 (full text currently unavailable; cited according to: Greenberg, Kee, and Weeramantry, *International Commercial Arbitration*, para. 4.176).
23 Minoli, »Key Note«, 4; cited according to Straus, »A Network of Arbitration Associations«, 492.

- Parties that agree on hybrid arbitration choose a form of institutional arbitration, not ad hoc arbitration. However, advantages of predictability and efficiency commonly associated with institutional arbitration are largely lost when agreeing on one institution and another institution's rules.
- In contrast to other arbitration clauses deemed pathological for ambiguity, a hybrid arbitration clause clearly conveys a choice for one institution and another institution's rules.
- Nevertheless, hybrid arbitration clauses raise issues of interpretation and operability or performance that diminish their efficiency. All efforts to accommodate these issues by interpretation or contract adaptation should first reflect the interests of the parties, but also those of the institution designated to administer the arbitration.
- Institutions are involved in arbitrations to differing degrees. These differences in control also influence their attitudes towards attempts by parties to opt out of all or some of their rules. Overall, institutional rules are negotiable contract terms.
- Institutions are not obliged to administer arbitrations under modified or even entirely different arbitration rules. They may either refuse to accept the parties (counter-)offer for an Administration Contract according to the parties' terms or terminate such contract at least until the constitution of an arbitral tribunal.
- Institutions are allowed to apply other institutions' rules. Neither contract law, nor intellectual property or unfair competition law prohibit such market conduct.
- Whether and to which extent an institution is capable to administer an arbitration under another institution's rules depends on the availability of functional equivalent actors to perform the required tasks.
- Decisive for such functional equivalence is not only a comparable organisational structure, but also experience with the kind of task required. The more controlling an institution is, the more difficult would it be for another institution to substitute its actors and functions.
- Only if and to the extent parties mutually agreed on the procedural steps to be taken during the arbitration, substituting institutional actors when administering hybrid arbitrations proceedings would not be a major issue.
- Enforcing hybrid arbitration agreements before state courts can raise difficulties. The current system of controlling and supporting state court competences under most arbitration laws does not sufficiently contemplate obstacles arising in an institutional setting.

- Contractual actions against institutions, if they overcome high liability thresholds, can only reasonably be directed at damages, not at specific performance or termination of the Administration Contract.
- The most probable causes of action against hybrid arbitration awards are challenges to the regularity of the arbitral procedure and/or the constitution of the arbitral tribunal.
- In recognition and enforcement proceedings, due attention should be given to the question if a party may be precluded or estopped from invoking grounds for challenge in light of a prior express agreement to hybrid arbitration. Moreover, it should only succeed if the irregularity reproached - *i.e.* the difference between the rules as agreed and the rules as applied - influenced the outcome of the case, the award.
- A hybrid arbitration agreement is an attempt by parties to shop for institutional rules of procedure and for an arbitral institution as two separate, unbundled products/services. Should an increase of this phenomenon prove market demand for institutional rules that are independent of a certain institution, institutions should consider cooperating rather than competing to meet such demand.

# Deutschsprachige Zusammenfassung (summary in German)

Um den deutschsprachigen Lesern die Orientierung zu erleichtern, wird an dieser Stelle zusammenfassend auf Deutsch in das Thema eingeführt (§22); zudem werden die wesentlichen Ergebnisse dargestellt (§23) und die Arbeitsthesen aufgeführt (§24).

## §22 Themeneinführung

Gegenstand der vorstehenden Untersuchung ist der Umfang der Parteiautonomie bei der Bestimmung von Verfahrensregeln für internationale institutionelle Schiedsverfahren. Insbesondere wird untersucht, ob die Wahl einer bestimmten Schiedsinstitution zwingend die Anwendung der Schiedsordnung dieser Institution nach sich zieht oder ob die institutionellen Schiedsordnungen im Ganzen oder nur bezüglich von Einzelregelungen dispositiv sind.

Können die Vertragsparteien ihre Streitigkeiten einer bestimmten Schiedsgerichtsinstitution unterstellen und zugleich die Schiedsordnung einer anderen Institution zur Anwendung bringen? Ist die Wahl einer solchen »*hybriden Schiedsklausel*« im Hinblick auf Verfahrensökonomie, Kosten und Anerkennung des Schiedsentscheides auch ratsam?

Die Arbeit gibt dabei auch Aufschlüsse über die Unterschiede zwischen einigen wesentlichen internationalen institutionellen Schiedsordnungen und zwischen institutionellen gegenüber Ad-hoc-Schiedsverfahren.

Aufhänger der Untersuchung ist der im Jahr 2009 zunächst vom Singapurischen High Court und dann vom Singapurischen Court of Appeals entschiedene Fall *Insigma Technology gegen Alstom Technology*.[1] Die Singapurischen Gerichte bestätigten die Zuständigkeitsentscheidung des Schiedsgerichtes und befanden, dass die dabei zugrunde liegende hybride Schiedsklausel nicht allein deshalb undurchführbar gewesen sei, weil die Parteien auf eine bestimmte Schiedsinstitution verwiesen haben (das Singapore International Arbitration Centre, SIAC), und zugleich die Schiedsordnung einer anderen Institution auf das Verfahren anwenden wollten (nämlich die

---

1    Hier zitiert als *Insigma v. Alstom*, [2008] SGHC 134; *Insigma v. Alstom*, [2009] SGCA 24.

Schiedsregeln der Internationalen Handelskammer, ICC, mit Hauptsitz in Paris).

Die Schiedsklausel lautete auszugsweise:

»Any and all such disputes shall be finally resolved by arbitration before the Singapore International Arbitration Centre in accordance with the Rules of Arbitration of the International Chamber of Commerce then in effect and the proceedings shall take place in Singapore and the official language shall be English.«

[Alle Streitigkeiten sollen endgültig im Wege des Schiedsverfahrens vor dem Singapore International Arbitration Centre gemäß der Schiedsordnung der Internationalen Handelskammer in der dann geltenden Fassung gelöst werden und das Verfahren soll in Singapur in englischer Sprache durchgeführt werden.]

Der angeführte Grund für die Wahl einer solchen hybriden Schiedsklausel war, dass die Parteien die bewährte und ihnen wohl bekanntere ICC-Schiedsordnung zur Anwendung bringen, aber zugleich von den geringeren Kosten eines SIAC-Schiedsverfahren profitieren wollten. Unter Berücksichtigung der daraus folgenden Schwierigkeiten für die im Schiedsverfahren obsiegende Partei, *Alstom Technology*, den gegen *Insigma Technology* erlassenen Endschiedsspruch in China zu vollstrecken, erwies sich dieser Ansatz allerdings zumindest im Nachhinein als Milchmädchenrechnung.[2] Die Arbeit untersucht aus verschiedenen Blickwinkeln und auf Grundlage eines rechtsordnungsübergreifenden, transnationalen Ansatzes, ob ein solches »*Rosinenpicken*« im internationalen Schiedsrecht jedenfalls zulässig ist, wenn es auch meist nicht ratsam scheint.

Als Reaktion auf diesen Fall und das Phänomen hybrider Schiedsklauseln aus institutioneller Sicht kann man, soweit eine Positionierung erkennbar ist, zwei Strömungen ausmachen: Die internationale Handelskammer (ICC) sowie das *International Centre of Dispute Resolution* der *American Arbitration Association* (AAA-ICDR) erachten die Möglichkeit der Vereinbarung und Durchführung hybrider Schiedsklauseln als Bedrohung für die institutionelle Schiedsgerichtsbarkeit und Angriff auf ihr Geschäftsmodell bzw. Ausnutzung ihrer Reputation und versuchen, ihre traditionelle

---

2    Der Hangzhou Intermediate People's Court versagte die Anerkennung und Vollstreckung aus verfahrensrechtlichen Gründen, *Alstom Technology v. Insigma Technology,* Az. 7/2011 (Chinesische Zitierweise: [2011]浙杭仲确字第7号) (Mittleres Volksgericht Hangzhou, Provinz Zhejiang, 6. Februar 2013, hier zitiert als *Alstom v. Insigma [Hz. IPC]*; Exzerpt auf Englisch nun veröffentlicht in [2014] XXXIX ICCA Y.B. Comm. Arb. 380; hier zusammengefasst und ausführlich diskutiert auf S. 480-487, §17C).

Vormachtstellung dagegen zu schützen. Entsprechend führte die Internationale Handelskammer bei Erlass ihrer seit 2012 geltenden Schiedsordnung in Artikel 1 Absatz 2 Satz 3 folgende Abwehrklausel ein:

> »Der Gerichtshof ist die einzige Institution, die zur Verwaltung von Schiedsverfahren nach der Schiedsgerichtsordnung, einschließlich der Prüfung und Genehmigung von danach ergangenen Schiedssprüchen, befugt ist.«

Das AAA-ICDR folgte diesem Beispiel, sodass die seit 2014 geltende Fassung seiner Schiedsordnung in Artikel 1 Absatz 3 Satz 4 folgendes bestimmt:

> »Arbitrations administered under these Rules shall be administered *only* by the ICDR or by an individual or organisation authorised by the ICDR to do so.«

> [Schiedsverfahren sollen nach dieser Schiedsordnung nur durch das ICDR oder eine Person oder Organisation verwaltet werden, die vom ICDR hierzu ermächtigt worden ist.]

Gegenläufig scheint die diesbezügliche Politik der *China International Economic and Trade Arbitration Commission (CIETAC)*, der internationalen Schiedsinstitution der Volksrepublik China, wie sie unter Betonung des hehren Prinzips - oder je nach Sichtweise: Deckmantels - der Parteiautonomie in Artikel 4 Absatz 3 der CIETAC-Schiedsordnung (Fassungen 2012 und 2015) zum Ausdruck kommt:

> »Where the parties agree to refer their dispute to CIETAC for arbitration but have agreed on a modification of these Rules or have agreed on the application of other arbitration rules, the parties' agreement shall prevail unless such agreement is inoperative or in conflict with a mandatory provision of the law as it applies to the arbitration proceedings. Where the parties have agreed on the application of other arbitration rules, CIETAC shall perform the relevant administrative duties.«

> [Wenn die Parteien vereinbaren, CIETAC für ein Schiedsverfahren anzurufen, aber sich auf Abweichungen von der CIETAC-Schiedsordnung oder die Anwendung einer anderen Schiedsordnung verständigt haben, so soll die Parteivereinbarung Vorrang haben, es sei denn, sie ist undurchführbar oder sie verstößt gegen das anwendbare Schiedsrecht. Wenn die Parteien die Anwendung einer anderen Schiedsordnung vereinbart haben, soll CIETAC die notwendigen Verwaltungsaufgaben ausführen.]

Die Problematik hybrider Schiedsverfahren gibt vor diesem Hintergrund auch Anlass, die Rechtsnatur von Bestimmungen internationaler Schiedsordnungen aus prozessualer, vertragsrechtlicher, urheber- und lauterkeitsrechtlicher Sicht ins Blickfeld zu nehmen.

Eine aktuelle Gerichtsentscheidung rückt das Thema hybride Schiedsvereinbarungen erneut in den Mittelpunkt der Aufmerksamkeit: Am 23. Januar 2015 wies das Stockholmer Berufungsgericht (*Svea Hovrätt*) in dem

Fall *Regierung der Russischen Föderation gegen I.M. Badprim S.R.L.*[3] einen Aufhebungsantrag gegen einen Schiedsspruch aus dem Jahr 2013 ab, der in einem durch das Schiedsinstitut der Stockholmer Handelskammer (*Stockholm Chamber of Commerce, SCC*) organisierten Verfahren unter - teilweiser - Anwendung der ICC-Schiedsordnung erging. Diese Entscheidung, die allerdings nur knapp begründet ist, bestätigt die wesentlichen Ergebnisse dieser Dissertation, wie einleitend[4] und abschließend angesprochen.[5]

## §23 Ergebnisse[6]

Wesentliches Ergebnis dieser Arbeit ist, dass die Wahl und Abänderung von institutionellen Schiedsordnungen eher auf faktische denn auf rechtliche Hürden stößt. Internationale Verträge und nationales Recht vermeiden die Regulierung der institutionellen Aspekte der Schiedsgerichtsbarkeit weitgehend. Ordnung, Kontrolle und Weiterentwicklung der institutionellen Schiedsgerichtsbarkeit sind privaten Akteuren überlassen, den Schiedsinstitutionen. Allerdings haben privatrechtlich verfasste und erlassene Schiedsordnungen keine Gesetzeskraft. Verbindlich werden sie nur kraft Vertrages und vertragliche Klauseln können wiederum durch vertragliche Vereinbarung modifiziert werden.

Der Grund, warum die Abbedingung institutioneller Schiedsregeln oder gar eine komplette Abwahl der Schiedsordnung der verwaltenden Institution problematisch ist, ist somit nicht, dass Schiedsordnungen oder ihren Vorschriften irgendein rechtlich »*zwingender*« Charakter zukäme. Er ist vielmehr in der komplexen vertragsrechtlichen Ordnung institutioneller Schiedsverfahren zu suchen. Das vertragsrechtliche Gerüst eines institutionellen Schiedsverfahrens bilden nicht allein die Schiedsvereinbarung und der Schiedsrichtervertrag, sondern zudem ein weiterer Vertrag mit der verwaltenden Schiedsinstitution. Auch hinsichtlich dieses Schiedsorganisationsvertrages gilt der Grundsatz der Vertragsfreiheit; ein Kontrahierungszwang für die Institution besteht nicht, insbesondere dann nicht, wenn die

---

3   Eine inoffizielle englische Übersetzung des Urteils ist über www.arbitration.sccinstitute.com/Swedish-Arbitration-Portal/Court-of-Appeal/Court-of-Appeal/Court-of-Appeal/ abrufbar.
4   Siehe oben, S. 37-39 (§1D).
5   Siehe oben, S. 495 (§19).
6   Sinngemäße deutsche Übersetzung von §19 [German translation of §19].

Parteien die Schiedsordnung dieser Institution nicht als allgemeine Geschäftsbedingungen akzeptieren.

Einerseits sind Schiedsvereinbarungen, welche Abweichungen zu wesentlichen Vorschriften der Schiedsordnung der gewählten Institution vorsehen und hybride Schiedsvereinbarungen, die sogar eine vollkommen andere Schiedsordnung statt der der angerufenen Institution als anwendbar bestimmen, nicht von vornherein unwirksam. Andererseits aber hängt ihre Durchführbarkeit entscheidend von der Einstellung, Unterstützung und Flexibilität der gewählten Schiedsinstitution hinsichtlich solcher Vertrags- und Verfahrensbedingungen ab.

Einige Schiedsinstitutionen nehmen die Abbedingung ihrer Schiedsordnung eher hin als andere. Weitgehend unnachgiebig ist diesbezüglich seit jeher der ICC-Schiedsgerichtshof. Hingegen haben sowohl das *AAA-ICDR* als auch der Londoner Internationale Schiedsgerichthof (*London Court of International Arbitration, LCIA*), die Parteiautonomie zunächst auch textlich über die Geltung ihrer Schiedsordnung erhoben. Uneingeschränkt galt dies jedenfalls bis zu den mit Revisionen ihrer Schiedsordnungen im Jahr 2014 teilweise eingeführten Einschränkungen. Der LCIA ist insofern insbesondere bemüht, Kontrolle über die Bildung des Schiedsgerichtes zu behalten, dürfte aber privatautonomen Verfahrensbestimmungen bezüglich anderer Aspekte des Schiedsverfahrens offener gegenüber stehen.

Die Schweizer institutionelle Schiedsgerichtslandschaft entwickelte sich von lose organisierten, dezentralen Schiedsgerichtsverwaltungen, angesiedelt bei den jeweiligen kantonalen Handelskammern, hin zu einem System, in dem eine große, zentrale Institution, die *Swiss Chambers' Arbitration Institution*, mit ihrem Schiedsgerichtshof die Mehrheit der internationalen institutionellen Verfahren unter einheitlichen Regeln, der Internationalen Schweizerischen Schiedsordnung (*Swiss Rules*), verwaltet. Zu erwarten ist, dass wesentliche Abweichungen von dieser Schiedsordnung mit einiger Skepsis durch die *Swiss Chambers' Arbitration Institution* betrachtet werden, denn diese hat als neue zentrale Institution ein nachvollziehbares Interesse an Vereinheitlichung, um das Label »*Swiss Arbitration*« weiterzuentwickeln und zu festigen.

Obwohl alle vorgenannten Institutionen bereit sind, Unterstützung von Schiedsverfahren nach der UNCITRAL-Schiedsordnung, welche eigentlich für Ad-hoc-Verfahren entwickelt worden ist, zu leisten, ist es eher unwahrscheinlich, dass sie dafür aufgeschlossen wären, Schiedsverfahren nach der Schiedsordnung einer anderen Institution zu verwalten. Die Kontrolle über die von ihnen verwalteten Verfahren und die guten Beziehungen zu der anderen Institution sollen nicht aufs Spiel gesetzt werden.

Unter der Schiedsordnung der *Deutschen Institution für Schiedsgerichtsbarkeit* (DIS) hat die Parteiautonomie ein besonderes Gewicht, da die DIS bei der Verwaltung von Schiedsverfahren große Zurückhaltung übt. Tatsächlich ist die Rolle der DIS weitgehend vergleichbar mit der einer ernennenden Stelle in Ad-hoc-Verfahren.[7] Wichtige Entscheidungen, wie die Bestimmung des Schiedsortes, Entscheidungen über Ablehnungsanträge gegen Schiedsrichter und selbst die Bestimmung des Honorars der Schiedsrichter, werden vollständig dem Schiedsgericht selbst überlassen. Auch ist eine vorläufige Zuständigkeitsentscheidung der Institution nach der DIS-Schiedsordnung nicht vorgesehen. Vor diesem Hintergrund scheint es denkbar, dass die DIS Schiedsverfahren auch dann annimmt, wenn die Parteien in wesentlichen Punkten von der DIS-Schiedsordnung abweichen wollen, und die Entscheidung darüber, wie diese Abweichungen behandelt werden sollen, der Vereinbarung zwischen dem Schiedsgericht und den Parteien oder der Entscheidung des Schiedsgerichtes überlässt. Wenn Parteien allerdings ein hybrides, von der DIS nach der Schiedsordnung einer anderen Institution verwaltetes Schiedsverfahren wünschen, stellt sich das Problem, dass die DIS keine vergleichbaren und hierfür hinreichend erfahrenen Akteure und Organe hat, um die Aufgaben und Funktionen nach Verfahrensordnungen auszuüben, welche eine starke Kontrolle und Mitbestimmung der Institution vorsehen, wie zum Beispiel die ICC-Schiedsordnung. Entsprechend ist es wahrscheinlich - jedenfalls ratsam - dass die DIS in einem solchen Fall bereits von vornherein klarstellt, dass sie nicht bereit ist, institutionelle Organe nach der gewählten Schiedsordnung zu ersetzen oder Dienste anzubieten, die die DIS-Schiedsordnung selbst nicht vorsieht. Nichtsdestotrotz könnten, wenn die Parteien dem zustimmen oder wenn das Schiedsgericht das für angemessen hält, solche Vorschriften der gewählten Schiedsordnung Anwendung finden, die mit dem DIS-Schiedsverfahrenssystem kompatibel sind, also insbesondere solche Vorschriften, die eine institutionelle Implementierung nicht verlangen. Diese Situation wäre dann vergleichbar mit einer, in der die Parteien eine institutionelle

---

7    Zu Zwischenformen zwischer institutioneller und Ad-hoc-Schiedsgerichtsbarkeit siehe oben auf Seiten 146-157 (§7C); vgl. auch Schlosser, *Das Recht der internationalen privaten Schiedsgerichtsbarkeit*, 139, Rn. 181 (den Deutschen Ausschuss für Schiedsgerichsbarkeit - DAS, Vorgänger der DIS - als Institution für halborganisierte Schiedsverfahren deutschen Zuschnitts qualifizierend).

Schiedsordnung als auf ihr Ad-hoc-Schiedsverfahren anwendbar wählen (vereinzelt als »*wild cat arbitration*« bezeichnet).[8]

Von SIAC und CIETAC ist bekannt, dass diese Institutionen der Verwaltung von hybriden Schiedsverfahren in der Vergangenheit bereits zugestimmt haben, insbesondere der Verwaltung von Schiedsverfahren nach der ICC-Schiedsordnung. Die diesbezügliche Flexibilität des SIAC erntete einige Aufmerksamkeit in Folge des *Alstom–Insigma*-Verfahrens, welches in Fachkreisen gemischte Reaktionen hervorrief. Hingegen war die Bereitschaft des CIETAC, Verfahren nach ICC-Regeln zu verwalten, zunächst nur vom Hörensagen bekannt. 2012 fand sie dann Eingang in Artikel 4 Absatz 3 der CIETAC-Schiedsordnung. Obwohl diese beiden Institutionen ihren Sitz auf dem asiatischen Kontinent gemein haben, zeigen sich zwischen den Heimat-Rechtsordnungen beider Institutionen erhebliche Unterschiede hinsichtlich Akzeptanz und Verständnis der Prinzipien internationaler Schiedsgerichtsbarkeit. Während das singapurische Schiedsrecht die Parteiautonomie bereits seit langem hervorhebt, sind Deregulierung und Flexibilisierung des Schiedsrechtes in China noch im Entwicklungsstadium.

Zwei mit ihrem Standort verbundene Gründe mögen diese in Asien angesiedelten Institutionen im Hinblick auf ihre Offenheit gegenüber hybriden Schiedsverfahren beeinflusst haben: Erstens scheinen hybride Schiedsvereinbarungen tendenziell eher in Verträgen mit einer asiatischen Partei enthalten zu sein. Eine hypothetische Erklärung hierfür - die zu weiteren empirischen Untersuchungen herausfordern soll - könnte in dem besonderen Wachstum der asiatischen Volkswirtschaften einerseits und der traditionellen Stärke der westlichen Wirtschaft andererseits gesehen werden. Diese Konstellation vermag Parteien aus den verschiedenen Weltregionen dazu bewegen, hybride Schiedsvereinbarungen als Kompromiss zwischen der Wahl einer traditionellen, zum Beispiel europäischen Institution und einer im Aufschwung befindlichen asiatischen Institution zu vereinbaren. Missverständnisse über einen etwaigen - rechtlich tatsächlich zu vernachlässigenden - Zusammenhang zwischen Schiedsort, Verfahrensort und Sitz der Institution fördern eine solche Kompromisslösung weiter. Zweitens - und überraschenderweise - scheinen sowohl ein besonders liberales Schiedsrecht, wie es Gesetzgebung und Gerichte in Singapur proklamieren, als auch der sehr viel restriktivere Ansatz, der sich noch im chinesischen Schiedsrecht findet, Schiedsinstitutionen dazu zu verleiten, einigen Einfallsreichtum bei der Anwendung hybrider Schiedsvereinbarungen an den Tag zu legen. Akteure und Organe der die gewählte Schiedsordnung

---

8    Siehe oben auf Seiten 151-156 (§7C.IV).

herausgebenden Institution können nach dem Verständnis der genannten Institutionen schlichtweg durch eigene ersetzt werden. Aus SIAC's Sicht war es geboten, das *Alstom–Insigma* Verfahren anzunehmen und die Schiedsvereinbarung durchzusetzen, um der singapurischen schiedsfreundlichen Haltung Geltung zu verschaffen. Das Berufungsgericht gab ihm Recht.[9] Aus CIETAC's Perspektive ist die Verwaltung hybrider Schiedsverfahren dagegen ein Weg, Restriktionen des chinesischen Schiedsrechtes zu umgehen und den Parteien zu ermöglichen, nach der Schiedsordnung ihrer Wahl in China zu prozessieren ohne zugleich Artikel 16 und 18 des chinesischen Schiedsgesetzes zu verletzen, nach denen eine verwaltende *»Schiedskommission«* zu bestimmen ist. Das gilt, solange es noch nicht eindeutig geklärt ist, ob und unter welchen Voraussetzungen ausländische Institutionen - die sich von Schiedskommissionen nach chinesischem Verständnis hinsichtlich Aufbau und Funktion unterscheiden - Schiedsverfahren in China verwalten dürfen. Allerdings gibt es inzwischen zumindest eine Entscheidung des chinesischen Obersten Volksgerichtshofes, die eine diesbezügliche Öffnung anzukündigen scheint.[10]

Sicherlich mag sich der Eindruck aufdrängen, dass Institutionen, die Schiedsverfahren nach Schiedsordnungen anderer Institutionen verwalten, wie es SIAC mit dem *Alstom–Insigma* Schiedsverfahren getan hat, und wie es CIETAC nach seiner Schiedsordnung ankündigt, versuchen, von dem guten Ruf und Erfolg solcher anderen Institutionen und dem Aufwand, den diese in die Entwicklung ihrer Schiedsordnungen investiert haben, zu profitieren. Doch selbst wenn man diesen Aspekt im Blick behält, scheint die Durchführung hybrider Schiedsverfahren vertretbar. Insbesondere ist bloße Anwendung - nicht Nachahmung - selbst zu kommerziellen Zwecken weder eine Verletzung eines etwaigen Urheberrechtes der herausgebenden Institution an der Schiedsordnung noch ist ersichtlich, dass hierdurch Markenrechte verletzt werden. Auf Schutzrechte des geistigen Eigentums gestützte Ansprüche der eine Schiedsordnung herausgebenden Institution gegen eine andere Institution, die diese Schiedsordnung bei der Verwaltung hybrider Schiedsverfahren anwendet, dürften regelmäßig ins Leere gehen. Naheliegender ist es noch, die Verwaltung hybrider Schiedsverfahren als Anwendungsbereich des Rechts des unlauteren Wettbewerbes zu betrachten.

---

9  *Insigma v. Alstom*, [2009] SGCA 24.

10  *Longlide*, [2013] Min Si Ta Zi no. 13; zitiert nach Sun, »SPC Instruction Provides New Opportunities for International Arbitral Institutions to Expand into China«, 695 (Appendix 3); siehe auch Dong, »Open Door for Foreign Arbitration Institutions?«

Insbesondere Konzepte wie Ruf- oder Leistungsausbeutung (*misappropriation*) oder parasitäres Wettbewerbsverhalten (*parasitisme*) kommen einem hierzu in den Sinn. Alle diese Verhaltensweisen, wie sie in verschiedenen Rechtsordnungen definiert worden sind und in unterschiedlichem Ausmaß missbilligt werden, setzten aber immer ein besonderes, subjektives Element der »*Unlauterbarkeit*« voraus. Eine solche Hürde, die lauterbarkeitsrechtliche Ansprüche nehmen müssen, ist unabdingbar, wenn durch die Anwendung des Lauterkeitsrechtes die handfesteren Kriterien, Werte und Grenzen des geistigen und gewerblichen Sonderrechtsschutzes nicht unterlaufen werden sollen. Solange eine Institution sich vor allem deshalb bereit erklärt, Schiedsverfahren nach der Schiedsordnung einer anderen Institution zu verwalten, um den Parteien die Durchsetzung ihrer ansonsten undurchführbaren Schiedsklausel zu ermöglichen, kann diese schiedsfreundliche Haltung andere möglicherweise weniger löbliche Nebenmotive ausgleichen. Vor diesem Hintergrund kann die Verwaltung hybrider Schiedsverfahren nicht verboten sein. In diesem Zusammenhang macht es auch aus rechtlicher Sicht keinen Unterschied, ob die anzuwendende Schiedsordnung eine Exklusivitätsvorschrift enthält, wie Artikel 1 Absatz 2 der ICC-Schiedsordnung oder Artikel 1 Absatz 3 Satz 4 der AAA-ICDR-Schiedsordnung, da diese Vorschriften keinen Gesetzesrang genießen und nur gegenüber vertraglich mit den herausgebenden Institutionen verbundenen natürlichen oder der juristischen Personen Geltung beanspruchen. In diesen subjektiven Anwendungsbereich fallen andere Schiedsinstitutionen oder Parteien, die solche anderen Schiedsinstitutionen mit der Verwaltung ihres Schiedsverfahrens beauftragen, aber nicht.

Größtes und ernstzunehmendes Problem bei der Durchführung hybrider Schiedsklauseln ist nicht ein rechtliches, sondern ein praktisches: Können Organe, die die anzuwendende Schiedsordnung vorsieht, durch eine Institution ersetzt werden, die solche Organe nicht hat, und wenn ja, wie? Diese Arbeit schlägt vor, die Frage unter Anwendung des Kriteriums funktionaler Äquivalenz[11] zu lösen: Wenn der Sinn und Zweck einer bestimmten Vorschrift der anzuwendenden Schiedsordnung auch noch in adäquater Weise erreicht werden kann, wenn ein Organ der verwaltenden Institution die betreffende Aufgabe ausführt, kann dieses Organ das nach der Schiedsordnung zuständige Organ der herausgebenden Institution ersetzen. Funktionelle Äquivalenz ist dann leichter zu bejahen, wenn die Aufgabe der Institution nur darin besteht, eine Verfahrensvereinbarung der Parteien zu

---

11  Inspiriert von der zum internationalen Privatrecht entwickelten Substitutionstheorie, siehe oben auf Seiten 344-355 (§14A).

bestätigen. Hingegen sind höhere Anforderungen an die Vergleichbarkeit der jeweiligen institutionellen Organe zu stellen, wo die anzuwendende Schiedsordnung eine streitige Entscheidung durch die Institution vorsieht. In Abgrenzung zu der hier vorgeschlagenen Prüfung funktioneller Äquivalenz erscheint es unzureichend, nur darauf abzustellen, ob die verwaltende Institution ein ähnlich bezeichnetes Organ hat, wie das in der anzuwendenden Vorschrift der Schiedsordnung vorgesehene. Beispielsweise ist die Bezeichnung »*Court*« (Schiedsgerichtshof) kein geschützter Begriff und institutionelle Organe mit dieser Bezeichnung unterscheiden sich in Zusammensetzung und Funktionsweise erheblich. Nicht zu leugnende Unterschiede existieren bereits zwischen den jeweiligen Schiedsgerichtshöfen der ICC, des LCIA, des SIAC und der *Swiss Chambers' Arbitration Institution*. Die Absurdität der Annahme, solange ein Organ nur als »*Court*« bezeichnet wird, könnte es beispielsweise den ICC-Schiedsgerichtshof ausreichend spiegeln, um dessen Aufgaben wahrzunehmen, zeigt sich bei einem kurzen Blick in die neueste Fassung der CIETAC-Schiedsordnung. Mit der Revision von 2015 wurde der Begriff »*Secretariat*« schlichtweg durch »*Court*« ausgetauscht, ohne dass hiermit wesentliche Veränderungen bei Zusammensetzung und Aufgaben des vormaligen Sekretariates, welches jetzt Gerichtshof heißt, einhergingen.

Während die Vereinheitlichung institutioneller Schiedsordnungen eine passende Strategie sein kann, dem Phänomen hybrider Schiedsvereinbarungen zu begegnen, sollte der Vereinheitlichungsprozess nicht auf begrifflicher Ebene stecken bleiben, wie es die 2015er Fassung der CIETAC-Schiedsordnung suggeriert. Vielmehr sollte die Tatsache, dass Parteien sich für so kontroverse Kompromisslösungen wie die hier diskutierten hybriden Schiedsklauseln entscheiden, um Vorteile verschiedener Schiedsinstitutionen und -systeme zu kombinieren, Schiedsinstitutionen zu verstärkter Kooperation und zum Austausch über ihre Erfahrungen mit Besonderheiten ihrer Schiedsordnungen motivieren. Wo weder »*zwingende*« Schiedsregeln noch der zivilprozessuale Rechtsweg ein solches »*procedure shopping*« verhindern können, sollten Kooperation und Harmonisierung passende Heilmittel sein - im Gegensatz zu verstärktem Wettbewerb und Protektionismus.

Wenn Schiedsinstitutionen die Effektivität der parteiautonomen Wahl institutioneller Schiedsgerichtsbarkeit stärken wollen, sollten sie zudem ihre Kräfte bündeln und auf eine Reform des internationalen und nationalen Schiedsrechts hinwirken, sodass es den Besonderheiten institutioneller Schiedsverfahren gerecht wird. Die meisten Schiedsgesetze basieren auf dem Modell der Ad-hoc-Schiedsgerichtsbarkeit, was diverse

Unsicherheiten bei der gerichtlichen Durchsetzung und Unterstützung institutioneller Schiedsverfahren nach sich zieht.

Daher haben auch verschiedene nationale Gerichte, die bisher mit der Wirksamkeit und Durchführbarkeit hybrider Schiedsvereinbarungen befasst waren, das Spannungsfeld zwischen Parteiautonomie und institutioneller Organisationsfreiheit unterschiedlich aufgelöst.

Die singapurischen Gerichte, die die Zwischenentscheidung zur Zuständigkeit im Fall *Alstom gegen Insigma*[12] überprüften, waren der Auffassung, dass es die Prinzipien des Vorranges der Parteiautonomie und effektiver Auslegung erforderten, nicht nur die Entscheidung der Parteien für ein hybrides Schiedsverfahren sondern auch SIAC's Auslegung der zu Grunde liegenden Schiedsklausel zu bestätigen. Mit ähnlicher Begründung wies auch das Stockholmer Berufungsgericht vor kurzem ein Rechtsmittel ab, dass gegen einen in einem (teilweise) nach der ICC-Schiedsordnung durchgeführten SCC-Schiedsverfahren ergangenen Endschiedsspruch eingelegt worden ist. Dabei wurde es als unstreitig angesehen, dass die SCC nicht die erforderliche organisatorische Struktur aufwies, um ein Schiedsverfahren in vollständigem Einklang mit der ICC-Schiedsordnung durchzuführen.[13] Mit ihren Entscheidungen legten sowohl die Singapurischen Gerichte als auch das Stockholmer Berufungsgericht ihr Augenmerk auf die Durchsetzung der generellen Wahl der Parteien, ihre Streitigkeit schieds- und nicht staatsgerichtlich zu lösen, und gewährten der verwaltenden Institution zu diesem Zweck weitgehende Freiheit bei der Durchführung der jeweils hybriden Schiedsvereinbarungen.

Im Gegensatz dazu betonte das mittlere Volksgericht (*Intermediate People's Court*) von Hangzhou, Volksrepublik China, in seiner Entscheidung[14] zu den im *Alstom–Insigma*-Verfahren ergangenen Endschiedssprüchen die Einzelheiten der Verfahrensvereinbarung der Parteien. Auf Grundlage des gerichtlichen Verständnisses dieser Einzelheiten versagte es den Schiedssprüchen die Anerkennung und Vollstreckung, weil es der Meinung war, dass SIAC die in der Schiedsklausel enthaltene Verfahrensvereinbarung zu frei interpretiert und angewendet hatte.

Die Widersprüchlichkeit dieser Entscheidungen zeigt auf, dass die Position der Schiedsinstitutionen auf dem schiedsrechtlichen Spielfeld

---

12  *Insigma v. Alstom*, [2008] SGHC 134; *Insigma v. Alstom*, [2009] SGCA 24.

13  *Regierung der Russischen Föderation gegen I.M. Badprim S.R.L;* siehe oben S. 503, Fn. 3.

14  *Alstom v. Insigma [Hz. IPC]; siehe oben* S. 480–487, §17C.

zwischen Parteien, Schiedsrichtern und Gerichten noch nicht hinreichend definiert ist. In dieser Arbeit wird die Empfehlung ausgesprochen, dass die verwaltende Schiedsinstitution daher versuchen sollte, in Zusammenarbeit mit den Parteien und den Schiedsrichtern über den Weg zu entscheiden, wie eine gewählte Schiedsordnung einer anderen Institution an das eigene System und die eigene Struktur angepasst werden kann. Aber selbst wenn die institutionelle Auslegung und Durchführung einer bestimmten Prozessregel im Einzelfall nicht ausdrücklich von einer Partei akzeptiert wird, sollten staatliche Gerichte im Interesse der Effektivität des Schiedsverfahrens nur eingreifen, wenn die die Verfahrensorganisation beanstandende Partei nachweist, dass die Einhaltung der betreffenden Verfahrensregel für sie von besonderem Interesse war. Während die Entscheidungen der singapurischen Gerichte und des Stockholmer Berufungsgerichts mit dieser Maxime im Einklang stehen, scheint die Entscheidung des Hangzhou Intermediate People's Court, den *Alstom–Insigma* Schiedssprüchen die Vollstreckbarkeit zu verweigern, weil eine - kleinere - Unregelmäßigkeit im Verfahren zur Bestellung des Schiedsgerichtes vorlag, nicht angemessen.

## §24 Thesen der Arbeit[15]

- Die Parteiautonomie als Grundprinzip internationaler Schiedsverfahren begründet eine Vermutung für die Wirksamkeit hybrider Schiedsklauseln.

- Nach normativ-hierarchischer Betrachtung hat eine Schiedsinstitution nicht die Rechtsetzungsmacht, um Parteien zu untersagen, ihre Schiedsordnung für ein Schiedsverfahren vor einer anderen Institution zu wählen.

- Hybride Schiedsverfahren sind institutionell, nicht ad hoc. Allerdings gehen die mit institutionellen Schiedsverfahren gemeinhin verbundenen Vorteile der Vorhersehbarkeit und Effektivität bei der Wahl hybrider institutioneller Schiedsgerichtsbarkeit weitgehend verloren.

- Abzugrenzen sind hybride Schiedsklauseln, welche klar eine Institution und die Schiedsordnung einer anderen Institution bestimmen, von Schiedsklauseln, die wegen Mehrdeutigkeit als defekt betrachtet werden.

- Allerdings ziehen auch hybride Schiedsklauseln Auslegungs- und Durchführbarkeitsprobleme nach sich, die ihre Effektivität schwächen.

---

15  Sinngemäße deutsche Übersetzung von §21 [German translation of §21].

Wenn solche Probleme durch effektive Auslegung oder Vertragsanpassung gelöst werden, sind neben den Interessen der Parteien auch die Interessen der zur Verwaltung des Schiedsverfahrens bestimmten Institution zu berücksichtigen.

- Schiedsinstitutionen nehmen in unterschiedlichem Ausmaß Einfluss auf das Verfahren. Die übliche Kontrolldichte beeinflusst auch die Toleranz der jeweiligen Institution gegenüber Versuchen, die anwendbare Schiedsordnung ganz oder teilweise abzuwählen. Grundsätzlich aber gilt: Schiedsregeln sind verhandelbare Vertragsklauseln.

- Schiedsinstitutionen sind nicht verpflichtet, ein Schiedsverfahren unter modifizierten oder gänzlich anderen Schiedsregeln durchzuführen. Sie können den Abschluss des Schiedsorganisationsvertrages in solchen Fällen ablehnen oder diesen zumindest bis zur Ernennung des Schiedsgerichtes sanktionsfrei kündigen.

- Schiedsinstitutionen dürfen Schiedsverfahren nach Schiedsordnungen anderer Institutionen verwalten. Weder Vertrags- noch Urheberrecht oder das Recht des unlauteren Wettbewerbs verbieten solches Marktverhalten grundsätzlich.

- Ob und in welchem Ausmaß eine Schiedsinstitution in der Lage ist, die Schiedsordnung einer anderen Institution anzuwenden, hängt davon ab, ob sie funktional äquivalente Organe hat, um die erforderlichen Aufgaben auszuführen.

- Entscheidend ist dafür nicht nur eine vergleichbare organisatorische Struktur, sondern auch die Erfahrung mit den erforderlichen Verfahrensschritten. Je strenger die durch eine Institution nach ihrer Schiedsordnung ausgeübte Kontrolle, umso schwieriger ist es für andere Institutionen, ihre Organe und Funktionen zu ersetzen.

- Nur wenn und soweit die Parteien sich über die einzelnen Verfahrensschritte einig sind, stellt die Notwendigkeit, institutionelle Organe zu ersetzen, keine größere Hürde für die Durchführbarkeit hybrider Schiedsklauseln dar.

- Hybride Schiedsklauseln mit Hilfe staatlicher Gerichte durchzusetzen, ist schwierig. Das aktuelle System staatlicher Kontrolle und Unterstützung von Schiedsverfahren in den meisten Rechtsordnungen berücksichtigt die Besonderheiten institutioneller Schiedsgerichtsbarkeit nicht ausreichend.

- Vertragsrechtliche Klagen gegen Schiedsinstitutionen können, wenn sie nicht schon an Haftungsbeschränkungen scheitern, sinnvollerweise nur auf finanzielle Entschädigung gerichtet sein, in der Regel aber nicht auf Erfüllung oder Beendigung des Schiedsorganisationsvertrages.

- Die erfolgversprechendsten Angriffsgründe gegen Schiedssprüche auf Grundlage hybrider Schiedsklauseln sind Rügen eines Verstoßes gegen das vereinbarte Verfahren und/oder die Zusammensetzung des Schiedsgerichtes.

- Im Anfechtungs- und Vollstreckungsverfahren sollte Augenmerk auf die Frage gelegt werden, ob die den Schiedsspruch angreifende Partei mit ihrer Rüge präkludiert/ausgeschlossen ist, weil sie zuvor ausdrücklich mit einem hybriden Schiedsverfahren einverstanden war. Zudem sollten nur Verfahrensunregelmäßigkeiten, die sich auf den Schiedsspruch ausgewirkt haben, zu einer Aufhebung bzw. Anerkennungs- und Vollstreckungsversagung führen.

- Eine hybride Schiedsvereinbarung ist der Versuch, die Schiedsordnung als Verfahrensordnung und die verwaltende Institution als zwei getrennte, ungekoppelte Rechtsprodukte/-dienstleistungen zu beziehen. Sollte dieses Phänomen vermehrt auftreten und sich dadurch eine entsprechende Nachfrage bestätigen, sollten Schiedsinstitutionen erwägen, zusammenzuarbeiten, um solcher Nachfrage ein adäquates Angebot gegenüberzustellen.

# Bibliography

AAA. »Administrative Fee Schedules (Standard and Flexible Fee)« *International Centre for Dispute Resolution*, n.d.

www.adr.org/aaa/ShowPDF?doc=ADRSTG_004338.

——., »About the American Arbitration Association (AAA) and the International Centre for Dispute Resolution (ICDR)« *Home | About AAA*, 2014.

www.icdr.org/icdr/faces/s/about.

Aden, Menno. »Auslegung und Revisibilität ausländischer AGB am Beispiel der Schiedsverfahrensordnung der Internationalen Handelskammer« *RIW* (1989): 607-11.

——. »Der Verfahrensverstoß des Schiedsgerichtsinstituts« *RIW* (1988): 757–63.

www.dresaden.de/A--Veroffentlichungen/II_-Juristische-Fachaufsatze/Verfahrens-verstoss_des_Schiedsgerichtsinstituts.pdf.

——. Internationale Handelsschiedsgerichtsbarkeit: Kommentar zu den Verfahrensordnungen. Heidelberg: Recht und Wirtschaft, 1988.

Aglionby, Andrew. »Arbitration Outside China: The Alternatives« *J. Int'l Arb.* 24, no. 6 (2007): 673–88.

Albrecht, Martin von. Amtliche Werke und Schranken des Urheberrechts zu amtlichen Zwecken in fünfzehn europäischen Ländern. Rechtswissenschaftliche Forschung und Entwicklung 340. Munich: VVF, 1992.

Allen, Tom. »Computer Software and Singapore's Law of Copyright« *EIPR* 16, no. 11 (1994): 500–505.

Allmeling, Anne. *Deutsche Scheidung mit Mullah. DW.DE*, 12 December 2011.

www.dw.de/deutsche-scheidung-mit-mullah/a-15595840-1.

American Dispute Resolution Center. »ADR Center | About Us«, n.d.

http://adrcenter.net/about.htm.

Andrew, Aglionby. »Notable Characteristics of Arbitration in China« In *Contemporary Issues in International Arbitration and Mediation*, edited by Arthur Rovine, 5:310–14. The Fordham Papers. New York: Boston: Leiden: Martinus Nijhoff, 2012.

Appel, Mark. »International Centre for Dispute Resolution (ICDR)« In *Arbitration World: Jurisdictional Comparisons*, 73–86. Thomson Reuters, 2012.

Arnold, Claudius. Amtliche Werke im Urheberrecht: zur Verfassungsmäßigkeit und analogen Anwendbarkeit des § 5 UrhG. Baden-Baden: Nomos, 1994.

Ashurst LLP. »Singapore High Court Considers Use of Other Institutional Rules by SIAC« *Arbflash*, January 2010.

www.ashurst.com/publication-item.aspx?id_Content=4920.

Bachmaier Winter, Lorena. »Art. 14« In *Comentarios a la ley de arbitraje de 2003*, edited by David Arias Lozano, 125–35. Cizur Menor: Thomson Aranzadi, 2005.

Bagner, Hans. »Article I« In *Recognition and Enforcement of Foreign Arbitral Awards: A Global Commentary on the New York Convention*, edited by Herbert Kronke, Patricia Nacimiento, Dirk Otto, and Nicola Christine Port, 19–36. The Hague: Kluwer Law International, 2010.

Baker & McKenzie and World Intellectual Property Organization. »Collecting Societies Handbook«, 2014.

www.collectingsocietieshb.com.

——«The Future of Copyright: If I Could Change One Thing (Video of the Full Event)« *Collecting Societies Handbook 2014*. London: King's College, 7 October 2014.

www.bakermckenzie.com/csh2014.

Von Bar, Christian, Eric Clive, Hans Schulte-Nölke, Hugh Beale, Johnny Herre, Jérôme Huet, Matthias Storme, et al., eds. *Principles, Definitions and Model Rules of European Private Law: Draft Common Frame of Reference (DCFR)*. Full. Munich: Sellier, 2008.

http://ec.europa.eu/justice/contract/files/european-private-law_en.pdf.

Basedow, Jürgen. »§ 305b BGB« In *Münchener Kommentar zum BGB*, edited by Franz Jürgen Säcker and Roland Rixecker. 7th ed. Munich: Beck, 2016.

Bassiri, Niuscha. »Art. 6 ICC SchO« In *Praxiskommentar ICC-SchO/DIS-SchO*, edited by Jan Heiner Nedden and Axel Benjamin Herzberg. Cologne: Otto Schmidt, 2013.

Baumbach, Adolf, Wolfgang Lauterbach, Jan Albers, and Peter Hartmann. *Zivilprozessordnung: mit FamFG, GVG und anderen Nebengesetzen*. 71st ed. Munich: Beck, 2013.

Van den Berg, Albert Jan. »111. Permanent Arbitral Bodies« In *Yearbook Commercial Arbitration*, edited by Albert Jan van den Berg, XXVIII:578, 2003.

——., ed. »Mandatory Rules: What's a Lawyer to Do?« In *Arbitration Advocacy in Changing Times*, 15:348–61. ICCA Congress Series 2010. Rio: The Hague: Kluwer Law International, 2011.

——. The New York Arbitration Convention of 1958: Towards a Uniform Judicial Interpretation. Deventer: Boston: Kluwer Law and Taxation, 1981.

www.newyorkconvention.org/publications/nyac-i.

Berger, Klaus Peter. »Aufgaben und Grenzen der Parteiautonomie in der internationalen Wirtschaftsschiedsgerichtsbarkeit« *RIW* (1994): 12–18.

——. »Sitz des Schiedsgerichts‹ oder ›Sitz des Schiedsverfahrens‹?« *RIW* (1993): 8-12.

——. The Creeping Codification of the New Lex Mercatoria. The Hague: Kluwer Law International, 2010.

Berger, Klaus Peter, Center for Transnational Law. *Private Dispute Resolution in International Business: Negotiation, Mediation, Arbitration*. The Hague: Kluwer Law International, 2006.

Bermann, George. »Introduction: Mandatory Rules of Law in International Arbitration« *Am. Rev. Int'l Arb.* 18. Mandatory Rules in International Commercial Arbitration (2007): 1–18.

Bermann, George, and Loukas Mistelis, eds. *Mandatory Rules in International Arbitration*. Huntington, N.Y.: Juris, 2011.

Bert, Peter. »CIETAC Administered Arbitrations: Internal Conflicts Cause Uncertainty« *Kluwer Arbitration Blog*, 7 November 2012.

http://kluwerarbitrationblog.com/blog/2012/11/07/cietac-administered-arbitrations-internal-conflicts-cause-uncertainty.

Bertrand, André. *Droit d'auteur*. 3rd ed. Paris: Dalloz, 2010.

BKP Rechtsanwälte. »Barbara Helene Steindl« Law Firm Website, n.d.

www.bkp.at/mag-barbara-helene-steindl.

Blackaby, Nigel, Constantine Partasides, Alan Redfern, and Martin Hunter. *Redfern and Hunter on International Arbitration*. 5th ed. Oxford: New York: Oxford University Press, 2009.

Blanke, Gordon. »Institutional versus Ad Hoc Arbitration: A European Perspective« *ERA Forum* 9, no. 2 (2008): 275–82.

———. »The New ADCCAC Arbitration Rules: Evolution or Revolution?« *Kluwer Arbitration Blog*, 8 October 2013.

http://kluwerarbitrationblog.com/blog/2013/10/08/the-new-adccac-arbitration-rules-evolution-or-revolution.

Bobei, Radu Bogdan. Arbitrajul intern şi internaţional: Texte. Comentarii. Mentalităţi. Bucarest: Beck, 2013.

Böckstiegel, Karl-Heinz. »Die Anerkennung der Parteiautonomie in der internationalen Schiedsgerichtsbarkeit« In *Wege zur Globalisierung des Rechts: Festschrift für Rolf A. Schütze zum 65. Geburtstag,* edited by Reinhold Geimer, 141–51. Munich: Beck, 1999.

———. »Einführung« In *Die neue ICC-Schiedsgerichtsordnung*, edited by Deutsche Institution für Schiedsgerichtsbarkeit, 7–9. Schriftenreihe der August Maria Berges Stiftung für Arbitrales Recht 22. Frankfurt am Main: Lang, 2012.

———. »Public Policy and Arbitrability« In *Comparative Arbitration Practice and Public Policy in Arbitration*, edited by Pieter Sanders, 1986:177–204. ICCA Congress Series 3. New York: The Hague: Kluwer Law International, 1987.

Böckstiegel, Karl-Heinz, Stefan Kröll, and Patricia Nacimiento, eds. »Annex II German Arbitration Law Prior to 1 January 1998« In *Arbitration in Germany: The Model Law in Practice*, 1115–22. Alphen aan den Rijn: Kluwer Law International, 2007.

Bohnet, Uwe. Das Markenrecht in der Volksrepublik China und Russland: eine rechtsvergleichende Studie unter Berücksichtigung der deutschen Rechtsentwicklung. Cologne: Heymann, 1996.

Bond, Stephen. »How to Draft an Arbitration Clause« *J. Int'l Arb*. 6, no. 2 (1989): 65-78.

Boo, Lawrence. »Arbitration« *SAL Ann. Rev. Sg. Cas*. 10 (2009): 53.

Börner, Achim-Rüdiger, and Ralf Oehmke. »Schiedsgerichtsklauseln in fortgeltenden deutsch-deutschen Wirtschaftsverträgen« *Der Betrieb* no. 44 (1993): 2217–20.

Born, Gary. *International Arbitration: Cases and Materials*. Alphen aan den Rijn: Kluwer Law International, 2011.

———. International Commercial Arbitration: Commentary and Materials. Alphen aan den Rijn: Kluwer Law International, 2001.

———. International Arbitration and Forum Selection Agreements: Drafting and Enforcing. 4th ed. Alphen aan den Rijn: Kluwer Law International, 2013.

———. *International Commercial Arbitration*. 2nd ed. Alphen aan den Rijn: Kluwer Law International, 2014.

———. *International Arbitration: Law and Practice*. Alphen aan den Rijn: Kluwer Law International, 2012.

———. »New Rules at the Singapore International Arbitration Centre« *Kluwer Arbitration Blog*, 14 May 2013.
http://kluwerarbitrationblog.com/blog/2013/05/14/new-rules-at-the-singapore-international-arbitration-centre.

Bredow, Jens. »Aus dem Tagebuch einer Schiedsgerichtsinstitution« *SchiedsVZ* 7, no. 1 (2009): 22–26.

Bredow, Jens, and Isabel Mulder. »Part III - Commentary on the Arbitration Rules of the German Institution of Arbitration (DIS Rules), Section 1 - Scope of Application« In *Arbitration in Germany: The Model Law in Practice*, edited by Karl-Heinz Böckstiegel, Stefan Michael Kröll, and Patricia Nacimiento, 664–69. Alphen aan den Rijn: Kluwer Law International, 2007.

———. »Part III - Commentary on the Arbitration Rules of the German Institution of Arbitration (DIS Rules), Section 18 - Challenge of Arbitrator« In *Arbitration in Germany: The Model Law in Practice*, edited by Karl-Heinz Böckstiegel, Stefan Michael Kröll, and Patricia Nacimiento, 720–24. Alphen aan den Rijn: Kluwer Law International, 2007.

Brem, Florian. Der ergänzende wettbewerbsrechtliche Leistungsschutz in Europa: eine vergleichende Untersuchung zum Schutz immaterialgüterrechtlich nicht geschützter Leistungen im deutschen, französischen, spanischen, italienischen und schweizerischen Recht. Berlin: Berliner Wissenschafts-Verlag, 2005.

Brick Court Chambers. *SIAC Rules: An Annotation*. Edited by Jonathan Hirst, Hilary Heilbron, and Klaus Reichert. Singapore: LexisNexis, 2014.

Brock, Dennis, and Laura Feldman. »Recent Trends in the Conduct of Arbitrations« *J. Int'l Arb.* 30, no. 2 (2013): 177–94.

Brower, Charles. »The Privatization of Rules of Decision« In *Law of International Business and Dispute Settlement in the 21st Century: Liber Amicorum Karl-Heinz Böckstiegel*, edited by Robert Georg Briner, Yves Fortier, Klaus Peter Berger, and Jens Bredow, 111–25. Cologne: Heymann, 2001.

Brower, Charles, and Charles Rosenberg. »The Death of the Two-Headed Nightingale: Why the Paulsson-van Den Berg Presumption that Party-Appointed Arbitrators Are Untrustworthy is Wrongheaded« *Arb. Int'l* 29, no. 1 (2013): 7–44.

Brown, Neville, L, John Bell, and Jean-Michel Galabert. *French Administrative Law*. Oxford: New York: Clarendon Press : Oxford University Press, 1998.

518

Bucher, Eugen. »Was macht den Schiedsrichter?: Abschied vom ›Schiedsrichtervertrag‹ - und Weiteres zu Prozessverträgen« In Grenzüberschreitungen: Beiträge zum Internationalen Verfahrensrecht und zur Schiedsgerichtsbarkeit, Festschrift für Peter Schlosser zum 70. Geburtstag, edited by Birgit Bachmann, Andreas Nelle, Christian Wolf, Stephan Breidenbach, Dagmar Coester-Waltjen, and Burkhard Heß, 97–118. Tübingen: Mohr Siebeck, 2005.

Bühler, Michael. *Handbook of ICC Arbitration: Commentary, Precedents, Materials.* 2nd ed. London: Thomson: Sweet & Maxwell, 2008.

Bühring-Uhle, Christian, Lars Kirchhof, and Gabriele Scherer. *Arbitration and Mediation in International Business.* 2 (revised). International Arbitration Law Library 5. Alphen aan den Rijn: Kluwer Law International, 2006.

Bundesministerium der Justiz und für Verbraucherschutz. »German Civil Code BGB« Translated by Neil Musset. *Gesetze Im Internet*, n.d.

www.gesetze-im-internet.de/englisch_bgb/index.html.

——. »Gesetz zur Förderung der Mediation und anderer Verfahren der außergerichtlichen Konfliktbeilegung (Englisch)« *bmj.de | Service | Broschüren*, n.d.

www.bmj.de/SharedDocs/Downloads/DE/pdfs/Gesetz_zur_Foerderung_der_Mediation_und_anderer_Verfahren_der_außergerichtlichen_Konfliktbeilegung_EN.pdf.

——.Entwurf eines Gesetzes zur Neuregelung des Schiedsverfahrensrechts, Bundestagsdrucksache 13/5274 (1996),

http://dipbt.bundestag.de/doc/btd/13/052/1305274.pdf.

Cabrol, Emmanuelle. »Observations« *Stockh. Int'l Arb. Rev.* no. 3 (20 February 2007): 160-65.

Cairns, David, and Alejandro Lòpez. »Spain's Consolidated Arbitration Law« *Rev. Esp. Arb.* (2012): 49-73.

Capps, Edward. Four Plays of Menander: The Hero, Epitrepontes, Periceiromene and Samia. Ginn and Company, 1910.

http://archive.org/details/fourplaysmenand00cappgoog.

Cavalieros, Philippe. »Note: Sentence arbitrale du 18 avril 2000 dans l'affaire CCI No.VB/99130, rendue à Budapest« *Rev. Arb.* no. 4 (2002): 1020-33.

——. »The Hungarian Arbitration Law: A Leap into the Past« *J. Int'l Arb.* 31, no. 2 (2014): 317-28.

Chan, Calvin. »Of Arbitral Institutions and Provisional Determinations on Jurisdiction, Global Gold Case« *Arb. Int'l* 25, no. 3 (2009): 403-26.

Chen, Luming, Wenhui Cui, and Jiadi Lui. »China - CIETAC ›Jurisdictional Turf War‹ Comes To An End?« *Conventus Law*, 25 May 2013.

www.conventuslaw.com/china-cietac-jurisdictional-turf-war-comes-to-an-end.

Cherpillod, Ivan. »Art. 2« In *Urheberrechtsgesetz (URG)*, edited by Barbara Müller and Reinhard Oertli, 2012.

Ch'eng, Te-chün, Michael J Moser, and Sheng-ch'ang Wang. *International Arbitration in the People's Republic of China: Commentary, Cases and Materials.* 2nd ed. Hong Kong: Butterworths Asia, 2000.

Cicoria, Cristiana. Nonprofit Organizations Facing Competition: The Application of United States, European and German Competition Law to Not-for-Profit Entities. Frankfurt am Main: Peter Lang, 2006.

CIETAC. *Selected Works of China International Economic and Trade Arbitration Commission Awards (1963-1988)*, Authorized English Version, Updated to 1993. China Law and Culture Publications. Hong Kong: Sweet & Maxwell, 1995.

——. »About Us | Introduction« *Home*, n.d.

www.cietac.org/index.cms

——. »Advantages of Arbitration« *Application for Arbitration*, 2013.

www.cietac.org/index/applicationForArbitration.cms

——. »Announcement on the Administration of Cases Agreed to Be Arbitrated by CIETAC Shanghai Sub-Commission and CIETAC South China Sub-Commission« *News*, 2 August 2012.

www.cietac.org/index/news.cms

——. »Announcement On Issues Concerning CIETAC Shanghai Sub-Commission and CIETAC South China Sub-Commission« *News*, 31 December 2012.

www.cietac.org/index/news.cms

——. »Home« Hong Kong Arbitration Center, 2013.

www.cietachk.org/portal/showIndexPage.do?pagePath=\en_US\index

——. »Organisation« *About Us*, n.d.

www.cietac.org/index/aboutUs.cms

——. »Panel of Arbitrators (Effective as from 1 May 2011)« *Arbitrators*, n.d.

www.cietac.org/index/arbitrators.cms

——. »Website«, n.d.

www.cietac.org

CIETAC Shanghai Commission and CIETAC South China Commission. »Joint Statement on CIETAC's Administrative Announcement« *Shenzhen Court of International Arbitration*, 4 August 2012.

www.sccietac.org/main/en/he/T115228.shtml.

Clapman, Andrew. *Human Rights in the Private Sphere*. Oxford : New York: Clarendon Press: Oxford University Press, 1996.

Clay, Thomas. *L'arbitre*. Paris: Dalloz, 2001.

——. »Note - Cour de cassation (1re Ch. civile) 20 février 2001« *Rev. Arb.* no. 3 (2001): 513-27.

Coe, Jack J. »From Anecdote to Data: Reflections on the Global Center's Barcelona Meeting« *J. Int'l Arb.* 20, no. 1 (2003): 11-22.

Cohen, Jerome. »Time to Fix China's Arbitration« *Far East. Econ. Rev.* 168, no. 2 (2005): 31-37.

Comité Francais de l'Arbitrage. »Les institutions d'arbitrage en France: Débats« *Rev. Arb.* no. 2 (1990): 375-80.

Conrad, Nicole, Peter Münch, and Jonathan Black-Branch, eds. International Commercial Arbitration: Standard Clauses and Forms: Commentary, 2013.

Coppo, Benedetta, and Stefano Azzali. »X v. Y, Award, CAM Case No. 6210, 4 May 2011, *A Contribution by the ITA Board of Reporters*« Kluwer Law International, 4 May 2011. KLI-KA-1138013.

Coulson, Robert. »The Future Growth of Institutional Administration in International Commercial Arbitration« In *The Art of Arbitration: Essays on International Arbitration - Liber Amicorum for Pieter Sanders, 12 Sept. 1912-1982*, edited by Albert Jan van den Berg and Jan Schultsz, 73-81. Kluwer Law International, 1982.

Craig, Laurence W., William W. Park, and Jan Paulsson. *International Chamber of Commerce Arbitration*. 3rd ed. Dobbs Ferry, NY: Oceana Publications, 2000.

Currie, Brainerd. »The Displacement of the Law of the Forum« In *Selected Essays on the Conflict of Laws*, 3-76. Durham: Duke University Press, 1963.

D'Agostino, Justin. »Key Changes to the CIETAC Arbitration Rules« *Kluwer Arbitration Blog*, 11 April 2012.

http://kluwerarbitrationblog.com/blog/2012/04/11/key-changes-to-the-cietac-arbitration-rules.

———. »The Aftermath of the CIETAC Split: Two Years On, Lower Courts Take Clashing Views on Arbitration Agreements and Awards- but Higher Courts Strive for Consistency« *Kluwer Arbitration Blog*, 2 May 2014.

http://kluwerarbitrationblog.com/blog/2014/05/02/the-aftermath-of-the-cietac-split-two-years-on-lower-courts-take-clashing-views-on-arbitration-agreements-and-awards-but-higher-courts-strive-for-consistency.

Dahm, Patrick. »International Arbitration: Why Wearing A Good Suit Makes All The Difference« *Linkedin*, 18 June 2014.

www.linkedin.com/today/post/article/20140618032252-175722208-international-arbitration-why-wearing-a-good-suit-makes-all-the-difference.

Davidson, Paul. »The International Federation of Commercial Arbitration Institutions« *J. Int'l Arb.* 5, no. 2 (1988): 131-38.

Davis, Benjamin G. »Pathological Clauses: Frédéric Eisemann's Still Vital Criteria« *Arb. Int'l* 7, no. 4 (1991): 365-88.

Delvolvé, Jean-Louis, Jean Rouche, and Gerald Pointon. *French Arbitration Law and Practice: A Dynamic Civil Law Approach to International Arbitration*. Alphen aan den Rijn: Kluwer Law International, 2009.

Department of Foreign Affairs, Trade and Development Canada. »Softwood Lumber - Dispute Settlement« *Export and Import Controls | Controlled Products*, 22 June 2013.

www.international.gc.ca/controls-controles/softwood-bois_oeuvre/other-autres/disp_Settlement-reglement_diff.aspx?lang=eng.

Derains, Yves, and Laurent Lévy, International Chamber of Commerce and ICC Institute of World Business Law. *Is Arbitration Only as Good as the Arbitrator?: Status, Powers and Role of the Arbitrator*. ICC Publication 714. Paris: ICC, 2011.

Derains, Yves, and Eric Schwartz. *A Guide to the ICC Rules of Arbitration.* 2nd ed. The Hague: Kluwer Law International, 2005.

Dezalay, Yves, and Bryant Garth. »Merchants of Law as Moral Entrepreneurs: Constructing International Justice from the Competition for Transnational Business Disputes« *L. & Soc. Rev.* 29, no. 1 (1995): 27-64. www.jstor.org/stable/3054053.

Díaz-Candia, Hernando. »El Rol Jurisdiccional de Los Árbitros y Su Constructiva Evolución: Deberes y Responsabilidad« *Rev. Esp. Arb.* no. 16 (2013): 79-105.

Dickinson, Andrew. »The Force Be with EU? Infringements of US Copyright in the English Courts (Lucasfilm v. Ainsworth)« *LMCLQ* (2010): 181-86.

Dicu, Catalina, and Elena-Valentina Preda. »Desemnarea tribunalului arbitral în cazul unui arbitraj instituționalizat organizat de Curtea de Arbitraj International de pe lângă Camera de Comerț și Industrie a României. Imposibilitatea constituirii tribunalului arbitral pe baza altor reguli decât Regulile de procedură ale CCIR« *Bizlawyer - Portalul Avocaturii de Business Din Romania,* 6 April 2013.

www.bizlawyer.ro/stiri/juridice/clauza-compromisorie.

Dietler, Hans. *Der Schiedsgerichtshof der Internationalen Handelskammer, seine Organisation und Verfahren.* Schweizerische Vereinigung für Internationales Recht 33. Zurich: Leipzig: Orell Füssli, 1935.

DIS. »About the DIS« *DIS Website,* n.d.

www.disarb.org/en/57/content/about-the-dis-id46.

——. »Cost Calculator (for 01 April 2014 and Later)« *Home,* n.d.

http://disarb.org/en/22/gebuehrenrechner2014/uebersicht-id0.

——. »DIS in eigener Sache« *BB-Beilage* no. 5 to no. 12, (1994): 3.

——. »DIS Secretariat«, n.d.

www.dis-arb.de/scho/9/content/secretariat-id8 (last accessed 31.12.2014: no longer available)

DIFC. »DIFC | LCIA Arbitration Centre«, 2008.

www.difcarbitration.com/index-2.html.

Ditchev, Alexandre. »Le ›contrat d'arbitrage‹: essai sur le contrat ayant pour objet la mission d'arbitrer« *Rev. Arb.* 1981 (1981): 395-410.

Dong, Arthur. »Does Supreme People's Court's Decision Open the Door for Foreign Arbitration Institutions to Explore the Chinese Market?« *Kluwer Arbitration Blog,* 15 July 2014.

http://kluwerarbitrationblog.com/blog/2014/07/15/does-supreme-peoples-courts-decision-open-the-door-for-foreign-arbitration-institutions-to-explore-the-chinese-market/#fnref-10034-1.

Draguiev, Deyan. »Unilateral Jurisdiction Clauses: The Case for Invalidity, Severability or Enforceability« *J. Int'l Arb.* 31, no. 1 (2014): 19-46.

Drahozal, Christopher R, and Richard W Naimark. *Towards a Science of International Arbitration: Collected Empirical Research.* New York: Kluwer Law International, 2005.

Dresden, Matthew. »Will the Real CIETAC Please Stand Up?« *China Law Blog*, 21 May 2013.

www.chinalawblog.com/2013/05/will-the-real-cietac-shanghai-please-stand-up.html.

Drexl, Josef. »Internationales Immatrialgüterrecht« In *Münchener Kommentar zum BGB*, edited by Franz Jürgen Säcker and Roland Rixecker. 6th ed. Munich: Beck, 2015.

———. »Internationales Lauterkeitsrecht« In *ibid*.

Dreyer, Gunda. »§ 5 UrhG« In *Urheberrecht*, edited by Gunda Dreyer, Jost Kotthoff, and Astrid Meckel. 3rd ed. Heidelberg: Müller, 2013.

Duffet, Brian, Bundesministerium der Justiz und für Verbraucherschutz. »The Act Against Unfair Competition« *Gesetze im Internet*, 2010.

www.gesetze-im-internet.de/englisch_uwg.

Dupuis, Georges, Marie-José Guédon, and Patrice Chretien. *Droit administratif.* 10th ed. Sirey. Paris: Dalloz, 2007.

ECOSOC. Report of the Committee on the Enforcement of Foreign Arbitral Awards, 18 March 1955, E/2704

———. Czechoslovakia: Amendment to Article 1, Conference on International Commercial Arbitration L.10, 26th Sess., 22 May 1958, E/CONF.26/L.10.

———. »Conference of International Commercial Arbitration, Summary Record of the Eight Meeting«, 26 May 1958. E/CONF.26/SR.8.

www.uncitral.org/uncitral/en/uncitral_texts/arbitration/NYConvention_travaux.html.

Egeler, Simone. Konsensprobleme im internationalen Schuldvertragsrecht. St. Gallen: Dike, 1994.

Ehle, Bernd, and Werner Jahnel. »Revision der Swiss Rules - erhöhte Effizienz und Flexibilität« *SchiedsVZ* 10, no. 4 (n.d.): 169-77.

Ehrenzweig, Albert Armin. Private International Law: a Comparative Treatise on American International Conflicts Law, Including the Law of Admiralty. Leyden: Dobbs Ferry, N.Y.: Sijthoff: Oceana, 1972.

Ehrenzweig, Albert Arnim. »Local and Moral Data in the Conflict of Laws: Terra Incognita« *Buff. L. Rev.* 16 (1967 1966): 55.

http://heinonline.org/HOL/Page?handle=hein.journals/buflr16&id=65&div=&collection=journals.

Eidenmüller, Horst. Ausländische Kapitalgesellschaften im deutschen Recht. Munich: Beck, 2004.

———. »Hybride ADR-Verfahren bei internationalen Wirtschaftskonflikten« *RIW* (2002): 1-11.

Eisemann, Frédéric. »La clause d'arbitrage pathologique« In *Arbitrage commercial: essais in memoriam Eugenio Minoli*, edited by Associazione Italiana per l'Arbitrato, 129-61, 1974.

Elster, Alexander Nikolaus. Gewerblicher Rechtsschutz: umfassend Urheber- und Verlagsrecht, Patent- und Musterschutzrecht, Warenzeichen- und Wettbewerbsrecht. Berlin: de Gruyter, 1921.

Enock, Roger, and Alexandra Melia. »Chapter 6: Ad Hoc Arbitrations« In *Arbitration in England: With Chapters on Scotland and Ireland*, edited by Julian. Lew, Harris Bor, Gregory Fullelove, and Joanne Greenaway, 89-104, 2013.

Erk, Nadja. *Parallel Proceedings in International Arbitration: A Comparative European Perspective*. International Arbitration Law Library 30. Kluwer Law International, 2014.

European Commission, Proposal for a Regulation of the European Parliament and the Council on the law applicable to non-contractual obligations, COM 427 final (2003), http://eur-lex.europa.eu/LexUriServ/LexUriServ.do?uri=COM:2003:0427:FIN:EN:PDF.

Fan, Kun. *Arbitration in China: A Legal and Cultural Analysis*. China and International Economic Law Series 5. Oxford: Hart, 2013.

Fauvarque-Cosson, Bénédicte, Denis Mazeaud, and Jean-Baptiste Racine, eds. European Contract Law Materials for a Common Frame of Reference: Terminology, Guiding Principles, Model Rules. Munich: Sellier, 2008. www.legiscompare.fr/site-web/IMG/pdf/CFR_I-XXXIV_1-614.pdf.

Fellhauer, Harry, and Heinz Strohbach. *Handbuch der internationalen Handelsschiedsgerichtsbarkeit*. Berlin: DDR Staatsverlag, 1969.

Fernando Mantilla Serrano. »Towards a Transnational Procedural Public Policy,« *Arb. Int'l* 20, no. 4 (2004): 333-53.

Ferrari, Franco, ed. Forum Shopping in the International Commercial Arbitration Context. Munich: Sellier, 2013.

Fichte, Johann Gottlieb. »Beweis der Unrechtmäßigkeit des Büchernachdrucks. Ein Räsonnement und eine Parabel« *Berlinische Monatsschrift* no. 21 (May 1793): 443-83. www.copyrighthistory.com/fichte.html.

Finder, Susan. »The Court's September 2013 Notice on the CIETAC Split: When Will Greater Transparency Come to the Court?« *Supreme People's Court Monitor*, 21 January 2014. http://supremepeoplescourtmonitor.com/2014/01/21/the-courts-september-2013-notice-on-the-cietac-split-when-will-greater-transparency-come-to-the-court.

Fischer-Lescano, Andreas. »Gutachten zu CETA: Schiedsgerichte rechtswidrig« Interview by Anne-Christine Herr. Legal Tribune Online, 12 November 2014. www.lto.de/recht/hintergruende/h/ceta-freihandelsabkommen-gutachten-schiedsgerichte-eu.

Fock, Soenke. Der unmittelbare wettbewerbsrechtliche Leistungsschutz: eine Untersuchung deutschen und US-amerikanischen Case-Laws. Cologne, Munich: Heymann, 2008.

Fouchard, Philippe. »Bibliographie - Réflexions sur le règlement d'arbitrage de la Chambre de commerce internationale - Les déviations de l'arbitrage institutionnel« *Rev. Arb.* no. 2 (1990): 527-28.

——. »Final Report on the Status of the Arbitrator« In *ICC International Court of Arbitration Bulletin*, 7:27-57. Paris: ICC, 1996. www.iccdrl.com/commissionreports.aspx.

——. L'arbitrage commercial international. Paris: Litec, 1965.

——. »Les institutions permanentes d'arbitrage devant le juge étatique (à propos d'une jurisprudence récente)« *Rev. Arb.* no. 3 (1987): 225-74.

——. »Note - Cour d'appel de Paris (1re Chambre A) 18 novembre 1987: Cour d'appel de Paris (1re Chambre A) 4 mai 1988: Tribunal de grande instance de Paris 23 juin 1988« *Rev. Arb.* no. 4 (1988): 657-657.

——. »Relationships between the Arbitrator and the Parties and the Arbitral Institution« *The ICC International Court of Arbitration Bulletin - Special Supplement* (1995): 12-23.

——. »Synthèse: Typologie des institutions d'arbitrage« *Rev. Arb.* no. 2 (1990): 281-309.

Foxton, David. »Book Review on Singapore Law on Arbitral Awards by Chan Leng Sun« *Arbitration* 78, no. 4 (2012): 410-11.

Franz Schwarz and Helmut Ortner. »Chapter III: The Arbitration Procedure - Procedural Ordre Public and the Internationalisation of Public Policy in Arbitration« In *Austrian Arbitration Yearbook*, edited by Christian Klausegger, Peter Klein, Florian Kremslehner, Alexander Petsche, Nikolaus Pitkowitz, Jenny Power, Irene Welser, and Gerold Zeiler, 133-220. Beck: Stämpfli & Manz, 2008.

Freyer, Dana. »Practical Considerations in Drafting Dispute Resolution Provisions in International Commercial Contracts: A US Perspective« *J. Int'l Arb.* 15, no. 4 (1998): 7-46.

Fry, Jason. »HKL Group Ltd v. Rizq International Holdings Pte. Ltd. and HKL Group Co. Ltd. v. Rizq International Holdings Pte Ltd« *J. Int'l Arb.* 30, no. 4 (2013): 453-62.

Fry, Jason, Francesca Mazza, and Simon Greenberg. The Secretariat's Guide to ICC Arbitration : A Practical Commentary on the 2012 ICC Rules of Arbitration. Paris: ICC Publishing, 2012.

Gaillard, Emmanuel. »Note - Cour d'appel de Paris (1re Ch. C) 22 septembre 1995 - Société Dubois et Vanderwalle v. société Boots Frites BV: Note - Cour d'appel de Paris (1re Ch. C) 11 janvier 1996 - Société Algotherm v. société DEP« *Rev. Arb.* no. 1 (1996): 106-8.

——. »Note - Cour de Cassation (1re Ch. Civile) 15 Juin 1994 - Communauté Urbaine de Casablanca v. Société Degrémont« *Rev. Arb.* no. 1 (1995): 92-101.

——. »Note - Cour de cassation (2e Ch. civ.) 10 mai 1995 - Société Coprodag et autre v. dame Bohin« *Rev. Arb.* no. 4 (1995): 618-21.

Gaillard, Emmanuel, and John Savage, eds. *Fouchard, Gaillard, Goldman on International Commercial Arbitration*. Kluwer Law International, 1999.

Gal, Jens. Die Haftung des Schiedsrichters in der internationalen Handelsschiedsgerichtsbarkeit. Tübingen: Mohr Siebeck, 2009.

Gamillscheg, Franz. *Der Einfluß Dumoulins auf die Entwicklung des Kollisionsrechts.* Berlin: Tübingen: de Gruyter: Mohr, 1955.

Ganea, Peter, and Thomas Pattloch. *Intellectual Property Law in China.* Edited by Max Planck Institute for Foreign and International Patent, Copyright and Competition Law. The Hague: Kluwer Law International, 2005.

Gaudet, Michel. »La coopération des juridictions étatiques à l'arbitrage institutionnel« *ASA Bull.* 6, no. 2 (1988): 90-122.

Geiger, Christophe. »Flexibilising Copyright: Remedies to the Privatization of Information by Copyright Law« *IIC* 39, no. 2 (2008): 178-97.

Geimer, Reinhold. *Internationales Zivilprozessrecht.* Cologne: Otto Schmidt, 2009.

Geisinger, Elliott, and Pierre Ducret. »Chapter 5: The Arbitral Procedure« In *International Arbitration in Switzerland - A Handbook for Practioners*, edited by Elliott Geisinger and Nathalie Voser, 73-106. 2nd ed. Alphen aan den Rijn: Kluwer Law International, 2012.

Geisinger, Elliott, and Julie Raneda. »Chapter 1: Legislative Framework« In *International Arbitration in Switzerland - A Handbook for Practioners*, edited by Elliott Geisinger and Nathalie Voser, 1-12. 2nd ed. Alphen aan den Rijn: Kluwer Law International, 2012.

Gerbay, Rémy. »Chapter 4: The London Court of International Arbitration« In *Arbitration in England: With Chapters on Scotland and Ireland*, edited by Julian. Lew, Harris Bor, Gregory Fullelove, and Joanne Greenaway, 89-104, Alphen aan den Rijn: Kluwer Law International, 2013.

———. »The Functions of Arbitral Institutions: Theoretical Representations and Practical Realities« Ph.D. thesis, Queen Mary University of London, 2014. https://qmro.qmul.ac.uk/xmlui/handle/123456789/8143.

Ghaffar, Arshad. »Rules and Legislation: The 2012 ICC Arbitration Rules« *Arbitration: Journal of the Chartered Institute of Arbitrators* 78, no. 2 (2012): 171-77.

Ginsburg, Tom. »The Culture of Arbitration« *Vand. J. Trans'l L.* 36, no. 4 (2003): 1335-45.

Girsberger, Daniel, and Pascal Ruch. »Part I: International Commercial Arbitration, Chapter 6: Pathological Arbitration Clauses: Another Lawyers' Nightmare Comes True« In *International Arbitration and International Commercial Law: Synergy, Convergence and Evolution*, edited by Stefan Kröll, Loukas Mistelis, Maria del Pilar Perales Viscasillas, and Vicky Rogers, 123-39. Alphen aan den Rijn: Kluwer Law International, 2011.

Glöckner, Jochen. »C. Erläuterungen zum Internationalen Lauterkeitsrecht« In *Gesetz gegen den unlauteren Wettbewerb*, edited by Henning Harte-Bavendamm and Frauke Henning-Bodewig. 3rd ed. Munich: Beck, 2013.

———. »Einleitung, D. Internationales Lauterkeitsprozessrecht« In *ibid.*

Glossner, Ottoarndt. »Das UN-Übereinkommen über die Anerkennung und Vollstreckung ausländischer Schiedssrüche vom 10. Juni 1958: 40 Jahre danach« In *Wege zur Globalisierung des Rechts: Festschrift für Rolf A. Schütze zum 65. Geburtstag*, 221-24, 1999.

———. »From New York (1958) to Geneva (1961) - a Veteran's Diary« In *Enforcing Arbitration Awards under the New York Convention: Experience and Prospects*, 5-9. New York: UN, 1999.
www.uncitral.org/pdf/english/texts/arbitration/NY-conv/NYCDay-e.pdf.

———. »Institutionelle Schiedsrichterernennung: das Besondere Komité des Europäischen Ubereinkommens über die Handelsschiedsgerichtsbarkeit von Genf vom 21. April 1961« In *Lebendiges Recht - Von den Sumerern bis zur Gegenwart : Festschrift für Reinhold Trinkner zum 65. Geburtstag*, edited by Friedrich Graf von Westphalen and Otto Sandrock, 555-59, 1995.

Goldman, Berthold. »Les Conflits de lois dans l'arbitrage international de droit privé« *Recueil des cours - Académie de Droit International de La Haye* 109, no. 2 (1963): 347-485.

Gottschalk, Eckart. »The Law Applicable to Intellectual Property Rights: Is the Lex Loci Protectionis a Pertinent Choice of Law Approach?« In *Conflict of Laws in a Globalized World*, edited by Eckart Gottschalk, Ralf Michaels, Giesela Rühl, and Jan von Hein, 184-219. Cambridge: Cambridge University Press, 2007.

Gottwald, Peter. Internationale Schiedsgerichtsbarkeit - Arbitrage international - International Arbitration: Generalbericht und Nationalberichte. Veröffentlichung der Wissenschaftlichen Vereinigung für Internationales Verfahrensrecht e.V. 9. Bielefeld: Gieseking, 1997.

Gottwald, Peter, and Heinrich Nagel. *Internationales Zivilprozessrecht*. 6th ed. Aschendorffs juristische Handbücher. Cologne: Beck, 2007.

Götz, Andreas. »Der Schiedsrichter zwischen Dienstleistungserbringung und Richtertätigkeit - Zum sogenannten Spruchrichterprivileg im System der Schiedsrichterhaftung« *SchiedsVZ* 11, no. 6 (2012): 311-17.

Graves, Jack, and Yelena Davydan. »Competence-Competence and Separability - American Style« In International Arbitration and International Commercial Law: Synergy, Convergence and Evolution - Liber Amicorum for Eric Bergsten, edited by Stefan Kröll, Loukas Mistelis, Maria del Pilar Perales Viscasillas, and Vicky Rogers, 157-78, 2011.

Greenberg, Simon. »Arbitral Award Scrutiny Under Scrutiny: An Assessment« In *Arbitral Institutions Under Scrutiny*, edited by Philipp Habegger, Gabrielle Nater-Bass, Daniel Hochstrasser, and Urs Weber-Stecher, 89-108. ASA special series 40. Huntington, New York: Juris, 2013.

Greenberg, Simon, Christopher Kee, and J. Romesh Weeramantry. *International Commercial Arbitration: An Asia-Pacific Perspective*. Cambridge: New York: Cambridge University Press, 2011.

Greenberg, Simon, and Flavia Mange. »Institutional and Ad Hoc Perspectives on the Temporal Conflict of Arbitral Rules« *J. Int'l Arb.* 27, no. 2 (2010): 199-213.

Greenblatt, Jonathan, and Peter Griffin. »Towards the Harmonization of International Arbitration Rules: Comparative Analysis of the Rules of the ICC, AAA, LCIA and CIETAC« *Arb. Int'l* 17, no. 1 (2001): 101-10.

Grierson, Jacob, and Annet van Hooft. *Arbitrating under the 2012 ICC Rules: An Introductory User's Guide*. Alphen aan den Rijn: Kluwer Law International, 2012.

Gusy, Martin F., James M. Hosking, and Franz T. Schwarz. *A Guide to the ICDR International Arbitration Rules*. Oxford: New York: Oxford University Press, 2011.

Habel, Arne. Contract Governance: eine verfassungsrechtliche und rechtsdogmatische Analyse zu vertraglichen und vertragsrechtlichen Regelungsstrukturen in Belangen des Gemeinwohls. Baden-Baden: Nomos, 2012.

Habscheid, Walther, and Edgar Habscheid. »Ende der West-Ost-Handelschiedsgerichtsbarkeit? Insbesondere zur deutsch-deutschen Schiedsgerichtsbarkeit« *DtZ* (1992): 370.

Hacking, David. »A New Competition: Rivals for Centres of Arbitration« *LMCLQ* (1979): 435-48.

Handig, Christian. »The ›Sweat of the Brow‹ is Not Enough!: More than a Blueprint of the European Copyright Term ›Work‹« *EIPR* 35, no. 6 (2013): 334-40.

Hantke, China. »China ist anders: Neue ICC-Schiedsklausel« *SchiedsVZ* 5, no. 1 (2007): 36-38.

Happ, Richard. »Arbitration Institutions and Centers« *Happ's Arbitration Links*, March 2012.

www.arbitration-links.de/00000099670ba0802.

Hasselblatt, Gordian. »§ 58 Rechtsbruch (§ 4 Nr. 11 UWG)« In *Handbuch des Wettbewerbsrechts*, edited by Michael Loschelder and Willi Erdmann. 4th ed. Munich: Beck, 2010.

Hausmaninger, Christian. »Rights and Obligations of the Arbitrator with Regard to the Parties and the Arbitral Institution: A Civil Law Viewpoint« *The ICC International Court of Arbitration Bulletin* Special Supplement (1995): 36-49.

Hausmann, Willi. »Der Schiedsrichtervertrag - Probleme der Haftung, der Erfüllung und der kollisionsrechtlichen Anknüpfung« Albert-Ludwigs University of Freiburg, 1979.

Hau, Wolfgang. »Fremdsprachengebrauch durch deutsche Zivilgerichte − vom Schutz legitimer Parteiinteressen zum Wettbewerb der Justizstandorte« In *Liber Amicorium Klaus Schurig zum 70. Geburtstag*, edited by Ralf Michaels and Dennis Solomon, 49-62, Sellier: Munich, 2012.

Hay, Peter, Patrick Borchers, and Symeon Symeonides. *Conflict of Laws*. 5th ed. St. Paul, Minnesota: West, 2010.

Heinz Strohbach. »Arbitration Between Foreign Trade Organisations of Socialist Countries and Parties from the Capitalist Economic Sphere« 4, no. 3. Pace L. Rev. (1984): 607.

http://digitalcommons.pace.edu/plr/vol4/iss3/4.

Hellner, Michael. »Unfair Competition and Acts Restricting Free Competition: A Commentary on Article 6 of the Rome II Regulation« *Yearbook of Private International Law* 9 (2007): 49-69.

Henning-Bodewig, Frauke. »Einleitung, F. Ausländisches Recht« In *Gesetz gegen den unlauteren Wettbewerb*, edited by Henning Harte-Bavendamm and Frauke Henning-Bodewig. 3rd ed. Munich: Beck, 2013.

Henning-Bodewig, Frauke. *International Handbook on Unfair Competition*. Munich: Portland: Beck: Hart, 2013.

Henning-Bodewig, Frauke. »Nationale Eigenständigkeit und europäische Vorgaben im Lauterkeitsrecht« *GRUR Int.* 59, no. 7 (2010): 549-63.

——. Unfair Competition Law: European Union and Member States. The Hague: Kluwer Law International, 2006.

Henning-Bodewig, Frauke, and Gerhard Schricker. »New Initiatives for the Harmonization of Unfair Competition Law in Europe« *EIPR* 24, no. 5 (2002): 271-76.

Henssler, Martin. »§ 627 BGB« In *Münchener Kommentar zum BGB*, edited by Franz Jürgen Säcker and Roland Rixecker. 6th ed. Munich: Beck, 2012.

Herbert Smith Freehills LLP. »The New CIETAC Arbitration Rules: A Move towards Internationalisation?« *Arbitration Notes*, 19 April 2012.

http://hsf-arbitrationnotes.com/2012/04/19/the-new-cietac-arbitration-rules-a-move-towards-internationalisation.

Hermes, Kai. »Die Schutzfähigkeit von besonderen AGB-Klauselwerken: eine juristisch-ökonomische Analyse am Beispiel von Versicherungs- und Finanzprodukten« Nomos, 2013.

Hill, Jonathan, and Adeline Swee Ling Chong. *International Commercial Disputes: Commercial Conflict of Laws in English Courts*. 4th ed. Studies in private international law. Oxford: Portland, Oregon: Hart Pub., 2010.

Hill, Richard. »Hybrid ICC/SIAC Arbitration Clause Upheld in Singapore« *Kluwer Arbitration Blog*, 10 June 2009.

http://kluwerarbitrationblog.com/blog/2009/06/10/hybrid-iccsiac-arbitration-clause-upheld-in-singapore.

Hilty, Reto, and Silvie Nérisson, eds. *Balancing Copyright - a Survey of National Approaches*. Berlin: New York: Springer, 2012.

Hirth, René-Alexander. »Schiedsordnung des SIAC« In *Institutionelle Schiedsgerichtsbarkeit: Kommentar*, edited by Rolf A. Schütze, IX. 2nd ed. Cologne, Munich: Heymann, 2011.

——. »SIAC Rules« In *Institutional Arbitration: Article-by-Article Commentary*, edited by Rolf Schütze. Munich: Oxford: Baden-Baden: Beck: Hart: Nomos, 2013.

Hirth, René-Alexander, and Adeline Munz. »CIETAC Schiedsvereinbarungen: Ein kompliziertes Unterfangen« *SchiedsVZ* 12, no. 1 (2014): 8-12.

Hochbaum, Johann-Friedrich. Mißglückte internationale Schiedsvereinbarungen: Zweckverfehlung bei internationalen Schiedsvereinbarungen nach deutschem Recht. Abhandlungen zum Recht der internationalen Wirtschaft 34. Heidelberg: Recht und Wirtschaft, 1995.

Hofbauer, Simone, Michael Burkart, Lara Bander, and Tari Mehtap. »Survey on Scrutiny of Arbitral Institutions« edited by Philipp Habegger, Daniel Hochstrasser,

Gabrielle Nater-Bass, and Urs Weber-Stecher. Vol. 40. ASA special series. Huntington, New York: Juris, 2013.

Hoffet, Franz. *Rechtliche Beziehungen zwischen Schiedsrichtern und Parteien*. Zürcher Studien zum Verfahrensrecht 98. Zurich: Schulthess, 1991.

Hoffmann, Bernd von. »Der internationale Schiedsrichtervertrag: eine kollisionsrechtliche Skizze« In *Festschrift für Ottoarndt Glossner zum 70. Geburtstag*, edited by Alain Plantey, Karl-Heinz Böckstiegel, and Jens Bredow, 143-53. Recht und Wirtschaft, 1994.

Hoffmann, Hermann. Kammern für internationale Handelssachen: Eine juristisch-ökonomische Untersuchung zu effektiven Justizdienstleistungen im Außenhandel. Recht und Gesellschaft. Baden-Baden: Nomos, 2011.

———. »Schiedsgerichte als Gewinner der Globalisierung? Eine empirische Analyse zur Bedeutung staatlicher und privater Gerichtsbarkeit für den internationalen Handel« *SchiedsVZ* 8, no. 2 (2010): 96.

Hofmann, Nathalie. »The Role of ADR Institutions: Mere Secretariat or Supervisory Body - Lessons Learned from Institutional Arbitration« In *The Role of Consumer ADR in the Administration of Justice: New Trends in Access to Justice under EU Directive 2013/11*, edited by Michael Stürner, Fernando Gascon Inchausti, and Remo Caponi, 103–14. Munich: Sellier, 2015.

Holtzmann, Howard, and Donald Francis Donovan. »National Report for the United States of America (2005)« In *International Handbook on Commercial Arbitration*, edited by Jan Paulsson, at USA 1-96. ICCA Handbook, lslf. Kluwer Law International, 1984.

Hong Kong International Arbitration Centre. »Model Clauses« *Arbitration*, 2014. www.hkiac.org/en/arbitration/model-clauses.

Horn, Norbert. »Zwingendes Recht in der internationalen Schiedsgerichtsbarkeit« *SchiedsVZ* 6, no. 5 (2008): 209-22.

Horton, David. »The Mandatory Core of Section 4 of the Federal Arbitration Act« *Virg. L. Rev. - In Brief* 96, no. 1 (April 2010): 1-8. http://papers.ssrn.com/abstract=1569783.

Horvath, Günther, Christian Konrad, and Jenny Power. Costs in International Arbitration: A Central and Southern Eastern European Perspective. Vienna: Linde, 2008.

Huber, Peter. »Das Verhältnis von Schiedsgericht und staatlichen Gerichten bei der Entscheidung über die Zuständigkeit« *SchiedsVZ* 1, no. 2 (2003): 73-75.

Hübner, Heinz. »Sinn und Möglichkeiten retrospektiver Rechtsvergleichung« In *Festschrift für Gerhard Kegel zum 75. Geburtstag 26. Juni 1987*, edited by Hans-Joachim Musielak and Klaus Schurig, 235-52. Stuttgart: Kohlhammer, 1987.

Hwang, Michael. »Insigma Technology Co Ltd v. Alstom Technology Ltd, Court of Appeal, [2009] SGCA 24, 2 June 2009, *A Contribution by the ITA Board of Reporters*« Kluwer Law International, n.d.

www.kluwerarbitration.com/document.aspx?id=ipn91441.

——. »Insigma Technology Co Ltd v. Alstom Technology Ltd, Singapore High Court, Originating Summons No 13 of 2008, 14 August 2008, *A Contribution by the ITA Board of Reporters*« Kluwer Law International, n.d.

——. »Unknown v. Oceanic Shipping & Singapore Tankers (The ›Titan Unity‹), Supreme Court of Singapore, High Court, Case Date 19 December 2013, *A Contribution by the ITA Board of Reporters*«, n.d. KluwerArbitration.com (at KLI-KA-144001.pdf).

ICC. »About the Commission on Arbitration and ADR« *About ICC | Policy Commissions | Arbitration and ADR*, n.d.

www.iccwbo.org/About-ICC/Policy-Commissions/Arbitration.

——. »Historic Opening of Arbitration Centre Set to Advance Palestine/Israel Commercial Dispute Resolution« *News | Articles*, 18 November 2013.

www.iccwbo.org/News/Articles/2013/Historic-opening-of-arbitration-centre-set-to-advance-Palestine/Israel-commercial-dispute-resolution.

——. ICC Uniform Customs and Practice for Documentary Credits. ICC Publication 500. ICC Publishing, 1993.

——. »List of Current Court Members« About ICC | Organisation | ICC International Court of Arbitration, n.d.

www.iccwbo.org/About-ICC/Organisation/Dispute-Resolution-Services/ICC-International-Court-of-Arbitration/List-of-Current-Court-Members.

——. »National Committees Connections Gateway« *Worldwide Membership*, n.d.

www.iccwbo.org/worldwide-membership/national-committees.

——. »Secretariat of the Court« *Organisation | About ICC*, n.d.

www.iccwbo.org/About-ICC/Organization/Dispute-Resolution-Services/ICC-International-Court-of-Arbitration/Secretariat-of-the-Court.

——. »Standard ICC Arbitration Clauses«, n.d.

www.iccwbo.org/Products-and-Services/Arbitration-and-ADR/Arbitration/Standard-ICC-Arbitration-Clauses.

——. »The Merchants of Peace« *History | About ICC*, n.d.

www.iccwbo.org/about-icc/history.

——. »Traders Warned about Non-Existent ICC Instruments Quoted on Internet« *Articles*, 1 April 1999.

www.iccwbo.org/News/Articles/1999/Traders-warned-about-non-existent-ICC-instruments-quoted-on-Internet.

——, Committee on International Commercial Arbitration. »Enforcement of International Arbitral Awards: Report and Preliminary Draft Convention« 13 March 1953. Paris.

www.newyorkconvention.org/userfiles/documenten/texts-history/87_preliminarydraft1953.pdf.

———. »2012 Statistical Report of the International Court of Arbitration« *Bulletin of the International Court of Arbitration* 24, no. 1 (2013): 5-18.

———. »Copyright and Trademarks«, n.d.

www.iccwbo.org/copyright-and-trademarks.

———. »Cost Calculator« *Arbitration*, n.d.

www.iccwbo.org/Products-and-Services/Arbitration-and-ADR/Arbitration/Cost-and-payment/Cost-calculator.

———. »Cost of Arbitration in Detail (articles 36 and 37)« *Arbitration*, n.d.

www.iccwbo.org/products-and-services/arbitration-and-adr/arbitration/cost-and-payment/cost-of-arbitration-in-detail-(articles-36-and-37).

———. »ICC Singapore« National Committees & Groups, n.d.

www.iccwbo.org/Worldwide-Membership/National-Committees/ICC-Singapore.

———. »Ten Good Reasons to Choose ICC Arbitration«, n.d.

www.iccwbo.org/Products-and-Services/Arbitration-and-ADR/Arbitration/Introduction-to-ICC-Arbitration/Ten-good-reasons-to-choose-ICC-arbitration.

ICCA. »Chapter II: Request for the Enforcement of an Arbitration Agreement« In *ICCA's Guide to the Interpretation of the 1958 New York Convention: A Handbook for Judges*, edited by Pieter Sanders, 36-65. ICCA, 2011.

———. »IIIrd Congress, Venice October 1969: Program of Congress Sessions« *Conferences and Congresses*, n.d.

www.arbitration-icca.org/media/0/12127373396070/venice_combined.pdf.

ILA, Committee on International Commercial Arbitration, Final Report to Public Policy as a Bar to Enforcement of International Arbitral Awards, 2002,

www.newyorkconvention.org/publications/full-text-publications/general/ila-report-on-public-policy-2002.

Illmer, Martin. »Anti-Suit Injunctions und nicht ausschließliche Gerichtsstandsvereinbarungen (zugleich Anmerkung zu Court of Appeal, 13.7.2009 - [2009] EWCA Civ. 725 - Deutsche Bank AG and Another v Highland Crusader Offshore Partners LP and Others)« *IPRax* 32, no. 5 (2012): 406-13.

Institut de Droit International - 1ère commission. »Resolution« In *La substitution et le principe d'équivalence en droit international privé*. Santiago, 2007.

www.idi-iil.org/idiE/resolutionsE/2007_san_01_en.pdf.

Izor, Sean. »Insigma Revisited: Singapore High Court Finds Arbitration Clause to Be Operable« *Kluwer Arbitration Blog*, 25 February 2013.

http://kluwerarbitrationblog.com/blog/2013/02/25/insigma-revisited-singapore-high-court-finds-arbitration-clause-to-be-operable.

Jarrosson, Charles. »Le rôle respectif de l'institution, de l'arbitre et des parties dans l'instance arbitrale« *Rev. Arb.* no. 2 (1990): 381-94.

Jasserand, Catherine, and Bernt Hugenholtz, *Using Copyright to Promote Access to Public Sector Information - A Comparative Survey*, Institute for Information Law, University of Amsterdam, June 2012, www.ivir.nl/publications/jasserand/WIPO_June_%202012.pdf.

Jayme, Erik. »Ausländische Rechtsregeln und Tatbestand inländischer Sachnormen: Betrachtungen zu Ehrenzweigs Datum-Theorie« In *Gedächtnisschrift für Albert A. Ehrenzweig*, 35-49, 1976.

———. »Report« In *Substitution et principe d'équivalence en droit international privé*, 72:1-94. Annuaire de l'Institut de droit international. Santiago, Chile: Paris: A. Pedone, n.d. www.idi-iil.org/idiF/annuaireF/2007/Jayme.pdf.

Jiménez-Blanco, Gonzalo, and Lucas Osorio Iturmendi. »Los Llamados ›Árbitros de Parte‹« *Rev. Esp. Arb.* 2013, no. 18 (2013): 63-122.

Johnston, Graeme. »Party Autonomy in Mainland Chinese Commercial Arbitration« *J. Int'l Arb.* 25, no. 5 (2008): 537-44.

———. »The Best Providers for Asian Arbitrations« In *Arbitration in Singapore and Germany: Recent Developments*, edited by Karl-Heinz Böckstiegel, Klaus Peter Berger, and Jens Bredow, 41-48. Schriftenreihe der Deutschen Institution für Schiedsgerichtsbarkeit 25. Cologne: Heymann, 2009.

Joseph, David. Jurisdiction and Arbitration Agreements and Their Enforcement. 2nd ed. London: Sweet & Maxwell, 2010.

Kadner Graziano, Thomas. »L'européanisation du droit privé et de la méthode comparative - Étude de cas (Annexe 1)« In *Le contrat en droit privé européen*, 317-32. Basel: Brussels: Paris: Helbing Lichtenhahn: Bruylant: LGDJ, 2010.

Kamina, Pascal. *Film Copyright in the European Union*. Cambridge University Press, 2002.

Kaplan, Neil, Jill Spruce, and Michael J Moser. *Hong Kong and China Arbitration: Cases and Materials*. Hong Kong: Singapore: Butterworths, 1994.

Karrer, Pierre A. »Naives Sparen birgt Gefahren : Kostenfragen aus Sicht der Parteien und des Schiedsgerichts« *SchiedsVZ* 4, no. 3 (2006): 113-19.

———. »Swiss Rules« In *Institutional Arbitration: Article-by-Article Commentary*, edited by Rolf A Schütze. Munich: Oxford: Baden-Baden: Beck: Hart: Nomos, 2013.

Karton, Joshua. The Culture of International Arbitration and the Evolution of Contract Law. Oxford: Oxford University Press, 2013.

Kassis, Antoine. Réflexions sur le règlement d'arbitrage de la chambre de commerce internationale: les déviations de l'arbitrage institutionnel. Paris: Librairie Génerale de Droit et de Jurisprudence, 1988.

———. »The Questionable Validity of Arbitration and Awards Under the Rules of the International Chamber of Commerce« *J. Int'l Arb.* 62 (1989): 79-100.

Kathpalia, Sujata. »Is Arbitration Being Colonized by Litigation? - Practitioners' Views in the Singapore Context« In *Discourse and Practice in International Commercial Arbitration: Issues, Challenges and Prospects*, edited by Vijay Bhatia, Christopher

Candlin, and Maurizio Gotti, 263-83. Law, language and communication. Farnham, Surrey, England: Burlington, VT: Ashgate Publishing, 2012.

Kaufmann-Kohler, Gabrielle. »Globalization of Arbitral Procedure« *Vand. J. Trans'l L.* 36, no. 4 (2003): 1313-33.

Khadjavi, Amir. ICC-Schiedsordnung und deutsches Schiedsverfahrensrecht: Kompatibilität institutioneller Schiedsgerichtsbarkeit mit nationalem Recht in verfahrensrechtlicher Hinsicht. Konstanz: Hartung-Gorre, 2002.

Kirby, Jennifer. »Insigma Technology Co. Ltd. v Alstom Technology Ltd.: SIAC Can Administer Cases Under The ICC Rules?!?« *Arb. Int'l* 25, no. 3 (2009): 319-28.

Kirchner, Jörg. »Schiedsgerichtsbarkeit in Berlin - zum Begriff des ›Wegfalls‹ eines ständigen Schiedsgerichts gem. § 1033 Nr. 1 ZPO« *DtZ* 3, no. 9 (1992): 270-72.

Klass, Nadine. »Das Urheberkollisionsrecht der ersten Inhaberschaft: Plädoyer für einen universalen Ansatz« *GRUR Int.* 56, no. 5 (2007): 373-86.

— –. »Ein interessen- und prinzipienorientierter Ansatz für die urheberkollisionsrechtliche Normbildung: Die Bestimmung geeigneter Anknüpfungspunkte für die erste Inhaberschaft« *GRUR Int.* 57, no. 7 (2008): 546.

Klein, Frédéric-Edouard. »La Convention européenne sur l'arbitrage commercial international« *Rev. crit. DIP* 51, no. 4 (1962): 621-40.

Kleinheisterkamp, Jan. »The Impact of Internationally Mandatory Laws on the Enforceability of Arbitration Agreements« *WAMR* 3, no. 2. LSE Legal Studies Working Paper no. 22/2009 (2009): 91-120.
http://ssrn.com/abstract=1496923 or http://dx.doi.org/10.2139/ssrn.1496923.

Kniprath, Lutz. »Neue Schiedsordnung der Chinese International Economic and Trade Arbitration Commission (CIETAC)« *SchiedsVZ* 3, no. 4 (2005): 197-206.

Kobayashi, Bruce, and Larry Ribstein. »Law as Product and Byproduct« *J. L. Econ. & Pol.* 9, no. 4 (2013): 521.
http://heinonline.org/HOL/Page?handle=hein.journals/jecoplcy9&id=553&div=&collection=journals.

——. »Private Lawdrafting, Intellectual Property, and Public Laws« In *Regulatory Competition in Contract Law and Dispute Resolution*, edited by Horst Eidenmüller, 43-65, Munich: Beck, 2013.

Köhler, Helmut, and Joachim Bornkamm. Gesetz gegen den unlauteren Wettbewerb: Elektronische Ressourcen, Preisangabenverordnung, Unterlassungsklagengesetz, Dienstleistungs-Informationspflichten-Verordnung. Munich: Beck, 2014.

Konrad, Sabine, and Robert Hunter. »LCIA Rules« In *Institutional Arbitration: Article-by-Article Commentary*, edited by Rolf A Schütze. Munich: Oxford: Baden-Baden: Beck: Hart: Nomos, 2013.

Kreindler, Richard. »Chapter 2, §2.05: The Role of State Courts in Assisting Arbitral Tribunals Confronted with Guerrilla Tactics« In *Guerrilla Tactics in International*

*Arbitration*, edited by Günther Horvath and Wilske Stephan, 102-16. International Arbitration Law Library 28. Kluwer Law International, 2013.

———. »Impending Revision of the ICC Arbitration Rules: Opportunities and Hazards for Experienced and Inexperienced Users Alike« *J. Int'l Arb.* 13, no. 2 (1996): 45-116.

Kreutzer, Till, and Benjamin Roger. »Copyright Protection of Standard Contracts (Schutzfähigkeit von Musterverträgen), District Court Stuttgart (Landgericht Stuttgart), 6 March 2008, *Kluwer Copyright Cases*« Kluwer Law International, n.d. www.kluweriplaw.com/CommonUI/document.aspx?id=KLI-EUIPC-08339001-DE-cr.

Kröll, Stefan. »Chapter 2, Part II: Commentary on Chapter 12 PILS« In *Arbitration in Switzerland: The Practitioner's Guide*, edited by Manuel Arroyo, 2013.

———. »Die Entwicklung des Rechts der Schiedsgerichtsbarkeit 2005/2006« *NJW* 60, no. 11 (2007): 743-49.

———. »Recourse against Negative Decisions on Jurisdiction« *Arb. Int'l* 20, no. 1 (2004): 55-72.

———. »Chapter I: Issues Specific to Arbitration in Europe, The European Convention on International Commercial Arbitration - The Tale of a Sleeping Beauty« In *Austrian Yearbook on International Arbitration*, edited by Christian Klausegger, Peter Klein, Florian Kremslehner, Alexander Petsche, Nikolaus Pitkowitz, Jenny Power, Irene Welser, and Gerold Zeiler, 1-22. Beck: Stämpfli & Manz, 2013.

Kropholler, Jan. »Anmerkung zu BGH JZ 1983, 903« *JZ* (1983): 905-7.

———. Internationales Privatrecht - einschliesslich der Grundbegriffe des internationalen Zivilverfahrensrechts. 6th ed. Tübingen: Mohr Siebeck, 2006.

Kuckenburg, Joachim. »Vertragliche Beziehungen zwischen ICC, Parteien und Schiedsrichter« In *Status, Aufgaben, Rechte und Pflichten des Schiedsrichters*, edited by Jens Bredow with Deutsche Institution für Schiedsgerichtsbarkeit, 78-102. DIS-Materialien 1. Bonn: DIS, 1997.

Kühne, Günther. »Methodeneinheit und Methodenvielfalt im Internationalen Privatrecht« In *Liber Amicorium Klaus Schurig zum 70. Geburtstag*, edited by Ralf Michaels and Dennis Solomon, 129-46, Sellier: Munich, 2012.

Kühner, Detlev. »Survie de la clause compromissoire en cas de disparition de l'institution d'arbitrage - l'exemple de la DIS, note sous Paris, Pôle 1 - Ch. 1, 20 mars 2012« *Rev. Arb.* no. 4 (2012): 808-10.

———. »Zur Wirksamkeit einer Schiedsklausel, in der auf eine nicht mehr existierende Schiedsinstitution verwiesen wird« *SchiedsVZ* 11, no. 4 (2013): 238-40.

Kunz-Hallstein, Hans Peter. »Die Beteiligung internationaler Organisationen am Rechts- und Wirtschaftsverkehr: Unter besonderer Berücksichtigung der Probleme des Schutzes des geistigen und gewerblichen Eigentums« *GRUR Int.* 89, no. 12 (1987): 819-33.

Laas, Bernhard. Der wettbewerbsrechtliche Schutz von Geschäftsmethoden: der Leistungsschutz nach der Reform des UWG. Munich: Utz, 2004.

Labes, Hubertus. »Zusammenfassung der Podiumsdiskussion« In *Recht und Praxis der internationalen Schiedsgerichtsbarkeit in Staaten Zentral- und Ost-Europas*, edited by Karl-Heinz Böckstiegel. Schriftenreihe der Deutschen Institution für Schiedsgerichtsbarkeit 13. Cologne: Berlin: Heymann, 1998.

Lachmann, Jens-Peter. *Handbuch für die Schiedsgerichtspraxis*. 3rd ed. Cologne: Otto Schmidt, 2008.

De La Fontaine, Jean, and Percy J Billinghurst. *A Hundred Fables of La Fontaine*. New York: Greenwich House, 1983.

eBook available at: www.gutenberg.org/files/25357/25357-h/25357-h.htm.

Lalive, Pierre. »Arbitration - The Civilized Solution« *ASA Bull.* 16, no. 3 (1998): 483-97.

———. »Note: Cour d'appel de Paris (1re Ch. A), 15 septembre 1998: Société Cubic Defense Systems Inc. c/ Chambre de commerce internationale« *Rev. Arb.* no. 1 (1999): 113-20.

———. »Transnational (or Truly International) Public Policy and International Arbitration« In *ICCA, Comparative Arbitration Practice and Public Policy in Arbitration*, edited by Pieter Sanders, 257-320. ICCA Congress Series 3. New York: The Hague, 1987.

Landau, Toby. »The Day Before Tomorrow: Future Developments in International Arbitration - Transcript of the 2009 International Arbitration Lecture« *Clayton Utz Annual International Arbitration Lecture*, 2009.

www.claytonutz.com/ialecture/2009/transcript_2009.html.

Landolt, Philip. »Chapter 49: Antitrust Arbitration under the ICC Rules« In *EU and US Antitrust Arbitration: A Handbook for Practioners*, edited by Gordon Blanke and Phillip Landolt, 1763-1898. Kluwer Law International, 2011.

Lauber-Rönsberg, Anne. »Kollisionsrecht« In *Beck'scher Online-Kommentar Urheberrecht*, by Philipp Möhring and Käte Nicolini, edited by Hartwig Ahlberg and Horst-Peter Götting. 3rd ed. Munich: Beck, 2013.

http://beck-online.beck.de/?vpath=bib-data/komm/BeckOK_UrhR_3/UrhG/cont/beckok.UrhG.Kollisions-recht.glA.glII.htm.

Lau, Christopher. »Conference Report Madrid: Options for the Resolution of International Commercial Disputes, Including the Drafting of Dispute Resolution Clauses« *IBA Arbitration News* 15, no. 1 (March 2010): 13-15.

———. »Singapore« In *Practitioner's Handbook on International Commercial Arbitration*, edited by Frank-Bernd Weigand, 693-748. Oxford: Oxford University Press, 2009.

Lau, Christopher, and Christin Horlach. »Party Autonomy - The Turning Point?« *Dispute Resolution International* 4, no. 1 (May 2010): 121-30.

Lazareff, Serge. »Le bloc-notes: de l'excès de réglementation« Edited by Alexis Mourre. *Les Cahiers de l'Arbitrage* 3. Gazette du Palais (July 2006): 9-11.

LCIA. »LCIA Arbitration«, n.d.

www.lcia.org//Dispute_Resolution_Services/LCIA_Arbitration.aspx.

——. »LCIA Services in Ad Hoc Proceedings«, n.d.

www.lcia.org/Dispute_Resolution_Services/LCIA_Services_in_adhoc_proceedings.aspx.

——. »Members of the LCIA Court« *LCIA*, n.d.

www.lcia.org/LCIA/Members_bios.aspx

——. »Organisation« *About Us*, 2014,

www.lcia.org/LCIA/Organisation.aspx.

——. »The Case for Administered Arbitration«, n.d.

www.lcia.org/Dispute_Resolution_Services/The_Case_for_Administered_Arbitration_.aspx.

——«Schedule of Arbitration Costs (LCIA)« *Dispute Resolution Services*, n.d.

www.lcia.org//Dispute_Resolution_Services/schedule-of-costs-lcia-arbitration.aspx.

LCIA India. »Home«, 2012.

www.lcia-india.org.

LCIA-MIAC. »LCIA-MIAC Arbitration Centre«, 2013.

www.lcia-miac.org.

Lembcke, Moritz. »IV. - Andere Verfahren: Schlichtung« In *Kommentar zum Mediationsgesetz*, edited by Roland Fritz and Dietrich Pielsticker, 810-21. Luchterhand: Wolters Kluwer, 2013.

Lettl, Tobias. *Das Neue UWG*. Aktuelles Recht für die Praxis. Munich: Beck, 2004.

Leverenz, Kent. Gestaltungsrechtsausübungen durch und gegen Personenmehrheiten. Berlin: Duncker & Humblot, 1995.

Lewald, Hans. *Règles générales des conflits de lois: contributions à la technique du droit international privé*. Institut für Internationales Recht und Internationale Beziehungen der Juristischen Fakultät Basel 3. Basel: Helbing Lichtenhahn, 1941.

Lewinski, Silke von. »§ 57 Grundlagen« In *Handbuch des Urheberrechts*, edited by Ulrich Loewenheim and Bernhard von Becker. Munich: Beck, 2010.

Lew, Julian. »Does National Court Involvement Undermine the International Arbitration Process?« *Am. Univ. Int'l L. Rev.*24, no. 3 (2009 2008): 489-538.

——. »The Law Applicable to the Form and Substance of the Arbitration Clause« In *Improving the Efficiency of Arbitration Agreements and Awards: 40 Years of Application of the New York Convention*, 114-45. ICCA Congress Series 9. Paris, 1998.

——. »Achieving the Dream: Autonomous Arbitration« *Arb. Int'l* 22, no. 2 (2006): 179-203.

Lew, Julian, and Loukas Mistelis, eds. Arbitration Insights: Twenty Years of the Annual Lecture of the School of International Arbitration, 2007.

Lew, Julian, Loukas Mistelis, and Stefan Kröll. *Comparative International Commercial Arbitration*. The Hague: New York: Kluwer Law International, 2003.

Lindacher, Walter. »Die internationale Dimension lauterkeitsrechtlicher Unterlassungsansprüche: Marktterritorialität versus Universalität« *GRUR Int.* 57, no. 6 (2008): 453-59.

Lin, Xiuqin, and Tieguang Liu. »China« In *Balancing Copyright*, edited by Reto Hilty and Silvie Nérisson, 255-84. Berlin: New York: Springer, 2012.

Lionnet, Klaus. »Der Schiedsrichtervertrag« In *Status, Aufgaben, Rechte und Pflichten des Schiedsrichters*, edited by Jens Bredow with Deutsche Institution für Schiedsgerichtsbarkeit, 64-77. DIS-Materialien 1. Bonn: DIS, 1997.

———. »The Arbitrator's Contract« *Arb. Int'l* 15, no. 2 (1999): 161-69.

Lionnet, Klaus, and Annette Lionnet. Handbuch der internationalen und nationalen Schiedsgerichtsbarkeit: systematische Darstellung der privaten Handelsschiedsgerichtsbarkeit für die Praxis der Parteien. 3rd ed. Stuttgart: R. Boorberg, 2005.

Liu, Joe, and Teresa Cheng. »Enforcement of Foreign Awards in Mainland China: Current Practices and Future Trends« *J. Int'l Arb.* 31, no. 5 (2014): 651-73.

Liu, Kung-Chung, Xinliang Tao, and Eric Wang. »The Use and Misuse of Well-Known Marks Listings« *IIC* no. 6 (2009): 685-97.

Liu, Lear, and Clarisse von Wunschheim. »Judicial Side Effects of the CIETAC Split: A Confusing Maze with a Happy End?« WunschArb, n.d.

http://issuu.com/wunscharb/docs/j189_wunsch_arb_cietac_vp4.

Lledó Yagüe, Francisco. In *Comentarios a la ley de arbitraje: ley 36/1988, de 5 de diciembre*, edited by Rodrigo Bercovitz Rodríguez-Cano and Santiago Álvarez González, 138 et seq. Madrid: Tecnos, 1991.

Loewenheim, Ulrich. »§ 8 Schutzumfang« In *Handbuch des Urheberrechts*, edited by Ulrich Loewenheim and Bernhard von Becker. Munich: Beck, 2010.

Logan, Lisa. »The Emperor's New Clothes? The Way Forward: TV Format Protection under Unfair Competition Law in the United States, United Kingdom and France: Part 1« *ELR* 20, no. 2 (2009): 38-43.

www.ifla.tv/format%20rights%20article%20Part%201.pdf.

———. »The Emperor's New Clothes? The Way Forward: TV Format Protection under Unfair Competition Law in the United States, United Kingdom and France: Part 2« *ELR* 20, no. 3 (2009): 87-92.

www.ifla.tv/format%20rights%20article%20Part%202%20%28PDF%29.pdf.

Lögering, Martin. »VII. - Andere Verfahren: Schiedsgerichtsbarkeit« In *Kommentar zum Mediationsgesetz*, edited by Roland Fritz and Dietrich Pielsticker, 872-99. Luchterhand: Wolters Kluwer, 2013.

Lörcher, Gino. »Wie zwingend sind in der internationalen Handelsschiedsgerichtsbarkeit zwingende Normen einer ›dritten‹ Rechtsordnung?« *BB-Beilage* no. 17 to no. 27 (1993): 3-8.

Lörcher, Gino, and Thorsten Lörcher. »§ 45 - Durchsetzbarkeit von Mediationsergebnissen« In *Handbuch Mediation: Verhandlungstechnik, Strategien, Einsatzgebiete*, edited by Fritjof Haft and Katharina von Schlieffen, 1119-34. 2nd ed. Munich: Beck, 2009.

Lörcher, Torsten, Guy Pendell, and Jeremy Wilson, CMS Legal, eds. »International Arbitration - an Overview« In *CMS Guide to Arbitration Online*, 2012

http://eguides.cmslegal.com/pdf/arbitration_volume_I/CMS%20GtA_Vol%20I_OVERVIEW.pdf.

Lundstedt, Lydia. »Gerichtliche Zuständigkeit und Territorialitätsprinzip im Immaterialgüterrecht: geht der Pendelschlag zu weit?« *GRUR Int.* 50, no. 2 (2001): 103-11.

Lu, Song. »The New CIETAC Arbitration Rules of 2012« *J. Int'l Arb.* 29, no. 3 (2012): 299-322.

De Ly, Filip. »Conflict of Laws in International Arbitration - an Overview« In *Conflict of Laws in International Arbitration*, edited by Franco Ferrari and Stefan Kröll, 3-16. Munich: Sellier, 2011.

Magnusson, Annette. »A Call from an Arbitration Activist« *Kluwer Arbitration Blog*, 23 September 2014.

http://kluwerarbitrationblog.com/blog/2014/09/23/a-call-from-an-arbitration-activist.

Marenkov, Dmitry. »DIS-Herbsttagung ›Die neue ICC-Schiedsgerichtsordnung‹« *SchiedsVZ* 10, no. 1 (2012): 33-40.

Marx, Claudius. Deutsches, europäisches und internationales Markenrecht. Neuwied: Luchterhand, 2007.

Mason, Paul. »Whether Arbitration Rules Should Be Applied by the Issuing Arbitral Institution« *Lexis Nexis Emerging Issues Analysis* 1149 (2009).

www.lexisnexis.com/legalnewsroom/international-law/b/commentry/archive/2008/05/20/whether-arbitration-rules-should-be-applied-by-the-issuing-arbitral-institution.aspx.

McIlwrath, Michael. »Can Arbitration Keep Up? Singapore Ratchets Up Forum Competition«, 31 October 2013.

http://kluwerarbitrationblog.com/blog/2013/10/31/can-arbitration-keep-up-singapore-forum-competition.

M., E. »Bibliographie - Handelsrechtliche Schiedsgerichts-Praxis H.S.G« *Rev. Arb.* 3, no. 1 (1986): 145.

Meeran, Ahn. »The 2012 International Chamber of Commerce Rules of Arbitration: Meeting the Need of the International« Arbitration Community in the 21 St Century« *YB Arb. & Med.* 4 (2012): 370-82.

Meili, Friedrich. »Argenträus und Molinäus und ihre Bedeutung im internationalen Privat und Strafrecht« *BöhmsZ* 5 (1895): 452-73.

Merkin, Robert M. *Arbitration Law1.* 2 vols. London: New York: Lloyd's of London Press, 1991.

Metzger, Axel. »Zum anwendbaren Urheberrecht bei grenzüberschreitendem Rundfunk« *IPRax.* 26, no. 3 (2006): 242-246.

Mezger, Ernst. »Das Europäische Übereinkommen über die Handelsschiedsgerichtsbarkeit« RabelsZ 29 (1965): 231-301.

Michaels, Ralf. »Die Struktur der kollisionsrechtlichen Durchsetzung einfach zwingender Normen« In *Liber Amicorium Klaus Schurig zum 70. Geburtstag*, edited by Ralf Michaels and Dennis Solomon, 191-210, Sellier: Munich, 2012.

———. »Dreaming Law without a State: Scholarship on Autonomous International Arbitration as Utopian Literature« *Lond. Rev. Int'l L.* 1, no. 1 (2013): 35-62.

http://lril.oxfordjournals.org/content/1/1/35.full.pdf+html.

——. »Rollen und Rollenverständnisse im transnationalen Privatrecht« Duke University School of Law, 2011.

http://scholarship.law.duke.edu/faculty_scholarship/2449.

——. »Rollen und Rollenverständnisse im transnationalen Privatrecht« In *Paradigmen im internationalen Recht: Implikationen der Weltfinanzkrise für das internationale Recht*, by Bardo Fassbender, 175-227, 175-227, 2012.

Minoli, Eugenio. »Key Note« In *Cooperation between Arbitration Organisations*. Venice, 1969.

Molinaeus, Carolus. Conclusiones de statutis et consuetudinibus localibus. Hannover, 1604.

Moller, Hans. »Schiedsverfahrensnovelle und Europäisches Übereinkommen über die internationale Handelsschiedsgerichtsbarkeit« *Neue Zeitschrift für Gesellschaftsrecht* (2000): 57-72.

Morgan, Robert. »International Arbitration in Hong Kong« In *Internationale Schiedsgerichtsbarkeit*, by Peter Gottwald, 421-505, 421-505, 1997.

Moser, Michael, and Yu Jianlong. »CIETAC and Its Work: An Interview with Vice Chairman Yu Jianlong« *J. Int'l Arb.* 24, no. 6 (2007): 555-64.

Moses, Margaret. *The Principles and Practice of International Commercial Arbitration*. Cambridge : New York: Cambridge University Press, 2008.

Mourre, Alexis. »Are Unilateral Appointments Defensible? On Jan Paulsson's Moral Hazard in International Arbitration« *Kluwer Arbitration Blog*, 5 October 2010.

http://kluwerarbitrationblog.com/blog/2010/10/05/are-unilateral-appointments-defensible-on-jan-paulsson%E2%80%99s-moral-hazard-in-international-arbitration.

——. »Institutional Arbitration Rules: Do They Deserve More Deference from the Judiciary? - Comments on *Tecnimont* and Other Cases« In *The Practice of Arbitration: Essays in Honour of Hans van Houtte*, edited by Patrick Wautelet, Thalia Kruger, and Govert Coppens. Oxford: Hart, 2012.

Muir Watt, Horatia. »Note - Cour de cassation (1re Ch. civ.), 1er février 2005« *Rev. Arb.* no. 3 (2005): 693.

Müller-Freienfels, Wolfram. »Der Schiedsrichtervertrag in kollisionsrechtlicher Beziehung« In *Liber amicorum Ernst J. Cohn: Festschrift für Ernst J. Cohn zum 70. Geburtstag*, 147-62. Heidelberg: Recht und Wirtschaft, 1975.

Münch, Joachim. »§ 1025 ZPO« In *Münchener Kommentar Zur Zivilprozessordnung*, edited by Wolfgang Krüger and Thomas Rauscher. 4th ed. Munich, 2013.

——. »§ 1029 ZPO« In *ibid.*

——. »§ 1032 ZPO« In *ibid.*

——. »§ 1035 ZPO« In *ibid.*

——. »§ 1040 ZPO« In *ibid.*

——. »§ 1042 ZPO« In *ibid.*

——. »§ 1043 ZPO« In *ibid.*

——. »vor § 1034 ZPO« In *ibid.*

Muñoz Sabaté, Luis. »El reglamento de la institución arbritral a la luz de la Nueva Ley de Arbitraje« *Anuario de Justicia Alternativa* no. 535-48 (2004).

Musielak, Hans-Joachim. »Einleitung« In *Kommentar zur Zivilprozessordnung: mit Gerichtsverfassungsgesetz*, edited by Hans-Joachim Musielak. 12th ed. Munich: Vahlen, 2015.

Naciemento, Patricia. »Konfliktlösung nach allgemeinen Schiedsordnungen, insbesondere ICC (International Chamber of Commerce), AAA (American Arbitration Association) und DIS (Deutsche Institution für Schiedsgerichtsbarkeit)« *ZUM* 48, no. 11 (2004): 785-93.

Nakamura, Tatsuya. »The Place of Arbitration - Its Fictitious Nature and Lex Arbitri« *Mealey's Int'l Arb. Rep.* 15, no. 10 (October 2000): 23-29.

Nater-Bass, Gabrielle. »'Prima Facie': Zuständigkeitsentscheide in internationalen Schiedsgerichtsverfahren aus der Sicht der Parteien« *ASA Bull.* 20 (2002): 608-22.

Nedden, Jan Heiner, and Axel Benjamin Herzberg. »Art. 1 ICC SchO« In *Praxiskommentar ICC-SchO/DIS-SchO*, edited by Jan Heiner Nedden and Axel Benjamin Herzberg. Cologne: Otto Schmidt, 2013.

──., eds. *Praxiskommentar ICC-SchO/DIS-SchO*. Cologne: Otto Schmidt, 2013.

Nesbitt, Simon. »LCIA Arbitration Rules, Article 1, The Request for Arbitration« In *Concise International Arbitration*, edited by Loukas Mistelis, 402-5. Alphen aan den Rijn: Kluwer Law International, 2010.

──. »LCIA Arbitration Rules, Article 5, Formation of the Arbitral Tribunal« In *ibid.*

──. »LCIA Arbitration Rules, Introductory Remarks« In *ibid.*

Nettlau, Harry. Die kollisionsrechtliche Behandlung von Ansprüchen aus unlauterem Wettbewerbsverhalten gemäß Art. 6 Abs. 1 und 2 Rom II-VO. Frankfurt am Main: Peter Lang, 2013.

Ng-Loy, Wee Loon. *Law of Intellectual Property of Singapore*. Singapore: Thomson Sweet & Maxwell Asia, 2008.

──. »Singapore« In *Balancing Copyright*, edited by Reto Hilty and Silvie Nérisson, 829-51. Berlin: New York: Springer, 2012.

Nicholas, Geoff, and Constantine Partasides. »LCIA Court Decisions on Challenges to Arbitrators: A Proposal to Publish« *Arb. Int'l* 23, no. 1 (2007): 1-41.

Nicholls, Anthony Cheah, and Christopher Bloch. »ICC Hybrid Arbitrations Here to Stay: Singapore Courts' Treatment of the ICC Rules Revisions in Articles 1(2) and 6(2)« *J. Int'l Arb.* 31, no. 3 (2014): 393-412.

Nielen, Michael, and Micaela Schork. »G. Zivilrechtliches Verfahren« In *Handbuch Marken- und Designrecht*, edited by Maximiliane Stöckel, 287-342. Erich Schmidt Verlag, 2013. http://public.eblib.com/EBLPublic/PublicView.do?ptiID=1213082.

Nordemann, Wilhelm. »Ersatz des immateriellen Schadens bei Urheberrechtsverletzungen« *GRUR* 82, no. 5 (1980): 434-36.

Oechsler, Jürgen. »Die Idee als persönliche geistige Schöpfung: Von Fichtes Lehre vom Gedankeneigentum zum Schutz von Spielideen« *GRUR* 111, no. 12 (2009): 1101-7.

Oetiker, Christian, and Sabine Burkhaler. »Swiss Chambers' Court of Arbitration and Mediation (SCCAM)« In *Institutional Arbitration: Tasks and Powers of Different Arbitration Institutions*, edited by Pascale Gola, Claudia Götz Staehlin, and Karin Graf, 233-52. Schulthess: Sellier, 2009.

Oetting, Torsten. *Der Schiedsrichtervertrag nach dem UML im deutschen Recht unter rechtsvergleichenden Aspekten.* Rechtswissenschaftliche Forschung und Entwicklung 425. Munich: VVF, 1994.

Office of Public Sector Information, Minister of the Cabinet Office, and United Kingdom. *The Future Management of Crown Copyright.* Command Papers 4300. London: Her Majesty's Stationery Office, 1999.

www.opsi.gov.uk/advice/crown-copyright/future-management-of-crown-copyright.pdf.

Öhlberger, Veit. »Chapter I: The Arbitration Agreement and Arbitrability - China-Related Contracts: What to Consider When Agreeing on CIETAC Arbitration« In *Austrian Arbitration Yearbook*, edited by Christian Klausegger, Peter Klein, Florian Kremslehner, Alexander Petsche, Nikolaus Pitkowitz, Jenny Power, Irene Welser, and Gerold Zeiler, 113-45. Beck: Stämpfli & Manz, 2009.

Ohly, Ansgar. »Anmerkung Zu Urteil: ›Hartplatzhelden.de‹. » *Gewerblicher Rechtschutz und Urheberrecht* 113, no. 5 (2011): 439-40.

——. »Einführung, B. Internationale Aspekte« In *Gesetz gegen den unlauteren Wettbewerb*, edited by Ansgar Ohly, Olaf Sosnitza, and Henning Piper. Munich: Beck, 2010.

——. »Schadensersatzanspruche wegen Rufschädigung und Verwässerung im Marken- und Lauterkeitsrecht« *GRUR* 109, no. 11 (2007): 926.

——. »UWG § 4« In *Gesetz gegen den unlauteren Wettbewerb*, edited by Ansgar Ohly, Olaf Sosnitza, and Henning Piper. Munich: Beck, 2010.

Onyema, Emilia. International Commercial Arbitration and the Arbitrator's Contract. London: New York: Routledge, 2010.

Oon & Bazul LLP. »The New International Chamber of Commerce ('ICC') Rules 2012: Hybrid Arbitration Agreements & Emergency Arbitrator Provisions« *E-Update March 2012*, March 2012.

www.oonbazul.com/assets/image/eupdates/ICC%20Rules%20-%20March%20E%20update%203.pdf.

Ortolani, Pietro. »The Role of Arbitration Institutions in China« *Transnational Dispute Management (TDM)* 10, no. 4 (1 September 2013).

www.transnational-dispute-management.com/article.asp?key=1971.

Oscar Wilde. »The Picture of Dorian Gray«, 1890.

www.gutenberg.org/ebooks/4078.

Pabst, Steffen. »vor § 23 EGGVG« In *Münchener Kommentar zur Zivilprozessordnung*, edited by Thomas Rauscher and Wolfgang Krüger. 4th ed. Munich: Beck, 2013.

Palandt, Otto. *Bürgerliches Gesetzbuch: mit Nebengesetzen.* 72nd ed. Beck'sche Kurz-Kommentare 7. Munich: Beck, 2013.

Paris - the Home of International Arbitration. »Glossary of Arbitration Terms«, n.d. www.parisarbitration.com/glossary.php.

Park, William. »Arbitration's Protean Nature: The Value of Rules and the Risks of Discretion« *Arb. Int'l* 19, no. 3 (2003): 279-301.
www.arbitration-icca.org/media/0/12554337959080/park_freshfields_protean_nature.pdf.

——. »Why Courts Review Arbitral Awards« In *Law of International Business and Dispute Settlement in the 21st Century: Liber Amicorum Karl-Heinz Böckstiegel*, edited by Robert Georg Briner, Yves Fortier, Klaus Peter Berger, and Jens Bredow, 595-606. Cologne: Heymann, 2001.
www.williamwpark.com/documents/Why%20Courts%20Review%20Awards.pdf.

Patocchi, Paolo Michele, and Tilman Niedermaier. »UNCITRAL-Schiedsordnung« In *Institutionelle Schiedsgerichtsbarkeit: Kommentar*, edited by Rolf A. Schütze, IX. 2nd ed. Cologne, Munich: Heymann, 2011.

Paulsson, Jan. »Arbitration Unbound: Award Detached from the Law of Its Country of Origin« *The International and Comparative Law Quarterly* 30, no. 2 (1981): 358-87.

——. »Are Unilateral Appointments Defensible?« *Kluwer Arbitration Blog*, 2 April 2009.
http://kluwerarbitrationblog.com/blog/2009/04/02/are-unilateral-appointments-defensible.

——. »Delocalisation of International Commercial Arbitration: When and Why It Matters« *International and Comparative Law Quarterly* 32, no. 1 (January 1983): 53-61.

——., ed. International Handbook on Commercial Arbitration: National Reports and Basic Legal Texts. lslf. Alphen aan den Rijn: Kluwer Law International, 1984.

——. »Moral Hazard in International Dispute Resolution« Inaugural Lecture. 29 April 2010. University of Miami School of Law.
www.arbitration-icca.org/media/0/12773749999020/paulsson_moral_hazard.pdf.

——. »Vicarious Hypochondria and Institutional Arbitration« *Arb. Int'l* 6, no. 3 (1990): 226-52.

Paulsson, Jan, Nigel Rawding, and Lucy Reed, eds. *The Freshfields Guide to Arbitration and ADR: Clauses in International Contracts*. Kluwer Law International, 2011.

Peking University Law Department. »Notice of the Supreme People's Court on Issues concerning the Proper Trial of Cases Involving Arbitration-Related Judicial Review« [最高人民法院关于正确审理仲裁司法审查案件有关问题的通知] Pkulaw.cn | Chinalawinfo, n.d.
http://en.pkulaw.cn/Search/SearchLaw.aspx?Effective=01

Pendell, Guy. »The Rise and Rise of the Arbitration Institution« *Kluwer Arbitration Blog*, 30 November 2011.
http://kluwerarbitrationblog.com/blog/2011/11/30/the-rise-and-rise-of-the-arbitration-institution.

Peter, Wolfgang. »Die neue Schweizerische Schiedsordnung - Anmerkungen für die Praxis« *SchiedsVZ* 2, no. 2 (2004): 57-65.

Petrochilos, Georgios. *Procedural Law in International Arbitration*. Oxford: New York: Oxford University Press, 2004.

Petsche, Markus. *The Growing Autonomy of International Commercial Arbitration*. Beitrage zum internationalen Wirtschaftsrecht 3. Munich: Sellier, 2005.

Pfeiffer, Thomas. »EuGH: Anti-suit injunction auch auf der Grundlage einer Schiedsvereinbarung unvereinbar mit Brüssel I-Verordnung (Anmerkung)« *Beck Fachdienst Zivilrecht LMK* no. 3 (2009): 276971.

De Pfeifle, María Elena Alvarez. Der Ordre Public-Vorbehalt als Versagungsgrund der Anerkennung und Vollstreckbarerklärung internationaler Schiedssprüche. Unter Berücksichtigung des deutschen, schweizerischen, französischen und englischen Rechts sowie des UNCITRAL-Modellgesetzes. Internationalrechtliche Studien. Berlin: Peter Lang, 2009.

Pflüger, Martin. »Aktuelle Informationen: Volksrepublik China - Erlass von Auslegungsbestimmungen des Obersten Volksgerichts hinsichtlich der Anwendung des Gesetzes gegen den unlauteren Wettbewerb« *GRUR Int.* 56, no. 8/9 (2007): 789-90.

Pflüger, Martin Johannes. *Der internationale Schutz gegen unlauteren Wettbewerb*. Schriftenreihe zum gewerblichen Rechtsschutz 168. Cologne: Heymann, 2010.

Picone, Paolo. »Les méthodes de coordination entre ordres juridiques en droit international privé« *RdC* 276 (1999): 9-296.

Pinsolle, Philippe. »Parties to an International Arbitration with the Seat in France Are at Full Liberty to Organize the Procedure as They See Fit - A Reply to Article Published by Noah Rubins« *Mealey's Int'l Arb. Rep.* 16, no. 3 (March 2001): 30.

Pisar, Samuel. »The Communist System of Foreign-Trade Adjudication« *Harv. L. Rev.* 72, no. 8 (1959): 1409-81.

Plassmann, Clemens. Bearbeitungen und andere Umgestaltungen in § 23 Urheberrechtsgesetz. Berlin: Berlin-Verlag - Arno Spitz, 1996.

Platte, Martin. »An Arbitrator's Duty to Render Enforceable Awards« 20, no. 3 (2003): 307-13.

Pluyette, Gérard. »Le Point de Vue Du Juge« *Rev. Arb.* no. 2 (1990): 353-66.

Poudret, Jean-François, and Sebastian Besson. *Comparative Law of International Arbitration*. Translated by Stephen Berti and Annette Ponti. 2nd ed. London: Sweet & Maxwell, 2007.

Prütting, Hanns. »Die rechtliche Stellung des Schiedsrichters« *SchiedsVZ* 9, no. 5 (2011): 233-39.

Putzo, Hans, Heinz Thomas, Rainer Hüßtege, Christian Sellier, and Klaus Reichold, eds. Zivilprozessordnung: FamFG, Verfahren in Familiensachen, GVG, Einführungsgesetze, EU-Zivilverfahrensrecht : Kommentar. Munich: Beck, 2013.

Queen Mary University of London, School of International Arbitration and PriceWaterhouseCoopers LLP. »International Arbitration Survey: Corporate Attitudes and Practices«, 2008.

www.pwc.co.uk/en_UK/uk/assets/pdf/pwc-international-arbitration-2008.pdf.

Queen Mary University of London, School of International Arbitration and White & Case. »International Arbitration Survey: Choices in International Arbitration«, 2010. www.whitecase.com/files/upload/fileRepository/2010International_Arbitration_ Survey_Choices_in_International_Arbitration.pdf.

Raape, Leo. *Internationales Privatrecht.* 5th ed. Berlin: Frankfurt am Main: F. Vahlen, 1961.

Racine, Jean-Baptiste. »La sentence d'incompétence« *Rev. Arb.* no. 4 (2010): 729-81.

Raeschke-Kessler, Hilmar, and Klaus Peter Berger. *Recht und Praxis des Schiedsverfahrens.* Cologne: RWS, 2008.

Rahmatian, Andreas. »Originality in UK Copyright Law: The Old ›Skill and Labour‹ Doctrine Under Pressure« *IIC* 44, no. 1 (1 February 2013): 4-34.

http://link.springer.com/article/10.1007/s40319-012-0003-4.

Rana, Rashda, and Michelle Sanson. *International Commercial Arbitration.* Sydney: Thomson Reuters (Professional) Australia, 2011.

Rathmann, Jens. »§ 23 EGGVG« In *Handkommentar zur Zivilprozessordnung*, edited by Ingo Saenger. 5th ed. Baden-Baden: Nomos, 2013.

Rauscher, Thomas. Internationales Privatrecht: mit internationalem und europäischem Verfahrensrecht. 2nd ed. Heidelberg: C. F. Müller, 2002.

———. »ZPO, Einleitung« In *Münchener Kommentar zur Zivilprozessordnung: mit Gerichtverfassungsgesetz und Nebengesetzen*, edited by Wolfgang Krüger and Thomas Rauscher. 4th ed. Munich, 2012.

Rawert, Peter. »Schiedsklausel (institutionsgebunden) - Anmerkungen« In *Beck'sches Formularbuch Bürgerliches, Handels- und Wirtschaftsrecht*, edited by Michael [Hrsg.] Hoffmann-Becking. 11th ed. Munich: Beck, 2013.

Real, Gustav K. L. Der Schiedsrichtervertrag: Inhalt und rechtliche Regelung im deutschen Recht mit rechtsvergleichenden Ausblicken. Cologne: Heymann, 1983.

Redfern, Alan, and Martin Hunter. *Law and Practice of International Commercial Arbitration.* 1st ed. London: Sweet & Maxwell, 1986.

Rehbinder, Manfred. »Kann für Allgemeine Geschäftsbedingungen Urheberrechtsschutz in Anspruch genommen werden?« Edited by Georg Roeber. *Benvenuto Samson zum 90. Geburtstag* (1978): 73-80.

Reimer, Dietrich. Zum Urheberrechtsschutz von Darstellungen wissenschaftlicher oder technischer Art, 1980.

Reiner, Andreas, and Christian Aschauer. »ICC Rules« In *Institutional Arbitration: Article-by-Article Commentary*, by Rolf A Schütze. Munich: Oxford: Baden-Baden: Beck: Hart: Nomos, 2013.

Renner, Moritz. Zwingendes transnationales Recht: zur Struktur der Wirtschaftsverfassung jenseits des Staates (Diss., Bremen, 2010). Baden-Baden: Nomos, 2011.

Republic of Latvia. »Šķīrējtiesu« *Register of Enterprises*, n.d.

www.ur.gov.lv/?t=3&a=172&v=lv.

Risse, Jörg. »Part III - Commentary on the Arbitration Rules of the German Institution of Arbitration (DIS Rules), Section 24 - Rules of Procedure« In *Arbitration in*

*Germany: The Model Law in Practice*, edited by Karl-Heinz Böckstiegel, Stefan Michael Kröll, and Patricia Nacimiento, 744-47. Alphen aan den Rijn: Kluwer Law International, 2007.

Rogers, W. V. H. *Winfield and Jolowicz on Tort*. London: Sweet & Maxwell, 2010.

Rose, Marianne. »The Tarnished Brand of CIETAC: Understanding the 2012 CIETAC Dispute« *J. Int'l Arb.* 31, no. 2 (2014): 139-82.

Roughton, Dominic. »Commencing Arbitration: Contemporary Paradoxes and Problems« In *International Arbitration: The Coming of a New Age?*, edited by Albert Jan, van den Berg, 174-93. ICCA Congress Series 17, n.d.

Rubino-Sammartano, Mauro. *International Arbitration: Law and Practice*. The Hague: Boston: Kluwer Law International, 2001.

Rubins, Noah. »The Arbitral Seat is No Fiction: A Brief Reply to Tatsuya Nakamura's Commentary« *Mealey's Int'l Arb. Rep.* 16, no. 1 (January 2001): 23-28.

Rühl, Giesela. »Party Autonomy in the Private International Law of Contracts: Transatlantic Convergency and Economic Efficiency« In *Conflict of Laws in a Globalized World*, edited by Eckart Gottschalk, Ralf Michaels, Giesela Rühl, and Jan von Hein, 153-83. Cambridge: Cambridge University Press, 2007.

Rüßmann, Helmut. »Zwingendes Recht in den Schiedsregeln einer Schiedsinstitution?« In *Festschrift für Rolf Stürner zum 70. Geburtstag*, edited by Alexander Bruns, Christoph Kern, Joachim Münch, Andreas Piekenbrock, Astrid Stadler, and Dimitrios Tsikrikas, 482-92. Tübingen: Mohr Siebeck, 2013.

Rüßmann, Helmut, and Kinga Timár. »The Laws Applicable to the Arbitration Agreement« In *Recht ohne Grenzen: Festschrift für Athanassios Kaissis zum 65. Geburtstag*, edited by Rolf A. Schütze and Reinhold Geimer, 837-59, 2012.

Rüthers, Bernd, Christian Fischer, and Axel Birk. *Rechtstheorie mit juristischer Methodenlehre*. Munich: Beck, 2011.

Sachs, Klaus, and Nils Schmidt-Ahrendts. »Diverging Concepts of the Principle of Competence-Competence?« In *New Developments in International Commercial Arbitration 2010*, edited by Christoph Müller and Antonio Rigozzi. Zurich: Schulthess, 2010.

Saenger, Ingo. »§ 1026 ZPO« In *Handkommentar zur Zivilprozessordnung*, edited by Ingo Saenger. 5th ed. Baden-Baden: Nomos, 2013.

———. »§ 1029 ZPO« In *ibid.*

———. »§ 1040 ZPO« In *ibid.*

———., ed. *Handkommentar zur Zivilprozessordnung*. 5th ed. Baden-Baden: Nomos, 2013.

———. »vor § 1025 ZPO« In *ibid.*

Salamon, Lester, and Helmut Anheier. *Defining the Nonprofit Sector: A Cross-National Analysis*. Manchester University Press, 1997.

Sanders, Pieter. »111. Field of Arbitration - Permanent Arbitral Bodies« In *Yearbook Commercial Arbitration*, edited by Pieter Sanders, I:208, 1976.

———. »Note on the Importance of the Place of Arbitration«, 26 September 1976. www.arbitration-icca.org/media/0/12741827220440/011.pdf.

——. Quo Vadis Arbitration? - Sixty Years of Arbitration Practice. The Hague: Kluwer Law International, 1999.

Sanders, Pieter, and Albert Jan van den Berg, eds. *International Handbook on Commercial Arbitration: National Reports and Basic Legal Texts.* lslf. Alphen aan den Rijn: Kluwer Law International, 1984.

Sandrock, Otto. »How Much Freedom Should an International Arbitrator Enjoy?: The Desire for Freedom from Law v. the Promotion of International Arbitration« *Am. Rev. Int'l Arb.* 3 (1992): 30-56.

Savigny, Friedrich Karl, von. Private International Law and the Retrospective Operation of Statutes: A Treatise on the Conflict of Laws and the Limits of Their Operation in Respect of Place and Time. 2nd ed. Clark, N.J: Lawbook Exchange, 2003.

Schack, Haimo. Internationales Zivilverfahrensrecht: Ein Studienbuch. 5th ed. Munich: Beck, 2010.

——. »Internationale Urheber-, Marken- und Wettbewerbsrechtsverletzungen im Internet - Internationales Privatrecht« *Multimedia und Recht* 3, no. 2 (2000): 59-65.

——. »Internationale Zuständigkeit bei Verletzung von Urhebervermögensrechten über Internet - Anmerkung zu C-170/12 (Peter Pinckney/KDG Mediatech AG)« *NJW* 66, no. 50 (2013): 3629-30.

——. *Urheber- und Urhebervertragsrecht.* 5th ed. Tübingen: Mohr Siebeck, 2010.

Schäfer, Erik, Herman Verbist, and Christophe Imhoos. *Die ICC Schiedsgerichtsordnung in der Praxis.* Internationale Wirtschaftspraxis 8. Bonn: Economica, 2000.

Schäfer, Manuela. Die Verträge zur Durchführung des Schiedsverfahrens - Analyse und Vergleich zweier Lösungsmodelle am Beispiel des deutschen und US-amerikanischen Rechtsraums. Vol. 1. 2 vols. Saarbrücker Studien zum Privat- und Wirtschaftsrecht 64. Frankfurt am Main: Peter Lang, 2010.

Schewe, Christoph. »Schiedsgerichtsbarkeit in Lettland« *SchiedsVZ* 11, no. 3 (2013): 160-66.

Schiedermair, Gerhard. *Vereinbarungen im Zivilprozess.* Bonner rechtswissenschaftliche Abhandlungen 33. Bonn: L. Röhrscheid, 1935.

Schiffer, Jan. »Zwingende Normen einer ›dritten‹ Rechtsordnung in der internationalen Handelsschiedsgerichtsbarkeit?« *BB-Beilage* no. 12 to no. 5 (1994): 22-24.

Schilling, Alexander. »§ 6 DIS SchO« In *Praxiskommentar ICC-SchO/DIS-SchO,* edited by Jan Heiner Nedden and Axel Benjamin Herzberg. Cologne: Otto Schmidt, 2013.

——. »Art. 4 ICC SchO« In *Praxiskommentar ICC-SchO/DIS-SchO,* edited by Jan Heiner Nedden and Axel Benjamin Herzberg. Cologne: Otto Schmidt, 2013.

Schlaepfer, Anne Véronique, and Angelina Petti. »Chapter 2: Institutional versus Ad Hoc Arbitration« In *International Arbitration in Switzerland - A Handbook for Practioners,* edited by Elliott Geisinger and Nathalie Voser, 13-24. 2nd ed. Alphen aan den Rijn: Kluwer Law International, 2012.

Schlosser, Peter. »§ 1025 ZPO« In *Kommentar Zur Zivilprozessordnung,* edited by Friedrich Stein and Martin Jonas. Vol. 9. 22nd ed. Tübingen: Mohr Siebeck, 2002.

——. »Anti-suit injunctions zur Unterstützung von internationalen Schiedsverfahren« *RIW* 52, no. 7 (2007): 486-92.

———. »Comparative International Commercial Arbitration (Book Review)« *SchiedsVZ* 1, no. 6 (2003): 279-81.

———. Das Recht der internationalen privaten Schiedsgerichtsbarkeit. 2nd ed. Tübingen: Mohr, 1989.

———. »vor § 1025 ZPO« In *Kommentar Zur Zivilprozessordnung*, edited by Friedrich Stein and Martin Jonas. Vol. 9. 22nd ed. Tübingen: Mohr Siebeck, 2002.

Schmidt-Ahrendts, Nils, and Philipp Höttler. »Anwendbares Recht bei Schiedsverfahren mit Sitz in Deutschland« *SchiedsVZ* 9, no. 5 (2011): 267-76.

Schmidt, Christian. »Anti-suit injunctions im Wettbewerb der Rechtssysteme« *RIW* (2007): 492-98.

Schmidt-Szalewski, Joanna. »Der Unterschied zwischen der Klage wegen Verletzung gewerblicher Schutzrechte und der Wettbewerbsklage in der französischen Rechtsprechung« *GRUR Int.* 46, no. 1 (1997): 1-10.

Schmitthoff, Clive Maximilian. Clive M. Schmitthoff's Select Essays on International Trade Law. BRILL, 1988.

———. »Nature and Evolution of the Transnational Law of Commercial Transactions« In *Transnational Law of International Commercial Transactions*, edited by Clive Maximilian Schmitthoff and Norbert Horn, 19-31, 1982.

Schneider, Christof Alexander. Die Kollision Allgemeiner Geschäftsbedingungen im internationalen geschäftsmännischen Verkehr. Hamburg: Kovač, 2012.

Schneider, Michael E. »The Essential Guidelines for the Preparation of Guidelines, Directives, Notes, Protocols and Other Methods Intended to Help International Arbitration Practioners to Avoid the Need for Independent Thinking and to Promote the Transformation of Errors into Best Practices« *Liber Amicorum En L'honneur de Serge Lazareff* (2011): 563-67.

Schöldström, Patrik. The Arbitrator's Mandate: A Comparative Study of Relationships in Commercial Arbitration under the Laws of England, Germany, Sweden and Switzerland. Stockholm: Jure, 1998.

Schotten, Günther, and Cornelia Schmellenkamp. *Das internationale Privatrecht in der notariellen Praxis*. 2nd ed. Munich: Beck, 2007.

Schramm, Dorothée, and Elliott Geisinger. »Article II« In *Recognition and Enforcement of Foreign Arbitral Awards: A Global Commentary on the New York Convention*, edited by Herbert Kronke, Patricia Nacimiento, Dirk Otto, and Nicola Christine Port, 37-114. Kluwer Law International, 2010.

Schreiber, Peter. »Wettbewerbsrechtliche Kennzeichenrechte?« *GRUR* 111, no. 2 (2009): 113-18.

Schultz, Thomas. Transnational Legality: Stateless Law and International Arbitration, 2014.

Schulz, Gernot. »UrhG § 5« In *Urheberrechtsgesetz, Urheberrechts-wahrnehmungsgesetz, Kunsturhebergesetz: Kommentar*, edited by Thomas Dreier and Gernot Schulze. 4th ed. Munich: Beck, 2013.

———. »UrhG § 14« In *ibid.*

Schulz, Markus, and Tilman Niedermaier. »Unwirksame Schiedsklausel in Franchise-verträgen durch Wahl des Tagungsortes im Ausland? Besprechung von drei OLG-Entscheidungen in Anerkennungs- und Vollstreckungsverfahren« *SchiedsVZ* 7, no. 4 (2009): 196-203.

Schurig, Klaus. Kollisionsnorm und Sachrecht: zu Struktur, Standort und Methode des internationalen Privatrechts. Berlin: Duncker & Humblot, 1981.

Schütze, Rolf A. »Die Bedeutung des effektiven Schiedsortes im internationalen Schiedsverfahren« In *Grenzen überwinden - Prinzipien bewahren: Festschrift für Bernd von Hoffmann zum 70. Geburtstag am 28. Dezember 2011*, edited by Herbert Kronke and Karsten Thorn, 1077-86, 2011.

———. *Institutional Arbitration: Article-by-Article Commentary*. Munich: Oxford: Baden-Baden: Beck: Hart: Nomos, 2013.

———. Institutionelle Schiedsgerichtsbarkeit: Kommentar. 2nd ed. Cologne, Munich: Heymann, 2011.

———. »International Commercial Arbitration, Commentary« *SchiedsVZ* 12, no. 1 (2014): 30.

Schütze, Rolf A, Dieter Tscherning, and Walter Wais. Handbuch des Schiedsverfahrens: Praxis der deutschen und internationalen Schiedsgerichtsbarkeit. Berlin: New York: W. de Gruyter, 1990.

Schwab, Karl Heinz. »Schiedsrichterernennung und Schiedsrichtervertrag« In *Festschrift für Gerhard Schiedermair zum 70. Geburtstag*, edited by Gerhard Lüke and Othmar Jauernig, 499-515. Munich: Beck, 1976.

Schwab, Karl, Gerhard Walter, and Adolf Baumbach. Schiedsgerichtsbarkeit: Systematischer Kommentar zu den Vorschriften der Zivilprozessordnung, des Arbeitsgerichtsgesetzes, der Staatsverträge und der Kostengesetze über das privatrechtliche Schiedsgerichtsverfahren. 7th ed. Munich: Basel: Beck: Helbing & Lichtenhahn, 2005.

Schwartz, Eric A. »Choosing Between Broad Clauses and Detailed Blueprints« In *Improving the Efficiency of Arbitration Agreements and Awards*, edited by Albert Jan van den Berg, 9:105-13. ICCA Congress Series. Paris: Kluwer Law International, 1999.

Schwarz, Matthias, and Ulrich Reber. »§ 21 Rechte zur unkörperlichen Verwertung« In *Handbuch des Urheberrechts*, edited by Ulrich Loewenheim and Bernhard von Becker. Munich: Beck, 2010.

Senftleben, Martin. »The Trademark Tower of Babel: Dilution Concepts in International, US and EC Trademark Law« *IIC* 40, no. 1 (2009): 45-77.

Severin, Adrian. »Consideratii asupra reglementarii arbitrajului in noul Cod de procedura civila - cu speciala privire la arbitrajul institutionalizat« *Dreptul* no. 1 (2011): 40-75.

———. »Considerations on the Regulation of Arbitration in The New Civil Procedure Code - with Particular Consideration of Institutionalized Arbitration« *International Journal of Law and Jurisprudence Online, Published by Union of Jurists of Romania and Universul Juridic Publishing House* I, no. 1 (2011). www.internationallawreview.eu/fisiere/pdf/Adrian-Severin-Articol_15.pdf.

Shanghai International Economic and Trade Arbitration Commission. »About Us« Shanghai International Economy and Trade Arbitration Commission - Shanghai International Arbitration Centre, 2013.

www.shiac.org/English/About.aspx.

Shiraz, Sabiha. »The New SIAC Rules 2007« In *Arbitration in Singapore and Germany: Recent Developments*, edited by Karl-Heinz Böckstiegel, Klaus Peter Berger, and Jens Bredow, 1-5. Schriftenreihe der Deutschen Institution für Schiedsgerichtsbarkeit 25. Cologne: Heymann, 2009.

Shore, Laurence. »Applying Mandatory Rules of Law in International Arbitration« *Am. Rev. Int'l Arb.* 18. Mandatory Rules in International Commercial Arbitration (2007): 91-101.

———. »The United States' Perspective on ›Arbitrability‹« In *Arbitrability: International and Comparative Perspectives*, edited by Loukas Mistelis and Stavros Brekoulakis, 69. Kluwer Law International, 2009.

Shyamkrishna, Balganesh. »The Uncertain Future of ›Hot News‹ Misappropriation After Barclays Capital v. Theflyonthewall.com« *Colum. L. Rev.* 112, no. 6 (2012): 134-46.

http://columbialawreview.org/wp-content/uploads/2012/06/134_Balganesh.pdf.

SIAC. »Board of Directors« *About Us*, n.d.

www.siac.org.sg/about-us/board-of-directors.

———. »CEO & Secretariat« *About Us*, 2014.

www.siac.org.sg/about-us/ceo-and-secretariat.

———. »Court of Arbitration« *About Us*, 2014.

www.siac.org.sg/about-us/ceo-and-secretariat.

———. »Estimate Your Fees« *Fees*, 2014.

www.siac.org.sg/component/siaccalculator/?Itemid=448.

———. »SIAC Model Clause« *Model Clauses*, n.d.

www.siac.org.sg/model-clauses/siac-model-clause.

———. »SIAC's New Governance Structure and Revised Rules of Arbitration« *SIAC | Home*, 1 April 2013.

www.siac.org.sg/index.php?option=com_content&view=article&id=429:siacs-new-governance-structure-and-revised-rules-of-arbitration-&catid=1:latest-news&Itemid=50.

———. »SIAC Panel« *Our Arbitrators*, n.d.

www.siac.org.sg/our-arbitrators/siac-panel#Top.

———. »Website«, n.d.

www.siac.org.sg.

———. »Why Choose Us«, n.d.

www.siac.org.sg/index.php?option=com_content&view=article&id=150&Itemid=63.

Smith, Murray L. »Contractual Obligations Owed by and to Arbitrators: Model Terms of Appointment« *Arb. Int'l* 8, no. 1 (1992): 17-39.

Sohn, Louis. »Arbitration in International Disputes: Ex Aequo et Bono« In *International Arbitration: Liber Amicorum for Martin Domke.*, edited by Pieter Sanders, 330-37. The Hague: Martinus Nijhoff, 1968.

Sonnenberger, Hans Jürgen. »EGBGB, Einleitung« In *Münchener Kommentar zum BGB*, edited by Franz Jürgen Säcker and Roland Rixecker. 5th ed. Munich: Beck, 2010.

South China International Economic and Trade Arbitration Commission. »About Us« South China International Economic and Trade Arbitration Commission - Shenzhen Court of International Arbitration, 2013.

www.sccietac.org/web/doc/about.html.

———. »SCIA 仲 通讯« no. 4 (10 January 2013).

www.sccietac.org/upload/20130131/2013131_1359624803620.pdf.

Spohnheimer, Frank. Gestaltungsfreiheit bei antezipiertem Legalanerkenntnis des Schiedsspruchs: Zugleich ein Beitrag zur Gewährung rechtlichen Gehörs in Schieds-verfahren und zur Aufhebung von Schiedssprüchen. Mohr Siebeck, 2010.

Stamer, Britta. Der Schutz der Idee unter besonderer Berücksichtigung von Unterhal-tungsproduktion für das Fernsehen. Baden-Baden: Nomos, 2007.

Steinbrück, Ben. Die Unterstützung ausländischer Schiedsverfahren durch staatliche Gerichte: eine rechtsvergleichende Untersuchung des deutschen, österreichischen, englischen, schweizerischen, französischen und US-amerikanischen Schiedsrechts. Tübingen: Mohr Siebeck, 2009.

Steindl, Barbara Helene. »Party Autonomy under the 2012 ICC Arbitration Rules« In *Party Autonomy versus Autonomy of Arbitrators*, edited by Alexander J Belohlávek and Nadezda Rozehnalová, 231-50. Czech and Central European Yearbook of Arbi-tration. Huntington, NY: Juris, 2012.

Stein, Erica. »Polimaster Ltd. v. RAE Systems, Inc.: My Place or Yours? But Not Both« *J. Int'l Arb.* 28, no. 3 (2011): 265-72.

Steingruber, Andrea Marco. *Consent in International Arbitration.* Oxford international arbitration series. Oxford: Oxford University Press, 2012.

Sterling, J. A. L. World Copyright Law: Protection of Authors' Works, Performances, Phonograms, Films, Video, Broadcasts and Published Editions in National, Interna-tional and Regional Law. London: Sweet & Maxwell, 2003.

Stieper, Malte. »Das Verhältnis von Immaterialgüterrechtsschutz und Nachahmungs-schutz nach neuem UWG« *Wettbewerb in Recht und Praxis* (2006): 291-302.

Straus, Donald. »A Network of Arbitration Associations« In *Arbitrage Commercial: Es-sais in Memoriam Eugenio Minoli*, edited by Associazione Italiana per l'Arbitrato, 487-94, 1974.

———. to Pieter Sanders, Letter. »Comments on Draft ›Commentary on UNCITRAL Ar-bitration Rules‹« 16 August 1976.

www.arbitration-icca.org/media/0/12741827871980/016.pdf.

Stricker-Kellerer, Sabine, and Michael J Moser. »CIETAC Rules« In *Institutional Arbitration: Article-by-Article Commentary*, edited by Rolf A Schütze. Munich: Oxford: Baden-Baden: Beck: Hart: Nomos, 2013.

——. »Schiedsordnung der CIETAC« In *Institutionelle Schiedsgerichtsbarkeit: Kommentar*, edited by Rolf A. Schütze, IX. 2nd ed. Cologne, Munich: Heymann, 2011.

Strieder, Joachim. Rechtliche Einordnung und Behandlung des Schiedsrichtervertrages. Cologne: Heymann, 1984.

Stubbe, Christian, and Paul Hobeck. »Genese einer Schiedsklausel« *SchiedsVZ* 1, no. 1 (2003): 15-23.

Stumpf, Michael. »Probleme beim Abschluß von Verträgen mit Betrieben in der DDR« *Betriebs-Berater* (1990): 157-60.

Stürner, Michael. Die Anfechtung von Zivilurteilen: eine funktionale Untersuchung der Rechtsmittel im deutschen und englischen Recht. Münchener Universitätsschriften 171. Munich: Beck, 2002.

Stürner, Michael, Fernando Gascón Inchausti, and Remo Caponi. The Role of Consumer ADR in the Landscape of Adjunction New Trends in Access to Justice under EU Directive 2013/11. Munich: Sellier, 2014.

Sun, Chan Leng. *Singapore Law on Arbitral Awards*. Academy Publishing, 2011.

Sun, Wei. »SPC Instruction Provides New Opportunities for International Arbitral Institutions to Expand into China« *J. Int'l Arb.* 31, no. 6 (2014): 683-700.

Sussman, Edna. »Final Step: Issues in Enforcing the Mediation Settlement Agreement« In *Contemporary Issues in International Arbitration and Mediation: The Fordham Papers*, edited by Arthur Rovine, 2:343-60. The Fordham Papers. New York: Boston: Leiden: Martinus Nijhoff, 2009.

www.sussmanadr.com/docs/Enforcement_Fordham_82008.pdf.

Swiss Chambers' Arbitration Institution. »Federal Statute on Private International Law« *Swiss International Arbitration Law*, n.d.

www.swissarbitration.org/sa/download/IPRG_english.pdf.

——. »Organisation« *Swiss Arbitration*, n.d.

www.swissarbitration.org/sa/en/organisation.php.

——. »Organisation«, n.d.

www.swissarbitration.org/sa/en/organisation.php.

Takla, Youssef. »Non-ICC Arbitration Clauses and Clauses Derogating from the ICC Rules« *The ICC International Court of Arbitration Bulletin* 7, no. 2 (December 1996): 7-.

Tallmo, Karl-Erik. »Beweis der Unrechtmäßigkeit des Büchernachdrucks. Ein Räsonnement und eine Parabel. Johann Gottlieb Fichte, 1793« *The History of Copyright: A Critical Overview With Source Texts in Five Languages*, n.d.

www.copyrighthistory.com/fichte.html.

Tang, Zheng Sophia. *Jurisdiction and Arbitration Agreements in International Commercial Law*. Routledge Research in International Commercial Law. London: New York: Routledge, 2014.

Tao, Jingzhou. *Arbitration Law and Practice in China*. Alphen aan den Rijn: Kluwer Law International, 2008.

——. »CIETAC Arbitration Rules, Chapter I, Article 4, Scope of Application« In *Concise International Arbitration*, edited by Loukas Mistelis, 518-20. Alphen aan den Rijn: Kluwer Law International, 2010.

——. »CIETAC Arbitration Rules, Chapter I, Article 6, Objection to an Arbitration Agreement And/or Jurisdiction« In *ibid*.

Templeman, John. »Towards a Truly International Court of Arbitration« *J. Int'l Arb*. 30, no. 3 (2013): 197-220.

Tevini, Anna. »Besonderheiten des chinesischen Schiedsverfahrensrechts« *SchiedsVZ* 8, no. 1 (2010): 25-31.

The Chamber of Commerce and Industry at the Russian Federation. »Commercial Arbitration in Russia (Historical)« *The International Commercial Arbitration Court*, n.d. www.tpprf-mkac.ru/en/-whatis-/history.

——. »List of Arbitrators« The International Commercial Arbitration Court, n.d. https://mkas.tpprf.ru/en/Arbitrators/

Theune, Ulrich. »DIS Rules« In *Institutional Arbitration: Article-by-Article Commentary*, edited by Rolf A Schütze. Munich: Oxford: Baden-Baden: Beck: Hart: Nomos, 2013.

Thorndon, Lord Cooke of. »Party Autonomy« *V.U.W L. Rev*. 30 (1999): 257-78. http://heinonline.org/HOL/Page?handle=hein.journals/vuwlr30&id=267&div=&collection=journals.

Thümmel, Roderich. »ICDR-IAR« In *Institutional Arbitration: Article-by-Article Commentary*. Munich: Oxford: Baden-Baden: Beck: Hart: Nomos, 2013.

Timmermann, Franz Hubert. »Anmerkung zu den Schiedssprüchen B 1 Nrn. 38, 40, 44 und 47« In *Rechtsprechung Kaufmännischer Schiedsgerichte*, edited by Kuno Straatmann and Peter Ulmer, 3:54-57. Hamburg Chamber of Commerce, 1984.

——. »Anmerkung zum Urteil des BGH vom 2.12.1982« In *Rechtsprechung Kaufmännischer Schiedsgerichte*, edited by Kuno Straatmann and Peter Ulmer, 4:17-18, 1988.

——. »Zur Auslegung der Klausel ›Hamburger freundschaftliche Arbitrage aufgrund der Waren-Vereinsbedingungen.'« *Praxis Des Internationalen Privat- und Verfahrensrecht* no. 3 (1984): 136-37.

Toope, Stephen J. *Mixed International Arbitration: Studies in Arbitration between States and Private Persons*. Edited by University of Cambridge and Research Centre for International Law. Cambridge: Grotius, 1990.

Le Tourneau, Philippe. Le parasitisme: agissements parasitaires et concurrence parasitaire, protection contre les agissements et la concurrence parasitaires, sauvegarde du savoir-faire, des informations, des données et des connaissances des entreprises. Paris: Litec, 1998.

Townsend, John. »Recourse against the Arbitrator after the Arbitral Award: An American Perspective« *The ICC International Court of Arbitration Bulletin* Special Supplement (1995): 115-20.

Trakman, Leon. »Arbitrating Options: Turning a Morass into a Panacea« *UNSW L.J.* 31, no. 1 (2008): 292.

http://search.informit.com.au/documentSummary:dn=150454963932996:res= IELHSS.

Trappe, Johannes. »Praktische Erfahrungen mit chinesischer Schiedsgerichtsbarkeit« *SchiedsVZ* 2, no. 3 (2004): 142-47.

Trittmann, Rolf. »Die wesentlichen Änderungen bei den Aufgaben des ICC-Schiedsgerichtshofs bzw. des ICC-Sekretariats« In *Die neue ICC-Schiedsgerichtsordnung*, edited by Deutsche Institution für Schiedsgerichtsbarkeit, 47-59. Schriftenreihe der August Maria Berges Stiftung für Arbitrales Recht 22. Frankfurt am Main: Lang, 2012.

Trittmann, Rolf, and Inga Hanefeld. »Part II - Commentary on the German Arbitration Law (10th Book of the German Code of Civil Procedure), Chapter II - Arbitration Agreement, § 1029 - Definition« In *Arbitration in Germany: The Model Law in Practice*, edited by Karl-Heinz Böckstiegel, Stefan Michael Kröll, and Patricia Nacimiento, 94-111. Alphen aan den Rijn: Kluwer Law International, 2007.

Turner, Peter. *A Guide to the LCIA Arbitration Rules*. Oxford: New York: Oxford University Press, 2009.

Tweeddale, Andrew, and Keren Tweeddale. *Arbitration of Commercial Disputes: International and English Law and Practice*. Oxford: Oxford University Press, 2005.

Ulrici, Bernhard. »Anhang zu § 278a - Mediationsgesetz« In *Münchener Kommentar zur Zivilprozessordnung: mit Gerichtverfassungsgesetz und Nebengesetzen*, edited by Wolfgang Krüger and Thomas Rauscher. 4th ed. Munich: Beck, 2012.

UNCITRAL. Recommendations to Assist Arbitral Institutions and Other Interested Bodies with Regard to Arbitration under the UNCITRAL Arbitration Rules, , 2010, UNCITRAL U.N. Doc. A/RES/67/90,

www.uncitral.org/pdf/english/texts/arbitration/arb-recommendation-2012/13-80327-Recommendations-Arbitral-Institutions-e.pdf.

Ungeheuer, Christina. Die Beachtung von Eingriffsnormen in der internationalen Handelsschiedsgerichtsbarkeit. Frankfurt am Main: New York: Peter Lang, 1996.

UN. »Status - European Convention on International Commercial Arbitration« *United Nations Treaty Collection*, n.d.

https://treaties.un.org/pages/ViewDetails.aspx?src=TREATY&mtdsg_no=XXII-2&chapter=22&lang=en.

Varady, Tibor. »On Appointing Authorities in International Commercial Arbitration« *Em. J. Int'l Disp. Res.* 2, no. 2 (1988): 311-57.

Varady, Tibor, Arthur Taylor Von Mehren, and John Barceló. *International Commercial Arbitration: A Transnational Perspective*. 4th ed. St. Paul, Minn.: West, 2009.

Veeder, Van Vechten. »ICCA 50th Anniversary Speech«, 2011.

www.arbitration-icca.org/media/0/13087091952910/v.v._veeder_speach.pdf.

———. »London Court of International Arbitration - The New 1998 LCIA Rules« In *Yearbook of Commercial Arbitration*, edited by Albert Jan, van den Berg, XXIII:366-68, 1998.

Van Venrooy, Gerd. *Internationalprivatrechtliche Substitution.* Konstanz: Hartung-Gorre, 1999.

Vidal, Dominique. *Droit français de l'arbitrage interne et international.* Paris: Gualino-Lextenso, 2012.

Vischer, Frank. Die rechtsvergleichenden Tatbestände im internationalen Privatrecht:Die Übereinstimmung der materiellen Rechtsinhalte als Voraussetzung des internationalen Privatrechtes - Die Bedeutung des Begriffes der Äquivalenz. Basel: Helbing & Lichtenhahn, 1953.

Vogt, Stephan A. »Der Schiedsrichtervertrag nach schweizerischem Recht« University of Zurich, 1989.

——. Der Schiedsrichtervertrag nach schweizerischem und internationalem Recht. Aachen: Shaker, 1996.

Voigt, Daniel. Idealvereine und andere Nonprofit-Organisationen im Wettbewerbsrecht. Cologne, Munich: Heymann, 2006.

Voit, Wolfgang. »§ 1025 ZPO« In *Kommentar zur Zivilprozessordnung: mit Gerichtsverfassungsgesetz*, edited by Hans-Joachim Musielak. 12th ed. Munich: Vahlen, 2015.

——. »§ 1029 ZPO« In *ibid.*

——. »§ 1032 ZPO« In *ibid.*

——. »§ 1035 ZPO« In *ibid.*

——. »§ 1040 ZPO« In *ibid.*

——. »§ 1042 ZPO« In *ibid.*

Voser, Nathalie. »Die wichtigsten Neuerungen der revidierten ICC-Schiedsordnung im Überblick« In *Die neue ICC-Schiedsgerichtsordnung*, edited by Deutsche Institution für Schiedsgerichtsbarkeit, 11-45. Schriftenreihe der August Maria Berges Stiftung für Arbitrales Recht 22. Frankfurt am Main: Lang, 2012.

——. »Harmonisation by Promulgating Rules of Best International Practice in International Arbitration« *SchiedsVZ* 3, no. 3 (2005): 113-18.

Wadlow, Christopher. *The Law of Passing-off: Unfair Competition by Misrepresentation.* London: Sweet & Maxwell/Thomson Reuters, 2011.

Waelde, Charlotte, Graeme Laurie, Kheria Smita, and Jane Cornwell. *Contemporary Intellectual Property: Law and Policy.* 3rd ed. Oxford: New York: Oxford University Press, 2013.

Wagner, Gerhard. »§ 826 BGB« In *Münchener Kommentar zum BGB*, edited by Franz Jürgen Säcker and Roland Rixecker. 6th ed. Munich: Beck, 2012.

——. »Anmerkung« *SchiedsVZ* 2, no. 6 (2004): 317-19.

——. »Part II - Commentary on the German Arbitration Law (10th Book of the German Code of Civil Procedure), Chapter I - General Provisions, § 1025 - Scope of Application« In *Arbitration in Germany: The Model Law in Practice*, edited by Karl-Heinz Böckstiegel, Stefan Michael Kröll, and Patricia Nacimiento. Alphen aan den Rijn: Kluwer Law International, 2007.

Waincymer, Jeffrey. *Procedure and Evidence in International Arbitration.* Alphen aan den Rijn: Kluwer Law International, 2012.

Walker, Hans-Peter. Die freie Gestaltung des Verfahrens vor einem internationalen privaten Schiedsgericht durch die Parteien. Zurich: P.G. Keller, 1968.

Walsh, Thomas, and Ruth Teitelbaum. »LCIA Court Decisions on Challenges to Arbitrators: An Introduction« *Arb. Int'l* 27, no. 3 (2011): 283-313.

Walter, Michel. »§ 58 Anwendbares Recht« In *Handbuch des Urheberrechts*, edited by Ulrich Loewenheim and Bernhard von Becker. Munich: Beck, 2010.

———. »§ 58 Anwendbares Recht« In *Handbuch des Urheberrechts*, edited by Ulrich Loewenheim and Bernhard von Becker. Munich: Beck, 2010.

Wang, Sheng Chang, and Lijun Cao. »Towards a Higher Degree of Party Autonomy and Transparency: The CIETAC Introduces Its 2005 New Rules« *Int'l Arb. L. Rev.* 8, no. 4 (2005): 117-23.

Waren-Verein der Hamburger Börse e.V. »Permanent Court of Arbitration«, 2013. www.waren-verein.de/en/permanent-court-of-arbitration.

Wegen, Gerhard, and Marcel Barth. »Die neue Schiedsgerichtsordnung des Singapore International Arbitration Centre (SIAC)« *SchiedsVZ* no. 2 (2008): 86-89.

Wild, Gisela. »Anmerkung: Zur urheberrechtlichen Schutzfähigkeit von Anwaltsschriftsätzen« GRUR 88, no. 10 (1986): 741–42.

Oscar Wilde, »The Picture of Dorian Gray,« first published in Lippincott's Monthly Magazine on 20 June 1890 as a short novel, eBook 13-chapter-version available at www.gutenberg.org/ebooks/4078.

Wilke, Mark. »Prozessführung in administrierten internationalen Handelsschiedsverfahren: eine rechtsvergleichende Untersuchung der internationalen Schiedsordnung der AAA sowie der Schiedsordnungen der DIS und der ICC« Augsburg, 2005. http://opus.bibliothek.uni-augsburg.de/opus4/frontdoor/index/index/docId/123.

Wilske, Stefan. »§ 1042 ZPO« In *Beck'scher Online-Kommentar ZPO*, edited by Christian Wolf and Volkert Vorwerk. 9th ed. Munich: Beck, 2013. http://beck-online.beck.de/?vpath=bib-data/komm/BeckOK_ZPR_9/cont/BeckOK.ZPR.htm.

Wilske, Stefan, and Lars Markert. »Entwicklungen in der internationalen Schiedsgerichtsbarkeit im Jahr 2010 und Ausblick auf 2011« *SchiedsVZ* 9, no. 2 (2011): 57-64.

Wilske, Stephan. »Part IV - Selected Areas and Issues of Arbitration in Germany, ICC Arbitration in Germany« In *Arbitration in Germany: The Model Law in Practice*, edited by Karl-Heinz Böckstiegel, Stefan Michael Kröll, and Patricia Nacimiento, 809-36. Alphen aan den Rijn: Kluwer Law International, 2007.

WIPO. *Guide to the Berne Convention for the Protection of Literary and Artistic Works (Paris Act, 1971)*. WIPO Publication 614. Geneva: WIPO, 1978, ftp://ftp.wipo.int/pub/library/ebooks/wipopublications/Guide-Berne-Convention-wipopub615E.pdf.

WIPO and Paris Union for the Protection of Intellectual Property. »Joint Recommendation Concerning Provisions on the Protection of Well-Known Marks« In

*Thirty - Fourth Series of Meetings of the Assemblies of the Member States of WIPO.* Vol. 888 (E). Geneva, 2000.

www.wipo.int/export/sites/www/freepublications/en/marks/833/pub833.pdf.

Wolf, Christian. »§ 1025 ZPO« In *Beck'scher Online-Kommentar ZPO*, edited by Christian Wolf and Volkert Vorwerk. 9th ed. Munich: Beck, 2013.

http://beck-online.beck.de/?vpath=bib-data/komm/BeckOK_ZPR_9/cont/BeckOK.ZPR.htm.

———. *Die Institutionelle Handelsschiedsgerichtsbarkeit.* Münchener Universitätsschriften. Munich: Beck, 1992.

Wolf, Christian, and Sven Hasenstab. »Hybride Verfahrensgestaltung internationaler Schiedsverfahren« *RIW* (2011): 612-19.

Wolff, Reinmar. »Grundzüge des Schiedsverfahrensrechts« *Juristische Schulung* 48, no. 2 (2008): 108.

www.uni-trier.de/fileadmin/fb5/prof/BRZIPR/veranstaltungen/zpo2/jus2008_108.pdf.

Wu, Yi Yi, and Nancy Sun. »CIETAC Issues 2012 Arbitration Rules but CIETAC Shanghai Issues Own Rules Too« Law Firm Website. *Minter Ellision Lawyers | Alert*, 14 May 2012.

www.minterellison.com/publications/cietac-issues-2012-arbitration-rules.

Yen, Alfred C. »The Danger of Bootstrap Formalism in Copyright« *JIPL* 5 (April 1998): 453-65.

http://works.bepress.com/alfred_yen/20.

Yoshida, Ikko. »History of International Commercial Arbitration and Its Related System in Russia« *Arb. Int'l* 25, no. 3 (2009): 365-402.

Yuan, Bin. »[案例分析]---国际商事仲裁中  合仲裁条款效力研究——以两起  型 仲  案件为实例« [Case Study - on the efficiency of mixed arbitration clauses in international commercial arbitration - with two typical example arbitration cases], n.d. (only in Chinese)

http://ningbo.dachenglaw.com/researchs/research/30835.html?view=/ningbo/template/print.ftl&id=c140d377db84461aa029c81969b861ff.

Yuen, Peter. »Arbitration Clauses in a Chinese Context« *J. Int'l Arb.* 24, no. 6 (2007): 581-96.

Yu, Jianlong. »Arbitrators: Private Judges, Service Providers, or Both? - CIETAC's Perspective« *Stockh. Int'l Arb. Rev.* no. 3 (2007): 1-13.

Zhou, Jian. »Arbitration Agreements in China: Battles on Designation of Arbitral Institution and Ad Hoc Arbitration« *J. Int'l Arb..* 232 (2006): 145-70.

Zhu, Meiting. Gewerblicher Rechtsschutz in der VR China, Cologne: Germany Trade and Invest, 2008.

Živković, Patricia. »Hybrid Arbitration Clauses Tested Again: Can the SCC Administer Proceedings under the ICC Rules?« *Kluwer Arbitration Blog*, 9 June 2015,

http://kluwerarbitrationblog.com/blog/2015/06/09/hybrid-arbitration-clauses-tested-again-can-the-scc-administer-proceedings-under-the-icc-rules.

Zuberbühler, Tobias, Christoph Müller, and Phillipp Habegger, eds. *Swiss Rules of International Arbitration: Commentary*. Zurich: The Hague: Schulthess : Kluwer Law International, 2005.

Ben-Zvi, Linda. *Women in Beckett: Performance and Critical Perspectives*. Urbana: University of Illinois Press, 1990.

Zweigert, Konrad, and Hein Kötz. *An Introduction to Comparative Law*. 3rd ed. Oxford: New York: Clarendon Press : Oxford University Press, 1998.

# Primary sources

## *Treaties / conventions & multilateral declarations*

Berne Convention: Berne Convention for the Protection of Literary and Artistic Works of 9 September1886, completed at Paris on 4 May 1896, revised at Berlin on 13 November 1908, World Intellectual Property Organisation,

www.wipo.int/treaties/en/ip/berne/trtdocs_wo001.html.

ECHR: European Convention for the Protection of Human Rights and Fundamental Freedoms (as amended by Protocols Nos. 11 and 14), Council of Europe, entered into force 3 September 1953, 213 UNTS 222,

www.echr.coe.int/Documents/Convention_ENG.pdf.

European Arbitration Convention: Convention on International Commercial Arbitration, Economic Commission for Europe of the United Nations, entered into force 21 April 1961, 484 UNTS 364,

www.jus.uio.no/lm/europe.international.commercial.arbitration.convention.geneva.1961.

IACHR: Inter-American Convention on Human Rights, Organization of American States, entered into force 18 July 1978, 1144 UNTS 123,

www.cidh.oas.org/Basicos/English/Basic3.American%20Convention.htm.

ICCPR: International Covenant on Civil and Political Rights, UN, entered into force 23 March 1976, 999 UNTS 171,

www.ohchr.org/EN/ProfessionalInterest/Pages/CCPR.aspx.

New York Convention: United Nations Convention on the Recognition and Enforcement of Foreign Arbitral Awards (New York Convention), UN, entered into force 7 June 1959,

www.newyorkconvention.org/texts.

Paris Agreement: Paris Agreement relating to Application of the European Convention on International Commercial Arbitration, Council of Europe, 17 December 1962,

http://conventions.coe.int/Treaty/en/Treaties/Html/042.htm.

Paris Convention: Paris Convention for the Protection of Industrial Property, World Intellectual Property Organization, entered into force 20 March 1883,

www.wipo.int/treaties/en/text.jsp?file_id=288514.

SLA: Softwood Lumber Agreement between the Goverment of Canada and the Government of the United States of America, entered into force 12 September 2006, E105072,

www.treaty-accord.gc.ca/text-texte.aspx?id=105072&lang=eng.

TRIPS: Agreement on Trade-Related Aspects of Intellectual Property Rights, World Trade Organisation entered into force 1 January 1996,

www.wto.org/english/docs_e/legal_e/27-trips.pdf.

Universal Declaration of Human Rights: Universal Declaration of Human Rights, UN Doc. A/810 (1948) 71,

www.ohchr.org/EN/UDHR/Pages/Language.aspx?LangID=eng.

WIPO Copyright Treaty: Copyright Treaty, World Intellectual Property Organisation, entered into force 20 December 1996,

www.wipo.int/treaties/en/ip/wct/trtdocs_wo033.html.


## EU legislation (Regulations & Directives)

Advertising Directive: Directive 2006/114/EC of the European Parliament and of the Council of 12 December 2006 concerning misleading and comparative advertising (codified version) of 12 December 2006 (O.J. 2006 L 376, 21-27),

http://eur-lex.europa.eu/legal-content/EN/TXT/?uri=CELEX:32006L0114.

Brussels-I-Regulation: Council Regulation (EC) No 44/2001 of 22 December 2000 on jurisdiction and the recognition and enforcement of judgments in civil and commercial matters of 22 December 2000 (O.J. 2001 L 12, 1-23),

http://eur-lex.europa.eu/legal-content/EN/TXT/?uri=CELEX:32001R0044.

Brussels-Ia-Regulation: Regulation (EU) No. 1215/2012 of the European Parliament and of the Council of 12 December 2012 on jurisdiction and the recognition and enforcement of judgments in civil and commercial matters of 12 December 2012 (Official Journal 2012 L 351, 1–32),

http://eur-lex.europa.eu/LexUriServ/LexUriServ.do?uri=OJ:L:2012:351:0001:0032:en:PDF.

Mediation Directive: Directive 2008/52/EC of the European Parliament and of the Council on certain aspects of mediation in civil and commercial matters of 21 May 2008 (O.J. 2008 L 136, 3-8),

http://eur-lex.europa.eu/legal-content/en/ALL/?uri=CELEX:32008L0052.

Rome-II-Regulation: Regulation (EC) No 864/2007 of the European Parliament and of the Council of 11 July 2007 on the law applicable to non-contractual obligations of 11 July 2007 (O.J. 2007 L 199, 40-49),

http://eur-lex.europa.eu/legal-content/en/ALL/?uri=CELEX:32007R0864.

Rome-I-Regulation: Regulation (EC) No 593/2008 of the European Parliament and of the Council of 17 June 2008 on the law applicable to contractual obligations of 17 June 2008 (O.J. 2008 L 177, 6-16),

http://eur-lex.europa.eu/legal-content/en/ALL/?uri=CELEX:32008R0593.

Unfair Commercial Practices Directive: Directive 2005/29/EC of the European Parliament and of the Council of 11 May 2005 concerning unfair business-to-consumer commercial practices in the internal market and amending Council Directive

84/450/EEC, Directives 97/7/EC, 98/27/EC and 2002/65/EC of the European Parliament and of the Council and Regulation (EC) No 2006/2004 of the European Parliament and of the Council of 11 May 2005 (O.J. 2005 L 149, 22-39), http://eur-lex.europa.eu/legal-content/EN/TXT/?uri=CELEX:32005L0029.

*National legislation, regulations and instruments issued by state organs*

## Belgium

CJ: Code judiciaire [Judicial code], 10 October 1967, as last amended on 28. February 2014,
   www.droitbelge.be/codes.asp#jud.

## England & Wales, United Kingdom

Arbitration Act 1950: Arbitration Act, 28 July 1950, ch. 27, 14 Geo. VI,
   www.legislation.gov.uk/ukpga/1950/27/pdfs/ukpga_19500027_en.pdf.
Arbitration Act 1996: Arbitration Act, 17 July 1996, ch. 23,
   www.legislation.gov.uk/ukpga/1996/23/contents.
Copyright Act: Copyright, Designs and Patents Act, 15 November 1988, ch. 48,
   www.legislation.gov.uk/ukpga/1988/48/contents.
Private International Law Act: Private International Law (Miscellaneous Provisions) Act, 1995, ch. 42,
   www.legislation.gov.uk/ukpga/1995/42/pdfs/ukpga_19950042_en.pdf.
Unfair Contract Terms Act: Unfair Contract Terms Act, 26 October 1977, ch. 50,
   www.legislation.gov.uk/ukpga/1977/50.

## France

C. Civ.: Code Civil [Civil Code],
   www.legifrance.gouv.fr/affichCode.do?cidTexte=LEGITEXT000006070721.
CPC: Code de Procédure Civile [Code of Civil Procedure], 1 January 1976, last amended on 9 September 2014,
   www.legifrance.gouv.fr/affichCode.do?cidTexte=LEGITEXT000006070716.
CPI: Code de la Proprieté Intellectuelle [Intellectual Property Code], 1 July 1992,
   www.legifrance.gouv.fr.

Décret portant réforme de l'arbitrage: Décret portant réforme de l'arbitrage [Decree reforming arbitration], 13 January 2011 (JORF no. 0011 777, text no. 9),

www.legifrance.gouv.fr.

Loi relative au contrat d'association: Loi relative au contrat d'association [Law on the contract of association], 1 July 1901,

www.legifrance.gouv.fr.

## Germany

BGB: Bürgerliches Gesetzbuch [Civil Code], in the version published on 2 February 2002, BGBl I 42, 2909: 2003 I 738, original date 18. August 1896, last amended on 29 June 2015, BGBl. I 1042,

www.gesetze-im-internet.de/bgb/index.html (with English translation).

EGGVG: Einführungsgesetz zum Gerichtsverfassungsgesetz [Introductory Act to the Law on the Organisation of the Judiciary], original date 27 January 1877, status as last amended on 23 June 2013, BGBl. I 2586,

www.gesetze-im-internet.de/gvgeg/index.html.

MarkenG: Markengesetz [Trademark Law], 25 October 1994, BGBl. I 3082: 1995 I 156: 1996 I 682, last amended on 19 October 2013, BGBl. I 3830,

www.gesetze-im-internet.de/markeng (with English translation).

SchiedsVfG.: Gesetz zur Neuregelung des Schiedsverfahrensrechts [Act modifying the arbitration law], 22 December 1997, BGBl. 1997 I 3224.

UrhG: Gesetz über Urheberrecht und verwandte Schutzrechte (Urheberrechtsgesetz) [Law on author's rights and neighbouring rights], original date 9 September 1965, BGBl. I 1237, last amended 5 December 2014, BGBl. I 1974,

www.gesetze-im-internet.de/urhg/index.html (with English translation).

UWG: Gesetz gegen den unlauteren Wettbewerb [Act against unfair competition], in the version published on 3 March 2010, BGBl. I 254, original date 3 July 2004, last amended on 1 October 2013, BGBl. I 3714,

www.gesetze-im-internet.de/uwg_2004/index.html (with English translation).

ZPO: Zivilprozessordnung [Code of Civil Procedure], in the version published on 5 December 2005, BGBl. I 3202, original date 12 September 1950, last amended on 8 July 2014, BGBl. I 890,

www.gesetze-im-internet.de/zpo (with English translation).

ZPO (old version): Zivilprozessordnung [Code of Civil Procedure], in the version published on 1 January 1964, BGBl.III 310-4, in force until 31 December1997.

## People's Republic of China

Decision concerning the Establishment of FTAC: Decision Concerning the Establishment of a Foreign Trade Arbitration Commission Within the China Council for the Promotion of International Trade, 6 May 1954, 215th Session of the Government Administration Council of The Central People's Government, English translation published in China International Economic and Trade Arbitration Commission, Selected Works of CIETAC.

Notice concerning the conversion of FTAC into FETAC: Notice concerning the Conversion of the Foreign Trade Arbitration Commission into the Foreign Economic and Trade Arbitration Commission, 26 February 1980, State Council, English translation published in China International Economic and Trade Arbitration Commission, Selected Works of CIETAC.

Notice Regarding Some Problems for the Implementation of the Arbitration Law: Notice Regarding Some Problems Which Need to Be Clarified for the Implementation of the Arbitration Law of the People's Republic of China, 8 June 1996, State Council,

www.cietac.org (English translation available under »References«).

Official Reply concerning the Renaming of FETAC into CIETAC: Official Reply concerning the Renaming of the Foreign Economic and Trade Arbitration Commission as the China International Economic and Trade Arbitration Commission and the Amendment of its Arbitration Rules, 21 June 1988, State Council, English translation published in China International Economic and Trade Arbitration Commission, Selected Works of CIETAC.

Plan for the Reorganisation of Arbitration Organs: Plan for the Reorganization of Arbitration Organs, 28 July 1995, State Council,

www.asianlii.org/cn/legis/cen/laws/pftroao466 (English translation).

SPC's Interpretation of Arbitration Law: Interpretation concerning Some Issues on Application of the Arbitration Law of the People's Republic of China, 23 August 2006, Supreme People's Court,

www.cietac.org (English translation available under »References«).

SPC's Interpretation on Unfair Competition: Interpretation on Some Matters about the Application of Law in the Trial of Civil Cases Involving Unfair Competition, 12 January 2007, Supreme People's Court,

www.wipo.int/wipolex/en/details.jsp?id=6558 (English translation).

SPC's notice on CIETAC split: Notice t on Issues concerning the Proper Trial of Cases Involving Arbitration-Related Judicial Review, 4 September 2013, Supreme People's Court,

http://lawinfochina.com/display.aspx?id=18089&lib=law (with English translation).

SPC's Circular on Foreign Arbitrations: Circular on Issues in the People's Courts' Handling of Foreign-related Arbitrations and Foreign Arbitrations, 28 August 1995, Supreme People's Court, English translation www.cietac.org (under »References«).

Unfair Competition Law: Law of the People's Republic of China Against Unfair Competition, 2 September 1993, promulgated by presidential order no. 10,

www.wipo.int/wipolex/en/details.jsp?id=849 (English translation).

Trademark Law: Trademark Law of the People's Republic of China, 30 August 2013 (last amendment), originally adopted at the 24th Session of the Standing Committee of the Fifth National People's Congress on 23 August 1982, revised for the first time on 22 February 1993, for the second time on 27 October 2001,

www.wipo.int/wipolex/en/details.jsp?id=13198.

## Romania

CPC: (Noul) Cod de procedură civilă [(New) Code of Civil Procedure], Monitorul Oficial I no. 485, 1 July 2010,

www.cameramures.com/CPC.pdf.

Law on the Chamber of Commerce of Romania: Legea privind Camerele de Comerţ din România [Law on the Chamber of Commerce of Romania], 3 December 2007 (Monitorul Oficial, pt. I no. 836),

http://arbitration.ccir.ro/engleza/legal.htm (English translation).

Modifying Act 2011: Legea pentru modificarea si completarea Legii camerelor de comert din Romania [Law modifying and complementing the Law on the Chamber of Commerce of Romanaia], 30 March 2011 (Monitorul Oficial, pt. I no. 224),

http://arbitration.ccir.ro/engleza/legal.htm (English translation).

## Russian Federation

Law on International Commercial Arbitration: Law on International Commercial Arbitration, No. 5338-I , 7 July 1993,

www.newyorkconvention1958.org/wp-content/uploads/2012/06/1993-07-07-RF-Law-on-Internaitonal-Commercial-Arbitraiton-en.pdf (English translation).

## Singapore

IAA: International Arbitration Act (Revised Edition), 31 December 2002, last amended on 1 June 2012,
http://statutes.agc.gov.sg.

## Spain

Ley de arbitraje: Ley de arbitraje [Arbitration Law], 23 December 2003, Boletín Oficial del Estado no. 309, 46097-109,
www.boe.es/diario_boe/txt.php?id=BOE-A-2003-23646.

Ley de reforma 2011: Ley de reforma de la ley de arbitraje y de regulación del arbitraje institucional en la Administratión General del Estado [Act on the reform of the arbitration law and the regulation of institutional arbitration in the General Administration of the State], 20 May 2011, Boletín Oficial del Estado no. 121, 50797-804,
www.boe.es/diario_boe/txt.php?id=BOE-A-2011-8847.

## Sweden

Lag om skiljeförfarande: Lag om skiljeförfarande [Arbitration Law], 1 April 1999,
www.ris.bka.gv.at/GeltendeFassung.wxe?Abfrage=Bundesnormen&Gesetzesnumm er=10001699&ShowPrintPreview=True.

## Switzerland

IPRG: Bundesgesetz über das Internationale Privatrecht [Federal Law on Private International Law], 18 December 1987, in the version of 1 July 2014, AS 1988 1776,
https://www.admin.ch/opc/de/classified-compilation/19870312.

URG: Bundesgesetz über das Urheberrecht und verwandte Schutzrechte [Federal law on author's rights and neighbouring rights], 9 October 1992, in the version of 1 January 2011, AS 1993 1798,
www.admin.ch/opc/de/classified-compilation/19920251.

UWG: Bundesgesetz gegen den unlauteren Wettbewerb [Federal law against unfair competition], 19 December 1986, in the version of 1 July 2014, AS 1988 223,
https://www.admin.ch/opc/de/classified-compilation/19860391/index.html.

## United States of America

(Revised) Uniform Arbitration Act: (Revised) Uniform Arbitration Act, 2000, originally enacted on 1955,

www.uniformlaws.org/shared/docs/arbitration/arbitration_final_00.pdf.

Copyright Law: Copyright Law and Related Laws of the United States of America (U.S.C. Title 17), originally enacted on19 October 1976,

www.gpo.gov/fdsys/browse/collectionUScode.action?collectionCode=USCODE.

FAA: United States Arbitration Act (including Federal Arbitration Act in its Chapter 1, originally enacted on 12 February 1925) (U.S.C. Title 9),

www.gpo.gov/fdsys/browse/collectionUScode.action?collectionCode=USCODE.

Restatement (Second) of Contracts: Restatement (Second) of the Law of Contracts, American Law Institute, 1981.

United States Trademark Act: United States Trademark Act, originally enacted on 5 July 1946 (U.S.C. Title 15),

www.gpo.gov/fdsys/browse/collectionUScode.action?collectionCode=USCODE.

## *United Nations Model Laws, principles and reports*

Note by the Secretariat: Note by the Secretariat: Model Law on International Commercial Arbitration: Revised Draft Articles I to XXVI, 14 December 1983, UNCITRAL YB XIV 78-85,

www.uncitral.org/pdf/english/yearbooks/yb-1983-e/yb_1983_e.pdf.

Rep. of the Secretary-General: Possible features: Report of the Secretary-General: Possible Features of a Model Law on International Commercial Arbitration, UNCITRAL, Working Group II, 14 May 1981, A/CN.9/207, UNCITRAL YB XII 75-93,

www.uncitral.org/pdf/english/yearbooks/yb-1981-e/yb_1981_e.pdf.

UNCITRAL Model Law: UNCITRAL Model Law on International Commercial Arbitration, 7 July 2006, originally enacted on 21 June 1985,

www.uncitral.org/uncitral/en/uncitral_texts/arbitration/1985Model_arbitration.html.

UNCITRAL Model Law (conciliation): UNCITRAL Model Law on International Commercial Conciliation, 24 July 2002,

www.uncitral.org/uncitral/en/uncitral_texts/arbitration/2002Model_conciliation.html.

UNCITRAL Model Law 1985: UNCITRAL Model Law on International Commercial Arbitration, 21 June 1985,

www.uncitral.org/uncitral/en/uncitral_texts/arbitration/1985Model_arbitration.html.

UNCITRAL Working Group on International Contract Practices, Report, 5th session: Report of the Working Group on International Contract Practices on the work of its fifth session (New York, 22 February-4 March 1983), UNCITRAL, 1983, A/CN.9/233, UNCITRAL YB XIV 60-78,

www.uncitral.org/pdf/english/yearbooks/yb-1983-e/yb_1983_e.pdf.

UNIDROIT Principles: UNIDROIT Principles of International Commercial Contracts, 2010,

www.unidroit.org/english/principles/contracts/principles2010/integralversionprinciples2010-e.pdf.

## *Arbitration rules & guidelines*

### AAA-ICDR

AAA-ICDR Rules (2014): International Arbitration Rules of the International Centre for Dispute Resolution, 1 June 2014,

www.icdr.org (under »Rules & Procedures«).

AAA-ICDR Rules (2009): International Arbitration Rules of the International Centre for Dispute Resolution, 1 June 2009

www.icdr.org (under »Rules & Procedures«).

### BCDR-AAA

BCDR-AAA Rules: BCDR-AAA Arbitration Rules 2010,

www.bcdr-aaa.org/en/rules-regulations/bcdr-aaa-arbitration-rulesenglish.html.

### CCIR

CCIR Rules (2014): Reguli de procedură arbitrală de Curţii de Arbitraj Comercial Internaţional [Arbitration Rules of the Court of International Commercial Arbitration], 5 June 2014,

http://arbitration.ccir.ro/engleza/Rules_of_arbitration_2014.pdf.

CCIR Rules 2013: Reguli de procedură arbitrală de Curţii de Arbitraj Comercial Internaţional [Arbitration Rules of the Court of International Commercial Arbitration], 6 March 2013, published in Monitorul Oficial [Official Monitor], pt. I no. 184,

http://arbitration.ccir.ro/engleza/rules.htm.

CCIR Organisational Rules 2014: Regulamentul privind organizarea şi funcţionarea Curţii de Arbitraj Comercial Internaţional [Rules on the organisation and operation of the Court of International Commercial Arbitration], 6 May 2014, published in Monitorul Oficial, pt. I no. 328.

CCIR Organisational Rules 2013: Regulamentul privind organizarea şi funcţionarea Curţii de Arbitraj Comercial Internaţional [Rules on the organisation and operation of the Court of International Commercial Arbitration], 6 March 2013, published in Monitorul Oficial [Official Monitor], pt. I no. 184.

## CIETAC

CIETAC Rules (2015): Arbitration Rules, 1 January 2015,
www.cietac.org/index/rules.cms.

CIETAC Rules (2012): Arbitration Rules, 1 May 2012
www.cietac.org/index/rules.cms.

CIETAC Rules (2005): Arbitration Rules, 1 May 2005
www.cietac.org/index/rules.cms.

## DIFC-LCIA

DIFC-LCIA Rules: DIFC-LCIA Arbitration Rules, 17 February 2008,
www.difcarbitration.com/arbitration/rules_clauses/index.html.

## DIS

DIS Rules: DIS-Schiedsgerichtsordnung [Arbitration Rules] 98, 1 June 1998
www.disarb.org/en/16/rules/dis-arbitration-rules-98-id10.

DIS-UNCITRAL Rules: UNCITRAL Arbitration Rules - Administered by the DIS, 1 May 2012,
www.disarb.org/en/16/rules/uncitral-arbitration-rules-administered-by-the-dis-id32.

## Hamburger Freundschaftliche Arbitrage [Hamburg Friendly Arbitration]

Hamburg Local Commodity Trade Usage: Platzusancen für den hamburgischen Waren-handel [Local Trade Usage for Commodity Exchange in Hamburg],
www.hk24.de/en/fairplay/arbitration/347708/arbitrage2.html.

# IBA

IBA Guidelines on Conflicts of Interest : Guidelines on Conflicts of Interest in International Arbitration, Arbitration Committee of the International Bar Association, 22 May 2004,

www.ibanet.org/Publications/publications_IBA_guides_and_free_materials.aspx.

IBA Guidelines on Party Representation: IBA Guidelines on Party Representation in International Arbitration, Arbitration Committee of the International Bar Association, 25 May 2013,

www.ibanet.org/Publications/publications_IBA_guides_and_free_materials.aspx.

IBA Rules on the Taking of Evidence: IBA Rules on the Taking of Evidence in International Arbitration, Arbitration Committee of the International Bar Association, 29 May 2010,

www.ibanet.org/Publications/publications_IBA_guides_and_free_materials.aspx.

# ICAC

ICAC Rules: Rules of the International Commercial Arbitration Court, approved by Order No. 76 of the Chamber of Commerce and Industry of the Russian Federation, 18 October 2005 as amended by the Order No 28 of the Chamber of Commerce and Industry of the Russian Federation of 23 June 2010,

http://mkas.tpprf.ru/en/documents.

# ICC Court

ICC Rules (2017): Rules of Arbitration of the International Court of Arbitration as amended in 2017, 1 March 2017, ICC Publication 880-3 ENG,

https://iccwbo.org/dispute-resolution-services/arbitration/rules-of-arbitration/

ICC Rules (2012): Rules of Arbitration of the International Court of Arbitration, 1 January 2012, ICC Publication 850 E,

http://internationalarbitrationlaw.com/about-arbitration/international-arbitration-rules/2012-icc-arbitration-rules/

ICC Rules (1998): Rules of Arbitration of the International Court of Arbitration, 1 January 1998, ICC Publication 808

www.jus.uio.no/lm/icc.arbitration.rules.1998.

ICC Rules (1988): Rules of Conciliation and Arbitration of the International Court of Arbitration, 1 January 1988, ICC Publication 447

www.jus.uio.no/lm/icc.conciliation.arbitration.rules.1988/doc.html.

ICC Appointing Authority Rules: Rules of ICC as Appointing Authority, 1 January 2004,

www.iccwbo.org/products-and-services/arbitration-and-adr/appointing-authority/rules-of-icc-as-appointing-authority.

## LCIA

LCIA Rules (2014): Arbitration Rules, 1 October 2014,
www.lcia.org/Dispute_Resolution_Services/lcia-arbitration-rules-2014.aspx.
LCIA Rules (1998): Arbitration Rules, 1 January 1998,
www.lcia.org/Dispute_Resolution_Services/LCIA_Arbitration_Rules.aspx.
LCIA Constitution: Constitution of the Court, 2011,
www.lcia.org/LCIA/Constitution_of_the_Court.aspx.

## LCIA India

LCIA India Rules: LCIA India Arbitration Rules, 17 April 2010,
www.lcia-india.org/Arbitration.aspx.

## LCIA-MIAC Arbitration Centre

LCIA-MIAC Rules: LCIA-MIAC Arbitration Rules, 1 October 2012,
www.lcia-miac.org/arbitration/arbitration-rules.aspx.

## Paris - the Home of International Arbitration (ad hoc rules)

Paris Arbitration Rules, n.d., current version available at:
http://parisarbitration.net/en/materials.

## SCCAM

Swiss Rules (2012): Swiss Rules of International Arbitration, 1 June 2012,
www.swissarbitration.org.
Swiss Rules (2004): Swiss Rules of International Arbitration, 1 January 2004,
www.swissarbitration.org.

SCCAM Internal Rules: Internal Rules of the Court of Arbitration, 21 May 2012,
www.swissarbitration.org.

## SCIA / SCIETAC

SCIA Rules (2016): Arbitration Rules of the South China International Economic and
Trade Arbitration Commission, 1 December 2016,
www.sccietac.org/web/doc/rules_list.html.

SCIA Rules (2012): Arbitration Rules of the South China International Economic and
Trade Arbitration Commission, 1 December 2012,
www.sccietac.org/web/doc/rules_list.html.

## SHIAC / SIETAC

SHIAC Rules (2015): Arbitration Rules of the Shanghai International Arbitration
Centre, 1 May 2015,
www.shiac.org/SHIAC/arbitrate_rules_E.aspx.

SHIAC Rules (2014): Arbitration Rules of the Shanghai International Arbitration Centre, SHIAC, 1 May 2014,
www.shiac.org/140418EN.pdf.

SHIAC Rules (2013): Arbitration Rules of the Shanghai International Arbitration Centre, 1 May 2013,
www.shiac.org/upload/day_130407/201304071023539471.pdf.

CIETAC Shanghai Rules (2012): Arbitration Rules of the China InternationalEconomic
and Trade Arbitration Commission Shangahi Commission, 1 May 2012,
www.shiac.org/upload/day_130413/201304130221249912.pdf.

## SIAC

SIAC Rules (2016): Arbitration Rules, 1 August 2016, 6th edition,
http://www.siac.org.sg/our-rules/siac-rules-2016

SIAC Rules (2013): Arbitration Rules, 1 April 2013, 5th edition,
www.siac.org.sg/our-rules/siac-rules-2013

SIAC Rules (2010): Arbitration Rules, 1 July 2010, 4th edition,
www.siac.org.sg/our-rules/siac-rules-2010

SIAC Rules (2007): Arbitration Rules, 1 July 2007, 3rd edition,
www.siac.org.sg/our-rules/siac-rules-2007

SIAC Rules (1997): Arbitration Rules, 22 October 1997, 2nd edition,
www.siac.org.sg/our-rules.

SIAC Domestic Rules (2002): Domestic Arbitration Rules, 1 September 2002,
2nd edition,
www.siac.org.sg/our-rules.

SIAC Practice Note (2014): Practice Note for Administered Cases, 2 February 2014, 01/14,
www.siac.org.sg/our-rules.

SIAC Practice Note for UNCITRAL Cases (2014): On case administration, appointment of arbitrators & financial management for cases under the UNCITRAL Rules 2010, 1 February 2014,
www.siac.org.sg/our-rules.

## UNCITRAL

UNCITRAL Rules (2010): UNCITRAL Arbitration Rules, 15 August 2010, Gen. Ass. Res. 65/22, with new article 1 para. 4 adopted in 2013,
http://www.uncitral.org/pdf/english/texts/arbitration/arb-rules-2013/UNCITRAL-Arbitration-Rules-2013-e.pdf.

UNCITRAL Rules (1976): UNCITRAL Arbitration Rules, 15 December 1976, Gen. Ass. Res. 31/98,
http://www.uncitral.org/pdf/english/texts/arbitration/arb-rules/arb-rules.pdf.

## Waren-Verein der Hamburger Börse

Waren-Verein Conditions & Rules: Geschäftsbedingungen, Schiedsgerichtsordnung, Verfahrensordnung für Sachverständige [Conditions of Business, Arbitration Rules, Rules for Experts of the Hamburg Commodity Exchange Board], 1 March 2011,
www.waren-verein.de/de/conditions-of-business-arbitration-rules-rules-for-experts